Bruno Olsson
A Grammar of Coastal Marind

Mouton Grammar Library

Edited by
Georg Bossong
Bernard Comrie
Patience L. Epps
Irina Nikolaeva

Volume 87

Bruno Olsson

A Grammar of Coastal Marind

—

DE GRUYTER
MOUTON

ISBN 978-3-11-112077-5
e-ISBN (PDF) 978-3-11-074706-5
e-ISBN (EPUB) 978-3-11-074712-6
ISSN 0933-7636

Library of Congress Control Number: 2021936232

Bibliographic information published by the Deutsche Nationalbibliothek
The Deutsche Nationalbibliothek lists this publication in the Deutsche Nationalbibliografie; detailed bibliographic data are available on the Internet at http://dnb.dnb.de.

© 2022 Walter de Gruyter GmbH, Berlin/Boston
This volume is text- and page-identical with the hardback published in 2021.
Printing and binding: CPI books GmbH, Leck

www.degruyter.com

Acknowledgements

This grammar is a completely revamped and expanded revision of my doctoral dissertation (Olsson 2017). My fieldwork was mainly carried out in the remarkable village of Wambi, where I was hosted by Paulus Yolmend and †Yustina Mahuze, and I am deeply grateful to them and their large family for their generosity and willingness to let me take part in their lives. For countless hours of linguistic discussion and transcription of recordings, I am indebted to the stellar team of Pau Yolmend (grandson of my host Paulus Yolmend), Alo Yolmend (Paulus and Yustina's second youngest son), Sepi Yolmend (the village secretary) and Ricky Basik-Basik (son of the village chief). In the villages of Buti and Payum, I was fortunate to work with the eminently knowledgeable †Petrus Kilub Gebze and Damianus Gebze. Special thanks are due to Rafael Samkakai and Sela Gebze in Duhmilah, who hosted me during my first field trip and who adopted me into the wallaby clan.

In Merauke, I benefitted enormously from the help of Budi Yolmend (Paulus and Yustina's eldest son) and his family. I am grateful to Kalasina Agaki and her late husband, †Nurman Nurhasan, and the rest of their family, who were my hosts in Merauke from my second trip and onwards, and especially to their son Dedi Agaki, whose impressive ability to navigate both the Marind and Indonesian realms became a guiding light. During my first trip, I was hosted by the Missionaries of the Sacred Heart while visiting Merauke, who kindly provided me with a room and gave me access to the mission archive. I am very grateful to Father Kees de Rooij and former Archbishop Nicolaus Adi Seputra for their help and generosity.

I owe particularly heartfelt thanks to František Kratochvíl, whose extensive supervisory efforts made my fieldwork and writing possible. For their comments on aspects of the manuscript, I wish to thank Luke Adamson, Danielle Barth, Matt Carroll, Bernard Comrie, Alec Coupe, Nick Evans, Sebastian Fedden, Kate Lindsey, Marianne Mithun, Naomi Peck, Ger Reesink, Phill Rogers, Edgar Suter, Timothy Usher, Bernhard Wälchli, and my students in LING3031 Papuan Languages.

Contents

Acknowledgements — V

List of maps, tables and figures — XVII

Abbreviations and conventions — XXI

1	**Preliminaries** — 1	
1.1	General information — 1	
1.1.1	Structural profile — 1	
1.2	Relationships with other languages — 5	
1.2.1	The Marindic languages and the Anim language family — 5	
1.2.2	The Marindic languages — 7	
1.2.3	Language contact — 14	
1.3	The Marind people — 15	
1.3.1	Geography — 15	
1.3.2	Ethnographic remarks — 15	
1.3.3	Demography — 17	
1.3.4	Socioeconomic setting, subsistence — 18	
1.4	Previous research — 19	
1.5	This grammar — 21	
1.5.1	The fieldwork — 21	
1.5.2	The corpus — 21	
2	**Phonology** — 24	
2.1	Segmental phonology — 24	
2.1.1	Consonants — 24	
2.1.2	Vowels — 31	
2.2	Phonotactics — 33	
2.2.1	Epenthetic /a/ — 34	
2.3	Suprasegmentals — 35	
2.4	Metrical structure — 35	
2.4.1	Insertion of pretonic epenthetic /a/ — 37	
2.4.2	Syncopation of antepretonic /a/ — 38	
2.5	Morphophonemic alternations — 39	
2.5.1	Antepenultimate vowel gradation — 39	
2.5.2	Plosive Nasalisation — 41	
2.5.3	Loss of /d/ — 42	
2.5.4	Loss of /h/ — 43	
2.5.5	Vowel sequences in verb prefixes — 45	

2.5.6	Optional /amo/-metathesis —— 46	

3 Nominals, their morphology and derivation —— 48
3.1 The nominal word classes —— 48
3.1.1 Nouns as a word class —— 48
3.1.2 Adjectives as a word class —— 49
3.1.3 Other nominal subtypes —— 51
3.2 Noun morphology —— 54
3.2.1 Overt marking of gender/number —— 54
3.2.2 Reduplication —— 57
3.3 Adjective morphology —— 58
3.3.1 The suppletive adjective 'small' —— 60
3.3.2 Bound adjectives —— 61
3.4 The numeral system —— 61
3.5 Morphology of kinship terms —— 63
3.5.1 Consanguineal relatives —— 65
3.5.2 Affinal relatives —— 67
3.6 Compounding —— 68
3.6.1 Types of compounds —— 70
3.7 Derived nominals —— 73
3.7.1 Verb stems used nominally —— 74
3.7.2 Deverbal instrument nouns —— 76
3.7.3 Participles —— 76

4 Pronouns and demonstratives —— 84
4.1 Personal pronouns —— 84
4.2 Demonstratives —— 86
4.2.1 Standard demonstratives —— 87
4.2.2 Emphatic demonstrative —— 91
4.2.3 Property demonstratives —— 94
4.3 Interrogative pronouns —— 95
4.3.1 *enda?* 'Where are you going?' (etc.) —— 96
4.4 The pro-word *ago* —— 97
4.4.1 In compounds —— 97
4.4.2 'What's-it-called' —— 97
4.4.3 Expressing purpose —— 99
4.5 The pro-name *eyal* —— 99

5 Nominal gender —— 101
5.1 Overview of gender agreement —— 102
5.2 Assignment —— 104
5.2.1 Assignment of animates —— 105

5.2.2	Assignment of inanimates — 106	
5.2.3	Referential gender — 109	
5.2.4	Gender doublets — 112	
5.3	More on agreement — 113	
5.3.1	Agreeing targets — 113	
5.3.2	Further remarks on the plural–Gender IV affinity — 115	
5.3.3	Agreement controllers — 118	
6	**Adpositions and particles — 120**	
6.1	Postpositions — 120	
6.1.1	*lek* 'from' — 124	
6.1.2	*ti* 'with' — 125	
6.1.3	*ni* Privative 'without' — 127	
6.1.4	*hi* Similative 'like' — 128	
6.1.5	*nanggo(l)* 'for, towards' — 130	
6.1.6	*en* Possessive-Instrumental — 131	
6.1.7	*se* 'only' — 132	
6.1.8	*nde* 'at' — 133	
6.1.9	*awe* 'for' — 133	
6.1.10	Denominal locational postpositions — 134	
6.2	Prepositions — 135	
6.2.1	*mbi* 'like' — 135	
6.2.2	*yah, yahaa* 'until' — 136	
6.3	Particles — 137	
6.3.1	*ndom* 'also' — 137	
6.3.2	*ay* Vocative, Yes/no-question, etc. — 137	
6.3.3	*a* — 138	
6.3.4	*ma* — 139	
6.3.5	*awi* 'what about…' — 140	
6.3.6	*mahut* 'on the other hand' — 140	
6.3.7	Adversative *yah* — 141	
6.4	Interjections — 143	
6.4.1	General interjections — 143	
6.4.2	Post-sneeze interjections — 145	
7	**The syntax of phrases — 146**	
7.1	The structure of noun phrases — 146	
7.1.1	Tight, left-branching NPs — 146	
7.1.2	Loose nominal expressions — 148	
7.2	NPs with and without demonstratives — 149	
7.2.1	Uses of bare NPs — 150	
7.2.2	Prenominal demonstratives — 151	

7.2.3	Postnominal demonstratives —— 152
7.3	Numerals —— 154
7.4	Postpositional phrases —— 156
7.5	Possession —— 158
7.6	Postposed markers —— 161
7.6.1	The Associative Plural *ke* —— 161
7.6.2	Intensifier *ya* 'real; very' —— 163
7.6.3	Additive *ap* 'also' —— 164
7.7	Quantification —— 165
7.7.1	*isi* 'other, some' —— 165
7.7.2	*mbya* 'all, completely' —— 167
7.7.3	Amount quantification —— 169
7.8	Coordination —— 170
8	**Overview of the verb —— 172**
8.1	Verbs as a word class —— 172
8.2	Macrostructure of the verb complex —— 173
8.3	Affix ordering in the prefixal complex —— 176
8.3.1	Multi-class prefixes and paradigmatic alignment —— 178
8.3.2	Affix mobility —— 178
8.3.3	Further remarks on position class systems —— 183
8.4	Structure of the verb stem —— 184
8.5	The outer suffixes —— 185
9	**Participant indexing I: The Actor, Dative and Genitive prefixes —— 187**
9.1	Overview of participant indexing —— 187
9.1.1	General and typological characteristics —— 187
9.1.2	The place of participant indexing in the verb complex —— 189
9.2	Actor indexing —— 190
9.2.1	Form of the Actor prefixes —— 190
9.2.2	Uses of the Actor prefixes —— 198
9.3	Dative indexing —— 204
9.3.1	Form of the Dative prefixes —— 205
9.3.2	Functions of Dative indexing —— 207
9.4	Genitive indexing —— 212
9.4.1	Form of the Genitive prefixes —— 213
9.4.2	Functions of Genitive indexing —— 214
9.5	The role-neutral 1pl prefix *e-* —— 217
9.6	Inclusory and associative indexing constructions —— 219
9.6.1	Inclusory plural —— 219
9.6.2	Associative indexing —— 220

10	**Participant indexing II: Undergoer alternations** —— 221	
10.1	Overview of Undergoer indexing —— 221	
10.1.1	Indexing of transitive O and patientive S —— 222	
10.1.2	The middle indexing pattern —— 223	
10.2	Undergoer stem alternations —— 224	
10.2.1	Classification of verbs as invariant or alternating —— 226	
10.2.2	Paradigmatic structure of alternating verbs —— 228	
10.2.3	Glossing of verb stems distinguishing number of inanimates —— 230	
10.3	Inflectional classes —— 230	
10.3.1	Class 1: Prefixing verbs —— 231	
10.3.2	Class 2: Infixing verbs —— 231	
10.3.3	Class 3: Suffixing verbs —— 240	
10.3.4	Class 4: Double-marking verbs —— 240	
10.4	Stem alternations according to gender of inanimates —— 242	
10.5	Verbal suppletion according to participant number —— 244	
10.5.1	Paradigmatic structure of suppletive verbs —— 248	
10.5.2	Number vs. pluractionality in verbal suppletion —— 250	

11	**The system of Verb Orientation** —— 253	
11.1	The Orientation prefixes —— 254	
11.1.1	Overview —— 254	
11.1.2	Neutral Orientation ø-, k- —— 257	
11.1.3	Object Orientation m- —— 262	
11.1.4	Directional Orientation k- —— 268	
11.1.5	Locational Orientation nd- —— 276	
11.1.6	Restrictive Orientation s- —— 278	
11.2	Discourse function of the pre-verbal constituent —— 280	
11.2.1	Expressing constituent focus —— 280	
11.2.2	In topic-comment structures —— 283	
11.3	Some morphosyntactic issues —— 286	
11.3.1	Incompatibility of Orientation prefixes with certain clause types —— 286	
11.3.2	Competition for the pre-verbal position —— 289	
11.4	Givenness marker tV-, t- —— 291	
11.4.1	Form of the Given prefix —— 292	
11.4.2	Gender agreement with the Given prefix —— 293	
11.4.3	Function of the Given prefix —— 294	

12	**Valence classes** —— 297	
12.1	Avalent verbs —— 299	
12.1.1	Plain avalent verbs (Type 0a) —— 299	
12.1.2	Avalent verbs with frozen Dative index (Type 0b) —— 299	
12.2	Monovalent verbs —— 299	

12.2.1	Plain intransitive verbs (Type 1a) —— 300	
12.2.2	Patientive intransitives (Type 1b) —— 301	
12.2.3	Middle intransitives (Type 1c) —— 304	
12.2.4	Dative Experiencer intransitives (Type 1d) —— 305	
12.3	Divalent verbs —— 306	
12.3.1	Alternating (Type 2a)/invariant (Type 2b) transitives —— 306	
12.3.2	Middle transitive (Type 2c) —— 307	
12.3.3	Dative O transitives (Type 2d) —— 308	
12.3.4	Genitive O transitives (Type 2e) —— 309	
12.3.5	Complex pseudo-transitives (Type 2f) —— 309	
12.4	Trivalent verbs —— 310	
12.4.1	Ditransitives with secundative indexing (Type 3a) —— 311	
12.4.2	Alternating (Type 3b)/invariant (Type 3c) ditransitives —— 311	
12.4.3	Middle ditransitive 'beg for' (Type 3d) —— 312	
12.5	Patient-preserving lability —— 312	
12.5.1	P-lability and the middle indexing template —— 314	
12.5.2	P-labile verbs and patientive intransitives —— 316	
13	**Valence-changing constructions** —— 319	
13.1	Applicatives —— 319	
13.1.1	Overview of applicative constructions —— 319	
13.1.2	Morphosyntactic properties of applicative arguments —— 321	
13.1.3	Dative indexing of applicative objects —— 324	
13.1.4	Use of the Instrumental applicative (*k-* WITH) —— 326	
13.1.5	Use of the Comitative applicative (*k-* WITH) —— 330	
13.1.6	Use of the Accompaniment applicative *e-* —— 333	
13.1.7	Use of the Allative applicative *ind-* —— 336	
13.1.8	Use of the Separative applicative *is-* —— 339	
13.2	The Reciprocal —— 344	
13.3	Expressing reflexive and causative situations —— 351	
14	**Tense and aspect** —— 354	
14.1	Overview of the tense-aspect system —— 354	
14.1.1	The basic ingressive–durative distinction —— 354	
14.1.2	Temporal interpretation of verb forms —— 357	
14.1.3	Remarks on the aspectual classification of verbs —— 358	
14.2	Functions of tense-aspect affixes —— 361	
14.2.1	The Past Duratives *d-* and *-ti* —— 361	
14.2.2	The Non-Past Imperfective *-e, -et* —— 365	
14.2.3	The Extended *-la* —— 368	
14.2.4	Continuative *anVpand-* —— 374	
14.2.5	The Perfect *mend-* —— 376	

14.2.6	The Habituals —— 381	
14.2.7	The Futures —— 385	

15	**Mood, attitude and engagement —— 396**	
15.1	The Counterfactual *-um* —— 396	
15.2	The Frustrative *um-* —— 399	
15.3	Speaker attitude prefixes —— 402	
15.3.1	The Actualis *b-* —— 403	
15.3.2	The Mirative *bam-* —— 407	
15.3.3	The Affectionate *bat-* —— 410	
15.3.4	The Self-interrogative *bah-* —— 412	
15.3.5	The Presentative *hat-* —— 415	
15.4	Engagement marking: The Deictic prefixes —— 418	
15.4.1	Shape of the Deictic prefixes —— 418	
15.4.2	Realignment of attention —— 419	

16	**Distribution of events in time and space —— 423**	
16.1	Pluractionality —— 423	
16.1.1	General remarks —— 423	
16.1.2	The Pluractional prefix —— 424	
16.1.3	Inherently Pluractional verbs —— 427	
16.1.4	Functions of Pluractional forms —— 429	
16.2	The Repetitive *i-* —— 433	
16.3	The Prioritive *ka-* —— 435	
16.3.1	Expressing a preceding event —— 435	
16.3.2	Similative use —— 437	
16.4	The Remote *an-* —— 438	
16.5	The Contessive *ap-* —— 438	
16.5.1	Marking contact with surface/off of the ground —— 439	
16.5.2	Attenuative use —— 441	
16.5.3	Lexicalised uses of the Contessive —— 443	
16.6	The Inessive —— 444	
16.6.1	Form of the Inessive —— 444	
16.6.2	Use of the Inessive —— 446	
16.7	The Venitive *-em* —— 448	

17	**The Auxiliary, copula clauses and light verbs —— 452**	
17.1	Form and function of the Auxiliary *wa* —— 452	
17.1.1	Form of the Auxiliary —— 452	
17.1.2	Lexical uses —— 455	
17.2	The Auxiliary predicating a preposed verb stem —— 457	
17.2.1	Predication of verb compounds —— 457	

17.2.2	Restrictive focus on verb stems: 'only/just Verb' —— 459	
17.2.3	The Verb-*ti*–Auxiliary construction —— 460	
17.3	The Auxiliary predicating a postposed verb stem —— 461	
17.3.1	The Thetic Predication construction —— 461	
17.3.2	The Predicated Manner construction —— 464	
17.4	The copula and copula clauses —— 467	
17.4.1	Morphology of the copula —— 467	
17.4.2	Nominal and adjectival predication —— 470	
17.4.3	Locative predication —— 472	
17.4.4	Predicative possession: *to have* —— 473	
17.4.5	Copula marking topics —— 474	
17.5	Light verbs —— 474	
17.5.1	*ola* 'be' —— 475	
17.5.2	*win* and *ay* 'become' —— 476	
17.5.3	*onggat* 'become.PLA' —— 477	
18	**Basic clausal syntax —— 479**	
18.1	Grammatical relations —— 479	
18.2	The minimal sentence —— 481	
18.3	Constituent order —— 482	
18.3.1	Arguments —— 482	
18.3.2	Focused constituents —— 482	
18.3.3	Topics —— 485	
18.4	Pre-verbal adverbials —— 487	
18.4.1	*mbya* ø- Negation —— 488	
18.4.2	*ndom* ø- 'still' —— 489	
18.4.3	*oso m-* 'just about to V, just V-ed' —— 490	
18.4.4	Ingressive *ye m-* 'start to V' —— 490	
18.4.5	*anep mayay m-* 'therefore' —— 491	
18.4.6	*tanama k-* 'again' —— 492	
18.4.7	*lun k-* 'without hesitation, straight away' —— 493	
18.4.8	*hindun s-* 'keep on V-ing' —— 493	
18.5	Secondary predication —— 493	
18.6	The Presentational construction —— 497	
19	**Non-declarative speech acts —— 500**	
19.1	Commands —— 500	
19.1.1	Singular and plural imperatives —— 500	
19.1.2	The Jussive *anam-* —— 501	
19.1.3	The Hortative *mat-* —— 503	
19.1.4	The Prohibitive series: *tamohat-* etc. —— 504	
19.1.5	The Relinquitive *adeh* —— 507	

19.2	Polar questions —— 508	
19.2.1	Present Polar Question *Vk-* —— 508	
19.2.2	Past polar question *ap-* —— 509	
19.2.3	Sentence final *ay* —— 510	
19.3	Content questions —— 511	
19.3.1	Morphology of content questions —— 511	
19.3.2	Types of content questions —— 514	
19.3.3	Self-interrogative questions —— 520	
20	**Combinations of clauses** —— 522	
20.1	Subordinate clauses —— 522	
20.1.1	Morphosyntax of subordinate clauses —— 522	
20.1.2	Functions of subordinate clauses —— 529	
20.2	Clause combining by means of *ago* QUOT —— 541	
20.2.1	Reported speech —— 541	
20.2.2	*kumay-mayan* 'inside-speech': reported thought and its extensions —— 543	
20.3	Sequential clause linkage —— 545	
20.3.1	The *epe te-nd-...- V* construction 'at that point, V' —— 549	
20.3.2	Consequential-culminative use of Directional *k-* —— 550	

Appendix: Texts —— 552

Bibliography —— 573

Index —— 585

List of maps, tables and figures

Maps

Map 1   The Anim languages —— 6
Map 2   Marindic and neighbouring languages —— 7

Tables

Tab. 1.1   Correspondences reflecting proto-Marindic *ɣ —— 11
Tab. 1.2   Correspondences reflecting proto-Marindic *j —— 11
Tab. 1.3   Correspondences reflecting proto-Marindic *w —— 11
Tab. 1.4   Correspondences reflecting proto-Marindic *r —— 11
Tab. 1.5   The 9 main clans and some prominent totems —— 16
Tab. 1.6   Population figures —— 19
Tab. 1.7   Codes used in corpus examples —— 23

Tab. 2.1   Consonants —— 24
Tab. 2.2   Minimal pairs for the consonant phonemes —— 29

Tab. 3.1   Temporal nouns —— 53
Tab. 3.2   Overt gender on nouns —— 55
Tab. 3.3   Gender agreement on adjectives —— 59
Tab. 3.4   Gender agreement on three colour adjectives —— 59
Tab. 3.5   Gender agreement on 'small' —— 60
Tab. 3.6   Numerals —— 62
Tab. 3.7   Consanguineal kin terms —— 65
Tab. 3.8   Affinal kin terms —— 67
Tab. 3.9   Verb stems used as nouns —— 75
Tab. 3.10   Lexicalised participles —— 80

Tab. 4.1   Personal pronouns —— 84
Tab. 4.2   Basic demonstratives: gender/number forms —— 86
Tab. 4.3   Property demonstratives: gender/number forms —— 86

Tab. 5.1   Gender assignment of some body parts —— 109
Tab. 5.2   Gender assignment of some common plants —— 110
Tab. 5.3   Overview of agreement targets and their exponents —— 114

Tab. 6.1   Postpositions —— 121

Tab. 6.2	Denominal postpositions —— 121
Tab. 8.1	Paradigm of *lay* 'talk, tell' —— 182
Tab. 8.2	The outer suffixes —— 185
Tab. 9.1	The Actor prefixes —— 191
Tab. 9.2	The Dative prefixes —— 205
Tab. 9.3	The Genitive prefixes —— 213
Tab. 9.4	The Genitive prefixes with *gan* 'hear' —— 214
Tab. 10.1	Summary of the four inflectional classes —— 225
Tab. 10.2	Proportion of alternating stems across some semantic classes —— 227
Tab. 10.3	Class 1 Prefixing verbs —— 232
Tab. 10.4	Class 1 Prefixing verbs displaying irregularities —— 232
Tab. 10.5	Regular infixing verbs —— 236
Tab. 10.6	Some infixing verbs with irregular 3SG.U stems —— 239
Tab. 10.7	Infixing *tuk*-verbs —— 241
Tab. 10.8	Some infixing *tuk*-verbs with irregular 3SG.U stems —— 241
Tab. 10.9	Suffixing verbs —— 242
Tab. 10.10	Double-marking verbs —— 242
Tab. 10.11	Inanimate gender stems that are identical to animate stems —— 243
Tab. 10.12	Some inanimate-only verbs with partly unpredictable Gender III stems —— 244
Tab. 10.13	Some inanimate-only verbs with stems in -*k* and -*b* —— 245
Tab. 10.14	Some inanimate-only verbs with unpredictable III vs. IV stems —— 246
Tab. 10.15	'Paired' verbs: Inanimate-only verbs with related animate verbs —— 247
Tab. 10.16	Suppletion according to participant number —— 248
Tab. 11.1	Overview of the Orientation prefixes and their uses —— 255
Tab. 11.2	Uses of the Neutral Orientation prefixes —— 262
Tab. 11.3	Uses of the Object Orientation prefix *m*- —— 267
Tab. 11.4	Uses of the Directional Orientation prefix *k*- —— 275
Tab. 12.1	Valence patterns —— 298
Tab. 12.2	Some patientive intransitive verbs —— 301
Tab. 12.3	Some intransitive middle verbs —— 305
Tab. 12.4	Two types of standard transitive verbs —— 307
Tab. 12.5	P-labile verbs —— 318
Tab. 13.1	Standard and applicative Dative indexing —— 325
Tab. 13.2	Paradigm of *ihon* 'run away' with Separative *is*- —— 327
Tab. 13.3	Some frequent Comitative verbs —— 330

List of maps, tables and figures — XIX

Tab. 14.1 Overview of tense-aspect morphology —— 355
Tab. 14.2 Punctual-durative verb pairs —— 360
Tab. 14.3 Some Extended stems with resultative meaning —— 371
Tab. 14.4 Gender forms of the Continuative prefix —— 375
Tab. 14.5 The General Future —— 390
Tab. 14.6 The Non-Asserted Future —— 390

Tab. 15.1 The Deictic verb prefixes —— 418

Tab. 16.1 Inherently Pluractional verbs and suppletive plural stems —— 429
Tab. 16.2 Some verb pairs differing in the presence of Contessive *ap-* —— 443

Tab. 17.1 The copula —— 468

Tab. 18.1 Constituent order in a sample of three texts —— 483

Tab. 19.1 The Prohibitive —— 505
Tab. 19.2 The Prohibitive + Contessive —— 506
Tab. 19.3 The Prohibitive + Genitive —— 507
Tab. 19.4 Semantic categories in content questions —— 515

Tab. 20.1 Syntactic roles of relativised nominals —— 533

Figures

Fig. 2.1   The vowel inventory —— 31

Fig. 5.1   Exponents of agreement on two targets —— 103
Fig. 5.2   Some gender doublets —— 112

Fig. 8.1   Position classes of the prefixal complex —— 177
Fig. 8.2   Structure of morphologically complex verb stems —— 184

Fig. 9.1   Overview of the position of participant indexing within the prefixal complex —— 190

Fig. 15.1 Use of the Presentative *hat-* —— 416
Fig. 15.2 Use of the Deictic verb prefix —— 420
Fig. 15.3 Another use of the Deictic verb prefix —— 421

Fig. 17.1 The Thetic Predication construction —— 461

Fig. 17.2   The Predicated Manner construction —— 465

Fig. 18.1   The Presentational construction —— 497

Fig. 20.1   Pitch track and waveform for example (1079) —— 528
Fig. 20.2   Pitch track and waveform for example (1080) —— 528
Fig. 20.3   The Subordinate Predicated Manner construction —— 537
Fig. 20.4   Pitch track and waveform for example (1125) —— 547

Abbreviations and conventions

The interlinearisation of examples follows the Leipzig Glossing Rules, except that the prefixal complex is separated orthographically from the verb stem by a blank step (§1.1.1.2, §8.2).

The inherent gender of a noun that acts as the controller of agreement is indicated within parentheses, e.g. dog(II).

Names of language-specific categories and constructions are capitalised in the text (e.g. Gender II, the Accompaniment prefix, the Predicated Manner construction).

Gloss	Label	Explanation
[…]	Boundaries of subordinate clause	
(m)	Malay/Indonesian word	
1, 2, 3	1st, 2nd 3rd person	
SG, PL	singular, plural	
2|3	2nd or 3rd person	
I, II, III, IV	Genders I, II, III and IV	Chapter 5
3PL>1	3pl Actor acts on 1st person	§9.2.2.3
Ø	Zero verb stem (copula)	§17.4
A	Actor	§9.2
ACPN	Accompaniment	§13.1.6
ACT	Actualis	§15.3.1
AFF	Affectionate	§15.3.3
ALL	Allative	§13.1.7
APL	Associative plural	§7.6.1
CONT	Continuative	§14.2.4
CT	Contessive	§16.5
CTFT	Counterfactual	§15.1
DAT	Dative	§9.3
DEP	Dependent	§20.1.1.1
DIR	Directional Orientation	§11.1.4
DIST	Distal (demonstrative)	§4.2.1
DIST	Distal (verb prefix)	§15.4
DUR	Past Durative	§14.2.1
EXT	Extended	§14.2.3
FRUS	Frustrative	§15.2
FUT	Future	§14.2.7
GEN	Genitive	§9.4
GIV	Given	§11.4
HAB	Habitual	§14.2.6
HORT	Hortative	§19.1.3

SLF.INT	Self-interrogative	§15.3.4
IMP	Imperative	§19.1.1
INESS	Inessive	§16.6
INGRS	Ingressive	§18.4.4
INSTR	Instrumental	§6.1.6
IPFV	Non-past Imperfective	§14.2.2
JUS	Jussive	§19.1.2
LOC	Locational Orientation	§11.1.5
MIR	Mirative	§15.3.2
NAFUT	Non-Asserted Future	§14.2.7
NEG	Negative	§18.4.1
NTRL	Neutral Orientation	§11.1.2
NPST	Non-past	§17.4.1
OBJ	Object Orientation	§11.1.3
ONLY	Restrictive Orientation	§11.1.6
PERF	Perfect	§14.2.5
PL.IMP	Plural Imperative	§19.1.1
PLA	Pluractional	§16.1
POSS	Possessive	§6.1.6
PRI	Prioritive	§16.3
PRNM	Pro-name	§4.5
PROH	Prohibitive	§19.1.4
PRWD	Pro-word	§4.4
PROX	Proximal (demonstrative)	§4.2.1
PROX	Proximal (verb prefix)	§15.4
PRS	Present	
PRSTV	Presentative	§15.3.5
PST	Past	
PTCL	Particle	§6.3
PTCP	Participial	§3.7.3
Q	Polar question	§19.2
QUOT	Quotative	§20.2
RCPR	Reciprocal	§13.2
RE	Repetitive	§16.2
REM	Remote (demonstrative)	§4.2.1
REM	Remote (verb prefix)	§16.4
RLQ	Relinquitive	§19.1.5
ROG	Interrogative	§19.3.1
SEP	Separative	§13.1.8
U	Undergoer	§10.1
VEN	Venitive	§16.7
WITH	Instrumental-Comitative	§13.1.4, §13.1.5

Kinship abbreviations (§3.5)

B	brother
C	child
D	daughter
E	elder
F	father
G	grand- (e.g. GC grandchild)
H	husband
M	mother
P	parent
S	son
W	wife
Y	younger
Z	sister

1 Preliminaries

1.1 General information

The Coastal Marind language is spoken by ca. 7,000–9,000 people in Southern New Guinea. The 27 villages in which the language is spoken are situated on the coast of the Arafura Sea and along the Kumbe river, on territory that today belongs to Indonesia. The term 'Marind' is also used to denote a larger ethnic group consisting of speakers of the other Marindic languages (Bush Marind and Upper Bian Marind) as well as some neighbouring groups who speak unrelated languages (such as Marori) but who were (and are) under strong cultural and political influence of the larger Marindic-speaking group (van Baal 1966).

The origin of the word *marind* (in the Eastern dialect of Coastal Marind) or *malin* (in the Western dialect described here) is unknown. It is perhaps related to the name Maro, which is one of the main rivers in the Marind territory.

The Marindic languages are members of the Anim family (Usher and Suter 2015), a group comprising at least 15 languages spread across the linguistically diverse southern lowlands. It is likely that the Anim family will prove to be related to other languages in New Guinea, as a member of the so-called Trans-New Guinea family. Although the details of such relationships remain to be worked out, it is clear that the Marindic languages (and probably Anim in general) are typologically very different from other Trans-New Guinea languages (Wurm 1982: 95, Evans 2012: 117). For an overview of the languages of the Southern New Guinea area, see Evans et al. (2018a).

This grammar describes the Western dialect of Coastal Marind, as it is spoken in the villages Wambi and Duhmilah, and, with minor variations, in the surrounding villages. For information on the Eastern dialect, see Drabbe (1955).

1.1.1 Structural profile

1.1.1.1 Phonology
Coastal Marind has a relatively simple phonology (Chapter 2), like many other Papuan languages. There is a standard 5-vowel inventory /a e i o u/. The 19-member consonant inventory is slightly more unusual since it contrasts plain and prenasalised stops (e.g. /p b mb/) and contains the preaspirated/voiceless glides /ʰj ʰw/. There is no lexical tone. Stress is generally root-final and primarily realised by pitch. Lengthening is not distinctive.

1.1.1.2 Verbs
Verb morphology is extremely complex. I describe the verb structure as consisting of two independent phonological words — the 'prefixal complex' and the verb stem —

which together form the verb complex (Chapter 8). The prefixal complex is a tight-knit affix cluster that may contain exponents of a wide range of inflectional categories, including: person/number indexing of agent-, recipient- and possessor-like participants, various types of aspectual morphology, two types of future marking, several applicative-like categories, various types of commands, marking of polar question as well as content questions, and an array of other markers that resist easy labelling. The inflectional categories are ordered according to a position class template, without any hierarchical structure or head-like elements (which could have motivated a description of the affix cluster as an inflecting auxiliary). Concatenation of the affixes involves complicated morphophonological processes. These are always predictable, however, and the following verb stem does not trigger any lexically specified affix suppletion, since it is phonologically separated from the prefixal complex.

The verb stem is itself host to a number of grammatical categories, such as Comitative and Pluractional prefixation. The exponents of these categories are generally more irregular than the affixes of the prefixal complex and their form as well as their meaning must sometimes be lexically stipulated. The verb stem is often followed by a suffix; this suffixal class primarily expresses aspectual notions.

In the interlinear glossing I separate the prefixal complex from the verb stem by means of a blank step, which indicates that they are independent phonological words. I add a trailing hyphen after the prefixal complex to indicate that the affix cluster forms a grammatical unit together with the ensuing stem. Examples:

(1) a. *katal ip-i-namb-ap-   ig-made*
money DIST:I/II.PL-3PL>1-1.GEN-CT- beg:2|3PL.U-PRS.HAB
'They usually ask me for money.'

b. *ndom-ago men-b-u-n-ind-a-y-   kama⟨y⟩in*
bad-PRWD:III PERF-ACT-2SG.A-1.DAT-ALL-1.DAT-1PL- make⟨2SG.U⟩
'You have done something bad to us.' [W19:0072]

When citing examples from this grammar, authors may follow this convention, or they may choose to remove the blank step between the prefix cluster and the stem, as in (2a), or remove the trailing hyphen, as in (2b), according to their own preferences.

(2) Alternative renditions of example (1a)

a. *katal ip-i-namb-ap-ig-made*
money DIST:I/II.PL-3PL>1-1.GEN-CT-beg:2|3PL.U-PRS.HAB

b. *katal ip-i-namb-ap   ig-made*
money DIST:I/II.PL-3PL>1-1.GEN-CT beg:2|3PL.U-PRS.HAB

The most complicated exponence is exhibited by the stem alternations realising person/number of the patient-like argument, which is present in ca. 50% of all verbs, and must be lexically specified as either prefixing, infixing, suffixing or double-marking depending on the inflectional class of the verb. Alternations according to the patient-like argument combine with the three types of person/number markers of the prefixal complex to form an intricate indexing system. The system exhibits semantic alignment, and displays a fundamental distinction between the agent-like participant of e.g. 'dance' and 'hit' from the patient-like participant of 'fall' and 'hit'. Participant indexing in the verb distinguishes three persons and two numbers, although 2nd and 3rd person plural is conflated in most paradigms (Chapter 9).

1.1.1.3 Nominals

The vast majority of nominals are invariant, so there is no case or number marking on nouns (Chapter 3). Exceptions are: kinship terms, which inflect for possessor, a subset of adjectives agreeing according to gender/number, and handful of frequent nouns that exhibit overt gender gender/number marking (e.g. *anem* 'man', *anum* 'woman', *anim* 'people').

Nouns are assigned to one of four genders: male humans (Gender I), female humans and all animals (Gender II), and inanimates (divided between Genders III & IV) – see Chapter 5. Beyond adjectives, gender agreement is found in a wide range of targets, such as demonstratives, interrogative pronouns, a small group of agreeing postpositions, and some of the verbal categories realised in the prefixal complex. Members of Genders I & II (i.e. all animates) combine gender agreement with expression of singular/plural number, whereas inanimates make no number distinction. A particularly complex issue in the description of gender agreement is its interaction with participant indexing in the verb stem (§10.4).

In addition to the subset of agreeing adjectives, gender is reflected in participles, which are productively derived from verbs by means of suffixation. There are no productive nominalisation strategies, but verb stems (stripped of the preceding affix cluster) are often used in the syntactic slot associated with nominals, and could be seen as zero-derived verbal nouns. Frequent use is made of compounds, which can be built from nouns, adjectives, verb stems, and other categories.

1.1.1.4 Syntax

Constituent order in Coastal Marind is relatively free, and is never used on its own to distinguish participant roles (Chapter 18). There is a weak tendency to place arguments and adjuncts before the verb complex. The most important syntactic position of the clause is the slot immediately preceding the verb complex, which has among its functions that of hosting a constituent that is assigned focus (Chapter 11). This dedicated focus slot interacts with a set of prefixes ('Orientation prefixes') in the prefixal complex which marks the role of the focused constituent. For example, the Neutral ø- marks the verb as oriented towards a focused constituent expressing the S/A-argument (3a), whereas the Object m- marks the verb as oriented towards a focused O-argument (3b).

(3) a. Answer to: 'Who hit him/her?'

      ehway   ø-a-   *w-amuk*
      father:3   NTRL-3SG.A-   3SG.U-hit

      'Father hit him/her.'

b. Answer to: 'Who did s/he hit?'

      ehway   m-a-   *w-amuk*
      father:3   OBJ-3SG.A-   3SG.U-hit

      'S/he hit Father.'

As this example suggests, the Orientation system functions according to a nominative-accusative basis, and interacts with the semantically aligned participant indexing system to create an elaborate set of valence classes (Chapter 12).

Noun phrase syntax is weakly developed (Chapter 7). Adjectival modification is mainly carried out by means of compounding (e.g. *yalet-anem*, lit. 'evil-man'; compounds are head-final) or by means of syntactically independent adjectival expressions used e.g. as secondary predicates (§18.5). Demonstratives used as determiners may be preposed (*upe nggat* 'that dog'), postposed (*nggat upe*), or circumposed (*upe nggat upe*) without any perceivable contrast in meaning. Adnominally used postpositional phrases precede the head noun, as in (4). When an agreeing postposition — such as *ni* 'without' in (4b) (in its Gender I form *ne*) — heads an adnominal PostP, the controller of gender agreement is the higher noun (*anem* 'man') and not the noun inside the PostP (*katal* 'money').

(4) a. *Mapi en bawan*   b. *katal ne anem*
    M. POSS clan   money(IV) without:I man(I)
    'the clans of the Mapi people'   'a man without money'

Coastal Marind does not use subordinate clauses to express e.g. reported speech (or thought). Instead the quotative particle *ago* is used, followed by a verbatim rendition of the quoted utterance or thought. I give two translations for example (5): one using direct discourse, and one using indirect discourse (with shifted deicticals). Both correspond to the *ago*-strategy in Coastal Marind.

(5) mesiwag nok ø-nak-o-   ayi ago
    old.woman 1   NTRL-1.A-3SG.DAT- say QUOT

   "e=   ka-p-e-   n-alaw   sayam"
   PROX= DIR-FUT:1.A-1PL- 1.U-search wallaby

   'I said to my wife: "Here we will look for wallabies".'
   'I told my wife that we were going to look for wallabies there.'   [W12:0027]

A general subordinate clause-construction can be used adverbially or to describe a referent. The adverbial and referential uses are not distinguished overtly, so an alternative translation of (6) is 'When that dog was sick yesterday, did it die?'. As indicated by the bracketing, the referent 'dog' is expressed inside the subordinate clause here; the head may also occur in the main clause, with the relative clause used paratactically and placed either before or after the rest of the sentence (see Chapter 20).

(6) wis   nggat   elel a-d-ø-   ola   upe,   ap-ø-   kahwid?
    [yesterday dog(II) sick DEP-DUR-3SG.A- be:3SG.U DIST:II] PST.Q-3SG.A- die:3SG.U

   'The dog that was sick yesterday, did it die?'

Switch-reference structures and serial verb constructions, often said to be characteristic of Papuan languages, are absent in Coastal Marind.

1.2 Relationships with other languages

In this section I describe the place of Marindic within the Anim family (§1.2.1) and situate Coastal Marind within the Marindic subgroup (§1.2.2). Finally, some brief information on language contact is given (§1.2.3).

1.2.1 The Marindic languages and the Anim language family

Coastal Marind and the other Marindic languages are members of the Anim language family. This family (named after the recurrent word *anim* 'people') was first identified by Usher and Suter (2015), and groups together a number of languages spoken across the South Papuan lowlands.

Usher and Suter recognise four subfamilies within Anim, as shown in Map 1. The Marindic languages are members of the westernmost branch of Anim, which also includes the poorly known languages Yaqay and Warkay-Bipim, spoken to the northwest of the Marind territory. The genealogical relationships between Marindic, Yaqay and the Lake Murray languages, spoken in Papua New Guinea to the northeast of Marind, have long been noted in the literature (Usher and Suter 2015: 133), but the relatedness

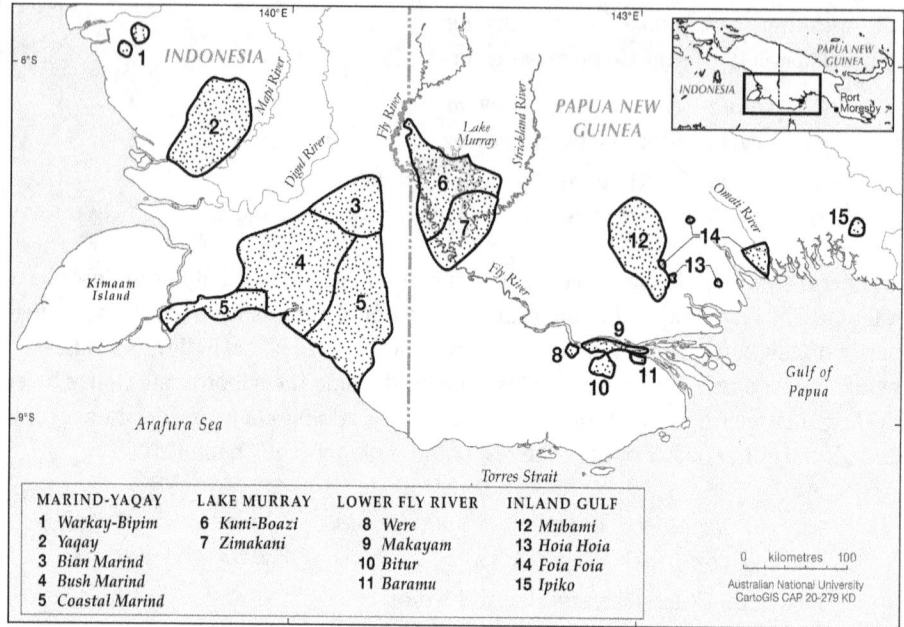

Map 1: The Anim language family

of these languages and the eastern branches (Lower Fly River and Inland Gulf) was first established in Usher and Suter's important work.

The pronominal forms reconstructed for the Anim subfamilies, e.g. Proto–Marindic-Yaqay 1sg *nok, 2sg *oy, resemble the person forms that have been reconstructed for the so-called Trans-New Guinea super-family (e.g. 1sg *na, 2sg *ŋga in Ross 2005). Linguists have proposed various incarnations of this language family, typically including an enormous number of languages from all over New Guinea, and reaching down to a time-depth that makes the application of the comparative method difficult. In this respect Trans-New Guinea is comparable to e.g. the Nostratic family that has been proposed for languages of Eurasia. More precise knowledge about the place of Anim within Trans-New Guinea is probably not to be expected within the near future. There are, however, other families within the proposed Trans-New Guinea phylum that feature interesting similarities with Anim (e.g. Ok, which shows striking parallels in its gender system; Usher and Suter 2015: 137, Olsson 2019b: 217–219). This suggests promising directions for future investigations of the wider relationships of the Anim family.

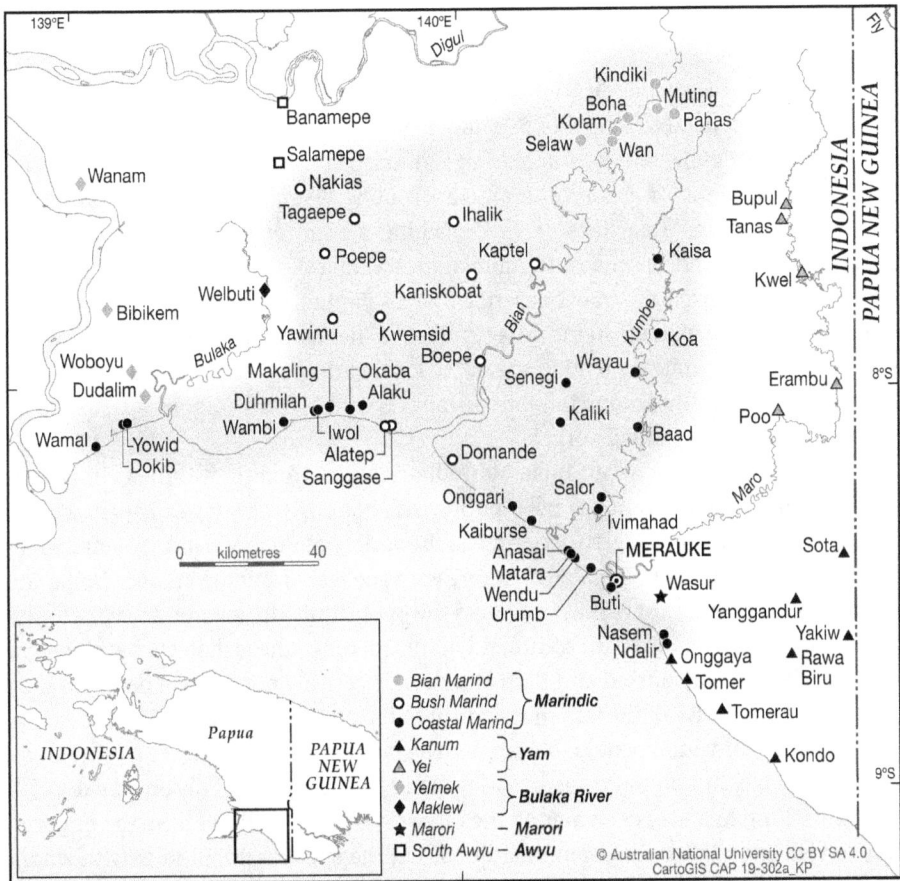

Map 2: Marindic and neighbouring languages

1.2.2 The Marindic languages

I consider there to be three distinct languages within the Marindic subgroup: Coastal Marind (whose Western dialect is described in this grammar), Bush Marind and Upper Bian Marind (or Bian Marind). The approximate extent of the Marindic-speaking area is shown by the shading in Map 2.

Coastal Marind is spoken along the Kumbe river and along the coast, except for three villages at the mouth of the Bian river. Bush Marind is spoken in 9 villages in the hinterland north of Okaba. In addition, the inhabitants of the three villages at the mouth of the Bian (Sanggase and its satellite village Alatep to the west, and Domande to the east) speak what seem to be somewhat divergent varieties of Bush Marind; these villages are in intense contact with Coastal Marind. Coastal Marind and Bush Marind are closely related.[1]

Bian Marind is spoken in 7 villages on the upper course of the Bian river, and is more distantly related to the other two languages.

The Eastern dialect of Coastal Marind is described in an early grammar by Geurtjens (1926), in Drabbe's masterful grammar (Drabbe 1955) and in the impressive dictionary by Geurtjens (Geurtjens 1933). The addition of my own work on the language (e.g. Olsson 2017 and the present grammar, describing the Western dialect) possibly makes Coastal Marind the 'most described' of all Papuan languages. Coastal Marind is an endangered language in the villages close to the district capital Merauke, where speakers of all generations tend to speak the local variety of Malay instead of Marind. Language use is still vigorous in more distant Coastal Marind communities, such as Wambi, where I did my fieldwork.

Very little is known about Bush Marind, and apart from the wordlists in Lebold et al. (2010) no information has been published about this language.[2] I spent a week in 2015 in Sanggase and Alatep, working on the variety of Bush Marind spoken there. I also spent a few hours in Merauke working with speakers from the villages Domande and Ihalik. It is unfortunate that I only had the opportunity to work on the varieties of Bush Marind spoken in the far south and far north. Since these dialects have been in contact with Coastal Marind and Bian Marind respectively one can suspect that they are not representative of the varieties spoken in the core of the Bush Marind area.

It seems that young people in Alatep, Sanggase and Domande have a good grasp of the language, but prefer to speak Malay amongst themselves. I observed extensive code-switching to Malay even among the oldest speakers. I did not have the opportunity to visit any of the villages in the inland, but the speaker from Ihalik with whom I worked reported that the local language remains vigorous in all generations in her village, which is the most remote of the Bush Marind-speaking communities.

For Bian Marind there is a short description of the verb (Drabbe n.d. 27–45) and an unpublished wordlist (Drabbe 1947), as well as more recent unpublished wordlists collected by Peter Jan de Vries of the SIL. I spent two weeks in Muting in 2016 working with speakers of Bian Marind. The youngest confident speakers of the language whom I met were in their 40s, so Bian Marind is clearly an endangered language.

---

1 In Olsson (2017), I referred to 'Central Marind' (because of its location between the Bian and Coastal groups) for what I now call Bush Marind. I am not aware of any Marind names that map exactly onto the linguistic boundaries, but *deg-anim* 'bush-people' and *deg-mayan* 'bush-speech' are often used to refer to the inhabitants of the inland villages and the varieties spoken by them, although these terms exclude the three Bush Marind-speaking villages on the coast.
2 Drabbe (1955) contains a short wordlist from Domande, probably the least representative of the Bush varieties. There are also scattered remarks on lexical features in Geurtjens (1933).

1.2.2.1 Languages vs. dialects

My designation of Coastal Marind, Bush Marind and Bian Marind as three separate languages differs from the views of the previous literature. Early observers, such as Geurtjens (1926, 1933) and Drabbe (1955) lump the three units together as dialects of a single language. These researchers operated with a very different idea of what counts as a dialect, and all modern scholars have identified Bian Marind as a language separate from the other two units. This is the stance taken by van Baal (1966: 11) and Voorhoeve (1975: 358), as well as all later sources. I agree with the classification of Bian Marind as a separate language, and will not elaborate further on it here. In the following pages I will mainly discuss evidence that Coastal and Bush Marind are best described as two distinct languages, and not as divergent dialects.

No researchers have suggested that Coastal and Bush Marind should be considered separate languages. The only source that discusses the status of Bush vs. Coastal Marind is the dialect survey by Lebold et al. (2010), and I will discuss their findings in brief here. As customary in the reports produced by SIL International, the survey team gauged the dialect situation by (i) asking speakers about perceived similarity and intercomprehension between varieties, and (ii) computing lexical similarity using wordlists.[3]

The survey reports that speakers in the coastal villages (from Alaku in the east to Wambi in the west) consider the inhabitants of the inland villages (Ihalik, Kaptel, etc.) to speak a dialect different from theirs, and vice versa — but not a different language (see Lebold et al. 2010: 23). This finding agrees with my own experience. All villagers that I asked in Wambi told me that the Marind people of the inland speak the same Marind language as themselves, albeit with a different accent (Malay *logat*) that gets more broken (*tamba rusak*) as one travels up north. However, speakers also claim that the Bian people are speakers of a different dialect, although all modern outside observers consider Bian Marind to be a distinct language. This is seen in Lebold et al.'s survey, which reports that speakers in 6 out of 7 coastal and inland villages consider Bian Marind to be a different dialect of the same language. This shows that the local idea of what it means to 'speak the same language' has more to do with ethnic and political unity than linguistic similarity, and should not serve as a basis for a language/dialect distinction in the sense used by linguists.[4]

---

[3] A short wordlist containing 69 items was used in 11 villages (6 Coastal-speaking and 5 Bush Marind-speaking villages), and a long wordlist containing 240 words was used in 3 villages (1 Coastal-speaking and 2 Bush Marind-speaking villages). These wordlists appear to be designed by the SIL specifically for use in Papua, and contain basic vocabulary as well as some typically Papuan terminology ('sago', 'cassowary', etc.).

[4] I have no systematic information on mutual intelligibility. According to my observations, adult villagers in Wambi and Sanggase have no major problems communicating, but the variety of Bush Marind spoken in Sanggase is much more similar to Coastal Marind than the other inland varieties are. Inhabitants from the two villages often have opportunities to interact, and thereby get used to each other's

The results of Lebold et al.'s lexicostatistical investigation are somewhat ambiguous. The team finds that the lexical similarity between the Bush varieties and the Coastal varieties west of the Bian river are too close to be considered different languages: the lowest score is 65% similarity (for Kaptel and Alaku), which is above the 60% threshold used by the survey team. However, lower scores are observed for the Coastal villages east of Bian (39–56% similarity with Bush Marind). My interpretation of this is that Lebold et al. managed to capture the difference between Bush Marind and the eastern varieties of Coastal Marind, whereas the differences between Bush Marind and the geographically close western Coastal varieties are masked by a few cases of lexical diffusion from Bush Marind that show up in the short word lists they use.

All varieties of Coastal Marind are very similar grammatically, and differ clearly in this respect from the known varieties of Bush Marind. This suggests that Coastal Marind is a distinct language, but that its western varieties have been influenced by Bush Marind, which makes the differences between the languages difficult to identify from short word lists. In the following subsections I give some examples of features that distinguish the languages, and some that appear to have been diffused over the language boundaries.

1.2.2.2 Sound changes

It is difficult to find clear examples of phonological innovations that respect the boundaries of the three Marindic languages, or that distinguish the more closely related Bush Marind and Coastal Marind from Bian Marind. Here I will present some of the more important consonant correspondences between the languages, represented by the varieties spoken in Ihalik and Kaptel (for Bush Marind), Wambi and Buti (for Coastal Marind), and Wan (for Bian Marind). The Kaptel data is from Lebold et al. (2010); the rest was collected by me. The proto-phonemes and sound changes given here follow Usher and Suter (2015: 126–133).[5]

An innovation that separates Bush Marind from the other two languages is the debuccalisation of proto-Marindic *ɣ into a glottal stop (Table 1.1). The original velar

---

speech. Some Wambi villagers claimed that they can understand the speech of the inland people, although they also admitted that it is difficult.

[5] For a fuller picture of sound correspondences within Marindic, see the "Marind" section of Usher's monumental *newguineaworld* project (Usher 2020). I am grateful to Timothy Usher for generously sharing his sound correspondences and for discussing them with me. The data presented here represent a fraction of what is known about sound changes in Marindic and other branches of Anim thanks to Usher's work. As of 2020, his data sets on Marindic could be accessed on https://sites.google.com/site/newguineaworld/families/trans-new-guinea/fly-river/marind-yakhai/marind. The interpretations in Olsson (2017: 33–35) differed slightly from Usher's reconstructions, but these details will have to be left for future comparative work.

Tab. 1.1: Correspondences reflecting proto-Marindic *ɣ

	Bush (Ihalik)	Bush (Kaptel)	Coastal (Wambi)	Coastal (Buti)	Bian
	ʔ	∅/ʔ	ɣ	h	ɣ
NIGHT	ʔap	ap	ɣap	hap	ɣap
LIE DOWN	ʔal	–	ɣali	hari	ɣali
EAT	ʔi	ey	ɣi	hi	ɣi
WALLABY	–	–	saɣam	saham	saɣam
INSIDE	kumoʔ	kumaʔ	kumaɣ	kumah	kmaɣ

Tab. 1.2: Correspondences reflecting proto-Marindic *j

	Bush (Ihalik)	Bush (Kaptel)	Coastal (Wambi)	Coastal (Buti)	Bian
	-h	-h	-h	-z	-z
NAME	igih	igih	igih	igiz	igiz
BOW	mih	mih	mih	miz	miz
	-ʰj-	-ʰj-	-ʰj-	-z-	-z-
WIFE:3	uʰjum	εʰjum	uʰjum	uzum	uzum
BIRD	uʰjub	uʰjub	uʰjub	uzub	uzub

Tab. 1.3: Correspondences reflecting proto-Marindic *w

	Bush (Ihalik)	Bush (Kaptel)	Coastal (Wambi)	Coastal (Buti)	Bian
	h	h	h	v	v
VILLAGE	milah	milah	milah	mirav	milav
WALLABY	waleh	waleh	waleh	warev	walev
FIRE	takoh	təkah	takah	takav	tekav
MANY/ALL	utih	?	otih	otiv	utiv
CANOE	yahun	?	yahun	yavun	yavun

Tab. 1.4: Correspondences reflecting proto-Marindic *r

	Bush (Ihalik)	Bush (Kaptel)	Coastal (Wambi)	Coastal (Buti)	Bian
	l	l	l	ɾ	l
FUR	lul	lul	lul	ɾuɾ	lul
RIVER	lik	leki	aliki	ɾiki	liki

fricative was retained in Bian Marind as well as Coastal Marind, where it underwent an independent process of debuccalisation into /h/ in the Eastern dialect.

Other changes show clear evidence of areal diffusion across the language borders. Table 1.2 shows the fate of proto-Marindic *j, which is occluded to /z/ in Bian Marind and the Eastern dialect of Coastal Marind, but changed into /h/ or /ʰj/ (depending on the context) in Bush Marind and the adjacent Western dialect of Coastal Marind. The same areal pattern is seen in the development of proto-Marindic *w, which became /v/ in Bian Marind and the Eastern dialect of Coastal Marind, and /h/ in Bush Marind and the Western dialect of Coastal Marind.

Proto-Marindic *r is realised as a retroflex [ɽ] in the Eastern dialect of Coastal Marind, but as lateral [l] in all other varieties (Table 1.4).

The three languages differ drastically in their phonotactics, with Bush Marind, and especially Bian Marind, permitting consonant clusters that are impossible in Coastal Marind, e.g. Bian Marind [kmaɣ] 'inside' (Coastal Marind kumaɣ), [mhuk] 'Crowned Pigeon' (Coastal mahuk) and [bhik] 'pig' (Coastal basik). Bush Marind permits similar clusters in derived environments.

1.2.2.3 Grammar

It is clear that Bian Marind and Bush Marind share the general structural profile of the better known Coastal Marind: a complex verb structure with a prefix cluster and intricate stem alternations, and an almost complete absence of nominal morphology — these traits seem to be found across the Anim family. I was also able to elicit the same four genders in Bush Marind and Bian Marind as in Coastal Marind, using nouns such as 'man' (Gender I), 'woman' (II), 'stomach' (III) and 'nose' (IV) and so on.[6] Beyond these similarities it is clear that Bian Marind has a more complex person/number system, adding dual number in the 3rd person (Drabbe 1954). Since there is general agreement that Bian Marind is a separate language, I will only add some information about grammatical differences between Coastal and Bush Marind here. (The data is taken from the variety spoken in one of the northernmost villages, Ihalik.)

Bush Marind has a remarkably small pronoun inventory, consisting of *nok* 'I, we' and *oʔ* 'you (sg/pl)'. The lack of a 2pl pronoun distinguishes it from the inventory of Coastal Marind; cf. Western dialect *nok* 'I, we', *oɣ* 'you (sg)', *yoɣ* 'you (pl)'. The lack of number also recurs in participant indexing, in which plural number for 1st and 2nd person arguments is indicated by special, role-neutral prefixes. These have the shape *e-* for both 1st and 2nd person (realised as *y-* in coda position), but apparently appear in different slots in the prefix template, since they can co-occur (7b). Compare

---

[6] Gender assignment seems to be remarkably consistent across the languages, so that the genders match across languages even when the nouns are not cognate: for example, none of the words for 'stomach' are cognate (Coastal *yandam*, Bush *ibus*, Bian *yamu*), yet all are Gender III — matching genders were also found with the other few dozens of nouns that I was able to check for gender.

this situation with Coastal Marind, which only uses a role-neutral plural prefix for 1st person arguments (8).

(7) Bush Marind (Ihalik variety)

a. *ab-o-da-y-*   *n-idih*
PERF-2.A-ASPECT-1PL- 1.U-see
'You (sg) have already seen us.'

b. *ab-o-d-e-y-*   *n-idih*
PERF-2.A-ASPECT-2PL-1PL- 1.U-see
'You (pl) have already seen us.'

(8) Coastal Marind (Wambi variety)

a. *mend-o-y-*   *n-idih*
PERF-2SG.A-1PL- 1.U-see
'You (sg) have already seen us.'

b. *mend-e-y-*   *n-idih*
PERF-2PL.A-1PL- 1.U-see
'You (pl) have already seen us.'

These examples also indicate other differences in the inflectional systems of the languages. For example, the Bush Marind prefix *ab-* does not appear to be cognate with (what I assume is) its Coastal counterpart, the Perfect *mend-*. There is also a common prefix *d-* (or *da-*) in Bush Marind, which seems to be cognate with the Coastal prefix *d-* ('Past Durative') but the two prefixes seem to have different meanings in the two languages (cf. its absence in the Coastal examples above).

Other important differences are illustrated in the following examples. Apart from the non-cognacy of the Imperative affixes (Bush *nda-/nd-*, Coastal *ah-* and *-em*), the examples show that the distribution of suppletive verb stems differs between the languages, as it is not triggered by 2nd person plural subjects in Bush Marind (the suppletive stem *naʔam* 'many come' only occurs with 3pl subjects in Bush Marind).

(9) Bush Marind (Ihalik variety)

a. *nda- ma!*
IMP- come
'Come!' (2sg addr.)

b. *nd-e- ma!*
IMP-2PL- come
'Come!' (2pl addr.)

(10) Coastal Marind (Wambi variety)

a. *ah- man!*
IMP- come
'Come!' (2sg addr.)

b. *ah- nayam-em!*
IMP- come.PL-PL.IMP
'Come!' (2pl addr.)

The discrepancies seen in these examples seem to be representative of the overall divergence between the verb systems of Bush Marind and Coastal Marind. Providing tentative glosses for these simple forms in Bush Marind is relatively straightforward using the analysis of Coastal Marind as a basis, but becomes non-trivial as soon as longer forms are considered. These differences present the strongest reasons for considering Bush Marind and Coastal Marind to be separate languages rather than divergent dialects of a single language. The grammatical systems of the Eastern and Western dialects of the Coastal Marind language are almost identical in their morphological structure – despite being phonologically quite divergent – and do not come close to the differences between Bush Marind and Coastal Marind seen in the examples above.

1.2.3 Language contact

The Coastal Marind language has had an important influence on the smaller, unrelated languages spoken by neighbouring groups. This is clear for the Bulaka River family, consisting of the languages Yelmek and Maklew spoken at the western border of the Coastal Marind area, and especially for the isolate Marori, spoken at the eastern border. These groups assimilated to Marind culture, adopted the Marind clan system, and followed the Marind cults (van Baal 1966: 13–16). Lexical diffusion from Coastal Marind into the Bulaka River languages and Marori can be seen from the 388-term wordlists collected in the Yamfinder database (Carroll et al. 2016). In the wordlist from the Welbuti village, where Maklew (of the Bulaka River family) is spoken, I identified 24 words that are likely loans from Coastal Marind (6%), whereas the Marori list contained 63 (16%) likely loans from Coastal Marind.[7] There also seem to be some grammatical calques from Marind in Marori, judging from published materials on the language (e.g. Arka 2012, 2015). The Kanum people to the east maintained friendly relationships with their Marind neighbours but their language does not show much linguistic influence: in the 388-term wordlist for Ngkolmpu (a language of the Yam family) I only found 6 Marind loans (2%).

I am not aware of any major influence of other languages on Coastal Marind. Today the Marindic languages, like all other languages of the region, are under pressure from Malay, in the form of the local variety of Malay as well as the Indonesian standard language. Wambi, the village where I carried out most of my fieldwork, is probably one of the few Marind villages where Malay is used relatively little, and especially so by younger people. Although the teachers in the village school (the majority of which are migrants from other parts of Indonesia) only use Malay/Indonesian during instruction, I found that many young people are uncomfortable speaking Malay and rarely engage in longer stretches of code-switching (which their parents' generation often do). This situation differs from the one in the nearest neighbouring village, Duhmilah, which has a larger proportion of non-Papuan migrants and better road connection to the sub-

---

[7] Certain lexical domains in Marori seem to be completely dominated by Marind loans. For example, I counted 17 Coastal Marind loans among the 26 sago-related terms in Hisa et al. (2017).

district capital Okaba. All young people in Duhmilah are fluent speakers of Coastal Marind, but code-switch to a large extent, with some even preferring to use Malay only.

1.3 The Marind people

This section contains some brief remarks on the geographical setting (§1.3.1), culture (§1.3.2), demography (§1.3.3) and the socioeconomic setting (§1.3.4).

1.3.1 Geography

The Trans-Fly area (named after the Fly, the largest river in the region) is the alluvial lowland that makes up the southernmost part of New Guinea. The area is dominated by savanna, grasslands and monsoon forest, and is largely devoid of the tropical rainforest that covers the rest of New Guinea. The landscape, with its wallabies and eucalyptus trees, is ecologically a part of northern Australia, isolated in a region that lost its land connection to Australia after the last ice age (Evans 2012). There are two distinct seasons: *sandawi-kiwal*, the South-Eastern Monsoon, which brings cool, dry air from Australia during April–November, and *muli-kiwal*, the North-Western Monsoon, in November–March, largely coinciding with heavy rainfall.

The area in which the Marindic languages are spoken is situated in the southwestern part of the Trans-Fly, and stretches along the coast approximately from the swampy Kolopom Island in the west to the international border with Papua New Guinea in the east, and far inland along rivers and swamps. The flat, dry area around the district capital Merauke, located at the mouth of the Maro river, is a fairly monotonous combination of peatland, savanna and swamps that are inundated during the rainy season. About 40–50 kms inland, the flat expanses give way to small hills covered in lush vegetation, as in the inland area where the Bian Marind language is spoken. Today the areas north and northwest of Merauke are dominated by settlements inhabited by migrants from other parts of Indonesia, and large parts of the land have been made into oil palm and sugar cane plantations. The area where I carried out my fieldwork lies west of the large Bian river. This part of Marind territory has been subject to little development and in-migration, due to the distance from the district capital and the limited accessibility.

1.3.2 Ethnographic remarks

The reader is referred to van Baal (1966) for information about Marind ethnography. Here I will only summarise a few important features of Marind history and culture.

Tab. 1.5: The 9 main clans and some prominent totems

	Clan		Totems
	Western dialect	Common spelling	
i.	Gebhe	Gebze	Coconut
ii.	Kayhe	Kaize	Cassowary
	Ndiken	Ndikend	Stork
	Samkakay	Samkakai	Wallaby
iii.	Mayuhe	Mahuze	Dog, sago
iv.	Balagayhe	Balagaize	Eagle
	Yolmen	Yolmend	Sea, stingray
	Basik-Basik	Basik-Basik	Pig
	Kahol	Kahol	Crocodile, betel

When the Dutch established a military presence in South New Guinea (1902) there were around 50 politically independent sub-tribes that identified as Marind. Despite significant cultural and lingustic differences, and a lack of central authorities, the Marind subtribes managed to maintain intra-village peace and collaborated in the organisation of large headhunting parties that set out to find their victims far beyond the limits of the Marind territory, mainly north of the Digul river and in present-day Papua New Guinea. Headhunting was spiritually motivated, and its goals included the collection of *pa-igih* 'head-names', i.e. names taken from the victims and given to Marind children at home, as well as kidnapping of children who then were brought up as Marind children (van Baal 1966: 695–764). Although headhunting was discontinued under pressure from the Dutch, all Marind people that I met are well aware of this aspect of Marind history, and one speaker even demonstrated the decapitation technique used by his ancestors. Many Marind people retain head names that they have inherited.

The Marind clan system shows some local variation. In Table 1.5 I list the nine main clans recognised in the western coastal area, along with some of their most prominent totems. The table gives the name of each clan as it is pronounced in the western dialect of Coastal Marind, as well as the spelling that I judge to be the most common. The spelling is supposed to be standardised across the Marind population, and is based on the Eastern dialect (spoken around the provincial capital Merauke), so the suffix *-he* (probably 'descendants', cf. *na-he* 'my-grandchildren') is written '-ze', the final *-d* in *-nd* is retained, and so on. These patrilineal clans can be grouped into four separate phratries (numbered i–iv in the table; cf. van Baal 1966: 39). There is still a preference for phratry exogamy in Wambi, although I am not sure how strictly it is enforced. The moiety distinction mentioned by van Baal does not seem to have any practical significance in contemporary Marind life.

Although the influence of the clan partition on e.g. marriage and land rights seems to be in general decline, the Marind people still hold on to their totems, which are dearly loved. Totemic relationships are an endless source of self-expression, nicknames, jokes and philosophical speculations. Symbols relating to one's totems are drawn on walls and carved into important possessions. Dogs are strictly named in line with the inventory of dog names belonging to one's clan. Motorcycles are also given names befitting the clan of their owners: since I had been adopted into the Samkakai clan, my motorcycle was given the name *ndom-yakeh*, literally 'bad-catch', referring to the fact that a wallaby that has been badly caught will free itself, attack the hunter or dog with its sharp claws, and then take off at high speed.

The majority of the Coastal Marind population adhere to the Roman Catholic faith, with Protestants present in just a few villages (e.g. Alatep, where they are the majority). The villagers in Wambi are not particularly devout, and Paulus Yolmend (my host father in Wambi), who was in charge of the Sunday mass, often preached to a congregation of mostly small children and a few women. Church service is exclusively held in Malay, although a small women's choir occasionally performed songs in Marind. Some of the most popular songs are about *Woliw*, a syncretic figure combining features of traditional Marind culture heroes with Christ. The millenarian movements and cargo cults known from other parts of New Guinea seem to be absent from this region.

Traditional organised religion appears to be on the verge of extinction in Wambi. Most villagers identify as followers of the *mayo* cult, but the last Mayo celebrations were held in the mid 1990s, after a longer hiatus, and the present generation appears unsure of its capability to revive the traditions, now that the elders behind the revival of the 1990s are gone.[8] The only traditional rite that has survived relatively unchanged into the present is the all-night mourning song cycle, the solemn *yalut*, followed by a feast meal the following day, the *yamu*.

1.3.3 Demography

Speakers of the three Marindic languages, all of which consider themselves to be ethnic Marind people, inhabit 45 present-day villages. The largest language, Coastal Marind, is spoken in 26 villages distributed along the coast and in the Kumb river valley. Government sources[9] report a population of 17,718 for the Coastal villages in 2016. This figure includes villages with large non-Marind populations (mostly migrants

---

8 The reader is advised to consult Corbey (2010) for documentation of the spectacular cult celebrations of the early colonial period. Todd Barlin, an American-Australian art collector and traveller, documented the Mayo celebrations held in Wambi in 1994, and is planning to archive these recordings with the South Australian Museum (Todd Barlin, pers. comm.).

9 In the form of a spreadsheet that an employee at the district government in Merauke provided me with. These figures are presumably based on reports from the heads of the respective villages.

from other parts of Indonesia) such as Urumb and Okaba, so a reasonable guess is that there are around 15,000 ethnic Marind living in these 27 villages. The SIL reports lower population figures: the sources to which I had access (Kriens 2003, Sohn et al. 2009, Lebold et al. 2010) give a population of 7,095 for 16 of the Coastal Marind villages; extrapolating this figure to the remaining Coastal Marind villages gives a total of around 12,000. The data are given in Table 1.6. In the tables, cells with minus signs represent missing figures (in the case of SIL data) or villages that are counted as part of some other village (in government figures; for example, Anasai is merged with Wendu for government purposes).

The vitality of Marind varies between vibrant (in the villages furthest from the district capital) to critically endangered (basically all villages east of the Bian river). Assuming that 60% of the Coastal Marind population speak the Coastal Marind language we arrive at estimates of between 7,000 (based on SIL figures) and 9,000 (based on the government figures) speakers of Coastal Marind.

1.3.4 Socioeconomic setting, subsistence

The main staples of Marind people are sago, and, along the coast, coconut. All families are in charge of one or several sago gardens, sometimes far away from the village, along with some simple plantations where tubers and bananas are grown. A description of sago processing, based on my observations and interviews with villagers, is in Olsson (2017: 561–565). Many villagers also grow *wati* (kava, Piper methysticum), for trading as well as for recreational use.

Fish is abundant in coastal villages such as Wambi, and seafood can be gathered on the mudflat during low tide. Fish can also be gathered from the swamps during the dry season, often by simply picking them up by hand. The native sweet water fish are rapidly being replaced by intrusive species such as the climbing perch (Anabas testudineus, Local Malay *ikan betik*), and many young people reported never having seen many of the fish species I collected for my lexical file. Other protein sources come from hunting of wallabies, pigs and bandicoot. Pigs (and occasionally wallabies) are taken captive and saved for feasts, although never bred.

There have been unsuccessful attempts to grow rice in Wambi, and there is little enthusiasm for agricultural innovations. The main cash sources are copra, which is produced by cutting ripe coconuts in half and smoking them, and trade with swim bladders and sea cucumbers, which are found along the coast or gathered illegally across the border in Papua New Guinea. The trade itself is completely controlled by non-Marinds, primarily Makassarese migrants, and none of the villagers seemed to be sure what the copra, swim bladders and sea cucumbers were used for. The income from these activities are used to buy e.g. tobacco, coffee and dried betelnut from the three or four dry-goods stores in Wambi (again, run by Makassarese migrants). Trade

Tab. 1.6: Population figures.
*Asterisks mark villages with large proportions of non-Marind people.

Upper Bian Marind			Coastal Marind		
Village	SIL	Gvmt	Village	SIL	Gvmt
Boha	272	317	Buti	–	–
Kindiki	350	355	Dokib	–	597
Kolam	300	302	Kaiburse	–	397
Muting*	916	1,263	Nasem*	–	675
Pahas	260	312	Ndalir	–	–
Selaw	376	528	Wamal	–	768
Wan	435	418	Yowid	–	535
			Anasai	–	–
Bush Marind			Wendu*	–	944
Village	SIL	Gvmt	Baad	331	428
Domande	–	804	Ivimahad	454	1,019
Boepe	100	–	Kaisa	324	658
Ihalik	378	385	Kaliki	343	535
Kaniskobat	226	350	Koa	331	431
Kaptel	243	424	Onggari	410	614
Kwemsid	338	677	Senegi	365	499
Nakias	293	267	Wayau	350	530
Poepe	–	–	Matara	444	777
Sanggase	526	662	Salor*	–	–
Tagaepe	390	427	Urumb*	650	968
Yawimu	508	624	Alaku	351	499
			Alatep	250	438
			Duhmilah	353	343
			Iwol	239	224
			Makaling	500	667
			Okaba*	–	1,229
			Wambi	1,400	1,238

with dried, imported betelnut has almost completely replaced locally planted betelnut.

1.4 Previous research

The standard work on Marind culture and religion is van Baal (1966), largely based on Wirz (1922/1925) and on correspondence with Father Jan Verschueren, a prominent Catholic missionary in the area. Good summaries can be found in van Baal (1984) and Knauft (1993).

The most important early work on the Marind language was carried out by the Dutch missionaries, who were present in the region from 1905. A Dutch–Marind dictionary was completed by van de Kolk and Vertenten (1922). The work was continued by

Hendrik Geurtjens after their departure, who published a substantial Marind–Dutch dictionary (Geurtjens 1933). Geurtjens' dictionary contains ca. 4500 entries (many of them divided into sub-entries), and a wealth of useful information, especially for the reader who has the patience to weed out the tiresome etymological speculations that seem to have been a driving force between Geurtjens' work.

Geurtjens published a rather amateurish grammar (Geurtjens 1926), a work that suffers from a lack of proper morphemic analysis, and appears to be based on a Latin grammar model. Drabbe, in the preface to his own grammar, acknowledges that Geurtjens' work is unsatisfactory, but points out that linguistic research on Papuan languages was just in its infancy at the time, so that Geurtjens had little to build upon in his pioneering efforts. Also, the knowledge of Malay among the Marind must have been sparse, making the task of grammar writing even more difficult.

Petrus Drabbe's grammar of the Eastern dialect of Coastal Marind (Drabbe 1955) is an extraordinarily rich source of data on the language, on which he worked between 1952–1954. Drabbe had spent 20 years in the Moluccas doing linguistic and missionary work before coming to Dutch New Guinea in 1935, where he spent 25 years working on a large number of languages, resulting in a long list of valuable publications that testify to his analytical skills.

Drabbe's grammar provides an astonishing amount of information on the complex morphology of the language, with some attention paid to morphosyntactic phenomena at the clause level. The appendix contains 9 texts with Dutch translation, two of which are glossed (see Olsson 2021 for glossed versions of the texts with English translations). It is unfortunate that Drabbe did not employ the same glossing technique elsewhere in the grammar, because this would have made his extremely dense presentation much more user-friendly. Some of the most outstanding achievements in Drabbe's work are: the analysis of the four genders (1955: 17–24, 79–82) and the complex person/number prefixes (pp. 28–31, passim), the person alternations in the verb stem (pp. 68–78), the extremely complicated formation of content questions in the Eastern dialect (pp. 113–121) and the detailed discussion of auxiliary verbs (pp. 85–100). None of these topics — with the exception of stem alternations, which are thoroughly documented in Geurtjens' dictionary — had received any satisfactory treatment in previous work. It is regrettable that Drabbe's Marind grammar has had so little impact on later literature,[10] which probably is explained by the compact presentation, the complexity of the language, and, perhaps most of all, the fact that Drabbe wrote in Dutch.

---

10 In October 2020, Google Scholar listed 48 publications as citing Drabbe (1955), none of which discussed data from Drabbe in any detail.

1.5 This grammar

1.5.1 The fieldwork

I started my doctoral studies in Singapore in 2013 with a vague idea that I was going to study some language spoken in Indonesian Papua. Since I would only have three years after completed coursework to devote to actual research, it seemed suitable to work on a language that had some previous research, so that I did not need to start from scratch. The choice therefore fell on Coastal Marind, which had extensive documentation from the Dutch period, and was relatively easy to access.

I carried out three trips to Merauke during my doctoral studies: October–November 2014, April–October 2015, and August 2016–January 2017, totalling ca. 13 months. The first, short trip was spent entirely in Merauke, where I tried to establish contacts and did some preliminary work with speakers of the Eastern and Western dialects of Coastal Marind. The longer trips were spent mostly in Wambi, which was my main field site, except for a three-week stay in Duhmilah, and week-long stays in Sanggase and Muting. I also went on shorter expeditions to Dokib and Yowid (west of Wambi). I was required to return from the village to Merauke every month in order to get my permits renewed, first at the immigration authorities and then at the police station, which meant that ca. 10 days of each month were spent waiting in Merauke. This would have been extremely frustrating without the large Wambi diaspora living in the outskirts of Merauke (in Payum, Nasem and Buti), which allowed me to keep up the work on the language while waiting for the paperwork to go through. After my PhD, I made two trips to the region to work on the Yaqay language (June 2018 and March–May 2019), during which I was able to transcribe several previously collected Marind recordings and gather additional data.

1.5.2 The corpus

The transcribed corpus consists of 45 recordings, totalling 9 hours and 45 minutes of annotated, time-aligned video recordings, containing approx. 40,000 words spread over 9,354 transcription segments (roughly corresponding to intonation units). The entire corpus has Malay and English translations. Transcription was done in ELAN.

Most of the recordings were made in Wambi (tot. 6 h 43 mins), the remainder in Duhmilah (1 h 50 mins) and Makaling (1 h 13 mins). Speakers vary in age from ca. 16 to 75 years. The corpus mainly represents middle-aged and elder speakers: ca. 4 h are dominated by 30–60-year-olds, 3 h 20 mins by speakers over 60, and 2 h 25 mins by speakers under 30. The corpus (Olsson 2015) is archived with the Pacific and Regional Archive for Digital Sources in Endangered Cultures (PARADISEC).

In corpus examples a code is given pointing to the recording from which the data is taken. A code such as W01:0001 identifies the recording (W01) and the line number

(0001). A list of recording codes and the corresponding archive items is given in Table 1.7. The initial letter in the recording code identifies the village of the recording: W = Wambi, D = Duhmilah and M = Makaling.

The varieties spoken in Wambi and the neighbouring village Duhmilah are practically identical, so I frequently use examples from Duhmilah when there is no appropriate Wambi data to cite. The variety of Coastal Marind spoken in Makaling shows some minor divergences from the Duhmilah/Wambi varieties, and I have generally avoided using examples from my Makaling subcorpus in this grammar. I went through all data from Makaling with a speaker of the Wambi variety, asking him to point out any detail that differed from his own variety. In a few instances I have cited Makaling data that the speaker identified as conforming to the Wambi variety.[11]

Examples without a code are taken from my collection of notes, representing elicitation and observed usage. My goal in writing has been to avoid using elicited and overheard data as much as possible, and instead base the description on video-recorded attestations of spontaneous language use. Often this has not been possible, sometimes because some crucial point is not yet attested in corpus data, or because the available corpus attestations are too complex to be suitable as illustrations.

---

[11] In addition to the spontaneous data I used the Family Problems picture task (San Roque et al. 2012) as the basis of one recording. This source is given a code like other corpus items, but I indicate in the top line of such examples that they are taken from the picture task.

Tab. 1.7: Codes used in corpus examples and corresponding items in the PARADISEC collection

Code	Item in Olsson (2015)
D01	20141121_SagoStory
D02	20150419_IsaiasNdikenStork
D03	20150423_IsaiasNdikenNdumai
D04	20150514_AdrianaKinamdeSago
D05	20150514_AgusYolmenHunting
D06	20150514_YustBasikHeadhunting
D07	20150515_KrisSamkakaiWew
D08	20150516_BamaiNdikenDuhmilah
D09	20150519_FamilyProblems
D10	20150602_AgusYolmenHunting
D11	20150603_BamaiNdikenStork
D12	20141028_FamilyProblems
D13	20150520_SagoPounding1
D14	20150520_SagoPounding4
M01	20150520_ErikGebzeHuntingMkl
M02	20150520_LiboAlulekHuntingMkl
M02	20150520_LiboAlulekHuntingMkl
M03	20150520_MaksiGebzeFunnyMkl
M04	20150520_MartinusAlulekFunMkl
M05	20150520_VillageMeetingMkl
W01	20150628_AloSamkakaiHunting
W02	20150628_AloYolmenHunting
W03	20150628_AloYolmenHunting2
W04	20150705_BedaSamkakaiWati
W05	20150824_WambiBoysSitting
W06	20150827_CleaningWell
W07	20150830_YakobaYolmenFishing1
W08	20150830_YakobaYolmenFishing2
W09	20150904_PaulinaSamkakaiFight
W10	20160908_PaulusYolmend
W11	20160916_Conversation
W12	20160921_PaulusYolmend
W13	20160923_NggehBalagaihe
W14	20160923_Wakatiiwag
W15	20160923_YustinasTrip-01
W16	20160923_YustinasTrip-02
W17	20160927_MbohaMagpieGoose
W18	20160927_OdiliaGebzeFeast
W19	20160927_OdiliaGebzeYamu
W20	20161017_MbokeYolmend
W21	20161017_YustinaMahuze
W22	20161026_YustinaMahuzeNet
W23	20150628_DengaHunting
W24	20150501_PayumConvo

2 Phonology

This chapter is a brief description of the phonology of Coastal Marind. I discuss the phonemes and their realisation in §2.1. Phonotactics, stress and the syllable canon are described in §2.2, §2.3 and §2.4. §2.5 describes some morphophonemic alternations.

2.1 Segmental phonology

2.1.1 Consonants

The consonant inventory of the Western dialect of Coastal Marind — the variety described in this grammar — is given in Table 2.1. When the orthography uses different symbols than the International Phonetic Alphabet, the graphemes are given inside the less/greater-than symbols <...>.

Tab. 2.1: Consonants

	Labial	Alveolar	Palatal	Velar	Glottal
Voiceless plosive	p	t		k	
Voiced plosive	b	d		g	
Prenasalised plosive	m͡b <mb>	n͡d <nd>		ŋ͡g <ngg>	
Nasal	m	n			
Fricative		s		ɣ	h
Voiced approximant		l	j <y>	w	
Voiceless approximant			ʰj <hy>	ʰw <hw>	

Consonants are articulated in five places: labial, alveolar, palatal, velar and glottal. Plosives are produced at the labial, alveolar and velar places of articulation, with each place distingushing three manners: voiceless /p t k/, voiced /b d g/ and prenasalised voiced stops /m͡b n͡d ŋ͡g/.

There are bilabial and alveolar nasal phonemes /m n/; the velar nasal /ŋ/ is restricted to toponyms (e.g. *Ngomab* [ŋomab] and *Wabengom* [wabeŋom]) and two terms for flora and fauna (*binga* [biŋa] 'grass sp.', *manga* [maŋa] 'fish sp.'). These are perhaps loanwords from some unidentified neighbouring language; I consider [ŋ] to be a marginal phoneme at most. Note that the sound [ŋ] is common in coda position in native words, where it is the realisation of the phoneme /ŋ͡g/.

In addition to the alveolar voiceless and glottal fricatives /s h/, the dialect described here also has the voiced velar fricative /ɣ/.[1]

Coastal Marind has one liquid, realised as a lateral approximant /l/ in the Western varieties.

Two sets of approximants are given. The voiced set /j/ and /w/ could perhaps be analysed as phonetic realisations of corresponding front and back vowels instead of phonemic approximants. There is a corresponding pair of pre-aspirated/devoiced approximants /ʰj ʰw/ (see §2.1.1.4).

All consonants may appear in both initial and final position, with the exception of the prenasalised stops /mb nd ŋg/, which have been simplified to plain nasals [m n ŋ] in final position. More detailed remarks on distribution are given in the following subsections. A full list of minimal sets is found in Table 2.2, after the description of the consonant segments.

2.1.1.1 Stops

The voiceless stops /p t k/ are unaspirated. The voiced stops /b d g/ are fully voiced in all positions; measurements show negative voice onset times of 100ms or more even in utterance-initial position. Word-finally, both series can have an unaspirated release, or be unreleased, without any phonemic significance.

The third series of stops are the prenasalised /mb nd ŋg/. Phonetically, the prenasalised stops are sequences of a voiced stop preceded by a homorganic nasal. The main reason for treating the prenasalised series as unitary phonemes rather than clusters /m/ + /b/ is that it allows us to make the generalisation that no tautosyllabic consonant clusters are allowed in Coastal Marind (with the exception of stop+glide clusters, §2.2).

Word-initially, the nasal segment is short and can be difficult to perceive, so /mbam/ 'louse' could be transcribed [ᵐbam]. Medially, the nasal segment is considerably longer: e.g. /ambam/ 'to wrap up', pronounced [ambam]. Despite this lengthening in medial position, it will be seen in §2.4 that for the purposes of syllabification, both the nasal and stop segments of /mb/ are contained within the onset of the second syllable: [a.mbam].

The prenasalised stops /mb nd/ contrast with plain nasals in initial position, e.g. *mbam* 'louse' vs. *mam* 'chip of sago bark' and *ndalaw* 'brolga' vs. *nalaw* 'to search (1.U)'.

---

[1] There is no consensus among speakers of the Western dialect how to write the phoneme /ɣ/. In the occasional text message and on social media I have mostly observed <h>, so that the word /ɣeɣ/ 'land' is written <heh>, which has the advantage of matching the Eastern dialect form *heh* (this dialect has merged *ɣ and *h). For the community dictionary I suggested the use of the digraph <gh> to represent /ɣ/, which is the solution found in the Dutch missionary materials (and still in use among some speakers). A short dictionary compiled and printed by a local school teacher employs the tetragraph <ghr̀> (i.e. a g, h and r followed by a grave accent), but this invention does not seem to have gained wider usage. For the linguist's orthography used in this grammar I have opted for the unambiguous <ɣ>.

The contrast is also found medially: e.g. *ambam* 'to wrap' vs. *amam* 'pity' ; or *kanda* 'tree sp.' vs. *kana* 'egg'. As stated above, there appears to be no native vocabulary in which a velar nasal /ŋ/ contrasts with the prenasalised velar stop /ŋ͡g/; however, all speakers contrast these sounds in a minimal pair such as *mangga* 'mango' (a Malay loan) and *manga* 'fish sp.' (possibly also a loan).

There is no contrast between prenasalised stops and plain nasals in final position: no words end in [mb nd ŋ͡g]. The reason for this is that final prenasalised stops have been reduced so that only the nasal segment is pronounced. Synchronically, this is most clearly seen within inflectional morphology. For example, the 2sg Genitive prefix is /amb-/, but before a word boundary (such as the one separating the prefixal complex from the verb stem, marked by a hyphen '-' followed by a blank space; see §8.3) it is realised as [am], as in (11a). If a vowel-initial prefix is added, the stop segment in /mb/ is pronounced, as in (11b).

(11) a. /mend-a-amb-   ihon/   →   [me.ˈndam i.hon]
         PERF-3SG.A-2SG.GEN- run:3SG.U   'yours ran away'

    b. /mend-a-amb-i-   ihon/   →   [me.nda.ˈmbi i.hon]
         PERF-3SG.A-2SG.GEN-RE- run:3SG.U   'yours ran away again'

No [b] occurs with a prefix that ends in underlying /m/, e.g. the Frustrative *um-*: cf. /mend-a-um-i- ihon/ (PERF-3SG.A-FRUS-RE- run:3SG.U) 's/he already ran away in vain again', pronounced [me.ndu.ˈmi i.hon].

Final simplification of the prenasalised stops is a dialectal feature. In Wambi, the words 'big', 'eye' and 'walk' are pronounced [sam], [kin] and [meŋ], with final nasals and no oral stop segment, while speakers of the Eastern dialect pronounce these words with full prenasalised stops (Eastern [samb], [kind] and [meŋ͡g]). In Wambi, the original prenasalised stops in these words are retained in lexicalised compounds such as *sambanem* 'big man, important person etc.' (< 'big' + *anem* 'man') and *kindiput* 'eyebrows' ('eye' + *put* 'feather') where the stop segments are unmistakably present, since the following vowel causes them to syllabify in onset position. Outside such fossilised compounds, 'big' and 'eye' are always [sam] and [kin], so there is no need to posit synchronic underlying forms with final prenasalised stops for these words.[2]

---

[2] One speaker of the Western variety (from Duhmilah) insisted that these words are 'actually' pronounced [samb] 'big', [kind] 'eye' and [meŋ͡g] 'walk', with clearly audible stop segments finally, and that they should be spelled accordingly, even when writing the Western dialects. During the same session, the speaker also claimed that the correct pronunciation of other words such as *in* 'middle' likewise is [ind], which turns out to be etymologically incorrect since all other dialects also have [in], even the dialects that preserve the prenasalised stops in final position. The prescriptive judgement that replacing final nasals with corresponding prenasalised stops is a more correct way of speaking and writing the language was not expressed by any other speakers, so I have not adopted this suggestion in the practical orthography.

On the other hand, words pronounced with final [ŋ], such as [meŋ] 'walk' are best represented phonemically as /meŋg͡/. Since [ŋ] is never contrastive, it should be treated as an allophone of /ŋg͡/ in final position.

2.1.1.2 Nasals
The nasals /m n/ show no allophonic variation.

2.1.1.3 Fricatives
The fricatives /s h/ show no allophonic variation. The glottal /h/ occurs in onsets as well as codas, as in *hoh* [hoh] 'war', but /h/ in coda position is rare word-internally, and occurs mainly in derived environments, as when the prefixed verb stem /i-hayaman/ 'PLA-enter.water' is realised [ihyaman] due to syncopation of the first /a/ (see §2.4.2).

The voiced velar fricative /ɣ/ is often articulated as a corresponding approximant, without any friction, in casual speech. In carefully articulated speech, the friction is clearly audible.

The phoneme /ɣ/ is absent from the Eastern varieties, but this difference has not gained the status of important shibboleth in the way that the liquids [l]~[ɾ] have (see §2.1.1.5).[3]

2.1.1.4 Approximants
The glides /j w/ are presented as distinct phonemes in Table 2.1. Alternatively, they can be regarded as allophones of the mid and high vowels /u/ and /i/ in non-nucleus position. Under this more abstract approach, words such as *kay* 'road' and *kaw* 'stick' are derived from forms with underlying high vowels: /kai/→[kaj] and /kau/→[kaw].

Support for the vowel approach comes from some derived forms in which high vowels alternate with glides. Some verb stems index the Undergoer by means of person/number prefixes (§10.3.1). The 3sg prefix is *w-* before a vowel-initial stem (e.g. *w-alok* 'stab him/her') but *o-* or *u-* before consonant-initial stems (e.g. *o-nggat* 's/he becomes.PLA', *u-sak* 'fight him/her'). If [w] is derived from a high vowel /u/, it also explains why the *u*-initial stem *um* 'go habitually' lacks the 3sg prefix *w-*, despite being vowel-initial: the underlying form /u-um/ is realised as [um] since the two identical vowels merge.

I note the possibility of this more abstract description, but the glides are retained in Table 2.1 as representative of the speech sounds of Coastal Marind. They can be

---

[3] Speakers in Wambi are clearly aware of /ɣ/ as characteristic of their dialect, however: when I had trouble understanding a small girl's (ca. 2 years) speech because of her use of /h/ in place of /ɣ/, a bystander commented 'Yes, she is still speaking *layuk-mayan*', i.e. Eastern dialect, where /ɣ/ has merged with /h/.

considered derived if one favours descriptive economy over avoidance of abstract representations.

The second set of glides /ʰj ʰw/ are the voiceless/preaspirated counterparts to /j w/. These sounds are unusual in the New Guinean context, and I am not aware of any Papuan language outside Coastal Marind for which they have been described. In careful speech, /ʰj ʰw/ are realised as preaspirated approximants [ʰj ʰw]. In casual speech they are better characterised as devoiced approximants without any distinct aspiration phase.

If the plain glides /j w/ are described as the phonetic realisation of abstract high vowels (as mentioned above), then one could speculate that the devoiced/preaspirated glides should be described as high vowels preceded by /h/. According to this description, [ʰj] is the phonetic realisation of the sequence /hi/ and [ʰw] the realisation of /hu/. This analysis appears appealing given certain stem pairs showing alternations between e.g. *hw* and *hu*, such as *ihwaluk* 'dangle inanimate' and *ihuleb* 'dangle animate (3SG.U)'. According to the high vowel approach, the former would be derived from an abstract form /ihualuk/→[ihwaluk].

However, several problems arise if one considers *hw* to be derived from underlying /hu/. One problem is that there is no productive process deriving stem forms such as *ihwaluk* and *ihuleb* (see e.g. §10.4), so little would be gained by stating that they are related by some abstract stem /ihu(a)l-/. A second problem is the existence of unrelated words such as *ihw* 'cry' and *ihu* 'ripe', in which [ʰw] contrasts with [hu]. It is not clear how both of these words could be derived from underlying /ihu/. Because of problems like these I consider the devoiced/preaspirated glides to be unitary phonemes.

2.1.1.5 Liquid

When asked what distinguishes their dialect from those of other villages, Marind speakers will likely give a response involving the realisation of the liquid, which is the most important shibboleth dividing the variety described here, with [l] as the sole native liquid, from those spoken in the east, in which the corresponding phoneme is pronounced as a retroflex flap [ɽ].

A second liquid has been introduced through Malay, and /r/ is now often heard in Malay words such as *rusa* 'deer', *gereja* 'church', *ranger* 'pick-up truck' and *drainasi* (or *garinasi*) 'drainage', along with other foreign sounds such as [dʒ]. Malay /r/ can be said to be the most integrated of the non-native sounds since it is common in Christian names such as *Kris*, *Markus* or *Kasimirus*, although short, /r/-less forms of the longer names (*Mako*, *Kasim*) are used in daily speech.

See Table 2.2 for minimal and near-minimal pairs distinguishing the consonants described above. Each set in the table gives pairs distinguishing two phonetically similar sounds in initial, medial and final position, where possible.

Tab. 2.2: Minimal pairs for the consonant phonemes

Segments	Phonemic	Gloss	Comment
/b/ – /p/	/bal/	'hole'	
	/pal/	'bark, skin'	
	/bobo/	'coconut shell'	near-minimal
	/popo/	'bubble'	
	/ab/	'armpit'	
	/ap/	'also'	
/d/ – /t/	/dahiɣ/	'to bite'	
	/tahiɣ/	'to spit out food'	
	/udup/	'young sago leaf'	
	/utup/	'lip'	
	/tad/	'to cause to burn'	
	/tat/	'arrow shaft'	
/g/ – /k/	/gaw/	'freshwater turtle; stupid'	
	/kaw/	'mushroom'	
	/age/	'what's-his-name'	
	/ake/	'gambier'	
	/lalag/	'bird sp. (Torresian Crow)'	
	/lalak/	'to reach for s.t.'	
/b/ – /m͡b/	/bum/	'earthquake'	
	/m͡bum/	'inner gills (of fish)'	
	/bobo/	'coconut shell'	near-minimal
	/m͡bom͡bo/	'taut'	
	—	(No contrast in coda)	
/d/ – /n͡d/	/de/	'tree'	
	/n͡de/	'in, at'	
	/kadib/	'to feel, squeeze'	near-minimal
	/kan͡di/	'unripe'	
	—	(No contrast in coda)	
/g/ – /ŋ͡g/	/gal/	'tree sp.'	
	/ŋ͡gal/	'young coconut'	
	/sagid/	'mane of pig'	
	/saŋ͡gid/	'to shake'	
	—	(No contrast in coda)	

Continued on next page

Tab. 2.2 – *Continued*

Segments	Phonemic	Gloss	Comment
/m/ – /m̬b/	/mo/	'muddy water'	
	/m̬bo/	'crocodile's tail'	
	/amam/	'pity'	
	/am̬bam/	'to wrap'	
	—	(No contrast in coda)	
/n/ – /n̬d/	/nalaw/	'to open eyes (1.u)'	
	/n̬dalaw/	'brolga'	
	/kono/	'urine'	
	/kon̬do/	*Kondo*, a place east of Merauke	
	—	(No contrast in coda)	
/ɣ/ – /h/	/ɣod/	'to vomit'	
	/hod/	'plans to leave'	
	/aɣan/	'to branch off'	
	/ahan/	'yourself'	
	/kahuɣ/	'to speak non-fluently'	
	/kahuh/	'many to bring out'	
/l/ – /d/	/lo/	'to root up ground'	
	/do/	'blood'	
	/kilub/	'catfish'	
	/kidub/	'bird sp. (White-bellied sea eagle)'	
	/gel/	'tree sap'	
	/ged/	'to stick in between'	
/j/ – /ʰj/	/jom/	'ditch'	
	/ʰjom/	'to fuck'	
	/ɣajam/	'tree sp.'	
	/ɣaʰjam/	'your (sg) wife'	
	/kabaj/	'bird sp. (Eastern Osprey)'	
	/kabaʰj/	'large wallaby'	
/h/ – /ʰj/	/haman/	'to sit (pl)'	near-minimal
	/ʰjamin/	'to call (pl)'	
	/ahak/	'to spread out sago paste'	near-minimal
	/ʰjaʰjak/	'to split wood'	
	/hoh/	'fighting, war'	near-minimal
	/oʰj/	'tree sp.'	
/w/ – /ʰw/	/waj/	'shooting star'	
	/ʰwaj/	'to paddle'	

Continued on next page

Segments	Phonemic	Gloss	Comment
	/kewaj/	'break'	
	/keʰwaj/	'paddle' (n.)	
	/kiw/	'crocodile'	near-minimal
	/iʰw/	'to cry'	
/h/ – /ʰw/	/haman/	'many to sit'	
	/ʰwaman/	'to take off clothes'	
	/aha/	'house'	
	/aʰwa/	'red clay'	
	/isih/	'many to become cooked'	near-minimal
	/siʰw/	'sago mixed with banana'	

Tab. 2.2 – *Continued*

2.1.2 Vowels

Coastal Marind has a simple 5-vowel system, shown in Figure 2.1. A minimal quintuplet:

/in/ 'middle'
/un/ 'white hair'
/en/ 'POSS'
/on/ 'liver'
/an/ 'mother'

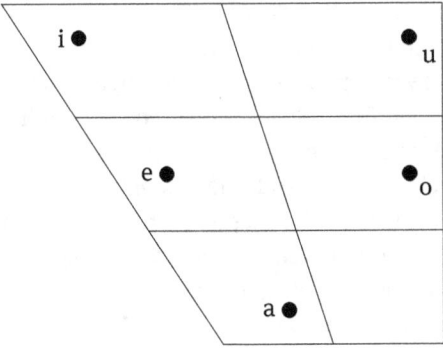

Fig. 2.1: The vowel inventory

2.1.2.1 The marginal vowel /ɐ/

In addition to the five core vowels there is a marginal near-open central vowel /ɐ/. This vowel would be considered a phoneme on distributional grounds, because there are four minimal pairs in which it contrasts with /a/:

/ɐ/		/a/	
/wɐj/	'sago grub'	/waj/	'shooting star'
/kɐj/	'Sulphur-crested cockatoo'	/kaj/	'road, path'
/bɐbob/	'plant sp.'	/babob/	'jellyfish'
/bɐk/	'to perforate'	/bak/	'outside'

There is also the near-minimal pair /bɐbɐ/ 'turtle sp.' and /baba/ 'Coix Lacryma-jobi'. I elicited these five pairs (none of which appears to contain loanwords) several times with speakers of different generations and genders; everybody makes a clear distinction between the two vowels in these words. I was not able to identify systematic occurrences of /ɐ/ in any other words in the language, despite spending considerable time working on the issue. In fact, one speaker made the observation that a word such as *pa* 'head' can be pronounced either [pa] or [pɐ] without any difference in meaning; this is confirmed by my corpus recordings, in which both pronunciations can be heard, even within a single recording of the same speaker.

For now I will conclude that that /ɐ/ in the pairs above is some sort of quasi-phoneme with limited contrastive function. I will leave it to future research to come up with a more satisfactory account of its status.

2.1.2.2 Vowel sequences

In the Western dialect of Coastal Marind described here, the only vowel sequences found in underived environments have /i/ as the first vowel. Examples: *sali̯a* 'immature cassowary', *naki̯en* 'greed', *kapi̯og* 'palm cockatoo', *ti̯un* 'wake s.b. up (3SG.U)'. Sequences with /e/ as the first vowel can arise in the concatenation of verb prefixes, see §2.5.5. These phonemic vowel sequences with initial /i/ or /e/ are heterosyllabic, so *salia* is pronounced [sa.li.ˈa], or more commonly, [sa.li.ˈja], with an onset-forming transitional glide. Other vowel sequences are not attested. See further §2.5.5, which describes processes involving adjacent vowels in the prefixal complex of the verb.

Historically, vowel sequences that existed in an earlier stage of Marind have been broken up by the insertion of glides in the Western dialect, as in *mayan* 'speech, language' from proto-Marindic **mean* (still pronounced *mean* in the Eastern dialect). Earlier word-final sequences **ai* and **au* are now pronounced with final glides, e.g. *amay* 'ancestor' (still *amai* in the Eastern dialect).

2.1.2.3 Vowel allomorphy

The non-low vowels are often affected by a preceding velar fricative /ɣ/. The vowels /i u o/ are diphthongised into [aɪ] and [aʊ], while the vowel /e/ is lowered to [æ]. These pronunciation variants are optional; the diphtongised/lowered versions are probably articulatory simplifications due to the retracted position of the tongue required for the articulation of /ɣ/. Below are examples of the variants for each of the four affected vowels.

(12) a. /ɣi/ → [ɣi] ~ [ɣaɪ] 'eat, drink'
     b. /ɣokun/ → [ɣokun] ~ [ɣaʊkun] 'put inside'
     c. /ɣujeh/ → [ɣujeh] ~ [ɣaʊjeh] 'shiver'
     d. /ɣe/ → [ɣe] ~ [ɣæ] 'rain'

The orthography used in this grammar disregards this variation and uses the combinations <yi>, <yo>, <yu>, <ye>.

2.2 Phonotactics

The dominant syllable canon in Coastal Marind is CV(C), and, word-initially, #V(C):

(13) a. CV /pa/ → [pa] 'head'
             /dalo/ → [da.lo] 'mud'
         CVC /bob/ → [bob] 'swamp'
             /kulwam/ → [kul.wam] 'Papuan black snake'
     b. #V /e/ → [e] 'scar'
           /ambaj/ → [a.m̪baj] 'leech'
         #VC /ad/ → [ad] 'father'
             /abna/ → [ab.na] 'theft'

An additional type of syllable has the shape CGV, i.e. with a glide /w j/ intervening between the initial consonant and the vowel. This CG-cluster only occurs when the initial consonant is /k/. The words in which it occurs are always polysyllabic, with the CG- cluster in the first syllable. Closed syllables *CGVC do not occur. Examples:

(14) CGV /kwemek/ → [kwe.mek] 'morning'
         /kwagin/ → [kwa.gin] 'to throw'
         /kjasom/ → [kja.som] 'girl'
         /kjaɣaʰjab/ → [kja.ɣa.ʰjab] 'to pull bowstring'

The frequent word *mbya* 'NEG' is exceptional, since it contains a CG-cluster in a monosyllabic word, and with an initial consonant other than /k/: /m̪bja/. (See §18.4.1 for the origin of this word.)

Syllables with final GC-clusters (CVGC) are marginal in monomorphemic words. Examples with final GC are *sews* [sews] 'back' and *nggays* [ŋ͡gajs] 'peer, mate'. This syllable structure occurs more often in derived environments, e.g. in verbs with the common (non-productive) ending -wn, such as *tamewn* [ta.mewn] 'to kick' and *yadewn* [ya.dewn] 'to leave'.

Syllables with initial consonant clusters *CCV(C) do not occur. The same is true for syllable-final CC clusters, with some minor exceptions. The words *ebta* ['eb.ta] 'sago thatch' and *abna* ['ab.na] 'theft' have the variants [ebt] and [abn] when uttered in isolation. The penultimate stress suggests that both words are historically derived forms.

2.2.1 Epenthetic /a/

Some languages of south New Guinea are described as having reduced, non-phonemic vowels that are inserted by epenthesis to break up underlying consonant clusters. In these languages it is common for words to lack underlyingly specified vowels altogether — syllable nuclei are then provided by the epenthetic vowels (see e.g. the Yam languages Komnzo and Nen; Döhler 2016: 79, Evans and Miller 2016: 341). This is not the case in Coastal Marind — vowels are better described as being fully lexically specified. However, the term 'epenthetic' will be used here to account for the phonemic, unreduced vowel /a/ occurring in various morphophonologically conditioned environments.

Given the constraints on syllable structure described above, many instances of the vowel /a/ can be described as epenthetic vowels assuring that e.g. consonant clusters do not occur. This is the case with prefixes of the shape C-, e.g. Comitative–Instrumental *k-* (15). Compare vowel-initial stems such as *k-og* 'do with'.

(15) /k-deh/   → [ka.deh]   'shoot with (3SG.U)'
      /k-hajad/ → [ka.ha.jad] 'play with'
      /k-man/   → [ka.man]   'come with, bring'

Before a glide /j w/ epenthesis will occur to prevent a closed syllable containing a CG-cluster, i.e. /a/ is only inserted if the glide-initial stem is monosyllabic (16a). If the base word is polysyllabic (e.g. GV.CVC) epenthesis is not required, since the prefixation of *k-* will produce an initial open syllable (*k*GV.CVC), as in (16b).

(16) a. /k-jum/   → [ka.jum]   'go habitually with (2|3PL.U)'
         /k-was/   → [ka.was]   'shoot (at s.b.) with (3SG.U)'
     b. /k-jasib/ → [kja.sib] 'hit with (2|3PL.U)'
         /k-walok/ → [kwa.lok] 'stab with (3SG.U)'

The presence of epenthetic /a/ is further discussed in the section on metric structure (§2.4.1).

2.3 Suprasegmentals

Stress in Coastal Marind is characterised by higher pitch on the stressed syllable, so it could alternatively be labelled (pitch) accent. There are no tonal contrasts in Coastal Marind.

The predominant stress pattern is for the last syllable of a monomorphemic word to be stressed. Uttered in isolation — without phrasal intonation superimposed — the pitch of the last syllable will then be the same as, or slightly higher than, that of the first, unstressed syllable. Examples of final-stress bearing words are *kana* [kaˈna] 'egg' and *patul* [paˈtul] 'boy'.

A less frequent pattern in (synchronically) monomorphemic words is for the penultimate syllable to bear stress, as in /ˈa.lo/ 'worm' and /ˈuk.na/ 'fear'. A likely explanation is that these words are historically derived forms. This is clearly seen in words such as /ˈuk.na/ 'fear' and /ˈab.na/ 'theft' which probably are derived by means of a no longer productive suffix *-na*. Other cases of penultimately stressed nouns which likely represent derived forms are:

(17) /alíki/ → [a.ˈli.ki] 'river' cf. *lik* 'river to flow' (verb)
 /ɣásti/ → [ˈɣas.ti] 'old man' cf. *ɣas* 'beard', *ti* 'with'

2.4 Metrical structure

This section describes the types of syllable sequences that may be used to form words. Two processes ensure that illegal syllable sequences do not occur: Pretonic Epenthesis (§2.4.1) and Antepretonic Syncopation (§2.4.2).

As stated in the previous section, stress falls on the final syllable of roots, with penultimate stress possible on forms that are (historically or synchronically) derived by suffixation. Stress is insensitive to syllable weight. However, it will be shown in this section that the distribution of different types of syllables is restricted by the placement of stress, so that closed syllables are not allowed in the position preceding the syllable carrying the stress. Furthermore, in many cases the presence or absence of the vowel /a/ reflects the avoidance of certain dispreferred sequences of syllable types.

There are two types of syllables: *heavy syllables* will be defined as any syllable with a consonant in the coda position (VC, CVC, CGVC, CVG, etc.); *light syllables* are those without any final consonant (V, CV, CGV).

Let us first look at some possible combinations of light and heavy syllables in the word. Some common patterns with word-final stress are in (18). As expected, single-syllable words can be light or heavy (18a–b). The stressed final syllable can also be preceded by one or more light syllables (18c–d). However, we generally do not find words where the stressed syllable is preceded by a heavy syllable (18e–f). A heavy syllable is only possible as the third syllable counting backwards from the stressed syllable (18g).

(18) Final stress

    a.   CV́(C)   *li* [li] 'live coal', *sok* [sok] 'spear'
    b.   V́(C)   *e* [e] 'scar', *in* [in] 'middle'
    c.   CV.CV́(C)   *kana* [ka.'na] 'egg', *ndalom* [nda.'lom] 'foam'
    d.   CV.CV.CV́(C)   *patale* [pa.ta.'le] 'grave', *sasodeh* [sa.so.'deh] 'cold'

    e.   *CVC.CV́(C)
    f.   *CV.CVC.CV́(C)

    g.   CVC.CV.CV́(C)   *galgala* [gal.ga.'la] 'shoulders', *kipletok* [kip.le.'tok] 'to tie'

It is important to note that words such as *yandam* 'stomach' and *kambet* 'ear' are not instances of the pattern *CVC.CVC; the consonants in the middle of these words are prenasalised plosives /mb nd/ and syllabify as the onset of the second syllable — [ɣa.'ndam] and [ka.'mbet] respectively — giving the allowed syllable structure CV.CVC.

There is a smallish number of words showing the pattern in (18e), e.g. *kulwam* 'Papuan black snake', *yayhuy* 'hornbill'. The word *kulwam* must be a loan from the related Upper Bian language, where *kulwam* means 'snake'.

Thus, the data in (18) suggest that there is a restriction preventing heavy syllables from occurring in the pretonic position. The same pattern is observed in the less frequent words with penultimate stress. The data in (19) show that the restriction on light/heavy syllables is according to their position relative to the stressed syllable, and not to their absolute position in the word. The heavy syllables in (19b–c) are permissible since they are stressed. Again, words with a heavy syllable preceding the stressed syllable are not attested (19d).

(19) Penultimate stress

    a.   (C)V́.CV   *yaba* ['ja.ba] 'big', *eho* ['e.ho] 'ripe'
    b.   (C)V́C.CV   *abna* ['ab.na] 'theft', *gomna* ['gom.na] 'fang'
    c.   (C)V.CV́C.CV   *kadakda* [ka.'dak.da] 'Adam's apple', *galigla* [ga.'lig.la] 'scales'

    d.   *(C)VC.CV́C.CV

We can formulate the restriction seen in (18) and (19) as a constraint:
– Avoid heavy syllables in pretonic position.

The next section discusses the consequences of this constraint for morphology.

2.4.1 Insertion of pretonic epenthetic /a/

Whenever affix concatenation would result in a heavy syllable immediately preceding the stressed syllable (e.g. *CVC.CV́C, cf. (18e)), a vowel /a/ will be present in the 'output' form forming a light pretonic syllable (CV.Ca.CV́C). This ensures that the output does not violate the constraint against heavy syllables in pre-tonic position (cf. previous section). This pattern will be illustrated by prefixing verb morphology, reduplicated forms, and comparative data.

It is common to find instances of /a/ in the prefixal morphology of the verb (see §8.3) that are not licensed by any of the prefixes themselves. Some straightforward examples of such epenthetic /a/'s were seen in §2.2, where /a/ was inserted between the prefix *k-* and a stem beginning with a consonant (*kaman* 'come with'; cf. *[kman]). The more complicated examples in (20) have the same unlicensed /a/, as seen in the bracketed output forms. The morphemic make-up of the prefixal complex is given to the left of the arrow; note that output [a] lacks any corresponding segment in the morphemic line-up. We can explain the presence of /a/ in these forms as a result of the constraint against heavy pretonic syllables. Note that the final syllable of the prefixal complex carries the stress; if /a/ had not been present, the output forms would have had a heavy syllable preceding the stressed syllable, e.g. *[mak.'ka ya.li] in (20a).

(20) a. /mak-ka-   yali/   →   [ma.ka.'ka ya.li]
         FUT:1.A-PRI-   lie.down   'I will lie down first.'

     b. /mend-b-a-ap-   balen/   →   [me.n̪da.'bap ba.len]
         PERF-ACT-3SG.A-CT- finish   'S/he has finished.'

Reduplication is not productive in contemporary Coastal Marind, but a large number of lexicalised forms systematically show reduplication with /a/ intervening between the reduplicant and the base (the asterisks in the Base column mark hypothetical unattested forms). The insertion of /a/ between a stressed syllable and a preceding heavy syllable follows the pattern seen above in morpheme concatenation: it prevents illegal output forms such as *CVC.CV́C.

(21)   Base   Reduplicated form   Gloss
   a.   *pod   podapod   [po.da.'pod]   cf. *[pod.'pod]   'lizard sp.'
   b.   pal 'skin' ? palapal   [pa.la.'pal]   etc.   'thin'
   c.   *yul   yulayul   [yu.la.'yul]   'coconut flower'
   d.   *dap   dapadap   [da.pa.'dap]   'skin disease sp.'

Another morphological process that depends on insertion of epenthetic /a/ is infixation of Undergoer markers into verb stems, as described in §10.3.2.

A final illustration comes from comparative data. The avoidance of heavy pretonic syllables is one of many features distinguishing Coastal Marind from the closely related Bush Marind. Below I contrast some forms from the Wambi dialect (the variety described in this grammar) with the variety of Bush Marind spoken in the village Sanggase. The Sanggase variety (like other varieties of Bush Marind) does not have any constraint against words of the shape CVC.CV́C, i.e. the pattern that is absent in Wambi and other villages where Coastal Marind is used. Compare the cognate forms given below:

(22)

		Coastal Marind		Bush Marind		Gloss
	a.	*namakad*	[na.ma.'kad]	*namkad*	[nam.'kad]	'thing'
	b.	*ipani*	[i.pa.'ni]	*ipni*	[ip.'ni]	'fish sp.'
	c.	*isala*	[i.sa.'la]	*esla*	[es.'la]	'sitting platform'
	d.	*nalakam*	[na.la.'kam]	*nalkam*	[nal.'kam]	'child'

2.4.2 Syncopation of antepretonic /a/

Examples (18) and (19) above showed that a heavy syllable is permissible in the antepretonic syllable (e.g. CVC.CV.CV́C) but not in the pretonic position (e.g. *CVC.CV́C). In this section, it will be shown that the former pattern is not only permissible, but also *preferred*, compared to the syllable sequence CV.CV.CV.CV́(C), i.e. three light syllables preceding the stressed syllable.

According to this preference, speakers will prefer to syncopate the vowel in the 2nd syllable (boldfaced) of the sequence CV.**CV**.CV.CV́(C) to form the preferred sequence CVC.CV.CV́(C). This only applies if the relevant vowel is an /a/ however; we can say that /a/ is the only syncopatable vowel in the language. The preference can be stated as follows:

– If possible, let the antepretonic syllable be heavy by syncopating /a/.

The effects of this preference are mostly found within the prefixal complex — roots are rarely longer than two syllables, so it is mostly vacuous outside affixation. A clear example is in (23): here, the prefix sequence would have the expected output ?[a.na.ma.'m̪bap], but the application of syncope to the boldfaced /a/ gives the preferred sequence VC.CV.CV́C:

(23) /an**a**m-a-am̪b-ap- hajad/ → [an.ma.'m̪bap ha.jad]
       JUS-3SG.A-2SG.GEN-CT- shut.up   'Shut yourself up!'

Other examples are:

(24) a. /t-mak-n-e-ap-   ʰwil/ → [tam.ka.ˈnep ʰwil]
       GIV-FUT:1.A-REM-1PL-CT- walk   'We will go over there.'
    b. /ah-bat-e-ka-   man/ → [abteˈka man]
       IMP-AFF-APPL-PRI-   come   'Bring him/her first!'

(Note also the insertion of epenthetic /a/ in (24a) preventing formation of a cluster *tm-.)

Outside verb morphology, syncopation of /a/ is found in certain lexicalised compounds that derive from the concatenation of two bi-syllabic words, the first of which ends in /a/. The final vowel of the first word is syncopated according to the pattern CV.Ca.CV.CVC→CVC.CV.CVC. Two examples are given below:

(25)   Etymology   Present-day forms
    a. */oŋgat-itit/ 'coconut-root'   → [uŋg.ti.ˈtit] 'root of coconut tree'
    b. */kata-pale/ 'scrub.fowl-ridge'   → [kat.pa.ˈle]   'scrubfowl mound'

This is not a productive pattern in compounds, however: a typical compound such as *takah-unum* (lit. 'fire-tongue') 'flame' has the main stress on the last syllable of the first member, and is not syncopated to *[ˈtak.hu.num].

2.4.2.1 Optional deletion of initial /a/

A marginal process which is perhaps related to /a/-syncopation is the loss of initial /a/ in items of the shape /a.σ.σ/, as in (26). This process is completely optional but is fairly common in casual speech, especially in the high-frequency word 'water'.

(26)   Long form   Short form
    a. *adaka*   [a.da.ˈka]   [da.ˈka]   'water'
    b. *amamun*   [a.ma.ˈmun]   [ma.ˈmun]   'entire'

2.5 Morphophonemic alternations

In this section I list some processes that are important for the description of morpheme concatenation.

2.5.1 Antepenultimate vowel gradation

In words of three syllables or more, the mid vowels /e o/ alternate with the high vowels /i u/ in the antepenultimate syllable. For example, in verb stems with a root vowel /o/

the alternant *u* is found if the 1.U infix *-n-* is present, as this adds one syllable to the stem (27). (The process of infixation is described in §10.3.2; the only thing to note for now is that the forms on the right are one syllable longer than the forms on the left.)

(27)   3SG.U   1.U
  a.   og⟨e⟩b   uga⟨n⟩ab   'bury'
  b.   kol⟨e⟩wn   kula⟨n⟩awn   'laugh at'
  c.   hoy⟨e⟩b   huya⟨n⟩ab   'make s.b. shut up'
  d.   lok⟨e⟩h   luka⟨n⟩ah   'peek'

An alternative analysis would be that these verb stems actually have an underlying /u/ which is lowered to [o] in the left column. This analysis must be wrong, since there are many verb stems with /u/ in this position (28).

(28)   3SG.U   1.U
  a.   luy⟨e⟩b   luya⟨n⟩ab   'name s.b.'
  b.   mungg⟨e⟩h   mungga⟨n⟩ah   'hum, buzz'   etc.

This shows that the simplest analysis must be raising of /o/, and not the other way around.

The same process is observed with verb stems that have an /e/ in the initial syllable in the 3SG.U form (29). The vowel is raised to [i] when the 1.U infix ⟨n⟩ is plugged into the stem, since this causes the syllable with /e/ to be pushed into the antepenultimate position.

(29)   3SG.U   1.U
  a.   kes⟨e⟩h   kisa⟨n⟩ah   'spit at'
  b.   kwehw⟨e⟩b   kwihwa⟨n⟩ab   'intercept'
  c.   men⟨e⟩h   mina⟨n⟩ah   'grunt in sleep'
  d.   hwes⟨e⟩wn   hwisa⟨n⟩awn   'have a good look at'

Antepenultimate gradation also applies to inflectional morphology. The prefixal complex that precedes the verb stem forms a phonological word on its own, so prefixes that contain /o/ or /e/ are affected by heightening if the vowel of the prefix occurs in the antepenultimate syllable counting from the end of the prefixal complex. Example (30) shows a sequence of prefixes occurring before the 1st person stem of the verb 'beg'. This verb indexes the person from whom the actor begs something by means of the Genitive prefix series; in this example, the 3rd person Genitive prefix *omb-*. In (30a), this prefix is followed by material that causes its vowel to be in the penultimate syllable, so the vowel /o/ surfaces as [o]. In (30b), the Frustrative prefix *um-* ('in vain') is added, which causes the /o/ in *omb-* to end up in the antepenultimate syllable. This triggers antepenultimate heightening, so /o/ is realised as [u] in the output form.

(30) a. /nak-om̰b-e-ap-   n-ig/ →   [na.ko.'m̰bep nig]
         1.A-3SG.GEN-1PL-CT-   1.U-beg   'We begged him/her for it'

     b. /nak-om̰b-um-e-ap-   n-ig/ →   [na.ku.m̰bu.'mep nig]
         1.A-3SG.GEN-FRUS-1PL-CT- 1.U-beg 'We begged him/her in vain'

The alternative analysis — saying that /u/ is the basic allomorph in the prefixes above, but that it is lowered in the penultimate syllable of the prefixal complex — must be wrong, because the Frustrative *um-* surfaces unaltered in this position, as in (30b) above, and (31) below:

(31) /nak-um-ap- atin/   →   [na.ku.'map atin]
     1.A-FRUS-CT- stand.up   'I tried to stand up.'

Heightening is also present in some words that appear to be historically reduplicated (mostly names of flora and fauna):

(32)   Base   Reduplicated form   Gloss
   a.   *yon   yunayon   [ɣu.na.'ɣon]   'infant'
   b.   *tol   tulatol   [tu.la.'tol]   'bird sp.'
   c.   *pod   pudapod   [pu.da.'pod]   'lizard sp.'
   d.   *ley   liyaley   [li.ya.'ley]   'flying squirrel'
   e.   *pes   pisapes   [pi.sa.'pes]   'grass sp.'
   f.   *nanggen   nangginanggen   [na.ŋ͡gi.na.'ŋ͡gen] 'ant sp.'

2.5.2 Plosive Nasalisation

This alternation is restricted to the prefixal complex, where it occurs quite frequently. When concatenation of morphemes causes a morph ending in one of the plosives /p t k/ to occur before /b/, the resulting sequence is realised as [m̰b] instead of the unacceptable *[pb], *[tb] or *[kb]. The resulting prenasalised plosive syllabifies as the onset of the following syllable (implying that the sequence is phonemicised rather than a sequence [m]+[b]). Examples (33a–c) show Plosive Nasalisation affecting the final /p t k/ of *ndap-* (FUT), *mat-* (HORT) and *nak-* (1.A) before /b/-initial prefixes.

(33) a. /ndap-bat-a-   kaʰwid/ → [nda.'m̰bat ka.ʰwid]
         FUT-AFF-3SG.A-   die:3SG.U   'he will die, poor one'

     b. /mat-bat-   aheb/   → [ma.'m̰bat a.heb]
         HORT-AFF-   eat:3SG.U   'Please let me eat it.'

     c. /m-h-ak-b-e-   hi/   → [ma.ha.'m̰be hi]
         OBJ-ROG-1.A-ACT-1PL- eat:IV.U   '(What) did we eat?'

The same process of nasalisation, but at the alveolar place of articulation, appears if a prefix ending in a plosive occurs before /d/. The only prefix of the shape *d-* is the Past Durative, and the only prefix ending in a plosive that can occur before the Past Durative is the 1st person Actor prefix *nak-*, so this process is restricted to the prefix sequence /nak-d-/. The /k/ is nasalised into [n] and the sequences is phonemicised as [nd], as shown in (34).

(34) /nak-d-e- naɣat/ → [na.'nde naɣat]
 1.A-DUR-1PL- be.moving 'we went'

Before prefixes starting with consonants other than /b d/ there is no Plosive Nasalisation, and sequences /p t k/ followed by other consonants are broken up by an epenthetic [a] according to the general phonotactic requirements (§2.2), as in (35).

(35) a. /nda-p-ka- na-ʰwala/ → [nda.pa.'ka na.ʰwala]
  LOC-FUT:1.A-PRI- 1.U-be 'I will be (there) first'
 b. /mat-ka-p- kahos/ → [ma.ta.'kap ka.hos]
  FUT:1.A-PRI-CT- chew.betel 'Let me chew betelnut first'
 c. /k-ak-hat- Ø/ → [ka.ka.'hat]
  PRS.NTRL-1.A-PRSTV- be.NPST '(Here) I am'

Nasalisation before the triggers /b d/ is restricted to the voiceless plosive targets /p t k/. The only voiced plosive target that could appear in this context is the Past Durative *d-*, which attaches before /b/-initial prefixes such as *b-* (ACT) and *bat-* (AFF). However, *d-* is always deleted (§2.5.3) before nasalisation can occur.

2.5.3 Loss of /d/

The Past Durative prefix *d-* is involved in an important phonological process affecting the prefixal complex: the loss of /d/ before /b/ (other plosives are retained in nasalised form before /b/, cf. §2.5.2). This means that *d-* is never present when one of the four *b*-initial prefixes from position class −11 is employed (see §15.3). Since the use of Past Durative *d-* is obligatory with many verbs in past-time contexts (e.g. *um* 'go repeatedly' or *tel* 'be lying'; see §14.2.1), a strictly morphemic approach would describe *d-* as being 'underlyingly' present in forms such as (36). Compare that example to (37), in which /d/ is retained since it is not followed by a /b/-initial prefix. The second lines in the examples provide morphemic representations of the input to *d*-deletion and other phonological processes.

(36) ndabat-   umti
    /nd-**d**-**bat**-ø-   ø-um-ti/
    LOC-DUR-AFF-3SG.A-   3SG.U-go-DUR
    'he, poor one, went (there) repeatedly'   [D03:0084]

(37) ndadap-   katelti
    /nd-**d**-ø-ap-   ka-tel-ti/
    LOC-DUR-3SG.A-CT- INESS-be.lying-DUR
    'she was lying inside (there)'   [W10:0124]

In the Eastern dialect of Coastal Marind, which lacks the process of *d*-deletion, the form of the prefixal complex corresponding to (36) would be *ndadabat-*, showing both Past Durative *d-* and Affectionate *bat-* intact.[4]

In order to keep abstraction at a minimum, I adopt the convention of never glossing verbs as having a 'deleted' Past Durative *d-* present, even in cases such as (36) where there are semantic reasons for stipulating a zero morph. Such artificial solutions are typical of morphemic approaches — a better description is to treat a prefixal complex of the shape *ndabat* as realising either the feature set [+Affectionate, −PastDurative, ...] or [+Affectionate, +PastDurative, ...], without having to take decisions on invisible morphs.

2.5.4 Loss of /h/

In certain contexts within the prefixal complex, /h/ is dropped.

2.5.4.1 Before consonant

When a prefix ending in /h/ precedes a consonant-initial prefix, /h/ is generally lost. In this regard, /h/ differs from other consonants which would trigger epenthesis in the same context (§2.2). The prefixes that are affected by loss of /h/ are the Imperative *ah-* (38), the Dependent *ah-* (39), the Interrogative *h-* (40), and the Proximal *eh-* (41).

(38) a. /ah-na- og/ →   ana-og!
         IMP-1.DAT- give   'Give me!'
     b. /ah-bat- man/ →   abat-man!
         IMP-AFF- come   'Come, poor one!'

---
4 Cf. paradigms in Drabbe (1955: 128 and passim).

(39) a. /ah-mo- uma⟨ɣ⟩ah/ → amo-umaɣah
       DEP-2SG.A.FUT- go⟨2SG.U⟩ 'If you go...'

   b. /ah-p-a-a- aɣi/ → apa-aɣi
       DEP-FUT-3SG.A-2SG.DAT- say 'If s/he tells you...'

(40) a. /h-b-a- was/ → ba-was?
       ROG-ACT-3SG.A- sew '(Who) sowed it?'

   b. /h-nak-b-e- naɣat/ → nambe-naɣat?
       ROG-1.A-ACT-1PL- be.moving.PL '(With whom) did we go?'

(41) a. /eh-nak-e-ap- laɣ-e/ → enakep-laɣe
       PROX:III-1.A-1PL-CT- speak-IPFV 'what we're saying'

   b. /ih-nak-e- haman-la/ → inake-hamata
       PROX:I/II.PL-1.A-1PL- sit.PL-EXT 'where we are sitting'

The deletion of /h/ in the Imperative shows variation in one context: the common combination *ah-ka-* (IMP-PRI-) has the variants [aka] and [ahaka], i.e. the /h/ can optionally be followed by epenthetic vowel /a/ instead of being elided. Examples are *aka-og!* or *ahaka-og!* 'Do it first!'; however, initial /a/ is usually elided in this high-frequency sequence — *haka-og!* — according to the principle in §2.4.2.1.

2.5.4.2 Optional deletion of intervocalic /h/

The loss of /h/ within the prefixal complex is a common feature, and it is especially prevalent in casual, allegro speech. Deletion of /h/ is only possible when it occurs between two identical vowels. This means that /h/ can be deleted in contexts such as /aha/, /oho/, etc., but must be retained between different vowels such as /oha/ or /ahe/. It also seems that intervocalic /h/ is mostly deleted where it is redundant, i.e. where the inflectional feature that it realises is recoverable from the surrounding context.

The redundancy feature can be illustrated by the Presentative prefix *hat-* (with a meaning similar to French *voilà*; see §15.3.5). Since no other prefix with a similar distribution to *hat-* ends in a /t/, the initial /h/ can be deleted without giving rise to any ambiguity in the parsing of the prefixes, as shown by the short and long output variants in (42a). In the case of *hat-*, deletion of intravocalic /h/ seems to be obligatory in non-stress bearing syllables: there are no corpus attestations of 'long forms' retaining the /h/ of *hat-* when the prefix makes up a non-final syllable of the prefixal complex (42b).

2.5 Morphophonemic alternations — 45

(42) a. /k-hat-ø-   yet/   →   kahat-yet or kat-yet
        PRS.NTRL-PRSTV-3SG.A-   walk
        '(There) s/he is walking.'

   b. /k-hat-ø-ap-   mil-e/   →   katap-mile
        PRS.NTRL-PRSTV-3SG.A-CT- be.sitting-DUR
        '(There) s/he is sitting.'

The same distribution of intravocalic /h/ is observed with the prefix combination *h-…b-* used in information questions. The complicated morphological details are discussed in §19.3.1; here it will suffice to note that the vowel after *h-* usually 'spreads' to the position before the prefix, so that *h-* ends up surrounded by identical vowels. Examples such as (43a) seem to be in free variation, while long forms with *h-* in the penultimate syllable of the prefixal complex (?*mohobap*), are unattested in corpus data.

(43) a. /ma-h-o-b-   ɣi/   →   mohob-ɣi? or mob-ɣi?
        OBJ-ROG-2SG.A-ACT-   eat
        '(What) did you eat?'

   b. /ma-h-o-b-ap-   idih-e/   →   mobap-idihe?
        OBJ-ROG-2SG.A-ACT-CT-   see:3SG.U-IPFV
        '(What) are you looking at?'

2.5.5 Vowel sequences in verb prefixes

Various patterns are observed when morpheme concatenation within the prefixal complex (§8.3) results in two adjacent vowels. It was observed in §2.1.2.2 that the only permitted vowel sequences /V_1V_2/ are those in which V_1 = /i/. Thus, when a prefix ending in /i/ is followed by a vowel-initial prefix, the sequence surfaces unaltered, as in (44).

(44) /ah-i-o-   aɣi/ →   ahio-aɣi!
       IMP-RE-3SG.DAT- say   'Tell him/her again!'

Other combinations trigger changes preventing illegal vowel sequences.
    VOWEL COALESCENCE. This is restricted to the Allative *ind-* and Separative *is-*. When a prefix ending in /o/ is followed by one of these /i/-initial prefixes, the sequence /oi/ merges into *u*:

(45) a. /ndamo-ind- man/   →   ndamun-man
        FUT:2SG.A-ALL- come   'You will come towards it.'

   b. /o-is-   iʰja⟨ɣ⟩on/   →   us-ihyayon
        2SG.A-SEP-   run.away⟨2SG.U⟩   'You ran away from it.'

GLIDE FORMATION. If V_1 is a non-high vowel, and V_2 is /e/ or /i/ which is not followed by other prefixes within the prefixal complex, the sequence is pronounced as Vy (46a–b). Three common verb prefixes are affected by this alternation: the Repetitive *i-* (§16.2), the Accompaniment *e-* (§13.1.6) and the 1st Person Plural *e-* (§9.5).

(46) a. /nak-o-e-   aɣi/ →   nakoy-ayi
         1.A-3SG.DAT-1PL- say   'We told him/her.'
     b. /a-mo-i-   kabed/ → amoy-kabed
         DEP-FUT:2SG.A-RE- ask   'if you ask again'

GLIDE INSERTION. A transitional glide *y* is inserted between /e/ and a following back vowel /o u/, as in (47a–b). (To facilitate morpheme segmentation, I have adopted the convention of omitting such transitional glides in the orthography used elsewhere in this grammar.)

(47) a. /e-o-   aɣi/ →   eyo-ayi
         2PL.A-3SG.DAT- say   'You (pl) told him/her.'
     b. /e-um-   aɣi/ →   eyum-ayi
         2PL.A-FRUS-   say   'You (pl) almost said it.'

DELETION. When two identical vowels are adjacent, one is deleted (there are no phonemic long vowels in Coastal Marind), as in (48a). In sequences of non-identical vowels that are not covered by any of the processes mentioned so far, the vowel that is lower in height is deleted, e.g. /o/ in the sequence /ou/ (48b), /e/ in the sequence /ei/ (48c), but /a/ in the sequence /oa/ (48d).

(48) a. /o-o-   aɣi/   → o-ayi
         2SG.A-3SG.DAT-   say   'You told him/her.'
     b. /o-um-   ɣod/   → um-yod
         2SG.A-FRUS-   vomit   'You almost threw up.'
     c. /ndame-ind-   umah/ → ndamin-umah
         FUT:2PL.A-ALL-   go:2|3PL.U 'You (pl) will go towards it.'
     d. /mak-o-ap-   idih/ → makop-idih
         FUT:1.A-3SG.DAT-CT- see:III.U   'I will watch it for him/her.'

2.5.6 Optional /amo/-metathesis

This process applies to the sequence /amo/ in the prefixal complex when it is followed by at least two other syllables (e.g. /a.mo.σ.σ/). It can be thought of as vowel metathesis /amo/ to /oma/ which then undergoes regular antepenultimate vowel gradation (§2.5.1) and syncope (§2.4.2): /o.ma.σ.σ/→u.ma.σ.σ→[um.σ.σ].

(49) /n̪d**amo**-na-ka-ap- og/ →   nd**um**nakap-og!
      FUT:2SG.A-1.DAT-PRI-CT- give   'You'll give it to me!'

However, speakers are inconsistent in the application of this process, and the basic /amo/ sequences are mostly left intact, except for the Prohibitive prefixes where it regularly occurs (see §19.1.4).

3 Nominals, their morphology and derivation

This chapter describes the category of nominals and its subtypes (§3.1). Morphology in the nominal domain is very limited, and most morphological patterns in nouns (§3.2) and adjectives (§3.3) are non-productive. The basic numerals reach to four, and nouns for 'hand' and 'foot' allow counting up to twenty (§3.4). Possessor marking on kinship terms is irregular and often expressed by suppletive words (§3.5). Compounding, on the other hand, is a productive pattern and serves various purposes (§3.6). The last section describes three types of derived nominals (§3.7).

3.1 The nominal word classes

The label 'nominal' is used here as a cover term for entity-denoting words and property-denoting words, which are similar in their ability to form referring expressions, and in their inability to combine with the inflectional material that characterises verbs (i.e. the prefixal complex). Properties of nouns are described in §3.1.1. It is not clear that a separate class of adjectives needs to be distinguished, as discussed in §3.1.2. Some other minor categories can also be considered sub-types of nominals, since all of their members can head NPs: kin terms, numerals, demonstratives and pronominals.

3.1.1 Nouns as a word class

Nouns are invariant and have no inflectional morphology. They are conventionally assigned to one of four genders: Gender I (male humans), Gender II (female humans, and all animals) and Genders III or IV (inanimates); see Chapter 5. Gender and (for animates) number are reflected in agreement and/or indexing on verbs and other agreeing targets, not on the nouns themselves. Compare: *nggat upe* (dog DIST:II) 'that dog' vs. *nggat ipe* (dog DIST:I/II.PL) 'those dogs'.

The only exceptions are so-called overt-gender nouns, a small group of nouns for which gender and number are reflected by a change in the stem-final vowel. The gender-marking vowels in these nouns must have arisen through the same umlaut process that gave rise to alternating vowels in the final syllable of agreeing adjectives, although the resulting pattern depends on the lexeme (see the next section, as well as §3.2.1 and §3.3).

Overt-gender nouns can be thought of as being derived from a root with a general meaning, e.g. *anVm* (with the general meaning 'person') from which nouns with more specific meaning are obtained by assigning them to a gender and plugging in the corresponding vowel: *anem* 'man', *anum* 'woman', *anim* 'people'.

It could be argued that these forms are inflectional variants of one lexeme ('person'), but for most other overt-gender nouns it is better to describe the individual gender forms as lexicalised, because they exhibit various irregularities in meaning and form. This is further discussed in §5.2.3.1. Therefore, the generalisation that nouns lack inflectional morphology remains robust.

Proper names share most of their distributional possibilities with standard nouns: for example, they can be determined by demonstratives (*Maria upe* 'that Maria') and occur in possessive constructions with *en* 'POSS' (*Wodim en Maria* 'Wodim's [daughter] Maria'). The main difference with lexical nouns is that proper names may occur with the Associative Plural *ke* or *keti* (§7.6.1), a property they share with kinship terms.

3.1.2 Adjectives as a word class

It is not entirely clear if there are any grammatical criteria that systematically distinguish the semantic class of property words (*yaba* 'big', *kanil* 'heavy', *kunayhi* 'black', *dohi* 'red', etc.) from nouns. I will list some commonalities before addressing potential differences. The candidates for adjective-hood will be referred to as 'property words' in order not to anticipate the final verdict on their status.

3.1.2.1 Commonalities with nouns

Like nouns, property words modify other words by being the first member of a compound with the modified word as the head. Examples of compounds with property words as the first members are: *yaba-basik* 'big pig', *kosi-basik* 'small pig', *dohu-basik* 'brown (lit. red) pig'. These are structurally identical to standard noun+noun compounds such as *basik-muy* 'pig meat'. See further §3.6.

There is no structural difference between the predication of property words (e.g. *waninggap* 'good') and predication of nouns (e.g. *mboy* 'widow'). Both kinds of words require the support of the copula (§17.4) or a copula-like verb such as 'become' to be predicated:

(50) a. *waninggap menda-b-ø- w-in*
       good   PERF-ACT-3SG.A- 3SG.U-become
       'S/he is well.' (e.g. recovered after illness)

   b. *mboy menda-b-ø- w-in*
       widow PERF-ACT-3SG.A- 3SG.U-become
       'She is a widow.'

Like all other nominals, property words can head NPs (or rather, referring phrases), such as *kunayhi ipe* 'the black ones' in (51). (Gender agreement in *kunayhi* 'black' will be addressed further below.) In traditional (and transformational) grammar such structures (including also the preceding NP *Geb en* '[the ones] of Geb') would be described as involving ellipsis of a head noun. (Here, it would be the head of a compound — *kunayhi-basik* 'black pigs' — that has to be ellipsed.) I prefer to state these facts by saying that property words (as well as some postpositional phrases) may head referring phrases on their own, without support from a noun, as long as the presence of the property word is sufficient for successful interpretation.

(51) sam-basik k-a-   Ø,   ipe   ti-k-a-   Ø
     big-pig   PRS.NTRL-3SG.A- be.NPST DIST:I/II.PL GIV:I/II.PL-PRS.NTRL-3SG.A- be.NPST
     Geb en,   kunayhi   ipe
     G.   POSS black:I/II.PL DIST:I/II.PL
     'It's big pigs, those are the ones belonging to the Geb[ze clan], the black ones.'
     [M02:0032]

Although the possibility of heading a referring phrase seems to exist for almost all property words (but see §3.3.2 for obligatorily bound adjectives), it is not much exploited in actual discourse. I have only found a handful of expressions such as 'the black ones' in the corpus, meaning that there are large distributional differences between thing words (which usually head referring phrases) and property words (typically used as modifiers or copula complements).

The three non-criteria discussed so far — acting as a modifier, requiring a copula for predication, and heading an NP — are familiar from other languages that have been claimed to lack a distinction between nouns and adjectives (e.g. Quechua, Weber 1989: 35–36). I now turn to criteria that might be used to distinguish property words from nouns.

3.1.2.2 Differences with nouns

Unlike standard nouns, property words are not assigned to a gender. This is probably the strongest argument for distinguishing a separate class of adjectives in Coastal Marind (and it is a classic argument for positing adjective classes in languages with gender; see e.g. Dixon 2004: 12–13).

The gender criterion is not unproblematic, however, since approximately a dozen nouns lack conventional gender assignment, and instead take their gender from the associated discourse referent (§5.2.3). For example, the noun *agey* 'bait' triggers Gender II agreement if it refers to a worm (cf. *alo* 'worm', Gender II), but Gender III if it refers to a piece of meat (*muy* 'meat', Gender III). If lack of conventionalised gender membership is the decisive criterion for noun- vs. adjectivehood, we must conclude that *agey* 'bait' is an adjective. This is a counterintuitive conclusion since *agey* is more similar in its meaning to thing words such as 'food' than property words such as 'red'. I have no observations of *agey* as a noun modifier, so its distribution seems more noun-like too. There are almost 1,000 nouns for which I have documented the conventional gender assignment, so it seems motivated to disregard the small group of exceptional nouns lacking inherent gender, and to conclude that it is necessary to distinguish nouns from adjectives because the former have fixed gender. I will still consider some additional criteria.

The presence of gender inflection is not useful for distinguishing an adjective class. As explained in §3.3, words such as *kunayhi* 'black' and *papes* 'small' signal agreement through changes in the stem final vowel, which makes them different from (almost all) nouns. However, only 16 property words exhibit agreement, whereas all others property words are invariant; applying this criterion would exclude invariant words such as *waninggap* 'good', *yaba* 'big' and *kanil* 'heavy' from the adjective class, despite these being some of the most frequent modifying words in my corpus. Thus, the presence of gender agreement does not pick out any class of words corresponding to an intuitive notion of adjective.

A more subtle criterion is provided by the degree modifier *ya*. This frequent word is used after the word it modifies, and translates as 'real' combined with thing words (*anim ya* 'real people', *mayan ya* 'real language, truth'), and as 'very' with property words (*kanil ya* 'very heavy', *papes ya* 'very small'). This semantic difference is sometimes cited as a good diagnostic for noun vs. adjectivehood (Dixon 2004: 13). I would suggest that this is an artefact of translation into English, and that the actual function of *ya* is to indicate that something scores high in prototypicality, or signals an 'undeniable instance' of the property/referent. (The difference is also not present in local Malay, where *ya* translates as *betul* 'true' with both property and referring words.) See also §7.6.2.

To summarise, we can say that syntactic criteria do not necessitate a distinction between nouns and adjectives in Coastal Marind. A counter-argument comes from conventionalised gender assignment, which motivates separating nouns from adjectives, but with the caveat that this diagnostic is problematic for the small number of nouns that lack fixed gender assignment. In this grammar, the fixed gender criterion is treated as diagnostic of an adjective class, but I acknowledge that the evidence is somewhat weak. It seems that the distributional differences between entity-denoting and property-denoting words in Coastal Marind are not strongly reflected in morphosyntactic differences between the two semantic classes.

Note that adjective-like expressions can be derived from (some) nouns using the postpositions *hi* 'like', *ti* 'with', and *ni* 'without' (as discussed in §6.1), and from (some) verbs by means of the Participial suffixes *-la* and *lek* (§3.7.3).

3.1.3 Other nominal subtypes

3.1.3.1 Ability nominals
Two high-frequency words express ability and knowledge, and the lack thereof: *mayay* 'can, know' and *mbaymbay* 'cannot, not know', as shown in (52–53). These words must

be nominals, because they are predicated by means of the copula, to express a state ('knows', 'didn't know' etc.), or the light verb *win* 'become', to express a change-of-state ('realise', 'become unable' etc.). They lack other properties of standard entity-denoting nouns, however, such as the ability to form compounds or appearing in contexts that trigger gender agreement.

(52) Explaining the meaning of the word *nak*.

epe   nak   mbaymbay   k-a-   Ø,
DIST:I vine   cannot   PRS.NTRL-3SG.A- be.NPST

namaya nak   mayay ndame-ø-   w-in
now   vine   know   FUT-3SG.A-   3SG.U-become

'He doesn't know what *nak* ('vine') is, but now he will know what *nak* is.'

[W13:0209]

(53) *anim   mayay   tapahat-ø- in,*
people   know   PROH-3SG.A- become:2|3PL.U

nahan   inah   sa-p-e-   Ø   nok   mayay
1.EMPH   two   ONLY-FUT:1.A-1PL-   be.NPST 1   know

'Don't let other people know, only the two of us should know.'   [D03:0103]

In stative predications with the ability nominals, the participant who knows, is unable etc. (the knower) is indexed on the copula, as shown by the 1st person agreement in (53) above. If *win* 'become' is used to express the corresponding change-of-state, it patterns like a patientive verb (§12.2.2), and indexes person/number of the knower by means of the Undergoer affixes, and the Actor prefix defaults to 3sg, as seen in (53) and (55). The ability nominal functions as the complement of the copula or light verb. The adjunct expressing the entity, skill, word etc. that is known or unknown can be a noun, as in (52), or a phrase headed by a nominally used verb stem, as with *ndakla ne lohwis* 'climbing down without using a bamboo pole' in (54).

(54) *ndakla   ne   ka-lohwis   mayay   k-a-   Ø*
bamboo.pole   without:I INESS-descend.PLA   can   PRS.NTRL-3SG.A-   be.NPST

'It's possible to climb down [into the well] without a bamboo pole.'

[W06:0196]

To express knowledge of a state-of-affairs, a reported speech construction, introduced by the quotative *ago* is used (55) (cf. §20.2.1).

Tab. 3.1: Temporal nouns

Deictic		Times of the day		Other	
nanawis	'day before yesterday'	*kwemek*	'morning'	*mandin*	'long time ago'
wis	'yesterday'	*yanid*	'day, mid-day'	*alinde*	'in the future'
namaya	'now, today'	*usus*	'afternoon'	*agonde*	'later'
yapap	'tomorrow'	*yap*	'evening, night'	*adida*	'a short while'
yopo	'day after tomorrow'	*in-yap*	'midnight'	*hyuw*	'long time'
				hindun	'forever'

(55)   *mayay*   *menda-b-ø-e-*   *n-in*   *ago,*
       know   PERF-ACT-3SG.A-1PL-   1.U-become   QUOT

       amay   *keti ipe*   *ti-k-a-*   *nayam*
       ancestor   APL   DIST:I/II.PL   GIV:I/II.PL-PRS.NTRL-3SG.A-   come.PL

       'Then we realised that grandfather and the others were coming.'   [W21:0174]

The use of nominals to express 'can', 'cannot' etc. is shared with other languages of Southern New Guinea area, such as Komnzo and Nmbo (Yam; Döhler 2016: 356, Kashima 2020: 268), and Ende (Pahoturi River; Lindsey 2019: 159), but it is found in other parts of New Guinea as well (e.g. Momu; Honeyman 2017: 127).

3.1.3.2 Temporal nouns

Words expressing temporal deixis, times of the day and durations are nouns, belonging to Gender III. Some common temporal nouns are listed in Table 3.1. The deictic day-names reach two days into the past and future, but the words for 'day before yesterday' and 'day after tomorrow' are flexible in their reference and can sometimes refer to anytime from two up to a few days from today. Coastal Marind lacks the symmetrical day-names reported for some Papuan languages, in which the same lexical item expresses e.g. 'yesterday' and 'tomorrow' (i.e. 'one day from today').[1] The postposition *hi* 'like' (§6.1.4) is added when the reference of the day-name is calculated from a point in time other than the time of speech, as in *yapap hi* 'the next day' (French *le lendemain*).

3.1.3.3 The mass/count distinction

Two diagnostics single out mass nouns (or nouns used with a mass sense). The first is amount quantification with *sam* 'big, much' (56) rather than *otih* 'many' (§7.7.3).

---

1 As found in e.g. Kobon (Davies 1981: 140), Usan (Reesink 1987: 70), Yimas (Foley 1991), Komnzo (Döhler 2016: 111) and Eibela (Aiton 2016: 67). Such systems are fairly rare world-wide but are found in e.g. Hindi (Tent 1998), and it is not clear that they are especially prevalent in Papuan languages.

(56) muy sam k-a-namb-e-   Ø   ay?
     meat big PRS.NTRL-3SG.A-1.GEN-1PL- be.NPST Q
     'We got lots of meat, right?'   [W11:1117]

The second is the use of durative aspectual inflection (such as the Durative *d-*, §14.2.1) on a punctual verb with a non-plural S/O participant. A punctual verb such as *hawa* 'emerge' (which normally describes the onset of the motion event, i.e. 'start to emerge') can only describe a durative action if its subject is plural, as in 'many people started to emerge', or if it is converted into a durative verb by means of the Exended *-a* ('be emerging', §14.2.3). If the subject is a mass noun, however, the punctual base verb *hawa* can express a durative situation, e.g. a liquid, smoke or fire coming out of something, or wind blowing, as in (57).

(57) muli   menda-d-a-p-   hawa
     north.western.monsoon(III) PERF-DUR-3SG.A-CT-   emerge:III.U
     'The north-western monsoon was already blowing.'   [W12:0028]

Some flexibility can be noted, especially with respect to the first diagnostic, and many nouns seem to permit both mass and count conceptualisations. In (58) the speaker used *otih* 'many' to quantify *tamuy* 'food', which usually would occur with *sam* to express 'lots of food'. The preceding context makes it clear that the speaker is referring to varieties of food, which motivates the use of *otih*.

(58) The ancestors survived on bush foods, but "now we eat bananas, taro, sweet potato":

     tamuy otih k-a-   Ø   namaya
     food many PRS.NTRL-3SG.A- be.NPST now
     'There are many [kinds of] food nowadays.'   [W13:0155]

Quantification of mass nouns with numerals shows similar flexibility, at least if the relevant measure is contextually or conventionally available, as in *adaka inah* 'two [bottles/jerrycans etc. of] water'.

3.2 Noun morphology

3.2.1 Overt marking of gender/number

Marind nouns are morphologically invariant, so the nominal categories gender and number are reflected on agreeing targets, but not on the noun itself. There is, however, a small number of exceptional nouns that signal gender and number overtly, by means of changes in the stem-final vowel. I list all such nouns in Table 3.2.

Tab. 3.2: Overt gender on nouns

	I sg	II sg	I/II pl	III	IV
a.	an**e**m 'man'	an**u**m 'woman'	an**i**m 'people'	an**e**m (in compounds)	an**i**m (in compounds)
b.		namak**u**d 'animal'	namak**i**d 'animals'	namak**a**d 'thing(s)'	namak**i**d 'thing(s)'
c.	nam**e**k 'clanmate (m)'	nam**u**k 'clanmate (f)'	nam**i**k 'clanmates'		
d.	nan**i**h 'face (m)'	nan**u**h 'face (f)'	nan**i**h 'faces'		
e.	wanangg**i**b 'son'	wanangg**u**b 'daughter'	wanangg**a** 'children'		
f.	amnangg**i**b 'married man'		amnangg**a** 'married men'		
g.	nahy**a**m 'my husband'	nahy**u**m 'my wife'			
h.	ey**a**l 'a certain man'	ey**u**l 'a certain woman'		ey**a**l 'a certain thing'	
i.		wayukl**u** 'young woman'	wayukl**i**(k) 'young women'		

All of these nouns appear to be built from a skeletal stem into which a vowel is inserted once gender is assigned. The vowels themselves (in boldface) vary, with the most consistent pattern shown by the vowel /u/ marking Gender II (cf. e.g. Gender II form *upe* of the Distal demonstrative). Historically, overt gender marked by stem-final vowels arose through umlaut triggered by postposed gender-marking articles of the shape -V (Usher and Suter 2015). The original articles have disappeared in the Marindic languages, but they are still attested in other branches of the Anim language family.

Note that a noun is said to exhibit overt gender only if there is at least one other corresponding noun in another gender. For example, the noun *yayhuy* 'hornbill' (II) does not show overt gender, despite having the stem-final vowel /u/ (characteristic of Gender II), because there are no corresponding nouns such as **yayhey* or **yayhiy* in other genders.

The only noun stem for which overt gender can be considered productive — with one form for each gender value, and predictable meaning according to the gender — is *anVm* 'person'. This set includes *anem* 'man', *anum* 'woman' and *anim* 'people', but also forms in Genders III (*anem*) and IV (*anim*) that are found in some compounds referring to inanimate entities, e.g. *nene-anim* 'bell' (IV). Such compound formation is especially common for persons, so that a compound *X-anVm* means roughly 'person who does X'. For example, *abna* 'theft' is the base of the compounds *abna-anem* '[male] thief' (I) and *abna-anum* '[female] thief' (II). But the Gender II form *abna-anum* is also used to refer to e.g. a dog who steals food, since animals are also in Gender

II. Other examples of common compounds that are used for both women and animals are *emel-anum* 'woman/animal that keeps asking for food' (< *emel* 'hunger') and *ukna-anum* 'cowardly woman/animal' (< *ukna* 'fear').

The fact that the stem *anVm* appears in expressions denoting inanimate items, and the form *anum* in expressions denoting animals, means that the glosses 'person' and 'woman' are too narrow. One way to solve this problem is to state that *anem*, *anum*, etc. mean 'man', 'woman', and so on, in their independent uses, and that there is a second, bound word *-anVm* whose function is to head compounds with various (sometimes idiosyncratic) meanings, and that this bound word agrees in gender with whatever referent the compound is used for.[2]

There is also a fairly productive stem *namakVd*, giving *namakud* 'animal' (plural *namakid* 'animals'), as well as two words for 'thing': *namakad* (III) and *namakid* (IV). The Gender III word is of more general use, but the Gender IV *namakid* is used to refer to e.g. items of modern technology, which are mostly in Gender IV (for example, my laptop was sometimes referred to as *namakid ipe* 'that thing'). I have never heard the expected Gender I form *namaked*, but speakers that I asked reported that the word exists, and can be used about a male, although they did not agree on its precise meaning.

I note that the productivity of overt gender with these two stems poses a lexicological problem: should the various forms be merged into two super-lexemes *anVm* and *namakVd*, without gender and with underspecified meanings, or should they be divided into multiple, fully specified lexemes such as *anem* 'man' (Gender I), *anum* 'woman' (Gender II), *-anVm* (used in compounds), and so on? I prefer to remain agnostic on this issue since it has little practical consequence (it concerns only two stems), but I do follow the multiple-lexeme approach in the Coastal Marind dictionary (giving *anem* and *anum* separate entries, with usage notes explaining the use of e.g. *-anVm* in compounds) in order to avoid unnecessarily abstract dictionary entries.

The other nouns with overt gender/number are restricted to Genders I and II, with some accidental gaps. For example, the words *eyal* and *eyul* (Genders I and II respectively) mean something like 'a certain man/woman' (used to avoid uttering a person's name; §4.5), but lack a plural form.[3] Similarly, *nahyam* and *nahyum* mean 'husband' and 'wife', but there is no plural form **nahyim* 'spouses'. The issue of how to treat these nouns in the construction of a dictionary does not arise: they are clearly sepa-

---

[2] Interestingly, some animal names are compounds headed by *anem* 'man', e.g. *sanggal-anem* 'kite sp.', *ndaman-anem* 'fish sp.'. Despite the Gender I form *-anem*, these words follow all other nouns denoting animals and trigger agreement according to Gender II. It is likely that these nouns are a remnant of an earlier stage of Marind, in which animals were divided between Genders I and II (this is still the case in other branches of the Anim family) and that their previous assignment to Gender I remains visible in the form *-anem*, but that the more recent reassignment to Gender II is reflected in agreement.
[3] A plural form is reported for the Eastern dialect by Geurtjens (1933: 111), giving the triplet *eher* (I), *ehur* (II), *ehir* (I/II.pl).

rate lexemes, to be listed in separated dictionary entries, just like e.g. Spanish nouns with overt gender such as *hermano* 'brother' and *hermana* 'sister'.

Note finally that the exceptional noun 'child' (in the sense 'prepubescent human') has suppletive number forms: *nalakam* 'child' and *isahih* 'children'.

3.2.2 Reduplication

Reduplication is not a productive pattern in Coastal Marind (unlike in e.g. Malay), but there are many words that appear to have been derived by reduplication historically, as well as a few common expressions that can be reduplicated in certain adverbial contexts. There are also a few kin terms that express plurality by means of reduplication (§3.5).

In the lexicon, reduplicated forms are especially common as names for flora and fauna. Many are reduplicative orphans, without any known source form. For example, *nduknduk* means 'firefly', but there is no known word *nduk*. For others there is a clear etymology, although the motivation remains unclear: for example, I have not yet understood how *kambetkambet*, a plant species with edible fruits, is related to *kambet* 'ear'. For only a small number of reduplicated words are there plausible accounts of the motivation behind the form, provided to me by speakers. Examples are *ihilihil*, a plant whose characteristic red flowers look just like *ihil*, a kind of earrings worn as a traditional decoration; and *nggatnggat* 'fern', so named because the young fronds are furled just like a dog's (*nggat*) tail.

A few nouns may be reduplicated to form adverbial expressions. There are not enough attestations to say how productive this pattern is, and what semantic effects are involved. The noun *yanid* 'day' clearly has a distributive meaning 'every day' when it is reduplicated, as in (59). With other nouns the only function of reduplication seems to be that of deriving an adverbial expression e.g. *ye-ye* 'during the rain' from *ye* 'rain', as in (60). Other attested examples are *dino-dino* 'in the dark' (from *dino* 'dark'), *mayan-mayan* 'while talking' (from *mayan* 'speech, language').

(59) yanid-yanid ka-d-na- i-sak-ma
 day-REDUPL DIR-DUR-3PL.A- 2|3PL.U-hit.PLA-PST.HAB
 'Every day they would kill [a pig].' [W18:0272]

(60) yoy ye-ye m-e-d- nayat Pau ti
 2PL rain-REDUPL OBJ-2PL.A-DUR- be.moving.PL P. with:I/II.PL
 'You went with Pau during the rain.' [W19:0425]

Many ideophones ("marked words that depict sensory imagery"; Dingemanse 2012: 655) contain two identical CV-syllables, e.g.

gigi	'sound of thunder'
yoyo	'splashing in water; sound of rumbling in stomach'
lili	'high-pitched noise, e.g. rustling of dry leaves, splashing of water'
nene	'sound of e.g. bells ringing, mosquitos humming'
papa	'sound of firewood popping'
tataya	'sound of smacking/munching while eating'

These reduplicated (or partly reduplicated, in the case of *tataya*) words seem to be iconic in that they denote sounds that have duration in time; ideophones describing instantaneous bursts of sounds have only one syllable, e.g. *sik* 'psst, denotes the fricative sound made to get someone's attention' and *te* 'the sound of popping a louse between one's nails'. All known Coastal Marind ideophones are sound-imitating, and they do not form a separate word class. Morphosyntactically they behave like other nouns, and trigger agreement in Gender III, and can fill argument slots in the clause, as shown in (61), which has *papa* as the A-argument of the second clause.

(61) mend-an-d-e- n-alit-a, yah takah-papa
     PERF-1.A-DUR-1PL- 1.U-call-EXT but fire-popping.sound

ø-d-ø-e- yahwiy-a
NTRL-DUR-3SG.A-2|3PL.DAT- eat-EXT

'We were calling out for them, but the noise from the fire covered (lit. ate) our calls.' [D05:0090]

3.3 Adjective morphology

Adjectives as a word class separate from nouns were discussed in §3.1.2. There is a subclass consisting of 16 adjectives in the Western dialect of Coastal Marind that agree in gender/number; this is reflected through change in the stem-final vowel.[4] The same kind of exponence was observed for a small set of nouns with 'overt gender' in §3.2.1. The pattern of variable stem-final vowels in adjectives is also a result of a process of umlaut triggered by postposed gender articles in an earlier stage of Marind (Usher and Suter 2015).

---

[4] Some additional agreeing adjectives are reported for the Eastern dialect of Coastal Marind in Drabbe (1955) and Geurtjens (1933): (i) *erakV* (Drabbe, p. 22) or *erakVk* (Geurtjens, p. 115) 'playful, lascivious', no known cognate in the Western dialect; (ii) *akhatV* 'wild' (Drabbe p. 22, not in Geurtjens), no known cognate in the Western dialect; (iii) *kanVr* 'heavy' (Drabbe p. 23), corresponding to invariant (i.e. non-agreeing) *kanil* in the Western dialect; (iv) *memeVn* 'whole, entire' (Drabbe p. 23, Geurtjens p. 242), invariant *amamun* in the Western dialect. Of the agreeing adjectives in the Western dialect, two are unattested in the material on the Eastern variety: *VhV* 'ripe' and *yayayVy* 'sharp'.

3.3 Adjective morphology

Tab. 3.3: Gender agreement on adjectives

Gloss	I sg	II sg	I/II pl	III	IV
'light (weight)'	ak*e*k	ak*u*k	ak*i*k	ak*a*k	ak*i*k
'mid-size'	samlay*e*n	samlay*u*n	samlay*i*n	samlay*a*n	samlay*i*n
'short'	dahwag*e*s	dahwag*u*s	dahwag*i*s	dahwag*i*s	dahwag*i*s
'long'	wagat*o*k	wagat*o*k	wagit*u*k	wagat*o*k	wagit*u*k
'old, ancient'	tanam*e*	tanam*u*	tanam*i*	tanam*a*	tanam*i*
'thin'	halah*e*l	halah*u*l	halah*i*l	halah*a*l	halah*i*l
'thin'	palap*e*l	palap*u*l	palap*i*l	palap*a*l	palap*i*l
'sturdy'	tag*e*	tag*u*	tag*i*	tag*a*	tag*i*
'soft'	–	yahy*u*hy	yah*i*h	yahy*a*hy	yah*i*h
'sharp'	–	–	–	yayay*a*y	yayay*i*y
'dull'	–	–	–	yanday*a*l	yanday*i*l
'ripe'	–	–	–	eho	ihu

Table 3.3 gives the gender forms for 12 of the 16 agreeing adjectives, with the alternating stem-final vowels in boldface. The general pattern of exponence is: Gender I *-e-*, Gender II *-u-*, Gender III *-a-*, Gender IV and the plural of Genders I & II *-i-*. The only exceptions are *dahwagVs* 'short', which has *-i-* in Gender III, *wagVtVk* 'long', which is *wagatok* in all genders except *wagituk* in Gender IV and I/II plural, *VhV* 'ripe' which has the forms *eho* (III) and *ihu* (IV). This adjective, along with 'sharp' and 'dull', is only compatible with nouns that denote inanimates, which explains the lack of forms in Genders I & II (since these genders contain animate nouns). I was unable to get a Gender I form of 'soft'; the Gender II form *yahyuhy* can be used about animals (which are in Gender II).[5]

There are three native colour terms in Coastal Marind, all of them derived from combinations of nouns and the similative postposition *hV* 'like'. This postposition agrees in gender, but it has a distinct shape only in Gender II, *hu*, whereas it is *hi* in all other combinations. The forms of the lexicalised colour adjectives ending in *-hV* are in Table 3.4.

Tab. 3.4: Gender agreement on three colour adjectives

Gloss	I sg	II sg	I/II pl	III	IV
'white'	kohi	kohu	kohi	kohi	kohi
'red'	dohi	dohu	dohi	dohi	dohi
'black'	kunayhi	kunayhu	kunayhi	kunayhi	kunayhi

---

[5] Drabbe (1955: 22) gives the Gender I form *hazez* from the Eastern dialect, with the Dutch gloss *zacht*, *week* 'soft, weak'. The expected cognate form **yahyehy* was not accepted by speakers of the Western dialect described in this grammar.

3.3.1 The suppletive adjective 'small'

The most interesting agreement forms are those of 'small'. This adjective is suppletive, and the cells of its paradigm are filled by no less than three unrelated stems: the singular stem *papes* and the two plural stems *isahih* and *wasasuy*. The paradigm of 'small' is given in Table 3.5.

Tab. 3.5: Gender agreement on 'small'

	I	II	III	IV
SG	papes	papus	papes	papis
PL	isahih	isahih	wasasuy	isahih

The most remarkable observation about 'small' is that this lexeme makes a distinction that no other agreeing target makes in the language: it distinguishes number of inanimates. Recall that it generally is Gender I (male humans) and Gender II (female humans, all animals) that have the ability to trigger plural agreement forms when the referent is plural; nouns denoting inanimates (divided between Genders III and IV) trigger agreement in gender but make no distinction between singular and plural. 'Small' is exceptional, because in addition to the suppletive plural stem *isahih* used for animates in Genders I and II (the word *isahih* is also a noun meaning 'children, young of animals', with the singular *nalakam* 'child'), the lexeme also provides stems for the plurals of inanimates: *wasasuy* for plurals of Gender III, and (again) *isahih* for plurals of Gender IV. This means that 'small' makes a distinction that no other adjective does, giving two extra cells in its paradigm, so it can be said to be overdifferentiated (Bloomfield 1933: 223–224, Corbett 2007: 31) with respect to the feature gender/number.[6,7]

---

[6] Corbett (2007: 32, fn. 44), citing Heath (1981), gives a parallel examples from Mara, an Australian language of the Northern Territory. In Mara, plural marking with non-humans is found with three suppletive adjectives: 'small', 'big' and 'other', whereas plural marking elsewhere is restricted to human referents.

[7] The overdifferentiation observed with 'small' begs the question of the diachronic origin of the plural stems. The only piece of evidence I have is the existence of a verb stem that is very similar in shape to the Gender III plural form *wasasuy*, viz. *asasiy*. This verb seems to be archaic, and the speaker found it difficult to explain its meaning, giving me the cryptic gloss "this is when you sit alone, and there are birds or children surrounding you, making noise". I find the combination of plural and small ('birds or children') in this gloss suggestive of a connection with an adjective meaning 'many small'. The similarity in shape suggests a possible common origin in a stem *$VsVsVy$ (the *wa-* segment in *wasasuy* is an innovation in the Western dialect, cf. Eastern cognate *usasuh*). An origin as a verb entailing plurality of the subject could provide a plausible explanation for the introduction of this number distinction in an adjective paradigm. Unfortunately, not much is known about the other plural stem, *isahih*, other than reconstructed proto-Coastal Marind form */isahij/.

3.3.2 Bound adjectives

A small number of adjectives may not appear in predicative contexts unless they are compounded with the 'pro-word' *ago* (see §4.4). The only known adjectives that always display this behaviour are *ndom* 'bad', *tanama* 'old' and *noy* 'new, young'. In addition, *kosi* 'little' is almost always compounded, but the non-compounded use is also accepted and attested.

Compare the independent adjective *waninggap* 'good' in (62a) with the bound adjective *ndom* 'bad' in (62b).

(62) a. waninggap ya k-a-   Ø
        good   real PRS.NTRL-3SG.A- be.NPST
        'It is very good.'

   b. ndom-ago   ya k-a-   Ø
        bad-PRWD:III real PRS.NTRL-3SG.A- be.NPST
        'It is very bad.'

It is possible that *ndom* 'bad' and *tanama* 'old' are bound in their use as adjectives to avoid ambiguity with the adverbs *ndom* 'still' and *tanama* 'again'. Compare *ndom-ago ka* 'It is bad' with *ndom ka* 'It still exists'. The adjective *kosi* 'little' is also commonly used as an adverbial meaning '(to V) a little' (cf. §7.7.3), then always without *ago*.

3.4 The numeral system

Numerals are similar to nouns and other nominal categories in that they may head referring phrases: *hyakod upe* 'that one', *inah ipe* 'those two', although their most common use is that of modifying nouns. In their use as attributive modifiers they differ from other common modifying elements (nouns and adjectives) in being in relatively loose apposition to the modified word, instead of compounded with it (§7.3).

In contemporary Coastal Marind, native numerals are only used up to five or six. Speakers occasionally point out that Coastal Marind has words for counting all the way to twenty. Most people can, with some effort, produce some or all of these numerals, but I have never heard them used (even by older speakers).

Table 3.6 lists all numerals up to twenty. The simplex numerals *hyakod* 'one' and *inah* 'two' provide the etymological sources of the numerals *inhyakod* 'three' (< *inah+hyakod*) and *inahinah* 'four' (< *inah+inah*).

The higher numerals are formed by combinations of the lower numerals, the body parts *sangga* 'hand' and *tagu* 'foot', and the words *lay* '(one) side, (the other) side', *mbya* 'all, total' and *balen* 'finish, run out'. For example, 'five' is *mbya-lay-sangga*,

Tab. 3.6: Numerals

Numeral	Etymology	Gloss	Numeral	Etymology	Gloss
hyakod		'1'	tagu-hyakod	(foot+1)	'11'
inah		'2'	tagu-inah	(foot+2)	'12'
inhyakod	(1+2)	'3'	tagu-inhyakod	(foot+3)	'13'
inahinah	(2+2)	'4'	tagu-inahinah	(foot+4)	'14'
mbya-lay-sangga	(all-side-hand)	'5'	mbya-lay-tagu	(all-side-foot)	'15'
lay-sangga-hyakod	(side-hand+1)	'6'	lay-tagu-hyakod	(side-foot+1)	'16'
lay-sangga-inah	(side-hand+2)	'7'	lay-tagu-inah	(side-foot+2)	'17'
lay-sangga-inhyakod	(side-hand+3)	'8'	lay-tagu-inhyakod	(side-foot+3)	'18'
lay-sangga-inahinah	(side-hand+4)	'9'	lay-tagu-inahinah	(side-foot+4)	'19'
sangga-balen	(hand-finish)	'10'	tagu-balen	(foot-finish)	'20'

which can be given the literal gloss 'all [of the fingers from] the hand [on one] side', while 'six' is *lay-sangga-hyakod* 'hand [on one] side [plus] one', and so on. 'ten' is formed from 'hand' plus the verb stem 'finish, run out', i.e. 'the hands, finished'. The counting then continues according to the same pattern, but with *tagu* 'foot' instead of 'hand', all the way to twenty.

The same counting system was documented for the Eastern dialect of Coastal Marind by Geurtjens (1926: 18–19) and Drabbe (1955: 26). Today it is clearly becoming obsolete, and some speakers, when showing their counting skills, hesitantly produced forms such as *inah-inah-hyakod* 'two+two+one' for 'five', and *inah-inah-inah* 'two+two+two' for 'six'. Such arithmetic neologisms reflect the fact that reciting numbers in Marind is a rather unnatural exercise, and all speakers clearly prefer to use Malay for this purpose.

Speakers often code-switch to Malay even for expressing lower numerals. Malay requires that a numeral classifier be present in order to count a noun, so one of the three Malay classifiers *orang* (for humans, from the noun *orang* 'person'), *ekor* (for animals, < 'tail') or *buah* (for things, < 'fruit') is usually present after the numeral, as in (63). In both instances the numeral expression (*empat ekor, satu ekor*) is separated from the counted noun (*rusa* 'deer'). This follows the native pattern of relatively loose apposition of the numeral and the noun (see §7.3).

(63) rusa   empat   ekor   m-ak-e-   i-sak,
     deer(m) four(m) tail(m) OBJ-1.A-1PL-   2|3PL-hit.PLA

   nok satu   ekor   ma-no-d-   ahwik⟨e⟩h-a   rusa
   1   one(m) tail(m) OBJ-1.A-DUR-   carry⟨3SG.U⟩-EXT   deer(m)

   'We killed four deer, [and] I carried one deer.'   [W02:0092-0093]

There are some non-numeric uses of the lowest numerals. For example, *hyakod* is used in the expression *hyakod a* (the status of *a* is unclear) meaning 'together' (64), and in *mbya-hyakod* 'same' (literally 'all-one'), as in (65). The numeral *inhyakod* 'three' can also express 'a few', as in (66).

(64) hyakod a   k-an-d-e-   nayat
     together   DIR-1.A-DUR-1PL- be.moving.PL
     'We went together.'   [W10:0027]

(65) tis ka   mbya-hyakod   menda-b-ø-   ay
     that's.it all-one   PERF-ACT-3SG.A-   become
     'That's it, now we're even.'   [D03:0102]

(66) *inhyakod* a-d-ø-   *ibotok-a*   *epe,*   *nok ø-nak-e-*   *kama⟨n⟩in,*
      [three   DEP-DUR-3SG.A-   put.PLA:III.U-EXT   DIST:III] 1   NTRL-1.A-1PL- make⟨1.U⟩

      nok ø-nak-e-   *atug*
      1   NTRL-1.A-1PL-   scrape.coconut

      'The few [coconuts] that were lying around, we prepared them, we scraped them.'   [W19:0054]

3.5 Morphology of kinship terms

Most of the terms used for addressing and speaking about relatives in Coastal Marind are organised into person paradigms. Several of the kinship terms that distinguish person are suppletive, a phenomenon that seems to be particularly common in the languages of New Guinea (Baerman 2014). For example, the word *kak* is used to address or talk about one's own paternal aunt (i.e. my father's sister). A different word, *yahwyak*, is used to talk about the paternal aunt of an addressee (e.g. 'Where's your aunt?'). Finally, *ehwyak* is used to refer to someone else's aunt, i.e. 'his/her/their aunt' (in addition, this word is also used instead of *yahwyak* if the addressee is plural, i.e. 'Where's your (pl) aunt?').

Person forms of kinship terms are usually referred to by linguists as marking possession, although I prefer to avoid this use in the context of kinship terms. Here are the full paradigms of 'father's sister' and 'grandchild':

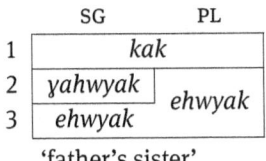
'father's sister'

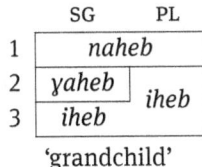
'grandchild'

In these paradigms we can distinguish two stems that are preceded by person prefixes: *-hwyak* 'father's sister' and *-heb* 'grandchild' (such stems never occur independently). The person prefixes *na-* (1st person) and *ya-* (2sg) are identical to the Undergoer prefixes found in the subclass of prefixing verb stems (§10.3.1). As suggested by the forms *ehwyak* and *iheb*, the prefixes found in 2pl and 3rd person forms are more variable. I will return to this point below.

The use of a suppletive word for the 1st person term (*kak* is unrelated to the stem *-hwyak* of the other persons) is found with several of the kin terms. Almost all of the suppletive words are shorter (one syllable instead of two) than the regular terms in the same paradigm, and some are also segmentally simpler (cf. *kak* 'aunt' vs. regular *yahwyak* 'your aunt'), making them look like child language variants. (See Dahl and Koptjevskaja-Tamm 2001 on vocative, "ego-centric", kin terms becoming suppletive paradigm members.) It appears that all such suppletive terms are extended beyond just the 1st person/term of address use, so e.g. *kak* may be used in a possessive construction such as *oy en kak* (2SG POSS aunt) 'your aunt'. Speakers clearly prefer to use the suppletive 'vocative' words in 2nd person contexts, because the regular 2nd person forms sound harsh, "like you're angry", as one speaker put it.

Tables 3.7 and 3.8 give all kin terms that are part of person paradigms. Other terms, e.g. *oha-anem* 'sister's son', are invariant and lack distinct person terms.

The person from whose point of view a kinship term is to be understood is traditionally known as the 'ego', but I prefer to call this reference person the 'anchor' instead. It would be strange to use the term ego for Coastal Marind since the Marind kinship terms are marked for 1st, 2nd and 3rd person (*ego* is the Latin 1st person singular pronoun).

REMARK ON 3RD PERSON/2PL FORMS. Inspecting the tables, it is clear that most 1st person and 2sg forms are mutually interpredictable (disregarding the suppletive 1st person forms): to get the 2sg form, one replaces the *n-* of the 1st person with *y-*, and vice versa. But the forms used for 2pl and 3rd person are more unpredictable. It is possible to segment out at least four different recurring prefixes: (i) *i-* as in *i-heb* 'his/her[8] grandchild'; (ii) *ih-* as in *ih-ibi* 'her brother's child'; (iii) *hi-* as in *hi-nabay* 'his/her daughter's husband (etc.)'; and (iv) *e-* as in *e-hway* 'his/her father'. In addition, there is *u-* in *u-hyum* 'his wife' and *wa-* in *wa-hok* 'his/her mother's brother'. I am not aware of any straightforward rules predicting the choice between the four main prefixes, and there is even a minimal pair differing only in the prefix: *i-ham* 'his/her grandparent', *e-ham* 'her husband'. One could perhaps state that the default prefixes are *i-* (before consonant-initial stems) and *ih-* (before vowel-initial stems), with the rest having exceptional *hi-* or *e-*. These differ from the Undergoer prefixes found on prefixing verbs (cf. the similarity with 1st and 2nd person *na-* and *ya-*) which are mostly *w-*,

---

[8] In glosses, I translate the 2pl/3rd person forms with 'his/her', skipping the 2pl and 3pl possessors.

Tab. 3.7: Consanguineal kin terms

Gloss	1, term of addr.	2sg	2pl, 3
F, FB	ad	yahway	ehway
F, FB pl	nahwin	yahwin	ihwin
M, MZ sg	an[a]	yahu	wah
M, MZ pl	nahwisah	yahwisah	ihwisah
MB sg	yay	yahok	wahok
MB pl	wahok-nahwin	wahok-yahwin	wahok-ihwin
FZ sg	kak	yahwyak	ehwyak
FZ pl	nahwyak-nahwyak	yahwyak-yahwyak	ehwyak-ehwyak
B, FBS	namek	yanamek	namek
Z, FBD	namuk	yanamuk	namuk
FZC, MZC, MBC sg	onos/nasu	yanos	ihanos
FZC, MZC, MBC pl	onos-onos	yanos-yanos	ihanos-ihanos
BC[b] sg	kemlay	yibi	ihibi
BC[b] pl	kimbakem	?	ihibi-wanangga
GC sg	naheb	yaheb	iheb
GC pl, GP pl	nahe	yahe	ihe
GP sg	amay	yahyam	iham
twin, born-same-day	nggays	yatom	itahyom, ihatom

[a] There is also *nahu* 'my/our mother', which I have never heard used.
[b] Only with female anchor.

o-/u- or zero (cf. Table 10.3 on p. 232), so it is unclear if the forms are diachronically related.

The two following subsections treat the kin terms and their use in more detail.

3.5.1 Consanguineal relatives

Consanguineal kin terms with distinct person forms are listed in Table 3.7.

THE PARENTS. There are no terms corresponding to English *mother* and *father* in Coastal Marind, because the closest equivalents also include the sisters of the mother and the brothers of the father, respectively. Thus, *ad* is used as a term of address to one's own father but also to one's paternal uncles, and *an* is used for one's own mother and also one's maternal aunts. Both of these are suppletive stems; there is also a suppletive 2pl/3rd person term *wah* 'his/her mother (etc.)'. The regular 1st person *nahu* 'my/our mother (etc.)' (cf. Geurtjens 1933: 334, entry *wah*) seems to have fallen out of use. It is common to specify the relative age of an uncle/aunt refer to by the terms *ad/an* by using the words *es* 'behind', *in* 'middle' and *mayay* 'front', e.g.: *es-ad* 'my/our youngest paternal uncle', *es-yahway* 'your.sg youngest paternal uncle', *es-ehway* 'his/her/your.pl youngest paternal uncle'.

There are special plural terms *nahwin* 'my/our fathers (etc.)' used to refer to one's father and his brothers as a group. The corresponding plural terms for the mother and her sisters (*nahwisah* etc.) are probably based on the word for 'fathers' plus the word *sah* 'married woman' (i.e. *nahwisah* < *nahwin* + *sah*). Both sets can be used as respectful terms for any group of elder men or women.

THE UNCLES AND AUNTS. There are only kin terms for the father's sister, *kak*, and the mother's brother, *yay*, since the other aunts and uncles are classified as one's parents. Like the terms for the parents, these are suppletive 1st person forms. The expected regular 1st person form of *kak* — *nahwyak* — is not used for the father's sister, but by a woman to refer to her husband's mother, whereas the expected 1st person form of *yay* — *nahok* — is used to address one's husband's elder brother (see below).

There are corresponding plural terms: the ones for 'mother's brothers' are made up of 2pl/3rd person form *wahok* and the words for 'fathers (etc.)' (e.g. *ihwin*); the ones for 'father's sisters' are reduplicated forms *yahwyak-yahwyak* 'your father's sisters' etc.

SIBLINGS AND COUSINS. The terms *namek* (m) and *namuk* (f) (plural *namik*) are best translated 'clanmate', and can be used to address one's siblings, one's father's brother's children, or anybody else who is a member of the same clan as oneself. Since clan membership follows the patriline, the children of one's paternal uncle will always belong to the same clan as oneself. There are 2sg forms *yanamek* 'your clanmate' etc., but no special 2pl/3rd person forms. The standard *namek* is used for this purpose.

With one's siblings, however, the terms *namek* etc. are fairly infrequent, and there is instead a small sub-system of compound terms indicating relative age. The system is built on the words *anem* 'man' and *anum* 'woman' (plural *anim* 'people'), combined with *es* 'behind', *in* 'middle' and *mayay* 'front' (this was also seen with the uncles and aunts above).

es-anem	'younger brother'	*es-anum*	'younger sister'
in-anem	'middle brother'	*in-anum*	'middle sister'
mayay-anem	'elder brother'	*mayay-anum*	'elder sister'

It is primarily the terms on *es-* and *mayay-* that are used as terms of address; the terms on *in-* 'middle-' are used to refer to the second sibling in a set of three, or the third in a set of five, etc.

All cousins that are not classified with one's siblings fall under the term *onos*, i.e. the children of mother's brother and sister, and of father's sister.

CHILDREN AND NEPHEWS. The terms for one's children lack person forms: *wananggib* 'son', *wananggub* 'daughter', *wanangga* 'children'.[9] These are also used by a woman about her sister's children, and by a man about his brother's children. These words

---

9 There is also *hib* and *hub*, apparently meaning 'son' and 'daughter' respectively, but these are poorly attested (archaic?).

Tab. 3.8: Affinal kin terms.
Self-reciprocal terms are indicated thus: X↔Y, meaning that X and Y use the term about each other.

Gloss	1, term of addr.	2sg	2pl, 3
H	*nahyam*	*yahyam*	*eham*
W sg	*nahyum*	*yahyum*	*uhyum*
W pl	*nahyus*	*yahyus*	*ihus*
DH↔WP, YZH↔WEZ sg	*nabay*	*yanabay*	*hinabay*
DH↔WP, YZH↔WEZ pl	*nabay-nabay*	*yanabay-yanabay*	*hinabay-hinabay*
SW, YBW[a] sg	*nikna*	*yikna*	*ihikna*
SW, YBW[a] pl	*nikun*	*yikun*	*ihikun*
HM	*nahwyak*	*yikna*	*ihikna*
HF	*pap*	*yakna*	*ehakna*
HEB	*nahok*	*yakna*	*ehakna*
YZH↔WEB sg	*manday*	*yamanday*	*himanday*
YZH↔WEB pl	*manday-manday*	*yamanday-yamanday*	*himanday-himanday*
WYB, WYZ sg	*sahok*	*yahyamok*	*ihamok*
WYB, WYZ pl	*sahok-sahok*	*yahyamok-yahyamok*	*ihamok-ihamok*
EZH	*mbit*	*yambit*	*ihambit-ehway*
WZH	*nakom*	*yakom*	*hinakom*

[a] YBW: only with female anchor.

only have the sense 'offspring', not 'pre-pubertal human'. For the latter sense there are words such as *isahih* 'children, young (of animals)' and *yunayon* 'infant'.

For her brother's children, a woman uses the term *kemlay* (plural *kimbakem*), and they call her *kak* in return. A man refers to his sister's son as *oha-anem*, and his sister's daughter as *uho* (both lacking person forms), and they address him as *yay*.

GRANDCHILDREN AND GRANDPARENTS. Grandchildren are referred to by *naheb* (plural *nahe*) etc. There is a special term of address, *amay*, used by grandchildren to address their grandparents, and by people in general as a respectful term for any elder person. (During my stay in Wambi, this is how I addressed my host Paulus Yolmend and his wife Yustina Mahuze.) The plural terms for grandchildren (*nahe* etc.) are also used to refer to one's grandparents, and, in particular, more distant ancestors.

The vocative term *nggays* is not strictly a term for a relative, but can be used for friends or clanmates of the same age. The members of my host family said that this term, and especially the non-vocative person forms, refers to someone who was born on the same day as oneself. It can also be used about twins, although I have only recorded *inah-lik* (lit. two-from) in this meaning.

3.5.2 Affinal relatives

Affinal kin terms with distinct person forms are listed in Table 3.8.

SPOUSES. The terms for husband, *nahyam*, and wife, *nahyum*, are perhaps originally derived from a single stem meaning 'spouse', since they only differ in the stem-final vowel, although Usher and Suter (2015: 113) reconstruct separate stems as far back as proto-Anim. There are plural forms for 'wives' (*nahyus* 'our wives' etc.), but I am not aware of any corresponding terms for 'husbands' (*amnangga* 'married men' can be used instead). The Marind do not practice polygamy, so the 2sg form *yahyus* 'your wives' is only used in joking contexts.

SPOUSES' PARENTS, AND BROTHERS- & SISTERS-IN-LAW. The term used between a husband and his parents-in-law is *nabay* (plural *nabay-nabay*). This is a self-reciprocal term, so the parents-in-law also address their son-in-law with the same word. It is used in the same way between the husband and his wife's elder sister.

The son's wife is referred to as *nikna* by the parents of the husband. In return, she addresses her mother-in-law as *nahwyak* (cf. 'father's sister' above), and her father-in-law as *pap*. Note that the non-address forms of *nahwyak* are identical with those of *nikna* (2sg *yikna*, 2pl/3rd pers. *ihikna*), whereas the non-address forms of *pap* are identical to those used to refer to the husband's elder brother, which has the term-of-address *nahok* (cf. 'mother's brother' above).

The term *nikna* is also used by a woman to address her younger brother's wife, who then replies using *isane* (no person forms).

A man uses *manday* (plural *manday-manday*) to address his wife's elder brother, and the brother uses the same term in response. For the younger siblings of the wife, *sahok* (plural *sahok-sahok*) is used, and the siblings reply using *mbit* (I have not recorded any plural form). Some other affinal terms are: *ne* 'elder brother's wife', *uha-anum* 'younger brother's wife (male anchor)', *es-lek* 'husband's younger brother', *es-luk* 'husband's younger sister' (all without person forms).

Finally, two men who are married to two sisters call each other by the term *nakom*. This kin term is widely distributed throughout the Southern New Guinea area, and has apparently been borrowed into several different families (e.g. Komnzo *nakum*, Yelmek/Maklew *nakom*, both unrelated to Marind). It is probably a borrowing into Marind as well, with the person forms *yakom* and *hinakom* being formed by analogy from *nakom*.

3.6 Compounding

The pattern referred to as compounds in this grammar combines two lexical elements, such that the rightmost is the morphosyntactic head of the expression (determining e.g. gender agreement on agreeing modifiers of the compound), and usually also a hyperonym of the compound itself. For example, the compound *awe-hayaw* 'fish bone' triggers Gender III agreement since *hayaw* 'bone' belongs to Gender III (*awe* 'fish' is Gender II), and *hayaw* is also a hyperonym (i.e. a more generic term) of *awe-hayaw*, since the compound as a whole denotes a more specific subtype of its head *hayaw* 'bone'.

A compound forms a lexical element in itself and can constitute the input to a new compound, so e.g. *da-yol* 'sago beating' can be part of the compound [*da-yol*]-*say* 'sago beating place', and so on. This means that compounds can be infinitely recursive, although I have not documented any examples beyond first-level embedding.

A compound forms a grammatical unit, so neither of the members of the compound can be modified by demonstratives, numerals, etc.; such modification is only applicable to the compound as a whole. Compare (67a) with the impossible structure in (67b):

(67) a. *awe-hayaw ya*   b. *[awe ya]-hayaw*
          fish-bone   real   fish real-bone
          'a real fish bone'   'bone of a real fish'

Phonologically, on the other hand, a compound is not an isolated unit, so the processes described as applying within phonological words in Chapter 2 (such as epenthesis and vowel gradation) apply separately to each member of a compound, and not to the compound as a whole.

These features of compounds in Coastal Marind make them similar to structures labelled 'compounds' in various grammatical traditions (see e.g. Bauer 2001). The main difference between Coastal Marind compounds and compounds in English (and other European languages) lies in their use, because compounding is in Coastal Marind often the only available equivalent for syntactic modifier-head structures in English.

This is most striking in the domain of adjectival modification. Attributively used adjectives in Coastal Marind cannot be used as syntactic modifiers inside an NP, only as the first member of a compound. Thus, the equivalent to English *a big fish* is literally 'big-fish' in Coastal Marind. As with any compound, the individual parts cannot take syntactic modifiers (cf. the preceding example), so the only way to express 'a very big fish' in Coastal Marind is as in (68a), literally 'a real big-fish'.[10]

(68) a. *yaba-awe ya*
          big-fish   real
          'a very big fish'

      b. *[yaba ya]-awe*
          big   real-fish

---

[10] Drabbe (1955: 24) cites structures such as *kez ha onggat*, (lit. 'tall very coconut') from the Eastern dialect of Coastal Marind, but this unattested ordering was rejected by the speakers of the Western dialect with whom I worked.

3.6.1 Types of compounds

In the following subsections I list some representative compounds found in the corpus.

3.6.1.1 Noun+noun compounds
This is the most common type of compound.

(69)
Compound	Gloss	Meaning
nggat-muy	dog-meat	'dog meat'
do-imu	blood-smell	'smell of blood'
anggip-bal	nose-hole	'nostril'
weli-ban	stingray-stinger	'stinger of a stingray'
olam-aha	maternity-house	'maternity hut'
nu-say	sleep-place	'bed'
de-tagu	wood-foot	'sandals'
kiwal-mayan	wind-speech	'telephone'
pale-yahun	land-canoe	'motorcycle'

Some subpatterns deserve mention:
- Compounds with *es* 'back, behind', *in* 'middle' and *mayay* 'first, front' as first member. These are common with kinship terms, with which they specify relative age (*es* being the youngest): *es-anum* (back-woman) 'younger sister', *mayay-anim* (front-people) 'elder siblings', etc. They are also used to subdivide Marind villages such as Wambi, which stretch along the beach: *es-milah* (back-village) or *es-Wambi* is the eastern part of the village, and *mayay-milah* (front-village) or *mayay-Wambi* is the western part.[11]
- Compounds referring to places characterised by some plant species are formed with the words *yah* and *bak* as their heads. It seems that *yah* has no use outside such compounds; *bak* means 'outside, the area around the house'. Examples: *suba-yah* 'bamboo grove', *bus-yah* 'eucalyptus grove', *kasim-yah* 'place with lots of *kasim* grass'; *da-bak* 'sago plantation', *onggat-bak* 'coconut grove', *badi-bak* 'banksia (sp.) grove'.
- There is a large number of compounds headed by forms of *anVm* 'person'. A boy who has just learned to walk is a *meng-anem* (*meng* is a noun meaning 'walk'), and a boy who just learned to talk is a *mayan-anem* (*mayan* 'speech, language'). Indonesians (i.e. non-Papuans) are referred to as *pu-anim* '*pu*-people', the meaning of *pu* being unclear (one speaker said it refers to the sound made by rifles, *pu!*).

---

[11] See van Baal (1966: 217–221) for a thorough discussion of the association of *es* with young/east and *mayay* with old/west and mythological correlates of these pairings.

Other examples: *mih-anem* 'soldier, police man' (*mih* 'bow'), *ukna-anem* 'coward' (*ukna* 'fear'), *Belanda-anim* 'Dutch people'. There are also some animal names and terms for inanimate things ending in *anVm*: *sanggal-anem* 'kite sp.' (*Sanggal* is the name of a river), *ndaman-anem* 'large fish sp.' (the meaning of *ndaman-* is unknown), *mom-anim* 'grass sp.' (*mom* 'mucus'), *nene-anim* 'bell' (probably imitative).

3.6.1.2 Adjective+noun compounds

Recall that this pattern is used to combine attributive adjectives with nouns. Many combinations are completely lexicalised, such as the expression for 'coffee' below.

(70)	Compound	Gloss	Meaning
	kosi-aliki	small-river	'small river'
	keh-onggat	tall-coconut	'tall coconut palm'
	noy-anim	new-people	'young people'
	dohi-anem	red-man	'fair-skinned man; albino'
	kunayhi-adaka	black-water	'coffee'
	ndom-bekay	bad-heart	'disappointed, unhappy'

3.6.1.3 Verb+noun compounds

Such compounds denote entities associated in some way with the action described by the verb stem. This pattern is particularly productive with *anVm* 'person', forming expressions similar to e.g. English agent nominalisations: *sasayi-anem* (lit. 'work man') 'worker'. Other examples:

(71)	Compound	Gloss	Meaning
	kahos-anem	chew.betel-man	'man who chews betelnut'
	umuh-anum	go:3SG.U-woman	'deceased woman'
	lemed-anum	stand.PLA-woman	'lazy woman'[12]
	kahos-emel	chew.betel-hunger	'betel abstinence'
	kimamub-sangga	clench.fist-hand	'clenched fist'
	tanin-ndon	tie.things-rope	'rope for tying up things'
	inohal-mayan	swear-language	'swearing'

---

[12] The pluractional stem *lemed* can mean 'come to a standstill repeatedly' so a *lemed-anum* is perhaps a woman who keeps stopping when she is supposed to work/walk.

3.6.1.4 X+adjective compounds

Compounds in which another element qualifies an adjectives appear to be rare, with only a few examples:

(72)

Compound	Gloss	Meaning
yaba-wagatok	big-long	'very long'
papes-yaba	small-big	'somewhat big'
ndom-yel	bad-tasty	'bad-tasting'
kitul-yel	cockroach-tasty	'disgusting'

3.6.1.5 X+verb compounds

It is common for verb stems to be compounded with their O-argument or some expression filling an adverbial role (e.g. instrument). Examples:

(73)

Compound	Gloss	Meaning
takah-l-ahum	firewood-PLA-carry.firewood	'carrying of firewood'
onggat-kapet	coconut-climb.PLA	'climbing of coconut trees'
suba-taman	bamboo-shoot	'shooting with bow & arrow'
mahut-kayanad	far.away-tide.recede	'very low tide'
mangga-ihwim	mango(m)-become.dark	'thick shade of mango trees'

Typical contexts for the use of such compounds are as complements of the words *mbaymbay* 'not able' and *mayay* 'able' (§3.1.3.1), as in (74), or in agentive compounds with *anVm* 'person', as in (75). Since these expressions describe habitual or repeated actions, it is usually the so-called Pluractional verb stem (glossed PLA) that appears in the compound.

(74) onggat-kapet   mayay ek-o-   Ø   oy?
     coconut-climb.PLA able   PRS.Q:I-2SG.A- be.NPST   2SG
     'Do you know how to climb coconut trees?'

(75) mobil-   k-um-   anem
     car(m)   WITH-go.PLA:3SG.U- man
     'chauffeur' (lit. 'car-drive-man')

A verb stem occurring in a compound must be in the appropriate person, number and/or gender form. What form is appropriate depends on the valence template associated with the verb (§12). For many verbs agreement will be with the O-argument with which the stem is compounded, as in the next example, in which the verb 'finish' is realised by its plural stem *ba⟨h⟩in*, since it is used with an O-argument from Gender IV. Compare this with the verb *kamin* 'make' in (77), which agrees according to a different valence template and selects a stem that agrees with the A-argument rather than the O with which it is compounded.

(76) katal-   i-ba⟨h⟩in-   namakad
     money(IV)- PLA-finish⟨IV.U⟩-   thing
     'thing that makes money disappear' (i.e. alcohol)

(77) tamuy-   kama⟨n⟩in   nd-ak-ap-   balen
     food(III)- make⟨1.U⟩   LOC-1.A-CT-   finish:III
     'I finished making the food/I finished the food-making.'   [W20:0296]

In addition to the common 'object-verb' compounds there are a few exocentric compounds headed by verbs, e.g. *katane-huhu* (sun-emerge.PLA) 'the east' and *yahun-ibotok* (canoe-put.PLA) 'place in swamp where canoes are kept'.

3.6.1.6 Backwards compounds

A few compounds appear (at least from an English perspective) to reverse the modifier-head order of other compounds, placing the hyperonym as the first member of the compound. For example, the compound *de-takah* means 'firewood' and has the noun *takah* 'fire' as its rightmost element, modified by *de* 'wood', so literally 'wood-fire'. The explanation for this pattern is that *takah* also can be used alone to mean 'firewood', especially in stereotypical contexts in which it is easy to distinguish it from the 'fire' meaning (e.g. 'go to the forest and fetch *takah*'). In other contexts, the compound with the modifier *de* 'wood' may be used, to specify that reference is made to the 'wooden' type of *takah*.

Other examples:

(78) | Compound | Gloss | Meaning |
      |------------|--------------------|--------------------|
      | *de-onggat* | tree-coconut | 'coconut palm' |
      | *nggol-unum* | tip-tongue | 'tip of the tongue'|
      | *mit-unum* | base-tongue | 'tongue base' |
      | *pal-ake* | skin/bark-gambier | 'gambier bark' |

3.7 Derived nominals

There are three patterns that derive nominals from verb stems: bare verb stems used as nouns (§3.7.1), instrument nouns derived by the Instrumental *k*-prefix (§3.7.2), and participles (basically deverbal adjectives; §3.7.3).

3.7.1 Verb stems used nominally

As described in Chapter 8, the verb stem is the unit that together with the prefixal complex forms the verb complex in Coastal Marind. For a verb stem to be able to occur in nominal uses, it must be stripped of the material in the prefixal complex (mainly inflection-like prefixes marking person, tense-aspect-mode, etc.).

Coastal Marind is relatively generous in permitting bare verb stems to be used in syntactic slots that are typically filled by nouns, without the presence of any nominalising morphology. However, this possibility is mostly employed for grammatical purposes, e.g. in structures in which the verb stem is predicated by the Auxiliary or semantically 'light' verbs such as *win* 'become' (see e.g. §17.2). Here is an example of the verb stem *yi* 'eat', heading a compound with *kosi* 'little', and predicated by the Auxiliary *wa*:

(79) awe   kosi-yi   s-a-   w-a
      fish little-eat ONLY-3SG.A-   3SG.U-AUX
      'S/he only ate a little of the fish.'
      (lit.) 'S/he only did little-eating of the fish'

This use of *yi* is clearly nominal, since the stem appears in a compound and lacks any of the inflectional prefixes (cf. the prefixes preceding the Auxiliary). The stem is not used referentially, it just fills a slot in a skeletal construction with a literal meaning 'only do a little V-ing'.

Although verb stems frequently occur in positions typically occupied by nouns, there is no widespread use of verb stems as heads of fully referential NPs: out of more than 600 verbs I am only aware of a dozen or so that regularly are put to use as standard nouns, some of which are listed in Table 3.9. In all of these cases the verbal use is much more frequent than the nominal use, so it seems warranted to treat these as verb stems put to use as nouns, and not the other way around. Note that several of these verb stems may exhibit morphological alternation expressing various grammatical categories, but in their use as nouns they are completely fixed. For example, the form *hwetok* is the 3rd person Undergoer stem of the verb 'to think', with other possible forms such as 1st person *hwitanuk* 'to think about me/us', but it is only the stem *hwetok* that is used as a noun.

All nominally used verb stems trigger agreement in Gender III (for an example, cf. agreement with *weheb* 'to wait' in ex. (948) on p. 471).

Examples of verb stems *kahos* (80a), *omos* (80b) and *sinik* (80c) used as NPs:

(80) a. eee   kahos   mbya   k-a-namb-   Ø-e
          INTERJ chew.betel   NEG   PRS.NTRL-3SG.A-1.GEN- be.NPST-IPFV
          'Oh, I don't have any betelnut.'   [W21:0080]

Tab. 3.9: Verb stems used as nouns

	As verb stem	As noun
esol	'to make noise'	'noise'
yanakeh	'to cook'	'cooking'
yod	'to vomit'	'vomit'
hwetok	'to think'	'thought'
kahek	'to climb, to rise'	'height'
kahos	'to chew betelnut'	'betelnut'
nasak	'to fight each other'[a]	'fight'
omos	'to spread out (mat etc.) on ground'	'mat (etc.) on ground'
pig	'to become daylight'	'heat from sun'
sasayi	'to work'	'work'
sinik	'to carry'	'things being carried'
tak	'clear, become empty'	'source, well, dug-out hole'

[a] This is a fossilised use of the Reciprocal stem *nasak* 'fight each other' (see §13.2) of the verb *usak* 'fight'.

    b. *omos   lahwalah k-an-d-ap-   ibotok*
       spread.out on.top   DIR-1.A-DUR-CT- put.PLA:III.U
       'I put [the sago] on top of the spread out [leaves].'   [W20:0176]

    c. *ipe   sinik sam ya   ø-d-ø-em-   ola*
       DIST:I/II.PL carry big real NTRL-DUR-3SG.A-2|3PL.GEN- be:III.U
       'They had lots of stuff to carry.' (lit. 'Their things to carry were really big')
       [W03:0049]

One descriptive bird name is a compound headed by a verb stem: *kumay-kasanak* (a darter or cormorant). Its segmentation is in (81). This lexicalisation is exceptional since deverbal agentive expressions usually are compounds headed by *anVm* (see the section on compounds, §3.6.1.3).

(81) *kumay- ka-sanak*
       inside- INESS-search.for.fish

      (lit.) 'search for fish inside [the water]'

3.7.2 Deverbal instrument nouns

There is a small set of nouns denoting various kinds of tools that are derived from corresponding verb stems by means of the Instrumental prefix *k-* (*ka-* before a consonant).[13] Examples:

(82)   *ka-yahwek*   'sago beating stick'   < *yahwek* 'beat, pound'
        ka-nalaw   'mirror'   < *n-alaw* '1.U-see'
        k-ehway   'paddle'   < *e-hway* 'PLA-paddle'

There have been attempts by Marind speakers to coin words for some modern items using the Instrumental derivation, which suggests that it remains productive to some degree. As far as I know none of these have caught on, however, so speakers use Malay words instead. All examples that I have listed are compounds of the shape Object+*k*-Verb, such as:

(83)   *pa- k-ihatuk*   'hat, helmet'   < *pa* 'head', *i-hatuk* 'PLA-cover'
        tatih- k-yalok   'comb'   < *tatih* 'hair (IV)', *y-alok* 'IV.U-stab'
        de- k-usak   'hammer'   < *de* 'wood (III)', *u-sak* 'III.U-hit.PLA'

A corresponding applicative prefix *k-* exists in the verbal domain, and adds an instrument NP to the clause — see §13.1.4.[14]

3.7.3 Participles

Participles are productively derived from verb stems, and have several functions, including attributive modification of nouns and predication of a property (typically a resultative state). It is this similarity to adjectives that motivates the use of the label 'participle' (cf. Haspelmath 1994, Shagal 2019).

3.7.3.1 Form of participles
Participles are derived from verb stems through suffixation of the appropriate Participial suffix (also §3.7.3):

---

13 Drabbe (1955: 22) lists some more deverbal instrument nouns for the Eastern dialect of Coastal Marind, most of which appear to have fallen out of use by now.
14 It is possible that instrument nouns (such as *ka-yahwek* 'sago beating stick') are better described as applicative verb stems (meaning 'beat sago with s.t.') that have been made into nouns through zero derivation. But since there is no general process in the language for converting verb stems into entity-denoting nouns, I think it is better to consider the instrumental nominaliser *k-* and the verbal applicative *k-* to be diachronically related, but synchronically heterosemous, prefixes.

I.sg	II.sg	III	IV, I/II.pl
-la	-luk	-la	-lik

This means that *-la* forms participles in Gender I singular (i.e. describing one male human) and Gender III (most inanimates), *-luk* participles in Gender II singular (i.e. one animal or female human), and *-lik* for Gender IV (some inanimates) and plurals of Genders I & II. Agreement in participles functions the same way as in agreeing adjectives, so an attributively used participle agrees with the modified head noun etc. (see the following subsection for examples). Cf. also Chapter 5 for general information about the gender system.

There are two reasons for describing these markers as suffixes rather than postpositions: (i) they attach to a single word (a verb stem) and not a phrase, and (ii) they trigger a phonological change in a stem with final /n/, viz. /n/→[t]. This makes them similar to other affixes in the language (which often trigger phonological changes in surrounding material) and makes them different from postpositions, none of which have such effects. As shown in (84), the postposition *lik* 'from' added to the noun *mandin* 'long ago' does not trigger any change in the final /n/, whereas the homophonous Participial suffix *-lik* causes the final nasal in the verb stem *kiska⟨h⟩in* 'stack.on.top⟨2|3PL.U⟩' to be realised as [t].

(84) a. /mandin lik/ → *mandin lik* 'the ones from long ago'
     b. /kiskahin-lik/ → *kiskahitlik* '(having been) stacked on top of e.o.'

The Participial suffix attaches to a bare verb stem, so none of the inflection-like material that makes up the prefixal complex may enter into a participle. The data in (85a) gives an example of a predicatively used verb stem, which is preceded by the prefixal complex (here with the Perfect *mend-*, the Actualis prefix *b-*, and the zero marking 3sg Actor), whereas the participle in (85b) consists of a verb stem without the prefixal material. The use of the Participial suffix *-la* means that this participle can be used as an adjective describing a human male, which belongs to Gender I; since the Gender III form is also realised by *-la* it could also describe e.g. a dead tree belonging to Gender III.

(85) a. *menda-b-ø-   kahwid*   b. *kahwid-la*
        PERF-ACT-3SG.A- die:3SG.U   die:3SG.U-PTCP:I
        'S/he is dead.'   'dead' (human male)

However, any affixes or morphological alternations that are used to form verb stems may also be present in participles (such morphology is part of the stem itself, as opposed to the prefixes of the prefixal complex, which are phonologically separate from the verb stem).

As an example, let us take the verb stem *tahuk* 'stick to a surface', which can be used for e.g. glueing a piece of paper to a wall, and from which a participle such as *tahuk-la* 'stuck to a surface' (Gender III) can be formed. The stem *tahuk* allows the derivation of a pluractional stem by means of the prefix *i-*, giving *itahuk*, meaning roughly 'stick to a surface in several places'. This derived stem has a corresponding participle *itahuk-la* 'stuck to a surface in several places'. Further derivational morphology can be added, such as the Inessive *k-* (used for actions taking place in a circumscribed location, e.g. inside a house), giving the stem *kitahuk* 'stick to a surface in several places indoors' and the corresponding participle *kitahuk-la* 'stuck to a surface in several places indoors'.

The verb stem is also the locus of person/number/gender indexing of the so-called Undergoer argument (Chapter 10), and the alternations that realise this category are retained in participles. For example, the verb 'stick to a surface' uses the stem *tahuk* for Undergoers of Gender III (e.g. pieces of paper), but a modified stem *tahyohyab* if the Undergoer belongs to Gender IV (e.g. a bank note). If the participle is used to modify such a noun, the appropriate form is *tahyohyab-lik* 'stuck to a surface (IV)' (recall that the shape of the Participial suffix is *-lik* in Gender IV).

The retention of stem-deriving morphology in the input to participle formation contrasts with the inability of any material from the prefixal complex to be included in a participle. For example, one cannot add the 1st person Actor prefix *no-* to *tahuk-la* in order to express 'stuck to a surface by me', because the prefix *no-* is part of the prefixal complex and is not used in the derivation of verb stems. (The expression of an agent with a participle would require an instrumental phrase with the postposition *en*, e.g. *nok en* 'by me'; see below.)

COMPOUNDS HEADED BY PARTICIPLES. Like other nominals, participles can be the head of compounds (they also function as adjectival modifiers in compounds, as discussed further below). The modifiers compounded to participles that are attested in my corpus provide adverbial specification, e.g. location, as in (86a),[15] or time, as in (86b). (I separate the members of the compound by means of a trailing hyphen here to distinguish them from the affixes.)

(86) a. in-   ka-tak-la
       middle- INESS-become.empty-PTCP:III
       'clearing in the middle'

   b. noy- mat-la
       new- come-PTCP:I
       '[male] new-comer'

---

[15] The expression *in-katakla* is used in Wambi to refer to the empty corridor that runs between the two rows of houses arranged along the beach in the part of the village where I live.

EXPRESSION OF AN AGENT. The internal syntax of phrases headed by participles demands further research, so I will only comment on the expression of the participial agent here. Such a participant may be realised as a phrase formed with the Instrumental-Possessive postposition *en*. This is shown in the next example, in which the phrase *nahan en* 'by myself' serves to express the agent of the participle *yayohla* 'planted'.

(87) ehe namaya nahan en yayoh-la k-a- Ø,
here now 1.EMPH INSTR plant.PLA-PTCP:III PRS.NTRL-3SG.A- be.NPST

de otih ehe
tree(III) all PROX:III

'Here they were planted by myself, all these trees.' [W18:0252]

The polyfunctional postposition *en* is used to mark both instruments and possessors. I gloss *en* as INSTR in its use marking a participial agent, since this makes it possible to distinguish it from the possessive use, which is possible with participles used as nouns:

(88) nahan en lod-la
1.EMPH POSS make.windshield-PTCP:III

'my own windshield'

Whether the postposition *en* is used to express the agent or possessor of the participle is presumably made clear by the context. The speaker with whom I translated (87) stated that *nahan en* refers to the person who planted the trees, regardless of their present owner, but I have not explored this ambiguity further.

3.7.3.2 Functions of participles

AS NOUNS. Such nouns denote entities that are produced as a result of the event described by the base verb. For example, the verb *ahak* 'spread out sago in banana leaves and wrap it up' is the base of the participle *ahakla*, formed with the Gender III Participial suffix *-la*, which is the noun used to refer to such packages of wrapped-up sago.

Another common example is the participle *kahosla*, which is used to refer to the red residue from chewing betel (*kahos* 'chew betel') which is spat out after the desired effect has been achieved. Referentially used participles such as *ahakla* and *kahosla* can fill the same syntactic slots as standard nouns, as in the following example, or example (163) on p. 130.

Tab. 3.10: Lexicalised participles

Base verb	Participle	Gender	Gloss
lod 'make windshield'	lodla	III	'windshield'
kum 'bear fruit'	kumla	III	'fruit'
ayan 'branch off'	ayatla	III	'branch'
keswan 'wash'	keswatla	III	'laundry'
aluy 'wound to form'	alula	III	'wound'
kakim 'plait hair'	kakimlik	IV	'plait'
yahwab 'hit, pound flat'	yahwablik	IV	'k.o. arrow'

(89)   ado   kahosla mata-ka- haliɣ
       INTERJ betel.spit HORT-PRI- spit

'Oh, just let me spit out the betelnut first.'   [W11:0400]

Other examples of participles that are commonly used as referential expressions are listed in Table 3.10. Some show clear signs of lexicalisation, e.g. the irregular loss of /ɣ/ in *alula* 'wound' (cf. *aluy* 'wound to form'; I have only observed the form *aluyla* in elicitation) or the unpredictable meaning of *yahwablik* 'arrows with a metal arrowhead' (from the verb *yahweb* 'pound, hit', i.e. 'thing that has been pounded flat').[16]

Gender membership of lexicalised participles follow the general tendencies of gender assignment (Chapter 5), so it is not surprising that the hair-related participle *kakim-lik* 'plait' is in Gender IV (cf. *tatih* 'hair', IV), etc. There do not seem to be many lexicalised participles denoting animates, so all of the nouns given in Table 3.10 are in Genders III and IV (the inanimate genders).

There are also several nouns that appear to be participles historically, although their origin has been obscured by phonological erosion and/or the loss or meaning change of the base verb.[17]

ADJECTIVAL USE. Participles are used either attributively or predicatively to describe a noun as being in a state resulting from the event expressed by the base verb. The participle-deriving suffix agrees in gender/number with the noun that is describes.

Like most other nominal modifiers, including standard adjectives, participles are compounded to their head noun in their attributive use. The data in (90) nicely il-

---

[16] *yahwablik* is a Gender IV noun, and the stem *yahwab* is the form of *yahweb* used with an Undergoer argument from this gender. Different types of arrows are assigned to either Gender III or IV, but I am not aware of the basis of this choice.

[17] For example, *wayuklu* 'young girl' turns out to derive from a participle **wayuk-luk* (cf. plural *wayuk-lik*) of the verb *wayuk* 'turn'. The motivation for this comes from the characteristic hairdo that was given to girls when they reached puberty, involving parts of coconut leaves braided ('turned') into the hair; cf. the description in Geurtjens (1933), p. 335, entry *Wahoek*.

lustrate the meaning difference that arises in compounds with the participle *dahipla* 'drunk' vs. the base verb stem *dahip* 'get drunk': the compound with participle in (90a) is used to refer to a man who is drunk, whereas the compound with the bare stem in (90b) would be used to refer to someone who gets drunk habitually (but who is not necessarily drunk right now).

(90) a. *dahip-la- anem*
       get.drunk:3SG.U-PTCP:I- man(I)
       'drunk man'

   b. *dahip- anem*
       get.drunk:3SG.U- man(I)
       'drunkard, alcoholic'

The next examples illustrate the predicative use of participles.

(91) *dahip-la k-a- ∅ epe*
     get.drunk:3SG.U-PTCP:I PRS.NTRL-3SG.A- be.NPST DIST:I
     'He is drunk.'

(92) *tamuy kamit-la ∅-d-a- ola*
     food(III) make-PTCP:III NTRL-DUR-3SG.A- be:III.U
     'The food was ready.' [W15:0067]

Predicative participles also occur in a construction similar to the English Perfect, as discussed in §14.2.5.3.

Since a participle describes a state (rather than an action) of the noun that it modifies, it follows that most attributively used participles are oriented towards the patient of the base verb, because it is usually the case that the patient of a transitive or intransitive verb undergoes a more prominent change than a participant with the semantic role of agent does. This means that speakers often use patient-oriented participles such as *dahipla* 'drunk' as noun modifiers, whereas an agent-oriented description such as 'dancing' would require a relative clause construction ('a man who is dancing') rather than a participle.

Although attributive participles are most frequently patient-oriented, like the participles in (90–91), it must be stressed that the crucial parameter is not semantic role but the existence of a clear, new state affecting the modified noun. The data in the following examples show that participles can modify a noun that corresponds to the agent of its base verb, as long as the participant has undergone some change as a consequence of the event described by this verb.

For example, the verb *saletok* may be used intransitively with an agent participant who enters into a hiding position (by her own volition and control), and since this event entails a change-of-state ('being in hiding') it is possible to use the participle derived from *saletok* to the describe the agent being in this state, as in (93a).[18] It is also possible for some agent-oriented participles to be used as noun modifiers as long as they are combined with an adverbial-like element such as *noy* 'new, recent' in (93b). This gives a contrast that is familiar from European languages in which participial constructions such as **an arrived guest* are impossible, but *a newly arrived guest* is fine.

(93) a. sal⟨e⟩tok-luk-   anum
       hide⟨3SG.U⟩-PTCP:II- woman(II)
       'a hiding woman'

  b. noy- mat-la-   anem
     new- come-PTCP:I- man(I)
     'new-comer, newly arrived man'   [D03:0009]

Below are some more examples of attributively used participles. Note that the verb 'die' in (94a–b) is suppletive in the plural.

(94) a. kahwid-la-   anem
       die:3SG.U-PTCP:I- man(I)
       'dead man'

  b. yahwahwih-lik-   anim
     die:2|3PL.U-PTCP:I/II.PL- people
     'dead people'

  c. ay⟨e⟩b-la-   da
     scrape⟨III.U⟩-PTCP:III- sago(III)
     'scraped-off sago pith'

  d. kotib-luk-   basik
     get.lost:3SG.U-PTCP:II- pig(II)
     'pig that got lost'

  e. kalab-la-   kana
     peel:III.U-PTCP:III- egg(III)
     'peeled egg'

---

18 It would not be possible to use a participle to describe the transitive agent of the same verb, i.e. 'a woman who is hiding something', since the transitive use does not entail a change-of-state of the agent, only of the transitive patient.

3.7 Derived nominals

DEPICTIVE USE. Participles are used as participant-oriented adjuncts, describing an action that the relevant participant is involved in at the time of the situation expressed by the main verb. This is the same use as that of converbs in many languages.

Participles used as adjuncts are placed in the syntactic slot immediately before the verb complex. The role of the participant involved in the action expressed by the participle is reflected in the use of one of the so-called Orientation prefixes on the verb (described in Chapter 11). The facts are complicated, but for now they can be summarised thus: if the subject of the participle functions as the S/A-argument of the main verb, the verb is prefixed by means of the Neutral Orientation prefix (ø- in non-present time contexts). If the subject of the participle functions as the O-argument of the main verb, another Orientation prefix is used, e.g. the Object prefix *m*- or the Directional prefix *k*-.

The difference is illustrated below. In the elicited example in (95), the subject of the participle *ihw-luk* 'while crying' is the S/A-argument of the main verb *yet*, so the Neutral ø-prefix is used on the verb. In (96), an overheard utterance, it is clear from the use of the Object prefix *m*- that the participant roles differ, and that the agent of the event corresponding to the participle ('shooting') is the O-argument of the main verb 'look, watch'. Note also the gender agreement with the participial subject in both examples.

(95) ihw-luk   ø-no-d-   yet
    be.crying-PTCP:II NTRL-1.A-DUR- be.moving
    'I (female) was walking along crying.'

(96) mes   w-as-lik   m-a-p-   hyadih-e
    old.coconut(III) III.U-shoot-PTCP:I/II.PL OBJ-3SG.A-CT- see:2|3PL.U-IPFV
    'He is watching them shoot at old coconuts.'

I consider this use of participles to be an instance of the more general construction type called secondary predication. See §18.5 for discussion.

In addition to their participant-oriented use, participles also occur with a following verb marked with the Object Orientation to express a reason or cause, as in (97). This use is not participant-oriented so the Participial suffix takes the default Gender III form *-la*. The use of the Object Orientation prefix *m*- with expressions of reason/cause is described in §11.1.3.5.

(97) ye   ay-la   m-a-p-   hu-h-a-m,
    rain(III) become:III.U-PTCP:III OBJ-3SG.A-CT- emerge-2|3PL.U-EXT-VEN

    hatuk m-a-   y-alaw-a-m
    cover OBJ-3SG.A- 2|3PL.U-search-EXT-VEN

    '[The mosquitos] are coming in because it started to rain, they are looking for shelter.'

4 Pronouns and demonstratives

4.1 Personal pronouns

There are only three personal pronouns, distinguishing 1st and 2nd person, plus singular and plural for the latter. There is also a corresponding set of emphatic pronouns, showing the same person/number distinctions. Both series are listed in Table 4.1.

Tab. 4.1: Personal pronouns

	PLAIN		EMPHATIC	
	SG	PL	SG	PL
1	nok		nahan	
2	oy	yoy	ahan	ihan

Note that there are no 3rd person pronouns. This vacancy is filled by demonstratives (§4.2).

The dearth of pronominal forms contrasts with the extensive participant indexing in the verb complex (Chapter 9), which fills the function that grammatical case marking might have in a dependent-marking language.

The lack of a number distinction only in the 1st person of the independent pronouns is typologically unusual (Corbett 2000: 56ff, Siewierska 2004: 92ff). The presence of an I/we-distinction has even been suggested to be universal (see Cysouw 2003: 81–84). On the paradigm level, the Coastal Marind personal pronouns clearly falsifiy such a putative universal. On the system level, however, Coastal Marind is no exception since a special role-neutral verb prefix *e-* is obligatorily present whenever the clause contains a 1pl argument, as in (98) (the prefix *e-* is described in §9.5). This means that the absence of a number distinction in the 1st person pronouns rarely results in ambiguity.

(98) nok nak-e- ayak-e
     1   1.A-1PL- go.inland-IPFV
     'We're going inland.' [W20:0222]

The pronouns have the same syntactic distribution as phrases headed by nouns. For example, pronouns may function as arguments, as in (99), or be the complement of e.g. the possessive postposition *en*, as in *oy en nggat* 'your (sg) dog' or *ahan en mayan* 'your (sg) own language'.

https://doi.org/10.1515/9783110747065-004

(99) yoy   m-ak-ind-e-   awat-a-m   nok
      2PL   OBJ-1.A-ALL-1PL-   run.PL-EXT-VEN   1
      'We came here to get you.'   [W10:0209]

The 1pl prefix *e-*, as in (98) and (99) above, is not available to disambiguate the number reference of a 1st person participant in contexts where this participant functions as an adjunct (rather than an argument of the verb). In such contexts the Associative Plural marker *ke* (or its variant *keti*, §7.6.1) is usually added to *nok* or *nahan*, e.g. *nok keti en nggat* 'our dog(s)', as opposed to *nok en nggat* 'my dog(s)'.

Personal pronouns are sometimes modified by demonstratives, such as the Proximal *ihe* combining with the 2pl pronoun *yoy* in (100). This usage is not well understood at present, but it is perhaps a way of signalling that the pronouns introduces a new topic ('As for you women here, ...').

(100) In a story, the protagonist is addressing some women he chased down from a tree.

      yoy   ihe,   ihe   iwag   ihe,   yoy   ihe   eham
      2PL   PROX:I/II.PL PROX:I/II.PL woman   PROX:I/II.PL 2PL   PROX:I/II.PL husband:2PL

      ek-ø-   ø-e?
      PRS.Q:I-3SG.A- be.NPST-IPFV
      'You, you women, do you have a husband?'   [D01:0218]

The emphatic pronoun series (*nahan, ahan*, etc.) are typically used contrastively, to stress that the referent(s) alone should do something, without the participation of others. Typically this would be in contrast to other participants explicitly mentioned, or in contrast to some expectation that others might participate, as in (101).

(101) The speaker is lending a boat to the addressee.

      yahun   epe   mate,   nahan   mak-e-   ka-dhetok   yapap   kwemek
      canoe(III)   DIST:III let.it.be   1.EMPH   FUT:1.A-1PL- WITH-return   tomorrow   morning
      'Just leave the boat there, we will bring it back ourselves tomorrow morning.'
                                                                                          [W10:0175]

In example (102) the use of the emphatic series is part of a standard reply used to defer decision-making to the addressee. It almost conveys a mild reproach, e.g. 'It's up to *you* — why would *I* know?'. An even stronger sense of annoyance is conveyed by the forceful use of *ahan* in (103).

(102) Speaker was asked if she wants a bucket of water.

      ahan   s-o-   ø   mayay!
      2SG.EMPH   ONLY-2SG.A- be.NPST   knowing
      'It's up to you!' (lit. 'Only yourself know!')   [W06:0096]

(103) The addressee had ordered the speaker to get some bamboo, then changed his mind and told them not to get it.

mayay   ahan   ø-d-o-na-y-   lay!
first   2SG.EMPH   NTRL-DUR-2SG.A-1.DAT-1PL-   tell

'It was *you* who told us [to get it] in the first place!' ('And now you're telling us not to — make up your mind!')   [W06:0219]

For 3rd person reference there is a special set of emphatic demonstratives used in emphatic contexts, but this series also has various other functions not shared by the emphatic pronouns — see §4.2.2.

4.2 Demonstratives

The four sets of basic demontratives are in Table 4.2. All demonstratives have an initial gender marking vowel *V-*, except the emphatic set *anVp*, in which the vowel is in the final syllable.

Tab. 4.2: Basic demonstratives: gender/number forms

	PROXIMAL *Vhe*		DISTAL *Vpe*		REMOTE *Vhan*		EMPHATIC *anVp*	
	SG	PL	SG	PL	SG	PL	SG	PL
I	ehe	ihe	epe	ipe	ehan	ihan	anep	anip
II	uhe		upe		uhan		anup	
III	ehe		epe		ehan		anep	
IV	ihe		ipe		ihan		anip	

In addition to the four basic sets, property demonstratives are derived from the Proximal *ehe* and Distal *epe* by adding the element *-tago* or *-tagol* (Table 4.3), e.g. *ehetago* or *ehetagol* 'like this'. The variants with and without final *-l* are in free variation.

Tab. 4.3: Property demonstratives: gender/number forms

	VhetagV(l) 'like this'		*VpetagV(l)* 'like that'	
	SG	PL	SG	PL
I	ehetage(l)	ihetagi(l)	epetage(l)	ipetagi(l)
II	uhetagu(l)		upetagu(l)	
III	ehetago(l)		epetago(l)	
IV	ihetagi(l)		ipetagi(l)	

The Coastal Marind demonstratives are used in three main grammatical functions: as independent referring expressions ('this one'), determiners ('this dog') and adverbials ('here, there'). Demonstratives agree in gender with the antecedent or head noun in the first two uses, whereas adverbially used demonstratives are invariant and appear in the Gender III forms per default (*ehe* 'here' etc.). The functions and the meaning of the different demonstratives are described in the following subsections.

4.2.1 Standard demonstratives

An example of the independent use of the Distal *epe*-demonstratives to express a verb argument is in (104), in which the plural form *ipe* realises the O-argument of the clause. The Distal *Vpe*-series is the most frequently used option for endophoric reference (i.e. reference to things mentioned elsewhere in the discourse) in texts and can probably be regarded as a default choice in this function.

(104) ipe   epe   k-ak-e-   yad⟨a⟩wn,   Karel k-a-   Ø
      DIST:I/II.PL there DIR-1.A-1PL- leave⟨2|3PL.U⟩   K.   PRS.NTRL-3SG.A-   be.NPST
      'We left them there, Karel [and the others].'   [W08:0033]

The textual uses of the Proximal *ehe*-series are not well understood at present. An excerpt from a narrative illustrating their use is in (105). The relevant referents, 'the boys from Sanggase', have appeared several times during a longer stretch of the preceding text, and are referred to by lexical means (*Sanggahe-patul*) in the first line of this excerpt. In the second line, anaphoric reference to them is made twice, in both instances by means of the Proximal *ehe*-demonstratives.

(105) Some boys from the Sanggase village had helped the speaker and his family cross a river, but then started stalking them.

       Sanggahe-patul namaya epe   k-e-na-y-p-   esoh,
       S.-boy   now   there DIR-3PL>1-1.DAT-1PL-CT- follow

       ihe   iwag   nanggol m-e-na-y-p-   esoh ihe
       PROX:I/II.PL   woman   for   OBJ-3PL>1-1.DAT-1PL-CT- follow PROX:I/II.PL

       'Now the Sanggase boys followed us there, they followed us for our women.'
                                                                           [W10:0179-0180]

More detailed study of information flow management in Coastal Marind narratives will be necessary to say more about the choice between Proximal and Distal demonstratives in endophoric reference.

Situational uses (also called exophoric uses, i.e. for reference to the physical surroundings of the speaker and hearer) of Distal vs. Proximal demonstratives are easier to understand. The utterance in (106) is from a face-to-face conversation, in which the speaker, Kolum (a ca. 15 years old boy), calls out to a passer-by (ca. 5 metres away) informing him/her that the people sitting with Kolum are drinking *wati* (kava). The use of the Proximal *ihe* is clearly motivated by the spatial configuration of the referents, which are close to the speaker but further away from the hearer.

(106) Said to a passer-by:

ihe   wati   anipand-an-   yi-e
PROX:I/II.PL kava(III) CONT:I/II.PL-3PL.A-   drink:III.U-IPFV

'These [people] just keep on drinking kava.'   [W05:0102]

The Remote *ehan*-series is only attested as determiners and adverbials, not as independently referring expressions.

In their use as determiners, demonstratives can appear postposed to the noun, e.g. *yap epe* 'that night' in (107), preposed, as in *epe anem* 'that man' (108), or circumposed, as in *ipe duwet ipe* (109).[1] The preposing option is much less frequent than the other two (see §4.2 for discussion).

(107) *yap   epe   ebta   k-ak-e-y-   haman*
      night(III) DIST:III sago.thatch(IV)   DIR-1.A-1PL-ACPN-   sit.PL

'That night we sat [making] sago thatch roofing.'   [W20:0276]

(108) The speaker describes how he waited in vain for his friend during a hunt.

epe   anem   mandin   mend-a-p-   ihe⟨n⟩ab
DIST:I   man(I) long.ago   PERF-3SG.A-CT-   pass⟨1.U⟩

'That man had already gone past me long ago.'   [W02:0058]

(109) *a-na-   og   ipe   duwet   ipe!*
      IMP-1.DAT-   give   DIST:IV   money(m)(IV)   DIST:IV

'Give me that money!'   [W19:0398]

The Proximal, Distal and Remote series may be used adverbially to refer to locations. Often the demonstrative is placed in the syntactic slot immediately before the verb complex, with one of the so-called Orientation prefixes (Chapter 11) prefixed to the verb, specifying whether the demonstrative marks e.g. the source or goal of movement. In (110), *epe* 'there' combines with the Directional prefix (§11.1.4.1), since it marks the goal of *haman* 'many assume a sitting position'. Cf. also (104) above.

---

1 The word *duwet* is ultimately from Dutch *duit*, and is used alongside Coastal Marind *katal* to refer to money.

(110) ah- naŋam, epe ka-p-e- haman
      IMP- come.PL there DIR-FUT:1.A-1PL- sit.PL
      'Come, we will sit over there.' [W18:0183]

The meaning difference between the Proximal *ehe*-series, the Distal *epe*-series and the Remote *ehan*-series is not particularly clear. When prompted, speakers say the *ehe* is used about something in the immediate vicinity, *epe* about something a bit further away, and *ehan* about something really far away.

These intuitions receive little support from the corpus data and my own observations. It is true that the Proximal series is used for deictic reference to e.g. items held by or sitting next to the speaker, whereas the Distal *epe*-series is unattested in such contexts. But the Proximal *ehe*-series may also be used for pointing out distant things (e.g. an aeroplane in the sky, or a herd of deer in the distance), perhaps as long as they are sufficiently salient or within the attention of the addressee. In line with Enfield's (2003) study of Lao demonstratives I hypothesise that the Distal series can be understood as meaning 'not here', while hearers infer that the Proximal *ehe*-series refer to things either close to the speaker or things that are within the field of attention, regardless of the physical distance involved, an inference that is made because the speaker chose not to use the Distal series.

Speakers' intuitions about the semantics of the Remote *ehan*-series are more difficult to reconcile with observed use. There are two problems: (i) although *ehan* is said to mean 'very far away', speakers also use the Distal *epe*-series (and, to some extent, the Proximal *ehe*) for very distant referents, e.g. for objects at the horizon, or for referents in other villages; and (ii) the Remote *ehan*-series is sometimes used for reference to the space in the immediate vicinity of the speaker, i.e. to express 'here'. The second observation is especially surprising since we expect the Proximal series to be used for 'here'-reference — recall that the Distal *epe*-series is unattested in this use.

I would like to make the very preliminary suggestion that these uses can be explained if the Remote series means something similar to 'far from the addressee' or perhaps 'inaccessible to the addressee'. Consider the following observed examples in support of this.

The exchange in (111) happened as Yakoba, a young girl in my Wambi host family, and I were walking in the village. As we walked I was (as usually) watching the ground in front of me for snakes and pointed objects, so I failed to locate the referent (*ad* 'father') in Yakoba's first utterance. In response, she said *ehan* 'over there' and pointed in a direction approximately 90° to my left, where her father was coming out of the vegetation about 50 m. away.

(111) 1. ad   ep-a-p-   hawa-em
         father DIST:I-3SG.A-CT- emerge:3SG.U-VEN

      2. [huh?]

3. (Pointing:) *ehan*
                    REM

1. (Yakoba:) 'Father is coming hither.'
2. (me:) [looks up, does not see Father.]
3. (Yakoba:) 'Over there.'

Now contrast this with how one would express 'Pass the ball to me!' as exclaimed during a football game, to draw the attention of a player elsewhere on the field. The most natural option is the Remote demonstrative *ehan*, as in (112), which is a frequent exclamation during all football games played by children in Wambi.

(112)   *ehan nanggol! ehan nanggol!*
        REM   for   REM   for
        '[Pass the ball] over here, over here!'

If the Remote demonstrative series means 'way over there', it is impossible to understand why *ehan* is used both in (111) and (112), since the latter example means 'way over here', not 'way over there'. If instead we assume that *ehan* means 'far from you, where you're not looking', it is possible to make sense of both utterances as instructions to the addressee to switch their attention to some distant object or location indicated by the speaker. (This description is similar to the analysis of the Deictic prefix series given in §15.4.)

This analysis is also compatible with *ehan* used for referents in e.g. other villages and far-away places. Example (113) was uttered to me by a man in Duhmilah, who was comparing the sago processing methods in use along the coast with those of the inland (see Olsson 2017: 561–565 for information about sago processing among the Marind). The speaker gestured to the north, approximately in the direction of Yawimu, a village a few hours (by motorcycle) from Duhmilah and Wambi, whose inhabitants belong to the culturally and linguistically distinct inland group of Bush Marind people, whereas the villagers in Wambi and Duhmilah identify as Coastal Marind.

(113)   *deg-anim   ihan,   Yawimu, mbya ka-n-is-ap-   o-tad-e*
        forest-people   REM:I/II.PL   Y.   NEG   PRS.NTRL-3PL.A-SEP-CT-   PLA-burn-IPFV
        'The forest people over there, in Yawimu, they don't bake [the sago loaves].'
                                                                              [D14:0001]

The use of the Remote *ihan* instead of the Distal *ipe* could reflect the fact that the referent (the Yawimu village and its inhabitants) is unknown and visually inaccessible to me, and perhaps also underline the cultural distance separating it from the coastal villages — although this is speculative.

4.2.2 Emphatic demonstrative

The emphatic demonstrative series *anep* has the same uses as the emphatic pronouns (§4.1), plus a few more. Like their pronominal counterparts, they are used in the S/A role to express that the referent does something without the participation or help of others, as in (114). Compare this to the use of an emphatic pronoun in e.g. (101) above.

(114) Describing how the bishop from Merauke inaugurated a new church.

anep	*ø-a-*	*kab*	*gereja-kay,*	*ah-ø-*	*k⟨y⟩amin*	*anim*
EMPH:I	NTRL-3SG.A-	open	church(m)-door	[DEP-3SG.A-	enter⟨2|3PL.U⟩	people]

'He himself opened the church door, when people entered.'   [W16:0057]

When speakers use the emphatic series in the sense 'without involvement of others', they often choose to reinforce this meaning by adding modifiers such as *kudaya* 'alone', as in (115–116). Such reinforcement does not seem to occur with the emphatic pronouns *nahan* 'myself' etc. This is perhaps because the other unrelated uses (see below) of the *anep*-series have made these forms somewhat semantically bleached.

(115) Asking about a hunter bringing back a pig.

anep   kudaya   ø-a-   w-asib   ay?
EMPH:I   alone   NTRL-3SG.A- 3SG.U-hit Q

'Did he kill it himself?'   [D05:0041]

(116) Comment about a cigarette.

anep   kudaya ø-a-   lahway
EMPH:III alone   NTRL-3SG.A- become.extinguished

'It went out by itself.'

The emphatic demonstratives are found as the complement of some postpositions with an emphatic-reflexive meaning. The phrase *anep nanggo* 'for himself' in (117) is used by the speaker to contrast the community spirit of old days, when food was shared with other villagers, with the individualism of today.

(117)   *anep   a-me-ø-   w-alaw   epe,*
        [EMPH:I DEP-FUT-3SG.A-   3SG.U-search DIST:III]

anep   nanggo   ma-me-ø-   w-alaw-a
EMPH:I   for   OBJ-FUT-3SG.A-   3SG.U-search-EXT

'If someone is searching for food, he will search just for himself.'   [W13:0714]

The rest of this section is devoted to the various other uses of the *anep*-series. These uses are much more common in the corpus than the 'without involvement of others'-function described above, but unfortunately most of them are poorly understood.

IN POSSESSIVE PHRASES. When such phrases have a demonstrative as the possessor ('his/her/its/their X') speakers seem to prefer to use the emphatic *anep* demonstrative in lieu of the plain demonstratives (*epe, ehe*) to express the possessor.[2] The use of the emphatic *anep* is not associated with any kind of emphasis in such contexts, and it is used regardless of whether the possessor is co-referential with some argument of the verb (e.g. the S/A-argument) or not. An example:

(118) yis-kah   a-mo-   yayahwig epe,   anep   en   nak
       [sweet.potato(III) DEP-FUT:2SG.A- plant:III.U   DIST:III] EMPH:III POSS vine(III)
       mo-   yayahwig
       FUT:2SG.A-   plant:III.U

'If you plant sweet potatoes, you have to plant their vine.'   [W13:0223]

DISCOURSE PARTICLE. Emphatic *anep* is commonly found in clause-initial position, and then serves to express some discourse function that unfortunately remains completely opaque. I had no success in my attempts do discuss this function of *anep* with speakers, so it will be left to future research to elucidate this common pattern.

Two corpus examples are provided below to give the reader a notion of the issues involved. The most noteworthy morphosyntactic feature of these examples is that *anep* agrees in gender with the subject of its clause. This is slightly surprising since the syntactic position of *anep* appears to be at the periphery of the clause, and there are no signs suggesting that it is in a modifier relationship to any noun.

(119) About drunk boys disrupting a celebration in a neighbouring village.

    1. sageru   lik   yap   ma-n-i-e-   aya⟨h⟩in
       alcohol(m)   from:I/II.PL night OBJ-3PL.A-RE-ACPN-   run.around⟨2|3PL.U⟩

---

[2] There are 34 attestations of these structures in the texual corpus: 28 of them (82%) employ the emphatic *anep*, whereas only 6 (18%) have the shape *epe en X* or *ehe en X*, despite the plain demonstratives being more than 6 times as frequent in the corpus as the emphatic ones overall (this, however, also includes their uses as determiners etc., and so is not directly comparable to their pronominal use in possessor phrases). For the personal pronouns (*nok* 'I, we' etc.), the plain pronouns predominate in possessive phrases, with only 9 out of 26 (35%) possessor phrases using the emphatic variants.

2. *anip   Wambi-patul ø-d-ø-i-   ya-hwala,*
   EMPH:I/II.PL W.-boy   NTRL-DUR-3SG.A-RE- 2|3PL.U-be

   yap   ma-n-   i-sak
   night OBJ-3PL.A- 2|3PL.U-hit.PLA

   1. 'At night [the police] were running around after drunk people again.'
   2. 'It was Wambi boys again, at night [the police] hit them.'

   [W18:0196-0197]

(120) a. *ehe   ad   tanama menda-b-ø-   dahetok*
         PROX:I father(I) again PERF-ACT-3SG.A- return

   b. *anep   yabe sasayi-anem   ø-d-a-   ola*
      EMPH:I   Gh.   work-man   NTRL-DUR-3SG.A-   be:3SG.U

   1. 'Father here already returned,
   2. because he had work to do in Ghabe Island.' (lit. 'was a work-man')

   [W18:0120]

It is unclear if the presence of the word 'because' (Malay *karena*), which was added by the speaker who helped me transcribe the latter example, is related to the presence of the word *anep*.

EXCLAMATIVE/EVALUATIVE: 'X INDEED!' Speakers often form evaluative exclamations of the shape adjective+*anep*, perhaps corresponding to something like 'Adj. indeed!' or 'How Adj.!'. For example, during a meal it is common to hear participants exclame *yel anep!* 'How tasty!'. The main differences between Adj.+*anep* and the construction *X ya* 'very X' is that the latter is also attested with nouns and other parts of speech (see §7.6.2), and that the construction with *anep* always occurs as independent utterances, not integrated within a larger syntactic structure.

Two corpus examples are below. The emphatic demonstrative shows agreement in gender/number according to the referent being described.

(121) Pau and Mili are discussing a recent hunting expedition.

   1. *adaka   epe   nd-an-d-e-   yi*
      water(III) there LOC-1.A-DUR-1PL- drink:III.U

   2. *adaka   halay anep!*
      water(III) clear EMPH:III

   1. (Pau:) 'We drank water there.'
   2. (Mili:) 'The water [was] really clear!'

   [W11:0649-0650]

(122) A vivid account of how the speaker spotted a deer and several wallabies during a hunt.

awi   sayam?   aneeee otih anip!
what.about wallaby(II) EXCLAM many EMPH:I/II.pl

'And what about the wallabies? Woooah so many!' [W11:0728-0729]

The emphatic demonstrative sometimes co-occurs with a verb marked by the Actualis *b-*, in a use that seems to emphasise the truth value of the proposition, somewhat like English 'indeed' — see §15.3.1.1.

4.2.3 Property demonstratives

As mentioned above, property demonstratives are formed by combining the plain demonstratives *ehe* 'this' and *epe* 'that' with the element *-tago*, giving e.g. *ehetago* 'like this' and *epetago* 'like that' (with Gender III agreement). A final *-l* is often added, without any known meaning contribution: *ehetagol* etc. The gender forms of the property demonstratives were given in Table 4.3 above.[3] In casual, allegro speech these demonstratives are often significantly reduced: e.g. *ehetagol* > *etal* 'like this'.

The most common use of the property demonstratives is situational: the speaker uses the demonstrative to refer to degree or quality (colour, measures, distance, etc.) of some property in the immediate surroundings, usually combined with a pointing gesture. For example, time of the day is usually expressed as in (123), with a gesture indicating a point in the sky (there are no watches in Wambi), whereas size of e.g. animals is conveyed by indicating a point on one's leg up to which a four-legged animal reached, as in (124). (Fish are measured as the distance between the tip of one's middle finger and a point indicated further up on one's arm.)

(123) Pointing to the sky.

ehetago   katane
like.this:III sun(III)

'at this time of the day' (lit. 'the sun like this') [W04:0055]

---

[3] I avoid segmentation of the property demonstratives in interlinear glosses, so instead of *e-hetag-o* 'III-like.this-III', I write *ehetago* 'like.this:III'. The origin of *-tago* is uncertain, but it is likely related to the 'pro-word' *ago* (see discussion in §4.4).

(124) kosi-basik   epe   nda-d-ø-   yi-la-ti,   kosi   mbya,
      small-pig(II) there LOC-DUR-3SG.A-   eat-EXT-DUR   small NEG

   uhetagul   menda-b-ø-   w-in
   like.this:II PERF-ACT-3SG.A-   3SG.U-become

   'A little pig was eating there, not little, it was already [big] like this.'
                                                                    [W11:0518]

Non-situational uses are rare. Example (125) is one of the few corpus examples of a property demonstrative employed to refer to a linguistic element of the surrounding discourse.

(125) I asked two villagers to stage an interview for me to record. Here, the interviewer complains that the interviewee is not providing sufficiently detailed answers.

   "ahak" se   tumat-ap-   y-a,   ndom-ago   k-a-   ø
   yes   only   PROH:2SG.A-CT-   2SG.U-AUX   bad-PRWD:III PRS.NTRL-3SG.A-   be.NPST

   epetago   epe
   like.that:III DIST:III

   'Don't just say "yes", it's no good like that.'   [D07:0005-0006]

Endophoric reference to other parts of discourse is usually realised through the important Predicated Manner Construction, described in §17.3.2. This contruction is also used to refer to mimicked action, e.g. 'do like this' (showing an action with e.g. one's hands). Property demonstratives can be used for reference to mimicked actions, but this usage is very rare in my corpus.

Note that the above examples instantiate different grammatical functions of the manner series. In (123) and (124) the demonstrative expressions are used as attributive modifiers, and show agreement according to the gender of the head noun: Gender III with *katane* 'sun', and Gender II with *basik* 'pig'. In (125) *epetago* functions as an adverbial and therefore automatically appears in Gender III, which is the default gender of agreeing targets (such as *epetago*) when they appear in non-agreeing contexts (e.g. used as an adverbial).

4.3 Interrogative pronouns

Marind has only three basic interrogative pronouns: *ta* 'who, what', *en* 'where, which', *entago* 'what kind, how many' (with the apparently synonymous variant *entagol*). All of these pronouns exhibit gender agreement marked by vowel alternations. The resulting gender forms are:

	I	II	III	IV, I/II.PL	
	ta	tu	ta	ti	'who, what'
	en	un	en	in	'where, which'
	entage(l)	untagu(l)	entago(l)	intagi(l)	'what kind, how many'

The latter is perhaps not morphologically basic since it can be analysed as a combination of *en* 'where, which' plus the element *-tago(l)*, which also occurs in property demonstratives (§4.2.3).

All other interrogative expressions are derived from these basic interrogative words, e.g. *ta lek* 'why, for what reason' (lit. 'from what') or *ta* plus a verb inflected with the Locational Orientation prefix *nd-*, giving a 'when'-question (see §11.1.5.2).

The question words are frequently used as modifiers within a larger interrogative phrase, e.g. *ta patul?* 'what boy?', *tu kyasom?* 'what girl?', *en milah?* 'which village?'. Interrogative words and phrases are always placed in the syntactic slot immediately preceding the verb complex, and have no functions outside content question constructions (they are not used as indefinite pronouns). The formation of content questions is complicated by the use of special interrogative morphology on the verb, as discussed in §19.3. Of special interest are manner questions ('How did you do it?') which are formed without any interrogative pronouns (see §19.3.2.5).

4.3.1 *enda?* 'Where are you going?' (etc.)

This interrogative word forms a complete utterance on its own, so it is not an interrogative pronoun but rather an interrogative pro-sentence.[4] Its most frequent use is as the standard exclamation *enda?* 'Where are you going?', which villagers use to interrogate all passers-by leaving the village or going somewhere away from their house (cf. Gil 2015: 280–282 on such greetings). The corresponding question upon return is fully compositional: *en ndohob-manem?* 'Where are you coming from?'.

It is also possible to use *enda?* as a short question about general location of some previously mentioned event, as in 'I fell with the motorbike' —'Oh, *enda?*' —'Over there on the beach'.

The appropriate answer to the conventionalised greeting *enda?* 'Where are you going?' depends on the social relationship between the interrogator and the passer-by, and the planned itinerary of the former. A minimal response, appropriate to answer e.g. some inquisitive children, is to say *epe* 'over there', casually lip-pointing to some unspecified location in the distance. With adults a more substantive response is re-

---

[4] This expression is somehow related to the interrogative pronoun *en* 'where' (*end* in dialects without final simplification of the prenasalised plosive /n̪d/). One might suspect that *enda* originated as a truncation of some longer phrase meaning 'Where are you going?', but no such phrase starts with *enda-* in contemporary Coastal Marind (e.g. *en mohob-umayahe* 'Where are you going?').

quired, with its length adjusted to the newsworthiness of one's plans: a short answer for familiar, unremarkable destinations, e.g. *Tinus mit* 'To Tinus' place' (Tinus has a small shop selling cigarettes and dried betelnut), and more detailed explanations for longer excursions. The asker then says 'Okay, keep going!' (as in example 767 on p. 398), or something to that effect, to signal their satisfaction with the response.

4.4 The pro-word *ago*

This is a multifunctional item, labelled 'pro-word' for want of a better term. Three of its functions are treated in turn in the subsections below: in compounds forming predicative adjectives and demonyms (§4.4.1), 'what's-it-called' (§4.4.2) and as a purposive marker (§4.4.3). For its use as a quotative index, see §20.2.

Note that *ago* is one of the few agreement targets that distinguish all four genders: *age* (I), *agu* (II), *ago* (III), *agi* (IV). The plural of Genders I and II is *agi*.

Alongside the four uses of *ago* outlined below, the same shape also appears as a part of the property demonstratives *ehetago* 'like this' and *epetago* 'like that' (§4.2.3). It seems reasonable to hypothesise that *ago* earlier functioned as a manner deictic meaning 'so' or 'such', but that this function is no longer available to the independent word *ago*. This origin would provide clear explanations for its use as a quotative (*S/he said so: "..."*) and purposive (cf. English *S/he did it so that...*), although perhaps less so for its other uses. The contemporary property demonstratives appear to consist of *ago* preceded by two layers of demonstratives: the element *-t-*, probably a reflex of the proto-Anim demonstrative root **tV* (Usher and Suter 2015), preceded by the innovated demonstratives *ehe/epe*.

4.4.1 In compounds

It was shown in §3.3.2 that *ago* is obligatorily appended to the small class of bound adjectives when they occur in predicative contexts (e.g. *noy-ago ka* 'It is new'). Another use as the head of compounds is with village demonyms, i.e. expressions denoting inhabitants of a village. Examples: *Wambi-agu* 'a woman from Wambi', *Sanggahe-agi* 'Sanggase villagers', *Duh-age* 'a man from Duhmilah' (this village name is a compound from *duh* 'beach' and *milah* 'village').

4.4.2 'What's-it-called'

In this extremely common use *ago* functions as a placeholder for an expression that the speaker has trouble remembering or formulating, just like English *whatchamacallit*, *what's-her-name*, and so on. Often speakers use it as a general marker of hesitation ('um...'). Note that the placeholder *ago* shows the gender value corresponding to that of the sought-after expression.[5]

(126) Referring to a place where hunters used to skin deer carcasses.

epe	*nd-a-d-na-*	*kaysa⟨h⟩ib-ma*	*ago,*
there	LOC-DEP-DUR-3PL.A-	skin⟨2|3.U⟩-PST.HAB	PRWD:III

anip	*en*	*ago*	*epe,*	*ugu*
EMPH:I/II.PL	POSS	PRWD:III	DIST:III	skin(III)

'there where they used to remove the what's-it-called, their um...skins.'

[W10:0071]

It is also common to use *ago* in self-repair, to mark that the material following *ago* replaces or clarifies something problematic just uttered. Example (127) shows this use in a repair sequence. In line 1, Pau self-initiates repair by using *ago* as a hesitation marker, and explicitly asks for correction by adding the final question particle *ay*. Mili provides the correction in line 2, which Pau echoes as *ago*-marked self-repair in line 3. (All placenames trigger Gender III agreement.)

(127) 1. | *epe* | *k-ak-e-* | *uma⟨n⟩ah,* | *ago* | *Moyga* | *k-ak-e-p-* | *i-hyaman* |
|---|---|---|---|---|---|---|
| there | DIR-1.A-1PL- | go⟨1.U⟩ | PRWD:III | M. | DIR-1.A-1PL-CT- | PLA-enter.water |

ay?
Q

2. *Mokob*
M.

3. *ago,* *Mokob*
PRWD:III M.

1. (Pau:) 'We went there, we went throught the water in um Moyga, right?'
2. (Mili:) 'In Mokob.'
3. (Pau:) 'I mean, in Mokob.'

[W11:0853-0855]

---

5 The presence of gender agreement on 'what's-it-called' or 'whatchamacallit', like that on interrogative pronouns such as *ta* 'who, what', is perhaps surprising since these words are used when the speaker lacks access to the relevant noun. Gender is clearly more predictable than phonological shape, but see (964) on p. 475 for an example of the wrong gender form *ago* (III) used as a placeholder for the Gender IV noun *kahil*. Cf. Feldman (1986: 44) for gender agreement on 'whatchamacallit' in Awtuw (Sepik) and Reid (1997) for Ngan'gityemerri (or Nangikurrunggurr), an Australian language of the Northern Territory.

4.4.3 Expressing purpose

In this structure *ago* appears with a noun referring to some entity that the agent hopes to acquire as a result of the action expressed by the verb. Since *ago* appears after the noun, it should perhaps be considered a postposition in this use. The combination is placed in the slot prceding the verb, which is marked by the Object Orientation *m-* (§11.1.3). There is no gender agreement in this context so *ago* appears in the default Gender III shape *ago*. This way of expressing purpose is less common than using a postposition such as *nanggo* 'for' (see §6.1.5).

(128) Observed, about a little girl.

wah ago m-a- ihw-e
mother(II) PRWD:III OBJ-3SG.A be.crying-IPFV

'She's crying for her mum.'

For clause combinations expressing purpose, see §20.2.2.

4.5 The pro-name *eyal*

This word, glossed PRNM, is used instead of the name of a person or thing. The citation form *eyal* is used for an anonymous male (Gender I) or item (Gender III, e.g. a village), and *eyul* for an anonymous female (Gender II). There are no forms for plural animates or Gender IV items.

Its main use is as a placeholder 'such-and-such' when the actual identity is irrelevant or unknown, as in the second line of the narrated dialogue in (129).

(129) 1. oy ta ka-h-o-b- Ø igih?
2SG who:I PRS.NTRL-ROG-2SG.A-ACT- be.NPST name

2. nok eyal ka-no- Ø nok
1 PRNM:I PRS.NTRL-1.A- be.NPST 1

3. epe igih epe, nda-p-ø-o- ayi,
DIST:I name DIST:I LOC-FUT-3SG.A-3SG.DAT- say

tis ka-me-ø- w-a kadahab epe
that's.it DIR-FUT-3SG.A- 3SG.U-AUX behead:3SG.U DIST:I

'[The headhunter would ask:] "What's your name?",
[The victim would reply:] "I'm such-and-such",
That name, he would say it to him, then he would behead him.'

[D06:0020–0022]

The pro-name can also be used to get around name avoidance with in-laws. If my sister-in-law is named *Babu* (also a noun meaning 'skin of baked sago loaf'), I can refer to her as *eyul* 'you-know-who'. Typically, more clarity is required, so I would refer to her either by the name of her husband (*Sami uhyum* 'Sami's wife', if my brother is named Sami), or by some circumlocution such as *da-pal* (lit. 'sago-skin').

5 Nominal gender

Coastal Marind has a gender system comprising four genders. I follow the conventions established by Drabbe (1955) and refer to them as Genders I–IV (only replacing Drabbe's Arabic numerals with Roman ones). The vast majority of nouns that I have recorded are conventionally assigned to one of the four genders, and always trigger agreement according to that gender.

The basis for gender assignment is animacy: all nouns denoting animate beings are assigned to Genders I and II, and inanimates to Genders III and IV. Within animates, Gender I contains male humans, while Gender II contains female humans and all animals (regardless of biological sex). In contrast, there is no obvious rationale (semantic or phonological) for the assignment of inanimates to Gender III and IV, but note that Gender III is considerably larger (452 recorded members) than Gender IV (195 members). There are also good reasons to consider Gender III a 'default' gender, because when agreeing targets (e.g. demonstratives) occur in syntactic contexts that do not allow agreement (e.g. in some adverbial positions) it is always the Gender III form of the target that is used.

Similar four-gender systems — featuring roughly one masculine, one feminine and two inanimate genders — are found throughout the Anim language family. Usher and Suter (2015) present data (from missionary-linguists Roland Fumey and Robert Petterson) showing evidence of four genders in the languages Kuni (of the Lake Murray subgroup) and Ipiko (of the Inland Gulf subgroup), and ongoing research by Phillip Rogers has unearthed four genders in Bitur (of the Lower Fly subgroup). During my own fieldwork I was also able to identify four genders in the other languages of the Marindic subgroup, i.e. Bush Marind and the Upper Bian language. It seems reasonable to conclude that four genders were present in the proto-Anim language and that they have been inherited — with some differences in assignment principles — by its present-day descendants.

Like Corbett (1991), I find Hockett's definition of gender as "classes of nouns reflected in the behaviour of associated words" (1958: 231) to be a useful starting point for the investigation. There is a small number of nouns in Coastal Marind that exhibit vowel alternations corresponding to assignment to different genders (with a predictable change in meaning), but it is the pervasive phenomenon of gender agreement in targets such as determiners, adjectives and verbs that makes it necessary to posit the category gender for Coastal Marind. I provide an overview of the reflection of gender in such 'associated words' in §5.1. The principles of gender membership are reviewed in more detail in §5.2. More detailed discussion of some agreement phenomena is in §5.3.

5.1 Overview of gender agreement

The aim of this section is to provide the basic data that demonstrate that Coastal Marind has a gender system. I will do this by showing agreement on two different targets: demonstratives used as determiners, and adjectives. Similar expositions of the Coastal Marind gender system have appeared in Foley (1986: 82–83, based on Drabbe 1955: 19) and in Corbett (1991: 116, based on Foley).

The data in (130) illustrate the behaviour of the Distal demonstrative *Vpe* when it functions as a determiner within a noun phrase. In (130a) the demonstrative appears in the shape *epe*, because it combines with the noun *patul* 'boy'. In (130b) it has the shape *upe*, because it occurs with the noun *kyasom* 'girl'. These nouns belong to Gender I and II, since they denote a male and a female human respectively. In (130c–d), plural reference is made, which causes the demonstrative to be realised as *ipe*. Since no distinction between Genders I and II is made in the plural, I gloss the *i*-form of the demonstrative as 'I/II.PL'. Note that the nouns themselves are invariant, so the number difference is only manifested in the agreement form of the determining element *epe*.

(130)   a.   *patul epe*   b.   *kyasom upe*
            boy(I)   DIST:I   girl(II)   DIST:II
            'that boy'   'that girl'

          c.   *patul ipe*   d.   *kyasom ipe*
            boy(I)   DIST:I/II.PL   girl(II)   DIST:I/II.PL
            'those boys'   'those girls'

Consider now the inanimate nouns in (131). The noun *da* 'sago, sago palm' in (131a) triggers the demonstrative *epe*, and the noun *bomi* 'termite mound' in (131b) triggers *ipe*. These forms happen to be homophonous with the demonstratives used for the Gender I noun in (130a) and with the plural forms in (130c–d). But the agreement pattern is different for the inanimate nouns 'sago' and 'termite mound' with respect to number: the forms in (131a–b) can be used for both singular and plural reference, whereas the animate nouns above required special plural forms of the demonstrative. The four different agreement patterns (or agreement classes) can be used as evidence suggesting four separate genders in the language.

(131)   a.   *da*   *epe*   b.   *bomi*   *ipe*
            sago(III)   DIST:III   termite.mound(IV)   DIST:IV
            'that sago palm'   'that termite mound'
            'those sago palms'   'those termite mounds'

We find further support for the four-gender analysis looking at other agreement targets, such as agreeing adjectives. Only a small subclass of 16 adjectives agree in gender, and it is somewhat difficult to find an adjective that is equally compatible with animate and inanimate referents (for example, the agreeing adjective meaning 'ripe' is only used with fruits and vegetables, never with animates). In (132) I illustrate adjectival agreement with *samlayVn*, 'mid-size, neither too big nor too small' an adjective that speakers found acceptable with both types of referents.

In its attributive use, the adjective is compounded with the noun. Agreement is signalled by a change in the stem-final vowel of the adjective, marked by boldface. The pattern of exponence differs slightly for different adjectives (cf. Table 3.3 in §3.3). As seen below, *samlayVn* shows almost the same pattern of exponence as the demonstrative *epe*: Gender I triggers the vowel *e*, Gender II *u*, while Gender IV and the plural of Genders I & II trigger *i*. The only difference is that this target lacks the homonymy between Genders I and III, and exhibits a distinct agreement form with the vowel *a* for Gender III.

(132) Agreement on the adjective *samlayVn* 'mid-size'

a.	samlay**e**n-patul	'mid-size boy'		(I)
b.	samlay**u**n-kyasom	'mid-size girl'		(II)
c.	samlay**i**n-patul	'mid-size boys'		(I/II.PL)
d.	samlay**i**n-kyasom	'mid-size girls'		(I/II.PL)
e.	samlay**a**n-da	'mid-size sago palm(s)'		(III)
f.	samlay**i**n-bomi	'mid-size termite mound(s)'		(IV)

The patterns of exponence exhibited by the two targets seen so far, *Vpe* 'that' and *samlayVn* 'mid-size', are diagrammed in Figure 5.1.

	SG	PL
I	e	i
II	u	i
III	e	
IV	i	

Vpe 'that'

	SG	PL
I	e	i
II	u	i
III	a	
IV	i	

samlayVn 'mid-size'

Fig. 5.1: Exponents of agreement on two targets

The four agreement patterns seen with these targets recur with all agreeing targets in the language, although with some differences in the exponent vowels. It will be seen in the following section that each pattern picks out a sufficiently large set of nouns to posit four full-fledged genders in Coastal Marind.

A final remark on the exponence pattern shown by the vowels is in place. It was noted that the vowel /i/ marks Gender IV, but also the plural of Gender I & II. This homophony pattern recurs systematically with all targets, and is potentially worrisome for the four-gender analysis. It is common to find nouns across languages that invariably trigger plural agreement, even in contexts of singular reference, e.g. English *scissors* or Russian *časy* 'clock'. Such nouns are called pluralia tantum, and are generally not considered to form a separate gender — they just happen to have a fixed number value. This suggests an alternative analysis of the Coastal Marind gender system, according to which Gender IV nouns like *bomi* 'termite mound(s)' do not form a separate gender, but are simply members of Genders I or II that happen to have a fixed plural value. I will address this issue in §5.3.2.

5.2 Assignment

At the end of my fieldwork, the lexical database contained ca. 1100 nouns, of which I had been able to identify the gender membership of 949. 25 nouns lack conventionalised gender assignment and trigger agreement according to the referent at hand, as discussed in §5.2.3. The remainder are nouns that I either did not have the opportunity to check for gender, or nouns for which I failed to get information about gender membership.

Below I repeat the semantic basis for assignment, along with numbers showing the distribution of the 949 nouns that could be assigned to genders:

I	male humans	16	(2%)
II	female humans, all animals	286	(30%)
III	inanimates	452	(48%)
IV	inanimates	195	(20%)

There is only a small number of nouns that exclusively denote either men or women, most of them kinship terms (e.g. *ad* 'father') or terms for age classes (e.g. *mesiwag* 'old woman'). This explains why Gender I (male humans) has so few members. The membership of Gender II is larger since it includes well over 200 animal names. More details on the assignment of nouns to genders are given in the following subsections.

5.2.1 Assignment of animates

5.2.1.1 Humans

The assignment of male humans to Gender I and female humans to Gender II has no known exceptions. Nouns that are assigned to Gender I include male-denoting kinship terms such as *yay* 'mother's brother', *pap* 'husband's father' and *mbit* 'elder sister's husband' etc., and male-denoting person terms such as *patul* 'boy', *yasti* 'old man', *mes-meakim* 'unmarried older man', *ewati* 'young man (of marriageable age)' etc. Nouns denoting female humans in Gender II include the kinship terms *ne* 'elder brother's wife', *kak* 'father's sister', *nikna* 'son's wife' etc., and person terms such as *kyasom* 'girl', *iwag* 'woman', *sah* 'married woman', and so on.

Other person-denoting nouns are not restricted to either sex, and may be used to refer to either a man or a woman. Examples are *yunayon* 'infant' and *onos* 'cousin', which trigger agreement in Gender I or II depending on whether the referent given in the context is male or female. In the dictionary I list members of this group of nouns (which also includes some nouns denoting inanimate things) as having 'referential gender' (see §5.2.3).[1]

5.2.1.2 Animals

Animals always trigger agreement in Gender II. This is true even when reference is made to a male animal (e.g. *gomna* 'male pig') and for most animals with anthropomorphic traits in stories. No special treatment is given according to shape, size or prototypicality: pigs and cassowaries belong to Gender II, just like lice, jellyfish and barnacles. In this respect Coastal Marind appears to differ from at least some other Anim languages, such as Bitur, in which animals are divided between the Masculine and Feminine genders (corresponding to Coastal Marind Genders I and II), although the principles behind the assignment are not entirely clear (Phillip Rogers, pers. comm.).[2]

---

[1] The distinction between human-denoting nouns as displaying inherent vs. referential gender is somewhat artificial, since it could be argued that all nouns for humans have referential gender — it just happens that some words, e.g. *yay* 'mother's brother', always have a male human as their referent and therefore invariably trigger Gender I agreement. This is a valid point since it captures the fact that gender assignment of humans is completely predictable (cf. German *Mädchen* 'girl', which is grammatically Neuter, not Feminine). Despite this, I choose to treat words such as *yay* 'mother's brother' as having conventionalised Gender I, since this makes the usage clearer, and avoids the counter-intuitive conclusion that Gender I has zero members.

[2] I suggest in Olsson (2019b: 207) that certain phonological patterns in Coastal Marind animal terms indicate that the assignment to Gender II is an innovation, and that these words were divided between Genders I and II at an earlier stage.

5.2.1.3 Border-line animates and animacy spillover

The real-world distinction between animate and inanimate entities is not always easy to draw, and when languages incorporate this distinction into their grammars it is often the case that some nouns are treated like animates despite denoting items that are clearly inanimate (see e.g. Corbett 1991: 20–21 for Algonquian languages). Here I will list some Coastal Marind nouns that denote inanimates, yet 'spill over' into Gender II, as if they were animals.

All words for stars and stellar constellations are assigned to Gender II. Giving stars animate status is motivated from a cosmological point of view, although it seems that different stars were traditionally considered to be men, women or animals (these finer mythological distinctions are apparently not reflected in gender). For example, the Milky Way is referred to as *ahyaki* 'snake' (I also heard *yalet-ahyaki* 'dangerous snake'). Betelgeuse has the Coastal Marind name *olib*, which is also the name of a small flatfish species. The three stars in Orion's Belt are boys spearing the *olib* fish (van Baal 1966: 295, fn113).[3] However, it appears that both *katane* 'sun' and *mandaw* 'moon' are treated as inanimates and assigned to Gender III, despite being male beings in the mythology (van Baal 1966: passim).[4]

The noun *at* 'skin mole' belongs to Gender II, as observed by Drabbe (1955: 17). This is perhaps motivated by the similarity between moles and animals living on the skin such as lice and ticks. Other skin conditions belong to Gender IV (e.g. *apupin* 'pimple'), as discussed below.

Kites are assigned to Gender II. I have only heard the Malay word *layang-layang* used for these flying objects, but one speaker said that he had heard a native term, although he could not recall it. The motivation for the gender assignment is perhaps the similarity with birds (the Malay term, however, comes from a verb meaning 'to fly' and is unrelated to birds).

In addition it can be mentioned that corpses remain animate, so the cadaver of a pig triggers Gender II agreement even after it technically has ceased to be animate.

5.2.2 Assignment of inanimates

All inanimates (except for the borderline cases mentioned in §5.2.1.3) are divided between Genders III and IV, with the majority (70%) of the nouns assigned to Gender III. It is not possible to devise hard and fast rules predicting membership of inanimates, so the best advice for a learner of Coastal Marind is to memorise all of the minority

---

[3] Drabbe (1955: 17) erroneously claims that stars are female in Marind mythology.
[4] Admittedly, it is hard to establish with absolute certainty whether the sun and moon belong to Gender III or Gender I, because the main morphological difference between the two is that Gender I nouns trigger *i*-forms in the plural, but I have never recorded 'sun' and 'moon' with plural reference in Coastal Marind discourse. This is a point for future investigation.

nouns belonging to Gender IV, and to treat the remaining nouns as Gender III by default. However, there are some tendencies in gender membership, to be outlined in the following subsections. Some of these admittedly have an ad hoc flavour, and it is possible that other linguists would discern other (robuster) patterns in the same data.

Semantic fields that are predominantly assigned to Gender III (e.g. abstracts, places, and weather phenomena) and Gender IV (e.g. skin conditions and body decorations) are listed in §5.2.2.1 and §5.2.2.2 respectively. Semantic fields that are split across Genders III and IV (mainly body parts and plants) are presented in §5.2.2.3.

5.2.2.1 Semantic fields predominantly in Gender III

Here I list categories whose members appear to be uniformly assigned to Gender III, with no known exceptions to date. Examples are given for each semantic field.

- ABSTRACTS AND INTANGIBLES: *dul* 'shame', *abna* 'theft', *emel* 'hunger', *ena* 'heat', *hi* 'song', *imu* 'smell', *sal* 'taboo', *ul* 'news, message', *mayan* 'speech, language', *hwetok* 'thought', *kambala* 'k.o. black magic', *kuy* 'head hunting', *nggathi* 'sing-sing', *bawan* 'clan'.
- PLACES, LANDMARKS: *bob* 'swamp', *aliki* 'river', *duh* 'beach, coast', *tutu* 'current', *etob* 'tide, ocean', *yahwayah* 'forest', *hekay* 'clearing', *makan* 'ground, land', *mamuy* 'savanna', *pale* 'land ridge', *poya* 'garden', *milah* 'village'. All placenames and locations.
- WEATHER PHENOMENA: *kiwal* 'wind', *wakeh* 'northern wind', *ahwadak* 'light breeze', *ye* 'rain', *malob* 'rainbow', *omom* 'clouds', *satap* 'dew', *laku* 'fog', *misalaw* 'clear, blue sky'.
- LIQUIDS: *ahwasi* 'tears', *gel* 'sap', *huhu* 'wound liquid, exudate', *kanola* 'semen', *kono* 'urine', *do* 'blood', *bub* 'milk' (also 'breast'), *adaka* 'water', *sa-halay* 'oil, petrol'.

Nouns in the following categories overwhelmingly fall into Gender III. Below are sample nouns, after which I list all known exceptions.

- TRADITIONAL ARTIFACTS: *akada* 'fish hook', *bakuma* 'big basket', *kalal* 'trap', *kandala* 'drum', *kipa* 'net', *mbasom* 'axe', *pandu* 'fan', *wad* 'basket strapped to head', *kehway* 'paddle', *aha* 'house', *mih* 'bow', *tangge* 'arrow', *ok* 'k.o. small arrow'.
    - Exceptions, in Gender IV: *kahil* 'tongs', *bayis* 'pestle', *imadeh* 'quiver', *nggim* 'bracer'. Several types of arrows, e.g.: *ambata* 'trident arrow', *kapan* 'blunt tip arrow'.
- MASSES: *sa* 'sand', *dalo* 'mud', *ahwa* 'red clay sp.', *ndahwe* 'edible clay sp.', *gumna* 'ashes', *wi* 'contents of fruit/shellfish', *kabel* 'fat, grease', *wah* 'steam, vapor', *lak* 'smoke', *takah* 'firewood' (also 'fire').
    - Exceptions, in Gender IV: *ndalom* 'foam', *kangging* 'layer of crushed seashells on the beach', *po* 'white clay sp.'.

5.2.2.2 Semantic fields predominantly in Gender IV

I have not been able to identify any semantic field that is entirely restricted to Gender IV.

- SKIN CONDITIONS: *apupin* 'pimple', *bunggi* 'boil', *tibol* 'large boil', *dapadap* 'skin disease (prob. Tinea Versicolor)', *gewa* 'k.o. itching rash', *kambi* 'skin disease (prob. Tinea Imbricata)', *mbilambil* 'skin disease (ringworm?)', *samani* 'scabies'.
  - Exceptions, in Gender III: *mam* 'skin disease (in dogs)', *mapo* 'disease causing sores in scalp'.
- BODY DECORATIONS: *himbu* 'feathered headdress', *mbalal* 'bracelet worn on upper arm', *panggo* 'pubic shell (traditionally worn by women)', *segos* 'rattan girdle', *baway* 'grass skirt', *kayso* 'feathered stick (worn on arm)', *kindali* 'nautilus shell (hung around neck)', *wale* 'k.o. bracelet', *ihil* 'k.o. earrings', *baba* 'necklace from seeds of Coix Lacryma-jobi'.
  - Exceptions, in Gender III: *ud* 'girl's traditional headwear', *sayu* 'pubic shell (traditionally worn by men)', *kalam* 'k.o. necklace'.
- MODERN TECHNOLOGY & TOOLS, ELECTRONIC APPLIANCES: *lahwalah-yahun* 'aeroplane', *yahun* 'ship' (if used in Gender III, this words means 'canoe'), *katal* 'money' (if in Gender III: 'stone'). Malay loanwords: *jarum* 'needle', *kunci* 'key', *sensor* 'chain saw', *bolpen* 'ballpoint pen', *HP* 'mobile phone', *spid* 'motorboat', *cas* 'power cord'.
  - Exceptions, in Gender III: *nggawil-yahun* 'motorcycle', *lampu* 'lamp' (<Malay).

5.2.2.3 Semantic fields divided between Genders III & IV

Two large semantic fields are split between the two inanimate genders: body parts (ca. 70% in Gender III, and 30% in Gender IV) and flora (60% Gender III, 40% Gender IV). Samples are given in Tables 5.1 and 5.2. The proportion of nouns in each gender mirrors fairly well the overall distribution of inanimate nouns in the language (approx. 70%–30% Genders III–IV). Synchronically there is no discernible semantic basis explaining why certain body parts or plants belong to one gender and not the other.

I have shown elsewhere (Olsson 2019b: 205–207) that the stem-final vowels /a/ and /i/ are over-represented in words of Gender III and IV respectively, a phonological skewing that arose through the same umlaut process that gave rise to overt gender in some nouns (§3.2.1). That the vowels show traces of this historical process can be shown with stastical measures, but it is not valid as a synchronic assignment principle. For example, most nouns in Gender IV do not have /i/ as their stem-final vowel, and many nouns with stem-final /i/ belong to Gender III.

Tab. 5.1: Gender assignment of some body parts

			Gender III			
ab	'armpit'	hin	'shin'	pangga	'buttocks'
anggip-bal	'nostril'	isalet	'little finger'	pe	'intestines'
atak	'groin'	isas	'footprint'	pela	'vagina'
babake	'mouth'	kabel	'fat'	pip	'cheek'
bayalim	'body odour'	kadakda	'Adam's apple'	sangga	'hand, arm'
bekay	'heart'	kaka	'afterbirth'	sews	'back'
bub	'breast; milk'	kambet	'ear'	tagu	'leg, foot'
bud	'ear lobe'	lul	'fur'	tah	'wing'
dakum	'navel'	manggat	'tooth'	tepod	'turtle's tail'
dam	'collar bone'	mbaku	'nape of neck'	tepod	'heel'
ete	'chin'	mom	'snot'	ugu	'skin'
yandam	'stomach'	muk	'elbow'	un	'white hair'
yas	'beard'	muy	'meat'	unum	'tongue'
yohwed	'hip'	na	'faeces'	upen	'fin'
yomu	'brains'	nay	'front of neck'	wabuy	'marrow'
gomna	'fang of pig'	ombo	'scrotum'	wahani	'body'
gon	'tail bone'	pa	'head'	wap	'thigh'
hayaw	'bone'	palapal	'temple'	utup	'lips'
			Gender IV			
bi	'rectum'	kindiput	'eyebrows'	sagit	'pig's mane'
bop	'bird's chest'	ko	'womb'	sakih	'wallaby's leg'
yambul	'upper part of arm'	mayos	'swim bladder'	saning	'ankle joint'
galgala	'shoulder'	mig	'knee'	suh	'vulva'
halahil	'lungs'	ndas	'nose bone'	talagi	'tendon'
ibayak	'kidneys'	nggil	'fin (of shark)'	talup	'cassowary claw'
itil	'nail/claw'	on	'liver'	tatih	'hair'
kalambit	'tendon'	put	'feather'	tiwna	'gums'
kasil	'breast bone'	sagasig	'Achille's tendon'	uhik	'penis'

5.2.3 Referential gender

As mentioned in §5.2.1.1 I treat nouns such as *yunayon* 'infant' (which can trigger Gender I or Gender II agreement depending on whether the referent is male or female) as exhibiting 'referential gender' (Dahl 2000). It is mostly nouns that denote humans (e.g. kinship terms, see §5.2.1.1) that lack inherent gender, but also a small number of inanimate nouns. So far the following have been recorded:

– *oyak* 'pillow, headrest'. Any suitable item can be used as a headrest for a nap. The word *oyak* triggers III agreement if one uses, say, some rolled up clothes (*wanugu*, III) and Gender IV if a coconut leaf stalk (*bing*, IV) is used.
– *agey* 'bait' is Gender II if a worm (*alo*, II) is used, Gender III if the bait is a piece of meat (*muy*, III).

Tab. 5.2: Gender assignment of some common plants

	Gender III		
ake	'gambier (Uncaria gambir)'	napet	'banana'
bagaw	'ginger'	od	'sugar cane'
balok	'yam sp.'	onggat	'coconut'
bus	'eucalyptus'	sawalu	'casuarina sp.'
da	'sago'	sote	'palm sp.'
yalah	'mangrove (Rhizophora sp.)'	suba	'bamboo'
gal	'Nauclea orientalis'	ukap	'k.o. galangal'
gelud	'Excoecaria agallocha'	umasa	'kunai grass (Imperata cylindrica)'
ihw	'lemongrass'	wakati	'Hibiscus tiliaceus'
kan	'tree sp.'	wati	'kava (Piper methysticum)'
kanis	'betel palm (Areca catechu)'	wiwi	'mango sp.'
kin-de	'chilli pepper'	yaluwa	'Barringtonia asiatica'
	Gender IV		
badi	'tree sp. (Banksia sp.?)'	ngganggin	'croton sp.'
elel	'floating fern sp.'	nggatnggat	'fern sp.'
yabo-kambet	'croton sp.'	ndik-isas	'croton sp.'
kambali	'seaweed sp.'	nggeh	'palm sp.'
kasuk	'Planchonia papuana'	pak	'cordyline (?)'
kem	'taro (Colocasia esculenta)'	pale-yowi	'garlic'
kiwin	'tree sp. (Melaleuca sp.?)'	payum	'candlenut tree (Aleurites sp.)'
kondo-nini	'croton sp.'	salingga	'tree sp. (Pandanus sp.)'
lug	'Terminalia catappa'	song	'thin bamboo sp.'
mamat	'water lily sp.'	tup	'rattan'
nggalnggamil	'creeper sp.'	wimap	'coconut with sweet husk'

- *nen* 'shoot for planting; animal for raising' is Gender III if it refers to e.g. a cutting from a kava plant (*wati*, III), and Gender IV if a taro corm (*kem*, IV) is being planted. The word *nen* is also used for e.g. pups and piglets, especially when given as gifts for someone to raise, and it then triggers Gender II agreement (animals are always Gender II).

5.2.3.1 Overt gender

The reader is referred to §3.2.1 for a list of nouns exhibiting overt gender marking — such as *anem* 'man' (I), *anum* 'woman' (II), *anim* 'people' (I/II.pl) etc. — along with some discussion of e.g. their lexemic status. If these nouns are considered to be forms of general lexemes such as *anVm* 'person', then they should also be considered a subset of the nouns exhibiting referential gender.

For example, the stem *namakVd* exhibits overt gender marking and could perhaps be glossed 'non-human entity'. The Gender II form *namakud* means 'animal' (plural *namakid* 'animals'), while the Gender III *namakad* and Gender IV *namakid* both mean 'thing' and are used for unspecified items corresponding to each gender. Thus, I have heard *namakad* used as a euphemism for *pela* 'vagina' (III) and *namakid* as a euphemism for *uhik* 'penis' (IV). The latter uses are clearly instances of referential gender; it is more unclear whether *namakud* 'animal' is a part of the same pattern or should be considered a separate lexeme.

5.2.3.2 Inherited gender

A handful of nouns receive their gender specification through a subtype of referential gender, which I call inherited gender (following Evans 1994). The clearest cases are the nouns *igih* 'name', *abab* 'reflection, shadow' and *nanVh* 'face' (Gender II *nanuh*, all other genders *nanih*). These nouns 'inherit' the gender value of the referent to which they are attached, so *igih* 'name' triggers Gender I agreement if it refers to the name of a man (*igih epe* 'that [male] name'), Gender II agreement if it refers to the name of a woman or a named animal (*igih upe* 'that [female/animal] name'), and so on. The following commonly heard questions show gender agreement reflected on the interrogative pronoun:

(133) a. igih   ta   ka-ha-b-ø-   Ø?
         name what:I   PRS.NTRL-ROG-ACT-3SG.A-   be.NPST
         'What's his name?'

    b. igih   tu   ka-ha-b-ø-   Ø?
         name what:II   PRS.NTRL-ROG-ACT-3SG.A-   be.NPST
         'What's her/its name?'

According to the speakers I consulted, the agreement on the interrogative pronoun is also observed when the name of an inanimate entity is asked for, so *ta* 'what:III' should be used to ask about any item that one knows/assumes to be in Gender III, and *ti* 'what:IV' for a Gender IV item. I do not have any spontaneous data bearing on this issue, but it seems unlikely that this (prescriptive) rule is followed with any strictness, since the gender of unfamiliar items is generally hard to predict.

Corbett (2006: 48), discussing data from the Australian language Nungali, suggests that pairs of nouns with inherited gender might be treated as derivationally related instead of obeying special assignment principles. If this was done for the Coastal Marind nouns we would end up with lexemes such as *nanuh* (II) 'face of woman or animal' and *igih* (III) 'name of entity belonging to Gender III'. These glosses are oddly specific in their reference to the distinctions of the gender system, so I believe that it is better to retain the gender inheritance analysis and describe a lexeme such as *nanVh* as having the more general meaning 'face', and so on.

5.2.4 Gender doublets

There are several instances of nouns with identical phonological shape belonging to different genders and having different meanings. Some of these are just accidental homonyms, e.g. *wah* 'his/her mother' (Gender II) and *wah* 'steam, vapor' (Gender III). For others there seems to be a semantic connection, suggesting that the meaning of one noun is a (metaphorical) extension of the other noun, and that the shift in meaning is accompanied by assignment to a different gender.

Consider the following two pairs: the Gender II noun *ambay* 'leech' corresponds to the homonymous Gender IV noun *ambay* 'uvula', and alongside the Gender II noun *saley* 'shrimp' there is the Gender IV homonym *saley* 'coconut inflorescence'. It seems likely that the animal terms (in Gender II) are primary in this case, and that they have been the sources of metaphorical extensions based on shape: the uvula is somewhat similar to a leech attaching to the palate, and the coconut flower is shaped approximately like a shrimp, with the bent spathe resembling the shell, and the spikelets sticking out of the spathe corresponding to the shrimp's legs. Some more doublets are listed in Figure 5.2.

alalin	II	'tapeworm'	manggon	III	'coconut shell'	
	IV	'noodles'		IV	'knee cap'	
saley	II	'shrimp'	ndakindaki	II	'firefly'	
	IV	'coconut inflorescence'		IV	'bioluminescence'	
kayahwek	II	'fish sp. (sawfish)'	ambay	II	'leech'	
	III	'sago beating stick'		IV	'uvula'	
kaniskanis	II	'beetle sp.'	tup	III	'bow string'	
	III	'plant sp.'		IV	'rattan'	
katal	III	'stone'	yahun	III	'canoe'	
	IV	(i) 'stone used in leaf oven'		IV	'ship'	
		(ii) 'money'				
koy	II	'crustacean sp.'				
	III	'lime (calcium oxide)'				

Fig. 5.2: Some gender doublets

It is interesting to note that for many of the doublets that I have found in which the innovative member denotes an inanimate, this member is assigned to Gender IV, like in the case of 'uvula' and 'coconut inflorescence'. Other examples for which I judge the IV noun to be innovated are e.g.: 'tapeworm' (II) > 'noodles' (IV), 'stone' (III) > 'money' (IV), 'coconut shell' (III) > 'knee cap' (IV). This is suggestive of some metaphorical principle that adds new members to Gender IV, although there are not enough examples to elucidate the details behind this principle. There are also exceptions, for 'bow string'

(III) is most likely an extension of the word 'rattan' (IV), since rattan often serves as the material for making bow strings.

5.3 More on agreement

5.3.1 Agreeing targets

The set of ageement targets is rather diverse, and includes e.g. demonstratives, some pronouns, a subset of adjectives, some postpositions, and four of the inflectional verb prefixes that occur in the prefixal complex. Table 5.3 provides a list of the targets, with cross-references to sections providing more information. (The table excludes the over-differentiating adjective 'small', see §3.3.1 for discussion.)

Table 5.3 also charts the vowels that realise agreement on the various targets. The main observations to be drawn are that the most consistent exponence is found with Gender II (realised by *u*) and Gender IV (realised by *i*; the Gender IV forms are always identical to the plural of Genders I and II). Genders I and III exhibit more inconsistency in the choice of vowels: Gender I alternates between *e*, *a* and *i*, and Gender III between *e*, *o*, *a*, *i*. Since the exponent vowels for Gender I and III often merge (as in the demonstratives) it is necessary to take e.g. standard adjectives, which distinguish the two genders, into consideration to prove that the two genders are indeed distinct.

5.3.1.1 Gender and participant indexing

The aspects of gender agreement discussed so far in this chapter make up a relatively straightforward part of Coastal Marind grammar. The same can unfortunately not be said about the interaction between gender and participant indexing in the verb. Participant indexing refers to the marking of person/number of arguments through four categories realised in various locations of the verb complex: (i) the Actor prefix series (§9.2), (ii) the Dative prefix series (§9.3), (iii) the Genitive prefix series (§9.4) (all in the prefixal complex), and (iv) alternations in the verb stem marking the Undergoer (Chapter 10).

The indexing of animate arguments offers no surprises, with three persons and two number (sg/pl) distinguished throughout the indexing system. Gender of animates (i.e. Genders I and II) is not reflected in participant indexing, so there is for example only one 3sg Actor prefix *a-*, used regardless of whether the indexed participant is male (Gender I) or female/animal (Gender II).

The behaviour of inanimates (i.e. nouns in Genders III and IV) is much more complicated and poses some problems in terms of synchronic description (e.g. morphemic glossing) as well as diachronic origins. The main facts can be summarised as in the following three points:

Tab. 5.3: Overview of agreement targets and their exponents

Category	Item	I	II	III	IV, I/II.pl
Demonstratives (§4.2.1)	Vpe, Vhe, Vhan	e	u	e	i
Emphatic demonstr. (§4.2.2)	anVp	e	u	e	i
Proword (§4.4)	agV	e	u	o	i
Interrogative pronouns (§4.3)	tV 'what'	a	u	a	i
	Vn 'where, which'	e	u	e	i
	VntagV(l)	e...e	u...u	e...o	i...i
Agreeing adjectives (§3.3)	wagVtVk 'long'	a...o	a...o	a...o	i...u
	VhV 'ripe'	–	–	e...o	i...u
	Colour adjectives	i	u	i	i
	Other adjectives	e	u	a	i
Agreeing postpositions (§6.1)	tV 'with', hV 'like'	i	u	i	i
	nV 'without'	e	u	i	i
	lVk 'from'	e	u	e	i
Participial suffix (§3.7.3)	-la/-lV(k)	-la	-lu(k)	-la	-li(k)
Verb prefixes (§8)	anVpand- (CONT)	e	u	e	i
	Vp-, Vh- (DIST, PROX)	e	u	e	i
	Vk- (PRS.Q)	e	u	e	i
	tV- (GIV)	e	u	e	i
Verb stem (§10.4)	U. alternations				
Indexing prefixes (§9.2.2.4)	A. prefixes etc.				

1. The distinction between Genders III and IV is not reflected in Dative and Genitive indexing. It can be probably be argued that indexing with this series is restricted to animate participants, although more research on this issue is required (see §9.2.2.4).
2. Actor indexing is generally insensitive to the distinction between Genders III and IV, with the exception of some intransitive verbs, with which a Gender III subject triggers 3sg Actor prefix (a-), and a Gender IV subject triggers the 3pl Actor prefix (n-) (see §9.2.2.4).
3. In Undergoer indexing, the form of the verb stem used with inanimate participants depends on whether the verb is morphologically invariant or alternating (§10.2.1). An invariant verb uses the same stem regardless of gender membership. With an alternating verb the usage is as follows. A Gender III participant triggers either (a) the same stem as used with an animate 3sg participant, or (b) a distinct, derivationally related stem used specifically for inanimates of Gender III. This choice is lexical and must be memorised for every alternating verb. A Gender IV participant always triggers the same stem as non-1st person plural animates, i.e. the stem glossed '2|3pl'.

The fact that inanimates in Gender III are indexed by means of the same forms as 3sg animates, and, in particular, the fact that the plural of animates is indexed by the same forms as inanimates in Gender IV create difficulties for glossing: how should a verb stem such as *hyadih* — the form of the verb 'see' which is used when the Undergoer is either (a) a 2nd or 3rd person plural animate, or (b) one or more items in Gender IV — be glossed? As discussed in §10.2.2 I favour readability over faithfulness to the logic of the Coastal Marind system and choose to gloss such stems '2|3PL.U' when they index a plural animate, and 'IV.U' when the participant is an inanimate of Gender IV. Forcing two different glosses on forms that are systematically identical fails to capture the important affinity between Gender IV and animate plurals, but it makes the content of example sentences easier to parse for the reader. I provide some remarks on this gender/number conundrum below (§5.3.2).

Since the details of Gender III and IV encroaching on person/number indexing require a basic understanding of the indexing system, I will postpone discussion of the formal correlates until Chapters 9 and 10. The most complicated issue — indexing of inanimate Undergoers by means of stem alternations — is discussed at length in §10.4. Indexing of inanimate arguments by the prefixes in the prefixal complex (i.e. Actor, Dative and Genitive indexing) is limited and usually defaults to 3sg marking, as described in §9.2.2.4.

5.3.2 Further remarks on the plural–Gender IV affinity

In this section I show that the distinction between Genders III and IV is reflected in two contexts that hardly can be described as agreement targets for gender: number suppletion of verb stems (§5.3.2.1) and the choice of comitative strategies (§5.3.2.2). I draw some preliminary conclusions in §5.3.2.3.

5.3.2.1 Gender and suppletive verb stems

The formal identity of forms indexing animate plurals and Gender IV even extends to verbs that are entirely suppletive (§10.5.1). Consider the following facts. The verb 'come' is suppletive according to number, and uses the stem *man* 'one to come' with a singular animate subject, but the unrelated stem *nayam* 'many to come' with a plural animate subject (these stems make no further person distinctions). But if the subject is inanimate, the singular stem *man* is used if it belongs to Gender III, whereas the plural stem *nayam* is triggered if the subject belongs to Gender IV.

(134) lahwalah-yahun ipe   ti-ka-hat-ø-   nayam
aeroplane(IV)   DIST:IV GIV:IV-PRS.NTRL-PRSTV-3SG.A- come.PL

'An aeroplane is coming there.'
'Aeroplanes are coming there.'

Any attempt to describe the identical forms triggered by animate plurals and inanimates in Gender IV as being a pattern of accidental homophony collapses when confronted with such data (a similar case is the suppletive adjective 'small', §3.3.1). It is perfectly likely that the shared exponent *i* (in e.g. demonstratives and adjectives) is a case of accidental homophony between animate plurals and Gender IV, since the language has only five vowels to choose from, to be divided across four genders. But the use of the plural stem *nayam* (as opposed to singular *man*) is impossible to treat as a case of chance similarity.

5.3.2.2 Gender and comitatives

Marind has two morphological techniques that allow the verb to add a comitative participant as an argument: the Comitative *k-* (prefixed to the verb stem; §13.1.5) and the Accompaniment *e-* (prefixed within the prefixal complex; §13.1.6). Both of these are applicative prefixes, since they add an object-like argument to the verb. The main difference between the two is that the Comitative *k-* is used when the comitative argument is an inanimate item, whereas the Accompaniment *e-* is used when it is an animate. This means that the role of the comitative participant in the event is usually quite different depending on its animacy. A verb prefixed by means of the Comitative *k-* is typically used about an inanimate item being brought somewhere, e.g. 'go with NP, bring NP', or held while the agent assumes a position, e.g. 'sit down holding NP'. The Accompaniment *e-*, on the other hand, is usually used about chasing an animal (literally 'run with NP'), or assuming a position in somebody's company ('sit down together with NP'). The different uses of the two prefixes — which at first sight seem to involve animacy and not gender — are illustrated in the following examples:

(135)   *tamuy   mano-   k-ambid*
        food(III)   FUT:1.A-   WITH-sit
        'I am going to sit down and eat.' (lit. 'sit down with food')

(136)   About two adult ducks and their ducklings.
        ipe   wanangga   ma-n-e-   hamat-a
        DIST:I/II.PL   children(I/II.PL)   OBJ-3PL.A-ACPN-   sit.PL-EXT
        'They are sitting with their children.'   [W11:1027]

Looking at more data, this picture turns out to be incomplete. When the comitative argument is a noun belonging to Gender IV, it must co-occur with the Accompaniment *e-*, despite being inanimate. Verbs in this context do not mean 'chase', 'sit down together with' etc., but have exactly the same meaning as verbs prefixed with Comitative *k-*. Example (137) illustrates this, again with the verb *ambid* 'sit down'.

(137) manday   e=   k-ø-i-e-   ambid ebta
      brother.in.law PROX= DIR-3SG.A-RE-ACPN- sit   sago.thatch(IV)

'Brother-in-law sat down here [and plaited] sago thatch again.'
(lit. 'sat down with sago thatch') [W20:0292]

The fact that the Accompaniment *e-* treats Gender IV nouns as if they were animate is surprising since neither of the two applicative prefixes interact with gender in any other way. Unlike true agreement targets they make no distinction between e.g. Genders I and II — the only interaction with gender is that the Accompaniment prefix lumps Gender IV nouns together with humans and animals. This provides further evidence that the identical agreement exponents for (plural) animates and Gender IV nouns is not accidental, because these two categories are grouped together even in constructions that are completely unrelated to the gender-indicating vowel changes seen in typical agreement targets.

5.3.2.3 Gender IV and the four-gender analysis

The way that Gender IV nouns interact with verbs exhibiting number suppletion and with comitative inflection in the verb complex challenges the traditional description of Coastal Marind as having four genders. The four-gender description states that the nouns in Gender III and IV are inanimates, and lack grammatical number. As we have seen, Gender IV nouns are treated as animates, and trigger plural agreement, which is difficult to reconcile with the tenets of the four-gender description.

As I pointed out in Olsson (2019b) one solution is to abandon Gender IV as a gender of its own, and instead describe the former Gender IV nouns as members of Gender I/II that are lexically specified as plural-only. This parallels the treatment traditionally given to so called pluralia tantum in European languages: nouns such as Italian *forbici* 'scissors' or Russian *sani* 'sledge' invariably trigger plural agreement, but are described as having a fixed number value, not as belonging to a separate gender. Although the morphological facts make the pluralia tantum analysis seem adequate for Coastal Marind, there are good arguments against it: (i) it is counter-intuitive since ca. 30% of inanimates would be reclassified as pluralia tantum, as opposed to between handful and a few dozen pluralia tantum in European languages; (ii) the robust generalisation that inanimates in Coastal Marind lack number makes it strange to claim that a large part of the inanimates nevertheless are lexically specified for plurality; (iii) it would wreak havoc to the semantic basis for gender assignment (animates in Gender I & II, inanimates in Genders III & IV) since 30% of the inanimates would be assigned to Genders I/II (and, incidentally, lexically specified as plural).

A more radical solution would be to dispense with the (eurocentric?) notion of gender for the description of Coastal Marind, and instead base the description of agreement and indexing patterns on the features of animacy and/or sex, combined with a partly lexically fixed plural feature. In such a system one might define former Gender

III nouns as being [+inanimate, –plural], and former Gender IV nouns as [–inanimate, +plural], which would capture their similarity with the [–inanimate, ±plural] nouns denoting animates. This description undoubtedly captures the logic of the Coastal Marind system better than a traditional four-gender analysis, but adopting it would result in a much less user-friendly grammar, as well as making cross-linguistic comparison involving Coastal Marind more difficult. For this reason I will not pursue the issue here. I retain the four-gender analysis presented in Drabbe (1955) while noting that its treatment of the relationship betwen Gender IV and inanimate plurals is unsatisfactory.

5.3.3 Agreement controllers

Coastal Marind has a large array of possible controllers (i.e. NPs that trigger agreement in agreeing targets), some of which are of typological interest.

Agreement in the nominal domain offers few surprises: demonstrative determiners (§4.2) agree with the head noun, as do the subclass of agreeing adjectives (§3.3).

The agreement on agreeing postpositions (§6.1) is more spectacular. Adpositions agreeing in gender have been documented for various languages (cf. Corbett 2006: 46, Brown and Chumakina 2014), but it appears to be rare for adposition agreement to be triggered not by the governed noun (i.e. the complement of the adposition) but by the head noun that the adpositional phrase modifies (in an attributive use) or by an argument of the higher clause (if the phrase is used as an adjunct). It is shown in §6.1 that this is precisely the situation in Coastal Marind: see for example (150) on p. 126 for the adjunct use, and (151) for the attributive use. It appears to be more common that adpositions agree with their complement, so that *from* in *from school* agrees with *school*, but this never occurs in Coastal Marind (see e.g. Evans 2000 for adpositions agreeing with the subject in the Iwaidjan languages spoken in Australia; cf. also Chumakina et al. forthcoming).

The largest diversity in terms of possible controllers is found within the verb complex. Gender agreement is possible in multiple parts of the verb complex, e.g. in prefixes such as the Continuative *anVpand-* or Present polar question *Vk-*, as well as in the verb stem. Unlike some languages, which restrict gender agreement on the verb to controllers filling a specific role (e.g. subject or absolutive), Coastal Marind allows gender agreement to be controlled by any argument of the verb: attested controllers include S-, A- and O-arguments, recipients (indexed by the Dative prefix series) and 'affected possessors' (indexed by the Genitive series). The selection of one argument as the controller (in clauses with more than one argument) seems to be dependent on discourse prominence. For examples, see the sections on the the Given prefix *tV-* (§11.4), the Continuative *anVpand-* (§14.2.4), the Deictic *Vp-*/*Vh-* (§15.4), and the Present polar question *Vk-* (§19.2.1).

5.3.3.1 Gender resolution

Resolution rules state the agreement value taken by a target when the controllers are conjoined NPs (Corbett 1991: 264). The only available data on resolution rules concern indexing on verbs when the controller is a mix of inanimates from Genders III and IV. All speakers that I asked agreed that the verb stem corresponding to Gender III is the only option in such contexts. Example (138) illustrates a combination of Gender III and Gender IV patient-like participants. The use of Gender III Undergoer indexing is not surprising since Gender III has other features suggesting a default status (mainly, being the form used in non-agreeing contexts).

(138) *paya,   ayiy,   wad   ka-no-d-   bak⟨e⟩h*
      coconut.fibre(III) pinches(IV) basket DIR-1.A-DUR- put⟨III.U⟩
      'The coconut fibres and the pinches, I put them in the basket.' [W20:0026]

6 Adpositions and particles

This chapter describes postpositions (§6.1), two preposition-like markers (§6.2), an assortment of particle-like items (§6.3) and some common interjections and exclamations (§6.4).

6.1 Postpositions

The class of postpositions can be defined extensionally as the 13 items listed in Table 6.1. Grouping these together as one category is convenient since all of them serve to express relational notions (e.g. 'in the house') and/or oblique participant roles ('with a stick'), i.e. functions that are commonly expressed by adpositions and cases cross-linguistically. I prefer the label 'postpositions' rather than 'cases' since none of these items trigger any segmental changes in the preceding material, and since they combine with the preceding material on the phrase-level rather than on the word-level:

(139) a. nok en aha kumay   b. uhe   an   ti
         [1 POSS house]_NP inside   [PROX:II mother(II)]_NP with
         'in my house'   'with this lady'

As suggested by the information in the table, the postposition class is internally quite heterogeneous, and its members appear to form a category squish which would allow for further subdivisions depending on what criteria one considers to be diagnostic. In the table, the four items at the top could perhaps be described as derivational markers deriving property expressions, whereas the four items at the bottom could be described as regular nouns that speakers sometimes employ to describe locational relationships; the ones in the middle would fall somewhere between these two extremes.

I see no point in getting embroiled in category-splitting discussions here, but I believe that it is useful to spell out the parameters that distinguish the postpositions explicitly, so that other linguists who wish to provide alternative classifications have the data to do so. After the discussion of these features, individual subsections provide miniature sketches of the meaning and use of the various postpositions.

ALWAYS POSTPOSITION. Most members of the postposition class are easily identified as postpositions in all their uses. Five of the postpositions are heterosemous and are also used independently as regular nouns (Table 6.2). The nominal use is likely the diachronically earlier use, so a noun that originally meant 'base of tree' later ac-

Tab. 6.1: Postpositions

		Always post-position	Attributive use	Heads referential phrase	Gender agreement
lek	'from'	yes	yes	yes	yes
ti	'with'	yes	yes	yes	yes
hi	'like'	yes	yes	yes	yes
ni	'without'	yes	yes	yes	yes
nanggo(l)	'for, towards'	yes	yes	yes	no
en	Possessive	yes	yes	yes	no
en	Instrumental	yes	yes?	no	no
se	'only'	yes	no	no	no
nde	'at'	yes	no	no	no
awe	'(search) for'	no	no	no	no
mit	'near'	no	no	no	no
lahwalah	'above, on top'	no	no	no	no
kumay	'inside'	no	no	no	no
kala	'below, under'	no	no	no	no

Tab. 6.2: Denominal postpositions

	As postposition	As noun
awe	'(search) for'	'fish; game'
mit	'near'	'base (of tree or body part)'
lahwalah	'above, on top'	'top, upper side'
kumay	'inside'	'inside'
kala	'below, under'	'depression in ground'

quired a more general relational use as a postposition.[1] The purposive postposition *awe* '(search) for' appears to be (diachronically) related to the noun *awe* 'fish; game', as explained in §6.1.9.

The only morphosyntactic criteria that distinguish nouns used as postpositions (e.g. *kumay* in *aha kumay* 'in the house') from nouns used as the head of compounds (*hayaw* 'bone' in *awe-hayaw* 'fish bone') are: (i) postpositions take NPs as their complements, possibly containing NP-internal modifiers preposed to the head noun, whereas the heads of compounds only accept other words or other compounds as the first member of the compound; and, (ii) a postposition heading a postpositional phrase may not occur independently (without its complement) whereas the head of a compound also is a free lexeme that can appear on its own. (Of course, this criterion presupposes that

---

[1] The relational use of nouns is restricted to these words, and other nouns that one could imagine being used to indicate spatial relations (e.g. *nggol* 'top of tree', *elet* 'far end of something', *sews* 'back of human/animal', etc.) have no corresponding postpositional use.

the postpositional use of heterosemous items like *mit* 'near' can be distinguished from the corresponding noun.)

ATTRIBUTIVE USE. About half of the postpositions may be used attributively, heading a phrase that modifies a noun. This was already seen in e.g. (139a) above, where the possessive postposition *en* heads the phrase *nok en* 'of me', which in turn modifies the noun *aha* 'house', giving *nok en aha* 'house of me/my house'. Other examples of attributively used postpositions:

(140) a. *wambad nanggo yanid*
make.plantbed for day
'a day for making plantbeds'

b. *teb ti katal*
hole with:IV money(IV)
'holed money' (Papua New Guinea 1-kina coins)

The other postpositions do not allow this use, so one cannot say e.g. *aha kumay katal to mean 'the money inside the house'. This would require a relative clause to be literally translated from English.

The instrumental use of the postposition *en* is indicated as 'yes' plus a question mark in Table 6.1, since it cannot be used attributively with nouns, but is commonly used to modify nominally used verb stems, e.g.:

(141) Observed; I was trying to light a cigarette.
korek en o-tad mayay k-o- Ø oy?
lighter(m) with PLA-burn knowing PRS.NTRL-2SG.A- be.NPST 2SG
'Do you know how to light using a lighter?'

The unit *korek en otad* forms an NP and could be given the literal translation 'lighting with a lighter'.

HEADS REFERENTIAL PHRASE. With the exception of instrumental *en*, all postpositions that can be used attributively may also be used without a modified noun to head a referential phrase. The resulting structures could also be described as having an ellipsed head noun. For example, instead of referring to a coin as in (140b), one can say *teb ti* 'the one with a hole'.[2]

A corpus example of a referentially used postpositional phrase is in (142), in which *wis lek* '(lit.) from yesterday' is used to refer to a man who had been encountered the previous day. (Gender I agreement on *lek* and demonstrative *epe* identifies the referent as male).

---

[2] This expression is also used by Marind speakers as a rather vulgar insult.

(142) wis   lek   epe, epe   te-ø-ø-i-   man-em
      yesterday from:I DIST:I DIST:I GIV:I-NTRL-3SG.A-RE- come-VEN
      'The man from the day before, it was he who came again.'   [W19:0282]

GENDER AGREEMENT. This was already seen on the postpositions *ti* 'with' in (140b) and *lek* 'from' in (142) above. In addition, the postpositions *ni* 'without' and *hi* 'like' are agreement targets, while the remaining postpositions are invariant. However, *ti*, and *hi* only differentiate Gender II from the other gender/number values:

I.sg	II.sg	III	IV, I/II.PL	
ti	tu	ti	ti	'with'
hi	hu	hi	hi	'like'

ni 'without' adds one distinction and has two separate forms for Genders I and II singulars respectively, while conflating the other values:

I.sg	II.sg	III	IV, I/II.PL	
ne	nu	ni	ni	'without'

The forms of *lek* 'from' make the same number of distinctions as *ni* 'without', but conflate Gender III with Gender I:

I.sg	II.sg	III	IV, I/II.PL	
lek	luk	lek	lik	'from'

These four postpositions show agreement when they head a postpositional phrase used in one of the following contexts: (i) as an attributive modifier to a noun, as in (140b) above (agreement is with the modified noun); (ii) as a referential phrase, as in (142) above (agreement is according to the gender of the referent); (iii) as an adjunct, like the phrase *nu lik* 'from sleep' in (143) below. For adjunct targets the agreement trigger is usually the S/A-argument of the clause ('we', which triggers the Gender I/II plural form *lik*), but agreement can be with other arguments if the adjunct is a participant-oriented secondary predicate (see §18.5).

(143) namaya kwemek nd-ak-e-   u-timin   nu   lik
      now   morning LOC-1.A-1PL-   PLA-wake.up   sleep from:I/II.PL
      'Then in the morning we woke up from sleep.'   [W20:0114]

The following conclusions can be drawn from the above discussion of the features distinguishing the postpositions from each other. Postpositions such as *mit* 'at, by, near' or *kumay* 'inside', which lack all of the four features (cf. the summary in Table

6.1), are morphosyntactically close to nouns, and indeed also have uses as standard nouns (e.g. *mit* 'base of tree').

On the opposite side of the spectrum, postpositions such as *lek* 'from' and *ti* 'with' are very unlike nouns, and the expressions they form are more akin to adjectives: for example, *katal ti* 'with money' is the standard way to express 'rich' in Coastal Marind, and several common adjectives turn out to be lexicalisations of phrases with *hi* 'like' (e.g. *dohi* 'red' < *do* 'blood' + 'like', *dehi* 'hard' < *de* 'wood' + 'like'). Looking further afield, it is clear that the Participial suffix *-la* (§3.7.3) is grammaticalised from the postposition *lek*, and thus represents the next step on the path from independent to bound markers. From this discussion it should be clear that the class of postpositions as defined here easily could be fit into other classification schemes.

The following subsections provide information on the meaning of the different postpositions.

6.1.1 *lek* 'from'

This common postposition primarily marks various kinds of sources, as in (142) and (143) above. Two more examples are given below, with the postpositional phrases functioning as attributive modifiers:

(144)   a.   *wis   lek   mayan*
              yesterday(III) from:III speech(III)
              'yesterday's issue/problem'

   b.   *lay   lik   yambul*
         side(III)   from:IV   front.leg(IV)
         'the front leg on one side, one of the front legs'

It is also extended to mark reason/cause, as in (145), and, with nominals with action-like semantics such as *walak* 'running', simultaneous action (146).

(145)   About a woman who got startled by a noise and crashed into a mosquito net.
   ukna   luk   m-a-p-   ikyalun?
   fear   from:II   OBJ-3SG.A-CT-   jump
   'She jumped out of fear?'   [W11:0254]

(146)   *walak   lek   kam   k-a-   kw-ehw⟨e⟩b*
           running   from:I   pole   DIR-3SG.A-   INESS-intercept⟨3SG.U⟩
           'While running, he got stuck by a pole.'

Note that both of these adjuncts exhibit gender agreement with the S/A-arguments of their clauses. It seems that *lek*-phrases describing reasons, as in (145), are optional targets of agreement, as I have recorded several instances of *lek* appearing in its default Gender III form (failing to agree with any argument of the clause) in this context.

A participant-oriented adjunct such as *walak lek* in (146) agrees with the participant whose action it describes (and not necessarily the S/A-argument), as discussed further in §18.5.

6.1.2 *ti* 'with'

Four main uses of *ti* can be distinguished: (i) the comitative use ('come with, bring'); (ii) the adnominal proprietive use ('having X'); (iii) in inclusory constructions ('A including X'); and (iv) distributive ('one-by-one, one each').

The comitative use of *ti* is mostly found with motion verbs (147) and positional verbs (148).

(147) inah   yahun   ø-ø-um-   bamet-a-m   tamuy ti
      two   canoe(III) NTRL-3SG.A-FRUS-   run.PLA-EXT-VEN   food   with:III
      'Two trucks were going to come with food (but didn't).'   [W18:0191]

(148) Hunters shot repeatedly at a pig, but it didn't die.
      tangge   tu   ø-d-a-   itala
      arrow(III)   with:II   NTRL-DUR-3SG.A-   be.standing
      'It was standing with arrows.' (i.e. sticking out of its body)   [W11:0599]

The postpositional mode of expression exists in competition with the comitative use of the derivational WITH-prefix *k-* (§13.1.5), which licenses a bare NP expressing the theme argument. The corpus data suggest that speakers overwhelmingly opt for *k*-marked verbs to express comitatives. It seems that comitatives with *ti* are used when the presence of the theme (i.e. the brought item) is not dependent on the volition or control of the agent, as in (147) and (148) where the trucks and the pig, respectively, do not control the location of the theme arguments. The volitionality or control criterion is especially clear with non-agentive verbs such as 'fall', with which the postposition *ti* is the only option (such verbs do not allow *k*-prefixation). An example of this is in (149).

(149) The speaker and another lady were sitting on a platform when it suddenly broke.
      isala   ti   ø-ø-e-   hihi-n
      platform(III)   with:I/II.PL   NTRL-3SG.A-1PL-   fall.PLA-1.U
      'We fell with the sitting platform.'   [W19:0058]

Gender agreement on *ti* is with the participant that brings along the comitative theme. Compare the preceding examples with the form *ti* with e.g. (148) above, where agreement is with the pig (Gender II), or (150) below, with a female subject triggering the Gender II form *tu*.

(150) lahwalah-yahun tu ø-a- man-em
on.top-canoe(IV) with:II NTRL-3SG.A- come-VEN
'She came by aeroplane.'

The proprietive use of *ti* is clearest when it forms adnominal phrases, specifying something that the head noun owns, is adorned with, contains, and so on. As shown by the examples in (151) the postposition agrees in gender with the noun that the phrase modifies (agreement is never with the complement of the postposition).

(151) a. katal ti anem   b. yas tu awe
money(IV) with:I man(I)   beard(III) with:II fish(II)
'moneyed man, rich man'   'fish with beard' (e.g. a catfish)

Some other common expressions are *imu tu awe* (lit. 'fish with smell') 'rotten fish', *ena ti adaka* ('water with heat') 'hot water', *inahinah tagu ti yahun* 'canoe with four feet', i.e. a car.

Like some of the other postpositions, *ti* may head a referring phrase without the presence of a modified head noun. In (152), uttered by someone who was changing clothes, this is exemplified by the phrase *nanamos ti* '[the ones] with dirt', which is understood to refer to the clothes (*wanugu* 'clothes', is a Gender III noun).

(152) ehe nanamos ti ka-p-e-ka- n-a yokun
PROX:III dirt with:III DIR-FUT:1.A-1PL-PRI- 1.U-AUX put.inside.PLA:III.U
'The dirty ones, we'll put them in [the bags].' [W10:0475]

Some nouns are frozen head-less expressions formed with *ti*, e.g. *yasti* 'old man' (< *yas* 'beard' + *ti*), and perhaps *banati* 'echidna' (cf. *ban* 'spike, thorn').

In the inclusory use, a *ti*-marked phrase appears with a verb indexed for a plural argument. The phrase marked with *ti* is understood to be a member of the set corresponding to the plural index on the verb. This is seen in (153), which could be given the literal gloss 'We, including Pau, came.

(153) Pau ti ø-nak-e- nayam
P. with:I/II.PL NTRL-1.A-1PL- come.PL
'Pau and I came.'
'Pau, I, and others came'

Some more discussion of the inclusory construction is in §9.6.

Finally, *ti* is used with numerals to form distributive expressions, as in the following elicited examples. It is not possible to decide whether *ti* agrees with its complement in the distributive use, or defaults to the Gender III form, since the plural form for animates is identical to the Gender III and IV forms (all are *ti*).

(154) a. hyakod ti   ø-d-a-   huhu-h
         one   with NTRL-DUR-3SG.A- emerge.PLA-2|3PL.U

   'They went out one at a time.'

   b. inah ti   m-o-   yuka⟨h⟩in-e
      two   with OBJ-2SG.A- put.inside.PLA⟨2|3PL.U⟩-IPFV

   'You'll put them inside two at a time.' (e.g. fish into a bag)

6.1.3 *ni* Privative 'without'

This is the negative counterpart of *ti* 'with'. I have recorded it in two functions: (i) as a participant-oriented adjunct, especially with motion verbs, as in (155); and (ii) heading an adnominal phrase, as in (156).

(155) tamuy ni   ø-nan-d-e-   aya⟨n⟩it-a
      food   without:I/II.PL   NTRL-1.A-DUR-1PL- run.around⟨1.U⟩-EXT

   'We went without bringing food.'   [W18:0149]

(156) haman ne   meng   m-ak-e-   nayam epe
      sit.PL without:III   walk(III) OBJ-1.A-1PL- come.PL DIST:III

   'We walked without resting.' (lit. 'We walked a sitting-less walk')   [D05:0172]

Note that gender agreement in the latter example shows that *haman ne* 'without sitting' is a modifier of the noun *meng* and not a participant-oriented adjunct (in the latter use, agreement would have been with an argument of the verb, as in the immediately preceding example). The phrase *haman ne* also shows the common use of bare verb stems (i.e. without any of the inflectional material of the prefixal complex present) as the complement of a postposition. The following observed example shows the same adnominal use but with a noun as the complement of *ni*:

(157) I asked a Wambi villager what the people living across the border in Papua New Guinea are like.

   da   ni   anim   k-a-   ø,   nal ka-n-   yahwiy-e
   sago without:I/II.PL people PRS.NTRL-3SG.A- be.NPST yam DIR-3PL.A- eat-IPFV

   'They are sago-less people, they eat yams.'

Some other common expressions with *ni*: *mes ne milah* 'place/village without coconuts', *awe ne tamuy* 'food without fish' (e.g. only sago/rice), *de ne say* 'place without trees'. The last expression is a common way of referring to the beach and the coast in general, and Coastal Marind people often exclaim *de ne say a!* 'Oh, tree-less place!' during trips inland, or arriving back at the village after such a trip, to express their appreciation of the beach.

6.1.4 *hi* Similative 'like'

This postposition is used to form expressions meaning 'like X'. Like the structures discussed above, such phrases are used as a participant-oriented adjuncts, as in (158), or as modifiers of a nominal, as in (159).

(158)   Discussing a villager who is known for his excessive consumption of *wati* (kava).

sawanggi   hi   k-a-   yi-e   wati
evil.spirit(m) like:I PRS.NTRL-3SG.A- drink-IPFV kava

'He drinks kava like an evil spirit.' [W05:0020]

(159)   *basik hi   nanih*
        pig(II) like:I face(I)

'face like a pig'

As mentioned previously, there are some adjectives that clearly are fossilised expressions with *hi*:

dehi	'hard, solid'	< *de* 'wood' + *hi* 'like'
dohi	'red'	< *do* 'blood' + *hi* 'like'
koyhi, kohi	'white'	< *koy* 'slaked lime' + *hi* 'like'
kunayhi	'black'	< *kunay* '?'[3]+ *hi* 'like'

Two more constructions with *hi* deserve mention. First, *hi* is used in stories with deictic time expressions such as *wis* 'yesterday' and *yapap* 'tomorrow' to indicate that the time expression is to be interpreted with reference to narrated time, and not the time of speech. So *wis hi* means 'the previous day' and *yapap hi* means 'the next day'. A corpus example:

---

[3] There is no word *kunay* in contemporary Coastal Marind, and the etymological speculations in Geurtjens' dictionary (Geurtjens 1933: 218, entry: *Koenei*) are as usual of little help. None of the contemporary Coastal Marind words that one might suspect could be used to form a word meaning 'black' are similar to *kunay*, cf. e.g.: *suplakop* 'soot', *gumna* 'ashes'.

(160) 1. ago "mate, yapap mak-i-e- uma⟨n⟩ah"
       QUOT okay tomorrow FUT:1.A-RE-1PL- go⟨1.U⟩

   2. yapap hi tanama k-a- umah
      tomorrow like again DIR-3SG.A- go:2|3PL.U

   1. '[they said:] "Tomorrow we shall leave",
   2. and the next day they left again.' [W21:0220-0221]

Second, *hi* also occurs in a poorly understood use as a marker of similative clauses. Interestingly, *hi* does not attach after the material that it has scope over (the clause, in this case). Instead it is placed after the first element of the clause, as seen in (161), where *hi* appears after *anem* 'man'. The resulting meaning is not 'like a man', but (literally) 'as if a man told him'. (Unlike its English translation, the Coastal Marind clause shows no signs of being subordinate.)

(161) Locating a pig during the hunt.

   epe Vitalis ye m-a- kahek, anem hi ø-ø-o- ayi,
   there V. INGRS OBJ-3SG.A- climb man like:I NTRL-3SG.A-3SG.DAT- say

   kala nanggo u= k-at-ø- ø
   depression towards PROX:II= PRS.NTRL-PRSTV-3SG.A- be.NPST

   'Vitalis climbed, as if somebody told him, "[The pig] is down here".'
                                                                   [W11:0884]

What seems to be the same structure appears in one of the texts in Drabbe's grammar. Here the clause has an optative rather than similative meaning, perhaps contributed by the presence of the Non-Asserted Future, which has some irrealis-like uses (see §14.2.7). The speaker of the Western dialect (i.e. the variety described in this grammar) with whom I discussed this sentence said that the same use is found in the Western dialect as well, although I personally have not observed it. I give the original sentence in (162a), with the corresponding Western version in (162b). As shown in (162c), the gender agreement of *hi* is with the possessor.

(162) a. Eastern dialect: Drabbe 1955, p. 158, 4th line from the end

   waninggap-uzub ha, nok hi mak-ø-namb-i-e-ka-
   good-bird real 1 like:I/II.PL NAFUT-3SG.A-1.GEN-RE-1PL-PRI-

   ø-et!
   be.NPST-IPFV

   'What a beautiful bird! If it could only be ours!'

b. Western dialect; based on (a)

   waninggap-uhyub ya,   nok hi   mak-a-nmb-e-ka-   Ø-et
   good-bird   real 1   like:I/II.PL NAFUT-3SG.A-1.GEN-1PL-PRI- be.NPST-IPFV
   '[same translation as (a)]'

c. As (b), but female speaker:

   nok hu   mak-a-nmba-ka-   Ø-et
   1 like:II NAFUT-3SG.A-1.GEN-PRI-   be.NPST-IPFV
   'If it could only be mine!'

6.1.5 *nanggo(l)* 'for, towards'

The most frequent use of *nanggo* (or *nanggol*, with no discernible meaning difference) is as a general purposive marker, as in (163–164). It is especially common to find a nominally used verb stem as the object/complement of the postposition, as in (164), where the verb stem *lesad* 'draw water' together with its O-argument *adaka* 'water' make up the complement. An example of a *nanggo*-phrase used attributively was given in (140a) above.

(163) From a story, about a small leaf oven.

   inah ahakla   nanggol k-a-   kamem anep
   two wrapped.up.sago   for   DIR-3SG.A- suffice EMPH:III
   'It was sufficient for two packages of wrapped-up sago.'   [W18:0222]

(164) Listing the equipment needed for sago processing.

   bobo,   adaka lesad   nanggo
   coconut.shell   water draw.water for
   'a coconut shell, for drawing water'   [W20:0025]

Compare the use of *nanggo(l)* with that of *awe* 'for', described in §6.1.9.

There is also a spatial use of *nanggo(l)* marking goal of motion. The most frequent strategy for signalling a constituent as a goal is to place this constituent in the syntactic slot immediately preceding the verb, and add the Directional *k-* prefix to the prefixal complex (see §11.1.4.1). In cases where this strategy is unavailable, e.g. when the relevant constituent is placed after the verb, the postposition *nanggo(l)* is useful for flagging the goal role, as in (165).

(165) yahaa   anep   kay   ep-ø-   kagub-a   timan nanggol epe
      until [EMPH:III road(III) DIST:III-3SG.A- break:III.U-EXT   inland towards DIST:III]
      'all the way to where the road bends inland'   [W19:0030]

6.1.6 *en* Possessive-Instrumental

Possession can be marked by placing a postpositional phrase headed by *en* before the possessed noun. This structure is available for the expression of alienable (166a) and inalienable (166b–c) possession, as well as various other non-possessive associations (166d). Kin terms with person prefixes also may enter into this possessive construction, as in (166c). A second means for expressing possession in Coastal Marind, the Genitive prefixes on verbs, is described in §9.4.

(166) a. nok   en   katal
         1   POSS money
         'my money'

   b. anep   en   igih
      EMPH:I POSS name
      'his own name'

   c. ipe   en   iham
      DIST:I/II.PL   POSS 2|3pl:grandparent
      'their grandparent'

   d. manggon   en   li
      coconut.shell POSS ember
      'ember from coconut shells'

The postposition *en* provides one of two means of marking instruments in Coastal Marind (167). The other option is to use the applicative WITH-prefix on the verb stem, as discussed in §13.1.4.

(167) namakad   ye   m-ak-e-   kw-ayob   tenda   en
      thing(III) INGRS OBJ-1.A-1PL- INESS-cover:III.U tarpaulin(m)   INSTR
      'We covered the things with the tarpaulin.'   [W11:0488]

The postposition *en* is optionally used with the expressions *kamak* 'fast' and *alil* 'slow'. An example, from a hunting story:

(168) mate, mat-i-e-p- w-esoh-a-m alil en
okay HORT-RE-1PL-CT- 3SG.U-follow-EXT-VEN slow INSTR
'Okay, let's follow [the pig] slowly.' [W11:0874]

6.1.7 *se* 'only'

This postposition differs semantically from all other postpositions since it has a quantificational rather than relational meaning. I classify it as a postposition on distributional grounds, since *se* only occurs with a preceding NP over which it has scope (e.g. *nggat se* 'only dog(s)'), and never floated to other positions of the clause (cf. the quantificational particle *ap* 'also', which allows placement elsewhere in the clause).

The so-called Restrictive Orientation prefix *s-* 'only' (§11.1.6) has the same meaning as *se*, and it seems reasonable to assume that the prefix originated through the merger of the postposition *se* into the verb complex in contexts where *se* was placed immediately before the verb. Schematically, this development was: NP *se* Verb > NP *s*-Verb.

In today's Coastal Marind the prefix *s-* is used when the constituent in its scope is immediately before the verb complex (NP *s*-Verb), while the postposition *se* is used when the pre-verbal slot is occupied by other material (e.g. NP *se* X Verb), i.e. contexts where the incorporation of *se* into the verb complex was blocked by intervening material. For example, it is common that the negator *mbya*, which is obligatorily placed in the pre-verbal position, forces the speaker to use NP *se* instead of the tighter, prefixal variant NP *s-*, as in (169). See also example (261) further below.

(169) Instructing villagers to bring equipment for processing sago before a trip to another village where a mourning celebration was being held.

kayahwek ma-me- k-umah,
beating.stick OBJ-FUT:2PL.A- WITH-go:2|3PL.U

ehe nama yalut se mbya me- umah
here now mourning.song only NEG NAFUT:2PL.A- go:2|3PL.U

'You should bring sago beating sticks, now you're not going only for the mourning songs.' [W19:0041-0042]

6.1.8 *nde* 'at'

This postposition is mostly employed to mark static location, as in (170). It also occurs in some temporal expressions such as *epe nde epe* 'at that time' (*epe* is the Distal demonstrative), as in example (171).

(170) About the Marind before pacification.

hyakod	*milah*	*nde*	*mbya*	*ø-d-a-*	*ya-hwala*	*ehe*
one	village	at	NEG	NTRL-DUR-3SG.A-	2|3PL.U-be	here

'They didn't stay in one place.' (=they moved around) [D08:0004]

(171) The speaker is locating the time of a reminiscence with respect to a recent feast.

epe nde epe	*mbya*	*ø-na-*	*yanakeh*
at.that.point	NEG	NTRL-3PL.A-	cook

'At that point they hadn't started preparing the food [for the feast] yet.'
[W22:0003]

Like the postposition *se* 'only', the postposition *nde* provides one of the few clear instances in the language of a non-affixal item which has provided the source of an inflectional affix, viz. the Locational Orientation prefix *nd-* (§11.1.5). This prefix is used when the NP referring to the location is in the syntactic position immediately before the verb complex, whereas the postpositional structure NP+*nde* is used in all other positions. The two structures also differ in their meaning, since the prefic *nd-* can mark both (static) location and source, while the postpositional expression of source requires *lek* 'from'.

6.1.9 *awe* 'for'

Like *nanggo(l)*, *awe* has a purposive meaning, but is restricted to contexts involving motion. The phrase marked by *awe* corresponds to the item acquired as a result of the motion event.

(172) From a hunting story.

nama	*rusa*	*awe*	*ndame-ka-*	*n-ahik*
now	deer(m)	for	FUT:2PL.A-PRI-	1.U-accompany

'Now you will take me [to hunt] for deer.' [W01:0025]

The postposition is perhaps (diachronically) related to the noun *awe* 'game' (i.e. game in hunting). One could imagine that this noun was common with animal names in hunting-related contexts, e.g. 'to go [search for] pig-game', and that it somehow became reanalysed as a purposive marker in such contexts. As a postposition it extends beyond animal names, so if asked 'Where are you going?', one can answer e.g. *roko awe* '[To buy] cigarettes'.

6.1.10 Denominal locational postpositions

The denominal locatives and their source nouns were listed in Table 6.2. I include the four words *mit* 'near', *lahwalah* 'on top', *kumay* 'inside' and *kala* 'below' in this subclass, although the last item, *kala*, is fairly rare, with only a handful of recorded observations. There are perhaps other nominals that should be accorded membership among the postpositions but escaped my attention.

Phrases headed by the denominal postpositions may be used as independent adverbials expressing some spatial configuration, as the phrase *Anselmus mit* in (173), or be embedded under another postposition, as described in §7.4. Example (174) shows that a postpositional phrase in the position before the verb may occur with one of the Orientation prefixes, e.g. the Locational *nd-* marking static location (see §11.1.4).

(173)   uhyum   epe   nda-d-ø-   mil,   Anselmus   mit
       3SG:wife there   LOC-DUR-3SG.A- be.sitting A.   near
       'His wife was sitting there, at Anselmus' place.'   [W10:0349]

(174)   Commenting on a picture of an egg in a glass of water.
       kana   adaka   kumay   nd-a-   kahakut-a
       egg(III) water inside   LOC-3SG.A- put.inside:III.U-EXT
       'The egg is in the water.'

Of the four denominal postpositions, *mit* has the most interesting semantics. As noted above it appears to derive from the noun *mit* meaning 'base (of tree or body part[4]), but I give it the general gloss 'near' in its postpositional use. This translation works best in its use with inanimate complements, as in (175). With humans, *mit* marks either the place where someone lives, i.e. *X mit* 'at X's place/house', as in (173) above, or location more generally, as in *nok mit* 'where I am, near me'.

(175)   etob   yey   mit   menda-b-ø-   ay
       tide(III) land   near   PERF-ACT-3SG.A-   become:III.U
       'The tide was already near land.'   [W10:0295]

---

[4] The body part meaning is found in the compounds *mit-kambet* (lit. base-ear) 'base of the ear' and *mit-unum* 'tongue base'.

In (176) *mit* has a verb stem as its complement and expresses 'almost V'. It appears that this use is only possible with verbs that express events whose culmination is reached by degree, such as 'finish' (another attestation is with *pig* 'become bright/morning'). This construction is not used with punctual verbs such as 'fall' or 'shoot', which require prefixation of the Frustrative *um-* to express 'almost V' (§15.2).

(176) The speaker and others spent a day processing sago.
 balen mit k-a- hay
 finish near DIR-3SG.A- fall
 'It got almost finished.' (lit. 'It fell near finish') [W19:0351]

6.2 Prepositions

There are two frequent words that can be classified as prepositions: *mbi* 'like' and *yah* or *yahaa* 'until, all the way to'.

6.2.1 *mbi* 'like'

The meaning of the preposition *mbi* is close to that of the similative postposition *hi* (§6.1.4), but their uses differ. The postposition *hi* forms phrases that are used as adjuncts or adnominal modifiers, whereas structures introduced by the preposition *mbi* occupy a peripheral syntactic position, or form complete utterances on their own. A phrase introduced by *mbi* typically presents an entity or a situation serving as a comparison with (or example of) something in the surrounding discourse, like the English word *like* in the beginning of this clause. In (177), I had asked for the meaning of the word *nak* 'vine', and the speaker pointed to a nearby plant growing as a vine.

(177) mbi ehan, labu k-a- Ø
 like REM:III pumpkin(m)(III) PRS.NTRL-3SG.A- be.NPST
 'Like that one over there, that's pumpkin.' [W13:0211]

When the comparison involves a situation, *mbi* takes a subordinate clause describing the situation as its complement. The verb is marked as subordinate by the Dependent prefix *ah-* (if the clause has non-present time reference), or, as in (178), by the Proximal/Distal prefix series (with present time reference; see further §20.1).

(178) The speaker is expressing her disapproval of code-switching.

mahut	mbya	dehi,	mbi	namaya	ih-ak-e-	n-a	lay
other.hand	all	hard	like	[now	PROX:I/II.pl-1.A-1PL-	1.U-AUX	talk

malin-mayan	ehe
Marind-speech(III)	PROX:III]

'On the contrary, [it's better to speak] completely straight (lit. hard), like the way we're speaking Marind now.' [W13:0916]

The subordinate clause in (178) refers to the manner in which the activity is carried out, so the Predicated Manner construction described in §20.1.2.4 is used.

The preposition *mbi* has another complementiser-like use, in which it expresses mistaken thought, as in the second clause of the formula 'I did X, mistakenly thinking that Y', or 'I did X, as if it were the case that Y'. The verb in the clause functioning as the complement of *mbi* is not marked as subordinate, but always carries the Presentative prefix *hat-*, as in (179). This construction is rare in corpus data, but was also noted by Drabbe (1955: 126–127).

(179) From a hunting story. The speaker shot a wallaby, then realised that there were several other wallabies hiding in the tall grass.

mbya	ø-no-	hyadih	ipe	isi	ipe,
NEG	NTRL-1.A-	see:2|3PL.U	DIST:I/II.PL	other	DIST:I/II.PL

mbi	kudaya	ka-hat-ø-	ø
like	alone	PRS.NTRL-PRSTV-3SG.A-	be.NPST

'I didn't see the other ones, [mistakenly thinking] it was alone.' [W12:0224]

See §20.2.1 for the expression of reported thought more generally.

6.2.2 *yah, yahaa* 'until'

The versatile *yah* and *yahaa* mean 'all the way to, until', as in the common phrase *Kondo yah Digul* 'from Kondo all the way to the Digul', which decribes the geographical extension of ethnic Marind people (from the village Kondo in the east to the Digul river in the west).

The longer form *yahaa* is often more of a verbal gesture than a preposition. The final /a/ is typically lengthened for iconic purposes, suggesting the distance to the goal: *yahaaaaaa Merauke* 'all the waaaay...to Merauke'. Since /a/ appears to always be lengthened to some degree, I write it with two *a*'s in the orthography, just like Drabbe (1955) did in his grammar. Another example:

(180) hi   mend-am-b-e-   n-in,   yahaa kwemek
      song PERF-1.A-ACT-1PL-   1.U-become   until   morning
      'We danced, until the morning.'   [W18:0256-0257]

6.3 Particles

In this section I list some short, common words whose distribution makes them difficult to lump with any of the other categories.

6.3.1 *ndom* 'also'

The word *ndom* is a particle used with the meaning 'also', but only in contexts where the thing or person in the scope of 'also' is brought along somewhere (181). Its placement is usually pre-verbal, but other positions are possible, as in (182).

(181) da-yol-namakad   ndom   ø-me-   k-umah
      sago-beat.sago-thing also   NTRL-FUT:2PL.A-   WITH-go:2|3PL.U
      'You should bring equipment for processing sago also.'   [W19:0043]

(182) Asking a truck driver for a ride.
      nok mak-e-   uma⟨n⟩ah   ndom   ay,   Merauke   mak-e-   uma⟨n⟩ah
      1   FUT:1.A-1PL- go⟨1.U⟩   also   Q   M.   FUT:1.A-1PL- go⟨1.U⟩
      'Can we also go [with you]? We're going to Merauke.'   [W10:0054]

It is also common to hear *ndom* as a one-word answer to a question such as 'Did you go with Yakobus?' —*ndom* ('Yes, him too').

The general additive marker is *ap* 'too', described in §7.6.3. Note also the homophonous temporal adverb *ndom* 'still' (§18.4.2).

6.3.2 *ay* Vocative, Yes/no-question, etc.

When calling for somebody's attention, one adds the particle *ay* after their name or the appropriate kin term, etc.: *Onggat-Iwag ay!* 'Hey, Onggat-Iwag!', *ad ay!* 'Father!', *patul ay!* 'Boys!', *mesiwag ay!* 'You old woman!'.

A second use is in the formation of yes/no-questions, in which *ay* is added at the end of the utterance. This structure resembles an English tag question, so the material preceding *ay* is a standard declarative sentence which is turned into a question by the presence of the final particle.

(183)   A listener asks the story-teller for clarification.

    1.   menda-b-ø-o-   hahin   katal   ay?
        PERF-ACT-3SG.A-3SG.DAT- put:IV.U money(IV) Q

    2.   duwit   mbya   ø-ø-o-   hahin,
        money(m)   NEG   NTRL-3SG.A-3SG.DAT- put:IV.U

        ayi s-ø-o-   w-a
        say ONLY-3SG.A-3SG.DAT- 3SG.U-AUX

    1. (A:) 'He already gave him the money, is it?'
    2. (B:) 'He didn't give him the money, he just said [that he would].'
                                                                                   [W19:0411-0412]

A different construction can be used to formulate a question with two sentences providing two explicit alternatives, but in this case the particle *ay* is placed at the beginning of each sentence:

(184)   ay   e=   ka-p-e-   uma⟨n⟩ah pale-kay ehe,
          Q   PROX= DIR-FUT:1.A-1PL- go⟨1.U⟩   land-road PROX:III

          ay   e=   ka-p-e-   uma⟨n⟩ah duh?
          Q   PROX= DIR-FUT:1.A-1PL- go⟨1.U⟩   beach

          'Shall we walk by the road inland, or shall we walk by the beach?'   [W18:0140]

Finally, *ay* used alone is a common backchannel in conversation, perhaps something like 'oh, is that so' or 'right'.

6.3.3 *a*

This particle is used after NPs to set them off against the surrounding discourse, either in coordination/listing of NPs (§7.8), or in the marking of certain topic NPs.

It is not uncommon to find topics, which are realised in the periphery of the clause, marked by *a*, as in (185). The example gives information about a new participant in the context ('the boy'), which the speaker continues to talk about in the turns following this excerpt. This topic marking strategy contrasts with topics marked by demonstratives, although it is unclear what the pragmatic or semantic difference is between the two choices (see §18.3.3 for more information on topics).

(185) patul a   menda-bat-ø- o-nggat   yawal   namaya,
      boy   PTCL PERF-AFF-3SG.A- 3SG.U-become deceased now

      ehe   igih ta   ka-ha-b-ø-   ø-e?
      PROX:I name who:I PRS.NTRL-ROG-ACT-3SG.A- be.NPST-IPFV

      kadam ti   ø-bat-ø-   ola
      clubfoot with:I NTRL-AFF-3SG.A-   be:3SG.U

      'The boy, he is already dead now, what's his name? He had a clubfoot.'
      [W10:0640-0641]

6.3.4 *ma*

This sentence-initial discourse particle seems to be used to indicate mild consternation with something that was previously uttered. In my data it is mostly attested in self-repair, as in (186), where it presumably indicates the speaker's disapproval of their own verbal performance. (I know of no straightforward English gloss, so I add 'MA' to the translation.)

(186) The speaker realises that he has mixed up the chronology of the story.

      ma   ndom-ago,   obay mak-ap-   lay-e,   ehetagol   usus   katane ehe
      PTCL bad-PRWD:III wait FUT:1.A-CT- tell-IPFV like.this:III afternoon   sun(III) PROX:III

      'MA, [that's] wrong, wait I'll tell it [correctly]: it was this time of the afternoon.'
      [W10:0133]

The next example is not from self-repair. Here, one of the participants asked who had come on a trip, and he knew that I (Bruno, here referred to as *koyhi-pal* 'white skin') had been on that trip. When the addressee leaves me out of his answer (line 1), the other participant responds with a *ma*-marked question (line 2), presumably because the answer to his initial question had not been as informative as required.

(187) 1. bapa   Rum, nok, Bas
          father(m) R.   1   B.

      2. ma   ehe   koyhi-pal   ehe?
          PTCL PROX:I white-skin PROX:I

      3. mbit   ti   inah ah-ø-   awat-a-m
          brother.in.law with two   DEP-3SG.A- run.PL-EXT-VEN

      1. (A:) '[It was] Uncle Rum, me and Bas.'
      2. (B:) 'MA, and the white man here?'
      3. (A:) '[He and] brother-in-law were the ones who went here together.'
      [D07:0062-0064]

6.3.5 *awi* 'what about...'

The particle *awi* is used with a following NP, as in (188), or with a following (subordinate) hypothetical clause, as in (189). This forms a complete utterance, functioning as a question 'what about...' or 'what if...'.

(188) 1. nd-ak-e-   dahetok Sulina-Mit
           LOC-1.A-1PL-   return   S.-M.

       2. awi   patul?
           what.about   boy

       3. patul ipe   epe   nda-d-a-p-   hamat-a
           boy   DIST:I/II.PL   there LOC-DUR-3SG.A-CT-   sit.PL-EXT

       1. (A:) 'Then we returned to Sulina-Mit.'
       2. (B:) 'And how about the boys?'
       3. (A:) 'The boys, they were sitting there.' [W07:0011-0013]

(189) Discussing whether a bamboo pole could be used to climb down a well. One participant suggests that it could be made into a ladder by cutting steps in the wood.

       awi   tangga-tangga   a-mund-o-   kama⟨y⟩in-e?
       what.about   steps(m)   DEP-FUT:2SG.A:ALL-3SG.DAT-   make⟨2SG.U⟩-IPFV
       'What if you made steps in it?' [W06:0207]

6.3.6 *mahut* 'on the other hand'

This is the word *mahut* 'far away', which also serves as a much used discourse particle. It is used to introduce a contradiction to or a clarification of something said earlier, perhaps a bit like English *rather, on the contrary* or *on the other hand*. I choose 'other.hand' as a general gloss for the particle.

A common situation in which *mahut* occurs is various meta-linguistic corrections or clarifications corresponding roughly to the scheme *not X, but rather Y*, in which *mahut* fills the function of the *but rather* part. The constituent that follows *mahut* replaces or contradicts the constituent in the scope of negation of the previous clause. The word *mahut* forms a complete clause (or even utterance) with the following constituent.

(190) kaka   Kadoy mbya ø-d-a-   yet-ti,   mahut   Alo
       elder.sib(m)   K.   NEG   NTRL-DUR-3SG.A-   be.moving-DUR   other.hand   A.
       'It wasn't Kadoy that went, rather it was Alo.' [W11:0103-0105]

It is also common to use *mahut* with a clause following it, to suggest an alternative scenario. The clause that follows *mahut* often has a verb marked with the Counterfactual suffix *-um*, showing that the hypothetical scenario was not realised. Note that *mahut* is not necessary to form such irrealis hypotheticals (these only require the presence of *-um*); the contribution of *mahut* is perhaps something like 'it would have been better (if you had...)'.

(191) I drove to Okaba and bought petrol for the generator, but when I returned to Wambi at noon it turned out that the jerrycan that I tied to the motorbike had fallen. A bystander commented:

mahut   kwemek   ø-o-   kipalud-um   jeriken   dehi,
other.hand morning NTRL-2SG.A-   tie:III.U-CTFT jerrycan(m)(III)   hard

mbya   ø-a-   hay-um
NEG   NTRL-3SG.A-   fall:III.U-CTFT

'If you had tied the jerrycan hard in the morning, it wouldn't have fallen.'

Another example is in (192). Here a more literal translation could be 'I will be wet, it would have been better [=*mahut*] if I had gone in the beginning'.

(192) dubadub   ka-me-ø-   w-a   n-in,
      wet   DIR-FUT-3SG.A-   3SG.U-AUX   1.U-become

mahut   oso   nda-no-   uma⟨n⟩ah-um
other.hand   start LOC-1.A-   go⟨1.U⟩-CTFT

'I will be wet, I should have gone in the beginning [before it started raining]'
[W19:0426]

6.3.7 Adversative *yah*

The word *yah* is very frequent as an clause-initial particle with an adversative meaning, 'but, however'. Its meaning makes it useful for contrasting the meanings of two clauses, but I see no reason for calling it a conjunction rather than a particle. It also has various other uses, one of which (with the verb prefix *s-*) is described below.

(193) kala   epe   k-ø-um-e-   kw-atin,
      depression   there DIR-3SG.A-FRUS-ACPN-   INESS-stand

yah   mbya   ø-ø-e-p-   asa
but   NEG   NTRL-3SG.A-2|3PL.DAT-CT- bark

'[The dog] stopped them below there, but he didn't bark at them.'   [W11:0715]

THE ADVERSATIVE *yah s-* CONSTRUCTION. In this phraseological combination *yah* occurs immediately before the verb, which is prefixed with the Restrictive *s*-prefix (meaning 'only'; see §11.1.6). Like other uses of *yah*, the construction has an adversative meaning, although its precise interpretation is dependent on the context. In most of its attestations the pattern is used with change-of-state verbs to express that some situation holds contrary to expectation, especially with negative consequences:

(194) The speaker describes how he was sitting in a tree, having fled from an attacking pig. He attempts to throw sticks at the pig in order to make it go away. The plan backfires:

o,   upe   yaman yah s-a-   w-in
EXCLAM DIST:II   mean   PTCL ONLY-3SG.A- 3SG.U-become

'Oh! It became even angrier.'   [M02:0051]

With the *yah s-* construction it is common to add the Extended *-la* (realised as *-a* after non-vowels) and Venitive suffix *-em* 'hither' (realised as *-m* after a vowel) to the verb expressing a change-of-state; the meaning is that the realisation of the (unexpected/undesired) state is approaching:

(195) Cleaning a well.

kamak en,   adaka   kosi yah s-a-   ay-a-m
fast   with water(III) little PTCL ONLY-3SG.A- become:III.U-EXT-VEN

'Hurry up! There's only a little water left.' (lit. 'the water is becoming little')
[W06:0067]

The next two examples illustrate a very interesting extension of this construction. Its use can be understood as marking the reversal of the expected participant roles in a clause. For example, if somebody says, 'X did something to Y', and one wants to reply that in fact, 'it was Y who did something to X', one may use the *yah s-* construction to signal this reversal of the participant roles.

(196) 'Did she give it to you?'

mbya ø-ø-na-   og, yah s-ak-o-   og
NEG   NTRL-3SG.A-1.DAT- give   PTCL ONLY-1.A-3SG.DAT- give

'[No,] she didn't give to me, **I** gave to **her**.'

(197) Elder brother was teasing little brother; I jokingly said to elder brother 'Watch out, he'll hit you', to which elder brother replied:

mahut   yah sa-mo-   w-asib
other.hand PTCL ONLY-FUT:1.A-   3SG.U-hit

'On the contrary, **I** am the who will hit **him**.'

A corpus example is in (198). The speaker is complaining that his relatives who live in the other end of the village never come to visit him, although he often pays a visit to them. Note that *yah s-* construction is in the first clause in this example.

(198) yah   s-ak-ap-   apanawn-e,   yah   mbya   k-i-n-ind-a-
       PTCL ONLY-1.A-CT-   visit:2|3PL.U-IPFV PTCL NEG   PRS.NTRL-3PL>1-1.DAT-ALL-1.DAT-

y-um
2|3PL.U-go.PLA

'Although **I** go to visit **them**, they never come to me.' [W13:0886]

This use is remarkable since such metalinguistic corrections would be expected to make use of focus structures (cf. the boldface words in the English translation), but in these Coastal Marind examples there are not even any overt NPs that could be given prosodic prominence (the person indexes in the verb complex cannot be stressed to show contrastive focus). Apparently the use of the *yah s-*construction is sufficient to signal that the speaker wants to contrast this new information with the one previously given.

6.4 Interjections

6.4.1 General interjections

Here I list some common interjections and similar expressive items and describe their use.

ahak   This common interjection (often pronounced [aha?]) is used to answer 'yes' to a question.

ane   Used as a general expression of surprise ('Wow!'). Also response to behaviour of people or domestic animals that one finds anti-social or unacceptable for some reason, e.g. said to a child taking my notebook or to dogs entering the house during meal time.

aw   This interjection is used to get somebody's attention ('Hey you!'), or simply to greet someone ('Hello!'). It is common together with vocatives (*aw, Mili ay!* 'Hey, Mili!'), but is also used in response to vocatives, e.g. *Mili ay! —aw.* 'Hey Mili! —Yes/I'm here.'

aywa   Used to express melancholy, longing and endearment in general, e.g. when talking about somebody's upcoming departure ('*aywa*, you're going away from us'). To give a maximally pathetic effect, this word may be pronounced in the lower voice range of the speaker, with the final [a] lengthened and pronounced with an exaggerated vibrato (as if one's voice were cracking before bursting into tears). This interjection is also used in reaction to pictures of totemic animals and edible plants, e.g. pictures of kangaroos that I took in Australia (*aywa, sayam!* 'Oh my, wallabies!') or drawings of coconut palms (*aywa, onggat!* 'Oh my, coconuts!').[5]

eeee   Exclamation used when saying farewell, consisting of the vowel [e] pronounced with a rapidly rising pitch, often into the falsetto range of the speaker.

hayo   Used to chase away intrusive dogs, often in combination with a forceful [hə̃ə̃ə̃ə̃ə̃] (this is the only occurrence of a nasalised vowel that I am aware of in the language).

mate   This is a response meaning 'okay' but also 'whatever, never mind'.

mbya ka   This phrase has the literal translation 'It is not' (*mbya k-a-* Ø; NEG PRS.NTRL-3SG.A- be.NPST) and is used as a negative interjection/answer 'no'. It is also commonly used to avoid answering a content question, as in 'Where are you going? —*mbya ka*', i.e. 'Nowhere in particular/none of your business'.

pela   This is the most general swear word, literally meaning 'vagina', but used by all speakers as a relatively mild curse (perhaps something like English *Damn!*) expressing both planned and automatic responses to surprise, emotion, etc. The high discourse frequency and relative mildness of this expression contrasts with the metalinguistic, prescriptive, remarks given to me by speakers, who claimed that this word is very offensive and should not be used. Ironically, *pela* (usually pronounced *pele*) is used as an ubiquitous discourse particle in the Malay spoken in the district capital Merauke and adjacent areas (even by Javanese or Buginese migrants who might never have met a Marind person).

se   A response to positive surprises, e.g. throwing a stone at some distant object and unexpectedly hitting it.

way   A response to dangerous situations that could lead to people being injured, property damaged, etc. Like similar expressions in many other languages (e.g. Malay *awas*, Swedish *akta*, but none in English) this interjection is followed by a syntactic slot that can host a bare noun expressing either (i) the danger that should be avoided, as in *way nggat!* 'Watch out for the dog!' or *way na!* 'Watch out [so you don't step on the] poo!'; or (ii) the body part, belonging, etc. that risks being injured or damaged if one does not take immediate action, as in *way pa!* 'Be careful with your head!', *way buku!* 'Be careful with the book' (e.g. it might rain on it). Although the semantic role of the noun following *way* is underspecified (it refers either to the danger or to a thing being in danger) it is usually clear from the context which interpretation is the correct one. It is also common to add a clause after *way* expressing the imminent danger, e.g. '*way*, you might fall!'. Such clauses always have a verb inflected by means of the Non-Asserted Future, as discussed in §14.2.7.

---

5 The same interjection is apparently present in other languages in the area, cf. *aiwa* 'used to signal compassion', of the unrelated Komnzo language spoken across the border in Papua New Guinea (Döhler 2016: 154).

6.4.2 Post-sneeze interjections

When a person sneezes, it is common for that person or somebody in the vicinity to yell a series of special post-sneeze interjections, one after each sneeze. The interjections are specific to the clan of the person sneezing (cf. van Baal 1966: 193).[6] During my stays in Dumilah and Wambi I became familiar with sneezing interjections of the Samkakai clan (the clan of my adoptive father Rafael in Duhmilah), the Yolmend clan (the clan of my host in Wambi, Paulus, and his children), and the Mahuze clan (the clan of Paulus Yolmend's wife, Yustina). I give the interjections for these three clans below, in the prescribed order of utterance.

The words used in the interjections are associated in different ways with the totems of each clan (Samkakai: wallaby; Yolmend: the ocean; Mahuze: faeces and sago), although there are some uncertainties in their translations.

Post-sneeze interjections of the Samkakai clan:

1.	*wak a!*	*wak* 'tail'
2.	*mayadugu!*	'tail-part of a wallaby cut in halves'
3.	*pa ti!*	*pa* 'head', *ti* 'with', i.e. 'the part with the head'
4.	*sakih amay!*	*sakih* 'part of wallaby's leg', *amay* 'ancestor'

Post-sneeze interjections of the Yolmend clan:

1.	*bom ka!*	(unknown meaning)
2.	*pandapna!*	'pectoral fin of sting ray'
3.	*mbum!*	'gill (on fish)'
4.	*kudiwa!*	'small crab sp.'

Post-sneeze interjections of the Mahuze clan:

1.	*na-imu ti a!*	*na* 'faeces', *imu* 'smell', *ti* 'with'
2.	*kambu na kewayla!*	*kambu* '?', *na* 'faeces', *kewayla* 'broken'
3.	*ndom muy da*	*ndom* 'bad', *muy* 'meat', *da* 'sago'
4.	*kabkabo*	'ball of sago'

---

6 See also Evans (1992) for the same phenomenon in Bininj Gun-Wok, a language of northern Australia.

7 The syntax of phrases

7.1 The structure of noun phrases

Coastal Marind nominal syntax can be described as involving two different 'construals': a tight, strictly left-branching NP, in which the modifier always precedes the head, and a loose construal, in which a modifier can be placed after the head, or elsewhere in the clause, so that the expression is discontinuous. The choice between the two construals depends on information structure and syntactic roles. The tight NP is described in §7.1.1, and the loose nominal construal in §7.1.2.

7.1.1 Tight, left-branching NPs

The structure of the tight NP is extremely simple, and consists of the head slot, preceded by a single modifier slot. The basic structure of the tight NP can be diagrammed as follows:

Modifier	Head
Demonstrative Postpositional phrase Numeral Quantifier	Simple nominal Compound nominal

The head slot can be filled by a simple nominal element, such as a noun, or, more rarely, an adjective or numeral, or by a compound. There is no slot for an adjective phrase in this template, and adjective-noun compounds are used instead of attributive adjective phrases. The modifier slot is optionally filled by a demonstrative, an attributive postpositional phrase, a numeral or a quantifier. Pronouns (§4.1) do not enter the NP structure but rather replace it as a whole.

The following NPs contain a compound head preceded by a modifying demonstrative (199) and a simple head preceded by a numeral (200).

(199) [*epe kosi-aliki*]$_{NP}$
DIST:III small-river(III)
'that small river'

(200) [*inahinah yanid*]$_{NP}$
four day
'four days'

Examples (201–202) show NPs containing modifying postpositional phrases. The expression in (202) is a set phrase, but it follows the structure of the NP template.

(201) [[[mandin]~NP~ lik]~PostP~   anim]~NP~
      long.ago   from:I/II.PL people
      'people from long ago, old-timers'

(202) [[[inahinah tagu]~NP~ ti]~PostP~ yahun]~NP~
      four   foot   with:III canoe(III)
      'car' (lit. 'canoe with four feet')

Only two non-numeral quantifiers appear within the NP: *isi* 'other' (§7.7.1) and *mbya* 'all, completely' (§7.7.2). Other quantificational meanings are expressed outside the NP (e.g. amount quantification, §7.7.3; the particle *ap* 'also', §7.6.3).

The absence of a projecting adjectival phrase is a striking gap in the noun phrase syntax of the language. As mentioned above, this niche is taken by compounds, in which adjectives may occur as the first member, e.g. *noy-aha*, literally 'new-house'. An adjective that has entered into a compound is grammatically isolated, just like the first member of English compounds, and may not be further modified by expressions such as *ya* 'real, very', which is a common modifier with predicatively used adjectives–see discussion in §3.6.

Compounding as the only technique for adjectival modification is rare cross-linguistically, but far from unattested, and has been discussed (under the labels compounding, incorporation or pseudo-incorporation) by Dahl (2004: 225–236, 2015: 127–134) for various languages, and by Creissels for languages of sub-Saharan Africa (2018: 733–737). It has, to my knowledge, not been described for any other Papuan languages.

The lack of complex noun phrase structure poses few problems for speakers. The corpus example in (203) shows how precise description of a referent ('big red jerrycans standing like this') is achieved through a number of independent expressions standing in a paratactic relationship rather than as modifiers within a single complex noun phrase.

(203) *epe   nda-d-ø-   ilawewt-a-ti   ago,   jeriken,*
      there LOC-DUR-3SG.A-   put.PLA:III.U-EXT-DUR PRWD:III   jerrycan(m)(III)

      dohi-jeriken   sam   eh-ø-   w-a   ka-bak⟨e⟩h
      red:III-jerrycan(m)(III) big   PROX:III-3SG.A- 3SG.U-AUX   INESS-put⟨III.U⟩
      'There were standing what's-it-called, jerrycans, red jerrycans, big, standing like this.'   [W10:0104]

There are no noun-modifying relative clauses in Coastal Marind. The multifunctional subordinate clause construction (§20.1) can be used to narrow down reference, but it always appears in the periphery of the clause, and not within the NP.

7.1.2 Loose nominal expressions

The tight-knit NP described in §7.1.1 exists in competition with a much looser construal, in which an element acting as a semantic modifier of a head can be placed after the head, or even appear separated from the head elsewhere in the clause. I will refer to these construals as loose nominal expressions (or NEs), to distinguish them from canonical NPs. Loose NEs are attested with most types of modifying elements: demonstratives, postpositional phrases, numerals and one non-numeral quantifier (*isi* 'other').

The use of the loose construal depends primarily on the information-structural status of the expression and its parts. Loose construals are common when only the modifier is in focus, and therefore placed in the immediately pre-verbal position of the clause, while the head is placed elsewhere in the clause. I illustrate this with focused numerals in (204–205). The words making up the loose NEs have been underlined in the examples.

(204) <u>sayam</u> <u>hyakod</u> ma-no- deh
 wallaby one OBJ-1.A- shoot:3SG.U
 'I shot one wallaby.' [W12:0346]

(205) Niko <u>hyakod</u> m-a- deh <u>rusa</u>
 N. one OBJ-3SG.A- shoot:3SG.U deer
 'Niko shot one deer.' [D10:0024]

Another context that commonly features loose NEs are presentational sentences introducing novel participants into the discourse (206–207), again illustrated with numerals.

(206) <u>rusa</u> <u>inah</u> ø-d-a- wayamat-a
 deer two NTRL-DUR-3SG.A- stand.PL-EXT
 'Two deer were standing there.' [M01:0024]

(207) yah <u>iwag</u> e= nda-d-a-p- hamat-a ehe <u>inhyakod</u>
 but woman PROX= LOC-DUR-3SG.A-CT- sit.PL-EXT PROX three
 'But there were three women sitting there.' [D01:0176]

A general pattern seen in the distribution of loose NEs is that their referents are always topical, in the sense that the utterance as a whole provides information about the referent. If a referent ranks high in topicality or 'aboutness', and one or more modifiers are present, then the loose construal is possible, or sometimes even preferred to the tight NP. Loose construals are only possible with NEs filling argument roles in the clause, and adjuncts are always expressed by tight NPs, which probably reflects the low topicality of adjuncts. Compare the argument NEs in (204–205) above, for which the loose construal is natural, with the adjunct NP 'one night' in (208), which can only be expressed using the modifier-head order of the tight NP.

(208) [hyakod ɣap]_{NP} m-a-   yali
       one   night OBJ-3SG.A- lie.down
       'He slept here for one night.'   [W22:0012]

7.2 NPs with and without demonstratives

Referential NPs can be determined by demonstratives, placed either before, after, or on both sides of the expression that is being determined. The demonstratives are always used deictically, either exophorically, to point to a referent in the surroundings, or endophorically, to refer back to some previously mentioned referent.

The placement options are illustrated in (209) with the Distal demonstrative (stem *Vpe*) agreeing in Gender II with the head *nggat* 'dog'. The meaning difference between the three patterns of demonstrative ordering is very subtle, and the primary difference lies in syntactic distribution. Note that the pattern in (209d) requires the two demonstratives to be identical, so it is not possible to combine e.g. a preposed Proximal demonstrative with a postposed Distal demonstrative, nor is it possible to have non-matching agreement values.

(209) a.   nggat   'a/the dog'
      b.   upe   nggat   'the/that dog'
      c.   nggat   upe   'the/that dog'
      d.   upe   nggat   upe   'the/that dog'

The demonstratives differ from definite articles (such as English *the*) in that they always retain a deictic meaning element, instructing the hearer to make an effort to identify the referent by paying attention to some entity in the surroundings or in the preceding discourse. If no such effort is required, e.g. because the referent is highly predictable, known to everybody, unique, etc., adnominal demonstratives are not used (cf. Himmelmann 1996 on differences between articles and demonstratives). The textual uses of bare NPs are described in §7.2.1. The uses of preposed and postposed demonstratives are discussed in §7.2.2 and §7.2.3.

For the semantic distinctions between the three demonstrative series *ehe* (Proximal), *epe* (Distal) and *ehan* (Remote), see §4.2.1.

7.2.1 Uses of bare NPs

Noun phrases that are non-referential, like *basik* 'pig(s)' in (210), or non-specific, like *malin-anum* 'a Marind woman' in (211), are always bare.

(210) basik mbya ø-a- ya-law
pig NEG NTRL-3SG.A- 2|3PL.U-search
'They didn't search for pigs.' [W11:0839]

(211) This advice was given to me in the form "This is how you should say:"

malin-anum a-mo- kisa epe,
[Marind-woman(II) DEP-FUT:1.A- marry:3SG.U DIST:III]

ndame-ø- n-in malin-mayan mayay
FUT-3SG.A- 1.U-become Marind-language able

'If I marry a Marind woman, I will learn the Marind language.'

(The Distal demonstrative *epe* in the last example marks the preceding clause as a conditional — or rather, as a topic — and does not interact with the NP 'Marind woman', as shown by the lack of gender agreement.)

Bare noun phrases are also used to introduce new participants in a text, such as that referred to by *rusa* 'a deer' in the next example.

(212) rusa epe k-a-p- man-em ago epe,
deer(m)(II) there DIR-3SG.A-CT- come-VEN PRWD:III DIST:III

aliki-toh k-a-p- man-em
river-side(III) DIR-3SG.A-CT- come-VEN

'A deer came along there at the what's-it-called, it came along the river side.'
[W10:0134]

Note that the deer is also a participant of the second clause of the example above, but since the referent has already been established it is not expressed by any overt noun phrase in this clause (some linguists call this "zero anaphora"). Pronominally used demonstratives are also common in this function (see §4.2.1). But it is also possible to use bare noun phrases for subsequent mention, as in (213), where the participant *patul* 'boy' has already been mentioned in the immediately preceding discourse. Here it is presumably the high topicality of another participant (the husband) that prevents the use of zero or pronominal anaphora for reference to the boy.

(213) Preceding context: 'I told my husband: "Please carry the boy".'

tis ka, patul nd-a- yan⟨e⟩b, menda-b-ø-e- umuh
that's.it boy LOC-3SG.A- carry⟨3SG.U⟩ PERF-ACT-3SG.A-ACPN- go:3SG.U

'That's it, then he carried the boy, and went away with him.' [W20:0131]

Coastal Marind employs bare noun phrases in cases where the referent of an expression is obvious or known to everybody, for example because it is unique, like *mandaw* 'the moon' in (214), or because it is identifiable through association with some other entity in the discourse, like the body part *sagid* 'pig's mane' in (215), which clearly is associated with a pig talked about in the preceding discourse. This makes it clear that the Coastal Marind determiners are best described as demonstratives rather than definite articles. A language like English, which has articles, would typically use definite NPs in such contexts.

(214) *mandaw oso m-a-p- hawa*
moon(III) start OBJ-3SG.A-CT- emerge:III.U
'The moon was about to come out.' [W10:0216]

(215) *sagid m-o-ø- ya-deh isawa?*
pig.mane(IV) OBJ-2SG.A-3SG.DAT- IV.U-shoot maybe
'Maybe you shot the mane [of the pig]?' [D05:0021]

7.2.2 Prenominal demonstratives

Prenominally placed demonstratives fill the modifier slot within the tight NP structure (§7.1.1). Their NP-internal placement distinguishes them from the postposed demonstratives (§7.2.3), which are placed after the tight NP. The difference in placement is seen when an NP is embedded under a postposition, as in (216). The postposition takes a tight NP as its complement, and therefore only allows the presence of a preposed demonstrative in its complement.

(216) [*epe mayan*]$_{NP}$ *lek*
DIST:III speech(III) from
'because of that issue'

Only the Proximal and Distal demonstratives occur in the modifier position, while the Remote *ehan*-series only occurs postposed or in adverbial functions.

The preposed option, without support of a postposed demonstrative, is used mainly with relatively easily accessible referents, and is only attested with endophoric reference. The preposed option is less common than postposed or doubled demonstratives.

Preposed demonstratives are not used if another element fills the modifier slot in the NP, such as the numeral in (217), so NPs with a preceding modifier only allow postposed demonstratives.

(217) [inah iwag]_{NP} ipe
 two woman DIST:I/II.PL
 'those two women'

7.2.3 Postnominal demonstratives

Postposed demonstratives are used to point to expressions in the surrounding discourse context, and in face-to-face conversation to point to things in the physical surroundings. They are also optionally used to mark constituents that function as topics (§18.3.3). Combinations of preposed and postposed determiners are common, giving 'double demonstratives', as in *upe nggat upe* 'that dog' in (209d) above.

Syntactically, phrases marked by postposed demonstratives can only appear as clause-level constituents, and not embedded under postpositions, as seen by comparing the phrase in (216) above with the unacceptable (218).

(218) *mayan epe lek
 speech(III) DIST:III from
 (Intended:) 'because of that issue'

Phrases marked by postposed demonstratives are mainly found in the peripheries of the clause, either as initial topics, as in (219), or as utterance-final additions or afterthoughts (220). The precise functions of the demonstratives differ: in (219) it points to preceding discourse ('that issue, that we've been talking about', i.e. the so-called discourse deictic use of demonstratives; Himmelmann 1996: 224), and in (220) it points to the physical surroundings ('here where we are sitting').

(219) yah epe mayan epe, sawanggi ma-n- lu
 but DIST:III speech(III) DIST:III sorcery(m)(III) OBJ-3PL.A- call:III.U
 'But that issue, they are calling it sorcery.' [M05:0033]

(220) ihe Duh-agi e= k-a-p- hahin,
 PROX:I/II.PL D.-PROW:I/II.PL PROX= DIR-3SG.A-CT- put:2|3PL.U
 ehe milah ehe
 PROX:III village(III) PROX:III
 'The Duh-inhabitants ended up here, in this village.' [D08:0138]

The next example shows what has been called the recognitional use of demonstratives: "the intended referent is to be identified via specific, shared knowledge rather than through situational clues or reference to preceding segments of the ongoing discourse" (Himmelmann 1996: 230). The excerpt mentions two new participants, 'grandma Kudiwa' and 'that child', in an account of some recent events. The first speaker (speaker A) use the Distal demonstrative *upe* with both expressions, and I interpret this as a way to show that the hearers, and especially the co-narrator of the story (speaker B), are familiar with the referents. Speaker B seems to confirm this familiarity by providing the name of the child in the 2nd line.

(221) (A:) *amay   Kudiwa upe   menda-d-a-p-   mil,   upe   nalakam upe*
           ancestor K.   DIST:II PERF-DUR-3SG.A-CT-   be.sitting   DIST:II child   DIST:II

— (B:) *Maria*
        M.

1. (A:) 'Grandma Kudiwa was already sitting, [with] that child.' — (B:) 'Maria.'
[W19:0082]

Postposed demonstratives are not limited to NPs, but can appear after non-NP constituents such as postpositional phrases (222–223) and subordinate clauses (see §20.1).

(222) [*nahan aha   kumay*]$_{PostP}$ *ehe,   anep   malin-mayan*
       1.EMPH house(III) inside   PROX:III   EMPH:III   Marind-speech

       ø-mo-   lay
       NTRL-FUT:2SG.A-   speak

       'Here inside our house, you should speak Marind.'   [W13:0054]

(223) *epe   nda-no-d-   sambayang kudaya,* [*epe   ad   nanggo*]$_{PostP}$ *epe*
       there LOC-1.A-DUR-   pray(m)   alone   DIST:I   father(I)   for   DIST:I

       'I was praying there alone, for that man (lit. father)' (so that he would recover from his illness)   [W19:0434]

The Remote demonstratives, which are not used as preposed modifiers, can be used in the postposed position, pointing to some entity in the distance (224).

(224) *yay   ehan   mbya ø-bat-ø-   kahos*
       uncle(I)   REM:I NEG   NTRL-AFF-3SG.A-   chew.betel

       'Uncle over there isn't chewing betelnut.'   [W13:0230]

It was mentioned above that a referent, once it is established, is typically referred to by means of zero anaphora, a pronominally used demonstrative, or a bare noun phrase. But if it is likely that the referent is no longer 'active' in the mind of the hearer — e.g. because it has not been mentioned for a while — the speaker may choose to 're-activate' it by means of a demonstrative expression. This is the case with *yahun epe* 'that canoe' in (225), which is the 2nd mention of a canoe, separated from its 1st mention by approximately 20 lines (roughly corresponding to intonation units), during which several other topics were discussed.

(225) yahun   epe   ye   ma-n-   ahus   patul
      canoe(III) DIST:III INGRS OBJ-3PL.A- pull.out:III.U boy
      'The boys pulled out the canoe.'
      'The [aforementioned] canoe was pulled out by the boys.' [W10:0130]

It should be mentioned, however, that there are many examples of robustly established referents that nevertheless are realised by means of determined noun phrases. For example, the referent of *rusa upe* 'that deer' in (226) has already been the dominant topic of several preceding lines, yet the speaker opts for a demonstrative expression in this sentence. My intuitive understanding of this example is that it marks a new 'paragraph' in the narrative, and the expression *rusa upe* is used to announce that it will be the topic of this section (too). Topic-comment structures are further discussed in §18.3.3.

(226) Preceding context: some hunters shoot at a deer. The deer is described as having arrows sticking out of its skin, having been shot by other hunters at some previous occasion.

rusa   upe   kaka   Way   e=   k-ø-um-o-p-   w-a
deer(m)(II) DIST:II elder.sib(M)   W.   PROX=   DIR-3SG.A-FRUS-3SG.DAT-CT-   3SG.U-AUX
kayub   ago,   menda-ø-b-   deh
guess   QUOT   PERF-1.A-ACT-   shoot:3SG.U

'[About] that deer, Way wrongly thought like this: "I shot it".' [W11:1152]

7.3 Numerals

This section describes some syntactic features of numeral expressions; the basics of the numeral system were described in §3.4.

Like other modifiers, numerals are placed before the head in the tight NP (§7.1.1), but it is common to express combinations of numerals and nouns with the loose construal (§7.1.2), which permits the numeral to be separated from the semantic head.

The tight numeral-noun order is obligatory for adjuncts and NPs functioning as the complement of a postposition, but it occurs with argument NPs too, like *inah anim ipe* 'those two people' in the following example:

(227) Describing hunters trying to bring their catch back to the village.

inah	anim	ipe,	mbaymbay	k-a-	∅	sinik
two	people	DIST:I/II.PL	unable	PRS.NTRL-3SG.A-	be.NPST	carry

'Those two people, they can't carry it.' [W03:0050]

Adverbial expressions containing a numeral modifier always exhibit the preposing pattern, e.g. *hyakod yap* 'one night' in (208) above, or *hyakod say* 'one spot' in (228).

(228) About several deer shot by hunters.

hyakod	say	ka-d-ø-	hihi-h
one	place	DIR-DUR-3SG.A-	fall.PLA-2|3PL.U

'They fell in one spot.' [W01:0048]

Another phrase type that always shows numeral-noun order is measure phrases, specifying the quantity of something, such as *inah plastik* 'two plastic bags' in (229). Measure phrases, like amount quantifiers (§7.7.3), are clause level adjuncts and do not form a constituent with the corresponding noun.

(229) Betelnut had been buried in the ground.

nok	kanis	ye	ma-no-	kaw-eg	inah	plastik
1	betelnut	INGRS	OBJ-1.A-	INESS-dig	two	plastic.bag(m)

'I started digging up the betelnut, two plastic bags [of it].' [W21:0250]

As noted in §7.1.2, deviations from the tight numeral-noun order are associated with specific information-structural configurations, as when a numeral is placed in the pre-verbal position, which is the site of focused constituents (Chapter 11). A clear illustration of this is in next example, which was volunteered to me during elication of verbs meaning 'bite'. The numeral *inah* 'two' appears in the pre-verbal focus position, separated from its head noun *nggat* 'dog(s)' by the intervening A-argument *ahyaki* 'snake'.

(230)
nggat	ahyaki	inah	m-a-	y-alok
dog	snake	two	OBJ-3SG.A-	2|3PL.U-stab

'The snake struck two dogs.'

The option of placing the numeral 'two' in the pre-verbal position is particularly common, even when there is no particular emphasis on the numeral. This is just an optional way of indicating that the action was performed by a pair, i.e. the function that morphological dual marking (which is absent in Coastal Marind) has in many of the other languages of Southern New Guinea. Examples:

(231) The preceding context describes the whereabouts of the speaker's relatives, with whom he had travelled to Merauke. The speaker then turns to the activities of himself and his wife.

nahan kota   inah ø-nan-d-e-   nayat
1.EMPH town(m)   two   NTRL-1.A-DUR-1PL-   be.moving.PL
'[As for] ourselves, the two of us walked in town.'   [W10:0579]

(232) hinabay   ti   inah ø-nak-e-   uma⟨n⟩ah
      mother.in.law:3SG   with:I/II.PL   two   NTRL-1.A-1PL- go⟨1.U⟩
      'His mother-in-law and I went.'
      (lit. 'With his mother-in-law, the two of us went.')   [W22:0034]

Another type of deviation from the tight numeral-noun order is found in what might be called grammatically peripheral contexts. One typical instance is in lists. A set of instructions for someone heading for one of the dry-goods stores in the village could be given as follows, with each item on the list consisting of a noun followed by the numeral indicating the quantity:

(233) kopi   inah, od   inah, kertas   hyakod
      coffee(m) two   sugar two   rolling.paper(m)   one
      '[Buy] two [packages of] coffee, two [packages of] sugar, one [pack of] rolling paper.'

Combinations of numerals and 1st and 2nd person pronouns also have postposed numerals (234).

(234) a. nok inah   b. yoy inah
           1   two   2PL two
           'the two of us'   'the two of you'

7.4 Postpositional phrases

The internal syntax of postpositional phrases consists of an open complement slot, filled by a tight NP (§7.1.1), and a head slot, containing one of the postpositions listed in §6.1. The complement NP can contain premodifiers, such as a demonstrative, as seen in (216) above, or a numeral (235).

(235) [hyakod kalambu]_NP   kumaẙ
      one   mosquito.net(m) inside
      'inside one mosquito-net'

The complement can also be filled by a postpositional phrase, resulting in a sequence of two nested postpositional phrases. The inner phrase is always headed by one of the denominal postpositions, e.g. *kumaẙ* (also a noun meaning 'inside'; §6.1.10), and the outer one by one of the spatial/directional postpositions *lek* 'from', *nanggo* 'towards' or *nde* 'at'. Example (236) shows the combination *kumaẙ lek*, lit. 'from inside', and example (237) *mit nanggo*, lit. 'towards near'.

(236) ahak, namaẙa ø-bat-ø-   hawa
      yes   now   NTRL-AFF-3SG.A-   emerge:3SG.U

      [[penjara   kumaẙ]_PostP lek]_PostP
      prison(m)   inside   from
      'Yes, he just came out from the prison.'   [D09:0279]

(237) The speaker was going to join the addressees for a prayer meeting, but rain prevented her from leaving the house.

      nok   mbya   ø-no-   uma⟨n⟩ah   [[yoẙ   mit]_PostP nanggo]_PostP
      1   NEG   NTRL-1.A-   go⟨1.U⟩   2PL   near   towards
      'I didn't go to you.'   [W19:0433]

Postpositional phrases function syntactically as adjuncts (e.g. with adverbial functions) or as adnominally or attributively used modifiers. Examples of these uses, which vary according to the postposition, were given in §6.1. For example, the postpositions which may head phrases functioning as attributive modifiers are the following, with cross-references to examples:

lek	'from'	ex. (144)
ti	'with'	ex. (151)
ni	'without'	ex. (157)
hi	'like'	ex. (159)
nanggo(l)	'for'	ex. (164)
en	POSS/INSTR	ex. (166)

Of these, the first four postpositions have the ability to agree in gender. With attributively used postpositional phrases, the controller of agreement is invariably the noun that is modified by the postpositional phrases, i.e. the 'higher' noun. This is clear in the following example, since *lek* appears in its Gender II form *luk*, triggered by the modified head noun *anum* 'woman'.

(238) [*milah luk*]_{PostP} *anum*
village(III) from:II woman(II)
'woman from the village' [W18:0170]

7.5 Possession

In this section I provide an overview of the strategies that are used to express possession in Coastal Marind. Two adnominal strategies are used: a postpositional phrase headed by Possessive *en* expressing the possessor, and juxtaposition of the possessor and possessee.

Two types of indexing on the verb can express possession-like relationship: Dative indexing of owners of body parts (§9.3), and Genitive indexing of other possessors (§9.4). These are not adnominal, since the possessor and possessee are expressed as independent noun phrases, but they are mentioned in this section so that these common strategies can be compared with the adnominal strategies.

A possessor expression headed by *en* forms a standard postpositional phrase and forms a constituent with the following noun (the possessee). In (239), the PostP [[*yay Ndawil*]_{NP} *en*]_{PostP} 'uncle Ndawil's' modifies the head noun *aha* 'house' within the larger NP [[[*yay Ndawil*] *en*] *aha*]_{NP} 'uncle Ndawil's house'. As shown in (240), possessive phrases can be added recursively (although I have not recorded more than one level of recursion).

(239) *yay Ndawil en aha k-a- itala*
uncle Nd. POSS house PRS.NTRL-3SG.A- be.standing
'Uncle Ndawil's house is standing [here].' [W10:0371]

(240) *amay en yay en pula*
ancestor POSS uncle POSS taboo.spot
'grandpa's uncle's taboo spot' [W21:0324]

There are no particular restrictions on the type of ownership expressed by *en* (e.g. alienable/inalienable), so it is common with both juridical possession, as with the owned house in (239), and with kinship terms, as in *amay en yay* 'grandpa's uncle' in (240).

Like possessive constructions in other languages, structures with the Coastal Marind Possessive *en* have a much broader range than just marking possession. A general translation of expressions following the pattern *X en Y* is more accurately given as 'the Y associated with X' rather than 'X's Y'. For example, it is clear in example (241) — in which the speaker inquires about the whereabouts of a non-Papuan peddler with whom the addressees usually associate — that the relationship with the man is not one of possession, but general association. Similarly, the expression *sah en egog* in (242) does not refer to strict possession but rather association, 'the dance steps of the woman' (or 'the movements associated with the woman').

(241)   yoy   en   pu-anem   epe,   namaya   ek-ø-   um-e?
       2PL   POSS   Indonesian.man   DIST:I   now   Q:I-3SG.A-   go.PLA:3SG.U-IPFV
       'Your Indonesian, does he usually come here now?'   [W19:0367]

(242)   From a story in which a man teaches some other male villagers Western-style dancing.
       sah   en   egog   oy   ø-mo-p-   ka-ya-nggat
       married.woman   POSS   movement   2SG   NTRL-FUT:2SG.A-CT-   WITH-2SG.U-become
       'You will do the dance steps of the woman.'   [M03:0041]

Many kinship terms have person forms (§3.5), expressing the 'anchor' point from which the kinship relation is calculated, such as the 2nd person forms in *yahu a yahway* 'your mother and your father' in (243). This is usually sufficient for indicating the person reference of such forms, so they are used without additional possessor marking.

(243)   a-bat-   dahetok!   yahu   a   yahway   epe   nd-a-   Ø
       IMP-AFF-   return   2SG:mother   PTCL   2SG:father   there   LOC-3SG.A-   be.NPST
       'You go home! Your mother and father are there.'   [W10:0650]

But if explicit possessor marking needs to be indicated for a kinship term, the possessor can be marked either with the standard Possessive postposition *en*, or occur as a bare noun, juxtaposed before the kinship term. Example (244) shows the first option, first with a kinship term lacking anchor forms (*wanangga* 'children [offspring]'), and then with a kinship term that has them (*nahe* 'my/our grandchildren').

(244)   wanangga   en   wanangga   ipe,   nok keti   en   nahe   ipe
       children   POSS   children   DIST:I/II.PL 1   APL   POSS   grandchildren:1   DIST:I/II.PL
       'the children of the children, our grandchildren'   [W13:0004–0005]

Example (245) illustrates the juxtaposition strategy, with the kinship term *eham* 'her husband'. The juxtapposition strategy is strongly preferred with spouse terms, which are unattested with Possessive *en*. Expressions such as *Ndalom-Iwag eham*, literally 'Ndalom-Iwag husband', collocate strongly as speakers use them as avoidance terms for in-laws whose names they are not allowed to utter.

(245) From a hunting story.

> Ndalom-Iwag eham ye m-ø-in- umuh
> Nd.-I. husband:3SG INGRS OBJ-3SG.A-ALL- go:3SG.U
>
> 'Ndalom-Iwag's husband went after [the pig].' [W11:0600]

Other kinship terms that are recorded only in the juxtaposing structure are 'cousin' and 'husband's elder brother' in (246). On the other hand, many kinship terms are attested in the corpus with a Possessive *en*-phrase, e.g. *yay* 'uncle', *mayay-anem* 'older brother', *an* 'mother' and *kemlay* 'nephew', and some are attested with both strategies (*namek* 'clanmate').[1]

(246) In a story, a man introduces his wife to his *onos* 'cousin'.

> nok onos ya k-a- Ø ehe, oy yakna
> 1 cousin real PRS.NTRL-3SG.A- be.NPST PROX:I 2SG husband's.elder.bro:2SG
> k-a- Ø
> PRS.NTRL-3SG.A- be.NPST
>
> 'This is my cousin, your brother-in-law.' [W10:0418]

Body parts may enter into the postpositional structure (e.g. *anup en lul* 'its fur') but this option is mostly attested in reference to parts of dead slaughtered animals. The more frequent strategy is to index the owner of the body part on the verb by means of the Dative prefix series (see §9.3). This marking option is only available if the body part is an argument of the verb (and not e.g. part of an adjunct NP). It is very frequent in expressions such as 'X hit/shot Y in the [body part]', as in (247). Example (248) shows Dative indexing on the copula (consisting of the prefixal complex and a zero verb stem; see §17.4); a literal translation reflecting the Coastal Marind structure would be 'Good hands exist to me'.

(247) bekay ya s-ak-o- dahatuk
heart real ONLY-1.A-3SG.DAT- shoot
'I shot right in the [wallaby's] heart.' [W12:0222]

(248) nok waninggap-sangga k-a-na- Ø
1 good-hand PRS.NTRL-3SG.A-1.DAT- be.NPST
'My hands are good/I have good hands.' [W11:0229]

---

[1] My data do not support Drabbe's (1955: 103) claim that it is the kinship terms lacking person forms that appear in the juxtaposing pattern, as shown by *eham* in (245).

An equivalent structure is available for possessed non-body parts, using the Genitive prefixes (§9.4) on the verb instead of the Dative prefixes. In (249) the owner of *aha* 'house' is marked by means of the Genitive prefix. The difference between this example and an example such as (239) above, which uses the postpositional strategy, appears to be very subtle, and both strategies are common for marking owners of things as well as e.g. offspring and domestic animals in the corpus. Genitive marking is used in copula clauses as the standard way of expressing predicative possession, as in (250); see further §17.4.4.

(249) *Yambaya epe nda-d-ø-om- itala-ti aha*
Y. there LOC-DUR-3SG.A-3SG.GEN- be.standing-DUR house
'Yambaya's house was standing there.' [W10:0233]

(250) *tamuy mbya k-a-namb-e- Ø nok mayay nanggo*
food NEG PRS.NTRL-3SG.A-1.GEN-1PL- be.NPST 1 front for
'We don't have any food for later on.' [W10:0264]

7.6 Postposed markers

This section describes three elements that adjoin at the end of, or after, an NP. The Associative Plural *ke* attaches after names and kinship terms (§7.6.1). The intensifier *ya* 'very, real, etc.' combines with various expression types that express gradeable concepts (§7.6.2). The particle *ap* means 'also' (§7.6.3).

7.6.1 The Associative Plural *ke*

Noun phrases marked by the Associative Plural *ke* or *keti* "denote a set comprised of the referent of the nominal (the main member) plus one or more associated members" (Corbett 2000: 101; see also Moravcsik 2003). I adopt the convention of translating expressions of the shape *Yakobus ke* or *Yakobus keti* as 'Yakobus and the others'.[2] The set marked by the Associated Plural is indexed on the verb according the normal rules for person indexing, as shown in (251–252).

---

[2] The corresponding translation in local Malay is *Yakobus dorang*. *Dorang* is the 3rd person plural pronoun 'they', so literally 'Yakobus they'.

(251) menda-b-ø- dahetok-a-m, yay ke k-ø-e-p- esoh-a-m
PERF-ACT-3SG.A- return-EXT-VEN uncle APL DIR-3SG.A-2|3PL.DAT-CT- follow-EXT-VEN
'She already returned here, she followed uncle and the others.' [W19:0378]

(252) amay keti menda-b-na- hus
ancestor APL PERF-ACT-3PL.A- cross.river
'Grandpa and the others had already crossed the river.' [W15:0140]

The form *keti* is most likely a reinforcement of *ke* through the addition of *ti* 'with'. The forms are completely interchangeable and both forms are used by speakers of all ages in my corpus.

In my corpus data the Associative Plural is only attested with proper names, kinship terms, and 1st person pronouns. With 1st person pronouns *nok* 'I, we' and *nahan* 'myself, ourselves' it has a disambiguating function since these are unspecified for number. The addition of *ke* or *keti* is especially common when the 1st person pronoun is in a non-argument position, as in (253), in which it is possessor inside an NP. A 1st person that fills an argument position always has its number reference disambiguated by person indexing on the verb (presence/absence of the 1pl prefix *e-*), which obviates the need for the Assocative Plural.

(253) From a discussion about dried betelnut imported from Jayapura.
nahan ke en kahos epe, eyaw mend-am-b-e-p- ka-n-in
1.EMPH APL POSS betelnut(III) DIST:III unwilling PERF-1.A-ACT-1PL-CT- WITH-1.U-become
epe
DIST:III
'As for our own [traditional] betelnut, we don't care about it anymore.'
[W13:0115]

It is impossible to add the Associative plural to any other pronouns: **oy ke* 'you (sg) and the others' can only be expressed by the 2pl pronoun *yoy*.

I have not been able to find any context in which the Associative Plural can be used with standard lexical nouns. For example, I once heard the expression *Iyob ke* 'Iyob and the others' used to refer to Iyob, a prominent dog of the household, and some of the neighbour's dogs with which he often associates, but I was told that **nggat ke* 'the dog and the others' sounds strange and cannot be used. Similar lexical restrictions on associative plurals are found across languages (e.g. Daniel and Moravcsik 2013).

See also §9.6.2 for an alternative way of expressing associative plurality.

7.6.2 Intensifier *ya* 'real; very'

This is the all-purpose intensifier of Coastal Marind. It is placed after the word it modifies, e.g. *anim ya* 'real people'. There is some evidence that *ya* can float to other positions, at least in copula clauses, where it is attested clause-finally:

(254) The speaker is making fun of the shape of the addressee's head.

kata-pa   tu   k-a-   Ø   oy   ya
scrubfowl-head with:II PRS.NTRL-3SG.A- be.NPST 2SG real

'You have a real scrubfowl head.' [W11:0360]

The English translation of *ya* is completely context-dependent, so I will illustrate its use with various kinds of expressions as found in the corpus. The meaning 'real' with a noun was already seen in (254). With adjectives, *ya* means 'very' or 'really', i.e. indicates high degree (255).

(255) sa   yahyahy ya   k-a-   Ø
sand(III) soft:III real PRS.NTRL-3SG.A- be.NPST

'The sand is really soft.' [W06:0238]

A verb stem can be moved out of its usual position after the prefixal complex and modified with *ya* in a construction meaning 'to really Verb'. The stem+*ya* occurs immediately before the verb complex, which is headed by the Auxiliary, as in (256). The structure could be translated literally as 'I did real-seeing'.

(256) The speaker had been accused of lying about witnessing an earlier event.

mombali k-a-   Ø,   anep   idih   ya   ka-no-   n-a
nonsense PRS.NTRL-3SG.A- be.NPST EMPH:III see:3SG.U real DIR-1.A- 1.U-AUX

'That's nonsense, I really saw it.' [W06:0214]

With nouns denoting body parts, *ya* can indicate that one is referring to a spot that is really where the body part is, and not just close to it. This use is only attested with verbs of hitting, shooting, spearing, etc., as in (257), from a hunting story. This use of *ya* is synonymous with the use of the preposed modifier *mbya* shown in (275) below.

(257) bekay   ya   s-ø-o-   deh
heart(III) real ONLY-3SG.A-3SG.DAT- shoot:III.U

'He just shot it right in the heart.' [W02:0138]

The 'exact spot' use of *ya* is also found with nouns denoting places, as in the two following examples. All attestations of this use are with verbs of motion or position.

(258) [...] *yaba-kayi,   hekay   ya   ka-d-ø-   umak-a-ti*
      big-cassowary clearing real DIR-DUR-3SG.A- be.running-EXT-DUR
'a big cassowary, it was running right in the clearing.' [W11:0944]

(259) *uhe   yaba-rusa uhe,   anup   elet   ya   nda-d-a-p-   tel*
      PROX:II big-deer(II) PROX:II EMPH:II far.end real LOC-DUR-3SG.A-CT- be.lying
'This big deer, it was sleeping at the very far end [of the swamp].' [D05:0073]

With time expressions such as *kwemek* 'morning' and *usus* 'afternoon', *ya* narrows down reference to their most characteristic stage: *kwemek ya* 'early in the morning', *usus ya* 'late in the afternoon'. A corpus example:

(260) *usus   ya   menda-b-ø-   ay*
      afternoon(III) real PERF-ACT-3SG.A- become:III.U
'It's already late in the afternoon.' [W10:0359]

Nouns denoting body parts, locations, and stages of the day are clearly gradeable — something can be 'more or less' in a place, and one can debate when morning turns into noon — so it makes sense that Coastal Marind uses a single degree modifier to intensify these concepts.

Instead of describing *ya* as being polyfunctional (with multiple context-dependent interpretations) one could perhaps say that *X ya* means something like 'an undeniable instance of X': everybody would agree that 5pm is *usus* 'afternoon', and everybody would agree that the hunter in (257) hit the heart, and that the sand in (255) is soft, and so on. This approach to the meaning of *ya* undermines its ability to act as a test for distinguishing the word classes noun and adjective (cf. §3.1.2).

7.6.3 Additive *ap* 'also'

The additive particle *ap* 'also' is placed after the constituent over which it has scope:

(261) Discussing preparations for sago processing.
      nok nahan   ap   mano-   kaha⟨h⟩ib,   yoy se   mbya me-   yol
      1   1.EMPH also FUT:1.A- tie⟨IV.U⟩   2PL only NEG   NAFUT:2PL.A-   beat.sago
      wanangga
      children
'I myself will also put the [washing troughs (IV)] in place, it won't be only you children beating the sago.' [W19:0334]

(262) A hunting story. A wallaby was hiding in the tall grass, but the hunters didn't approach it.

Vitalis	ap	mbya	ø-a-p-	yanid,
V.	also	NEG	NTRL-3SG.A-CT-	move.forward

nggu	kumay	epe	mbya	ø-a-	kw-atin
grass.sp	inside	DIST:III	NEG	NTRL-3SG.A-	INESS-stand

'Vitalis didn't go forward either, he didn't stand in the *nggu* grass.' [W11:0745]

Example (263) shows that *ap* can be floated and placed after the verb. It is somewhat unclear what the scope or function of *ap* is in this sentence, but I assume that it refers to the fact that the truck-driving also occurred where the church was standing.[3]

(263) Preceding context: "The truck drove along the beach. An old church was standing there."

yahun	epe	k-a-	hwilug	ap
canoe	there	DIR-3SG.A-	travel.along.edge	also

'That's also where the truck drove along.' [W10:0492]

7.7 Quantification

There is no distinct quantifier word class in Coastal Marind, but several words have quantificational uses, as described below. The words *isi* 'other' (§7.7.1) and *mbya* 'all, completely' (§7.7.2) appear in the modifier slot within the NP, whereas the amount quantifiers described in §7.7.3 are clause-level adjuncts.

Other items with related meanings are *se* 'only' (§6.1.7) and *ap* 'also' (§7.6.3).

7.7.1 *isi* 'other, some'

This common modifier usually means 'other', as in (264). It usually occurs in the modifier slot preceding the modified noun, but also allows non-contiguous expression, as in (265).

(264)

ehe	isi	nggat	emba	k-a-	y-a	awan
here	other	dog	side	DIR-3SG.A-	2|3PL.U-AUX	run.PL

'The other dogs were running somewhere else [...]' [W11:0721]

---

[3] The translation I got for this sentence was *mobil juga lari di situ*, literally 'car also drive there'. The scope of Malay *juga* is ambiguous in such sentences.

(265) isi   ah-in-   uma⟨y⟩ah   ember
      other IMP-ALL-   go⟨2SG.A⟩   bucket(m)
      'Go get another bucket!'   [W06:0112]

Without a head nominal, *isi* singles out one referent, or a set of referents, from a larger group or sequence. In (266), the structure *isi..., isi...* means 'some [did X], others [did Y]':

(266) isi   kay   ø-a-   nayam,   isi   ku ti   ø-a-   nayam
      other road NTRL-3SG.A-   come.PL   other raft with NTRL-3SG.A-   come.PL
      'Some came by land, others came by rafts.'   [D08:0019]

As the first member of a nominal compound, *isi* has an evaluative function, roughly according to the pattern *isi-X* 'quite some X, an extraordinary X'. In (267) Yustina Mahuze had been recounting some feats of her eldest son, and calls him *isi-anem*, literally 'other-man'. In (268), from a story, the speaker had been describing how the villagers in Onggari (the official name; this village is called *Wanggali* in Wambi) had stared at them as they walked through the village at a time before inter-village travel became common. The speaker calls them *isi-kin* '(lit.) other-eye', perhaps something like English '[they were] all eyes', i.e. they kept on staring.

(267) The speaker is praising her son.
      Budi anep   isi-anem   ka-bat-ø-   ø
      B.   EMPH:I other-man(I)   PRS.NTRL-AFF-3SG.A-   be.NPST
      'Budi is really extraordinary.'   [W11:0139]

(268) Wanggali lik   isi-kin   k-a-   ø,   ado
      W.   from:I/II.PL   other-eye PRS.NTRL-3SG.A-   be.NPST INTERJ
      'The Onggari people like to stare at people, oh my!'   [W10:0352]

Compounded with a verb stem, *isi* can mean 'wrongly'. In the next example, taken from the same story as (268), the speaker realises that he made a mistake in the telling that needs to be corrected. This sentence features *isi* compounded with the nominally used verb stem *lay* 'tell', predicated by the Auxiliary, so a literal rendition could be 'I did other-telling to you'.

(269) mbya ka, isi-lay   s-ak-um-a-   n-a   epe
      no   other-tell   ONLY-1.A-FRUS-2SG.DAT-   1.U-AUX   DIST:III
      'Oh no, I told it to you wrongly.'   [W10:0113]

7.7.2 *mbya* 'all, completely'

The word *mbya* has two diametrically opposed functions: as a negator (§18.4.1), and as a quantifier-like element, described here.

In its quantifier-like use, *mbya* is always placed before the quantified nominal (a noun or adjective). A sentence of the form '*mbya* boys danced' means "Of those who danced, all were boys". A corpus example:

(270) nahe   ipe,   mbya kyasom ø-d-a-   ya-hwala
      ancestors:1 DIST:I/II.PL   all   girl   NTRL-DUR-3SG.A-   2|3PL.U-be
      'Those ancestors, they were all women.'   [D08:0109–0110]

The meaning of *mbya* in such contexts is very similar to *se* 'only' and the Restrictive verb prefix *s-* (i.e. 'The ancestors were women only'; §6.1.7, §11.1.6). But *mbya* differs subtly from *se* in the perspective taken, and focuses on the exhaustion of the set (all member of the set are women), whereas *se/s-* focuses on the exclusion of non-members (no non-women are members of the set). A consequence of this is that *mbya* only occurs with nominals that refer to plural participants or mass nouns, whereas *se/s-* can have scope over an expression referring to a single individual too.

The typical syntactic functions of *mbya*-phrases are as copula complements, as in (270) above, and in (271), or as secondary predicates (§18.5), as in (272–273). In both these functions, the meaning is that the *mbya*-phrase exhaustively describes the referent.

(271)   Describing an injured body part.
        tagu mbya talagi   ø-d-a-   ya-hwala
        foot all   tendon(IV) NTRL-DUR-3SG.A- IV.U-be
        'The foot was all tendons, only tendons remained of the foot.   [W10:0020]

(272)   Explaining why a sitting platform broke, causing the people on it to fall down.
        mbya yaba-anim   ø-nan-d-e-p-   hamat-a isala
        all   big-people NTRL-1.A-DUR-1PL-CT- sit.PL-EXT sitting.platform
        'We were all big people sitting on the platform.'   [W19:0091]

(273)   In a story, some children cut sticks for beating someone up.[4]
        mbya dahwagis ka-d-na-   l-esad-a
        all   short:III DIR-DUR-3PL.A-   PLA-cut:III.U-EXT
        'They cut them all short.'

---
4 From Drabbe (1955, p. 156, l. 18), adapted to the Wambi dialect in consultation with a speaker.

Despite the gloss 'all', *mbya* does not express universal quantification, which distinguishes it from *otih* (§7.7.3), which can be used as a universal quantifier 'all'. In (274), the unavailable meaning 'we ate all the meat' could be expressed with *otih*, or even more likely, with the verb *balen* 'finish'.

(274) mbya muy   m-an-d-e-   yi
      all   meat(III) OBJ-1.A-DUR-1PL-   eat:III.U

'We ate only meat, we had an all-meat meal.'
* 'We ate all the meat.'

Some common expressions with *mbya* are *mbya hyakod* 'same' (lit. 'all one') and *mbya sangga* (lit. 'all hands'), used about hunters returning from a hunt without any catch, i.e. 'empty-handed'. With temporal nouns, *mbya* has a distributive meaning: *mbya yanid* 'every day', *mbya kwemek* 'every morning'.

The phrase *mbya X* can also mean roughly 'straight at X, right in the X'. This is observed primarily with verbs involving motion towards an entity, such as a body part (275), but also to express location in the middle of some space, as with *mbya mamuy* 'in the middle of the savanna' in (276). Cf. *ya*, which also has this meaning (§7.6.2).

(275) mbya muy   e=   k-ø-o-p-   yayahwig
      all   meat(III) PROX.III= DIR-3SG.A-3SG.DAT-CT- plant:III.U

'He shot [the arrow] right here in the flesh.'   [W02:0135]

(276) yales-aha   epe   te-ka-hat-ø-   kw-itala,
      sago.thatch-house(III) DIST:III GIV:III-PRS.NTRL-PRSTV-3SG.A-   INESS-be.standing

      mbya mamuy   epe
      all savanna(III) DIST:III

'A house made from thatch is standing there, right in the middle of the savanna.'   [W10:0392]

In addition, *mbya* has a specialised use in reciprocal contexts (§13.2), in which it combines with an emphatic pronoun such as *nahan* 'ourselves'. The addition of this combination seems to emphasise that all the agent participants of the verb are part of the reciprocal action, and not just a subset.[5]

(277) mbya nahan   ye   ma-n-d-inm-i-e-   anetok
      all 1.EMPH   INGRS OBJ-1.A-DUR-RCPR-RE-1PL-   divide:III.U

'We started dividing [the food] amongst each other.'   [W18:0262]

---

[5] Expressions such as *mbya nahan* are very frequent in the (elicited?) reciprocal examples given by Drabbe (1955), but they are fairly rare in my corpus.

7.7.3 Amount quantification

The words *otih* 'many, all', *sam* 'big', *papes* 'small' and *kosi* 'small' are used as adjuncts to express amount ('a lot', 'a little'). They are usually, but not always, placed in the pre-verbal syntactic slot.

Large amount is indicated by means of the words *otih* 'many, all' (for count nouns) or *sam* 'big' (for substances). Compare the count noun *betik* (an intrusive fish species, *Anabas testudineus*) in (278a), with the mass noun *bensin* in (278b). Some nouns, such as *kanis* 'betelnut', permit conceptualisation as either individuable entities or as a substance, and may combine with either *otih* or *sam* (278c). (See also §3.1.3.3)

(278) a. betik   otih/*sam ka-mo-   lemeh!
         climbing.perch(m) many/big DIR-FUT:2SG.A- catch:2|3PL.U
         'Catch lots of climbing perch!'

   b. bensin sam/*otih ndom k-a-nam-   Ø
      petrol big/many still PRS.NTRL-3SG.A-1.GEN- be.NPST
      'I still have a lot of petrol.'

   c. kanis   sam/otih ka-mo-   ka-man-em!
      betelnut big/many DIR-FUT:2SG.A WITH-come-VEN
      'Bring lots of betelnut!'

The word *kosi* 'small' is used in the same way but for small amounts ('a little, a few'), and does not show any mass/count distinction.[6]

When the quantifier occurs in the syntactic slot before the verb and refers to the amount of the O-argument, as in (278a) and (278c), the verb takes the so-called Directional prefix *k-* instead of the usual Object prefix *m-* (see §11.1.4.5).

The quantifier *otih* is ambiguous between 'many' and 'all', a type of vagueness that is familiar from several Australian languages (most famously Warlpiri; Bittner and Hale 1995). In (279), a speaker translated *otih* as 'all', but the 'many'-interpretation is possible too, i.e. "the lemons, which were numerous, we gave to...".

---

6 It is also possible to use the word *papis* (identical to the Gender IV form of the agreeing adjective *papes* 'small', §3.3.1) in the sense 'a few', but this use is only attested in elicited data, while *kosi* is common in the corpus. Drabbe's (1955: 23–24) mention of amount quantifiers in the Eastern dialect suggests a more complex situation than in the Western variety described here, with contrasts such as *papis basik* 'a few pigs' vs. *basik papes* 'a small amount of pig [meat]'. I suspect, however, that Drabbe misinterpreted the placement of the amount quantifier in the pre-verbal position (e.g. [basik] [papes] Verb) as a fact of NP-internal syntax (i.e. [basik papes]_NP Verb), when in fact it is an instantiation of the standard Topic–Focus–Verb Complex template.

(279) namaya lemon   epe   otih   mend-am-b-o-y-   og   anep,
      now   citrus.fruit(III) DIST:III many PERF-1.A-ACT-3SG.DAT-1PL- give EMPH:I

      pu-anem   epe
      Indonesian.man(I)   DIST:I

      'Then we gave all the citrus fruits to him, that Indonesian.'   [W21:0084]

7.8 Coordination

Noun phrases can be coordinated by simply juxtaposing them, as with *nok Yambaya* 'Yambaya and I' in (280).

(280) nok Yambaya mayan m-an-d-e-p-   lay-a-ti   a   in-yap
      1   Y.   speech OBJ-1.A-DUR-1PL-CT-   talk-EXT-DUR PTCL middle-night

      'Yambaya and I talked until the middle of the night.'   [W10:0244]

There is a common particle *a* (§6.3.3), which is optionally used after NPs that are being listed, as with the two coordinated placenames *Mangang a Wiyeb a* 'Mangang and Wiyeb' in (281), or the three coordinands *sayam a tuban a duy a* 'wallaby, bandicoot, and black bandicoot' in (282).

(281) yaba-anim   Mangang a   Wiyeb a   epe   nda-d-ø-   ya-hwala
      big-people M.   PTCL   W.   PTCL   there LOC-DUR-3SG.A-   2|3PL.U-be

      ipe
      DIST:I/II.PL

      'Lots of people were there in Mangang and Wiyeb.'   [W21:0227]

(282) Budi yap   ma-d-ø-   yus   tuban-sep,   sayam   a
      B.   night OBJ-DUR-3SG.A-   bake bandicoot-leaf.oven wallaby PTCL

      tuban   a   duy   a
      bandicoot PTCL black.bandicoot PTCL

      'At night Budi made a leaf oven with the bandicoot [meat]: [there was] wallaby, bandicoot and black bandicoot.'   [W11:0138-0139]

Despite its use in such enumerations, *a* is not primarily a coordinator 'and', but rather a particle that delineates a constituent from the rest of the utterance, and it is used as a topic marker (§18.3.3), a marker of hesitation, etc. It can also demarcate NPs that express alternatives, as in (283–284).

(283) During an expedition inland, a man was injured and could not walk without assistance.

ehe	namaya	nda-m-b-e-	n-a	og?	anem-sinik	a,	namakad-sinik
here	now	LOC-FUT:1.A-ACT-1PL-	1.U-AUX	do	man-carry	PTCL	thing-carry

a?
PTCL

'How shall we do now? Carry the things or carry the man?'   [W21:0208-0209]

(284) *yah mak-ap- w-esoh-a-m yapap a yopo*
but FUT:1.A-CT- 3SG.U-follow-EXT-VEN tomorrow PTCL day.after.tomorrow

'Then I will follow, tomorrow or in a few days.'   [W18:0254]

8 Overview of the verb

This short chapter is concerned with the morphological building blocks forming the verb complex (or simply verb) in Coastal Marind. I will use this label to refer to the part of the clause in which a verbal root combines with grammatical (inflectional) material expressing tense, person indexing, and a variety of other grammatical meanings. As will be clear from the following description, the Coastal Marind verb complex consists of adjacent, but phonologically independent, units that together make up a grammatical verb unit. This makes the Coastal Marind verb different from the verbs of languages such as English or French, in which the label 'verb' is used for phonologically unitary words representing an inflectional form of a verbal lexeme (e.g. *sings*, or *brought* in *brought up*).

Below, I first describe verbs as a word class (§8.1). I then outline the general structure of the verb complex (§8.2), and describe the ordering of prefixes (§8.3), including exceptional variation in their ordering (§8.3.2), as well as the structure of the verb stem (§8.4). Finally, some remarks on the suffixes that may be added at the end of the verb complex are given (§8.5).

8.1 Verbs as a word class

This section discusses the criteria that identify verbal lexemes, and distinguish these from the other large word class in the language, nominals. This distinction is generally easy to make, based on morphosyntactic criteria, because only verbs have the ability to combine with the rich inflectional morphology that characterises Coastal Marind. The prefixal complex is a structure that immediately precedes the verb stem; it is auxiliary-like since it forms a separate phonological word, but affix-like since it lacks any part that could be described as a (morphological or syntactic) 'head'. It is the verb stem that is listed in the dictionary, stripped of the material in the prefixal complex. Most verb stems can be morphologically complex, with stem forms marking Undergoer indexing and categories such as the Inessive (§16.6), Pluractional (§16.1) and Applicative formation (§13.1.4, §13.1.5). None of these categories are available to nominals.

Some words are used both as verbs and nominals. For example, *sasayi* 'work' can be used as a verb stem after the prefixal complex, as in (285a), or as a noun heading a referring expression (285b). Since *sasayi* does not participate in any of the stem alternations (e.g. Undergoer indexing) that would unambiguously identify it as originally being a verb, it is not possible to tell whether the verbal or nominal use is primary.

(285)   a. ah- sasayi!   b. nok en   sasayi
           IMP- work   1   POSS work
           'Work!'   'my work'

Heterosemous lexical items such as *sasayi* 'work' are rare, so their existence is not a problem for the distinction between verbs and nominals. Other examples that I am aware of are:

	As nominal	As verb
pig	'sunshine, heat from sun'	'become day/bright'
esol	'noise'	'make noise'
sinik	'things being carried'	'carry things'
kahek	'height'	'climb'

Other seemingly ambiguous noun/verb words turn out to be deverbal lexicalisations, derived by zero-conversion, because closer inspection reveals that they contain frozen verb stem morphology. For example, the noun *nasak* 'fight(ing)' is the Reciprocal stem (see §13.2) of the verb *usak* 'hit many times, fight'; the noun *yayahwig* 'pole supporting the washing trough during sago processing' is the Gender III stem of a verb 'plant, stick into the ground' (the stem used for planted items in Gender IV is *yayhwituk*), and so on. See also §3.7.1.

8.2 Macrostructure of the verb complex

The Coastal Marind verb maximally consists of three different parts, which are partially phonologically independent of each other, but form a single grammatical unit. These are: (i) the *prefixal complex*, a highly complicated affix cluster; (ii) a *verb stem*, which is often morphologically complex; and (iii) a small set of *outer suffixes* attaching after the verb stem.

In the Marind orthography adopted here, I show the boundary between the prefixal complex and the verb stem by means of a hyphen, as in (286a). This example features morphological material from all three parts of the verb complex. In the interlinear glossing, I adopt the convention of writing the prefixal complex with a blank space separating it from the verb stem,[1] with the rightmost prefix followed by a final trailing hyphen indicating that the affix cluster forms a grammatical unit with the following verb stem despite being independent phonological words (see below). These conventions are shown in example (286b), which shows the morphemic segmentation and visualises the tripartite structure of the verb complex.

---

[1] I thank Phillip Rogers for suggesting this solution.

(286) a. ndapanay-kadhetokam
'S/he will bring it back for us.'

b.

ndap-	a-	na-	y-	ka-	dh⟨e⟩tok	-a	-m
FUT-	3SG.A-	1.DAT-	1PL-	WITH-	return⟨3SG.U⟩	-EXT	-VEN

prefixal complex — verb stem — outer suffix

verb complex

The main reason for separating the prefixal complex from the verb stem is the complete lack of phonological integration between the two: the prefixal complex is a phonological word of its own. The alternations described in §2.5 (e.g. presence of epenthetic /a/) are found both within the Prefixal complex and the verb stem, but always apply separately within these domains, and not across them.

For example, there are no situations in which the phonological shape of the verb stem affects the realisation of affixal material belonging in the prefixal complex, and vice versa.[2] This contrasts with the situation *within* these two domains: in morphemic segmenting and concatenation it will often be necessary to state that some affix takes on a different shape because of the surrounding affixes. For example, within the prefixal complex, the vowel /o/ (as in the 2sg Actor Future prefix *mo-*) merges with initial /i/ of a following prefix, resulting in *u*, as in (287) (cf. §2.5.5). No such fusion happens if the following /i/ occurs in the verb stem, since the two vowels would then be separated by the boundary of the phonological word (288).

(287) /mo-is-ap-   atin/   → [mu.sap a.tin]   'you will step on (it)'
      FUT:2SG.A-SEP-CT- stand

(288) /mo-   itawip/   → [mo i.ta.wip]   'you will extinguish (it)'
      FUT:2SG.A- extinguish   (not *[mu.ta.wip])

Prosodically, the prefixal complex and the verb stem pattern like nominal compounds (§3.6), and receive main prominence on the last syllable of the next-to-last phonological word, so that the last syllable of the prefixal complex is stressed. For the verb in (287) we get

(289)   [mu.ˈsap atin]   'you will step on (it)'

---

2 The only potential counterexample is the realisation of the 3pl Actor prefix *n-*, which often groups phonologically with the verb stem, as discussed in §9.2.1.3.

The outer suffixes themselves appear to be more closely bound to the preceding material and are treated as affixes. Although not subject to any phonological alternations (which suggests that they are phonologically independent), they seem to lack the independence of the other parts of the verb complex as they never take stress, and only occur when a preceding host (the verb stem) is present. (See Chapter 2 for more information on phonology.)

The linear order of prefixal complex and verb stem is fixed, and no other constituents of the clause can intervene between the two, so their phonological independence is not matched by any syntactic freedom. Note that the prefixal complex occurs alone, with a zero verb stem, in non-past copula clauses (290) (see also §17.4). The fact that the prefixal complex is retained even when the copula has no phonological realisation could be seen as further evidence for its morphological independence vis-à-vis the verb stem.

(290) nu-say   e=   ka-bat-ø-om-   Ø
      sleep-place PROX= DIR-AFF-3SG.A-3SG.GEN- be.NPST
      'Here's the poor one's bed.'   [D09:0060]

The lack of integration between the prefixal complex — which is the main locale for inflectional information in the language — and the associated verb stem is decidedly odd given the (reasonable) intuition that inflectional material should occur inside the verb word, ideally as affixes bound to a lexical root (as in European languages), or at least attached to some auxiliary-like element. Looking at verbs from other polysynthetic languages, it is evident that this intuition must be discarded. Witness, for example, the phonologically independent 'disjunct' and 'conjunct' domains in Athabaskan morphology (e.g. Sapir and Hoijer 1967, McDonough 2000 for Navajo), or the mismatches between the verbal and phonological words in Yimas (as discussed by Foley 1991: 81), Cree and Dakota (Russell 1999), Jarawara (Dixon 2002b) or Dalabon (Evans et al. 2008); see also Bickel and Zúñiga (2017) for discussion of multi-unit verbs in polysynthetic languages. Linguists are probably more ready to accept phonologically independent affix clusters in the nominal domain: think of articles, which commonly express grammatical features (e.g. definiteness, number, case) without being bound to the head noun, and often without having much in the way of a lexical root — yet few linguists would find it necessary to say that e.g. the German articles are a 'periphrastic' expression of those features. It is perhaps a helpful analogy to think of the Marind Prefix Cluster as a 'verb article' expressing features relevant to the following verb stem, just like the German article *dem* expresses the features definite, dative and singular in the NP *dem Garten* 'the garden'.

8.3 Affix ordering in the prefixal complex

In addition to their phonological realisation, the main issues in the description of affixes belonging to the prefixal complex are their syntagmatic order (i.e. which affix comes after which) and the paradigmatic oppositions into which they enter (which affixes are mutually exclusive). The main descriptive device that I will use in the account of the morphotactics is a system of linearly ordered position classes.[3] In such a system, strictly ordered affix classes are stipulated, such that members of a class may appear after members of the preceding class, and before members of the following class, whereas members belonging to the same position class are mutually exclusive and may not co-occur.

The position class system for the Coastal Marind prefixes is rather unwieldy, and contains 17 prefixal positions, shown in Figure 8.1. The classes are numbered from −17 up to −1, with −17 being the leftmost prefix position (furthest removed from the verb stem) and −1 being the rightmost position (closest to the stem). A well-formed verb is constructed by scanning the position class template from left, picking up the affixes that are required by the syntax and semantics, and then assembling them into a verb according to their relative position in the class template.

Horizontal lines indicate multi-class prefixes, which straddle several position classes, as explained in §8.3.1. Variable ordering of some prefixes occurs under certain conditions, as discussed in §8.3.2.

Two illustrative examples with prefixes from 5 different position classes each are in (291). The number corresponding to each class has been added below the morphemic glosses. Note that the prefixes are ordered as prescribed by the ordering of the position classes, and that no more than one member of each class is present in the prefixal complex.

(291) a. *a-   p-   a-   na-   y-   man*
         DEP- FUT- 3SG.A- 1.DAT- ACPN- come
         −15   −13   −10   −5   −3   (Stem)
         'if s/he brings him/her for me'

   b. *ta   ma-   h-   am-   b-   e-   og   -e*
       what OBJ- ROG- 1.A- ACT- 1PL- do   -IPFV
             −16   −14   −13   −11   −4   (Stem)   (outer suffix)
       'What are we going to do?'

---

3 See Bloomfield (1962) for a classic example of position classes in the North American descriptivist tradition. For a theoretically informed account of a Papuan morphological system in terms of position classes, see Inkelas (1993) on Nimboran (an isolate of Northwestern New Guinea). My description of the position class model takes inspiration from Crysmann and Bonami (2015).

Position	Label
-1	Contessive
-2	Prioritive / Distal
-3	Accompaniment
-4	1st person Plural
-5	Dative
-6	Repetitive
-7	Separative / Allative
-8	Frustrative
-9	Genitive
-10	3rd Actor — Reciprocal
-11	Speaker attitude
-12	Past Durative
-13	1st, 2nd Actor / General Future
-14	Interrogative / Jussive (*) — Prohibitive — Hortative (*), Imperative
-15	Dependent — Non-asserted Future
-16	Orientation — Polar Qs, Perfect, Deictic
-17	Given — Continuative

Position 0: (Verb stem)

Fig. 8.1: Position classes of the prefixal complex. Assignment is tentative for prefixes marked with (*).

8.3.1 Multi-class prefixes and paradigmatic alignment

Certain prefixes are paradigmatically opposed to members of several adjacent position classes. For example, whenever the Imperative prefix *ah-* (§19.1.1) is used, no prefix from position classes –17 to –12 may occur in the same verb form. The 'leftmost' position class whose members can follow the Imperative is class –11, which is home to the so-called Speaker Attitude prefixes such as the Affectionate *bat-* (giving a nuance of pity or affection to the sentence, 'poor one'):

(292) a-bat- nayam!
       IMP-AFF- come.PL

   'Come here, poor ones!'

I describe such multi-class prefixes as spanning several position classes. Multi-class prefixes are shown in the lower part of Figure 8.1 with horizontal lines indicating their positional range.

A notable fact about the Coastal Marind position class system is that many of the prefixes in Figure 8.1 are in paradigmatic opposition despite being syntagmatically distinct, i.e. belonging to different position classes. For example, the 1st, 2nd and 3rd person Actor prefixes (used to index the agent-like participant of verbs such as 'dance' and 'hit'; §9.2) are mutually exclusive and may not co-occur in the same verb form. However, the position class system in Figure 8.1 only predicts the paradigmatic opposition between the 1st and 2nd person prefix sets, since they are members of the same position class (class –13). The 3rd person Actor prefixes are positioned closer to the verb stem, in position class –10, which means that their incompatibility with the other Actor prefixes does not follow from the logic of the position class system.

Such mismatches between paradigmatic and syntagmatic oppositions are not unusual (for an illustration from Nepali, see Crysmann and Bonami 2015: 316–317). Other examples of paradigmatically opposed prefixes from separate position classes are the General Future prefixes (of class –13) & Past Durative *d-* (class –12), which are incompatible on semantic grounds, and the Dependent *ah-* (class –15) & Interrogative *h-* (class –14), which are incompatible since they are restricted to different syntactic contexts (subordinate clauses and content questions respectively). Such interdependencies must be posited independently of the position class template, which diminishes the predictive power of the approach somewhat.

8.3.2 Affix mobility

A reasonable expectation is that the ordering of morphs is stable — one would not expect to encounter a new English verb that places the Present 3sg *-s* before the stem instead of after it. The ordering of morphs in Coastal Marind is generally fixed, but

8.3.2.1 Affix reordering to optimise metric structure

Some inflectional prefixes show variable order, apparently in order to improve syllable shapes. Constraints on phonological well-formedness is a well-known factor affecting variability in affix ordering (e.g. Noyer 1994 and Y. Kim 2010).

First, consider the 1pl prefix *e-*, which is assigned to position class −4 in Figure 8.1. This prefix is a role-neutral person marker used whenever one of the arguments of a verb is 1st person plural (see §9.5). The 1pl prefix displays positional instability and occurs either before or after the prefixes of class −2 (the Prioritive *ka-* and Remote *an-*). I describe the prefix as belonging to position class −4, i.e. a position before the Prioritive *ka-* of class −2, but I will show that when placement of *e-* according to the position class system would lead to a clash with phonological requirements, the prefix 'moves' and is realised *after* the Prioritive *ka-* of class −2, i.e. in a position that does not follow from the ordering of the classes.

The data in example (293) show the placement of 1pl *e-* under normal circumstances. In (293a), the prefix occurs before the Prioritive *ka-*. Example (293b) shows 1pl *e-* preceded by the homophonous 2|3pl Dative prefix *e-*. The sequence /e-e-/ is realised [ej] (written *e-y-*), i.e. the 1pl *e-* is realised as a glide [j] (written *y-*) when it occurs after another tautosyllabic vowel (alternatively, it can be deleted).

(293) a. *epe nd-an-d-e-ka- hamat-a*
there LOC-1.A-DUR-1PL-PRI- sit.PL-EXT
'We were sitting there first.' [W03:0162]

b. *mak-e-y-p- esoh*
FUT:1.A-2|3PL.DAT-1PL-CT- follow
'We will follow you.' [W08:0008]

Recall from §2.4 that Coastal Marind avoids placing closed syllables in the penultimate position of the phonological word, whereas the final syllable of a word may be closed. This means that a sequence of prefixes that creates a closed penultimate syllable must be readjusted, usually by inserting epenetic /a/ (§2.4.1). But epenthesis does not occur when the placement of 1pl *e-*, in its realisation as [j], would create a closed penultimate syllable: instead the 1pl prefix is moved to a position where it does not create an illegal sequence of syllables.

This situation occurs if the Prioritive *ka-* (which always occurs in the final syllable of the prefixal complex) is used together with a vowel-final prefix such as the 2sg Dative *a-* (of position class –5). If 1pl *e-* is added to this sequence, the position class system predicts that it will be placed between 2sg Dative *a-* and Prioritive *ka-*, thereby creating a sequence /a-e-ka-/. This sequence would be realised as *aj.ka]_ω, i.e. as an illegal syllable sequence *VG.CV]_ω. In order to avoid this outcome, 1pl *e-* shifts its position and appears after the Prioritive, forming the acceptable sequence /a-ka-e/ → a.kaj]_ω.

Below are two examples illustrating this ordering, with the 2sg Dative *a-* (294a) and the 3sg Dative *o-* (294b).

(294) a. ehe   mak-is-a-ka-y-   hok
         here FUT:1.A-SEP-2SG.DAT-PRI-1PL- lie.down.PL
         'We will lie down here by you first.'

     b. mat-o-ka-y-p-   takin
        HORT-3SG.DAT-PRI-1PL-CT-   wait
        'Let's wait for her first.'   [W21:0165]

Apparently, the constraint against a pretonic heavy syllable is stronger than the faithfulness to the linear ordering of the affixes posited in Figure 8.1, as *ka-* and *e-* (realised as *y-*) appear to have switched positions. The same reordering also occurs with the Accompaniment *e-* of position class –3, under the same circumstances. Compare the following examples, in which the Accompaniment *e-* (or *y-*) has a comitative-like function:

(295) a. katal   a-bt-e-ka-   man!
         money   IMP-AFF-ACPN-PRI-   come
         'Please bring money first!'

     b. katal   a-bta-na-ka-y-   man!
        money   IMP-AFF-1.DAT-PRI-ACPN-   come
        'Please bring my money first!'

A similar case, in which exceptional affix ordering is motivated by phonotactic constraints, is the partial affixal metathesis affecting the 1st person Dative prefix *na-*, as described in §9.3.1.

Finally, there is considerable variation in the placement of 2nd person Actor prefixes, especially in combination with prefixes of the shape /C-/, such as the Durative *d-* and the Actualis *b-*. The 2nd person Actor prefixes would be expected to occur before these prefixes on the basis of the position template, but when these combinations would produce onset-less VC-syllables, the order is often reversed to produce a canonical CV sequence. A paradigm in which this 'deviating' ordering of 2nd person Actor prefixes occurs with both 2sg *o-* and 2pl *e-* is in Table 8.1. Here, all combinations of Actor and Dative prefixes are given, along with the Durative Past *d-* (of position class

–12). Note that the 1st person Actor prefix *nak-* (realised as *nan-*) occurs in its expected position before the Durative past, whereas the 2nd person Actor prefixes are place after *d-*, despite belonging to the same position class as 1st person *nak-* (class –13).

Cf. the Prohibitive paradigms for similar phenomena affecting the 2sg and 2pl prefixes (§19.1.4).

8.3.2.2 Affix reordering to avoid deletion: the Dependent floating *h*

The Dependent prefix *ah-* (which forms subordinate clauses, §20.1) is the sole member of position class –15, and almost always occurs as the leftmost prefix of a subordinate verb, before all other prefixes. In certain environments, however, the segment /h/ in *ah-* detaches and 'floats' into the onset of the final syllable of the prefixal complex, leaving the initial /a/ behind. This *h*-floating occurs before certain consonant-initial prefixes, i.e. in environments where /h/ would normally be lost due to the rules in §2.5.4, so this phenomenon allows /h/ to escape deletion, and resurface in the final, stressed syllable of the prefixal complex.

Consider first (296a), in which *ah-* appears unaltered, with /h/ retained, and (296b), in which /h/ is dropped. (The brackets in the gloss line indicate the boundaries of the subordinate clause.)

(296) a.   oy ah-o-d-   yet
            [2SG DEP-2SG.A-DUR- be.moving]
            'when you went'

       b.   kay a-no-d-   tak   nok
            [path DEP-1.A-DUR- make.way 1   ]
            'the path that I was making'   [M02:0655]

In (296a), /h/ is retained thanks to its position before the vowel-inital 2SG.A prefix *o-*. In (296b), /h/ is deleted because it occurs before the consonant initial 1.A prefix *no-*, and because there is not enough prefixal material after *no-* to allow /h/ to be rescued by floating into another syllable.

The deletion vs. *in situ* retention of /h/ in (296a–b) contrasts with the *h*-floating in (297). In (297a), the addition of the Contessive prefix *ap-* provides an extra syllable to which /h/ can float, while the /a/ stays behind, before the 1.A prefix (here, its allomorph *nak-*, realised as *nka-*; see §9.2.1.1). Similarly, the presence of the 3SG.DAT prefix *o-* at the end of the prefixal complex in (297b) provides a landing site for floated /h/, while /a/ remains before the Durative *d-*.

(297) a.   a-nka-h-ap-   mil-em
            [DEP-1.A-DEP-CT- be.sitting-VEN]
            'while I was sitting' (coming here on the motorcycle)

Tab. 8.1: Paradigm of *laɣ* 'talk, tell' showing combinations of Actor (in boldface) and Dative marking with Past Durative *d-*. (*) indicates forms in positions in which Actor prefixes occur in positions that deviate from the order stipulated by the position classes.

	1SG.DAT *na-*	1PL.DAT *na-...e-/y-*	2SG.DAT *a-*	2PL.DAT *e-*	3SG.DAT *o-*	3PL.DAT *e-*
1SG.A *nak-*	—	—	*nak-d-a-laɣ* 'I told you (sg)'	*nan-d-e-laɣ* 'I told you (pl)'	*nan-d-o-laɣ* 'I told him/her'	*nan-d-e-laɣ* 'I told them'
1PL.A *nak-...e-/y-*	—	—	*nan-d-a-y-laɣ* 'we told you (sg)'	*nan-d-e-y-laɣ* 'we told you (pl)'	*nan-d-o-y-laɣ* 'we told him/her'	*nan-d-e-y-laɣ* 'we told them'
2SG.A *o-*	*d-o-na-laɣ* (*) 'you (sg) told me'	*d-o-na-y-laɣ* (*) 'you (sg) told us'	—	—	*d-ø-o-laɣ* (*) 'you (sg) told him/her'	*o-d-e-laɣ* 'you (sg) told them'
2PL.A *e-*	*d-e-na-laɣ* (*) 'you (pl) told me'	*d-e-na-y-laɣ* (*) 'you (pl) told us'	—	—	*e-d-o-laɣ* 'you (pl) told him/her'	*e-d-e-laɣ* 'you (pl) told them'
3SG.A *a-*	*d-a-na-laɣ* 's/he told me'	*d-a-na-y-laɣ* 's/he told us'	*d-ø-a-laɣ* 's/he told you (sg)'	*d-ø-e-laɣ* 's/he told you (pl)'	*d-ø-o-laɣ* 's/he told him/her'	*d-ø-e-laɣ* 's/he told them'
3PL.A *n-*	*d-e-na-laɣ* 'they told me'	*d-e-na-y-laɣ* 'they told us'	*da-n-a-laɣ* 'they told you (sg)'	*da-n-e-laɣ* 'they told you (pl)'	*da-n-o-laɣ* 'they told him/her'	*da-n-e-laɣ* 'they told them'

b. *yay   a-d-a-h-o-   laɣ-ti*
   [uncle DEP-DUR-3SG.A-DEP-3SG.DAT- talk-DUR]
   'when uncle was talking to him' [W11:0368]

As seen in the interlinear glossing above, I follow a suggestion from the Leipzig Glossing Rules for the treatment of bipartite elements (Comrie et al. 2015, Rule 8) and simply repeat the category label (DEP-) for each part of the discontinuous morph.

8.3.3 Further remarks on position class systems

Whereas the position class approach has several advantages (such as restricting affix order in a straightforward way) it also presents some drawbacks. Firstly, the large number of position classes does not reflect the number of affixes that are found on verbs as used in actual discourse: no verb containing morphology from all 17 position classes has been attested, and verb forms with more than 7 or 8 prefixes are extremely rare. In fact, verbs inflected by means of only 2–4 prefixes probably make up the majority of the total number of verb forms in my corpus.

Secondly, there are many affix combinations that are ruled out independently of the restrictions following from the organisation of the position classes. In most cases there are clear semantic reasons explaining the incompatibility. For example, 2sg Actor *o-* and 3pl Actor *n-* belong to different position classes (−14 and −11 respectively), which makes them compatible on purely morphotactic grounds, but since person/number of Actor can only be marked once within a single verb it is impossible to employ both prefixes in one form.

Thirdly, many of the position classes in Figure 8.1 are set up to account for only one member (e.g. positions −1 and −6). This diminishes the value of the position class approach, since such single-member classes only serve to restrict syntagmatic ordering, and provide no information on paradigmatic oppositions.[4]

Position class systems have enjoyed a renaissance in the theoretical literature in the current century, and play an important role in the framework of Stump (2001). Major criticism against position classes as a descriptive device was given in Muysken (1986) and Rice (2000). Muysken points out that Yokoyama's (1951) 'slot matrix' cannot predict the variable affix ordering observed in Quechua, that numerous co-occurrence restrictions are unaccounted for, and that the slot matrix implies a flat structure rather than the hierarchical organisation that Muysken posits based on scope effects. The last point is crucial for Rice's deconstruction of the Athabaskan position class systems,

---

[4] Note also that there is generally no reason to consider empty positions in an inflected Coastal Marind verb to be filled by 'meaningful zeros' (e.g. there is no reason to consider an empty −6 position as marking a 'non-repetitive' meaning by means of a zero morph). The major exceptions are the 3sg Actor prefix ø- and the past tense allomorph of the Neutral Orientation; see §9.2.1.3 and §11.1.

which in her analysis follow from principles of scopal relations between quantifier-like affixes, thus minimising the need for arbitrary linear stipulation. Most of these considerations do not apply to Coastal Marind: even if some affixes could be said to have quantifier-like meanings (e.g. *s-* 'only', the Reciprocal *enam-* and prefixes with applicative-like functions such as Allative *ind-*), none of them display variable ordering or any other behaviour suggesting scopal relations within the inflectional morphology.

8.4 Structure of the verb stem

I use the label 'verb stem' for the morphological unit that appears after the prefixal complex, and to which outer suffixes such as the Imperfective *-e* (see §8.5) may attach. The verb stem is a site of considerable morphological complexity in itself, since it is the locus of Undergoer indexing (Chapter 10) and hosts several derivational categories. Here, the position of these affixes will be reviewed in brief.

The exponence of Undergoer indexing is treated in detail in Chapter 10. Of the affixes that appear attached directly to the verb stem, the Undergoer affixes are closest to the stem. Their position as prefixes, suffixes or infixes depend on the inflectional class of the verb (§10.3). The stem, including the Undergoer exponents, forms the base onto which the derivational affixes attach.

Four derivational categories are realised as affixes on the stem: the Comitative-Instrumental applicative (§13.1), the Pluractional (§16.1), and the Inessive (§16.6), which are prefixes, and the Extended (§14.2.3), which is a suffix. The applicative prefix and the Inessive are mutually exclusive and attach before the Pluractional prefix, so the relative position of these affixes can be diagrammed as in Figure 8.2.

Inessive *kw-* etc. Instrumental-Comitative *k-*	Pluract. *l-, e-* etc.	BASE	Extended *-la*

Fig. 8.2: Structure of morphologically complex verb stems

I label the four categories associated with the verb stem (except Undergoer indexing) derivational in order to distinguish them from the inflectional affixes of the prefixal complex and the outer suffix position. The main behavioural difference setting these two types of affixes apart is that the derivational affixes (but also the Undergoer affixes) move along with the stem in constructions that involve displacement of the stem, whereas all inflectional affixes stay in their original position, attached to the Auxiliary *wa*, which replaces the lexical verb stem in such constructions. See e.g. compounds

Tab. 8.2: The outer suffixes

Suffix	Label	Gloss	Description
-e, -et	Non-past Imperfective	IPFV	§14.2.2
-ti	Past Durative	DUR	§14.2.1
-em	Venitive	VEN	§16.7
-em	Plural Imperative	PL.IMP	§19.1.1
-um	Counterfactual	CTFT	§15.1
-ma	Past Habitual	PST.HAB	
-made	Present Habitual	PRS.HAB	§14.2.6
-motok	Future Habitual	FUT.HAB	

involving verb stems (§3.6), verb stems as the object of a postposition (§6.1) or verb stems predicated by the Auxiliary (§17.2).

8.5 The outer suffixes

In addition to the prefixal complex and the verb stem, the verb complex often contains a final suffix from a group of suffixes that I call the outer suffixes. These markers show relatively little integration with the preceding material and could perhaps be described as clitics instead of suffixes. I will go through their general characteristics below.

The outer suffixes are listed in Table 8.2, with references to sections describing their use. A maximum of one suffix from this affix class may occur within a single verb, i.e. the outer suffixes are mutually incompatible and can be described as making up one position class.

Phonologically the outer suffixes are rather loosely bound to the verb stem, whereas grammatically they are dependent on a preceding host and never occur independently. Thus, the outer suffixes behave like the prefixal complex and form a single phonological word, but an outer suffix may not form a grammatical word on its own. I will briefly review the relevant facts here.

The outer suffixes exhibit no contextual allomorphy (with the marginal exception of Venitive -em, see §16.7), and never trigger phonological changes in the preceding stem. Unlike the various affixes that derive verb stems the presence of an outer suffix never triggers epenthesis or syncope in the preceding stem. The presence of an outer suffix in the verb complex never triggers vowel gradation (§2.5.1) in the preceding stem, i.e. the addition of a syllable (or two, in the case of -made and -motok) does not affect the syllable count regulating vowel gradation in the stem.

In contrast, one could argue that in certain other respects the outer suffixes are more tightly attached to the preceding verb stem than the prefixal complex is to the following verb stem: (i) none of the outer suffixes can occur alone (e.g. *motok* may not be used as an independent word, only attached to a verb stem), whereas the prefixal complex frequently occurs independently (namely in non-verbal predication, where it functions as a copula; §17.4); (ii) there is never a (disfluency) pause between the stem and an outer suffix, whereas such pauses are frequent between the prefixal complex and the verb stem.

I let these latter facts take precedence in deciding to treat -*e* etc. not as postposed function words or clitics but as suffixes. This solution was also favoured by speakers in orthography discussions.[5]

---

[5] The speakers' preference to write the suffixes attached to the stem rather than separated from it is probably due to their shortness, and at least one speaker reported that it is better to write the longest suffix -*motok* as a separate word.

9 Participant indexing I: The Actor, Dative and Genitive prefixes

This chapter contains an overview of participant indexing on the verb (§9.1), and detailed descriptions of Actor (§9.2), Dative (§9.3), Genitive (§9.4) and role-neutral 1pl (§9.5) indexing. Special uses of indexing are described in the section on inclusory and associative indexing (§9.6).

Note that a terminological distinction is made between *indexing* and *agreement* in this grammar. Indexing is used only in relation to the verbal affixes in the four affix sites just mentioned. Agreement is used for agreement in gender among nominal targets, which primarily is manifested as stem-internal vowel-alternations in e.g. demonstratives and adjectives (Chapter 5), and for verb prefixes that show the same patterns of vowel alternations (e.g. the Continuative, §14.2.4).

9.1 Overview of participant indexing

9.1.1 General and typological characteristics

Four types of marking are used to index participants on the verb:
- The Actor (gloss: A) prefixes (§9.2) index the agent-like participant of transitive and intransitive verbs.
- The Dative (DAT) prefixes (§9.3) index recipients in transfer events.
- The Genitive (GEN) prefixes (§9.4) are used optionally to index the possessor of an S/O-argument.
- Undergoer (U) alternations in the verb stem index the patient-like participant of transitive and intransitive verbs.

In addition to these role-marking indexing categories, there is a role-neutral prefix *e-* which indexes a 1pl argument (§9.5).

In (298a–d) are four simple examples that illustrate different combinations of indexing types within single verb forms. All four verbs contain Actor prefixes, which is the only obligatory indexing category. Undergoer indexing is observed in examples (298b) and (298d), on the verbs *dahip* 'burn' and *usak* 'hit repeatedly, beat up' respectively. Example (298c) expresses a transfer event with the recipient indexed by the Dative prefix. In (298d), the affected possessor of the patient-like argument *nggat* 'dogs' is indexed by means of the Genitive prefix, while the Undergoer affix indexes the patient.

(298) a. Actor indexing
Budoy ø-a- ayi
B. NTRL-3SG.A- say
'Budoy said [it].' [W11:0082]

b. Actor + Undergoer indexing
koy ø-a- daha⟨y⟩ip
slaked.lime NTRL-3SG.A- burn⟨2SG.U⟩
'The slaked lime burnt you.' [W13:0095]

c. Actor + Dative indexing
nok ø-nak-o- ayi koyhi-anem
1 NTRL-1.A-3SG.DAT- say white-man
'I said [it] to Bruno.' [W08:0013]

d. Actor + Genitive + Undergoer indexing
nggat oy ø-o-nam- i-sak
dog 2SG NTRL-2SG.A-1.GEN- 2|3PL.U-hit.PLA
'You beat up my dogs.' [M02:0393]

Of these, the first three, which belong in the prefixal complex, are described in this chapter. Undergoer indexing, which is part of the verb stem, is described in its own chapter, Chapter 10. This section briefly outlines the system as a whole, and places it in areal and typological context.

Coastal Marind participant indexing can be described as exhibiting semantic alignment (Malchukov 2008), because the sole participant of an agentive intransitive verb, such as 'dance', is indexed by means of the Actor prefixes (299a), whereas the sole participant of a patientive intransitive verb, such as 'fall', is indexed by means of Undergoer indexing (299b). Other terms for this type of alignment are split intransitivity (Merlan 1985) and agentive alignment (Mithun 1991). There is no 'fluidity' in the Coastal Marind system: each intransitive verb indexes its participant according to one, and only one, pattern. For a list of patientive verbs, see §12.2.2.

(299) a. nok ø-no-d- mahay
1 NTRL-1.A-DUR- dance
'I danced.'

b. nok ø-a- hi-n
1 NTRL-3SG.A- fall-1.U
'I fell.'

Actor indexing is obligatory in all predicatively used verb forms (the only exceptions are commands formed with the Imperative *ah-* and the Hortative *mat-*). Verbs that lack an agent-like participant (such as certain avalent weather verbs, and patientive verbs) automatically appear with 3sg Actor indexing, as seen with 'fall' above (299b).

Dative and Genitive indexing primarily express recipient- and possessor-like roles, but a smallish number of verbs are lexically specified as having one or the other series as part of their indexing template (e.g. 'meet someone', which always indexes its O-argument by means of the Genitive series). Such verbs are listed in §9.3.2 and §9.4.2.

Undergoer indexing in the verb stem may be either prefixing, suffixing, infixing or, for certain verbs, a combination of these, as discussed at length in Chapter 10. The presence of Undergoer indexing is lexically restricted to about half of the verbal lexicon. The other verbs do not exhibit stem alternation according to the features of the patient-like participant. Various languages in the Trans-New Guinea family (to which the Anim languages probably belong; §1.2.1) restrict object indexing to a small subset of all transitive verbs (Suter 2018, Windschuttel 2018). Examples are Mian, which has seven verbs that take an object prefix (Fedden 2011: 265), or Usan, with three prefixing verbs (Reesink 1987: 108). Coastal Marind is an outlier in the Trans-New Guinean context, because it has extended this set to include hundreds of verbs. For a similar situation from a completely different part of the verb, compare the Nakh-Daghestanian language Archi, which restricts verb agreement to about a third of the verb lexemes (Chumakina and Bond 2016).

Participant indexing generally distinguishes two numbers (singular/plural) of 1st, 2nd and 3rd person, and, in the case of Undergoer alternation, gender, but usually not number, of inanimate arguments (§10.4). The gender of animates is not reflected in participant indexing. Coastal Marind, and probably most other Anim languages, differ from other languages of the South New Guinea area in the lack of a dual number category. Dual marking is found in the unrelated, neighbouring languages Marori (Arka 2012), Ngkolmpu (Yam; Carroll 2016) and Maklew (Bulaka River; Drabbe 1950). It is absent in Bush Marind and Yaqay, spoken north of Coastal Marind. Interestingly, the smallest Marindic language, Bian Marind, has a fully productive dual category, perhaps due to contact with neighbouring Yam languages.

9.1.2 The place of participant indexing in the verb complex

The exponents of all four types of participant indexing are tightly integrated into the rest of the verb morphology, exhibit various morphophonological changes, and, in the case of the Undergoer alternations in the stem, non-predictable realisations that require inflectional classes to be posited. The three prefixal series are part of the cluster of inflectional affixes called the prefixal complex (Chapter 8). The prefixal complex is separated from the following verb stem by a phonological word boundary, but note that the prefixes themselves occur tightly bound to each other and to other material within the prefixal complex. The participant indexing is not affected by the occurrence or omission of overt arguments in the clause.

9 Participant indexing I: The Actor, Dative and Genitive prefixes

																	Verb stem →
-17	-16	-15	-14	-13	-12	-11	-10	-9	-8	-7	-6	-5	-4	-3	-2	-1	
Given	Orientation	Dependent	Interrogative Jussive	**1st, 2nd Actor** Future	Durative	Speaker attitude	**3rd Actor**	**Genitive**	Frustrative	Separative Allative	Repetitive	**Dative**	**1st Person Plural**	Accompaniment	Prioritive Distal	Contessive	

Fig. 9.1: Overview of the position of participant indexing within the prefixal complex

The person categories that are realised within the prefixal complex — Actor, Dative and Genitive indexing — are spread across different sites in the morphological template posited in Chapter 8. Figure 9.1 is a simplified overview of the position classes of the prefixal complex (showing only single-class prefixes), with the prefixal indexing sets indicated by boldface. Note that the Actor prefixes belong to different classes: 1st and 2nd person are in class –13, whereas the 3rd person Actor prefixes belong to class –10, closer to the verb stem. More details on the position of the indexing prefixes relative to other prefixes are given in the respective sections below.

In addition to the three sets of role-marking prefixes there is a role-neutral 1pl prefix *e-*, whose position in class –4 of the prefix template can be seen in Figure 9.1. This prefix occurs in any verb that has a 1st person plural argument, regardless of its role. The role-indicating 1st person prefixes (e.g. the 1st person Genitive *nam-* in 298d above) do not mark number, but are interpreted as corresponding to a singular participant in the absence of 1pl *e-*. More information about the use of this prefix is given in §9.5.

9.2 Actor indexing

The set of Actor prefixes indexes the agent-like participants of both transitive and intransitive verbs. The formal aspects of Actor indexing are described in §9.2.1; the use of the prefixes is described in §9.2.2.

9.2.1 Form of the Actor prefixes

The Actor prefixes are shown in Table 9.1.

Tab. 9.1: The Actor prefixes

	SG	PL
1	no-, nak-	
2	o-	e-
3	a-, ø-	n-

As mentioned above, the 1pl prefix *e-* (§9.5) disambiguates number reference for the 1st person *nak-*prefix, but it is role-neutral and co-occurs with all types of person indexing, not only Actor prefixes, so it is not shown in Table 9.1.

A second prefix of the shape *e-* is used in contexts of a 3pl agent acting on a 1st person participant (of any role). This divalent prefix is described in §9.2.2.3.

The following subsections focus on the shape of the Actor prefixes, according to person: 1st (§9.2.1.1), 2nd (§9.2.1.2) and 3rd (§9.2.1.3).

9.2.1.1 1st person Actor: *nak-* (1.A)

The first person prefix has the most complicated allomorphy of the Actor prefixes. The alternations can be described as involving three allomorphs, *no-*, *nak-* and *ak-*, of which the latter two are affected by Plosive Nasalisation (to *nam-*, *nan-* etc.) according to the environment. The allomorphs are used according to the rules A–C.

(A) The allomorph *no-* is used whenever this prefix can be accommodated within the last syllable of the prefixal complex, as in (300a–b).

(300) a. /no-   dahetok/   →   *no-dahetok*
         1.A-   return   'I returned.'

      b. /mend-no-b-   dahetok/   →   *mendanob-dahetok*
         PERF-1.A-ACT- return   'I already returned.'

The environments where this occurs are: whenever 1.A is (i) followed by no other prefixes, or (ii) followed only by Past Durative *d-* or Actualis prefix *b-*.

In casual speech the allomorph *no-* is sometimes dropped, so that (300b) is realised *mendab-dahetok*. This only happens when there are other prefixes present before *no-* (such as the Perfect *mend-*), and is not possible with the other allomorphs described below.

(B) The allomorph *nak-* is used if additional morphology after the 1.A prefix prevents it from making up the onset and nucleus of the final syllable of the prefixal complex. This occurs whenever the ensuing affixal material consists of anything other than a single consonant -C- (the only prefixes with this shape are *b-* and *d-* mentioned in rule A).

(301) a. /nak-e- dahetok/ → nake-dahetok
    1.A-1PL- return   'We returned.'

   b. /nak-um-e- aɣi/ → nakume-aɣi
    1.A-FRUS-2|3PL.DAT- say   'I told them in vain.'

(C) The initial /n/ of the allomorph *nak-* is deleted whenever it is preceded by a consonant (other than /h/):

(302) /mend-nak-e aɣi/ → mendake-aɣi
   PERF-1.A-2|3PL.DAT- say   'I already told them.'

Preceded by a vowel, *nak-* remains intact. The Givenness-marking prefix *tV-* (described in §11.4) ends in a vowel, so *nak-* is preserved. The intervening Neutral Orientation prefix (§11.1.2) is realised as zero in past time contexts, so it does not affect the shape of *nak-*.

(303) *epe* te-ø-nak-e- ka-lahos
    DIST:III GIV:III-NTRL-1.A-1PL- WITH-smoke
   'That's [the tobacco] that we used for smoking.'   [W01:0069]

Preceded by a suffix ending in /h/ (either the Dependent *ah-* or the Proximal *eh-*), *nak-* remains intact and the /h/ is lost:

(304) /eh-nak-e-ap- laɣ-e/ → enakep-laɣe
   PROX:III-1.A-1PL-CT- talk-IPFV   'what we are saying.'

If *nak-* is used in this context, and if it is followed by two syllables, then its /a/-segment is deleted by Antepretonic syncope (§2.4.2), giving the form *nk-*:

(305) /a-nak-emb-e- gan/ → ankembe-gan
   DEP-1.A-2|3PL.GEN-1PL- hear   'what we heard about you(pl)/them'

Note that the /h/-segment of the Dependent *ah-* may escape deletion by floating forwards, as described in §8.3.2.2.

If the /k/ of the allomorphs covered in rules B and C is followed by a heterosyllabic /b/ or /d/, then the /k/ undergoes Plosive Nasalisation (§2.5.2). This means that /k/ becomes a nasal and assimilates to the place feature of the following plosive, becoming [m] before /b/ and [n] before /d/. This is shown for the sequence /kb/ in (306a), in which *nak-* is followed by the Affectionate prefix *bat-* (used to soften an utterance; §15.3.3), and for the sequence /kd/ in (306b), in which *ak-* (with initial /n/ deleted as per above) is followed by the Past Durative *d-* (§14.2.1).

(306) a. /nak-bat- dahetok/ → nambat-dahetok
       1.A-AFF-   return   'I returned.'

    b. /mend-nak-d-e- og/ → mendande-og
       PERF-1.A-DUR-1PL- do   'We already did it.'

The resulting nasal+plosive sequences behave like single segments (i.e. prenasalised plosives), so the syllabifications of the prefix sequences above are [na.m̰bat] for (306a) and [me.nda.n̰de] for (306b).

Positionally, the 1.A prefixes (along with the 2SG.A and 2PL.A prefixes) belong to class −13, which means that most other prefixes occur closer to the verb stem. Among the prefixes that may precede them are e.g. the Orientation prefixes (§11.1) and some of the prefixes expressing TAM-like notions such as the Perfect *mend-* (§14.2.5) and the Deictic series (§15.4). The rightmost prefix in the morphological template by which the 1st person Actor prefix can be preceded is the Interrogative *h-* of position class −14 (307). In this context the 1.A prefix is always realised as *am-*, since the prefix *h-* always occurs in combination with the Actualis prefix *b-* to mark a content question (§19.3).

(307) ta   ma-h-am-b-e-   og-e?
      what OBJ-ROG-1.A-ACT-1PL-   do-IPFV
      'What are we going to do?'

The leftmost prefix that can occur after the 1.A prefix is the Past Durative *d-* (of position class −12), as in (306b) above.

9.2.1.2 2nd person Actor: *o-* (2SG.A), *e-* (2PL.A)

The 2nd person Agent prefixes show no allomorphy, except that they predictably undergo Antepenultimate vowel gradation (§2.5.1) to *u-* and *i-* respectively in the third syllable counting from the end of the prefixal complex. This is illustrated in the (b)-examples below, in which the Affectionate *bat-* has been added to the prefixal complex (making the question sound softer), which causes 2nd person Actore prefixes to be realised in the antepenultimate syllable of the prefixal complex.

(308) a. /ap-o-ap-   balen/ → apop-balen?
         PST.Q-2SG.A-CT-   finish   'Did you finish?'

    b. /ap-o-bat-ap   balen/ → apubatap-balen?
       PST.Q-2SG.A-AFF-CT-   finish   'Did you finish?'

(309) a. /ap-e-ap-   balen/ → apep-balen?
         PST.Q-2PL.A-CT-   finish   'Did you (pl) finish?'

    b. /ap-e-bat-ap   balen/ → apibatap-balen?
       PST.Q-2PL.A-AFF-CT-   finish   'Did you finish?'

Note also that the sequence /oiC/ is realised [uC], which affects the 2SG.A prefix *o-* when it is followed by an *i*-initial prefix; cf. example (287) above.

9.2.1.3 3rd person Actor: *a-* (3SG.A), *n-* (3PL.A), *e-* (3PL>1)

The prefixes realising 3rd person Actors are members of position class −10, so they are closer to the verb stem than the 1st and 2nd person (which are in class −13). The Actor prefixes are mutually exclusive, despite belonging to separate classes, so it is not possible to combine e.g. a 1st person and a 3rd person Actor prefix within the same verb.

The following examples explain why it is necessary to describe the 3rd person Actor prefixes as members of position class −10. The verb in these examples — *yoman* 'approach' — can be used to mean 'meet X_{Gen}', with the subscript indicating that the O-argument is indexed by means of the Genitive prefixes (described in §9.4). In the forms below it occurs with a common prefix sequence consisting of the Perfect *mend-* and the Actualis *b-* (see §15.3.1 for this combination). The Actualis (along with the other so-called Speaker Attitude prefixes) belongs to position class −11, and the Genitive prefixes belong to position class −9, so the 3rd person prefixes must make up an intervening class, position class −10. Note that the prefix *e-* in (310c), glossed '3PL>1', is used whenever a plural 3rd person participant acts on a 1st person participant (see further §9.2.2.3 below).

(310) a. men-b-a-nam-   yoman
         PERF-ACT-3SG.A-1.GEN- approach
         'S/he already met me.'

     b. men-ba-n-em-   yoman
         PERF-ACT-3PL.A-2|3PL.GEN- approach
         'They already met you(pl)/them.'

     c. men-b-e-nam-   yoman
         PERF-ACT-3PL>1-1.GEN- approach
         'They already met me.'

Compare the forms above with corresponding 1st person Actor form in (311). The 1.A prefix (realised as *am-* in accordance with the principles in §9.2.1.1) is positioned before the Actualis prefix *b-*, since it belongs to a position class further away from the verb stem (position class −13).

(311) mend-am-b-am-   yoman
       PERF-1.A-ACT-2SG.GEN- approach
       'I already met you.'

9.2 Actor indexing — 195

Below I provide more information about the realisation of the 3rd person Actor prefixes.

3SG ACTOR: *a-*. If the 3sg Actor prefix is the only prefix making up the prefixal complex, it takes the shape *a-* (312a). If there are other prefixes present, and these prefixes consist of enough phonological material to make up one or more syllables on their own, the 3SG.A prefix is zero (written ø- in the morphematic segmentation) (312b). If the other prefixes that are used with the 3SG.A prefix are not sufficient to build a syllable, the Actor prefix will be *a-*, as in (312c), where the Directional Orientation prefix *k-* (§11.1.4) is insufficient to form a syllable by itself.

(312) a. *a- dahetok-e*
 3SG.A- return-IPFV
 'S/he's about to return.'

 b. *bat-ø- dahetok-e*
 AFF-3SG.A- return-IPFV
 'S/he's about to return.'

 c. *tanama k-a- dahetok*
 again DIR-3SG.A- return
 'S/he returned again.'

In all other contexts the 3SG.A allomorph is *a-*, but note that it often suffers deletion due to Syncope (§2.4.2), in which case it is written ø-.

3PL ACTOR: *n-*. The 3pl Actor prefix *n-* usually shows the expected behaviour with regards to epenthesis (cf. §2.2.1). Used alone, The segment *n-* is followed by epenthetic /a/ allowing it to make up a well-formed CV-syllable *na-* (313a). In contexts where the prefix can form a syllable with surrounding material it is realised as *n-* (313b–c).

(313) a. *na- dahetok-e*
 3PL.A- return-IPFV
 'They're about to return.'

 b. *ba-n- dahetok-e*
 ACT-3PL.A- return-IPFV
 'They're about to return indeed.' [W19:0326]

 c. *n-e- ayi*
 3PL.A-2|3PL.DAT- say
 'They said it to you(pl)/them.'

The behaviour of *n-* is more remarkable when it is preceded by two or more prefixes that together can form a closed syllable, and there are no inflectional prefixes following *n-*. In such contexts, *n-* does not syllabify with the other prefixes, and instead forms a phonological unit with the verb stem following to the right. This is remarkable since all other prefixes treat the boundary between the prefixal complex and the verb stem as the boundary between two phonological words, and never syllabify across it. It is as if the 3PL.A prefix ignores the word boundary and crosses freely to attach to the stem when there are no intervening prefixes blocking the movement across the border. Consider example (314), containing the three prefixes *m-*, *d-* and 3pl *n-*:

(314) da   ma-d-na-   w-alok
      sago(III) OBJ-DUR-3PL.A-   III.U-stab
      'They were felling the sago palm.'

If the 3PL.A prefix respected the phonological boundary we would expect syllabification to precede from right to left in the prefixal complex, with *d-* and *n-* forming a heavy syllable *dan*, and *m-* plus epenthetic /a/ adding a light syllable: *ma.dan-*. Instead, *n-* joins the verb stem (with insertion of epenthetic /a/) and *m-* and *d-* are left to syllabify on their own. The phonological grouping of (314) is

(315) (da)_ω (mad)_ω (nawalok)_ω

It is especially clear that *n-* must have crossed the word boundary when the verb stem is vowel initial, as this allows *n-* to occur without epenthetic /a/ (316a). A tautosyllabic cluster *dn* would be unacceptable, but does not arise since *n-* syllabifies as the onset of the first syllable of the stem (316b).

(316) a. awe ma-d-n-   ibingg⟨a⟩b-ti
         fish OBJ-DUR-3PL.A-   gather⟨2|3PL.U⟩-DUR
         'They gathered the fish.'

      b. (awe)_ω (mad)_ω (nibinggabti)_ω

The loss of epenthetic /a/ before a vowel-initial stem seems completely optional, and most instances of the prefix sequence above were transcribed as *madna-* rather than *madn-* before vowel-initial stems (the difference is difficult to tell in rapid speech).

This behaviour — attaching to the verb stem when no other prefixes intervene — is peculiar to the 3pl *n-*prefix. As discussed in §8.2, all other prefixes belonging in the prefixal complex form a tight morphophonological unit with other such prefixes, and do not 'jump across' to the ensuing verb stem.[1]

---

[1] Ger Reesink (pers. comm.) points out that the fact that the 3pl Actor prefix may group with either the prefixal complex or the verb stem is a sign of the unity of the Coastal Marind verb complex as a whole: "we're still dealing with a verb, albeit very complex morphologically".

3PL>1 *e-*. The prefix *e-* does not exhibit any allomorphy, but undergoes Antepenultimate gradation (§2.5.1) in the third syllable from the end of the prefixal complex (like most other prefixes containing mid vowels). In the following examples, the 1pl prefix *e-* is added at the end of the prefixal complex in (317b), which causes the 3PL>1 prefix to be in the antepenultimate position, and therefore raised from /e/ to [i]:

(317) a. /k-e-namb- yoman/ → *kenam-yoman*
       DIR-3PL>1-1.GEN- approach 'They met me.'

   b. /k-e-namb-e- yoman/ → *kinambe-yoman*
       DIR-3PL>1-1.GEN-1PL- approach 'They met us.'

Again, it is important to note that the 3PL>1 prefix *e-* belongs to position class −10 (like the other 3rd person Actor prefixes), whereas the 2nd person Actor prefixes are assigned to position class −13. This distinguishes the 3PL>1 prefix from the identical 2pl Actor prefix *e-*. The two *e-*prefixes appear to be identical if one compares two verb forms without any prefixes of the intervening position classes present:

(318) a. *yoy ø-e- na-sak*
       2PL NTRL-2PL.A- 1.U-hit
       'You hit me.'

   b. *isahih ø-e- na-sak*
       children NTRL-3PL>1- 1.U-hit
       'The children hit me.'

But once a prefix from an intervening position class — e.g. the Affectionate prefix of class −11 — is added, it becomes clear that the 2pl Actor prefix adjoins before the Affectionate, whereas the 3PL>1 prefix adjoins after it. This shows that the 2pl Actor *e-* and the 3PL>1 *e-* are distinct prefixes.[2]

(319) a. *yoy ø-e-bat- na-sak*
       2PL NTRL-2PL.A-AFF- 1.U-hit
       'You hit poor me.'

   b. *isahih ø-bat-e- na-sak*
       children NTRL-AFF-3PL>1- 1.U-hit
       'The children hit poor me.'

---

[2] It is possible that the 2PL.A *e-* and 3PL>1 *e-* share a common origin, since all other indexing sets (Dative and Genitive prefixes, Undergoer alternations in the stem) show pervasive syncretism between 2pl and 3pl (e.g. the 2|3pl Dative prefix *e-*, of position class −5).

9.2.2 Uses of the Actor prefixes

9.2.2.1 General remarks

The use of the Actor prefix series to index the agent-like participant of a verb can be observed in any of the examples in the preceding sections. In addition to the agent-indexing use, a 3sg Actor prefix is always used as a default with verbs that lack an agent-like participant, such as avalent verbs (320a) and patientive verbs (320b).

(320) a. *a-*   *pig-e*
           3SG.A-   become.bright-IPFV
           'It's about to become morning.'   [W13:0394]

      b. *mbya*   *ø-a-*   *yada⟨n⟩in*
          NEG   NTRL-3SG.A-   drown⟨1.U⟩
          'I didn't drown.'

The remainder of this section explains some complications in the usage of the 3rd person Actor prefixes: the choice between singular and plural prefixes (§9.2.2.2), the use of the divalent 3PL>1 prefix *e-* (§9.2.2.3), and indexing of inanimate agent-like participants (§9.2.2.4).

9.2.2.2 Conditions on 3rd person Actor indexing

The 3rd person Actor prefixes distinguish singular *a-* and plural *n-*. In some fairly common situations, however, the use of the sg/pl Actor prefixes does not correspond to the actual number of the indexed participants. The rules determining the prefix choice are explained in this section. These rules are complicated and quite counterintuitive, but they are important as they affect some of the most frequent verbs in the language, and their consequences are amply attested in corpus data.

In general, a plural agent participant is indexed by means of the 3PL.A prefix *n-*. The following two rules describe contexts in which the 3rd person Actor *singular* prefix is employed to index a *plural* agent participant. I also describe a set of exceptions to the two rules, in which indexing follows the general pattern, so that a plural participant is indexed by means of the plural prefix *n-*.

Because of the complexity of the rules, I will illustrate them with simple, elicited utterances.

RULE 1: ALWAYS 3SG WITH MIDDLE VERBS. If the agent is 3rd person plural, and the verb is a middle verb, then 3SG.A *a-* is used. There are ca. 40 verbs that index their agent-like participant according to the so-called middle pattern (cf. Table 12.3 on p. 305 for a list), meaning that the person/number features of a 1st or 2nd person agent are simultaneously indexed in the Actor prefix and in the Undergoer alternations of the verb stem (§10.1.2, §12.2.3). If the agent of a middle verb is 3rd person, however, 3SG.A is used regardless of the number of the agent. Compare the non-middle verb *dahetok* in (321) with the middle verb *kwamin* 'enter' in (322) for an illustration of this.

(321) a. a-   dahetok
         3SG.A-   return
         'S/he returned.'

   b. na-   dahetok
      3PL.A-   return
      'They returned.'

(322) a. a-   k⟨w⟩amin
         3SG.A-   enter⟨3SG.U⟩
         'S/he entered.'

   b. a-   k⟨y⟩amin
      3SG.A-   enter⟨2|3PL.U⟩
      'They entered.'

RULE 2: ALWAYS 3SG WITH SUPPLETIVE VERBS. If the agent is plural, and the verb exhibits stem suppletion according to the number of the agent, then 3SG.A *a-* is used. Some common verbs use a suppletive stem in the plural (§10.5). For 10 of these verbs, suppletion is triggered by the agent. One of these, the suppletive verb *ambid* 'sit' (plural *haman*) is used in (323) to illustrate that the 3SG.A is used with a 3rd person plural agent.

(323) a. a-   ambid
         3SG.A-   sit
         'S/he sat down.'

   b. a-   haman
      3SG.A-   sit.PL
      'They sat down.'

Note that suppletion according to participant number, as in (323), must be distinguished from suppletion according to event number/pluractionality, which does not affect 3rd person Actor indexing (see §10.5.2).

EXCEPTIONS TO RULES 1 & 2. In the following three circumstances, the rules above do not apply, and a 3rd person plural agent of a middle or suppletive verb is indexed by means of 3PL.A *n-*. All of these exceptions involve increased valence of the verb.
– If the clause has an additional argument that is indexed by the Dative prefixes on the verb

- If the clause has an additional argument that is indexed by the Genitive prefixes on the verb
- If the clause has an additional argument introduced by the Allative, Separative or Accompaniment applicatives

I will exemplify each of these exceptions. A Dative prefix on the verb can be used to index e.g. the owner of a body part, a benefactor etc. (see §9.3). The examples in (324), which are based on a clause in a narrative, show the middle verb *kwamin* 'enter' with the Dative prefix indexing the owner of a body part. Compare (322b) above with (324b), in which the 3PL.A *n-* reappears due to the presence of a participant indexed by the Dative prefix.

(324) a. nanggit ø-ø-o- k⟨w⟩amin anggip-bal
       mosquito NTRL-3SG.A-3SG.DAT- enter⟨3SG.U⟩ nose-hole
       'A mosquito entered his/her nose.'

   b. nanggit ø-n-o- k⟨y⟩amin anggip-bal
      mosquito NTRL-3PL.A-3SG.DAT- enter⟨3PL.U⟩ nose-hole
      'Mosquitos entered his/her nose.'

The Genitive prefixes (§9.4) mostly index possessors, but they can be used with 'sit' to express 'sit and wait for X$_{Gen}$'. Compare (323b) above with (325), which shows that the 3PL.A prefix *n-* reappears when a Genitive prefix is present on the verb.

(325) oy ma-n-amba-ka- hamat-a
      2SG OBJ-3PL.A-2SG.GEN-PRI- sit.PL-EXT
      'They are sitting waiting for you.'

The applicative prefixes described in §13.1 license the addition of an applicative argument. When one of the three applicatives that are marked within the prefixal complex (Allative *ind-*, the Separative *is-* and the Accompaniment *e-*) are used with a 3rd person plural agent, the 3PL.A prefix *n-* is used, even when the verb is a middle verb (326a) or suppletive (326b–c).

(326) a. oy ma-n-ind-a- k⟨y⟩amin
         2SG OBJ-3PL.A-ALL-2SG.DAT- enter⟨2|3PL.U⟩
         'They entered [in order] to get you.'

     b. oy ma-n-is-a- awan
        2SG OBJ-3PL.A-SEP-2SG.DAT- run.PL
        'They fled from you.'

c. oy   ma-n-a-y-   awan
   2SG OBJ-3PL.A-2SG.DAT-ACPN- run.PL
   'They chased you.'

Note that the Instrumental/Comitative applicatives, marked by the prefix *k-/i-* on the verb stem, do not pattern with the other applicatives in this respect. Even when adding this valence increasing prefix, the 3PL.A prefix *n-* may not be used with a middle verb (327a) or with a suppletive verb (327b).

(327) a. da   m-a-   i-k⟨y⟩amin
       sago OBJ-3SG.A- WITH-enter⟨2|3PL.U⟩
       'They brought in the sago.'

     b. da   m-a-   k-awan
       sago OBJ-3SG.A- WITH-run.PL
       'They ran away with the sago.'

It is difficult to imagine any synchronic logic behind these conditions on the 3PL.A prefix, especially as none of the rules above impact Actor indexing in the 1st or 2nd person.

9.2.2.3 Use of 3PL>1 *e-*

If a 3pl Actor acts on a 1st person (singular or plural), the Actor is indexed by means of the prefix *e-* (glossed 3PL>1) instead of the standard 3PL.A prefix *n-*. The formal realisation of the prefix was described at the end of §9.2.1.3 above, and some examples of its use were given in (318–319).

The formulation "3pl Actor acts on a 1st person" should be understood as referring to any scenario in which a verb has a 3pl agent triggering Actor indexing and a 1st person argument in any non-agent role. The 3PL>1 prefix occurs regardless of whether the 1st person participant is indexed by Undergoer alternations in the stem, as in (328), by the Dative prefixes (329) or by the Genitive prefixes (330).

(328) nok kudaya epe   k-e-   yada⟨n⟩awn
      1   alone   there DIR-3PL>1- leave⟨1.U⟩
      'They left me there alone.'   [W20:0132]

(329) napet ye   m-e-na-y-   og
      banana INGRS OBJ-3PL>1-1.DAT-1PL- give
      'They gave us bananas.'   [W11:0412]

(330) mayan   epe   mbya   k-e-nam-   i-hwagib-e
     speech(III) DIST:III NEG   PRS.NTRL-3PL>1-1.GEN- PLA-save:III.U-IPFV
     '[The children] are not paying attention to my advice.' (lit. 'They don't save my speech') [W18:0217]

The 3PL>1 prefix also occurs in cases in which a 1st person argument is not indexed by any other overt markers on the verb. This happens when a 1st person participant functions as the patient-like argument of an invariant verb (e.g. a lexeme that lacks the ability to index the Undergoer; Chapter 10), as witnessed by the elicited example in (331). Here the invariant verb *abun* 'bark' is used transitively, with a 1st person O-argument. The 3PL>1 prefix occurs even though the 1st person participant is not indexed on the verb, since the only requirement is that it is an argument.[3]

(331) nggat nok ma-d-e-   abun
     dog   1   OBJ-DUR-3PL>1- bark
     'Dogs barked at me.'

For the sake of completeness I add elicited examples below showing that *e-* does not occur in scenarios other than the 3pl>1 configuration. In (332a) a 3pl agent acts on a 2sg patient, so the standard 3PL.A *n-* is used. In (332b) the patient is a 3rd person, so again *n-* is used.

(332) a. nggat oy   ma-d-na-   abun
         dog   2SG   OBJ-DUR-3PL.A-   bark
         'Dogs barked at you.'

     b. nggat Yakoba ma-d-na-   abun
         dog   Y.   OBJ-DUR-3PL.A-   bark
         'Dogs barked at Yakoba.'

The 3PL>1 prefix does not occur if the agent is singular:

(333) nggat nok ma-d-ø-   abun
     dog   1   OBJ-DUR-3SG.A-   bark
     'A dog barked at me.'

---

3 Drabbe (1955: 63) notes the existence of the prefix *e-* in his grammar of the Eastern dialect of Coastal Marind, but seems to consider it some sort of morphophonologically conditioned allomorph of the standard 3PL.A prefix *n-*. An account such as "3PL.A *n-* becomes *e-* before *na-* (1.DAT) and *namb-* (1.GEN)" does not explain why *e-* also occurs (i) when the exponent of the 1st person argument is non-adjacent to the 3pl prefix (as when the verb stem is marked according to an Undergoer), and (ii) when the 1st person argument is not indexed at all, as in (331). My description of *e-* as marking the 3pl>1 scenario also solves the problems that Drabbe struggles with in the analysis of the Negative Future (1955: 70).

It should be pointed out that the 3PL>1 *e-* co-occurs with markers indexing the 1st person participant, rather than replacing them. This distinguishes the Coastal Marind prefix from the typical cases of transitive portmanteaux expressing person/number of both agent and patient (see e.g. Heath 1991, 1998).

9.2.2.4 Actor indexing of inanimates

The argument slots that correspond to Actor, Dative and Genitive indexing may, with some verbs, be filled by inanimate participants. When inanimate participants are used in these roles, however, the corresponding indexing prefixes default to 3sg. This can be seen as a consequence of the lack of a number distinction within inanimates (as reflected in gender agreement, Chapter 5). Examples (334a–b) shows that animate A-arguments trigger sg/pl Actor indexing, whereas inanimate A-arguments with the same verb (335) fail to trigger a number distinction in the Actor prefixes.[4]

(334) a. *Takolep epe k-ø-om- yoman*
T. there DIR-3SG.A-3SG.GEN- approach
'Takolep met him there.' [D11:0032]

b. *anim epe ka-n-om- yoman*
people there DIR-3PL.A-3SG.GEN- approach
'People met him there.'

(335) a. *yahun epe k-ø-om- yoman*
vehicle there DIR-3SG.A-3SG.GEN- approach
'The truck met him there.'

b. *yahun epe k-ø-om- ya-yoman*
vehicle there DIR-3SG.A-3SG.GEN- PLA-approach
'The trucks met him there.'

The last three examples were elicited based on (334a) and other very similar examples, but the principle that inanimate participants fail to trigger a sg/pl contrast in Actor indexing is robustly supported by corpus data and other elicited data.[5]

---

[4] Note that the *yahun* 'truck(s)' (lit. 'canoe') triggers the Pluractional prefix on the stem in the plural (335b). Pluractional marking (§16.1) is independent of Actor indexing, so it does not affect the point made here. Speakers always use Pluractional marking for several vehicles moving, which apparently is considered to be 'multiple events'. The Pluractional could be used with animate A-arguments in (334), e.g. in a habitual context, 'repeatedly met him'.

[5] Evidence for indexing of inanimates by the Dative and Genitive prefixes is much more sparse, primarily because it is difficult to find verbs for which these configurations make sense. I leave this for future research.

Consider now the category of gender. The gender values of inanimates are systematically reflected in nominal agreement targets (e.g. demonstratives; §5.3), but also in the Undergoer alternations described in the next chapter (in particular, §10.4). With such agreement targets, the inanimate nouns in Gender IV always trigger agreement or indexing forms that are identical to those triggered by animate plurals, despite lacking a number distinction (as discussed in §5.3.2). If this pattern extended to Actor indexing, we would expect an inanimate agent-like participant in Gender IV to trigger the 3PL.A prefix *n-* on the verb.

It turns out that this is indeed the case, but only for a small subset of the investigated verbs. Most verbs do not distinguish gender of inanimate agent-like participants, and they trigger invariant 3SG.A indexing on the verb. However, certain intransitive verbs, such as *esol* 'make noise' (336), employ 3SG.A indexing with a Gender III noun (336a), and 3PL.A with a Gender IV noun (336b). The nouns triggering agreement in these examples are loanwords, but both are in common use in the villages and have conventionalised gender assignment: *motor* 'motorcycle' in Gender III, *mesin* 'machine, generator' in Gender IV.

(336) a. *motor*   *epe*   *te-k-at-ø-*   *esol-e*
motorcycle(m)(III)   DIST:III   GIV:III-PRS.NTRL-PRSTV-3SG.A-   make.noise-IPFV
'The motorcycle is making noise.'

b. *yaba-mesin*   *ipe*   *ti-k-at-n-*   *esol-e*
big-machine(m)(IV)   DIST:IV   GIV:IV-PRS.NTRL-PRSTV-3PL.A-   make.noise-IPFV
'The generator is making noise.'

This is a remarkable extension of the systematic syncretism between Gender IV nouns and animate plurals, but it is not known why it is limited to intransitive verbs (for further discussion and examples, see Olsson 2017: 248–249, Olsson 2019b: 214–215).[6]

9.3 Dative indexing

The Dative prefixes are used to index a participant filling a role such as recipient, benefactor or possessor of a body part. Example:

(337) *katal*   *men-ba-n-o-*   *hahin*
money(IV)   PERF-ACT-3PL.A-3SG.DAT-   put:IV.U
'They already gave him the money.'   [W22:0124]

---

[6] Similar observations have been made for the other indexing prefixes, e.g. Gender IV nouns triggering 2|3pl Dative indexing. But the attestations are not sufficient to describe these phenomena in detail, so this will have to be addressed in future work.

Note that the ditransitive theme (the money) is indexed by means of Undergoer alternations in the verb stem, like standard O-arguments with monotransitive alternating verbs, whereas the recipient is indexed by a separate prefix set. In the typological literature this is known as indirective alignment (see also §11.1.3.2).[7]

The formal realisation of Dative indexing is described in §9.3.1, while the functional range of the Dative series is described in §9.3.2. I use the term 'Dative' since this is the label given to case forms and adpositions with similar semantics in traditional grammar.[8]

9.3.1 Form of the Dative prefixes

The Dative prefixes are shown in Table 9.2. The prefix *e-* realises both 2nd and 3rd person plural (glossed 2|3PL.DAT), a syncretism pattern that recurs in all indexing forms except the Actor prefixes (which distinguish 2pl *e-* and 3pl *n-*).

Tab. 9.2: The Dative prefixes

	SG	PL
1	na-	
2	a-	e-
3	o-	

As seen in Figure 9.1, the Dative prefixes belong to position class −5 in the templatic model of the prefixal complex. A paradigm containing the Dative prefixes was given in Table 8.1 above, showing combinations of the Dative series with the Actor prefixes and the Past Durative *d-*.

The only complication affecting the Dative prefixes concerns the 1st person prefix *na-*. Whenever this prefix co-occurs with any of the prefixes belonging to position classes −8 (i.e. the Frustrative *um-*), −7 (Separative *is-* and Allative *ind-*) and −6 (Repetitive *i-*), a kind of partial affixal metathesis occurs, in which the segment *n-* 'moves' leftwards, so that the added prefix appears between the segments of the discontinuous Dative prefix *n-...a-*. This differs from the non-1st person Dative prefixes, which are placed after the prefixes belonging to classes −8, −7 and −6, as predicted by the position class model.

---

[7] Marind is erroneously classified as aligning the recipient with the monotransitive O in Reesink's study of the 'give' event in Papuan languages (Reesink 2013: 260). I thank Ger Reesink for bringing this to my attention.
[8] Another possible term would be 'Indirect Object' prefix which would be misleading since it suggests that the prefix is limited to a specific syntactic configuration.

I illustrate this in (338), using the class −8 Frustrative prefix *um-* (expressing that an event almost happened, or that an activity was carried out in vain; see §15.2). The 3sg Dative prefix *o-* appears after the Frustrative in (338a), which is the expected ordering since the Dative prefix is a member of a position closer to the verb stem (class −5). If *o-* is replaced by the 1st person Dative *na-*, however, the special metathesis kicks in, giving discontinuous *n-um-a-* instead of the expected sequence **um-na-*. As with other instances of discontinuous morphs in the language (e.g. the Dependent *ah-*, §8.3.2), the category label ('1.DAT') is repeated under both substrings in the interlinear glosses (as per Comrie et al. 2015, Rule 8).

(338) a. *basik ø-ø-um-o- haniy*
pig NTRL-3SG.A-FRUS-3SG.DAT- bite
'The pig almost bit him/her.'

b. *basik ø-ø-n-um-a- haniy*
pig NTRL-3SG.A-1.DAT-FRUS-1.DAT- bite
'The pig almost bit me.'

(The Dative is used to index the owner of the bitten body part in the previous examples, cf. §9.3.2.)

The following examples contain corpus data illustrating discontinuous *n-...a-*. In (339) the Separative *is-* (signalling motion away from the participant indexed by means of the Dative; §13.1.8) intervenes between the segments of the 1st person Dative. Examples (340–341) show that more than one intervening prefix may be added between *n-* and *a-*. In these examples the Allative *ind-* (§13.1.7) signals motion towards the Dative participant, whereas the Repetitive *i-* (§16.2) in (341) serves to express 'again'.

(339) *men-b-ø-n-is-a-y- ihon*
PERF-ACT-3SG.A-1.DAT-SEP-1.DAT-1PL- run.away:3SG.U
'She already ran away from us.' [W19:0378]

(340) *nok m-a-n-um-ind-a- dahetok-a-m*
1 OBJ-3SG.A-1.DAT-FRUS-ALL-1.DAT- return-EXT-VEN
'He (tried to) came back towards me.' [W02:0197]

(341) *etob epe k-a-n-ind-i-a-y- man-em*
sea.water there DIR-3SG.A-1.DAT-ALL-RE-1.DAT-1PL- come-VEN
'There the sea water came towards us again.' [W07:0031]

The reason for the splitting of *na-* into *n-* and *a-* in these contexts is perhaps related to the avoidance of a heavy syllable in the penultimate syllable of the phonological word (see §2.4). The prefixal complex constitutes a phonological word, so speakers avoid prefix sequences resulting in shapes such as *CVC.CV]$_ω$ with a heavy penultimate CVC syllable (usually by insertion of epenthetic /a/, giving e.g. CV.C*a*.CV]$_ω$). Illegal sequences such as *um-na- (FRUS-1.DAT-), *ind-na- (ALL-1.DAT-), *is-na- (SEP-1.DAT-) and *a-y-na- (IMP-RE-1.DAT-) would result in heavy penultimate syllables whenever *na-* is in the final syllable of the prefixal complex, so the metathesis of *n-* could be seen as a way to replace the heavy penultimate syllables with well-formed CV.CV]$_ω$. However, it is not clear why the conflict between faithfulness to affix order and avoidance of heavy penultimate syllables could not have been solved by epenthesis (producing *um-a-na-* etc.) instead of the more radical metathesis of *n-…a-*.[9]

9.3.2 Functions of Dative indexing

The range of meanings expressed by the Dative prefix series is similar to the meanings of dative case forms and indirect object indexing in many languages. In addition to the productive uses, there are some verbs that must be lexically specified as indexing one of their participants by means of the Dative series, as listed in the end of this section.

The Dative prefixes index the recipient participant in a typical transfer event. The most neutral way of expressing such events is by means of the pro-verb *og* 'do', which is used as a three-place predicate 'give' if it appears with a Dative prefix (342).[10] The transfer verb *ikalen* 'send' also exhibits Dative indexing (343).

(342) kak Siana ka-n-o- og Cap Lang
       aunt S.   DIR-3PL.A-3SG.DAT- give C. L.
       'They gave aunt Siana the "Cap Lang" medicine.' [W09:0017]

(343) surat mak-o- ikalen Simon
       letter(m)(III) FUT:1.A-3SG.DAT- send:III.U S.
       'I'm going to send a letter to Simon.'

When verbs of putting and placing are used with a Dative participant they express transfer, e.g. the verb *aten* 'cause to stand' (cf. *atin* 'stand up') which expresses 'give animate to somebody' with Dative indexing (344), and placement verbs such as *bakeh* 'put vertically oriented object' (e.g. a bottle) which are commonly used to express giving instead of the more general *og* (345). Other verbs that may express transfer with

---

9 In Olsson (2017: 234) I erroneously claimed that the combination of the Repetitive *i-* and the 1st person Dative *na-* would not cause a penultimate heavy syllable, unless metathesis intervened. I thank Bernard Comrie for pointing out this error.

10 Do/give macrofunctionality seems to be rare across languages, but is attested in a number of languages in Northwestern New Guinea (Gil 2017).

the Dative series are e.g. *kwegen* 'throw' (> 'throw to') and *anetok* 'divide' (> 'divide among'), as in (346).

(344) nggat a-na- aten!
dog IMP-1.DAT- make.stand:3SG.U
'Give me a dog!'

(345) sopi ma-n-um-o- bakeh
sopi(m)(III) OBJ-3PL.A-FRUS-3SG.DAT- put:III.U
'They tried to give him *sopi* (an alcoholic beverage).' [D09:0205]

(346) From an account of a feast organised by the district governor in Merauke.
kwemek sam-yasti epe namakad k-a-na-y- an⟨e⟩tok
morning big-old.man(I) DIST:I thing(III) DIR-3SG.A-1.DAT-1PL- divide⟨III.U⟩
'In the morning the governor started dividing the things among us.'
[W18:0258]

An exception to this indexing pattern of recipients is the verb *koh* 'feed' which codes the feedee by means of prefixed Undergoer marking on the stem (cf. *na-koh* 'feed me/us', *ya-koh* 'feed you' etc.; see §10.1).

Verbs describing creation or production can be used with Dative indexing to mark the recipient of the produced goods (347).

(347) tangge nahe ø-d-e-na-y- sakud-ti
arrow(III) grandparents:1 NTRL-DUR-3PL>1-1.DAT-1PL- fasten.tightly:III.U-DUR
'Our grandparents made arrows for us.' [W13:0753]

A closely related use is the indexing of the recipient-like argument of verbs of speaking such as *ayi* 'say' and *kabed* 'ask':

(348) namaya, patul epe k-ak-e-y- ayi ago "[...]"
now boy there DIR-1.A-2|3PL.DAT-1PL- say QUOT
'Now we said to the boys: "[...]"' [W07:0019]

(349) nok ad k-ak-o- kabed, ago "[...]"
1 father DIR-1.A-3SG.DAT- ask QUOT
'I asked father, "[...]"' [W23:0033]

An exceptional verb that does not use the Dative series to index the addressee-like participant is *wig* 'beg somebody for something', which indexes the person being begged by means of a Genitive prefix, presumably since this participant is also the owner of the item asked for (§9.4).

Dative indexing is used with verbs meaning 'show', e.g.

(350) mate, mak-e-   uma⟨n⟩ah, kay mend-o-na-y-   uman
      okay   FUT:1.A-1PL- go⟨1.U⟩   way PERF-2SG.A-1.DAT-1PL- show
      'Okay, let's go, you have already shown us the way.' [W10:0651]

(351) About some suspects handing themselves over to the police.
      nanih ka-n-e-p-   lawetok
      face   DIR-3PL.A-2|3PL.DAT-CT- turn
      'They showed (lit. turned) them their faces.' (i.e. to the police) [W09:0124]

The Dative also extends to contexts in which an action is performed to communicate or signal something to somebody, although the verb in itself is not a verb of communication. Below this is seen with the verbs *kiwayeb* 'turn, spin' to mean 'wave one's hand at somebody' (352) and *yedak* 'pound repeatedly', which in the context of (353) refers to a hunter imitating the mating behaviour of wallabies by thumping the ground with his knee.

(352) From a hunting story: spotting a wallaby.
      mesiwag   es   nd-a-   man-em,
      old.woman behind LOC-3SG.A- come-VEN

      sangga   ye   m-ak-o-   kiway⟨e⟩b
      hand(III) INGRS OBJ-1.A-3SG.DAT- turn⟨III.U⟩
      'My wife was coming from behind, I started waving my hand at her.'
      (To make her stop.) [W12:0187]

(353) Still hunting for wallabies.
      mate, hyakod a-mo-   idih,   mak-o-   y⟨e⟩dak
      okay   one   DEP-FUT:1.A- see:3SG.U FUT:1.A-3SG.DAT- ⟨PLA⟩thump
      'Okay, if I see one, I will thump [the ground] at it.' [W12:0121]

When a body part is an argument of a verb, the owner of the body part is indexed by means of the Dative prefixes (cf. so-called external possession constructions in many languages; König and Haspelmath 1997). Actions and states involving body parts that often occur with this pattern are e.g. 'grasp', 'hit', 'shoot', 'hurt', '[body fluid] come out', and so on. Examples:

(354) Describing a picture in the Family Problems task.
   tagu   k-ø-o-   wa-hanid-a   namaya
   foot(III) DIR-3SG.A-3SG.DAT- III.U-grasp-EXT now
   'She is holding [the baby] by its feet.'   [D09:0215]

(355) About a sudden bout of food poisoning.
   ɣandam   ɣap   m-a-na-y-   keway
   stomach   night OBJ-3SG.A-1.DAT-1PL-   break
   (lit.) 'At night our stomachs broke.'   [W11:0925]

(356) uy,   nok mig   men-b-a-na-   awih,
      EXCLAM   1   knee(IV)   PERF-ACT-3SG.A-1.DAT-   hurt:IV.U
      ihe   ɣ⟨e⟩dak-la   epe
      PROX:IV   ⟨PLA⟩thump-PTCP:III   DIST:III
      'Ouch, my knee is already hurting, [from] thumping the ground.'   [W12:0227]

(357) Describing a deer being chased by dogs.
   anup   ndalom   menda-b-ø-o-   hu-h   upe   rusa
   EMPH:II foam(IV) PERF-ACT-3SG.A-3SG.DAT-   emerge-IV.U   DIST:II   deer(m)(II)
   'Foam was already coming out of the deer['s mouth].'   [W02:0194]

There is an important constraint on the indexing of the owner of a body part, namely that the owner indexed by the Dative prefix may not be co-referential with the agent indexed by means of the Actor prefix. To express such reflexive scenarios (e.g. 'I cut my hand') the Dative prefix is dropped, leaving the owner unindexed (literally 'I cut the hand'). See examples in §13.3.

In some expressions the Dative can be seen as signalling an experiencer of a mental or bodily state. Many such idioms involve metaphorical uses of body parts, like *bekay* 'heart' in (359), and are difficult to distinguish from the owner-of-body-part use of the Dative.

(358) k-a-na-   w-a   yalen
      DIR-3SG.A-1.DAT-   3SG.U-AUX   taste.bad
      'It tasted bad (to me).'

(359) Discussing another — less pleasant — village.
      ndom-bekay   epe   ka-d-a-na-   ay-ma   nok
      bad-heart(III)   there DIR-DUR-3SG.A-1.DAT-   become:III.U-PST.HAB   1
      'I used to feel unhappy there.'   [W19:0358]

The Dative may be used to index the beneficiary of an action. The central feature of this use is that the Dative participants do not have to carry out the action by themselves, because the agent does it on their behalf (360), so-called substitutive benefaction (Kittilä 2005). The semantic difference between the recipient and the benefactive uses is clearest in examples that involve no transfer of a gift (361–362).

(360)   mesiwag   mak-o-   kahos-e
        old.woman   FUT:1.A-3SG.DAT-   chew.betel-IPFV
        'I will chew betelnut for grandma.' (Grandma has no teeth.)

(361)   kay   a-na-   kab
        door   IMP-1.DAT-   open
        'Open the door for me!'   [D11:0015]

(362)   Asking a bystander to identify a stranger.
        waninggap   a-na-   idih!
        good   IMP-1.DAT-   see:3SG.U
        'Have a good look at him for me!'   [W10:0317]

The negative counterpart to the benefactive — the malefactive Dative — also occurs, expressing that the person is adversely affected by the event. (This use is difficult to render elegantly in English; here I add 'on me' etc. to the free translations).

(363)   yayew   k-a-na-   w-a   kepad   onggat   kahek-la
        climbing.rope(III) DIR-3SG.A-1.DAT-   3SG.U-AUX   break:III.U   coconut   climb-PTCP:I
        'The rope (tied around feet and trunk) broke on me while climbing coconut tree.'

(364)   nggat   tamuy   mak-a-na-   yi,   pen   ka-mo-   w-amuk
        dog   food(III)   NAFUT-3SG.A-1.DAT- eat:III.U   murder DIR-FUT:1.A-   3SG.U-hit
        'The dog might eat the food on me, (if so,) then I will kill it.'   [W06:0162]

(365)   Describing how a person tried to catch some ducklings he found in the bush.
        isi   e=   ka-da-n-o-   ka-huhu-h
        other   PROX=   DIR-DUR-3PL.A-3SG.DAT- INESS-emerge.PLA-2|3PL.U
        'The rest of them went out on him.'   [W11:1040]

Malefactive uses as in (364) above are often similar to the 'affected owner' use of the Genitive prefix series described in §9.4.2 below, because the adverse action affects some item owned by the Dative participant. The difference is that the use of the Genitive series implies ownership, whereas the malefactive use of the Dative series gives no particular information of the way in which the participant is involved in the event.

Some verbs must be lexically specified as indexing one of their arguments by means of the Dative series. I list the most important ones here. The following verbs are intransitive, so the Dative indexes the sole argument:

>
> | | |
> |---|---|
> | yek | 'X$_{Dat}$ becomes used to s.t.' |
> | kamob | 'X$_{Dat}$ becomes betel-drunk' |
> | isik | 'X$_{Dat}$ becomes full (from eating)' |
> | dahuk | 'X$_{Dat}$ dies' |
> | luhay | 'X$_{Dat}$ remains in a different place' |

Recall that all inflected verb forms contain Actor indexing according to my analysis, which defaults to 3sg with these intransitive verbs, e.g.

(366) adu   tis ka,   men-b-a-na-y-p-   l-isik
      EXCLAM that's.it PERF-ACT-3SG.A-1.DAT-1PL-CT- PLA-become.full
      'Oh my, that's it, we're already full.'   [W12:0162]

Other verbs are transitive, with the agent-like participant indexed by means of the Actor prefixes, and the patient-like argument indexed by means of the Dative prefixes:

> | | |
> |---|---|
> | takin | 'X$_A$ waits for Y$_{Dat}$' |
> | yina | 'X$_A$ helps Y$_{Dat}$' |
> | ikaway | 'X$_A$ hides by Y$_{Dat}$' |
> | kalalid | 'X$_A$ invites Y$_{Dat}$' |
> | kahoy | 'X$_A$ frightens Y$_{Dat}$' |
> | lemed | 'X$_A$ meet Y$_{Dat}$' |
> | hyom | 'X$_A$ fucks Y$_{Dat}$'[11] |
> | talun | 'X$_A$ gives Y$_{Dat}$ a push' |
> | dahuy | 'X$_A$ prevents Y$_{Dat}$ from leaving' |
> | wayuk | 'X$_A$ joins/associates with Y$_{Dat}$' |

These verbs are described as valence classes in §12.2.4 and §12.3.3 respectively.

9.4 Genitive indexing

The Genitive prefixes have a more limited range of uses than the Dative prefixes, and while the label 'Genitive' is less felicitous for some of these uses, it captures their most common function. In general terms, the Genitive prefixes index a participant which, although not directly involved in the action described by the verb, is affected by (or

---

[11] Note that the verb *hyom* is considered very vulgar; a politer expression used for 'have intercourse' is *kisa* 'grab', which is a standard transitive verb of the alternating class.

in some other way important to) the event qua possessor of one of the more central arguments.

There are also a few verbs that have Genitive indexing as a fixed part of their indexing template; the most common are *gan* 'hear' and *yoman* 'meet, reach', which always index their patient-like arguments by means of Genitive prefixes. Cf. the end of §9.4.2 below.

9.4.1 Form of the Genitive prefixes

The person/number combinations are expressed by the prefixes in Table 9.3. The Genitive prefixes are identical to the Dative prefixes (Table 9.2) except for the final segment *mb-*. Synchronically, however, the two series are clearly distinct, since the Genitive prefixes occur in a different position of the prefix template (position class −9) than the Dative prefixes (class −5), and may co-occur with them, as in (370) further below. The sequence *-mb-* does not have any other function.

Tab. 9.3: The Genitive prefixes

	SG	PL
1	namb-	
2	amb-	emb-
3	omb-	

Example (367) shows that a Genitive prefix is ordered before the Frustrative *um-* of position class −8; this example also shows that the /o/ in *omb-* undergoes Antepenultimate vowel gradation to [u] (§2.5.1).

(367) oso m-ak-umb-um-e- yoman
       start OBJ-1.A-3SG.GEN-FRUS-1PL- approach
       'We were almost reaching it.' [W02:0179]

The other phonological alternation affecting the Genitive prefixes is syllable-final simplification of the prenasalised plosive /m̪b/: when this segment (which is found in all members of the Genitive paradigm) cannot syllabify in onset position, it is simplified to [m] (cf. §2.1.1.1). This is observed in the paradigm given in Table 9.4, in which the Genitive prefix occurs in the end of the prefixal complex (left column) and followed by the Repetitive *i-* (of position class −6; right column).

Tab. 9.4: The Genitive prefixes: 'S/he_A will hear X_Gen'
ndap- = FUT, *ø-/a-* = 3SG.A, *e-* = 1PL, *gan* 'hear'.

	without Repetitive *i-*	with Repetitive *i-*
1SG	*ndap-a-nam- gan* 'S/he will hear me'	*ndap-a-namb-i- gan* 'S/he will hear me again'
2SG	*ndap-ø-am- gan* 'S/he will hear you'	*ndap-ø-amb-i- gan* 'S/he will hear you again'
3SG	*ndap-ø-om- gan* 'S/he will hear it'	*ndap-ø-omb-i- gan* 'S/he will hear it again'
1PL	*ndap-a-namb-e- gan* 'S/he will hear us'	*ndap-a-namb-i-e- gan* 'S/he will hear us again'
2PL	*ndap-ø-em- gan* 'S/he will hear you'	*ndap-ø-emb-i- gan* 'S/he will hear you again'
3PL	*ndap-ø-em- gan* 'S/he will hear them'	*ndap-ø-emb-i- gan* 'S/he will hear them again'

9.4.2 Functions of Genitive indexing

As stated above, the Genitive series indexes an owner of one of the other arguments of the verb. The possessed item is never a body part, since owners of body parts are indexed by means of the Dative prefix series (see §9.3.2). I am not aware of any other constraints on the possessed participant: both animates, as in (368), and inanimates, as in the observed example (369), co-occur with Genitive-marked verbs:

(368) *nalakam elel   ø-d-ø-om-   ola*
      child   sick   NTRL-DUR-3SG.A-3SG.GEN-   be:3SG.U
      'Her child was sick.'   [W09:0011]

(369) *de-roko   men-b-a-nam-   lahway,   takah   ø-na-ka-   og!*
      wood-tobacco(m) PERF-ACT-3SG.A-1.GEN- fire.go.out, fire   IMP-1.DAT-PRI- give
      'My cigarette went out, give me the lighter!'

The fact that Dative and Genitive index different types of 'possessors' is clear from cases where they co-occur within the same verb, indexing different participants. Example (370) is the utterance following (368) in an account explaining why a woman had to go to the aid post with her child. Although both sentences ostensibly are about the child, the Genitive prefix *omb-* marks the mother as being the 'affected owner' of the sick child, while the Dative prefix *o-* in (370) marks the child as being the 'affected owner' of the stomach. The prefixes have been marked with indices; the second, less idiomatic, translation reflects the participants corresponding to the respective prefixes.

(370) yandam k-ø-omb$_i$-o$_j$-   w-a   yadan
      stomach DIR-3SG.A-3SG.GEN-3SG.DAT- 3SG.U-AUX get.swollen
      'His$_i$ stomach was swollen.'
      'The stomach was swollen to [her$_i$ child$_j$].'   [W09:0012]

It is difficult to explicate in any detail the semantics that license the use of Genitive indexing. Examples (368–369) have an adversely affected possessor, but non-affected possessors also occur. For example, Genitive indexing is used to express predicative possession (371), or the whereabouts of people's belongings (372–373).

(371) mesiwag Babob mbya ø-d-ø-om-   ola   kahos
      old.woman B.   NEG   NTRL-DUR-3SG.A-3SG.GEN- be:III.U   betel(III)
      'Auntie Babob didn't have any betelnut.'   [W21:0250]

(372) aha   en   nda-ha-b-ø-om-   itala?
      house where LOC-ROG-ACT-3SG.A-3SG.GEN-   be.standing
      'Where is his/her house?'

(373) Said to child who was about to move elder brother's kava plants.
      wati   adeh m-ø-omb-ap-   ka-hat-a,   yap   ndame-ø- ikuwad
      kava(III) RLQ   OBJ-2SG.A-3SG.GEN-CT-   INESS-put:III.U-EXT   night FUT-3SG.A- drink.kava
      'Let his kava sit there (on the table), he'll drink it tonight.'

The entity that is owned by the Genitive participant is often the S-argument of the clause, as in (371–372) above, since verbs expressing predicative possession and location typically are one-place predicates, but it can also be in the O-role, as in (373), or as in (330) on p. 202. I have no information about a possessed entity filling the A-role of a Genitive-marked verb, but note that the possessed participant is not necessarily an argument of the verb, as witnessed by (1056b) on p. 516.

There is one remarkable use of the Genitive that involves no possession at all, and instead has a causal meaning, with the Genitive prefix indexing a participant that brings about the event described by the verb (374–376). This use is only attested with intransitive verbs. The addition of the Genitive causer does not affect the properties of the original argument of the verb, which appears with the same indexes on the verb, i.e. Undergoer indexing if the verb is patientive (374–375), or Actor indexing if the verb is agentive (376). The participant undergoing the caused change remains in the S-argument role, which is why I avoid labelling this a causative construction, opting for the vaguer label 'causal'. The added participant, if it is expressed pre-verbally as in (376), triggers the use of the Object Orientation on the verb, in analogy with the adverbials with causal meaning described in §11.1.3.5.

(374) Describing how some men beat a pig during a pig feast.

tis, menda-b-ø-em- kahwid basik
finished PERF-ACT-3SG.A-2|3PL.GEN- die:3SG.U pig

'That's it, they had made the pig die/the pig had died because of them.'

[W18:0067]

(375) Speaker complaining about a nearby child's handling of a kitten.

ndap-ø-om- kahwid, sangga lek ka-me-ø- kahwid
FUT-3SG.A-3SG.GEN- die:3SG.U hand from:III DIR-FUT-3SG.A- die:3SG.U

'It will die because of her, it will die from [being squeezed by] the hands.'

[W14:0147]

(376) In a story, some women trick a man into swimming around in a lake, looking for their reflection.

yoy m-ak-em- i-hyaman hyakod yanid ehe!
2PL OBJ-1.A-2|3PL.GEN- PLA-enter.water one day(III) PROX:III

'Because of you I swam for an entire day!' [D01:0211]

See also the remarks in §13.3 about the general lack of grammaticalised means of expressing causation in Coastal Marind.

The Genitive prefixes are part of the indexing template of the following verbs:

yoman   'X_A meets Y_{Gen}'
gan   'X_A hears Y_{Gen}'
wig   '$X_{A,U}$ begs Y_{Gen} for s.t.'
hayan   'Y_{Gen} becomes quiet'

Below are examples illustrating *wig* 'beg' (377) and *yoman* 'meet' (378). Note that *wig* 'beg' is a middle verb (§10.1.2), so the agent-like participant is indexed both by the Actor prefix and in the verb stem.

(377) yah a-me-ø- dahetok-a-m epe, kanis
but DEP-FUT-3SG.A- return-EXT-VEN DIST:III betel

ndam-omb-ap- y-ig
FUT:2SG.A-3SG.GEN-CT- 2SG.U-beg

'When he returns, you should ask him for betelnut.' [W20:0049]

(378) 1. in   e=   k-ak-em-   ka-yoman   ay?
        middle PROX= DIR-1.A-2|3PL.GEN- INESS-approach Q
        'I met you in the middle, right?'

   2. ahak epe k-u-namb-e-   ka-yoman   motor-kay
      yeah there DIR-2SG.A-1.GEN-1PL- INESS-approach motorcycle(m)-path
      'Yeah you met us there by the motorcycle path.'   [W11:0666-0667]

The verb 'sit' is used with the Prioritive *ka-* to mean 'wait' (lit. 'sit first'). The Genitive can be added to this combination, and then indexes a person for whom one is waiting (379).

(379) oy m-ak-amb-e-ka-   hamat-a
      2SG OBJ-1.A-2SG.GEN-1PL-PRI- sit.PL-EXT
      'We are waiting for you.'   [W19:0016]

This use is perhaps related to the 'causal' use of the Genitive prefixes ('We are waiting because of you').

9.5 The role-neutral 1pl prefix *e-*

The prefix *e-* (glossed 1PL) is obligatory whenever one of the arguments of a verb is a 1st person plural participant, regardless of whether this argument is indexed by means of the Actor, Undergoer, Dative or Genitive series. The 1st person indexes (Actor *nak-*, Dative *na-* etc.) do not distinguish singular from plural, just like the 1st person independent pronoun *nok* means both 'I' and 'we', but in the absence of the role-neutral 1pl prefix *e-* a 1st person index is interpreted as indexing a singular participant.

The prefix is illustrated (380), combined with all four types of participant indexing: 1pl Actor (380a), Undergoer (380b), Dative (380c) and Genitive (380d).

(380) a. nak-e-   nayam milah
        1.A-1PL- come.PL village
        'We came to the village.'   [W07:0047]

   b. etob   ø-ø-e-   tangga⟨n⟩ab
      sea.water NTRL-3SG.A-1PL- chase.away⟨1.U⟩
      'The (approaching) sea water forced us away.'   [W07:0026]

   c. ø-na-y-   ayi ago [...]
      3SG.A-1.DAT-1PL- say QUOT
      'He said to us that...'   [D07:0078]

d. roko   mbya   ø-d-a-namb-e-   ola
    tobacco(m)(III) NEG   NTRL-DUR-3SG.A-1.GEN-1PL-   be:III.U
    'We didn't have any smokes.'   [W02:0107]

The 1pl argument is indexed by *e-* even if the verb belongs to one of the classes of verbs that do not index person/number of the argument role filled by the 1st person participant in the clause. For example, the verb *kaguh* 'give birth' has a separate Pluractional stem *ewah* which is used whenever the Undergoer is plural. This Pluractional stem belongs to the invariant class of verbs (see §10.2.1). As opposed to the singular stem *kaguh*, which infixes a person/number marker reflecting the Undergoer (381a), the Pluractional stem *ewah* does not take any morphology signalling the person, number and role of the offspring (381b). The role-neutral 1pl *e-* still appears in (381b), as it is insensitive to the inflectional class of the stem, and only requires that the 1pl participant is an argument of the verb.

(381) a. u=   tu-ø-a-   kagu⟨n⟩ah
         PROX:II= GIV:II-NTRL-3SG.A-   give.birth⟨1.U⟩
         'It was she who gave birth to me.'

      b. u=   tu-ø-d-ø-e-   ewah
         PROX:II= GIV:II-NTRL-DUR-3SG.A-1PL-   give.birth.PLA
         'It was she who gave birth to us.'

Compare these elicited examples to example (971) on p. 480, in which the 1pl participant is an adjunct (i.e. a non-argument) and therefore does not trigger the use of 1pl *e-*.

The indexing of 1st person prefixes differs from other indexing of person, number and role in Coastal Marind in that the other indexes always express person, number and role within a single exponent. For example, the 2sg Actor prefix *o-* simultaneously expresses 2nd person, singular number and Actor role. For the 1st person, however, Actor *nak-* marks person but not number, and 1pl *e-* marks person and (plural) number but not role. The expression of first person by means of this type of 'non-cumulative' exponence is in fact the opposite of what would be expected from a cross-linguistic point-of-view: there is a strong tendency of 1st person person/number marking to be more opaque (i.e. expressed by person/number portmanteaux) than 3rd person cross-linguistically (Dressler and Barbaresi 1994: 60–64, Siewierska 2004: 93–94).

Note that the 1PL *e-* must be distinguished from 3PL>1 *e-* (§9.2.2.3), with which it can co-occur.

9.6 Inclusory and associative indexing constructions

In this section two special indexing patterns are mentioned.

9.6.1 Inclusory plural

It is common to express plurality of an argument by combining plural indexing in the verb with a phrase (typically just a name) marked by the postposition *ti* 'with' (§6.1.2). The *ti*-marked phrase picks out a member of the set indexed by the plural marking on the verb. Thus, a sentence of the form

$$(A_i) \quad X\text{-}ti \quad 3\text{PL.A}_i\text{-Verb}$$

can be literally translated as 'The group A, including X, Verbed', or, if A refers to a single participant, 'A and X verbed'. (The noun phrase referring to A can be left out if the identity of A is clear from context, as indicated by the parentheses.) Following Lichtenberk (2000) I call this the inclusory construction or inclusory plural.

Corpus examples of inclusory plurals are in (382). The relevant participants fill different argument slots: S-argument of *wayaman* in (382a), and patient-like argument of *mahid* 'get angry' in (382b). The superset ('we') is indexed accordingly on the verbs, with the A-prefix and a suppletive plural stem in (382a), and the Dative prefix in (382b) (indexing the patient-like argument by means of the Dative series is an idiosyncrasy of the verb *mahid*).

(382) a. nok Vitalis ti   ø-nan-d-e-   wayamat-a
      1   V.   with:I/II.PL NTRL-1.A-DUR-1PL- stand.PL-EXT
      'Vitalis and I were standing there.'   [W11:0863]

    b. Budoy ti   ma-bt-i-n-ind-a-y-   mahid
      B.   with:I/II.PL OBJ-AFF-3PL>1-1.DAT-ALL-1.DAT-1PL- get.angry
      'They got angry at me and Budoy.'   [W11:0961]

In these examples, context makes it clear that the supersets refer to two people (e.g. 'Vitalis and I') but the same clauses can be used with a superset of any cardinality, although this would correspond to different English translations ('Vitalis and the rest of us', etc.).

Note that the inclusory plurals are different from the use of *ti* to mark comitative constructions (see §6.1.2), since comitatives never trigger plural marking on the verb.

9.6.2 Associative indexing

A second special type of indexing consists of a noun phrase with singular reference (typically a proper name), which is indexed on the verb by means of a plural marker. This pattern is so far only attested with the Actor prefixes, and has the same meaning as the Associative Plural marker *ke* in the nominal domain (§7.6.1), i.e. 'X and those associated with X'.

Consider (383). The noun phrase *Rovina* refers to a girl named Rovina, but the Actor indexing on the verb is 3rd person plural *n-*. This mismatch gives rise to the associative reading 'Rovina and the others'.

(383)   tis ka,   Rovina   tanama   ka-n-   dahetok
        that's.it   R.   again   DIR-3PL.A-   return
        'That's it, then Rovina and the others went back again.'   [W09:0098]

10 Participant indexing II: Undergoer alternations

A patient-like participant of a transitive verb (e.g. the O-argument of 'hit') or intransitive verb (the S-argument of 'die') is generally indexed by means of Undergoer alternations in the verb stem, as described in this chapter. In example (384), the form *yamuk* is the 2nd person singular Undergoer form of the verb *wamuk* 'hit'.

(384)   no-   y-amuk
        1.A- 2SG.U-hit
        'I hit you.'

The general features of Undergoer indexing are covered in §10.1, including indexing of transitive O-arguments and patientive S-arguments (§10.1.1). An important quirk is that many common agentive intransitive verbs, such as motion verbs, exhibit a 'reflexive' indexing pattern, in which the agent is indexed simultaneously by the Actor prefix and Undergoer alternations — the so-called middle indexing pattern (§10.1.2).

The term *alternation* is used instead of 'affix', because the the exact locus of exponence (as a prefix, suffix or infix) is determined by the inflection class of the verb lexeme, and for some verb stems no segmentation is possible. The formal characteristics of verb stems are introduced in §10.2. A crucial observation is that the presence of Undergoer indexing is lexically restricted to about half of the verbal lexicon. Verb lexemes that participate in Undergoer indexing are *alternating*, and verb lexemes that do not are *invariant* (§10.2.1).

The four inflectional classes, distinguishing prefixing, infixing, suffixing and double-marking verb lexemes, are described in §10.3.

Alternating verbs that only select for inanimate S/O-arguments are treated in §10.4. These lack the full range of person/number stems of other verbs, and only reflect the gender of the Undergoer argument.

Finally, §10.5 describes verb suppletion according to the number of the S/O-argument, which affects more than a dozen verb lexemes.

10.1 Overview of Undergoer indexing

The morphology of Undergoer alternations is much more complex that the realisation of the indexing prefixes described in Chapter 9. In (385) I give four examples illustrating the four inflectional classes that need to be posited to account for the locus of Undergoer alternations; these examples show the 1st person stem forms. The four classes are: prefixing (a), infixing (b), suffixing (c), and double-marking (d) verbs — see further §10.3. Note that inflectional class membership does not correlate with semantics or valence, so there is no specific reason that e.g. the prefixing verb 'hit' in (385a) is transitive, or the suffixing verb 'fall' in (385c) intransitive, and so on.

(385) a. mend-a- n-amuk
PERF-3SG.A- 1.U-hit
'S/he already hit me.'

b. mend-a- yada⟨n⟩awn
PERF-3SG.A- leave⟨1.U⟩
'S/he already left me.'

c. mend-a- hi-n
PERF-3SG.A- fall-1.U
'I already fell.'

d. mend-a- n-usu-n
PERF-3SG.A- 1.U-heat-1.U
'I already became warm.'

The label Undergoer indexing is used in this grammar, instead of the more transparent 'object indexing' or 'patient indexing', for the following reasons. First, the set of participants that trigger Undergoer indexing do not correspond to any intuitive notion of syntactic object, so it is better to reserve the object label for the grammatical relation (§18.1). Second, although most participants that trigger Undergoer indexing bear the participant role of patient, there is no one-to-one correspondence between patients and the participants triggering Undergoer indexing. The patient-like participant of some verbs (such as *yina* 'help') are indexed with the Dative prefixes (§9.3), others (such as *yoman* 'meet'), with the Genitive prefixes (§9.4). If the verb is of the middle type (§10.1.2), its agent-like participant will be (co-)indexed by the Undergoer alternation.

The following three subsections outline the mapping between participant roles and Undergoer indexing for three types of verbs.

10.1.1 Indexing of transitive O and patientive S

The semantic role of patient corresponds to two argument roles: the O-argument of standard monotransitive verbs, and the S-argument of patientive intransitive verbs. This section summarises the mapping between these roles and Undergoer indexing.

If a verb describes an action that involves an agent-like participant acting on a patient-like participant, then the patient-like argument is indexed by means of Undergoer alternations. This can be seen in (385a–b) above and many other examples in this grammar. In the description of valence classes, these verbs belong to class 2a (§12.3.1).

The main exceptions to this rule are:
- Invariant verbs, which lack Undergoer stem forms (§10.2.1). Transitive verbs of this type belong to valence class 2b (§12.3.1).
- verbs such as *kamin* 'make', which exhibits the middle indexing pattern (§10.1.2). These belong to the valence class 2c (§12.3.2).
- transitive verbs with Dative or Genitive indexing of the patient (§9.3, §9.4). These belong to valence class 2d (§12.3.3) and 2e (§12.3.4) respectively.

Patientive intransitive verbs like *hi* 'fall' and *kahwid* 'die' index their sole argument by means of Undergoer alternations, which causes the Actor prefix to default to 3sg. Patientive verbs belong to valence class 1b, and are listed in §12.2.2. The main exceptions are:
- A small set of verbs, such as *yod* 'vomit', which are semantically patientive but index their sole argument by means of the Actor prefixes (listed in §12.2.2)
- A small set of 'Dative Experiencer' verbs, such as *isik* 'become full', which index their sole participant by means of the Dative prefixes (valence class 1d; §12.2.4)

10.1.2 The middle indexing pattern

Intransitive middle verbs are treated as a valence class in §12.2.3; in this section I will briefly describe and exemplify the indexing pattern of such verbs.

An alternating verb exhibits the middle indexing pattern if the agent-like participant is simultaneously indexed by means of the Actor prefix series in the prefixal complex and Undergoer alternations in the verb stem. A middle verb such as *umuh* 'go, take off' with, say, a 2nd person singular subject will display the 2sg Actor prefix *o-*, together with the 2sg Undergoer stem *uma⟨y⟩ah* (*umuh* belongs to the infixing class; §10.3.2). Middle verbs are the only verbs in which the stem alternates according to person/number of an agent-like participant rather than a patient. Since most middle verbs are intransitive and describe e.g. motion or posture, there is no patient-like argument for the stem to index.

In (386) a complete set showing all six person/number combinations of *umuh* 'go' is given.

(386) a. *menda-no- uma⟨n⟩ah* b. *mend-ak-e- uma⟨n⟩ah*
           PERF-1.A- go⟨1.U⟩   PERF-1.A-1PL- go⟨1.U⟩
           'I already went.'   'We already went.'

       c. *mend-o- uma⟨y⟩ah*   d. *mend-e- umah*
           PERF-2SG.A- go⟨2SG.U⟩   PERF-2PL.A- go:2|3PL.U
           'You already went.'   'You (pl) already went.'

       e. *mend-a- umuh*   f. *mend-a- umah*
           PERF-3SG.A- go:3SG.U   PERF-3SG.A- go:2|3PL.U
           'S/he already went.'   'They already went.'

The only exception to the pattern of matching indexing values in the Actor prefix and the verb stem is the 3pl form (386f). Middle verbs is one of the two contexts in which 3rd person indexing defaults to the 3sg Actor prefix *a-* (§9.2.2.2). The person reference of the form in (386f) remains unambiguous since the combination of the 3sg Actor prefix and a 2|3pl Undergoer verb stem does not occur in any other context.

10.2 Undergoer stem alternations

Coastal Marind verb lexemes can be divided into two groups: (i) verbs that exhibit stem alternations according to person/number (in the case of animates) and/or gender (in the case of inanimates) of the Undergoer argument (roughly a patient-like participant, see §10.1 for further clarification) and (ii) verbs that are invariant and employ the same stem regardless of the presence or absence of an Undergoer. Out of 627 investigated lexemes, 302 (or 48%) were identified as alternating. There is no way to predict with certainty whether a verb is invariant or alternating given only its meaning and/or transitivity, nor from inspecting the phonological shape of e.g. the stem chosen as the lemma in the dictionary (typically the 3sg stem form for alternating verbs), but there are nevertheless some clear correlations (§10.2.1).

For an illustration of an invariant and an alternating verb, compare the invariant 'bark' with the alternating 'shoot', here shown with three person/number combinations:

(387) Invariant verb
    a. nok ma-d-ø- abun
       'It was barking at me.'
    b. oy ma-d-ø- abun
       'It was barking at you (sg).'
    c. yoy ma-d-ø- abun
       'It was barking at you (pl).'

(388) Alternating verb
    a. nok ma-d-ø- n-as
       'S/he was shooting at me.'
    b. oy ma-d-ø- y-as
       'S/he was shooting at you (sg).'
    c. yoy ma-d-ø- y-as
       'S/he was shooting at you (pl).'

(In these examples, the prefix *ma-* is the Object Orientation, *d-* is the Past Durative, and ø- realises 3sg Actor.)

Alternating verbs are divided into four superclasses according to the locus of the morphological change within the stem. These classes are summarised in Table 10.1, along with the stems of one verb from each inflectional class. The largest class is Class 2, with more than 200 members, followed by Class 1, with 26 members, Class 3, with around 20 members and Class 4, with a handful of members. The exponents vary between the classes, but are largely predictable. Each class will be described in detail in §10.3.1–§10.3.4.

Alternating verbal lexemes are also classified according to the type of Undergoers they accept. Some verbs only admit animate Undergoers, and some only inanimate Undergoers. Others occur with both animate and inanimate Undergoers. Inanimates

Tab. 10.1: Summary of the four inflectional classes

	1. Prefixing 'u become tired'	2. Infixing 'chase away u'	3. Suffixing 'u crawl'	4. Double-marking 'snatch from u'
1SG|PL	n-ihwid	tangga⟨n⟩ab	lolo-n	n-aska⟨n⟩ab
2SG	y-ihwid	tangga⟨y⟩ab	lolo-y	y-aska⟨y⟩ab
3SG	w-ihid	tangg⟨e⟩b	lola-w	w-asaka⟨ø⟩b
2|3PL	ø-ihwid	tangg⟨ø⟩ab	lolo-h	y-aska⟨hy⟩ab

are always 3rd person, and do not distinguish singular and plural number, so they do not trigger person/number indexing. Instead, the verb stem alternates according to the gender of the inanimate Undergoer, i.e. either Gender III or Gender IV (see Chapter 5). An example of a verb that only occurs with inanimate Undergoers is given in (389).

(389) a. *nggat ø-ø-na-   haniy   sangga*
         dog   NTRL-3SG.A-1.DAT- bite:III.U hand(III)
         'A dog bit my hand.'

   b. *nggat ø-ø-na-   hanih   mig*
         dog   NTRL-3SG.A-1.DAT- bite:IV.U knee(IV)
         'A dog bit my knee.'

No other target in the language indexes both person/number of animates and the gender of inanimates. This renders the description of Undergoer alternations very complex, and it is difficult to predict whether a verb is alternating or invariant (§10.2.1); and for alternating verbs, whether it permits inanimate Undergoers (§10.2.2); and for such verbs, what the forms corresponding to Genders III and IV are (§10.4).

The following conventions are used when referring to alternating verb lexemes in the remainder of this chapter. When an English gloss of an alternating verb is given, it is given with the shorthand 'U' placed in the position in the English valence frame that best corresponds to the participant that is indexed on the Coastal Marind stem. For example, from reading the gloss 'snatch from U', the reader can gather that the stem indexes the participant who is deprived of a thing (and not the thing that is snatched away, or the agent who does the snatching). Secondly, I refer to alternating verb lexemes using the 3rd person Undergoer stem form as the lemma.[1]

---

[1] In the rare cases of verbs lacking a 3sg form, the 3pl stem is used as the lemma, e.g. *ibingg⟨ø⟩ab* 'gather⟨2|3PL.U⟩'.

10.2.1 Classification of verbs as invariant or alternating

It is not possible to tell with any certainty whether a given verb belongs to the invariant class or the alternating class from only looking at its meaning, or the shape of e.g. the stem chosen as the lemma in the dictionary. Syntactic transitivity does not predict the behaviour of a lexeme: typical transitive verbs include both invariant (*keway* 'break') and alternating (*walok* 'stab U') lexemes, just like intransitive verbs can be invariant (*ayak* 'go inland') or alternating (*oha* 'U go down to water'). As suggested by the last examples, it is easy to find pairs of verbs with similar or even synonymous meanings where one verb is invariant and the other alternating. For example, *kayam* 'look up' is invariant whereas *mikeh* 'U look to the side' is alternating, despite their similar meanings. The synonyms *dahuk* and *kahwid* both mean 'die', but only *kahwid* is alternating, and so on.[2]

Nevertheless, there are some clear tendencies, both semantic and formal, in the assignment to the alternating versus invariant classes. I will first consider the semantic correlates of the divide. The most important observation is that verbs that denote actions involving a 'highly affected' patient-like participant are often expressed by alternating verbs, whereas verbs on the other end of the transitivity spectrum (involving a participant that does not undergo any change, or involving no participants at all) typically correspond to invariant lexemes.

To get a feel for this, consider Table 10.2. This table lists some semantic verb classes according to the proportion of alternating stems in each class. (This selection was made entirely ad-hoc, by choosing some semantic fields that would allow straightforward classification of at least some verbs; other groupings would certainly be possible.) When counting the proportion of alternating lexemes in the semantic fields, it turns out that verbs of e.g. hitting and breaking are mostly alternating, while most verbs denoting sound emission (e.g. *kin* 'sing', *esol* 'make noise') and natural phenomena (*alalam* 'lightning to flash') are invariant.

This scale is partly similar to scales of transitivity proposed in typological studies (Tsunoda 1985, Haspelmath 2015), with more highly transitive verbs receiving a higher score. The main surprise is that three typically intransitive semantic classes turn out to have many alternating members (with the scores .40, .42 and .56). These classes consist of verbs that typically involve a single participant undergoing some self-initiated

---

[2] There are also several invariant verbs that are documented as alternating in older sources: for example, *kusatok* 'swallow' is invariant for contemporary speakers of the Western dialect of Coastal Marind, while Geurtjens (1933: 185) reports that its cognate in the Eastern dialect alternates according to the swallowee, e.g. Eastern *kausta⟨h⟩uk* 'swallow⟨2SG.U⟩' (used in a sentence such as 'the crocodile will swallow you'; the corresponding Western dialect form **kusta⟨y⟩uk* is not acceptable according to speakers). Surprisingly, at least one invariant verb, *hway* 'paddle, punt', whose Eastern cognate *vay* is given as invariant also in Drabbe's grammar (1955: 49), is claimed to be alternating by Geurtjens (1933: 328). I have no explanation for this. It seems unlikely that the verb ceased to be alternating in the short period between Geurtjens' and Drabbe's publications.

Tab. 10.2: Proportion of alternating stems across some semantic classes

Semantic field (*n* verbs)	Alternating
TYING (6)	1.00
HITTING (12)	.92
PUTTING (23)	.74
HOLD/CARRYING (23)	.70
BREAKING (15)	.67
CUTTING (22)	.59
POSTURE (18)	.56
NON-TRANSLATIONAL MOTION (26)	.42
TRANSLATIONAL MOTION (50)	.40
CONSUMING (9)	.33
COMMUNICATION (11)	.27
EMISSION OF SOUND (10)	.20
NATURAL PHENOMENA (16)	.0

change: posture verbs (e.g. *ambid* 'sit down'), verbs of non-translational motion (e.g. *atuk* 'flap wings') and translational motion (e.g. *ihon* 'run away'). The explanation for this pattern is that the alternating verbs in these classes exhibit the so-called middle indexing pattern, and index the sole participant by A- and U-affixing simultaneously. This is further discussed in §10.1.2.

Apart from the tendency of affected undergoer-actions to be expressed by alternating verbs, little can be offered in the way of semantic rules predicting invariant/alternating status. The only generalisation is probably that verbs that only combine with a very limited type of Undergoer participants are always invariant (this includes all verbs expressing natural phenomena). For example:

- Avalent verbs, e.g. *ihwim* 'become dark/night', *pig* 'become bright/day'.
- Verbs that only combine with a very narrow range of Undergoers, e.g. *ikuwad* 'drink wati'. Since *wati* (the local variety of kava, a mildly narcotic beverage) is inanimate (lacking number and person values) and always belongs to Gender III, there are no shifting feature values that could cause the stem to alternate. Other examples: *yol* 'pound sago', *itawip* 'extinguish fire', *lik* 'river to flow', *lod* 'make a windshield', *ayok* 'cover leaf oven' (the words for 'sago', 'fire', 'river', 'windshield' and 'leaf oven' are always Gender III); and *takun* 'make roof from sago thatch' ('sago thatch' is always Gender IV).

Note also that verbs that are borrowings from Malay remain invariant, e.g. *malayu* 'speak Malay', *sakola* 'attend school', *senter* 'shine flashlight'.

10.2.2 Paradigmatic structure of alternating verbs

Within the class of alternating verbs the paradigms can be grouped into four main patterns according to the number of cells that are filled by stem forms, and the layout of these cells. These patterns are orthogonal to the distinction between inflectional classes, so the different types of paradigm layouts are found both within e.g. the prefixing and infixing stem classes. (The number of lexemes exhibiting the paradigm pattern is indicated within parentheses.)

1. **Animate-only verbs ($n=56$)** only occur with animate Undergoers, i.e. humans and animals. They have stem forms distinguishing person and number. For example, *wihid* 'become tired' occurs only with animates (one could imagine metaphorical extensions to inanimates of Genders III and IV, but this has not been found so far).

wihid 'U become tired'

	SG	PL
1		*n-ihwid*
2	*y-ihwid*	*ø-ihwid*
3	*w-ihid*	

2. **Inanimate-only verbs ($n=72$)** are restricted to occurring with inanimate Undergoers and have only 2 cells, reflecting the gender of the Undergoer (III or IV; Genders I and II consist of animates). Inanimate-only verbs do not have person forms (since they cannot have 1st or 2nd person Undergoers) and do not distinguish number of the Undergoer. An example is the verb *awiy* 'hurt' which only occurs with body parts. Its complete paradigm is

awiy 'U hurt'

	SG	PL
III		*awiy*
IV		*awih*

The III form could be used with one or both hands (*sangga*, III) hurting, and the IV form with one or both knees (*mig*, IV) hurting.

3. **Unrestricted verbs ($n=143$)** are equally compatible with animate and inanimate Undergoers. The stem used for inanimates of Gender III is the same as the 3SG.U stem used for animates; the one used for inanimates of Gender IV is the same as the 2|3PL.U stem. An example is *hwagib* 'put away U'. This verb is common both for animates (in meanings such as put away a sleeping child, or euphemistically for burying the dead) and inanimates (e.g. *tamuy hwagib* 'put away food', III, or *katal hwagahib* 'save money', IV).

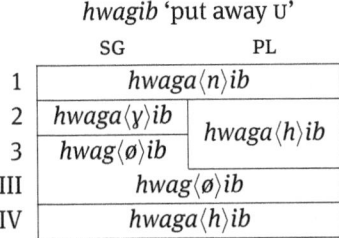

4. **Paired animate-inanimate verbs (*n*=31)** have one lexeme combining with an animate Undergoer (with a full set of person forms), and a second, derivationally related lexeme used with an inanimate Undergoer (with two stems, used for Undergoers of Genders III and IV). As with the unrestricted verbs, the stem used with inanimates of Gender IV is the same as the animate 2|3PL.U stem. An example is the verb *ambeh* 'wrap up (animate)' (e.g. a small child in a blanket, or fish in banana leaves) which is paired with *ambam* 'wrap up (inanimate)' (e.g. putting bandage around a body part). Both verbs share the stem *ambah*, used for 2|3PL.U animates and inanimates of Gender IV.

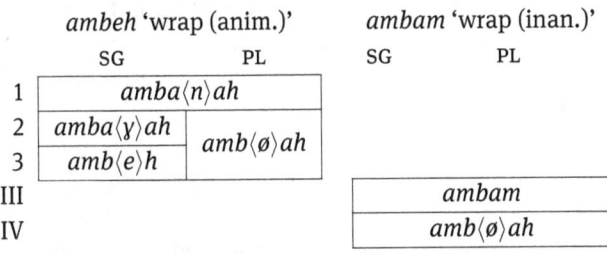

Setting aside the more complicated paired animate-inanimate verbs for now, we can represent the paradigm structures of the three other classes as follows. The Gender III stem of inanimate-only verbs is labelled Z to emphasise that it is always distinct from other stem forms, and the Gender IV stems of inanimate-only and unrestricted verbs are labelled D along with the 2|3PL.U stems with which they are systematically identical.

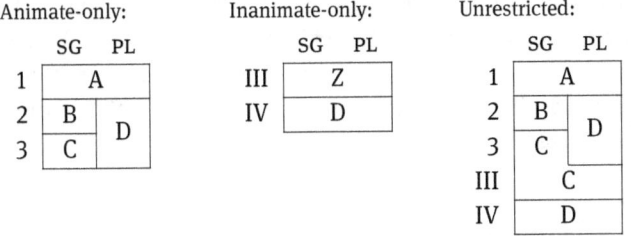

This situation leads to a labelling problem, most prominently for the D-cells. It would be misleading to use the label '2|3PL' for the stems used with inanimates (as these do not distinguish person, and — mostly — not number either), and using the label

'IV' when such stems are used with inanimates fails to convey the fact that they are systematically identical to the 2|3PL.U stems. Despite the fact that it does not reflect the system in an accurate way, I opt for the latter solution, and gloss a verb stem such as *hwaga⟨h⟩ib* 'put.away⟨IV.U⟩' if the indexing is triggered by an inanimate (e.g. *katal* 'money', IV) and 'put.away⟨2|3PL.U⟩' if it is triggered by animates (*awe* 'fish'). This difficulty does not arise for inanimate-only verbs, since stems such as *awih* 'hurt:IV.U' lack a corresponding use with animate plurals.

10.2.3 Glossing of verb stems distinguishing number of inanimates

Labelling stems used for Undergoers of Gender IV by means of 'IV.U' instead of '2|3PL.U' (despite their relatedness to the 2|3PL.U stems of animate-only and unrestricted verbs) turns out to be particularly useful for labelling stems belonging to lexemes for which part (or all) of the plural cells have been taken over by Pluractional stem forms, and/or show suppletion affecting part of the paradigm. The Pluractional (§16.1.2) is usually a separate derivational category available to many verbs, but in several lexemes it seems to have replaced the original non-Pluractional stems of the plural cells, so that there no longer exists a choice between Pluractional and non-Pluractional stems whenever the indexed participant is plural.

An example is the verb 'fall' which has the singular forms *hi-n* (1st person), *hi-y* (2nd person) and *hi* (3rd person), and the corresponding Pluractional stems *hihi-n*, *hihi-y* and *hihi* (to be used e.g. if one person falls multiple times). If this verb had regular plural forms, we would expect 1pl to be expressed by the stem *hi-n* as well (plus the role-neutral 1pl prefix *e-* in the prefixal complex), and the form *hi-h* to be recruited for the 2pl and 3pl parts of the paradigm (cf. other suffixing verbs such as 2|3pl *oha-h* 'go down to water'). Instead, 'fall' requires that the Pluractional stems *hihi-n* and *hihi-h* be used, regardless of whether falling occurred e.g. as a group or on different occasions involving different participants — the Pluractional forms have simply taken over this part of the paradigm. However, the Pluractional forms have only taken over the parts of the paradigm that actually involve a plural participant, which means that the form *hi-h* will be used to refer to a single item of Gender IV falling, and the 2|3pl form *hihi-h* extending to express that several items of Gender IV fall. For these verbs it would make even less sense to gloss the stem used with IV items in the singular as '2|3PL', since that form can never be used with 2nd or 3rd person plurals; the gloss 'IV' on the other hand, is unproblematic for such verbs.

10.3 Inflectional classes

The following subsections describe the four inflectional classes that are needed for verbs with stems distinguishing person and number forms. Verbs that only take an inanimate Undergoer and alternate according to gender (and not person) are more difficult to fit into the inflectional class schema — at least synchronically — so their discussion is postponed until §10.4.

10.3.1 Class 1: Prefixing verbs

Such verbs are listed in Tables 10.3 and 10.4. The part of the stem that follows the Undergoer prefix is referred to as the *final*, so that e.g. the stem *w-ahik* 'take him/her/it somewhere' consists of the 3SG.U prefix *w-* and the final *-ahik*. (The reason for not using terms such as 'Base' or 'Root' for the final will be clarified in §10.3.2.) Since the 3rd person stem is treated as the lemma, those stems have been given in the leftmost column, with 1st, 2nd and 2|3pl forms following to the right. The verbs are listed with vowel-initial finals first.

The morphological facts can be summarised as follows. The exponent of 3SG.U can be thought of as /o-/, generally realised as *w-* since almost all finals are vowel-initial, with the sequence /oa-/ realised as *wa-*. Before the final *-hwasig*, /o-/ undergoes regular gradation to *u-* in the antepenultimate syllable: *u-hwasig* 'U go up from sea'. Similarly, 2|3PL.U is expressed by /e-/ which surfaces as *y-* before all vowel-initial finals except the ones with initial /i-/, where the vowel sequence /ei-/ predictably is reduced to *i-*. The exponents for 1st person and 2sg are *n-* and *y-* respectively, followed by epenthetic /a/ in the case of consonant-initial finals.

A few prefixing verbs showing various irregularities are listed in Table 10.4. The irregularities are: realisation of 3SG.U by Zero and/or clipping part of the final (ø-*deh*, ø-*koh*, ø-*idih*); forms with unexpected prefixes such as *hya-dih* (2|3.U-see), *u-sak* (3SG.U-hit), *i-sak* (2|3PL.U-hit); the verb *k-w-amin* 'U enter' which apparently consists of a fossilised combination of a final *-amin* and the Inessive prefix *k-*, with the Undergoer prefix trapped in between. Since this verb no longer occurs without the *k-*, the Undergoer exponent is best described as an infix; I put this verb in the prefixing class since all other infixing verbs in the language have the infix at the right-edge of the stem.

The 26 prefixing verbs likely represent the most archaic type of Undergoer indexing in Coastal Marind.[3]

10.3.2 Class 2: Infixing verbs

This is the largest class with more than 150 members, some of which are in Tables 10.5, 10.6 and 10.7.

Infixing stems consist of an *initial* and a *final* (cf. §10.3.1), with the exponent of Undergoer indexing infixed between the two parts. This structure is a remnant of an

---

[3] See Olsson and Usher 2017 for a diachronic account of Coastal Marind Undergoer indexing.

Tab. 10.3: Class 1 Prefixing verbs

3SG.U	1.U	2SG.U	2|3PL.U	Gloss
w-a	n-a	y-a	y-a	Auxiliary (§17.1)
w-abayed	n-abayed	y-abayed	y-abayed	'u turn head'
w-ahanid	n-ahanid	–	y-ahanid	'gather u'[a]
w-agum	n-agum	y-agum	y-agum	'scold u'
w-ayasud	n-ayasud	–	y-ayasud	'u grow big'[a]
w-ahik	n-ahik	y-ahik	y-ahik	'take u somewhere'
w-ahun	n-ahun	y-ahun	y-ahun	'u be hungry'
w-alaw	n-alaw	y-alaw	y-alaw	'u open eyes'
w-alin	n-alin	y-alin	y-alin	'call out for s.b.'
w-alok	n-alok	y-alok	y-alok	'stab u'
w-amuk	n-amuk	y-amuk	–	'hit u'[b]
w-as	n-as	y-as	y-as	'shoot u'
w-asib	n-asib	y-asib	y-asib	'hit u'
w-esoh	n-esoh	y-esoh	y-esoh	'follow u'
w-ig	n-ig	y-ig	ø-ig	'u beg for s.t.'
w-ihid	n-ihwid	y-ihwid	ø-ihwid	'u become tired'
w-in	n-in	y-in	ø-in	'u become'
ø-um	n-um	y-um	y-um	'u go habitually'
o-la	na-hwala	ya-hwala	ya-hwala	'u be'
o-nggat	na-nggat	ya-nggat	e-nggat	'u become'
u-hwasig	na-hwasig	ya-hwasig	ya-hwasig	'u go up from sea'

[a] These verbs are only used with a plural Undergoer participant, so for animates only the 1st person and 2|3pl forms are used, while the 3sg form is used for inanimates in Gender III, and the 2|3pl form with inanimates in Gender IV.

[b] *wamuk* etc. means 'hit once' and cannot be used with a plural Undergoer. If several people are hit, *usak* 'hit, fight' is used. The verb *wamuk* cannot be used with inanimates, so there is no use for a potential plural form *yamuk* with inanimates in Gender IV. For inanimates (and animates), the verb *wasib* is used.

Tab. 10.4: Class 1 Prefixing verbs displaying irregularities

3SG.U	1.U	2SG.U	2|3PL.U	Gloss
ø-deh	n-adeh	y-adeh	y-adeh	'shoot u'[a]
ø-koh	n-akoh	y-akoh	y-akoh	'feed u'
ø-idih	n-idih	y-idih	hya-dih	'see u'
u-sak	na-sak	ya-sak	i-sak	'hit, fight u'
k-w-amin	ka-n-amin	ka-y-amin	k-y-amin	'u enter'[b]

[a] *deh* means 'shoot once' and can only be used with a singular Undergoer. The plural form *yadeh* is employed when the Undergoer participant belongs to Gender IV, e.g. such a body part. If the Undergoer is plural, the verb *was* 'shoot (several times)' has to be used.

[b] The prefix *k-* must be Inessive *k-*, attached to cranberry root *-amin*.

earlier system in which a lexical element (the initial) was predicated by means of an inflected auxiliary-like verb (the final). Some of these collocations fossilised, with the prefix on the final 'trapped' inside as an infix, and survive today as the monolexemic verbs discussed here.[4] Outside of these (non-productive) alternations the initials and finals have no functions in the language, so these labels are to be regarded as purely morphological notions that are useful for explicating patterns of allomorphy, and not as some kind of grammatical categories.

The main morphological division within the infixing class is between stems formed with finals of the shape -(V|G)C, such as -b, -h, -wn, -ib, -in and -ip (henceforth (V)C-finals; §10.3.2.1), and stems formed with the final -tuk (henceforth tuk-finals; §10.3.2.2). Within these two groups there are some further allomorphic subpatterns that can be seen either as dictated by inflectional (sub-)class membership, or derived by abstract rules. Below the major patterns in the Undergoer indexing will be presented, with statements on the deviations.

10.3.2.1 The (V)C-subclass

The infixed exponents of Undergoer indexing for (V)C-finals are

	SG	PL
1	-n-	
2	-y-	/-ʰj-/
3	/-e-/	

with the slashes indicating that these formants are subject to further changes according to the phonological environment, mainly deletion of /-e-/ or /-ʰj-/.

The stems corresponding to 1.U and 2SG.U are straightforwardly derived by infixing the exponent after the initial and before the final, with addition of epenthetic /a/ preventing illegal cluster formation and/or the formation of a closed stem-penultimate syllable (see §2.4 for general information about these processes). This can be illustrated by the verb 'leave U behind', which is composed of the initial yad- and the final -wn. Below are listed potential forms for 'leave me/us behind' and 'leave you (sg) behind'; note how the presence of epenthetic /a/ decides whether a form is acceptable.

---

[4] The diachronic process of entrapment (a term due to Ultan's seminal paper; see Ultan 1975) has been described for several languages and results in morphological systems similar to the Coastal Marind verb stems cross-linguistically, cf. Harris 2002, Nichols 2005 and Yu 2007: Chap. 5.

Input	Output	Gloss	Constraints violated
/ɣad ⟨n⟩ wn/ →	yada⟨n⟩awn	'leave 1.U'	(none)
	*yad⟨n⟩wn		Illegal cluster, closed penultimate
	*yad⟨n⟩awn		Closed penultimate
	*yada⟨n⟩wn		Illegal cluster
/ɣad ⟨ɣ⟩ wn/ →	yada⟨ɣ⟩awn	'leave 2SG.U'	(none)
	*yad⟨ɣ⟩wn		Illegal cluster, closed penultimate
	*yad⟨ɣ⟩awn		Closed penultimate
	*yada⟨ɣ⟩wn		Illegal cluster

1st and 2nd person stems formed with other (V)C-finals are assembled according to the same pattern, with the difference that the finals containing a vowel (-ib, -in, -ip) require no epenthetic /a/ to prevent cluster formation:

Input		Output	
/tam ⟨n⟩ b/	→	tama⟨n⟩ab	'1.U float to surface'
/tam ⟨ɣ⟩ b/	→	tama⟨ɣ⟩ab	'2SG.U float to surface'
/mik ⟨n⟩ h/	→	mika⟨n⟩ah	'1.U look to the side'
/mik ⟨ɣ⟩ h/	→	mika⟨ɣ⟩ah	'2SG.U look to the side'
/hwag ⟨n⟩ ib/	→	hwaga⟨n⟩ib	'put away 1.U'
/hwag ⟨ɣ⟩ ib/	→	hwaga⟨ɣ⟩ib	'put away 2SG.U'
/kas ⟨n⟩ ip/	→	kasa⟨n⟩ip	'scorch 1.U'
/kas ⟨ɣ⟩ ip/	→	kasa⟨ɣ⟩ip	'scorch 2SG.U'
/ɣad ⟨n⟩ in/	→	yada⟨n⟩in	'1.U drown'
/ɣad ⟨ɣ⟩ in/	→	yada⟨ɣ⟩in	'2SG.U drown'

An /a/ in the 2nd syllable of a disyllabic initial is usually lost in the 1st and 2nd person stems due to syncope (see §2.4.2):

Input		Output	
/ital ⟨n⟩ b/	→	itla⟨n⟩ab	'1.U roll around'
/ital ⟨ɣ⟩ b/	→	itla⟨ɣ⟩ab	'2SG.U roll around'
/kisak ⟨n⟩ h/	→	kiska⟨n⟩ah	'put 1.U to sleep'
/kisak ⟨ɣ⟩ h/	→	kiska⟨ɣ⟩ah	'put 2SG.U to sleep'

Note also that verb stems longer than two syllables are subject to vowel gradation (§2.5.1). Compare the fate of the vowel in the initials *og-* and *men-* in the forms for the 3rd person and 1st person:

/og ⟨e⟩ b/	→	og⟨e⟩b	'bury 3SG.U'
/og ⟨n⟩ b/	→	uga⟨n⟩ab	'bury 1.U'
/men ⟨e⟩ h/	→	men⟨e⟩h	'3SG.U to grunt'
/men ⟨n⟩ h/	→	mina⟨n⟩ah	'1.U to grunt'

The infix /-e-/ realising 3SG.U surfaces unchanged before the vowel-less finals (*-b, -h, -wn*). It is lost before the finals *-ib, -in* and *-ip*, as /e/ is elsewhere before /i/.

/ital ⟨e⟩ b/	→	ital⟨e⟩b	'3SG.U roll around'
/ɣad ⟨e⟩ wn/	→	ɣad⟨e⟩wn	'leave 3SG.U behind'
/kes ⟨e⟩ h/	→	kes⟨e⟩h	'spit on 3SG.U'
/hwag ⟨e⟩ ib/	→	hwag⟨ø⟩ib	'put 3SG.U away'
/kas ⟨e⟩ ip/	→	kas⟨ø⟩ip	'scorch 3SG.U'
/aɣ ⟨e⟩ in/	→	aɣ⟨ø⟩in	'3SG.U run around'

/-e-/ is also lost if the initial ends in a vowel:

| /kadi ⟨e⟩ b/ | → | kadi⟨ø⟩b | 'feel, squeeze 3SG.U' |
| /kaho ⟨e⟩ b/ | → | kaho⟨ø⟩b | '3SG.U capsize' |

(For clarity and consistence, the stems lacking any overt infixed segment are marked by an infixed Zero, ⟨ø⟩.)[5]

The 2|3PL.U forms are slightly more complicated. The 2|3PL.U infix must have been */-j-/ in an earlier stage of Coastal Marind (see §1.2.2.2), which corresponds to present-day *-h-, -hy-* or Zero depending on the environment. Here I present the synchronic alternation as being derived from an underlying /-ʰj-/, as this is a convenient way to represent the allomorphy. /-ʰj-/ is lost whenever an initial that ends in a consonant is combined with a vowel-less final (such as *-b, -h, -wn*). If the final contains the vowel /i/ (e.g. *-ib, -in* or *-ip*), the 2|3PL.U infix surfaces as *-h-*. It is realised as *-hy-* only if an initial ending in a vowel is followed by a vowel-less final.

---

[5] This device is used here to clarify the morphological differences between paradigm cells; in interlinear glossing such forms are treated as unsegmentable. For example, *italab* '2|3PL.U roll around' would be glossed 'roll.around:2|3PL.U', without infixed material, as opposed to 2nd person *itla⟨y⟩ab* 'roll.around⟨2SG.U⟩'.

/ital ⟨ʰj⟩ b/	→	ital⟨ø⟩ab	'2	3PL.U roll around'
/ɣad ⟨ʰj⟩ wn/	→	ɣad⟨ø⟩awn	'leave 2	3PL.U behind'
/kes ⟨ʰj⟩ h/	→	kes⟨ø⟩ah	'spit on 2	3PL.U'
/hwag ⟨ʰj⟩ ib/	→	hwaga⟨h⟩ib	'put 2	3PL.U away'
/kas ⟨ʰj⟩ ip/	→	kasa⟨h⟩ip	'scorch 2	3PL.U'
/aɣ ⟨ʰj⟩ in/	→	aya⟨h⟩in	'2	3PL.U run around'
/kadi ⟨ʰj⟩ b/	→	kadi⟨hy⟩ab	'feel squeeze 2	3PL.U'
/kaho ⟨ʰj⟩ b/	→	kaho⟨hy⟩ab	'2	3PL.U capsize'
/ɣo ⟨ʰj⟩ wn/	→	yo⟨hy⟩awn	'watch, guard 2	3PL.U'

The only exceptions are two verbs with vowel-final initials that realise 2|3PL.U as -h-:

| /ɣe ⟨ʰj⟩ b/ | → | ye⟨h⟩ab | '2|3PL.U slip' |
| /uti ⟨ʰj⟩ wn/ | → | uti⟨h⟩awn | 'wake 2|3PL.U up' |

The exponent -h- in the form yehab 'slip:2|3PL.U' follows from regular sound change of */j/ to h after e (cf. */ejam/ > eham 'her husband', */ejon/ > ehon 'border') whereas the -h- in utihawn seems to be a pure irregularity (cf. -hy- in kadihyab 'feel, squeeze 2|3PL.U'). For at least one other verb, there seems to be variation: both ihe⟨h⟩ab and ihe⟨hy⟩ab have been recorded as 2|3PL.U stems of the verb aheb 'pass by, overtake U' (this verb also has a slightly irregular 3SG.U stem instead of the expected *iheb).

Summing up, we can say that with the exception of such minor complications, the person forms of verbs with (V)C-finals are straightforwardly predictable given the shape of the initial, and the above statements account for the stem shapes the vast majority of infixing verbs with (V)C-finals. Table 10.5 provides the stems for some common verbs displaying regular infixing. The verbs are listed under their respective finals.

Tab. 10.5: Regular infixing verbs

3SG.U	1.U	2SG.U	2|3PL.U	Gloss
FINAL -b				
an⟨e⟩b	ana⟨n⟩ab	ana⟨ɣ⟩ab	an⟨ø⟩ab	'take u's place'
dah⟨e⟩b	daha⟨n⟩ab	daha⟨ɣ⟩ab	dah⟨ø⟩ab	'tide traps u'
ahe⟨ø⟩b	ihe⟨n⟩ab	ihe⟨ɣ⟩ab	ihe⟨h⟩ab	'pass, overtake u'
hoɣ⟨e⟩b	huya⟨n⟩ab	huya⟨ɣ⟩ab	hoɣ⟨ø⟩ab	'silence u'
hus⟨e⟩b	husa⟨n⟩ab	husa⟨ɣ⟩ab	hus⟨ø⟩ab	'pour water on u'
ihul⟨e⟩b	ihula⟨n⟩ab	ihula⟨ɣ⟩ab	ihul⟨ø⟩ab	'dangle u in air'
ital⟨e⟩b	itla⟨n⟩ab	itla⟨ɣ⟩ab	ital⟨ø⟩ab	'u roll around'
kadi⟨ø⟩b	kadi⟨n⟩ab	kadi⟨ɣ⟩ab	kadi⟨hy⟩ab	'feel, squeeze u'
kaho⟨ø⟩b	kaho⟨n⟩ab	kaho⟨ɣ⟩ab	kaho⟨hy⟩ab	'u capsize'

Continued on next page

Tab. 10.5 – Continued

kati⟨ø⟩b	kati⟨n⟩ab	kati⟨ɣ⟩ab	kati⟨hy⟩ab	'lift up ʊ'
kipas⟨e⟩b	kipsa⟨n⟩ab	kipsa⟨ɣ⟩ab	kipas⟨ø⟩ab	'whip ʊ against s.t.'
lisas⟨e⟩b	lissa⟨n⟩ab	lissa⟨ɣ⟩ab	lisas⟨ø⟩ab	'ʊ become deaf'
og⟨e⟩b	uga⟨n⟩ab	uga⟨ɣ⟩ab	og⟨ø⟩ab	'bury ʊ'
ol⟨e⟩b	ula⟨n⟩ab	ula⟨ɣ⟩ab	ol⟨ø⟩ab	'trade, exchange ʊ'
ot⟨e⟩b	uta⟨n⟩ab	uta⟨ɣ⟩ab	ot⟨ø⟩ab	'chase ʊ away'
sam⟨e⟩b	sama⟨n⟩ab	sama⟨ɣ⟩ab	sam⟨ø⟩ab	'ʊ turn (in spot)'
tah⟨e⟩b	taha⟨n⟩ab	taha⟨ɣ⟩ab	tah⟨ø⟩ab	'ʊ fill (a space)'
tam⟨e⟩b	tama⟨n⟩ab	tama⟨ɣ⟩ab	tam⟨ø⟩ab	'ʊ float to surface'
tangg⟨e⟩b	tangga⟨n⟩ab	tangga⟨ɣ⟩ab	tangg⟨ø⟩ab	'chase ʊ away'
tap⟨e⟩b	tapa⟨n⟩ab	tapa⟨ɣ⟩ab	tap⟨ø⟩ab	'ʊ fly up'
ye⟨ø⟩b	ye⟨n⟩ab	ya⟨ɣ⟩ab	ye⟨h⟩ab	'ʊ slip'
yed⟨e⟩b	yida⟨n⟩ab	yida⟨ɣ⟩ab	yed⟨ø⟩ab	'hit ʊ'
yin⟨e⟩b	yina⟨n⟩ab	yina⟨ɣ⟩ab	yin⟨ø⟩ab	'hit ʊ with fist'
FINAL -h				
ahwik⟨e⟩h	ahwika⟨n⟩ah	ahwika⟨ɣ⟩ah	ahwik⟨ø⟩ah	'put ʊ on shoulder'
amb⟨e⟩h	amba⟨n⟩ah	amba⟨ɣ⟩ah	amb⟨ø⟩ah	'wrap ʊ up'
asak⟨e⟩h	aska⟨n⟩ah	aska⟨ɣ⟩ah	asak⟨ø⟩ah	'ʊ be out of breath'
kes⟨e⟩h	kisa⟨n⟩ah	kisa⟨ɣ⟩ah	kes⟨ø⟩ah	'spit on ʊ'
kisak⟨e⟩h	kiska⟨n⟩ah	kiska⟨ɣ⟩ah	kisak⟨ø⟩ah	'put ʊ to sleep'
lok⟨e⟩h	luka⟨n⟩ah	luka⟨ɣ⟩ah	lok⟨ø⟩ah	'ʊ peek'
lond⟨e⟩h	lunda⟨n⟩ah	lunda⟨ɣ⟩ah	lond⟨ø⟩ah	'ʊ look greedily'
men⟨e⟩h	mina⟨n⟩ah	mina⟨ɣ⟩ah	men⟨ø⟩ah	'ʊ grunt'
mik⟨e⟩h	mika⟨n⟩ah	mika⟨ɣ⟩ah	mik⟨ø⟩ah	'ʊ turn head'
mungg⟨e⟩h	mungga⟨n⟩ah	mungga⟨ɣ⟩ah	mungg⟨ø⟩ah	'ʊ hum, buzz'
ol⟨e⟩h	ula⟨n⟩ah	ula⟨ɣ⟩ah	ol⟨ø⟩ah	'ʊ reach up'
yos⟨e⟩h	yusa⟨n⟩ah	yusa⟨ɣ⟩ah	yos⟨ø⟩ah	'ʊ jump along'
yuy⟨e⟩h	yuya⟨n⟩ah	yuya⟨ɣ⟩ah	yuy⟨ø⟩ah	'ʊ become startled'
FINAL -wn				
apan⟨e⟩wn	apna⟨n⟩awn	apna⟨ɣ⟩awn	apan⟨ø⟩awn	'go visit ʊ'
hwes⟨e⟩wn	hwisa⟨n⟩awn	hwisa⟨ɣ⟩awn	hwes⟨ø⟩awn	'examine ʊ' (?)
kol⟨e⟩wn	kula⟨n⟩awn	kula⟨ɣ⟩awn	kol⟨ø⟩awn	'laugh at ʊ'
yad⟨e⟩wn	yada⟨n⟩awn	yada⟨ɣ⟩awn	yad⟨ø⟩awn	'leave ʊ behind'
yo⟨ø⟩n	yo⟨n⟩awn	yo⟨ɣ⟩awn	yo⟨hy⟩awn	'watch, guard ʊ'
FINAL -ib				
hwag⟨ø⟩ib	hwaga⟨n⟩ib	hwaga⟨ɣ⟩ib	hwaga⟨h⟩ib	'put ʊ away'
kamb⟨ø⟩ib	kamba⟨n⟩ib	kamba⟨ɣ⟩ib	kamba⟨h⟩ib	'scratch ʊ'
kib⟨ø⟩ib	kiba⟨n⟩ib	kiba⟨ɣ⟩ib	kiba⟨h⟩ib	'make ʊ roll'

Continued on next page

Tab. 10.5 – Continued

kot⟨ø⟩ib	kuta⟨n⟩ib	kuta⟨ɣ⟩ib	kuta⟨h⟩ib	'u get lost'
kapangg⟨ø⟩ib	kapngga⟨n⟩ib	kapngga⟨ɣ⟩ib	kapngga⟨h⟩ib	'strangle u'
kas⟨ø⟩ib	kasa⟨n⟩ib	kasa⟨ɣ⟩ib	kasa⟨h⟩ib	'u lie on belly'
kaɣas⟨ø⟩ib	kaɣasa⟨n⟩ib	kaɣasa⟨ɣ⟩ib	kaɣasa⟨h⟩ib	'remove u's skin'
walimaɣ⟨ø⟩eb[a]	walimɣa⟨n⟩ib	walimɣa⟨ɣ⟩ib	walimɣa⟨h⟩ib	'bend u'
FINAL -in				
aɣ⟨ø⟩in	aɣa⟨n⟩in	aɣa⟨ɣ⟩in	aɣa⟨h⟩in	'u run around'
idag⟨ø⟩in	idga⟨n⟩in	idga⟨ɣ⟩in	idga⟨h⟩in	'lean u'
kam⟨ø⟩in	kama⟨n⟩in	kama⟨ɣ⟩in	kama⟨h⟩in	'u make'
ol⟨ø⟩in	ula⟨n⟩in	ula⟨ɣ⟩in	ula⟨h⟩in	'u hold on to s.t.'
FINAL -ip				
dah⟨ø⟩ip	daha⟨n⟩ip	daha⟨ɣ⟩ip	daha⟨h⟩ip	'u get drunk'
kas⟨ø⟩ip	kasa⟨n⟩ip	kasa⟨ɣ⟩ip	kasa⟨h⟩ip	'scorch u'
ɣun⟨ø⟩ip	ɣuna⟨n⟩ip	ɣuna⟨ɣ⟩ip	ɣuna⟨h⟩ip	'u catch fire'
sas⟨ø⟩ip	sasa⟨n⟩ip	sasa⟨ɣ⟩ip	sasa⟨h⟩ip	'u get burnt'

[a] In this form, /i/ is apparently lowered to [e] due to the preceding /ɣ/.

Tab. 10.6: Some infixing verbs with irregular 3SG.U stems

Initial	3SG.U	1.U	2SG.U	2|3PL.U	Gloss
tak(o|a)-	tako⟨ø⟩b	taka⟨n⟩ab	taka⟨y⟩ab	taka⟨hy⟩ab	'help U'
tal(o|a)-	talo⟨ø⟩b	tala⟨n⟩ab	tala⟨y⟩ab	tala⟨hy⟩ab	'keep U for s.b.'
um(u)-	umu⟨ø⟩h	uma⟨n⟩ah	uma⟨y⟩ah	um⟨ø⟩ah	'U go, take off'
kag(u)-	kagu⟨ø⟩b	kaga⟨n⟩ib	kaga⟨y⟩ib	kaga⟨h⟩ib	'break U'
ikal(e)-	ikale⟨ø⟩n	ikla⟨n⟩in	ikla⟨y⟩in	ikla⟨h⟩in	'send U'
kag(u)-	kagu⟨ø⟩n	kaga⟨n⟩in	kaga⟨y⟩in	kaga⟨h⟩in	'grab U'
kisak(u)-	kisaku⟨ø⟩n	kiska⟨n⟩in	–	kiska⟨h⟩in	'U be sandwiched'

A set of exceptional verbs is in Table 10.6. These verbs have initials ending in a vowel according to the 3SG.U forms; however, this vowel is lost in all other person forms, so that the 1, 2sg and 2|3pl forms verbs behave like the initial ended in -a or in a consonant.

Some verbs belonging to the (V)C-class (not shown in Table 10.5) have entirely unrelated stems that are used with a plural Undergoer participant: these suppletive verbs are *aheb* 'eat' (with the 1|2|3pl-stem *hi*); *yakeh* 'catch' (2|3pl *lemeh*, 1pl *lemem*); *ihon* 'run away' (1|2|3pl *awan*); *kaguh* 'give birth to' (1|2|3pl *ewah*); *kahekon* 'put inside' (2|3pl *yukahin*, 1pl *yukanin*); *kahwid* 'die' (2|3pl *yahwahwih*, 1pl *yahwahwen*). See further §10.5.

10.3.2.2 The *tuk*-subclass

The subclass of infixing verbs with the final -*tuk* is more difficult to segment than the (V)C-class. The 3SG.U exponent ⟨e⟩ is infixed before the final -*tuk*, but causes the vowel in the final to be lowered to [o] to agree in height:

Input		Output	
/kipl ⟨e⟩ tuk/	→	kipl⟨e⟩tok	'tie 3SG.U'
/law ⟨e⟩ tuk/	→	law⟨e⟩tok	'3SG.U turn around'

The corresponding plural stems have the 2|3PL.U exponent ⟨i⟩ infixed before the final, this time with the vowel /u/ intact:

/kipl ⟨i⟩ tuk/	→	kipl⟨i⟩tuk	'tie 2|3PL.U'
/law ⟨i⟩ tuk/	→	law⟨i⟩tuk	'2|3PL.U turn around'

Surprisingly, the 1.U and 2SG.U exponents ⟨n⟩ and ⟨y⟩ are not infixed before the final, but *inside* it, after the initial *t* of -*tuk*.[6] Note the distribution of epenthetic *a* in the out-

---

[6] The explanation for this is historical. For the infixing *tuk*-class, we can reconstruct an original auxiliary verb *-*tuk*, with regularly inflected forms *e-tuk, *na-tuk etc. When this auxiliary verb merged

put forms, preventing illegal clusters (e.g. *kipaltnuk) or heavy penultimate syllables (e.g. *kiplatnuk).

/kipl t ⟨n⟩ uk/	→	kiplata⟨n⟩uk	'tie 1.U'
/kipl t ⟨y⟩ uk/	→	kiplata⟨y⟩uk	'tie 2SG.U'
/law t ⟨n⟩ uk/	→	lawta⟨n⟩uk	'1.U turn around'
/law t ⟨y⟩ uk/	→	lawta⟨y⟩uk	'2SG.U turn around'

Some of the most common regular verbs belonging to this class are listed in Table 10.7. The *tuk*-class is overall remarkably regular. The infixed person exponents are identical throughout the class; only a handful of verbs have 3SG.U stems that replace the 3SG.U infix ⟨e⟩ with the vowels *a* and *o* (Table 10.8). These vowels were perhaps originally part of the initial and were lost in the other person stems. There is also the suppletive verb *katmetok* 'father (a child)' which has the plural stem *mamed* 'father several children'.

10.3.3 Class 3: Suffixing verbs

The four members of this class are listed in Table 10.9. The only irregularities are found in the 3sg stems. The origin of this class is uncertain.[7]

10.3.4 Class 4: Double-marking verbs

Six such verbs have been identified and are listed in Table 10.10.

---

with the preceding complement, the exponents of Undergoer indexing ended up in the penultimate syllable, as opposed to the other infixing classes, where it is in the final syllable (e.g. *tangga⟨n⟩ab* 'chase⟨1.U⟩'). Paradigmatic levelling motivated metathesis of the 1st person and 2sg forms into the final syllable of the stem, according to the following tentative outline:

(i) *sal + *na-tuk   > *salnatuk   > saltanuk   hide:1.U
     *sal + *ya-tuk   > *salyatuk   > saltayuk   hide:2SG.U
     *sal + *e-tuk   > saletok   hide:3SG.U
     *sal + *i-tuk   > salituk   hide:2|3PL.U

Evidence confirming this scenario come from the related language Bian Marind, where metathesis only affected 1st person stems (giving e.g. *kalad⟨n⟩uk* 'hide⟨1.U⟩') but left the 2sg infixes in their original, penultimate position (*kala⟨y⟩tuk* 'hide⟨2SG.U⟩') (data from Drabbe n.d.).

7 Timothy Usher (pers. comm.) suggests that this class derives from regular infixing verbs whose final (for some reason) eroded, leaving the Undergoer marker as a remaining suffix.

10.3 Inflectional classes

Tab. 10.7: Infixing *tuk*-verbs

3SG.U	1.U	2SG.U	2|3PL.U	Gloss
at⟨e⟩tok	atata⟨n⟩uk	atata⟨y⟩uk	at⟨i⟩tuk	'remove U'
dah⟨e⟩tok	dahta⟨n⟩uk	dahta⟨y⟩uk	dah⟨i⟩tuk	'turn U'
g⟨e⟩tok	agta⟨n⟩uk	agta⟨y⟩uk	g⟨i⟩tuk	'kill louse (=U)'
hw⟨e⟩tok	hwata⟨n⟩uk	hwata⟨y⟩uk	hw⟨i⟩tuk	'think about U'
hwahw⟨e⟩tok	hwahwta⟨n⟩uk	hwahwta⟨y⟩uk	hwahw⟨i⟩tuk	'rub U'
igl⟨e⟩tok	iglata⟨n⟩uk	iglata⟨y⟩uk	igl⟨i⟩tuk	'write U's name'
ikuh⟨e⟩tok	ikuhta⟨n⟩uk	ikuhta⟨y⟩uk	ikuh⟨i⟩tuk	'leave U'
kayn⟨e⟩tok	kayanta⟨n⟩uk	kayanta⟨y⟩uk	kayn⟨i⟩tuk	'turn to face U'
kipl⟨e⟩tok	kiplata⟨n⟩uk	kiplata⟨y⟩uk	kipl⟨i⟩tuk	'tie U'
lis⟨e⟩tok	lista⟨n⟩uk	lista⟨y⟩uk	lis⟨i⟩tuk	'cut U'
law⟨e⟩tok	lawta⟨n⟩uk	lawta⟨y⟩uk	law⟨i⟩tuk	'U turn around'
mas⟨e⟩tok	masta⟨n⟩uk	masta⟨y⟩uk	mas⟨i⟩tuk	'U lean forward'
sangg⟨e⟩tok	sangta⟨n⟩uk	sangta⟨y⟩uk	sangg⟨i⟩tuk	'shake U'
sal⟨e⟩tok	salta⟨n⟩uk	salta⟨y⟩uk	sal⟨i⟩tuk	'hide U'
tal⟨e⟩tok	talta⟨n⟩uk	talta⟨y⟩uk	tal⟨i⟩tuk	'U fall head first'
tangg⟨e⟩tok	tangta⟨n⟩uk	tangta⟨y⟩uk	tangg⟨i⟩tuk	'make U speak'
un⟨e⟩tok	unta⟨n⟩uk	unta⟨y⟩uk	un⟨i⟩tuk	'not recognise U'

Tab. 10.8: Some infixing *tuk*-verbs with irregular 3SG.U stems

3SG.U	1.U	2SG.U	2|3PL.U	Gloss
ambatok	amta⟨n⟩uk	amta⟨y⟩uk	amb⟨i⟩tuk	'take U on shoulders'
bakatok	bakta⟨n⟩uk	bakta⟨y⟩uk	bak⟨i⟩tuk	'turn U upside down'
yayotok	yayta⟨n⟩uk	yayta⟨y⟩uk	yay⟨i⟩tuk	'hold U tight'
ubatok	ubta⟨n⟩uk	ubta⟨y⟩uk	ub⟨i⟩tuk	'laugh at U'

This highly aberrant class contains verbs where the exponent of Undergoer indexing occurs in two sites of the stem. Only one verb, *w-asak⟨ø⟩ab* 'snatch something from U' can be segmented as having double overt exponents in more than two of the stems; the other verbs restrict the double marking to the 1st person and 2sg stems.

Some of these verbs likely originated as regular single-marking verbs, but a segment in the initial or final was reanalysed as an exponent of Undergoer indexing. For example, the verb 'bite' was probably a regular infixing verb, with the final *-iy*, which is common in verbs denoting mouth-related activities. The 1st person form would have been the expected **daha⟨n⟩iy* (here, the asterix marks a hypothesised form), but when the final *-y* in 2SG.U **daha⟨y⟩iy* was reinterpreted as a second marker of Undergoer indexing, an analogous 1st person form *daha⟨n⟩i-n* was innovated. Note that this reanalysis of the final was restricted to the 1st person and 2sg forms; *-iy* survives unaltered in the 3sg stem *dahiy* and the (suppletive) 2|3pl stem *isiy* (although the reanalysed *isi-h*, with 2|3 plural suffix *-h* is commonly heard).

Tab. 10.9: Suffixing verbs

3SG.U	1.U	2SG.U	2|3PL.U	Gloss
hawa	hu-n	hu-ɣ	hu-h	'U come out'
hi-ø	hi-n	hi-ɣ	hi-h	'U fall'
lol-aw	lolo-n	lolo-ɣ	lolo-h	'U crawl'
oha-ø	oha-n	oha-ɣ	oha-h	'U go coastwards'

Tab. 10.10: Double-marking verbs

3SG.U	1.U	2SG.U	2|3PL.U	Gloss
ik⟨u⟩baya	ik⟨n⟩ebe-n	ik⟨ɣ⟩ebe-ɣ	ik⟨e⟩be-h	'U disappear'
wa-sak⟨ø⟩ab	na-ska⟨n⟩ab	ya-ska⟨ɣ⟩ab	ya-ska⟨hy⟩ab	'snatch from U'
dah⟨ø⟩iɣ	daha⟨n⟩i-n	daha⟨ɣ⟩i-ɣ	isiɣ	'bite U'
kisa	kasa⟨n⟩i-n	kasa⟨ɣ⟩i-ɣ	—	'marry U'
lu	n-ulu-n	ɣ-ulu-ɣ	hyamin	'call U's name'
usu	n-usu-n	ɣ-usu-ɣ	isih	'U be heated'

10.4 Stem alternations according to gender of inanimates

In §10.2.2 it was claimed that alternating verb lexemes belong to one of four types, depending on whether they index animate and/or inanimate Undergoers. The three types that allow inanimate Undergoers are (i) inanimate-only verbs; (ii) unrestricted verbs, which allow both animate and inanimate Undergoers; and (iii) paired verbs, meaning that two different, but derivationally related, verbs are used with animate and inanimate Undergoers respectively. The paradigms for all these verbs will contain stems reflecting the gender (III or IV) of the inanimate Undergoer. In this section the shape of the stems exhibiting gender indexing is discussed.

One of the most pervasive features of gender agreement in Coastal Marind is that exponents of Gender IV (the second of the two inanimate genders) are homophonous with the forms used for animate (i.e. Genders I and II) plurals (as discussed in Chapter 5). For alternating verbs this means that most 2|3PL.U stems, e.g. *iklahin* 'send you (pl)/them', are also used with inanimates of Gender IV, e.g. *katal iklahin* 'send money'. In addition, the verbs that can combine with both animate and inanimate Undergoers ('unrestricted' verbs) usually have a 3SG.U stem that is identical to the stem used for inanimates of Gender III, e.g. *ikalen* 'send him/her' is also used with nouns such as *surat ikalen* 'send letter(s)' (Malay *surat* 'letter' is Gender III). In a formal account of Coastal Marind verb stem formation, this could be expressed by means of 'rules of referral': the stem filling the paradigm stem corresponding to inanimate Gender IV Undergoer is always taken from the cell for 2|3pl animate Undergoer, and (for unrestricted verbs) the Gender III stem is taken from the 3SG.U cell of the same verb. Table 10.11 lists

Tab. 10.11: Some verb stems whose inanimate gender stems are identical to animate 3SG.U and 2|3PL.U stems

III (=3SG.U)	IV (=2|3PL.U)	Gloss
oleb	olab	'exchange, sell U'
taheb	tahab	'U fill (a space)'
hwayob	hwayahyub	'hang U'
kadib	kadihyab	'feel, squeeze U'
ikubaya	ikebeh	'U disappear'
umuh	umah	'U go'
yunip	yunahip	'U catch fire'
idih	hyadih	'see U'

some verbs that have stems used with inanimates according to this pattern. Only the stems used with inanimates are given.

Other alternating verbs exclusively combine with inanimate Undergoer participants. Such inanimate-only verbs do not have stems for person/number combinations, only two stems distinguishing Gender III from Gender IV Undergoers. Despite lacking 2|3PL.U stems, it is clear that the Gender IV stems of these verbs are formed according to the pattern of 2|3PL.U stems of lexemes with full person paradigms. Consider the inanimate-only verb 'to pile up', which uses the stem *betok* for items in Gender III being piled up (e.g. scraped sago pith), and the stem *bituk* for items in Gender IV (e.g. money). These stems clearly follow the pattern of the *tuk*-subclass of infixing verbs (§10.3.2). Compare e.g. *g⟨e⟩tok* 'kill louse⟨3SG.U⟩', which has the 2|3PL.U stem *g⟨i⟩tuk* ('kill many lice'). The main difference between these verbs is that 'pile up' lacks person stems (there is no 1st person stem *bita⟨n⟩uk* 'pile us up' etc.), so the 'rule of referral' mentioned in the previous paragraph would not work for these lexemes.

Although some inanimate stems such as *betok* and *bituk* suggest a straightforward relationship to animate stems (such as *getok* and *gituk*), the correspondence turns out to be less direct for most verbs. A common pattern is for the Gender IV stem to look like a 2|3PL.U stem, while the Gender III stem shows some idiosyncrasy, or is even completely unrelated to the Gender IV stem and shows no formal resemblance to any 3SG.U stem. For an example of mildly idiosyncratic Gender III stems, consider the inanimate-only verbs listed in Table 10.12. The Gender IV stems follow the pattern of 2|3PL.U stems shown by regular infixing verbs with finals ending in *iC* (such as those listed in the end of Table 10.5). Before the *iC*-final, an *h* is infixed, just like for infixing 2|3PL.U stems. However, the Gender III stems below do not have the vowel *i* in the last syllable, making them look like the irregular verbs listed in Table 10.6.

For the majority of inanimate-only verbs, the forms of the two stems are much more unpredictable, although in some cases the same irregular derivational pattern is shared by several lexemes. The most frequent pattern holding between the Gender III and IV stems of such inanimate-only verbs is displayed by verbs that have a III stem

Tab. 10.12: Some inanimate-only verbs with partly unpredictable Gender III stems

III	IV	Gloss
kalab	kala⟨h⟩ib	'peel'
kayasub	kaysa⟨h⟩ib	'scratch'
hwilug	hwila⟨h⟩ig	'rub'
isug	isa⟨h⟩ig	'cut'
han	ha⟨h⟩in	'grasp; put'
amban	amba⟨h⟩in	'develop, sprout'

ending in -*k* and a IV stem ending in -*b* (often with *hy* before -*b*, like the 2|3PL.PL stems of infixing verbs ending in -*b*). Thanks to these verbs (so far 22 have been found) we can formulate a rule saying that if a verb alternates according to gender of an inanimate Undergoer and the Gender III stem ends in -*k*, then its Gender IV stem will end in *ab*. (Unfortunately there are various other irregularities in many of these verbs preventing the forms from being completely interpredictable.) All known verbs exhibiting the -*k* vs. -*b* pattern are listed in Table 10.13. Note that the first 6 verbs also have *hy* added before the -*b*.

Similar patterns are found with other verbs, but with at most a handful of lexemes participating in a pairing of stems ending in one segment with stems ending in another. Some such verbs are tabulated in Table 10.14, in which horizontal rules separate groups of verb that share a similar derivational pattern, e.g. verbs with Gender III stems ending in -*y* corresponding to Gender IV stems in -*h*, and so on.

For the paired verbs, i.e. verbs for which there in addition to the stems for inanimates of Gender III and IV also exists a morphologically related ('paired') animate verb, the same multiplicity of derivational patterns are observed for the inanimate verbs. For example, several show the frequent pattern of the Gender III stem ending in -*k* and the Gender IV stem in -*b*. However, the shape of the paired animate verb is always predictable from the shape of the IV stem (and vice versa), since the IV stem (with very few exceptions) is identical to the 2|3PL.U stem of the animate verb. Table 10.15 lists the known paired verbs, with the 3SG.U stem of the corresponding animate verb provided in addition to the two stems of each inanimate verb.

10.5 Verbal suppletion according to participant number

Several verbal meanings are expressed by means of morphologically unrelated verbs depending on whether the absolutive participant is singular or plural. By 'absolutive participant' is meant the S-argument of intransitive verbs and the O-argument of transitive verbs. For example, 'one person run away' is expressed by means of the verb *ihon*, whereas 'many run away' is expressed by the unrelated *awan*. The transitive verb *aheb* is used for 'eat one animate' (e.g. eat one sago grub, or one fish), while the verb *hi*

Tab. 10.13: Some inanimate-only verbs with stems in *-k* and *-b*

III	IV	Gloss
ahok	ihyohyab	pull out
panggak	panggahyab	unfold
sak	sahyab	wound or boil to disappear
eyak	iyahyab	release, untie
ihyayok	ihyahyab	break and shatter
kakak	kakahyab	get lost
ayahyak	ayahyab	liana to creep
alak	alab	chop off bark from tree
atak	atab	brush away/break up soil
ehwek	ehwab	get stuck
yahwek	yahwab	pound, slap
yanggak	yanggab	break, crush (e.g. glass)
yinik	yinab	hit at s.t.
hyahyak	hyahyab	split wood, coconut
ibangguk	ibinggab	gather
italak	italab	dip or roll in sand
kadahak	kadahab	cut off top of s.t.
kupuk	kupab	scatter, sow
sopak	sopab	accidentally touch wound/boil
tapak	tapab	stick out, protrude
tawak	tawab	shave hair on head
walawak	walawab	sharpen arrow/spear

'eat many' is used if several animates are consumed. (The number of the A-argument is irrelevant for transitive verbs, so *aheb* is also used for several people eating from one fish.)

The 16 concepts that are expressed by suppletive verb pairs are in Table 10.16. Verbs that are suppletive according to the S-argument (i.e. intransitive verbs) are on top, and verbs with the O-argument (transitive verbs) as trigger are listed below. Most of these verbs are among the most frequent verbs in my corpus.[8]

---

[8] The exceptions are *kaguh* 'give birth' and *katmetok* 'father (a child)', with 3 and 0 attestations respectively in texts. (Of the rest of the verbs, 'call' is the rarest, with 37 textual attestations, followed by 'catch', with 61 textual attestations.) The reason for 'give birth' and 'father (a child)' resisting regularisation (despite being relatively rare) is perhaps related to the fact that these verbs seem to be associated with quite different meanings with singular and plural participants. This is most striking with 'give birth': when discussing the meaning of this verb, several speakers claimed that the plural form *ewah* is used only about animals, as in a dog whelping, and not about humans (since humans usually give birth to a single child). However, the speakers' metalinguistic intuitions are clearly false in this case, since I have observed *ewah* used about humans in contexts where multiple births are referred to, e.g. talking about habits ('Women used to give birth in maternity huts') and ability ('She can't give birth, she is sterile'), but it is still interesting that speakers stress that the two stems have

Tab. 10.14: Some inanimate-only verbs with unpredictable III vs. IV stems

III	IV	Gloss
awiɣ	awih	'hurt'
baɣ	bah	'finish food/drink (etc.)'
haniɣ	hanih	'bite'
ihwaniɣ	ihwanih	'lick'
kamaniɣ	kamanih	'leave food/drink (etc.)'
makuɣ	makuh	'tree stump to stand; termite nest to stand'
kahaleb	kahlahib	'release, untie'
kasab	kasahib	'tear'
katab	katahib	'pluck fruit'
kigalab	kiglahib	'rip, tear'
kamaneb	kamnihyub	'leave (e.g. food/drink etc.)'
awad	awituk	'scoop up'
imanad	imnituk	'lengthen (rope etc.)'
kepad	kapituk	'break (rope)'
mamud	mamutuk	'grind, crush'
sakud	sakituk	'fasten tight-fitting item'
awin	awahin	'unload, take out'
kupan	kupahin	'take up grain-like substance'
otan	utahin	'fruits hang in abundance'
ɣombob	ɣombab	'cover plants with sea weed'
ayob	ayohyab	'cover'
ibotok	ibutuk	'put horizontally oriented objects'
letok	lituk	'wrap up sago in banana leaves'
aɣun	yaɣuhyawn	'tie in bundle'
ɣasug	ɣasahig	'scrape (fur, wood), shave hair'
yaɣahwig	yaɣhwituk	'plant, penetrate'
alalay	alalih	'become dry'
alam	alah	'get swollen'
ahwamun	ahuhyawn	'soak'
tanin	tanihah	'tie strap to firewood in order to carry it'
ahus	ahwasah	'pull out'

10.5 Verbal suppletion according to participant number

Tab. 10.15: 'Paired' verbs: Inanimate-only verbs with related animate verbs

	INANIMATE VERB			ANIMATE VERB
III	IV	Gloss	3SG.U	Gloss
halak	halab	'move, come loose'	haleb	's.b. become visible'
ibayak	ibayab	'make s.t. round'	ibayeb	's.b. become round'
ihwaluk	ihulab	'dangle s.t.'	ihuleb	'dangle s.b.'
matapek	matapab	'put s.t. in corner'	matapeb	'put s.b. in corner'
samek	samab	'turn s.t. (e.g. canoe)'	sameb	'animate turn'
husuk	husab	'pour water on s.t.'	huseb	'pour on s.b.'
tahuk	tahyohyab	'stick s.t. to surface'	tahob	'lean against'
tamak	tamab	'inanimate float'	tameb	'animate float'
kasid	kasituk	'tie s.t. in end of rope'	kasetok	'tie s.b.'
masud	masituk	'bend (wood etc.)'	masetok	'sit (etc.) folded'
salad	salituk	'hide s.t.'	saletok	'hide'
sanggid	sanggituk	'shake s.t.'	sanggetok	'shake'
kipalud	kiplituk	'tie s.t.'	kipletok	'tie s.b.'
hwahwid	hwahwituk	'rub s.t.'	hwahwetok	'rub s.b.'
kahakun	kahkahin	'put s.t. inside'	kahekon	'put (e.g. child) inside'
keswan	kiswahin	'wash (e.g. clothes)'	kiswahen	'wash (e.g. child)'
olan	ulahin	'hang (e.g. clothes)'	olin	'hang, hold on to s.t.'
kwagin	kugahin	'throw s.t.'	kwegen	'throw s.b.'
ambam	ambah	'wrap s.t.'	ambeh	'wrap s.b.'
elam	elah	'hang s.t. on shoulder'	eleh	'hang (e.g. wallaby)'
yuyam	yuyah	'be loose, wobble'	yuyeh	'shake, shiver'
ayad	ayab	'split s.t. lengthwise'	ayeb	'cut (e.g. fish)'
esad	esab	'cut s.t.'	eseb	'cut s.b.'
kandakab	kankahib	'pull s.t.'	kandakib	'pull (e.g. cow)'
kahwab	kahwahwib	'remove tight-fitting item'	kahwib	'release'
lalig	lalah	'string s.t. (e.g. seeds)'	laleh	'string (e.g. fish)'
bik	bituk	'take vertical item'	betok	'grab (e.g. hanging fish)'
ugaman	ogab	'bury s.t.'	ogeb	'bury'
yi	hi	'eat s.t.'	aheb	'eat (e.g. fish)'
hay	hih	'inanimate fall'	hi	'animate fall'

Tab. 10.16: Suppletion according to participant number.
'(+)' marks alternating verbs (3rd person stems shown). Stems within parentheses are durative forms derived from the punctual form above it.

Singular	Plural	Gloss	Trigger
ihon (+)	awan	'run away'	S
umak	(awat-a)	'be running'	S
ambid	haman	'sit down'	S
mil	(hamat-a)	'be sitting'	S
yali	hok	'lie down'	S
tel	(hok-a)	'be lying'	S
atin	wayaman	'stand up'	S
itala	(wayamat-a)	'be standing'	S
man	nayam	'come'	S
yet	nayat	'be in movement'	S
kahwid (+)	yahwahwih (+)	'die'	S
aheb (+)	hi	'eat animate'	O
kaguh (+)	ewah	'give birth to'	O
katmetok (+)	mamed	'father (a child)'	O
lu (+)	hyamin	'call (s.b.'s name)'	O
kahekon (+)	yukahin (+)	'put inside'	O

The list in Table 10.16 does not imply that there are 16 verbs that are suppletive for number in Coastal Marind. It is somewhat difficult to count the number of suppletive verbs, primarily because four of the meanings are expressed by different verbs in the singular depending on whether reference is made to the onset of the event (e.g. *ihon* 'run away, take off running') or to the ensuing situation (*umak* 'be running'), whereas this distinction is expressed morphologically (by means of the Extended suffix *-a*) in the corresponding plural verbs (*awan* 'many run away', *awat-a* 'many be running'). Since *ihon* and *umak* arguably should be considered separate lexemes, but *awan* and *awat-a* probably not, we end up with 16 singular verbs being in a suppletive relationship to 12 plural verbs.

10.5.1 Paradigmatic structure of suppletive verbs

Another source of complexity is the fact that different members of suppletive verb pairs often belong to different inflectional types. For example, *ihon* 'run away' is an al-

---

different meanings (nobody has ever claimed that e.g. 'one come' and 'many come' somehow mean different things). Similarly, 'father (a child)' probably has a connotation of promiscuity ('sleep around') in its plural version *mamed* that is absent from the single-occasion verb *katmetok* (this is speculative as I have not observed this verb used more than a handful of times). Such meaning differences have perhaps played a role in the evolution of these suppletive verbs.

ternating verb of inflection class 2 (infixing) with the 1.U stem *ihya⟨n⟩on* and the 2SG.U stem *ihya⟨y⟩on*, while the plural counterpart *awan* 'many run away' is an invariant verb, with a single stem used for 1st, 2nd and 3rd person plural. In Table 10.16 cells marked '(+)' indicate alternating verbs. Only two pairs, 'die' and 'put inside', have alternating verbs filling both the singular and plural halves of their paradigms.

The differing behaviours of the stems participating in the suppletive pairings mean that the resulting paradigms exhibit several different layouts. The simplest layouts are found with the verbs of sitting, lying and standing which are invariant and only occur with animate subjects:

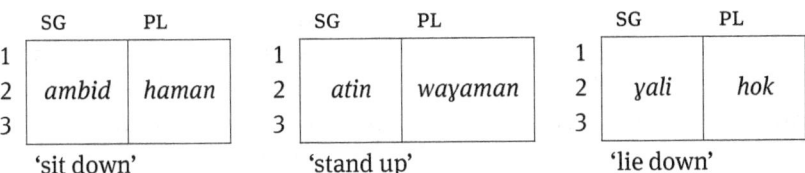

The paradigms for 'come' and 'be in movement' are more complex since they add cells for inanimate subjects. The stems used for inanimates of Gender IV are the same as the stems filling the plural cells of the paradigms (the inanimates do not have separate singular and plural stems). The use of a suppletive stem triggered by a difference in gender (III vs. IV) is quite surprising, but it conforms to the pattern observed in the paradigms of other alternating verbs, where the cells of inanimates of Gender III 'inherit' the stems used for 3SG.U, whereas the cells corresponding to Gender IV inherit the stems of the 2|3PL.U cells.

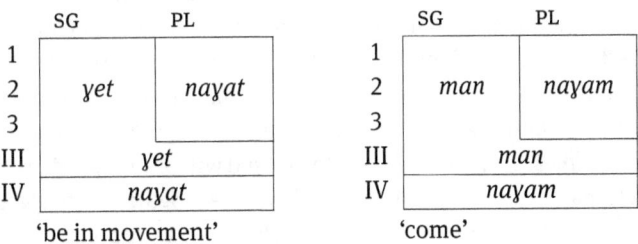

The paradigm structures become more complex when alternating stems are involved. Consider the pair *ihon* 'run away'/*awan* 'many run away', of which the first member is alternating and the second invariant, and the pair *kahwid* 'die'/*yahwahwih* 'many die', in which both participating stems are alternating. The resulting paradigms are:

	SG	PL
1	ihyanon	
2	ihyayon	awan
3	ihon	
III	ihon	
IV	awan	

'U run away'

	SG	PL
1	kahinad	yahwahwen
2	kahiyad	yahwahwih
3	kahwid	
III	kahwid	
IV	kahihad	

'U die'

The paradigm for 'die' shows one interesting difference from 'run away': the stem used for inanimates of Gender IV (*kahihad*, used for e.g. plants in Gender IV) is *not* the same as the stem used with animate 2|3PL.U stem *yahwahwih*. This is a remarkable exception from the general pattern of homophony between exponents of Gender IV and animate plurals. It is not clear why the plural verb for 'die', formed on a root *yahwahw-*, did not extend to inanimates of Gender IV, when the plural stem for 'run away', *awan*, did so. All other verbs that are compatible with both animate and inanimate Undergoers seem to exhibit the stem syncretism between Gender IV and 2|3PL.

10.5.2 Participant number versus pluractionality in verbal suppletion

Some of the verbs in Table 10.16 also participate in other pairings that resemble suppletion. Some of the singular stems have an aspectually durative counterpart, as mentioned above, and as discussed further in §14.1.3. There are also certain special stems that are used to express event plurality (referred to as Pluractional stems), rather than participant number. For example, corresponding to *ambid* (sg) and *haman* (pl) 'sit down' there is also the Pluractional *anik* 'sit down (on many occasions)'. Since the latter can be used with either singular or plural participants, it is not considered to be suppletive according to number. For other such verbs the relationship is more complicated: *kahek* 'climb' and *ihw* 'cry' are restricted to a singular participant, and the Pluractional stems *kapet* and *lihwanak* have to be used with plural participants. Again, since the Pluractional forms are also compatible with a singular participant (e.g. crying/climbing on several occasions) they are not classified as suppletive according to number (see §16.1.2 for a complete list).[9]

The difference between verbal suppletion triggered by participant number and paired verbs expressing pluractionality is not only semantic, but is also reflected in the behaviour of Actor indexing. The facts were described in §9.2.2.2, but will be repeated here. When used with a 3pl participant, intransitive verbs that are suppletive according to participant number, such as *man* 'come', occur with invariant 3sg Actor indexing (just like the so-called middle verbs, §10.1.2):

---

[9] This important point is overlooked by Drabbe, who states that pairs such as *kahek* 'climb' and *kapet* 'climb.PLA' are suppletive according to number (1955: 79).

(390) a. menda-b-ø-   man
       PERF-ACT-3SG.A- come
       'S/he came.'   [W15:0053]

   b. menda-b-ø-   nayam
       PERF-ACT-3SG.A- come.PL
       'They came.'   [W16:0020]

This special indexing pattern with 3rd person Actors is not found with verbs that have suppletive Pluractional stems (e.g. *kapet* 'climb'):

(391) a. menda-b-ø-   kahek
       PERF-ACT-3SG.A- climb
       'S/he climbed.'

   b. menda-b-na-   kapet
       PERF-ACT-3PL.A- climb.PLA
       'They climbed.'   [W08:0020]

A second difference is seen when the indexed participant belongs to Gender IV, which triggers plural marking across the system of Undergoer indexing. Thus, in (392) the Gender IV noun *lahwalah-yahun* 'aeroplane' requires the plural stem to be used, regardless of the cardinality of the referent(s) (cf. §5.3.2.1).

(392) Repeated from (134) on p. 115

   lahwalah-yahun ipe   ti-ka-hat-ø-   nayam
   aeroplane(IV) DIST:IV GIV:IV-PRS.NTRL-PRSTV-3SG.A- come.PL
   'An aeroplane is coming there.'
   'Aeroplanes are coming there.'

Gender does not affect the use of a suppletive stem expressing the Pluractional on the other hand. For example, the stem *takoy* 'fell a tree' is used to refer to the felling of a single tree belonging to either of the tree-containing genders (i.e. Genders III and IV), while the Pluractional stem *walok* 'fell several trees' is used when multiple felling events are referred to, regardless of gender of the trees.

This diagnostic can be used to show that a concept such as 'put inside', which has a paradigm similar to that of 'die' (above), is expressed by two separate verbs differing in pluractionality rather than a verb that is suppletive according to participant number. The complete set of forms expressing 'put inside' consists of no less than 9 different stem shapes: besides being composed of alternating verbs, the paradigm has paired animate-inanimate verbs filling the cells of the singular half: the animate 3SG.U stem *kahekon* has the inanimate counterpart *kahakun*, both belonging to the infixing inflectional class. In the Pluractional half of the paradigm both verbs are replaced by infixing stems formed from an unrelated root *yok-/yuk-*.

	NON-PLURACT.	PLURACTIONAL
1	kahkanin	yukanin
2	kahkayin	yukahin
3	kahekon	
III	kahakun	yokun
IV	kahkahin	yukahin

'put U inside'

Since the use of stems based on *yok-* is unaffected by the gender of inanimates (the stems *yokun* and *yukahin* are used with inanimates of Genders III and IV as long as several items are put inside) it is better to treat 'put inside' as being expressed by a non-Pluractional lexeme *kahekon* (etc.) and a corresponding Pluractional lexeme based on *yok-/yuk-*, rather than as a verb that is suppletive according to participant number (like 'die'). This is confirmed by semantics: although the meaning 'put one item inside several times' is unattested in my corpus, speakers reported that *yokun* (etc.), and not *kahakun*, would be used in such contexts. Stem alternations expressing event plurality are further described in §16.1.2.

11 The system of Verb Orientation

This chapter describes one of the most important morphosyntactic resources in Coastal Marind, the use of which has consequences for the constituent order and morphological shape of the verb in almost every clause. The structures discussed below, collectively treated under the rubric Verb Orientation, combine features of information structure and argument flagging in what appears to be a typologically unique way, although a similar system of prefixal focus marking has been described for the Papuan language Watam by Foley (1999). Some parallels also exist with symmetric voice systems as discussed by Austronesianists (e.g. Ross 2002), verbal focus marking in Bantu (Gibson et al. 2016), and with the voice-like systems of some Nilotic languages (e.g. Andersen 2015, from which I borrow the term 'orientation').

The most important factor governing the use of the Verb Orientation system is the function of the constituent placed immediately before the verb complex (henceforth the pre-verbal constituent). There are two facets of this: (i) how to choose a constituent to place before the verb, which is a question of how to package the information in a clause, and (ii) the grammatical and/or semantic role of the pre-verbal constituent, which governs the use of one of the five Orientation prefixes.

The following discussion will focus on the second issue first, and it will be shown that the Orientation prefixes have functions that are similar to grammatical case in dependent-marking languages, such as flagging a constituent as filling the role of S or A (i.e. the sole argument of an intransitive verb, or the agent-like argument of a monotransitive verb) or O (the patient-like argument of a monotransitive verb), in addition to various other uses, some of which are less suggestive of case marking. §11.1 is essentially a catalogue detailing some of the more frequent uses of the Orientation prefixes, and some readers may prefer to skim through these subsections.

The information-structural aspects governing what constituent ends up in the pre-verbal position are discussed in (§11.2), where it is shown that one of its main functions is the expression of focus, as shown by the obligatory pre-verbal placement of the questioned constituent in content (or *wh-*) questions, and of the corresponding constituent in answers to such questions.

§11.3 discusses some ways in which the Orientation system interacts with other grammatical subsystems in the language.

Finally, §11.4 describes the Givenness prefix *te-*, which is used when the constituent placed in the pre-verbal position contains a demonstrative.

11.1 The Orientation prefixes

11.1.1 Overview

As stated in §1.1.1.4, Coastal Marind is a language with relatively flexible constituent order, so it is up to the speaker to arrange the constituents in a clause in the way that best conveys the intended message. There is no case marking, and it is common to employ bare noun phrases (without adpositional marking) even for the expression of oblique roles. This lack of systematic coding of participant roles in the clause is to some extent compensated by the use of the Orientation prefixes, which signal the role of the pre-verbal constituent.

Example (393) shows some possible orderings of the three arguments of the verb 'to feed'. In each version of this (elicited) example, a different constituent is placed in the pre-verbal slot, with the result that a different Orientation prefix has to be employed. Throughout this chapter the constituent in the pre-verbal position is indicated by putting the corresponding material in the glosses within brackets. Where relevant, the role of the constituent is indicated by means of a subscript abbreviation (e.g. 'A' for the A-argument of the clause).

In (393a), the A-argument *patul* 'boy(s)' is in the pre-verbal position, triggering the use of the so-called Neutral Orientation prefix. The Neutral is *k-* in present tense contexts and zero in the non-present (i.e. in past and future contexts), with the zero allomorph indicated by means of 'ø-'. In (393b), the constituent *nggat* 'dog(s)' fills the same position, now with the Directional Orientation prefix marking its role as recipient in the clause. In (393c) the theme *muy* 'meat' fills the pre-verbal slot, which is signalled by the use of the Object Orientation prefix *m-* since it is the patient-like argument (or more specifically, the theme) of the clause. Note that the constituents that are in positions other than immediately before the verb complex are unmarked. The propositional content of the three versions is identical; the translations give a rough approximation of the difference in information structure between the three structures.

(393) a. *nggat patul ø-na- y-akoh muy*
dog [boy]_A NTRL-3PL.A- 2|3PL.U-feed meat

b. *patul nggat ka-n- y-akoh muy*
boy [dog]_R DIR-3PL.A- 2|3PL.U-feed meat

c. *patul muy ma-n- y-akoh nggat*
boy [meat]_T OBJ-3PL.A- 2|3PL.U-feed dog

Approximate translations:
a. 'It was the boys who fed meat to the dogs.'
b. 'It was the dogs that were fed meat by the boys.'
c. 'It was meat that the dogs were fed by the boys.'

Tab. 11.1: Overview of the Orientation prefixes and their uses

Role of pre-verbal constituent	Orientation prefix
Core arguments:	
S/A-argument	Neutral ø-/k-
O-argument of monotransitive verb	Object m-
Theme argument of ditransitive verb	Object m-
Recipient of ditransitive verb	Directional k-
Applicative arguments:	
Instrument licensed by k- (WITH-)	Neutral ø-/k-
Comitative argument	Object m-
Spatial adverbials:	
Path, goal of motion verb	Directional k-
Source of motion, (stative) Location	Locational nd-
Depictive secondary predicates:	
S/A-oriented	Neutral ø-/k-
O-oriented	Object m-
Various adverbials, e.g.:	
mbya NEG, *ndom* 'still'	Neutral ø-/k-
oso 'start', *ye* 'start'	Object m-
X *lek* 'because of X', X *nanggo(l)* 'for X'	Object m-
(Some) time expressions, e.g. 'at night'	Object m-
lun 'straight away', *tanama* 'again'	Directional k-
Restrictive Focus 'only X'	Restrictive s-

These clauses show no differences in transitivity or in the participant indexing on the verb. There is also no reason to consider one of the version to be derived or less basic than the others. Therefore it would be a mistake to liken these different options to alternations such as the English active-passive — the Coastal Marind system of Verb Orientation is more similar to what Dixon and Aikhenvald (1997) call "argument focusing constructions".

In addition to the Neutral, Object and Directional Orientation prefixes there are the Locational *nd-* and Restrictive *s-* Orientation prefixes. An overview listing some main functions of clause constituents and the corresponding Orientation prefixes is in Table 11.1. The uses of each prefix will be described in detail in the following sections; some general remarks will be given here.

There is no requirement that a clause must have a constituent placed before the verb in Coastal Marind. A complete clause can, and often does, consist of a single verb (394), or (more rarely) of an initial verb followed by other constituents (395). None of these examples exhibit Orientation prefixes as there are no pre-verbal constituents present.

(394) nak-e- uma⟨n⟩ah-e
 1.A-1PL- go⟨1.U⟩-IPFV
 'We're leaving.' [W07:0020]

(395) n-um-e-p- lesad epe lay nanggol epe
 3PL.A-FRUS-ACPN-CT- cross.river there side towards there
 '[The birds] were about to take [their young] over to the other side of the river.'
 [W11:1013]

In some types of discourse — especially narrative texts — it is commonly the case that the Orientation prefixes in addition to their function of flagging the role of the pre-verbal constituent assume the function of signalling certain inter-clausal relationships (§20.3), with the result that almost no verbs in such texts lack Orientation prefixes. Clauses lacking Orientation prefixes are much more frequent in spontaneous conversation, especially since many of the inflectional forms of the verb that are common in face-to-face conversation (the Imperative, the Deictic verb prefixes, yes/no-questions) are incompatible with Orientation prefixes (see §11.3.1).

Finally, a terminological note is called for. Since most of the Orientation prefixes correspond to a diverse set of functions it is difficult or impossible to find any single labels that appropriately encompass all of their uses. For example, the Neutral Orientation, which is used with a pre-verbal constituent functioning as the A of a transitive verb, as in (393a) above, is also used with the S of an intransitive verb (396a), with a bare NP expressing instrument (licensed by the use of the WITH-applicative), as in (396b), or when the clause is negated (396c). I use the label 'Neutral' for this Orientation, which in addition to its vagueness has the advantage of reflecting the status of the Neutral as the least marked of the five prefixes (with one of its two realisations being zero).

(396) a. nok ø-no- timin
 [1]_S NTRL-1.A- wake.up
 'I woke up.' [W11:0925]

 b. ndon ø-no-d- i-kipalud
 [rope]_Instr NTRL-1.A-DUR- WITH-tie
 'I tied with rope.'

 c. adaka mbya ø-no- lesad
 water [NEG] NTRL-1.A- draw.water
 'I didn't draw any water.' [W06:0095]

The other prefixes are similarly diverse in their uses, which prevents straightforward labelling; the reader is advised to think of the labels as purely mnemonic devices.

The following subsections describe the various uses of the five Orientation prefixes: the Neutral Orientation (§11.1.2), the Object Orientation (§11.1.3), the Directional Orientation (§11.1.4), the Locational Orientation (§11.1.5) and the Restrictive Orientation (§11.1.6). All of these prefixes make up a single position class (class –16) near the left edge of the prefix template (Chapter 8).

11.1.2 Neutral Orientation ø-, k-

11.1.2.1 With S/A-arguments

The use of the Neutral Orientation prefixes with S/A-arguments in the pre-verbal position was illustrated in (393a) and (396a) above.

Note that the use of the Neutral Orientation is not affected by the agentivity of an S-argument. In this way the alignment shown by the Orientation system differs from that of the participant indexing system (Chapter 9). The latter is is semantically aligned, and indexes the S-argument of an agentive verb such as 'dance' different from the S-argument of a patientive verb such as 'fall'. The Orientation system shows accusative alignment, so the Neutral Orientation is triggered by all S/A-arguments appearing in the pre-verbal position, regardless of agentivity. Here is an example of the Neutral Orientation triggered by the S-argument of 'fall':

(397) Sitting in the house. The speaker hears a motorcycle stopping on the beach, and looks out to see what is going on. (Yan is a passenger on the motorcycle.)

Yan topi ø-ø-o-p- hi-h
Y. [hat(m)(IV)]$_S$ NTRL-3SG.A-3SG.DAT-CT- fall-IV.U

'Yan's hat fell off.' (lit. 'to Yan the hat fell') [W11:0056]

The Neutral Orientation differs from the four other Orientation prefixes since it makes a distinction according to the tense of the clause: the Neutral is ø- (i.e. zero) in non-present contexts, i.e. past and future, and k- if the clause is in the present. Thus, both occurrences of the Neutral in (398) employ the zero allomorph since both clauses have past time reference. In examples (399–401) reference is made to the present, so the k-allomorph of the Neutral is used. Note that in all examples the constituent in the pre-verbal position fills the role of S- or A-argument of the verb.

(398) The speaker is scolding his children for building a bivouac and thereby making the game disappear from the area.

yoy ø-e- kama⟨h⟩in epe puk, deg yoy ø-e-
[2PL]$_A$ NTRL-2PL.A- make⟨2|3PL.U⟩ DIST:III bivouac(III) forest [2PL]$_A$ NTRL-2PL.A-
keway
destroy

'You made that bivouac, you ruined the forest.' [W10:0806]

(399) The speaker is instructing his son to show some visitors the way to a place called Kalaway.

namaya oy   k-o-   y-ahik-et   aaa   Kalaway
now   [2SG]_A PRS.NTRL-2SG.A-   2|3PL.U-accompany-IPFV   all.the.way.to K.

'Now you are taking them to Kalaway.'   [W10:0647]

(400) Specifying the name of a previously mentioned river.

Obol k-a-   lik-a
[O.]_S PRS.NTRL-3SG.A- river.flow-EXT

'The Obol river is flowing/That's the Obol river.'   [W11:0201]

(401) From a hunting story: the speaker had heard the bellowing of a deer.

isawa rusa   k-a-   kw-itala   nggu-bak   uhe
maybe [deer(II)]_S PRS.NTRL-3SG.A- INESS-be.standing   plant.sp-site PROX:II

'Maybe a deer is standing among the *nggu* grass here.'   [W11:0737]

The Neutral Orientation also employs the zero morph in future contexts, and is then followed by one of the prefixes from the General Future series (these are portmanteaux combining tense and person/number of Actor; see §14.2.7.1). The prefixes realising the 1st Future (which expresses standard future tense, as opposed to negated future) have longer allomorphs used when they are not preceded by any other prefix (e.g. 2SG.A Future *ndamo-*), and shorter allomorphs that are used when the future prefix is preceded by some other prefix (e.g. 2SG.A Future *-mo-*). Since a verb inflected for the 1st Future preceded by an S/A-argument is prefixed with the Neutral Orientation, the short allomorphs of the 1st Future are used, even though the Neutral Orientation is realised as zero in this context. Therefore it is important to distinguish the absence of the Neutral Orientation (e.g. when there is no constituent in the pre-verbal position), and the presence of the zero allomorph of the Neutral Orientation. An example:

(402) The speaker has a large amount of food to carry, and declares that the rice will be carried by the addressee.

mate, kanamin-kana ehe   oy   ø-mo-   ahwik⟨e⟩h
ok   rice(III)   PROX:III [2SG]_A NTRL-FUT:2SG.A-   carry⟨III.U⟩

'Ok, now you will carry the rice.'   [W03:0051]

In the following subsections I describe other uses of the Neutral Orientation.

11.1.2.2 With copula complements

In non-past contexts, the copula consists of the prefixal complex (featuring the appropriate set of prefixes) without any following verb stem (indicated by a zero in the segmentation). In the past, the verb *ola* 'to be' is used (see further §17.4). The copula is obligatorily preceded by the copula complement (i.e. *teacher* in the sentence *Bob is a teacher*; indicated by 'CC' in the glosses below). The copula is marked by the Neutral Orientation in nominal and adjectival predication. Examples:

(403) ey,   basik uhe   yaman-basik   k-a-   ∅
       EXCLAM pig(II) PROX:II [mean-pig]_CC   PRS.NTRL-3SG.A-   be.NPST
       'Ouch, this pig is a mean pig.'   [M02:0079]

(404) igih   Anes   ø-d-a-   ola
       name [A.]_CC NTRL-DUR-3SG.A-   be:3SG.U
       '[His] name was Anes.'   [W10:0123]

In locative predication the Locational Orientation *nd-* is used instead (see §11.1.5.1). If the clause describes a change-of-state ('become'), the Directional Orientation *k-* is used (§11.1.4.4).

11.1.2.3 With instruments

In addition to appearing when the pre-verbal constituent is an S/A-argument, the Neutral is employed when the pre-verbal constituent expresses an instrument. This treatment of an instrument is only possible if the verb stem is prefixed by means of the WITH-prefix *k-* (§13.1.4). The WITH-prefix has an applicative function and its presence allows the instrument role to occur with the Neutral Orientation, which otherwise is reserved for S/A arguments (405). See also example (396b) above.

(405) nok en   motor   k-a-   k-ihon-e
       [1   POSS motorcycle(m)]_Instr PRS.NTRL-3SG.A- WITH-run.away:3SG.U-IPFV
       'He's going away with my motorcycle.'

Although the obligatory presence of the *k*-prefix on the verb stem differentiates structures with a pre-verbal instrument from those with a pre-verbal S/A-argument, it is still interesting that both structures employ the Neutral Orientation marking. This is perhaps related to patterns of syncretism between instruments and agentive expressions (i.e. ergatives and agent phrases in passives) found in many languages (Stolz 2001).

As an alternative to the construction with a pre-verbal instrument licensed by the WITH-prefix on the verb stem speakers may use a periphrastic construction with a postposition such as the instrumental *en* 'with'. The periphrastic construction allows an instrument to be expressed in contexts that do not allow Orientation prefixes, such as the Imperative (§19.1.1). Compare the overheard example (406a), which employs the Neutral Orientation followed by the Future to form a command with a pre-verbal instrument, with the elicited example in (406b), using the periphrastic option, thus allowing the presence of the Imperative *ah-*.

(406) Dealing with an unfriendly dog.

  a. de ø-mo- k-u-sak!
    [wood]$_{\text{Instr}}$ NTRL-FUT:2SG.A- WITH-3SG.U-hit

  b. de en ah- u-sak!
    wood with IMP- 3SG.U-hit

  Both: 'Throw wood at it/hit it with wood!'

11.1.2.4 With secondary predicates controlled by S/A-argument

The Neutral Orientation is used when the pre-verbal position is filled by a constituent functioning as a depictive secondary predicate controlled by the S/A-argument.[1] In (407), the privative ('without') postposition *nV* forms a phrase providing information about the S-argument (with which it agrees in gender and number) and the phrase could be given the literal paraphrase *we, deprived of tobacco, went along*. Example (408) refers to a dog keeping its prey trapped while the rest of the hunting party failed to show up; context makes it clear that the depictive phrase 'all alone' is controlled by the A-argument (referring to the dog) and not the O-argument (the prey), thus motivating the use of the Neutral Orientation.

(407) *roko* *ni*   *ø-nan-d-e-* *aya⟨n⟩it-a*
   [tobacco(m) without:I/II.PL]$_{=S}$ NTRL-1.A-DUR-1PL- run.around⟨1.U⟩-EXT

  'We went without bringing any tobacco.'   [W02:0107]

(408) *kudaya* *ya* *ø-bat-ø-um-e-*   *itala-ti*
   [alone real]$_{=A}$ NTRL-AFF-3SG.A-FRUS-ACPN- be.standing-DUR

  'It$_i$ [the dog] was keeping them standing there all alone$_i$.' [W11:0721]

In the glosses the role of the argument about which the depictive phrase is providing information is indicated by subscripted '=S' for the S-argument etc. Depictive secondary predicates are further discussed in §18.5.

11.1.2.5 With adverbials

Certain adverbially used expressions such as *ndom* 'still', *namaya* 'just now' and the negator *mbya* are restricted to occurring in the pre-verbal position, and then invari-

---

[1] Drabbe omits S/A-oriented depictive predicates from his discussion of the Orientation prefixes (*schakelelementen* is his terminology) which leads to some erroneous statements, e.g. that the postposition *ti* 'with' always occurs without any Orientation prefix (Drabbe 1955: 48), when in fact it triggers Neutral or Object Orientation according to the role of the depictive phrase.

ably co-occur with the Neutral Orientation. It is not clear why these adverbials, which are not participant-oriented like secondary predicates are, should receive the same flagging as S/A arguments. Indeed, other types of adverbials co-occur with other Orientation prefixes, without any clear semantic explanation (see below). Examples are given with *ndom* 'still' in the present (409.1) and past (409.2) and *namaya* 'just now' in (410). Note that the word *namaya* also occurs with the general meaning 'now, at that point'; in that use it may occur in any syntactic position and does not trigger Orientation marking on the verb. Examples (411a–b) show negated clauses with past and present time reference respectively (see further §18.4.1).

(409) The speaker is describing events during a previous day's sago processing.

1. *ago* [...] *nok da*   *ndom k-a-nam-*   *b⟨e⟩tok-a*
   QUOT   1   sago(III) [still]   PRS.NTRL-3SG.A-1.GEN- pile.up⟨III.U⟩-EXT
   'I said: "My sago pith is still piled up."' (e.g., still lots to process)

2. *ayebla-da*   *epe,*   *ndom ø-d-a-*   *b⟨e⟩tok-a*
   scraped.off-sago DIST:III [still] NTRL-DUR-3SG.A- pile.up⟨III.U⟩-EXT
   'The scraped off sago, it was still piled up.'   [W20:0164–0165]

(410) The speaker looked out throught the door, at the sky.

omom   *namaya ø-ø-i-*   *ay*
cloud(III) [now]   NTRL-3SG.A-RE- become:III.U
'It just became cloudy again.'   [W11:0397]

(411) a. *udug mbya ø-nak-e-*   *i-hyaman*
    bath [NEG] NTRL-1.A-1PL- PLA-enter.water
    'We didn't bathe.'   [W15:0179]

b. *ukna mbya k-a-p-*   *e-nggat-made*
   fear [NEG] PRS.NTRL-3SG.A-CT- 2|3PL.U-become.PLA-PRS.HAB
   'They are never afraid.'   [W11:0255]

The uses of the Neutral Orientation prefixes are listed in Table 11.2 along with simple (mostly elicited or observed) examples in which the pre-verbal constituents and their equivalents in the English translations have been underlined.

Tab. 11.2: Uses of the Neutral Orientation prefixes (non-present ø-)

Role of pre-verbal constituent	Simple example
Arguments:	
S/A-argument	*nok no-ihwin* 'I cried'
S/A-oriented secondary predicate	*inah nake-umanah* 'The two of us went'
Instrument licensed by *k-* (WITH-)	*ayatip nod-katug* 'I scraped with a sea shell'
Various adverbial expressions:	
mbya NEG, *ndom* 'still', *namaya* 'just now'	*mbya no-deh* 'I didn't shoot'

11.1.3 Object Orientation *m-*

11.1.3.1 With O-arguments

The Object Orientation prefix *m-* is used when the constituent in the pre-verbal position is the O-argument of the clause, i.e. the most patient-like argument of a monotransitive verb (412–414).

(412)   da   ma-d-na-   yol
          [sago]$_O$ OBJ-DUR-3PL.A-   pound.sago
          'They were pounding sago.'   [W11:0423]

(413)   tamuy   m-ak-e-p-   balen
          [food(III)]$_O$ OBJ-1.A-1PL-CT-   finish:III.U
          'We finished the food.'   [W10:0673]

(414)   *Kaptel-anim wanangga ma-n-*   *y-ahik-a-m*
          K.-people   [children]$_O$ OBJ-3PL.A-   2|3PL.U-accompany-EXT-VEN
          'The Kaptel villagers were bringing their children.'   [W10:0109]

11.1.3.2 With ditransitive theme arguments

In Coastal Marind many verbs can be used ditransitively, as in the expression of a transfer event. The verb in such clauses has two non-subject arguments, and the Orientation marking differs according to whether the constituent expressing the theme (i.e. the gift) or the recipient is in the pre-verbal position. With a pre-verbal theme, the Object Orientation *m-* is used (415–416).

(415)   katal   m-ak-o-   og
          [money]$_T$ OBJ-1.A-3SG.DAT-   give
          'I gave him/her money.'

(416) *inahinah m-e-na-y-*   *og   kanamin-kana*
[four]ᴛ   OBJ-3PL>1-1.DAT-1PL- give rice
'They gave four [kilos] to us, of rice.'   [W03:0071]

It was noted in connection with example (393b) above that the recipient, when placed in the pre-verbal position, triggers the use of the Directional *k-* (see further §11.1.4.3, including discussion of counterexamples). Ditransitive constructions that exhibit the same marking for the monotransitive O and the ditransitive theme (or gift) are known in the typological literature as displaying indirective alignment (Siewierska 2003, Malchukov et al. 2010). Such typological classification of ditransitive constructions has focused on patterns of case flagging, so it is uncertain whether Coastal Marind as a whole should be classified as an 'indirective language' or rather as displaying neutral alignment (i.e. no case marking); what is clear is that the system of Verb Orientation treats the relevant arguments according to an indirective alignment.²

11.1.3.3 With secondary predicates controlled by O-argument

Depictive secondary predicates controlled by the S/A-argument were discussed in §11.1.2. A depictive phrase in pre-verbal position which is controlled by the O-argument occurs with Object Orientation *m-*; this is the case for *amamun* 'whole' in (417) referring to a deer being carried, and *kandi* 'raw' in (418) referring to a fish being eaten.

(417) *kaka*   *Kampanye amamun ma-d-ø-   sam⟨e⟩b-a-ti*
elder.sibling(m) K.   [whole]₌₀ OBJ-DUR-3SG.A- carry⟨3SG.U⟩-EXT-DUR
'Kampanye carried [the deer] whole.' (without cutting it up)   [W11:1205]

(418) (cf. also Drabbe 1955: 167, Text 5, line 13)
kandi   ma-d-ø-   ah⟨e⟩b-ti   awe
[raw]₌₀ OBJ-DUR-3SG.A- eat⟨3SG.U⟩-DUR fish
'S/he ate the fish raw.'

See §18.5 for more information about secondary predication.

11.1.3.4 With comitatives and other applicative arguments

A comitative argument (i.e. expressing a companion) that is licensed by the use of the WITH-prefix *k-* (§13.1.5) or the Accompaniment prefix *e-* (§13.1.6) is treated like a normal O-argument and triggers the Object Orientation if it is in the pre-verbal position. Note that this motivates the description of WITH-*k-* as having two distinct uses: licensing

---

2 For the alignment of participant indexing in ditransitive clauses, see §9.3.

an instrument (which corresponds to the use of the Neutral Orientation, see §11.1.2) and licensing a comitative object (using the Object Orientation). The Accompaniment *e-* has no corresponding instrumental use.

(419) epe   trek   epe   adaka   m-a-   ka-man
      DIST:III truck(m)(III) DIST:III [water]₀ OBJ-3SG.A- WITH-come
      'That truck brought water.'   [W10:0044]

(420) namaya isawa nggat m-ø-e-   umuh
      now   maybe [dog]₀ OBJ-3SG.A-ACPN- go:3SG.U
      'Maybe he brought the dogs along.'   [W10:0347]

Two prefixes of the prefixal complex, the Allative *ind-* (§13.1.7) and Separative *is-* (§13.1.8) mark applicative verbs. If the argument that is introduced by one of these prefixes is in the pre-verbal position the Object Orientation *m-* is used. The meaning of the resulting constructions could be glossed as *X m-....-ind-...V* 'Verb for X, in order to get X' and *X m-....-is-...- V* 'Verb from X, to avoid X'. This is illustrated for the Allative in (421). (See e.g. Table 13.2 for more examples with the Separative.)

(421) yoy   m-ak-ind-e-   awat-a-m   nok
      [2PL]₀ OBJ-1.A-ALL-1PL- run.PL-EXT-VEN 1
      'We came here to get you.'   [W10:0209]

It is also common for the Allative or Separative to be used with a pre-verbal constituent that is construed as a location rather than as a participant in the event. In such contexts the Directional *k-* is used instead of the Object Orientation, as in (447–448) further below.

11.1.3.5 With adverbials

Most of the expressions discussed in the preceding subsections could be thought of as O-arguments of their clauses. In addition, a variety of adverbial expressions occur with the Object Orientation. It is generally difficult to see any synchronic motivation behind this, since these adverbials have no special affinity with the O-argument.

With some motion verbs the Object Orientation *m-* appears with a bare NP in the pre-verbal position, which then expresses the goal of the movement.

(422) Merauke m-a-   umah
      [M.]_Goal OBJ-3SG.A- go:2|3PL.U
      'They left for Merauke.'   [W11:0180]

11.1 The Orientation prefixes — 265

Other motion verbs that are attested with Object Orientation marking the goal are *hwil* 'walk', *ihon* 'run away', *uhwasig* 'go up from water', *man* 'come', *wahik* 'accompany', *hus* 'cross (river)', *yet* 'be in movement'. Employing the same marking pattern for O-arguments and (some) goals is a well-known phenomenon in several European languages, e.g. the Latin Accusative in *Roma-m eo* 'I am going to Rome'. The Coastal Marind pattern also extends to mark NPs that are not strictly goals, but rather express the meaning 'go to do activity associated with X', e.g. *yandam* 'stomach'+*m*-[verb of going/sitting] 'to go/sit and defecate', *sawanggi* 'black magic' (<Malay *suanggi*)+*m*-[verb of going] 'go to do black magic'. The NP is commonly headed by a verb stem, and then has a general purposive meaning, as in

(423) kipa   i-k⟨i⟩sid   m-a-   umuh
       [net(III) INESS-⟨PLA⟩tie:III.U] OBJ-3SG.A- go:3SG.U
       'He went to tie a net.'   [W22:0015]

Adverbial phrases expressing cause and purpose occur with Object Orientation *m*- if the adverbial phrase is placed in the pre-verbal position. The examples below illustrate this for *X lek* 'because of X' (424), *X nanggol* 'for X, in order to X' (425) and *X awe* '(searching) for X' (426).[3]

(424) bayalim-imu   lek   m-a-   ambid
       [body.odour-smell from:III] OBJ-3SG.A sit.down
       '[The wallaby] stopped because of [smelling] the body-odour.'   [W11:0951]

(425) yi   nanggol m-e-   lesad-e   namaya otih ay?
       [drink for]   OBJ-2PL.A- draw.water-IPFV   now   all   Q
       'You're taking up all [this water] for drinking, are you?'   [W06:0185]

(426) tamuy   awe   ma-d-ø-   nayat-ti
       [food for] OBJ-DUR-3SG.A-   be.moving.PL-DUR
       'They went searching for food.'   [D12:0017]

The expression of cause by means of a *lek*-phrase alternates with a synonymous construction in which the cause is expressed as a companion licensed by the WITH-prefix *k*- on the verb stem, as in (427). A literal translation of (427b) would be 'it is screaming with hunger'. The use of the Object Orientation *m*- in (427b) follows the normal

---

[3] Drabbe (1955: 47) appears to claim that it is the presence of a postposition that triggers the use of Object *m*-. This is incorrect. In fact his own example (from the Eastern dialect of Coastal Marind) *de rek manod-og* 'I made it from wood' is contradicted by a parallel textual example with the Neutral Orientation on page 158, line 11.

use of comitative WITH-verbs (see above). One could speculate that the general use of the Object Orientation with cause/reason expressions (as in 424–425) is influenced by its occurrence in contexts such as (427b). Its use with expressions of purpose is more obviously related to the use of the Object Orientation with goals, discussed above.

(427) a. *emel   lek   m-a-   esol-e*
         [hunger from:III]   OBJ-3SG.A-   make.noise-IPFV

   b. *emel   m-a-   k-esol-e*
      [hunger]   OBJ-3SG.A-   WITH-make.noise-IPFV

   Both: '[The pig] is making noise because it is hungry.'

The Object Orientation *m-* also appears in expressions referring to the onset of an event. It forms *oso m-* 'just start to...' with the noun *oso* 'start, beginning' (428) (cf. §18.4.3). The frequent inceptive TAM-particle *ye* only occurs in the sequence *ye m-* (429) (§18.4.4).

(428) *adaka   oso   m-a-   kw-eyak*
      water(III)   [start]   OBJ-3SG.A-   INESS-release:III.U

   'The water was just about to disappear [from the swamps].'   [W03:0025]

(429) *mes   ye   ma-no-   n-alaw*
      ripe.coconut   [INGRS]   OBJ-1.A-   1.U-search

   'I looked/started looking for coconuts.'   [W20:0142]

Certain adverbially used NPs expressing calendrical units appear with the Object Orientation *m-* in past time contexts (430–431). Nominals attested in this construction include *yap* 'night', *kwemek* 'morning', *yanid* 'day', *usus* 'afternoon', *hyakod mandaw* 'one month'.

(430) *tuban   yap   m-ak-e-   y-as*
      bandicoot   [night]   OBJ-1.A-1PL-   2|3PL.U-shoot

   'At night we shot bandicoots.'   [W02:0086]

(431) *inahinah   yanid   m-an-d-e-   na-hwalah*
      [four   day]   OBJ-1.A-DUR-1PL-   1.U-be

   'We stayed there for four days.'   [W23:0018]

Other common temporal expressions never occur with the Object Orientation, e.g. *wis* 'yesterday' and *mandin* 'long ago', which typically are placed at the periphery of the clause, outside the pre-verbal position. It is tempting to explain this contrast as one involving more 'nouny' expressions ('night', 'morning' etc.) patterning with

Tab. 11.3: Uses of the Object Orientation prefix *m-*

Role of pre-verbal constituent	Simple example
Arguments:	
O-argument of monotransitive verb	*basik ma-deh* 'he shot <u>a pig</u>'
Theme argument of ditransitive verb	*dadami make-hahin*
	'I gave them <u>betel pepper</u>'
O-oriented secondary predicates	*kandi mad-ahebti* 'he ate him <u>raw</u>' (=(418))
Applicative arguments	*mes ma-kaman* 's/he brought <u>coconuts</u>'
	eham mis-ihon 's/he ran from <u>her husband</u>'
Various adverbial expressions:.	
Goal (with some motion verbs)	*Okaba ma-nahik* 's/he took me <u>to Okaba</u>'
	sageru-yi ma-umuh 'he went <u>to drink sageru</u>'
Expressions of cause, purpose	*nok nanggo ma-man* 's/he came <u>for me</u>'
Inceptive particle *ye*	*ye ma-kahek* 's/he <u>started</u> climbing'
with *oso* 'start, beginning'	*oso ma-ihwim* 'it was <u>just starting</u> to get dark'
Some temporal expressions	*kwemek map-hawa*
	's/he went home <u>in the morning</u>'
Other adverbials	*adida mano-man*
	'I came (to stay) <u>temporarily</u>'

O-arguments, while more adverb-like expressions ('yesterday') do not; however, this cannot be right as many expressions that are clearly non-nouny co-occur with the Object Orientation, e.g. *mbaymbay* 'unable, unknowing' in the expression '(come to a place) for the first time' (432), or *adida* 'temporarily, for a short while' (433). The ability of such items to participate in the Object Orientation-pattern seems to be an idiomatic feature of some expressions, and not due to any particular semantic commonality.

(432) *ane mame! mbaymbay ma-bat-ø- man-em ehe anem ehe*
oh my! [unknowing] OBJ-AFF-3SG.A- come-VEN PROX:I man(I) PROX:I
'Oh my! This man is coming here for the first time/not knowing the place.'
[W10:0342]

(433) *adida ma-no- man*
temporarily OBJ-1.A- come
'I came for just a short while (not intending to stay).'

The uses of the Object Orientation *m-* are listed in Table 11.3 along with simple (mostly elicited or observed) examples in which the pre-verbal constituents and their equivalents in the English translations have been underlined.

11.1.4 Directional Orientation *k-*

The function of the prefix *k-* ranges from the marking of various adverbial notions, mostly spatial in nature, to the flagging of the pre-verbal constituent as the recipient-like participant of a ditransitive verb. It is likely that its use in coding spatial relations is (diachronically) primary, so I will discuss its appearances with pre-verbal adverbials before describing its use with recipient arguments. In addition *k-* has important uses in clause combining, which are addressed in §20.3.

11.1.4.1 With spatial/directional adverbials

The Directional prefix is used when the pre-verbal constituent refers to the goal of motion, or the path along which a movement takes place. Thus, with verbs expressing motion towards an endpoint or entry into a posture, as in (434–437), the expression before the *k*-marked verb refers to the place in which the moving participant ends up as a result of the event.

(434) epe   k-a-   hi-n   nok
      [there]$_{Goal}$ DIR-3SG.A- fall-1.U 1
      'I fell there.'   [W03:0145]

(435) sam-milah epe   ka-mo-   yali
      [big-village there]$_{Goal}$ DIR-FUT:1.A- lie.down
      'I will sleep (lit. lie down) there in the main village.'   [W10:0225]

(436) pa   epe   k-ak-e-   kwagin
      head(III) [there]$_{Goal}$ DIR-1.A-1PL- throw:III.U
      'We threw the head there.'   [W10:0200]

(437) hyakod say   ka-mo-   ibotok
      [one   place]$_{Goal}$ DIR-FUT:2SG.A- put.PLA:III.U
      'You should put them together in one spot.'   [W20:0171]

Often the spatial adverbial is expressed by a bare NP, as in the examples above. It can also be expressed by a constituent headed by a postposition, as in (438–439).

(438) katpale   lahwalah ka-n-ap-   lun   napet
      [brush.turkey.mound on.top]$_{Goal}$ DIR-3PL.A-CT- plant banana
      'They planted bananas on top of a brush turkey mound.'   [W11:0980]

(439) "You can say like this if somebody asks why you didn't write down new words."

   pa   kumay   ka-no-   i-hwagib
   [head inside]_Goal DIR-1.A- PLA-save:III.U

   'I saved them inside my head.'

k- occurs with verbs that express the inception of movement, e.g. *man* 'come' (more accurately translated as 'take off hither' in Coastal Marind) and *umuh* 'go' (or rather 'take off, leave') when the pre-verbal constituent refers to the path along which the ensuing movement takes place (440–442).

(440) kay   k-a-   man-em
       [road]_Path DIR-3SG.A- come-VEN

       'He came by the road.'   [W01:0062]

(441) pale   ka-no-   uma⟨n⟩ah   epe
       [land.ridge(III)]_Path DIR-1.A- go⟨1.U⟩   DIST:III

       'I went by land.'   [W02:0128]

(442) Kalaway, epe   ka-mo-   oha-y
       K.   [there]_Path DIR-FUT:2SG.A- go.down.to.water-2SG.U

       'In Kalaway, there you go down.'   [W10:0626]

With verbs that do not have motion or entry into posture as part of their meaning, the Directional *k-* can be used to express the location of a punctual event denoted by the verb, as in (443–444).

(443) namaya epe   ka-bt-i-n-ind-a-y-   mahid   ihe
       now   [there]_Loc   DIR-AFF-3PL>1-1.DAT-ALL-1.DAT-1PL- become.angry PROX:I/II.PL

       'There they became angry at us.'   [W11:0961]

(444) bak   k-e-na-y-   og
       [outside]_Loc   DIR-3PL>1-1.DAT-1PL- give

       'They gave it to us outside.'   [W16:0046]

If the event referred to is durative, the Locational *nd-* must be used in the expression of place (§11.1.5). An exception to this is if reference is made to the path along which a durative movement takes place. In that case, the pre-verbal Path-expression is followed by a *k*-marked verb, as in (445). This is the same pattern as with the punctual verbs in (440–442) above. If the motion verb expresses a durative movement that does not take place along a Path the Locational Orientation *nd-* (§11.1.5) is used, as in (446), an overheard example reporting the play activities of some children.

(445) duh   ka-d-a-na-y-   umak
      [beach]ₚₐₜₕ DIR-DUR-3SG.A-1.DAT-ACPN- be.running
      'He drove us along the beach.'   [W10:0487]

(446) duh   nd-an-d-e-p-   ku-ya⟨n⟩it-a
      [beach]_Loc LOC-1.A-DUR-1PL-CT-   INESS-run.around⟨1.U⟩-EXT
      'We were running around on the beach.'

The expression of goal by means of the Directional *k-* is mostly used with pre-verbal constituents referring to stereotypical locations (e.g. geographical landmarks) and with deictic expressions ('here', 'there'). To express movement towards an animate the Allative *ind-* is usually added (§13.1.7):

(447) During a hunt, a pig tried to hide in the undergrowth. Iyob (a dog) followed it.
      yah nama Iyob anup   ya   ka-d-ø-in-   yet-ti
      but now   I.   [EMPH:II very]_Goal DIR-DUR-3SG.A-ALL- be.moving-DUR
      'But then Iyob was going straight towards it (*anup ya* 'itself'=the pig).'
                                                                       [W11:0565]

Somewhat confusingly, the Directional *k-* can also be used with the Separative *is-*, which has the opposite meaning of the Allative ('away'). The pre-verbal constituent typically refers to something fled from, as in (448). This use of *k-* is exceptional since the Locational Orientation *nd-* (§11.1.5) is used in most other contexts where the pre-verbal constituent expresses the source of movement.

(448) Looking for crabs in a swamp when the high tide entered.
      etob   k-ak-is-e-   awan
      [sea.water]_Source DIR-1.A-SEP-1PL- run.PL
      'We ran from the [approaching] sea water.'   [W07:0027]

11.1.4.2 Expressing actions on possessed body parts

Many verbs alternate between coding the pre-verbal participant by means of Directional *k-* and Object Orientation *m-*. This is expecially prominent with verbs describing actions on body parts, as in the three pairs in (449–451). The meaning difference between the (a)-sentences (with Directional *k-*) and the (b)-sentences (with Object *m-*) is subtle, and is perhaps similar to the alternation in English between *I hit his leg* and *I hit him on the leg* (the so-called "body-part possessor ascension alternation"; Fillmore 1970, Levin 1993: 71).

(449) a. *wap   k-ak-o-   wa-hanid*
       [thigh(III)]₀ DIR-1.A-3SG.DAT- III.U-grasp.PLA
       'I grabbed hold of [the deer's] thighs.'   [W11:1166]

   b. *sangga   m-enam- wa-hanid   ehe*
      [hand(III)]₀ OBJ-RCPR- III.U-grasp.PLA here
      'They are shaking hands.'   [D09:0263]

(450) a. *tagu   k-a-n-is-a-p-   ka-lemed*
       [foot]₀ DIR-3SG.A-1.DAT-SEP-1.DAT-CT- INESS-stand.PLA
       'He stepped on my foot.'   [W11:0935]

   b. *nggat tagu   m-a-na-p-   ihwaniy-e*
      dog [foot(III)]₀ OBJ-3SG.A-1.DAT-CT- lick:III.U-IPFV
      'The dog is licking my foot.'

(451) a. *kalambit ya   k-ø-o-   ya-deh*
       [tendon(IV) real]₀ DIR-3SG.A-3SG.DAT- IV.U-shoot
       'He hit [the pig] right at the [Achilles] tendon.'   [W03:0089]

   b. *isawa mbya ugu   m-ø-o-   deh*
      maybe [all skin(III)]₀ OBJ-3SG.A-3SG.DAT- shoot:III.U
      'Maybe he shot its skin only.'   [W11:1047]

The body parts are tentatively subscripted as O-arguments. More research will perhaps show that the pre-verbal constituents in the (a) vs. (b) variants bear different semantic roles.

11.1.4.3 With ditransitive recipient arguments

The Directional *k-* is used with ditransitive verbs if the pre-verbal constituent refers to the recipient (in a transfer event) or recipient-like participant (e.g. the addressee of verbs of communication). It is not surprising that the same marking is used to express goal (and related meanings) and recipient (cf. the English preposition *to* covering those two functions).

(452) *mayay nggus nok k-a-na-p-   kisak⟨e⟩h*
      first crab [1]ᵣ DIR-3SG.A-1.DAT-CT- lay.down⟨3SG.U⟩
      'First he gave me a crab.'   [W11:0298]

(453) *Alamem k-ø-o-   ayi ago, "menda-b-ø-   yali"*
      [A.]ᵣ DIR-3SG.A-3SG.DAT- say QUOT PERF-ACT-3SG.A- lie.down
      'He said to Alamem: "He has fallen asleep".'   [D01:0150]

It was observed in connection with examples (415–416) above that a pre-verbal constituent referring to the theme participant in a ditransitive clause patterns with the O-argument of a monotransitive clause and triggers the use of the Object Orientation prefix *m-*. The pair in (454a–b) shows the difference between a pre-verbal recipient-like argument (454a) and theme-like argument (454b), triggering prefixation with *k-* and *m-* respectively.

(454) a. *nok k-u-n-ind-a- tanggiy-e*
[1]$_R$ DIR-2SG.A-1.DAT-ALL-1.DAT- order-IPFV
'You keep giving me orders.' [W06:0108]

b. *namakad ma-n-um-ind-a- tanggiy-a*
[thing]$_T$ OBJ-3PL.A-FRUS-ALL-2SG.DAT- order-EXT
'They are ordering you [to get] things.' [W06:0131]

The description of Directional *k-* as flagging a pre-verbal recipient, and Object *m-* a pre-verbal theme, appears to be too simplistic, however, since there are a few attestations of *m-* appearing with a pre-verbal recipient. The contexts in which this marking variant is allowed are not understood at present. A (grammatically impeccable) corpus example is given in (455); attempts at eliciting analogous senteces failed as speakers preferred the Directional *k-* with the recipient argument in pre-verbal position.[4]

(455) *kak Ndalom-Iwag eham nok m-a-na- ayi*
aunt Nd.-I. 3:husband [1]$_R$ OBJ-3SG.A-1.DAT- say
'Aunt Ndalom-Iwag's husband told me.' [W11:0591]

11.1.4.4 In 'become'-clauses

In expressions meaning *X becomes Y*, with *Y* corresponding to a nominal, the Directional *k-* is used when the predicate nominal (i.e. the nominal describing the result of the change-of-state) is in the pre-verbal position. Examples:

(456) *wahani waninggap ka-p-a-na- ay*
body(III) good DIR-FUT-3SG.A-1.DAT- become:III.U
'My body will become well.' (from eating medicine)

---

4 Note that Drabbe's description (1955: 46–47) gives the impression that Object *m-* and Directional *k-* are interchangeable with a preceding recipient argument. This is incorrect according to my data.

(457) muy   kapalet k-a-   ay
     meat(III) dry   DIR-3SG.A- become:III.U
     'The meat became dry.'   [W11:1111]

(458) da   ay⟨e⟩b   sa-n-   y-a,
     sago(III) scrape⟨III.U⟩ ONLY-3PL.A- 2|3PL.U-AUX

     ipe   ay⟨e⟩b-anim   k-a-   in
     DIST:I/II.PL   scrape⟨III.U⟩-people DIR-3SG.A- become:2|3PL.U
     'They just scraped the sago pith, they became the sago scrapers.'
                                                                 [W19:0182–0183]

(459) From a story.[5]

     nanggit k-a-   in   yah, sayam-lul   ipe
     mosquito DIR-3SG.A- become:2|3PL.U   PTCL wallaby-fur(IV) DIST:IV
     'It turned into mosquitos, that wallaby fur.'   [D01:0161]

Compare the use of the Directional Orientation in change-of-state contexts with the use of the Neutral Orientation in stative copula clauses (§11.1.2.2).

11.1.4.5 With non-spatial adverbials

Certain adverbial expressions without any discernible spatial meaning (at least synchronically) occur in the pre-verbal position followed by Directional *k-* prefixed to the verb. This is true for expressions such as *hyakod a* 'together', *kosi* 'small' (in the sense 'a little'), *sam* 'big' (in the sense 'lots') and *otih* 'many, all'. These adverbials could perhaps be thought of as describing the 'extent' of the event; but note that e.g. *kudaya* 'alone' patterns with secondary predicates (cf. example 408) and not with 'together', despite expressing related meanings.

(460) hyakod a   k-an-d-e-p-   ka-hu-t-a   ay?
     [together] DIR-1.A-DUR-1PL-CT-   INESS-emerge-1.U-EXT Q
     'We went back together, right?'   [W11:0425]

(461) yah bing   kumay epe da   kosi   k-a-   kw-ambid
     but leaf.base inside DIST sago [little] DIR-3SG.A- INESS-sit
     'But in the output trough only a little sago settled.'   [W20:0071]

---

[5] The speaker is from Duhmilah (the village to the east of Wambi), where *lul* 'fur' takes Gender IV agreement, and not Gender III as in Wambi.

Interestingly, the use of the Directional *k-* in combination with *otih* 'many, all' only occurs when *otih* refers to the O-argument (462). When *otih* refers to the S/A-argument it patterns with secondary predicates and is followed by the Neutral Orientation prefix (463).

(462) otih   k-e-   i-sak?
      [many]₌ₒ DIR-2PL.A-   2|3PL.U-hit.PLA
      'Did you catch a lot (of fish)?'   [D07:0049]

(463) otih   ø-i-n-ind-a-   mahid
      [many]₌ₐ NTRL-3PL>1-1.DAT-ALL-1.DAT-   become.angry
      'All/many of them became angry at me.'

The common temporal adverbial *tanama* 'again' occurs followed by a verb prefixed with the Directional *k-*. This probably has a diachronic explanation: *tanama* is related to the adjective *tanama* 'old', so the original construction perhaps meant '(back) to the old (place/situation)' which acquired the meaning 'again'. Examples of *tanama* 'again':

(464) tanama   ka-n-   dahetok
      [again] DIR-3PL.A- return
      'They went home again.'   [W09:0015]

(465) tanama   k-ak-i-e-   yusig   usus   epe
      [again] DIR-1.A-RE-1PL-   make.fire   afternoon(III)   DIST:III
      'We lit [the leaf oven] again in the afternoon.'   [W03:0124]

Other expressions that always occur with Directional *k-* are the adverb *lun* (§18.4.7), in a construction meaning roughly 'straight away' (466), and the nominal *pen* 'murder' with the meaning 'to hit (etc.) somebody dead' (467).

(466) Petrus lun   k-a-   man-em
      P.   [straight.away] DIR-3SG.A- come-VEN
      'Petrus came straight away.'   [W11:0582]

(467) anem pen   ka-n-   w-amuk
      man   [murder] DIR-3PL.A- 3SG.U-hit
      'They killed a man.'

Tab. 11.4: Uses of the Directional Orientation prefix *k-*

Role of pre-verbal constituent	Simple example
Adverbial (spatial):	
Direction of motion	*epe ka-ambid* 'S/he sat down <u>there</u>'
Path	<u>duh</u> *kap-manem* 'S/he came along <u>the beach</u>'
Place of punctual event	<u>Okaba</u> *ka-nin* 'I was born in <u>Okaba</u>'
Arguments:	
Act on possessed body part	<u>muk</u> *kako-han* 'I grabbed his/her <u>elbow</u>'
R-argument of ditransitive verb	<u>Oskar</u> *kakop-oleb* 'I sold it <u>to Oskar</u>'
Various (non-spatial) adverbials:	
hyakod a 'together', *sam* 'lots'	<u>sam</u> *kamo-yi* 'You should eat <u>lots</u>!'
tanama 'again', *lun* 'straight away' (etc.)	<u>tanama</u> *kaki-yol* 'I pounded sago <u>again</u>'

11.1.4.6 Other uses

The Directional *k-* is used in meta-linguistic expression with verbs meaning 'call', 'say' etc. Example (468) shows a type of utterance that is extremely frequent in the linguistic socialisation of small Marind children: the speaker attracts the attention of a toddler, points to someone in the vicinity (or to him/herself) and instructs the child to call out the appropriate kinship term for this person. The kinship expression is in the pre-verbal position, and the verb is marked for Directional Orientation.

(468) Addressing a small child, pointing to the child's mother's brother (*yay*).

    yay   ka-mo-p-   lu!
    [uncle] DIR-FUT:2SG.A-CT- call:3SG.U

    'Say *yay* to him/call him *yay*!'

If the pre-verbal position is occupied by an expression referring to the entity being named (instead of the name itself), it behaves like a normal O-argument and triggers the use of the Object Orientation *m-* on the verb (469).

(469) Alamem nok m-e-   nulun-e
       A.   [1]$_O$ OBJ-3PL>1- call:1.U-IPFV

    'I am the one they call Alamem.'   [D01:0075]

The uses of the Directional Orientation *k-* are listed in Table 11.4 along with simple (mostly elicited or observed) examples in which the pre-verbal constituents and their equivalents in the English translations have been underlined.

11.1.5 Locational Orientation *nd-*

11.1.5.1 With adverbials expressing source/location

When flagging the role of the pre-verbal constituent, the Locational *nd-* has two functions: marking the location of a durative situation, and marking the source of punctual events. Thus, the meaning of this structure depends on the aspectual contrast durative vs. punctual (cf. §14.1.1). Examples of the Locational *nd-* marking location of durative situations:

(470) nok bak   nd-an-d-e-   hamat-a
      1   [outside]$_{Loc}$ LOC-1.A-DUR-1PL- sit.PL-EXT
      'We were sitting outside.'   [W16:0058]

(471) Kabaim nda-d-na-   nin-ma   ipe   sasayi-anim
      [K.]$_{Loc}$ LOC-DUR-3PL.A- sleep.PLA-PST.HAB DIST:I/II.PL work-people
      'They used to sleep in Kabaim, the workers.'   [W10:0039]

(472) hyakod epe   nd-a-   ka-tel-e
      one   [there]$_{Loc}$ LOC-3SG.A- INESS-be.lying-IPFV
      'One [deer] is lying there.'   [W01:0057]

(473) da   epe   nda-p-e-   yol   epe
      sago [there]$_{Loc}$ LOC-FUT:1.A-1PL- pound.sago there
      'We are going to pound sago there.'   [W20:0045]

In this use *nd-* is also common marking the copula in a locative predication. In (474) the copula consists of *nd-* followed by the 3SG.A prefix *a-*. The present tense copula has a zero verb stem (see §17.4).

(474) nanggit deg kumay   nd-a-   Ø   ipe   anip
      mosquito [forest inside]$_{Loc}$ LOC-3SG.A- be.NPST DIST:I/II.PL EMPH:I/II.PL
      'The mosquitos are inside the forest.'   [W11:0849]

In its function of marking the pre-verbal constituent as source, *nd-* is most often found with motion verbs, as in (475), but it is also frequent with non-motion verbs, as in (476–477).

(475) Mopa   nd-am-bat-e-   uma⟨n⟩ah
      [M.]$_{Source}$ LOC-1.A-AFF-1PL- go⟨1.U⟩
      'We went from Mopa.'   [W10:0537]

(476) nok Simson epe   nd-a-n-ind-a-   tanggiy
       1   S.   [there]_Source LOC-3SG.A-1.DAT-ALL-1.DAT- order
       'Simson sent me from there.'   [W02:0120]

(477) pal   oso   m-ak-e-p-   wayaman, epe   nd-ak-ind-a-y-   n-alaw,
       bridge start OBJ-1.A-1PL-CT- stand.PL [there]_Source LOC-1.A-ALL-2SG.DAT-1PL- 1.U-search
       ah-o-   umak-em
       [DEP-2SG.A- be.running-VEN]
       'We had just stopped at the bridge, from there we looked for you, when you came driving hither.'   [W20:0054]

Just like the Directional *k-*, the Locational *nd-* is mostly used with stereotypical locations (e.g. geographical landmarks) and with deictic expressions ('here', 'there'), especially in its function of marking motion away from a source. Speakers seem to prefer to use other marking options to express movement away from less typical entities. If the pre-verbal source is animate (e.g. 'flee from somebody') the Separative applicative *is-* is employed (§13.1.8), and the verb then takes the Directional *k-*, as in (448) above, or Object *m-*, as in (551) on p. 321. If the source is an inanimate non-landmark, the postposition *lek* can be added to unambiguously mark the pre-verbal constituent as a source, with Locational *nd-* still appearing on the verb:

(478) nok sambayang   lik   nd-ak-e-   hu-n
       1   [church.service(m) from:I/II.PL]_Source   LOC-1.A-1PL- emerge-1.U
       'We came out from the church service.'   [W15:0005]

(479) During a trip, the speaker and other villagers crossed a river, where a truck was waiting for them.
       belang-yahun   lik   nd-an-d-e-p-   ikyalun,
       [outrigger(m)-canoe   from:I/II.PL]_Source LOC-1.A-DUR-1PL-CT-   jump
       inahinah tagu ti   yahun   k-an-d-e-   ka-lemed
       [four   feet with canoe]_Goal   DIR-1.A-DUR-1PL-   INESS-stand.PLA
       'We jumped from the boat, and stood in the truck.'   [W15:0150]

The second clause in example (479) has a verb ('come to a standstill') marked with the Directional *k-* since the pre-verbal constituent is a goal.

11.1.5.2 In 'when'-questions and with calendrical units
The Locational Orientation is used in certain temporal expressions. It combines with an interrogative phrase headed by the general question word *ta* 'who/what' to form 'when'-questions (there is no word for 'when' in Coastal Marind; see §19.3.2.3):

(480) Alatep ta   nda-h-o-b-   yet?
      A.   [what]   LOC-ROG-2SG.A-ACT-   be.moving
      'When did you go to Alatep?'   [W11:0097]

(481) ta   katane nda-h-am-   man?
      [what   sun]   LOC-ROG-FUT:1.A:ACT- come
      'What time shall I come?'

The Locational *nd-* is also used when the pre-verbal constituent expresses a calendrical unit such as year, month or day:

(482) 1987   nd-a-   n-in
      [1987] LOC-3SG.A-   1.U-become
      'I was born in 1987.'

(483) yanid   epe   nd-ak-inm-e-ka-   n-idih
      [day(III)   DIST:III] LOC-1.A-RCPR-1PL-PRI- RCPR-see
      'On that day we met.' (lit. saw each other)   [W18:0114]

The Locational Orientation is not used with any other temporal expressions. Compare the Object Orientation prefix *m-* which is used with a broader range of time adverbials (§11.1.3.5). It is not clear how the use of *nd-* marking source/location (described in the preceding subsection) is related to its use with 'when?' and with calendrical units. Note that in its temporal use *nd-* combines freely with both durative verbs (such as *yet* 'go, be in movement' in example 480) and punctual verbs (such as *man* in example 481) whereas such verbs give rise to (static) location vs. source readings respectively when the Locational Orientation combines with a place adverbial.

11.1.6 Restrictive Orientation *s-*

The Restrictive Orientation means 'only', scoping over the pre-verbal constituent. This prefix differs from the other Orientation prefixes in being insensitive to the syntactic/semantic role of the pre-verbal constituent: for example, it occurs with the S-argument in (484) and with the O-argument in (485), roles that correspond to the use of the Neutral (§11.1.2) and Object (§11.1.3) Orientations respectively.

(484) sambayang   mbya   ø-nak-e-   uma⟨n⟩ah,   anip   amay   ke
      church.service(m)   [NEG] NTRL-1.A-1PL- go⟨1.U⟩   EMPH:I/II.PL   [ancestor APL]₅
      sa-d-ø-   nayat
      ONLY-DUR-3SG.A-   be.moving.PL
      'We didn't attend the church service, only grandpa and the others went.'
                                                                            [W15:0106]

(485) The speaker describes how she went home after processing sago.

ka	s-ak-ap-	ka-yad⟨e⟩wn
[sago.waste(III)]₀	ONLY-1.A-CT-	INESS-leave⟨III.U⟩

'I only left the waste pith.' [W20:0077]

Coastal Marind *s-* differs from the English quantifier *only* in being scopally unambiguous. No part of the clause other than the pre-verbal constituent can be interpreted as being in the scope of *s-*. For (485) this corresponds to the (written) English reading *I only left the wáste píth (and brought everything else)*; the reading *I only léft the waste pith (I didn't throw it away)* is impossible and would require pre-posing of the verb stem (see §17.2.2).

The Restrictive Orientation is used in some contexts where *only* does not occur in the English free translation. One interesting case is the expression of '(do something) *n* times' which consists of a numeral combined with *s-*.

(486) Describing how a truck brought people home from a feast in another village.

inhyakod	s-a-p-	u-dhetok
[three]	ONLY-3SG.A-CT-	PLA-return

'It went back and forth three times.' [W19:0244]

This is the normal way of expressing '*n* times', and there is no particular emphasis on the fact that something was done only *n* times and not more than *n* times (in the Malay translations offered during transcription, 'only' was never used). Note that there is a synonymous periphrastic expression with the particle *se* 'only': *hyakod se* 'once', *inah se* 'twice' etc.

Another use of the prefix *s-* is as part of a common construction in which the adversative particle *yah* 'but' fills the pre-verbal position. This combination has a contrary-to-expectation meaning, typically involving negative outcomes.

(487) Commenting on the water level in a well.

kosi	yah	s-a-	ay,	sam	ya	ø-d-a-	ola
little	[but]	ONLY-3SG.A-	become:III.U	[big	very]	NTRL-DUR-3SG.A	be:III.U

'There is a little water left, [before] there was a lot.' [W06:0019]

The literal translation of *yah* and *s-* would be 'but only', which never occured in the Malay translations given during transcription. It is probably best to think of this combination as having non-compositional semantics, as discussed in §6.3.7.

11.2 Discourse function of the pre-verbal constituent

The previous sections of this chapter were concerned with how the choice of an Orientation prefix depends on the function of the constituent placed in the pre-verbal position. In this section I will provide some clues as to how speakers choose what constituent to place in this position. The reader looking for hard and fast rules is likely to be disappointed: there are both pragmatic and grammatical factors involved in the choice of an occupant for this slot in the clause, and the precise nature of these factors is beyond what can be covered in a descriptive grammar. The following discussion is limited to the most prominent generalisations about the pre-verbal position. In §11.2.1 I describe the function of this syntactic slot as the position in which a focused constituent is placed. Pre-verbal constituents in topic-comment structures are discussed in §11.2.2.

It was mentioned above that a few expressions obligatorily appear in the pre-verbal position. This is true for e.g. the negator *mbya* and the temporal adverb *ndom* 'still'; further discussion of such purely grammatical constraints on pre-verbal placement is in §11.3. I am not aware of any 'deeper' synchronic explanation for the strict placement of these words, so it will just be treated as an idiosyncratic fact about *mbya* and *ndom*.[6]

11.2.1 Expressing constituent focus

In most contexts, the choice of what constituent to place in the pre-verbal position is governed by pragmatic concerns. This choice is part of the way the speaker models an utterance as to best structure the information to be conveyed to the listener. The most salient pragmatic function of the pre-verbal position is as the site of the constituent that is in focus. A focused constituent can be thought of as being highlighted by the speaker because it specifies which one of several possible alternatives holds, and that this information is relevant for the topic at hand. (For example, the utterance *The présidént ate the sandwich* specifies that it was the president and nobody else, while *The president ate the sándwich* highlights that it was a sandwich and nothing else; see Krifka 2008.) Another way of thinking about the focused part is as the more unpredictable piece of information in an utterance. The speaker then uses focus to contrast the unpredictable, most informative piece of information, with the information that is

---

[6] There is probably a diachronic explanations for the obligatory pre-verbal placement of the negator *mbya*. As discussed in §18.4.1, *mbya* originally only had the meaning 'all, completely' (which is still retained in its use as a nominal modifier today) and was used under focus in negated clauses as a generalizer '(not) at all'. This structure was the input to the familiar process called Jespersen's Cycle; the innovated negator *mbya* would then reflect its pre-verbal position from its original use as a focused generalising adverb.

shared with the addressee (the 'presupposed' part of the utterance; see Halliday 1967b, Lambrecht 1994).

If a constituent is in focus in Coastal Marind, it is usually in the pre-verbal position. Since this slot also can host non-focused constituents (for example, there are no reasons for considering the pre-verbal adverbial *ndom* 'still' to be focused), it would not be appropriate to label it as the 'focus slot'. Referring to this syntactic slot as the 'pre-verbal position' is neutral with respect to the function it is used to express.

The most conspicuous use of the pre-verbal position is as the site of the questioned element in a content question, and as the site of the corresponding constituent in the answer to such a question. These expressions can be considered to be in focus since they mark the point in the utterance where unpredictable information is requested or provided.[7] In Coastal Marind, these elements obligatorily occur immediately before the verb complex:

(488) 1. onggat ta   ø-b-ø-in-   kahek?
         coconut [who]$_A$ NTRL-ACT-3SG.A-ALL- climb
         'Who climbed for coconuts?'

     2. kaka   Budi ø-d-ø-in-   kahek
         [elder.sib(m) B.]$_A$ NTRL-DUR-3SG.A-ALL- climb
         'Budi climbed for coconuts.'   [W11:0082–0083]

Restricting the placement of the interrogative phrase to the pre-verbal position appears to be fairly common across languages, and it has even been claimed to be a characteristic feature of many SOV languages (A. H.-O. Kim 1988, but see also Herring and Paolillo 1995; Coastal Marind is at most mildly SOV). Content questions are further discussed in §19.3.

It is often helpful to think of a focused constituent in the pre-verbal position as providing an answer to a question that is not expressed, but nevertheless is implicit in the context (Krifka 2008). For example, the first speaker in the following exchange is trying to answer the implicit question *Who followed him?*, with the crucial piece of the response, *oy* 'you', in focus in the first turn, which is reaffirmed by the use of focused 'my nephew here' in the last turn.

(489) 1. oy   ø-o-d-   yet   ay?
         [2SG]$_S$ NTRL-2SG.A-DUR- be.moving Q

         oy   ø-o-d-o-p-   esoh ay?
         [2SG]$_A$ NTRL-2SG.A-DUR-3SG.DAT-CT- follow Q

---

[7] There is an enormous literature addressing the parallelisms between focus constructions and content questions; see e.g. Horvath (1986) and Cheng (1991) for classic studies within a generative framework.

2. *ahak*
   yeah

3. *ahak,   nama   kemlay   e=   te-ø-d-ø-o-p-   esoh*
   yeah   now   [nephew I:PROX=]_A GIV:I-NTRL-DUR-3SG.A-3SG.DAT-CT- follow

   1. (Aunt:) 'It was you who went, right? It was you who followed him?'
   2. (Nephew:) 'Yeah.'
   3. (Aunt:) 'Yeah, then my nephew here followed him.' [W22:0095–0097]

Another common use is that of 'replacing' a constituent in a previous utterance, as when the first speaker in the following exchange ('we felt the smell') is corrected by the second speaker ('*I* felt the smell'). Note how the 'information packaging' is completely different in the two turns. In the first turn, speaker A does not even express the first person experiencer 'we' by an overt noun phrase (since the identity of the smeller is not at issue), and the locative *epe* 'there' is in the pre-verbal position (but probably not focused; see §11.2.2.1 for this common feature in narrative texts). In the second turn, B repeats most of the content from the previous turn, but adds the 1st person pronoun *nok* placed in the pre-verbal position, as it is the crucial piece of information distinguishing her contribution from that of the previous turn.

(490) 1. *yah   nggus-imu   epe   k-a-na-y-   kw-esak*
         but   crab-smell [there]   DIR-3SG.A-1.DAT-1PL- INESS-hit

      2. *nok   k-a-na-   kw-ehek   nggus-imu   epe*
         [1]_Exper DIR-3SG.A-1.DAT- INESS-get.caught crab-smell DIST:III

      1. (A:) 'Then we felt the smell of crabs there.'
      2. (B:) 'It was *I* who felt the smell of crabs.' [W11:0282]

(The literal translations of these expressions are something like 'the smell hit us' and 'the smell got caught at me'; however, I label the pre-verbal constituent *nok* in the 2nd turn experiencer rather than location. The change in verbs — *kwesak* vs. *kwehek* — between the two turns is probably irrelevant to the point about the information packing.)

Another type of replacive focus, expression focus (the term is from Krifka 2008), is used in metalinguistic corrections, which are fairly frequent in the corpus.

(491) In a previous turn, the addressee had used the Malay word *rica* to refer to chilli pepper, instead of the native equivalent *kin-de* (lit. 'eye-tree', presumably because it stings in your eyes.)

   rica   tamohat-   lu   epe,
   [chilli.pepper(m)(III)] PROH:2SG.A- call:III.U DIST:III

   kin-de   ka-mo-   lu
   [eye-tree(III)] DIR-FUT:2SG.A- call:III.U

   'Don't call it *rica*! Call it *kin-de*!' [W11:0804]

In utterances in which the pre-verbal constituent is focused it is usually given some prosodic prominence, especially in cases in which focus is used to correct a previous utterance (and less so in e.g. content questions).

11.2.2 In topic-comment structures

In utterances in which the speaker mentions some topic and says something about this topic (so-called topic-comment sentences; see also §18.3.3), the constituent in the pre-verbal position is usually not focused, but forms a unit (the comment) together with the verb. (The pre-verbal constituent in a topic-comment sentence can be focused if the speaker wants to emphasise this part of the comment for some reason.)

This type of information-packaging strategy is easiest to demonstrate with examples showing nominal predication. In such clauses, the predicative expression (i.e. *teacher* in *He is a teacher* is always in the pre-verbal position, while the referential noun phrase (*He*), if it is expressed, appears in the periphery of the clause, e.g. as a left- or right-dislocated topic, as in (492) and (493) respectively.

(492) Talking about Wariso, a former school principal in Wambi. (Biak is an island off the northern coast of Papua.)

Wariso epe, Biak-anem ø-d-a- ola
W. DIST:I [B.-man] NTRL-DUR-3SG.A- be:3SG.U
'Wariso, he was Biakese/a Biak Islander.' [W21:0069]

(493) *ndom-milah k-a- Ø ehe*
[bad-village(III)] PRS.NTRL-3SG.A- be.NPST PROX:III
'This is a bad village.' [W19:0163]

I consider such structures to be instantiations of the more general topic-comment pattern since in these cases the pre-verbal constituent is not interpreted as focused, but rather it is packaged together with the verb complex into a comment unit which adds information about the topic.

The same structure is also common in standard predicative sentences, and I will give some examples with monotransitive clauses (having an A- and an O-argument) here. In examples (494–495) the A-arguments are topics, and the O-arguments together with the verb complex are packaged as comment units. As in the examples from nominal predication, the topic is found in a more peripheral position, either before (494) or after (495) the comment.

(494) My sister in Wambi had described how she was preparing the equipment for sago washing, and now turns to the activities of her husband:

manday   ehe,   da   k-a-p-   kahyab
brother.in.law(I) PROX:I [sago]₀ DIR-3SG.A-CT- remove.bark

'[As for] your brother-in-law, he cut the sago bark.'   [W20:0121]

(495) In the previous utterance the speaker mentioned a truck belonging to some road workers.

adaka   ma-d-ø-   k-umak-ti   trek
[water]₀ OBJ-DUR-3SG.A- WITH-be.running-DUR truck(m)

'It was bringing water, the truck.'   [W10:0042]

In (496) it is the O-argument (*upe Siska upe*) that is topical, and the A-argument (*age* 'what's-his-name') constitutes the comment together with the verb.

(496) The previous utterance introduced two new participants: "Siska and Yakub came along".

upe   Siska upe,   age   ø-a-   u-sak,   Paskalina eham
DIST:II S.   DIST:II   [PRWD:I]_A   NTRL-3SG.A-   3SG.U-hit   P.   husband:3SG(I)

'[As for] Siska, she had been beaten up by what's-his-name, Paskalina's husband.'   [W19:0266]

There is no reason to believe that the speakers wanted to put focus on the pre-verbal constituents in these examples; these constituents are placed in this slot because they belong together with the verb complex information-wise, as they are both part of the comment.

For clarity it must be stressed that the topic itself is not qualified to enter the pre-verbal position. The role of the topic constituent is never reflected in the Orientation prefix since these prefixes are sensitive only to the constituent in the pre-verbal slot. I interpret the following example as an instance of a left-dislocated topic, followed by a verb without Orientation marking. The topic, *namaya* 'today', is separated from the comment by means of the Proximal demonstrative *ehe* (this use of demonstratives was also seen in (492) and (494)).

(497) The speaker is announcing his plans for the day.

namaya ehe   no-   dahetok-e
now   PROX:III 1.A-   return-IPFV

'[As for] now, I'm going home.'   [W18:0082]

11.2.2.1 On the high frequency of pre-verbal locative adverbials.

It is an extremely common feature of narrative texts to place a locative adverbial in the pre-verbal position. In many cases the locative adverbial can be interpreted as in focus, as in (498), where the pre-verbal constituent *say* 'place' arguably is highlighted as it contrasts to alternative (more expected) locations (e.g. 'at home').

(498) The speaker and his friends found some ducklings in the forest. Some escaped, the rest they ate right away, instead of bringing them home.

    isi   say   k-ak-e-   yahwiy
    other [place]$_{Loc}$ DIR-1.A-1PL- eat
    'The others we ate on the spot.'   [W11:1036]

In general, however, the frequent placement of locative expressions in the pre-verbal position seems to follow a general text-building technique in narratives, in which the storyline progresses through the establishment of a series of topics, which are typically the names of places that the protagonists visit, each followed by a comment specifying what happened in this place. The following excerpt from a hunting story is rather typical in this regard:

(499) 1. yawelib, pale   k-ak-e-p-   nayam-em
       Gh.   [savanna]$_{Path}$ DIR-1.A-1PL-CT- come.PL-VEN

    2. Ulolya kay epe   k-ak-e-p-   hu-n
       U.   road [there]$_{Loc}$ DIR-1.A-1PL-CT- emerge-1.U

    3. yahaa   ago,   Alwetang onggat epe   nd-an-d-ind-e-
       all.the.way.to PRWD:III A.   coconut [there]$_{Loc}$ LOC-1.A-DUR-ALL-1PL-
       kapet
       climb.PLA

    4. Ambay a   age   Meka epe   k-inam-um-   na-sak
       A.   PTCL PRWD:I M. [there]$_{Loc}$ DIR-RCPR-FRUS- RCPR-hit.PLA

    1. 'In Ghawelib, we walked along the savanna,
    2. to Ulolya, there we went out along the road,
    3. to um Alwetang, there we climbed coconut trees,
    4. Ambay and um Meka almost started to fight there.'   [W01:0091–0094]

Since the names of the relevant places have already been mentioned in this example, they are referred to by placing *epe* 'there' in the pre-verbal position in turns 2–4. It is also possible to use pre-verbal *epe* even when the place has not been specified yet. This cataphoric use is common when the more specific locative expression is a heavy, multi-word constituent, since speakers prefer to place such constituents later on in the sentence. This is seen in the following example, where *epe* refers cataphorically to the entire expression 'in Yow...are standing', which is placed after the verb complex.

(500) The speaker is telling me where she had met her husband walking back to the village.

 epe   *k-ak-inam-e-*   *n-idih Yow duh epe, lug*
 [there]_{Loc}   DIR-1.A-RCPR-1PL-   1.U-see Y. beach there tree.sp(IV)

 ip-ø-   *ehaɣ-a*   *ipe,*   *mayay k-o-*   Ø   *oɣ?*
 DIST:IV-3SG.A- stand.PLA-EXT DIST:IV knowing PRS.NTRL-2SG.A- be.NPST 2SG

'We met there in Yow at the beach, where the *lug* (Terminalia Catappa) trees are standing, do you know?'   [W18:0097]

11.3 Some morphosyntactic issues in the description of the Orientation system

11.3.1 Incompatibility of Orientation prefixes with certain clause types

The Orientation prefixes are incompatible with several prefixes occurring close to the left edge of the prefixal complex. Following the templatic system in Chapter 8 we can describe this incompatibility as a matter of competition for slots in the position class system: a prefix such as the Imperative *ah-* may not co-occur with any of the Orientation prefixes since they would fill the same slot, and only one prefix may occur in a slot at any one time (the Orientation prefixes belong to position class –16 and the Imperative is a multi-class prefix covering all classes between –17 and –12, including class –16; cf. Figure 8.1). Since it is difficult to see any particular semantic or functional reason why a category like the Imperative should not be used with the Orientation system I will not attempt to find any 'deeper' explanation for this and the other incompatibilities. It is simply a rule of Coastal Marind morphosyntax.[8]

The prefixes that do not combine with Orientation prefixes are:
– most Prefixes used to form commands: the Imperative *ah-*, the Hortative *mat-* and the Prohibitive series (*tamohat-* etc.) (but not the Jussive *anam-*)

---

[8] Some of the impossible combinations could perhaps be explained diachronically. It is likely that some prefixes are incompatible with the Orientation prefixes because they are originally combinations of Orientation prefixes with other material that later merged into single, unanalysable prefixes. For example, the Perfect *mend-* and the Continuative *anepand-* could be hypothesised to have evolved from **me + nd-* and *anepa + nd-*, with the sequence *nd-* being the Locational Orientation prefix, and the preceding element some unknown material (perhaps adverbials). This would be an interesting topic for comparative reconstruction.

- the Non-Asserted Future, i.e. the Future series used under negation and in apprehensive contexts
- the polar question prefixes *ap-* (Past Polar Question) and *Vk-* (Present Polar Question)
- the Deictic series (*Vp-* etc.)
- the Perfect *mend-* and the Continuative *anepand-*.

Clauses in which the verb contains one of these prefixes lack the ability to express e.g. constituent focus, since such structures require an Orientation prefix on the verb. The constituent in the pre-verbal position of these clauses does not have any particular information-structural prominence.

The absence of Orientation prefixes is often compensated for by the use of postpositional marking in clauses that do not allow Orientation prefixes. For example, expressions that would use the Locational Orientation prefix *nd-* with a pre-verbal adverbial typically employ a periphrastic variant with a phrase headed by the postposition *nde* 'at, in' in contexts where Locational *nd-* is not allowed. The following example shows that a postpositional *nde*-phrase has to be used since the Prohibitive prefix is one of the prefixes that do not combine with Orientation marking:

(501) in-yanid   nde   tamohat-   uma⟨y⟩ah!
       middle-day at   PROH:2SG.A- go⟨2SG.U⟩
       'Don't go at noon!'

A constituent expressing a core argument of the clause, such as an S/A- or O-argument, may always occur before the verb in contexts that do not allow orientation prefixes, without requiring any postpositional flagging. The only difference from a clause with Orientation marking is that the pre-verbal constituent cannot be interpreted as in-focus, and that the lack of Orientation prefixes potentially makes the role of this argument ambiguous. The corpus examples in (502) show imperatives with an S-argument, O-argument and the R-argument of a ditransitive before verbs marked with the Imperative *ah-*, which does not allow Orientation marking.

(502) a. wanangga   ah-   hwehway-em!
          [children]$_S$ IMP- get.ready-PL.IMP
          'You children get ready!'   [W19:0381]

      b. Mili   sep   ah-   yad!
          M.   [leaf.oven]$_O$ IMP- uncover
          'Mili, open the leaf oven!'   [W11:0154]

      c. inhindah   ihe   ah-   ya-koh-em   tamuy!
          [guest   PROX:I/II.PL]$_R$ IMP- 2|3PL.U-feed-PL.IMP food
          'Give food to the guests!'   [W16:0017]

The same generalisation extends to applicative objects, i.e. O-like arguments introduced through applicative uses of e.g. the Comitative-Instrumental *k-* (503a) or Allative *ind-* (503b) may be used freely even when Orientation prefixes are absent.

(503) a. *yal   ah-   ka-nayam!*
         [banana.leaf]₀ IMP-   WITH-come.PL
         'Bring banana leaves!' [W18:0039]

    b. *piring   ah-in-   uma⟨y⟩ah!*
         [plate(m)]₀   IMP-ALL-   go⟨2SG.U⟩
         'Go get a plate!' [W06:0233]

The absence of Orientation prefixes indicating the role of the pre-verbal constituent does not seem to cause any major ambiguities in actual discourse, and I have for example not been able to locate any truly ambiguous Imperative clauses in the textual corpus.

There are several types of expression that require the presence of the Orientation prefixes, which means that they are incompatible with the prefixes listed above. For example, the instrumental use of the 'WITH-prefix' *k-* differs from its comitative use, seen in (503a) above, since the expression of an instrument in this construction always requires the use of the Neutral Orientation. Since Orientation marking is not available with e.g. the Imperative *ah-*, a command formed with the Future must be used instead (504b).

(504) a. **bolpen*   ah-   k-igletok!*
         [ballpoint.pen(m)]₍Instr₎ IMP-   WITH-write
         (intended:) 'Write with a ballpoint pen!'

    b. *bolpen   ø-mo-   k-igletok!*
         [ballpoint.pen(m)]₍Instr₎ NTRL-FUT:2SG.A-   WITH-write
         'Write with a ballpoint pen!'

Alternatively, a completely different construction is employed, such as the periphrastic variant using the postposition *en* 'with', as in (406) above.

Another structure that requires Orientation marking, and therefore is impossible with the prefixes listed above, is pre-verbal goal of motion. In §11.1.4 it was seen that the Directional *k-* is used to signal that an adverbial in the pre-verbal position expresses the goal of a motion event (e.g. 'throw at'). In a command formed with the Imperative prefix *ah-* this option is not allowed, since the presence of the Imperative prefix blocks the use of the Directional Orientation prefix. There is no corresponding postposition that can be used to flag this meaning periphrastically. Instead, the adverbial constituent must be placed in some other position, e.g. after the verb, as in (505a), or the command has to be formed with the Future instead of the Imperative, since the Future allows an Orientation prefix to be present (505b).

(505)   a.   *ah-ap-   ka-han   meja   lahwalah!*
             IMP-CT-   INESS-put [table(m)   on.top]_Goal

        b.   *meja   lahwalah   ka-mo-p-   ka-han!*
             [table(m)   on.top]_Goal   DIR-FUT:2SG.A-CT-   INESS-put

        Both: 'Put it on the table!' (e.g. a book)

Various other adverbial expressions are also incompatible with the Imperative (and other prefixes that fail to combine with Orientation marking), e.g. *mbya hyakod* 'same' (lit. 'all one') (506), in which the speaker expresses the command with a Future prefix instead. Charting the entire range of adverbial expressions that require an appropriate Orientation prefix to be present will be left for a future study, however.

(506)   Instructing people what to do with sago and scraped coconut.

        mbya   hyakod   ka-mo-   i-lwetok
        [all   one]   DIR-FUT:2SG.A-   PLA-turn:III.U

        'Mix them together!'   [W21:0013]

11.3.2 Competition for the pre-verbal position

§11.3.1 discussed some cases in which the Orientation prefixes are in conflict with other prefixes filling the same slots in the position class template of the verb complex. Other clashes, but of a syntactic nature, happen when two expressions that both require the pre-verbal position as their host are to be combined in the same clause. It seems that there are two different outcomes of this situation: either the two expressions simply cannot occur in the same clause (so that two clauses have to be used instead), or the conflict is resolved by putting one of the constituents in the pre-pre-verbal position, followed by the constituent that manages to make it into the pre-verbal position.

By 'expressions that require the pre-verbal position as their host' is meant expressions such as the temporal adverbial *ndom* 'still', which may not be placed elsewhere in the clause, or the negator *mbya*, which always occurs in the pre-verbal slot in its function as a negator. (As a nominal modifier, *mbya* means 'all, completely'; see §7.7.2. There is no alternative construction expressing negation to be used e.g. NP-internally, such as English *no books* or *none of them*).

By contrast, most other expressions that can be placed in the pre-verbal position can also occur elsewhere in the clause, possibly with adpositional marking flagging the role of the constituent. For example, adverbials occurring with the Locational Orientation nd- discussed in §11.1.5 are free to occur elsewhere in the clause, typically with the postposition *nde* 'in, at'. This is illustrated in examples (507–508), which contain adverbial constituents marked by *nde*. The reason for expressing the location with a postpositional phrase in these examples is that the pre-verbal position is occupied by *ndom* 'still' (507) and negative *mbya* (508) which both require being placed in the pre-verbal position.

(507) nok lay nde ndom ø-nan-d-e- na-hwala
1 side at [still] NTRL-1.A-DUR-1PL- 1.U-be
'We were still there on the other side of the river.' [W15:0059]

(508) da epe mahut nde mbya ø-nak-i-e- og, anep say epe
sago(III) DIST:III far at [NEG] NTRL-1.A-RE-1PL- do EMPH:III place(III) DIST:III
'We processed the sago not far from there, in that spot.' [W19:0136]

Other types of expressions that pattern with the negator *mbya* and *ndom* 'still' in requiring accommodation in the pre-verbal position are: adverbial expressions such as the inceptive particles *ye* and *oso* (which always combine with the Objective Orientation prefix *m-*, see §11.1.3.5), constituents expressing an instrument licensed by the use of Instrumental *k-* (see §11.1.2.3), and focused constituents, including the interrogative phrase in a content question (see §11.2).

We are now in position to ask what happens if we attempt to combine two expressions that can only be placed in the pre-verbal position in the same clause. The only available data showing such combinations involve the negator *mbya* in combination with an interrogative phrase. It turns out that speakers prefer to relegate the negator to the pre-pre-verbal position, while letting the focused interrogative phrase retain its usual position immediately before the verb complex. This structure is the only known instance in which *mbya* occurs outside the pre-verbal position and still expresses negation.[9]

(509) a. mbya ti ø-b-a- nayam?
NEG [who:I/II.PL]S NTRL-ACT-3SG.A- come.PL
'Who didn't come?'

---

[9] Note that the question in (509b) features a Malay verb, *dapat* 'get'. Like its English counterpart, this is a monotransitive verb casting the receiving participant as the A-like argument. There are no native verbs that allow this alignment: transfer verbs in Coastal Marind always treat the recipient as an O-like argument (triggering the Object Orientation prefix, and indexing by means of the U-affixes on the stem) or as a goal (triggering Directional Orientation, and indexing by means of the Dative prefix series). The exotic behaviour of this verb has no bearing on the points about the placement of the constituents in the example sentences.

b. *mbya ta   ø-b-a-   dapat?*
   NEG [who]ₐ NTRL-ACT-3SG.A- get(m)
   'Who didn't get any?'   [W11:0648]

Testing the behaviour of other expressions that require the pre-verbal position will be left for future research.

11.4 Givenness marker *tV-*, *t-*

The Givenness (or Given) prefix *tV-* or *t-* is the sole member of the leftmost position class in the templatic model of the prefixal complex (Chapter 8), which means that no other prefixes may precede it. The affixal status is less clear for the Given prefix than for other prefixes, which might be expected from a marker at the very edge of the prefixal complex. The Given prefix exhibits phonological behaviour that differentiates it from other prefixes, and some of this could be interpreted as evidence for word-hood rather than affix-hood (§11.4.1). However, other criteria identify it as an affix, and speakers never add a blank after the Given marker when writing in Coastal Marind. Therefore I treat it as a prefix in the orthography used in this grammar.

Understanding the function of the Given prefix requires a basic grasp of the system of Verb Orientation and the function of the syntactic slot immediately preceding the verb as the site focus of focused constituents, as described in the previous sections of this chapter. The Given prefix is employed whenever the focused constituent, occurring in the pre-verbal slot immediately before the Given prefix, is either (a) a demonstrative used as a 3rd person pronoun or (b) any other noun phrase determined by a demonstrative.

There are two demonstratives that commonly are used as pronouns and as determiners: Proximal *Vhe* and Distal *Vpe* (§4.2). When the Proximal *Vhe* is used as a pronoun ('this one') or as a postposed determiner (e.g. *nggat uhe* 'this dog') and occurs in the pre-verbal slot, it always appears in a reduced shape, with the final syllable *-he* deleted. I treat the remaining gender marking vowel as a clitic *V=*, leaning on the following verb. The Distal always occurs in its full form *Vpe*.

The presence of a focused constituent always triggers the use of one of the so-called Orientation prefixes (§11.1) on the verb, e.g. the Neutral *k-* (in contexts with present time reference) or *ø-* (in the non-present) corresponding to a pre-verbal constituent in an S/A role, or the Object *m-* corresponding to a constituent functioning as the transitive O. This means that the Givenness *t-* always occurs with an Orientation prefix present in the same verb form. We can devise the following mini-template for the structure in which the Given-prefix occurs:

| ... | DEM | *t-* | (*V-*) | ORIENTATION- | (other prefixes)- | VERB STEM |

Pre-verbal slot   Verb complex

The following corpus data will be used to illustrate the use of the Given prefix and its interaction with the material in the pre-verbal slot. These utterances are taken from a recording of the Family Problems picture task. The two speakers are watching and discussing a series of pictures. Here, the picture shows a policeman and a prisoner. One of the speakers points to the policeman and utters (510.1), 'This is the one who caught him'. The pronominal reference to the policeman is made by means of the Proximal clitic *e=* 'this one'. In line 3 (an intervening remark has been omitted in line 2) he shifts the attention to the prisoner and explains, using the same structure, 'This is the one that he caught' (or 'This one got caught'). Speakers often choose to use focus structures in contexts in which different participants are contrasted with each other. Since the in-focus expressions in this case are demonstrative forms, the Given prefix *tV-* must be used.

(510) 1. e=   te-ø-a-   yak⟨e⟩h   ehe
         PROX:I=   GIV:I-NTRL-3SG.A-   catch⟨3SG.U⟩   PROX:I
         'This is the one who caught him.'

   2. […]

   3. e=   ta-m-ø-   yak⟨e⟩h
         PROX:I=   GIV-OBJ-3SG.A-   catch⟨3SG.U⟩
         'This is the one that he caught.'   [D09:0028-0030]

As indicated by the notation '*tV-*', and as seen in (510.1), the segment *t-* may be followed by a vowel marking gender agreement. The vowels follow the same pattern as the initial vowels of the demonstratives: *e-* (Gender I and Gender III), *u-* (Gender II), and *i* (Gender IV, and the plural of Genders I/II). I do not consider this agreement marking vowel to be a prefix in its own right (i.e. belonging to a separate position class), since it can only occur if the segment *t-* is present. Using terminology from Harris (2016), the *t-V-* sequence can be described as a morphologically complex affix, with *t-* being a carrier affix hosting a dependent affix *V-*.

The distribution of the agreeing *tV-* versus non-agreeing *t-* is described in §11.4.2.

11.4.1 Form of the Given prefix

Some of the phonological behaviour of the Given prefix suggests that it forms a separate phonological word, distinct from the rest of the Prefixal Complex.

Firstly, consider the allomorphy of the 3sg Actor prefix, which always is realised as ø- if the other prefixes with which it occurs in the prefixal complex are sufficient to build a syllable. Otherwise it is realised as *a-*, for example if it is the only prefix present in the prefixal complex. The Given prefix and a following gender-marking vowel has the shape CV-, e.g. *te-* in (510.1) above. However, it is as if the Given prefix were invisible to the phonology, because the 3sg Actor prefix is always realised as *a-* when combined only with this prefix (the Neutral Orentation is always ø- in past time contexts, and does not affect the realisation of either prefix).

Secondly, recall from §2.4 that there are constraints on how open and closed syllables may be arranged within the phonological word in Coastal Marind. A closed penultimate syllable is avoided, so a word of the shape *CVC.CV is turned into an acceptable syllable sequence by means of epenthetic *a*-insertion: CV.C*a*.CV. However, the syllable formed by the given prefix escapes this constraint. In (511), the prefixal complex (preceded by the reduced demontrative clitic) forms a phonological word of the shape V.CVC.CV (*e.tam.da*), which goes against the prohibition of closed penultimate syllables.

(511) e=   ta-m-d-a-   w-alaw-a
       PROX:III= GIV-OBJ-DUR-3SG.A-   3SG.U-search-EXT
       'That's what he was looking for.'

This behaviour of the Given prefix suggests that it is phonologically detached from the rest of the prefixal complex. On the other hand, the fact that the exponent *m-* of the Object Orientation prefix syllabifies with the Given *ta-* suggests that they are part of the same phonological word, because consonants do not syllabify across word boundaries in Coastal Marind. The Object prefix *m-* is clearly a member of the prefixal complex, so the Given prefix must also be part of the prefixal complex, because otherwise they would not syllabify together. Note also that the Given prefix may not carry prosodic stress, which it would be expected to do if it were an independent word. The final result is ambiguous, with the Given prefix behaving partly as an independent word and partly as one of the affixes in the prefixal complex.

11.4.2 Gender agreement with the Given prefix

The presence of gender agreement depends on the choice of Orientation prefix, which in turn depends on the role of the focused constituent appearing in the pre-verbal slot (as described in §11.1.1). Gender agreement is obligatory with the Neutral Orientation *k-/ø-*, the Locational *nd-* and the Restrictive *s-* ('only'). It is usually absent with the Object Orientation *m-* (see below). There is no data on combinations of the Given prefix with the Directional Orientation *k-*.

The gender value shown by the agreeing segment in *tV-* is always the same as that of the preceding demonstrative. The exponence patterns are identical for the two targets so the resulting sequences are (with the Distal *epe*) *epe te-*, *upe tu-* and *ipe ti-*. The alliterative character of these sequences is even more prominent in allegro speech, where these common sequences usually are reduced to [epete], [uputu] and [ipiti] respectively (this is not reflected in the orthography).

The following examples show gender agreement with the Neutral Orientation.

(512) a. *epe te-k-a- deh-e*
DIST:I GIV:I-PRS.NTRL-3SG.A- shoot:3SG.U-IPFV
'He is the one who is going to shoot it.' [W02:0199]

b. *upe tu-k-a- deh-e*
DIST:II GIV:II-PRS.NTRL-3SG.A- shoot:3SG.U-IPFV
'She is the one who is going to shoot it.' [Elicited based on (a)]

c. *ipe ti-k-an- y-as-e*
DIST:I/II.PL GIV:I/II.PL-PRS.NTRL-3PL.A- 2|3PL.U-shoot.PLA-IPFV
'They are the ones who are going to shoot them.' [Elicited based on (a)]

Gender agreement is usually absent with the Object *m-*, as in (513). The insertion of epenthetic /a/ after *t-* prevents formation of a cluster *tm-*. Occasionally some speakers add gender agreement between *t-* and Object *m-*, as in (514). (All locations are assigned to Gender III.) This appears to be a completely optional variant; other attested examples of the verb 'go' in the same context lack agreement, without any noticeable difference in meaning.

(513) *epe mayan epe ta-m-an-d-ap- lay*
DIST:III speech(III) DIST:III GIV-OBJ-1.A-DUR-CT- talk
'That's the story that I told.' [W15:0187]

(514) *nok nama epe te-ma-no- uma⟨n⟩ah-e*
1 now there GIV:III-OBJ-1.A- go⟨1.U⟩-IPFV
'Now I'm going to go over there.' [W19:0018]

11.4.3 Function of the Given prefix

It was stated above that the main factor triggering the use of the Given prefix is the presence of a focused constituent that either consists of a demonstrative or is determined by a demonstrative. The function of demonstratives used as determiners can be regarded as an instruction to the hearer to retrieve the referent from the discourse context (§7.2). The hearer can be expected to have some familiarity with the referent, or at least access to it, e.g. because it has been mentioned before or because it is present in the physical surroundings.

The pragmatic notion of focus, on the other hand, has something of the opposite function: it singles out a piece of information because it is judged to be relatively unpredictable, and therefore informative. This is reflected in Van Valin and LaPolla's (1997: 205) account of focus structure, in which they rank different types of expressions according to their "markedness" as focal elements. Indefinite NPs are less marked than definite NPs, which are less marked than pronouns. (The most marked case would be a zero focus, which does not occur; cf. zero topics, which are common in grammatical analyses).

Van Valin and LaPolla's markedness of focal expressions corresponds directly to marking with the Given prefix in Coastal Marind: pronominally used demonstratives (corresponding to Van Valin and LaPolla's pronouns) always trigger Given marking when they are in focus, as do noun phrases with demonstrative determiners (corresponding roughly with Van Valin and LaPolla's definite NPs). It seems likely that the *tV*- prefix is a reflex of the Proto-Anim demonstrative root **tV* (reconstructed by Usher and Suter 2015: 118). This Proto-Anim demonstrative was replaced by *epe* in Coastal Marind, but apparently a remnant of it survives as part of the focus construction.

Below I give some further corpus examples to illustrate the use of *tV*-.

The next example exhibits a standard topic-comment articulation (§18.3.3), with the topical expression 'that house of ours' prosodically detached from the rest of the utterance (the comment). Within the comment, 'Father' is given focal prominence, since it is the fact that Father is the house-builder that is the crucial piece of information that the speaker wants to convey. The word *ad* 'father' is determined by the Distal demonstrative *epe*, presumably because the referent, who was not present at the time, had been discussed before the recording started. Since the focal expression is determined by a demonstrative, the verb is marked with Given *tV*-.

(515) epe   nok keti en aha,   ad   epe   te-ø-d-a-   ambad
      DIST:III 1 APL POSS house(III) father(I) DIST:I GIV:I-NTRL-DUR-3SG.A- build
      'That house of ours, it was Father who built it.'   [W18:0100]

A common strategy is to introduce a participant as a left-dislocated topic, which then is recast as a focused constituent in the comment: *As for X, it was S/HE who Verb-ed*. The following example is from a telling of some recent events. A truck had approached the speaker, and the driver turned out to be a man that she had encountered previously:

(516) wis   lek   epe,   epe   te-ø-ø-i-   man-em
      yesterday from:I   DIST:I DIST:I GIV:I-NTRL-3SG.A-RE-   come-VEN
      'The [man] from the day before, it was he who came again.'   [W19:0282]

Example (517) has a similar structure. A new referent (some wooden planks or poles) is mentioned in line 1. In line 2 *de* 'wood' is brought into focus, which triggers the use of *tV*- on the verb since it is determined by demonstratives.

(517) 1. *rusa   de   k-ø-um-   kapet,*
         deer(m) wood DIR-3SG.A-FRUS- climb.PLA

   a-d-ø-   ehwes-a-ti   de   beko   epe
   [DEP-DUR-3SG.A- put-EXT-DUR   wood   bulldozer(m)(III)]   DIST:III

   'The deer tried to climb the wood that was lying there by the bulldozer.'

2. *epe   de   epe   te-ø-na-   k-u-sak*
   DIST:III wood(III) DIST:III GIV:III-NTRL-3PL.A- WITH-3SG.U-hit.PLA

   Sanggahe-patul a,   epe   k-a-   kahwid
   S.-boy   PTCL   there DIR-3SG.A- die:3SG.U

   'With that wood they hit [the deer], the boys from Sanggase, and there it died.' [W10:0138-0139]

It is also very common for the focused expression to refer to something given in the surroundings, as in (518). The speaker shows her hand, describing how to receive the consecrated bread during the Eucharist. The focused expression is determined by the Proximal *ehe*, so the postposed demonstrative immediately before the verb is reduced to the gender-marking vowel only.

(518) *ehe   sangga   e=   te-ø-mo-   ka-han*
      PROX:III   hand(III) PROX:III= GIV:III-NTRL-FUT:2SG.A- WITH-take:III.U

   'You should take it with this hand.' [W16:0050]

12 Valence classes

This chapter describes the basic valence classes in Coastal Marind, as defined by the use of participant indexing (Chapter 9) and Orientation prefixes (Chapter 11). The valence classes are 'basic' in the sense that they do not include verbs that are formed by derivational morphology, e.g. the Comitative *k-* prefix. (The valence patterns of derived verbs are described in Chapter 13).

Some of the classes defined by comparing the behaviour of participant indexing and the Orientation system are quite marginal, and only contain one or a few members. For example, only one verb, *kayanad* 'become low tide' has been assigned to valence Class 0b ('Avalent verbs with frozen Dative index'). Other patterns are much more frequent and can probably be considered productive, e.g. those of standard monotransitive verbs. A class such as 2b (monotransitive verbs with invariant stems) readily accommodates Malay loan verbs and is perhaps better described as an open frame than as a class with a finite set of members. For simplicity, however, I label all of the patterns described here as 'classes'.

The classes are exemplified with verbs that commonly (or always) occur with the specific Orientation marking and indexing pattern prescribed by their class. This is a rather drastic simplification, because it would be more accurate to describe for each verb in the language whether or not it has the potential to follow the different valence patterns, and if so, with what consequences for meaning. This enormous task will be left for future research, and an idealised version where most verbs are members of only one class is presented here.

The classes to be described below are listed in Table 12.1. Sample verbs have been added to the table to illustrate the different classes, along with verb-specific role labels (e.g. 'Fallee' for the sole argument of 'fall').[1] Each role label is linked to the corresponding index set and to the Orientation prefix that the participant triggers when it is expressed in the pre-verbal position. For example, the Cryer participant of *ihw* 'be crying' triggers the Neutral Orientation prefix when expressed pre-verbally, and is indexed by means of the Actor prefix set.

Some verbs have an obligatory index (typically the default 3sg Actor prefix) but lack a corresponding participant, as when the verb is avalent (type 0 in the table). In such cases dashes are added to columns marking roles and Orientation prefixes. When a participant is not indexed on the verb, a dash is added to the Index set column.

---

[1] I refer to such fine-grained roles (rather than classic Fillmorean case roles; Fillmore 1968) to emphasise that the overall mapping from participant roles to index sets is often idiosyncratic (for example, the patient of *dahuk* 'die' is indexed by means of the Dative prefix set, whereas the patient of the synonymous verb *kahwid* 'die' is indexed by means of Undergoer alternations).

Tab. 12.1: Valence patterns

Type	Example verb	Gloss	Participant role(s)	Orientation	Index set
			AVALENT VERBS		
0a	*ihwim*	'become dark/night'	–	–	A[3SG]
0b	*kayanad*	'become low tide'	– –	– –	A[3SG] Dat[3SG]
			MONOVALENT VERBS		
1a	*ihw*	'be crying'	Cryer	Ntrl	A
1b	*hi*	'fall'	– Fallee	– Ntrl	A[3SG] U
1c	*hawa*	'emerge'	Emerger	Ntrl	A, U
1d	*kamob*	'become betel-drunk'	– Betel-Drunkee	– Ntrl	A[3SG] Dat
			DIVALENT VERBS		
2a	*wamuk*	'hit'	Hitter Victim	Ntrl Obj	A U
2b	*keway*	'break'	Breaker Broken object	Ntrl Obj	A –
2c	*kamin*	'make'	Maker Product	Ntrl Obj	A, U –
2d	*yina*	'help'	Helper Helpee	Ntrl Obj	A Dat
2e	*gan*	'listen'	Hearer Emitter of sound	Ntrl Obj (?)	A Gen
2f	*emel*_N *wahun*_V	'get hungry'	*emel* 'hunger' Sufferer	Ntrl Ntrl	A[3SG] U
			TRIVALENT VERBS		
3a	*koh*	'feed'	Feeder Feedee Food	Ntrl Dir Obj	A U –
3b	*oleb*	'sell'	Seller Buyer Goods	Ntrl Dir Obj	A Dat U
3c	*kabed*	'ask'	Asker Addressee Question	Ntrl Dir Obj	A Dat –
3d	*wig*	'ask/beg for'	Begger Addressee Goods	Ntrl Obj Obj	A, U Gen –

12.1 Avalent verbs

Avalent verbs do not take any arguments, so inflected forms of avalent verbs carry the 3sg Actor prefix by default. Two subclasses are distinguished.

12.1.1 Plain avalent verbs (Type 0a)

A small number of verbs belong to this class. Most of them refer to stages of the day (*alen* 'almost be day/sunrise', *pig* 'become day/bright', *ihwim* 'become night/dark') or natural phenomena (*alalam* 'lightning to flash'). Note the default 3sg Actor marking:

(519) menda-b-ø-   ihwim
       PERF-ACT-3SG.A-   become.dark
       'It's already dark.'   [W15:0100]

Most other expressions depicting natural phenomena belong to the class of monovalent verbs (Type 1a; §12.2.1) and appear with a fixed noun (e.g. *kiwal* 'wind') in combination with the verb (as in *kiwal ahwadak* 'wind to blow').

12.1.2 Avalent verbs with frozen Dative index (Type 0b)

This pattern, with the invariant 3sg Dative prefix *o-* in addition to the 3sg Actor prefix, is marginal, and is only frequent with the verb *kayanad* 'become low tide' (520). It also occurs with the verb *win* 'become' in an expression meaning 'become high tide', but then usually (but not always) combined with the noun *etob* 'sea, tide'.

(520) mahut k-ø-o-   kayanad-e
       far   DIR-3SG.A-3SG.DAT- low.tide-IPFV
       'The water goes down far at low tide.'

12.2 Monovalent verbs

Monovalent verbs take a single argument, and can be further subdivided into four subtypes according to by what means (e.g. by what prefix series) their sole argument is indexed in the verb complex. All monovalent verbs (regardless of the indexing type) behave the same way with regards to the Orientation system, since the constituent expressing the sole participant, when placed in the pre-verbal position, triggers the use of the Neutral Orientation prefixes (§11.1.2) in the verb complex.

12.2.1 Plain intransitive verbs (Type 1a)

Such verbs index their sole participant by means of the Actor prefix series. They have to be distiguished from the patientive intransitives (Type 1b, §12.2.2), which index the sole participant by Undergoer affixes in the verb stem. Most non-patientive intransitives involve an agent that instigates the action. Verbs that are typical in this regard are *mahay* 'dance', *ambid* 'sit down', *nahek* 'stay awake throughout the night', *yet* 'go, be in movement', and so on. In the following example, the 1st person Actor *no-* is prefixed to the verb, and the S-argument *nok* triggers the Neutral Orientation (expressed by zero ø- in past time contexts). Indexing by the Actor set and the use of the Neutral Orientation are the two defining characteristics of this class.

(521) Describing a hunting party.

 mayay ya nok ø-no-d- yet-ti
 first real 1 NTRL-1.A-DUR- be.moving-DUR
 'First of all, I went.' [W11:1028]

I also include intransitive verbs that only combine with some fixed (inanimate) S-argument, e.g. (*kiwal*) *ahwadak* '(wind) to blow'. All non-patientive intransitives are classified as 'plain intransitives'; the patientives are discussed in the next subsection.

A few common intransitive verbs are noteworthy because their translation equivalents in other languages would often allow transitive uses as well, whereas the Coastal Marind counterparts are strictly intransitive. These verbs are *alalay* '(become) dry', *huhu* 'boil' and *aluy* 'flame up, (lamp) turn on' (a fourth verb, *taheb* 'fill', belongs to the patientive class and is discussed in §12.2.2).

The strictly intransitive nature of these verbs is visible in command formation, since none of them allow a (transitive) command to be formed with the Imperative *ah-*. Instead the Jussive *anam-* must be used, so that the literal translation of the example in (522b) could be 'Make the water boil!'.

(522) a. **ah- huhu adaka!*
 IMP- boil water

 b. *anam-ø- huhu adaka!*
 JUS-3SG.A- boil water
 'Boil the water!'

The verb *huhu* 'boil' is identical to the Pluractional form of *hawa* 'emerge, come out', i.e. *huhu* 'come out repeatedly', so the meaning shift 'water come out repeatedly' > 'water boil' explains why this verb remains intransitive. (I am not aware of etymologies for the other verbs.)

Tab. 12.2: Some patientive intransitive verbs

kahwid	'die'	yunip	'catch fire'
ahwaleh	'still be hungry'	kweseb	'one's waist to get thin'
yuyeh	'become startled'	lahwaseb	'get stuck in mud'
hi	'fall'	sasip	'get burned'
tameb	'float to surface'	usu	'be heated'
yadin	'drown'	yeb	'slip'
ipih	'become constipated'	kotib	'get lost'
wayasud	'grow big'	ayip	'almost burn out'
alalay	'become dry'	ikubaya	'disappear'
kahob	'capsize'	taheb	'fill a space'
win	'become'		

12.2.2 Patientive intransitives (Type 1b)

The verbs in this class index their sole argument by means of Undergoer marking in the verb stem. The inflected verb form always carries an invariant 3sg Actor prefix.

Patientive verbs express events that the sole participant is affected by without being instigator or in control of the event. A typical patientive verb is *hi* 'fall', as in (523). Some other members of the class are listed in Table 12.2.

(523) *epe   k-a-   hi-n   nok*
       there DIR-3SG.A- fall-1.U 1
       'There I fell.'   [W03:0145]

The correlation between subclasses 1a–b of intransitive verbs and agentivity is not absolute, so a few verbs that express situations that could be seen as involving no or little control on the part of the S-argument are nevertheless members of the plain intransitive class (§12.2.1). This is true for *ihw* 'cry', *ihwin* 'burst into tears', *oyad* 'yawn', *yod* 'vomit', which treat their sole participant as an agent, and index it by means of the Actor prefix series.[2]

Since patientive verbs always exhibit Actor indexing, it could be argued that these verbs are standard transitive verbs meaning 'it fell me' (and not 'I fell') etc., with the patient as the O-argument and some (unspecified) force as the agent. I will now 'test' these two analyses (patientive intransitive versus standard transitive) by comparing two structures that are sensitive to the number of participants expressed in a clause, and it will be shown that the two tests give contradictory results: according to the use of Orientation prefixes, patientive intransitives behave like intransitive verbs, and according to the Prohibitive they behave like standard transitive verbs.

---

[2] It has often been noted that languages with semantic alignment show inconsistencies in their classifications of verbs; see e.g. Mithun 1991.

Recall from Chapter 11 that when an S- or A-argument is placed in the pre-verbal position, the verb must be prefixed with a Neutral Orientation prefix (ø- in non-present, k- in present time contexts). When the O-argument is placed in the pre-verbal position, the Object Orientation prefix m- is used instead. If the patientive intransitives are in fact transitive verbs we would expect the Object m- to be triggered by the patient-like argument. The following (elicited) examples show that this is not the case, for the verb hi 'fall' appears with the Neutral prefix, just like any other intransitive verb (524a–b). The Object prefix m- is completely ungrammatical (524c).

(524) a. ta   ø-b-a-   hi?
 who NTRL-ACT-3SG.A- fall:3SG.U
 'Who fell?'

 b. nok ø-a-   hi-n
 1   NTRL-3SG.A- fall-1.U
 'I fell.'

 c. *nok m-a-   hi-n
 1   OBJ-3SG.A- fall-1.U
 '(lit.) It fell me.'

Consider now the use of the Prohibitive prefix series. The Prohibitive distinguishes between 'Addressee-oriented' negative commands in which the Addressee is also the agent of the event (as in 'Don't you (sg) Verb!' expressed by the prefix *tamohat*-), and 'causative' or 'mediated' negative commands in which the Addressee is told to make the agent stop V-ing (as in 'Don't let him/her Verb!', expressed by the prefix *tapahat*-; see §19.1.4). Thus, the utterance in (525a) involves only one participant (other than the speaker), while the utterance in (525b) involves two: the Addressee and the agent of the verb *esol*.

(525) a. tamohat- esol!
 PROH:2SG.A- make.noise
 'Don't make noise!'

 b. tapahat-ø- esol!
 PROH-3SG.A- make.noise
 'Don't let him/her make noise!'

Compare the distribution of the Prohibitive prefixes with a patientive verb such as 'fall', presented in (526). Since the sole participant of patientive verbs is not indexed in the Actor prefixes, the Addressee-oriented *tamohat*-form may not be used. Instead the causative/mediated Prohibitive is employed, as in (526b). Thus, the formation of the Prohibitive treats patientive verbs as if they expressed two-participant events, as suggested by the literal translation to (526b).

(526) a. *tamohat- hi-y!
       PROH:2SG.A- fall-2SG.U
       (Intended: 'Don't fall!')

   b. tapahat-ø- hi-y!
       PROH-3SG.A- fall-2SG.U
       'Don't fall!' (lit. 'Don't let it fall you!')

We can conclude that the first diagnostic, that provided by the Orientation system, suggests that *hi* 'fall' is intransitive with the patient as the S-argument, whereas the second diagnostic, Prohibitive formation, treats it as a transitive verb with the patient as the O-argument, which reflects the fact that patientive verbs are always inflected by means of the 3sg Actor prefix.

The ambivalence between transitive and intransitive status of such 'transimpersonal' verbs (Malchukov 2008; the term is originally from Haas 1941) has been noted by several researchers (e.g. Keenan 1976) and can be thought of as a stage in the development of the patient-like argument from an object to a more subject-like argument. In this process, it is typically the syntactic subject properties (in Coastal Marind, this would correspond to the ability of S/A-arguments to trigger the Neutral Orientation prefix) that are aquired before the morphological alignment is reanalysed (as shown in Coastal Marind by the presence of 3sg Actor marking, and especially, by Prohibitive formation); see discussion in Malchukov (2008: 90). In the description of *hi* 'fall' and similar verbs, I let the facts of the Orientation system take precedence over the indexing, and treat them as a subtype of intransitive verbs.

12.2.2.1 The verb 'fill'.

One noteworthy patientive verb is *taheb* 'fill', because it shows that the valence properties of a verb can be quite different from those of its nearest English gloss. This verb has as its sole argument the entity that fills up some space (the 'filling entity'). Unlike English, the space that is being filled may not function as the O-argument of the clause, so *taheb* always indexes the filling entity by means of Undergoer marking inside the verb stem.

Thus, the first clause in (527) is intransitive, with *taheb* having a 1pl S-argument indexed in the verb. The NP *epe yahun epe* 'that truck (lit. canoe)' is best thought of as an adjunct.

(527) Referring to people standing on the back of a truck.

mbya ø-ø-e-p- taha⟨n⟩ab epe yahun epe,
NEG NTRL-3SG.A-1PL-CT- fill⟨1.U⟩ DIST:III canoe(III) DIST:III

ndom ø-d-a-p- tak
still NTRL-DUR-3SG.A-CT- be.empty

'We didn't fill the truck, there was still space.' [W15:0157]

Since English *fill* is transitive but Coastal Marind *taheb* a patientive intransitive, 'fill' is not really appropriate as a gloss. The Coastal Marind valence frame is better captured by e.g. 'become completely extended throughout a space', but I will stick to the gloss 'fill' for simplicity.

12.2.3 Middle intransitives (Type 1c)

Verbs index their S-argument according to the middle pattern if the person/number features are indexed in the Actor prefix and in the stem simultaneously. Approximately 40 verbs are lexically specified as middle-marking, almost all of which are primarily intransitive. For example, the middle verb *uhwasig* 'go up from water' used with a 1sg S-argument requires that the 1st person Actor prefix is used along with 1st person Undergoer marking on the verb stem, as in the following example (*uhwasig* is a prefixing verb, with the 1st person stem *nahwasig*).

(528) nok epe nda-no- na-hwasig
1 there LOC-1.A- 1.U-go.up.from.water

'I went up from there.' [W02:0065]

It follows from this definition that only verbs that exhibit stem alternations according to person/number of an argument (see Chapter 10) can be classified as middle-marking. As such, no invariant verbs belong to the group of verbs that index their S-argument according to the middle template, since a verb must exhibit co-referential indexing in both the Actor prefix and in the verb stem to count as middle indexing. Invariant verbs that index their sole argument by Actor prefixes are classified as plain intransitives, Type 1a (§12.2.1).

Drabbe (1955: 69) uses the label 'reflexive' for the middle indexing template. However, I opt for the label 'middle', because I believe that it is better to reserve the label 'reflexive' for constructions that express truly reflexive situations (such as 'vote for oneself', i.e. performing an action on oneself that is usually performed on others). There is no doubt that the middle indexing pattern originated as a reflexive construction in Coastal Marind, but it can no longer be used productively to express actions performed on oneself (for reflexives, see §13.3). For more information about the morphological aspects of the middle template, see §10.1.2.

Tab. 12.3: Some intransitive middle verbs

ihon	'run away'	idagin	'lean, cling'
italeb	'roll around'	meneh	'grunt'
kwamin	'enter'	munggeh	'hum, buzz'
lolaw	'creep, crawl'	olin	'hang/hold on to'
um	'go habitually'	sameb	'turn (in spot)'
umuh	'go, take off'	yakeh	'lie down on back'
lokeh	'peek'	tapeb	'fly up'
kasib	'lie down on stomach'	wabayed	'turn head back'
hawa	'emerge'	tahob	'lean against, cling to'
oleh	'reach up'	ayin	'run around'
yoseh	'jump along'	oha	'go down to beach'
taletok	'fall with head first'	uhwasig	'go up from water'
mikeh	'turn one's head'		

Intransitive verbs that index their S-argument according to the middle template are listed in Table 12.3. Most of these belong semantically to one of three types of events: translational motion (i.e. motion along a path), non-translational motion (moving e.g. a body part, while remaining in place) and posture verbs. (Since these are partly overlapping, I will not attempt a verb-for-verb classification). Typologically, these three categories are among the typical semantic domains that are expressed by middle forms across languages (Geniušienė 1987, Kemmer 1993).

Several languages of the Southern New Guinea region have been described as having special 'middle' indexing templates, for example the Yam languages Nen (Evans 2015b) and Komnzo (Döhler 2016), and the isolate Maori (Arka 2015). The existence of middle verbs in Coastal Marind is perhaps a consequence of some sort of areal preference in the lexicalisation of intransitive verbs. However, the 'middles' in the Yam languages are very different from the Coastal Marind indexing template: the Yam middles cover a much larger part of the lexicon (for example, the majority of intransitive verbs in Komnzo are middles; Döhler 2016: 230) and they are formed with dedicated middle affixes, and not through simultaneous use of (co-referential) Actor and Undergoer affixes as in Coastal Marind. In the latter respect Maori is more similar to Coastal Marind, by which it has been heavily influenced, since one of the Maori middle constructions described by Arka is signalled by means of co-referential subject and object affixes.

12.2.4 Dative Experiencer intransitives (Type 1d)

Such verbs have a single participant, indexed by means of the Dative prefix set. The Actor prefix is invariant 3SG. For most verbs the role of the sole participant is best described as an experiencer. Examples are: *kamob* 'become intoxicated from betel nut', *isik* 'become full (eating)', *yek* 'become used to, learn'. The common Dative Experiencer verb *dahuk* 'die' (used about animals) has a patient-like participant rather than an experiencer (other near-synonymous verbs, such as *kahwid* 'die', fall into the patientive intransitive class and index the S-argument through Undergoer alternations in the verb stem; §12.2.2). For another verb of this class, *luhay* 'S$_{Dat}$ remain in a different place' it is less clear how to classify the role of the S-participant indexed by the Dative.

Evidence that the affected participant of these verbs functions as an S-argument (rather than an O-argument, with the A omitted or unspecified) comes from elicited data. In (529) *nok* 'I, we' precedes a Neutral-marked verb, showing that the Neutral Orientation is used when the S-argument of a Dative Experiencer verb is placed in the pre-verbal position.

(529)   nok   ø-ø-na-y-p-   kamob
        1   NTRL-3SG.A-1.DAT-1PL-CT-   betel.drunk
        'We became intoxicated from betel nut.'

This is a small valence class, with only the five verbs cited above having been identified as members so far.

12.3 Divalent verbs

12.3.1 Transitive verbs with alternating (Type 2a) and invariant (Type 2b) stems.

Standard transitive verbs (with an agent-like and a patient-like participant) always occur with the Object Orientation prefix *m-* if the patient-like argument is in the pre-verbal position (see examples in §11.1.3.1).

The Coastal Marind verbal lexicon is split between verbs that exhibit stem alternations indexing person/number and/or gender of the patient-like participant (the Undergoer) and verbs that have invariant stems. This lexical division was described in §10.2. I define the valence classes based on participant indexing (in addition to the use of the Orientation prefixes), so transitive verbs that are alternating belong in one class (Type 2a), while verbs that are invariant, and fail to index their O-argument, belong to another (Type 2b).

The difficulties of predicting whether a given verb lexeme is alternating or invariant were discussed in §10.2.1. Almost all transitive verbs that can take an animate O-argument index this participant by means of stem alternations, and belong to class 2a. An example is *wamuk* 'hit'. One of the exceptions is *asa* '(dog) bark at (animal)' which does not index the O-argument and therefore belongs to valence class 2b. Verbs that occur with inanimate O-arguments are split between classes 2a and 2b: *kasab* 'rip, tear' is an alternating 2a-verb and alternates according to gender (with the stem *kasahib* used for inanimates in Gender IV, e.g. a rupiah banknote), while *keway* 'break'

Tab. 12.4: Two types of standard transitive verbs

Type 2a: Alternating		Type 2b: Invariant	
ayob	'cover'	ayaman	'split (sago) lengthwise'
ahus	'pull out'	aletok	'wrap (sago) in leaves'
ahwamun	'soak'	ambad	'erect (building)'
awad	'scoop up'	asa	'dog to bark at animal'
awin	'unload'	asoh	'chew wati'
betok	'pile up'	eyawn	'put down carried items'
eyak	'release'	ehwes	'pile wood'
yahwek	'pound'	yahwiy	'eat'
yasug	'scrape'	yanggaman	'break with foot'
haniy	'bite'	yaway	'cut up meat'
hwilug	'rub, rasp, grate'	yol	'beat sago'
hyahyak	'split'	hanituk	'lean'
ihwaniy	'lick'	hyahyag	'cut up meat'
isug	'cut'	kalemed	'put on garment'
kalab	'peel, dehusk'	keway	'break'
kasab	'tear'	kusatok	'swallow'
kepad	'break (rope)'	lahos	'smoke tobacco'
kupuk	'scatter'	omos	'spread out (mat etc.)'
mamud	'grind, crush'	takoy	'fell tree'
walawak	'sharpen (arrow)'	taman	'fire arrow'
keswan	'wash'	yaman	'sharpen (knife etc.)'
sanggid	'shake'	was	'sew'

is an invariant 2b-verb. There is no semantic explanation for this, so for many transitive verbs the learner must simply memorise whether it belongs to Type 2a or 2b. Some examples of verbs in the two classes are in Table 12.4.

12.3.2 Middle transitive (Type 2c)

There is only one clear example of a standard transitive verb (involving an agent acting on a patient) with participant indexing following the middle pattern (cf. intransitive middles in §12.2.3 above, and §10.1.2). This is the verb *kamin* 'make'. As seen in (530) this verb indexes its A-participant by both the Actor prefix and the Undergoer stem infix. Co-referential Actor and Undergoer indexing is the defining feature of middle verbs.

(530) *gambar   ma-no-d-   kama⟨n⟩it-a*
picture(m) OBJ-1.A-DUR- make⟨1.U⟩-EXT
'I took (lit. made) pictures'

Drabbe reports that this verb can index the O-participant if it refers to an animate, like the verbs in class 2a. I have not observed this usage, so I cite the only example given by Drabbe:

(531) Eastern dialect; adapted from Drabbe (1955: 69)
Allah ø-a- kama⟨n⟩in
God(m) NTRL-3SG.A- make⟨1.U⟩
'God made me.'

A candidate for inclusion in the middle transitive class is *walaw*, which can be used as a transitive verb with the meaning 'search for' (532). This verb is also used intransitively with the meaning 'open one's eyes'. This latter meaning likely reflects the original, intransitive, use of *walaw*, because many intransitive verbs denoting body actions (e.g. moving a body part) exhibit the middle indexing pattern (see §12.2.3). Presumably, the intransitive verb 'open one's eyes' was extended to a transitive use 'search for', and retained the original middle indexing pattern even as it acquired its transitive use.

(532) From a hunting story.
otih ap awe m-an-d-e- n-alaw
many too game OBJ-1.A-DUR-1PL- 1.U-search
'All of us were searching for animals.' [W23:0062]

12.3.3 Dative O transitives (Type 2d)

Such verbs have an agent and a patient-like participant, with the latter indexed by means of the Dative prefix set. Like the O-arguments of other transitive verbs, the constituent expressing the patient triggers the use of Object Orientation *m-* if it is placed in the pre-verbal position. Example with the verb *takin* 'wait':

(533) nok m-e-na-p- takit-a
1 OBJ-3PL>1-1.DAT-CT- wait-EXT
'They are waiting for me.'

Other verbs that pattern with *takin* are: *yina* 'help', *kalalid* 'invite', *kahoy* 'frighten', *lemed* 'meet', *hyom* 'fuck' and *talun* 'give s.b. a push', *dahuy* 'prevent s.b. from leaving'.

12.3.4 Genitive O transitives (Type 2e)

Only two verbs are known to index their O-argument with the Genitive prefix series, but both of these verbs, *gan* 'hear, listen' and *yoman* 'approach, meet', are relatively frequent. Example with *gan* 'hear, listen':

(534) *namaya rusa nahan ø-nak-om- gan*
now deer(m) 1.EMPH NTRL-1.A-3SG.GEN- hear
'Then I heard the deer myself.' [W11:0734]

For an example with *yoman* 'approach, meet' see (378) on p. 217.

The verb *gan* 'hear, listen' occurs in several valence frames. It can also be used as a plain intransitive verb (Type 1a), e.g. 'listen (to some unspecified stimulus)'. Another option is to use it transitively with an inanimate stimulus, such as *lala* '(high-pitched) noise' in (535). The stimulus (*lala*) is not indexed on the verb, so this use of the verb patterns with the invariant verbs of Type 2b.

(535) *oso m-ak-um- uma⟨n⟩ah lala epe nda-no- gan*
start OBJ-1.A-FRUS- go⟨1.U⟩ noise there LOC-1.A- hear
'I had just started to walk, [then] I heard a noise there.' [M01:0054]

It is more common to cast the stimulus as the O-argument of the verb, but to specify the source of the sound with the Genitive prefixes, as when the speaker in (536) links the stimulus (*gugu* 'thumping noise') to a previously mentioned wallaby. This construction, with the NP expressing the stimulus omitted, must have provided the source for the construction in which the emitter of the sound is the O-argument, retaining the indexing by means of the Genitive prefix series from the source expression.

(536) Hunters going after a wallaby.
mayay gugu mahut ya nd-an-d-omb-e- gat-a
first thumping.noise far real LOC-1.A-DUR-3SG.GEN-1PL- hear-EXT
'First we heard its thumping from very far away.' [W11:1074]

The Genitive coding of the transitive O can be understood as an extension of a situation in which only sound-denoting O-arguments were allowed with 'hear', which is the situation found in e.g. the highlands language Usan (Reesink 1987: 135).

12.3.5 Complex pseudo-transitives (Type 2f)

This interesting pattern is attested with a few complex verbal expressions, but more research is needed to establish how widespread it is. Coastal Marind has many idiomatic expressions denoting mental or bodily events such as 'become hungry', 'die', 'become sleepy', etc. These consist of a fixed nominal (e.g. *emel* 'hunger') and a verb, often with no discernible meaning (e.g. *wahun*, which only occurs in the expression 'become hungry'). In these expressions, the patient/experiencer is always indexed by means of Undergoer marking on the verb stem, and the Actor prefix is invariable 3SG. Therefore it seems reasonable to think of these verb expressions as standard transitives, with the fixed nominal (e.g. *emel* 'hunger') functioning as the A-argument, and the patient/experiencer functioning as the O-argument. A literal gloss for such an expression could be e.g. 'hunger affects me' (cf. Pawley et al. 2000 on similar idioms in the Papuan language Kalam).

However, if we compare the effect of pre-verbal placement of *emel* or the patient-like argument on the use of Orientation prefixes, we see that these expressions are not standard transitives. Recall that the A-argument of a standard transitive verb triggers the use of the Neutral Orientation, while the O-argument requires the Object Orientation prefix. With expressions such as *emel wahun* 'get hungry' we find the Neutral prefix with *both* the fixed nominal *emel* 'hunger', as in (537a), *and* the patient-like argument; in (537b) this is the interrogative *ta* 'who'.

(537) a. *emel ø-bat-ø- w-ahun*
hunger NTRL-AFF-3SG.A- 3SG.U-get.hungry
'S/he is hungry, poor one.'

b. *emel ta ø-b-a- w-ahun?*
hunger who NTRL-ROG-3SG.A- 3SG.U-get.hungry
'Who is hungry?'

Thus, it seems that these expressions are 'double-subject' expressions, since both *emel* 'hunger' and the patient-like argument *ta* 'who?' behave like S/A-arguments and trigger the Neutral Orientation. This pattern is not attested outside the class of idiomatic expressions with fixed stimulus-denoting nominals.[3]

12.4 Trivalent verbs

Most trivalent verbs express transfer events ('give something to somebody'). Such verbs have two object-like arguments: a theme (typically an inanimate) and a recipient-like participant (typically animate). The default pattern with respect to the Orientation prefixes is that a recipient placed in the pre-verbal position triggers the Directional *k*- on the verb (cf. §11.1.4.3), and the theme triggers the Object prefix *m*- (§11.1.3.2).

---

[3] The only other case is instrumental verbs derived with the applicative WITH-prefix, which also have two arguments that trigger the Neutral Orientation: the S/A-argument and the constituent expressing the instrument (§11.1.2.3).

12.4.1 Ditransitives with secundative indexing (Type 3a)

For this class, the recipient is indexed by means of Undergoer alternations in the verb stem, just like the O-argument of alternating transitive verbs (indexing and case flagging patterns treating the monotransitive O and the ditransitive recipient the same way are called *secundative* in e.g. Malchukov et al. 2010). The theme is not indexed in the verb complex.

This is a small class. The only transfer verb exhibiting this pattern is *koh* 'feed', as in example (393) on p. 254. In addition, I include the verbs *kwaneb* and *wasakab*, both roughly meaning 'snatch something from somebody', in this class. The animate who is deprived of something is indexed in the verb stems of these verbs, and the stolen item is unindexed, but triggers the Object Orientation prefix *m-* when placed in the pre-verbal position.

12.4.2 Standard ditransitives with alternating (Type 3b) and invariant (Type 3c) stems.

This is the major pattern for the expression of transfer and similar three-participant events. The verbs in these classes index the recipient-like participant by means of the Dative prefix series (§9.3), and only differ in whether they are lexically specified as having an alternating verb stem or not (cf. discussion in §12.3.1). If the verb is alternating the theme is indexed within the verb stem, as with *yadewn* in (538). Examples of invariant verbs used ditransitively are *og* 'do' (with the meaning 'give' in its ditransitive use) and *kabed* 'ask', which do not index the theme, and therefore belong to class 3c. The ditransitive use of *og* is illustrated in (539). For *kabed*, see example (349) on p. 208.

(538) The speaker found some jerrycans with fresh water hidden in the forest.
       adaka   ehe   nok k-e-na-y-   yad⟨e⟩wn   ipe   agi,
       water(III) PROX:III   1   DIR-3PL>1-1.DAT-1PL- leave⟨III.U⟩   DIST:I/II.PL   PRWD:I/II.PL
       Kaptel-anim
       K.-people
       'The water was left for us by um, Kaptel villagers.'   [W10:0108]

(539) *kipa   epe   nok ka-mo-na-   og*
       net(III) DIST:III   1   DIR-FUT:2SG.A-1.DAT- do
       'That fishing net, you will give to me.'   [W22:0066]

12.4.3 Middle ditransitive 'beg for' (Type 3d)

The frequent verb *wig* 'beg for' has a unique valence pattern: it indexes the A-participant according to the middle pattern (cf. the middle intransitives, §12.2.3) and indexes the person from whom one begs (i.e. the owner of the desired item) by means of the Genitive series. The theme is not indexed. Judging from corpus data the Orientation system treats the theme and the owner alike in deploying the Object prefix *m-* when either is placed in the pre-verbal position.

(540) kaka   Ambay m-ø-omb-ap-   w-ig   tangge ago, Ambay e!
      elder.sib(m) A.   OBJ-3SG.A-3SG.GEN-CT-   3SG.U-beg   arrow QUOT A.   PTCL
      'He asked Ambay for arrows, saying "Hey, Ambay!" '   [W02:0009]

12.5 Patient-preserving lability

In this section I discuss verbs that may occur in two different valence frames with a predictable difference in meaning between the two patterns. These alternations are uncoded, meaning that there is no added morphology on the verb (e.g. passive or causative markers) signalling the shift in valence. For coded alternations (e.g. applicative constructions) in Coastal Marind, the reader is referred to Chapter 13.

Many Coastal Marind verbs may be used according to two different valence patterns: one in which the verb is used transitively, with an agent-like participant (the A-argument) and a patient-like participant (the O-argument), and one in which the verb is used intransitively, with the sole argument having the semantic role of patient, so that the S-argument of the intransitive use corresponds to the O-argument of the transitive use. Compare *The referee$_A$ started the game$_O$* with *The game$_S$ started*. I refer to this possibility as patient-preserving lability (or P-lability; these terms are from Dixon 1994. Other researchers use the label 'causative-inchoative' alternation for the two uses of P-labile verbs). Verbs that behave like *start* and allow both uses are referred to as labile verbs.[4]

There is no requirement in Coastal Marind syntax that arguments be given overt syntactic expression (Coastal Marind allows 'pro-drop', as some linguists would put it), so one has to ensure that the seemingly intransitive use of a verb is not better described as the transitive use with the A-argument omitted (e.g. because it is recoverable from the context). In other words, one must ask whether the intransitive clause *The*

---

[4] P-lability contrasts with agent-preserving lability (or A-lability), as in *Mary is writing her dissertation*/*Mary is writing*. A-lability will not be discussed here.

games started is not in fact a transitive clause ∅_A *started the game*_O with a 'null' A-argument. Since the system of Verb Orientation (Chapter 11) tracks the syntactic role of the argument placed in the pre-verbal position by distinguishing S/A-arguments (which require the Neutral prefix *ø-* or *k-* on the verb; §11.1.2) from O-arguments (which require the Object prefix *m-*; §11.1.3), it is easy to distinguish the intransitive use of verbs from transitive uses with an omitted A-argument by observing examples with the patient-like argument in the pre-verbal position. A pre-verbal patient that triggers the Neutral Orientation on the verb signals that the pre-verbal argument is an S-argument and that the verb is intransitive; one that triggers the Object Orientation signals that it is an O-argument and that the verb is transitive. My identification of P-labile verbs is based on this diagnostic.

I will now apply this test to the verb *keway* 'break, ruin', and show that it is a labile verb. In (541a) *keway* is used as a standard transitive verb, corresponding to Type 2b in the valence classification outlined above (see §12.3.1). The A-argument *ahan* 'you, yourself' is in the pre-verbal position, so the Neutral Orientation prefix *k-* is borne by the verb. Compare this to the use in (541b), where the patient-like argument *yandam* 'stomach' is in the pre-verbal position. The verb form in (541b) also employs the Neutral Orientation prefix (here the allomorph *ø-*, because the verb has non-present time reference) rather than the Object Orientation *m-*. This shows that *yandam* in (541b) is an S-argument and not an O, and that this sentence represents an intransitive use of *keway*, and not a transitive use with an omitted A-argument. Just like its English counterpart *break*, Coastal Marind *keway* is a labile verb.

(541) a. Removing dirt from the well. The speaker complains that the addressee's cleaning efforts are doing more harm than good.

adaka ahan   k-o-   keway-a
water EMPH:2SG PRS.NTRL-2SG.A- break-EXT
'You are the one ruining the water!'   [W06:0038]

b. Said about a puppy that was throwing up.

yandam ø-bat-o-   keway
stomach NTRL-AFF-3SG.DAT- break
'Its stomach is upset.' (lit. 'The stomach broke to it')

The lability test is easy to apply across the verbal lexicon, and sometimes turns up a Coastal Marind verb that differs from its closest English counterpart in lability. For example, the English verb *drop* is clearly labile, and allows both transitive (*The dog dropped the bone*) and intransitive (*The bone dropped from its mouth*) uses. The closest Coastal Marind counterpart, *kahaleb* 'drop' allows the transitive use, as in (542a–b), but there is no intransitive use of this verb in which the patient is the S-argument (542c). Hence, a more accurate gloss of *kahaleb* would be 'let go of, cause to drop'.

(542) a. ta   ø-b-a-p-   kahal⟨e⟩b?
         who NTRL-ACT-3SG.A-CT- drop⟨III.U⟩
         'Who dropped it?'

   b. ta   namakad   m-o-b-ap-   kahal⟨e⟩b?
         what thing(III) OBJ-2SG.A-ACT-CT- drop⟨III.U⟩
         'What thing did you drop?'

   c. *ta   namakad   ø-b-a-p-   kahal⟨e⟩b?
         what thing(III) NTRL-ACT-3SG.A-CT- drop⟨III.U⟩
         Intended: 'What thing fell/dropped?'

Another example is the verb *tad* 'burn', which can be used transitively ('cause to burn') but not intransitively ('be consumed by fire'). Conversely, there are also Coastal Marind verbs that are labile whereas the closest English counterparts are not, e.g. *kakak* 'lose' which unlike English *lose* can be used intransitively in the sense 'get lost, disappear'.

Other verbs manifesting P-lability are listed in Table 12.5 (on p. 318); the following two subsections discuss some issues that arise when applying the notion lability to Coastal Marind.

12.5.1 P-lability and the middle indexing template

While labile verbs are straight-forwardly identifiable in Coastal Marind from the behaviour of the Orientation prefixes, things get more complicated once person marking is taken into account. As explained in Chapter 10, about half of the verb lexemes in the language use stem alternations to index the patient-like participant ('alternating verbs'). In its transitive use, a labile alternating verb such as *saletok* 'hide' indexes the O-argument in the verb stem, as in (543a). In its intransitive use, it is the S-argument that is indexed in the stem, as in (543b).[5] As described in §12.2.3, intransitive verbs that index their sole participant with co-referential Actor and Undergoer marking belong to the 'middle intransitive' valence class (Type 1c). Thus, the use of *saletok* 'hide' in (543a) corresponds to Type 2a verbs ('alternating transitive'), and the use in (543b) to Type 1c ('middle intransitive').

(543) a. katal   menda-b-ø-   sal⟨i⟩tuk!
         money(IV)   PERF-ACT-3SG.A-   hide⟨IV.U⟩
         'S/he has hidden the money.'

---

[5] It is important to note that this is not a reflexive construction, and it could not be used to express situations such as *Mary saw herself/voted for herself*. See §13.3.

b. *menda-b-ø-   sal⟨e⟩tok!*
   PERF-ACT-3SG.A- hide⟨3SG.U⟩
   'S/he has hidden/gone into hiding.'

Another example of an alternating labile verb is *kagub* 'break'. In its transitive use, the stem alternation indexes the patient-like participant (544a). The intransitive use follows the middle pattern, so the Actor prefix and the stem alternation simultaneously index the sole participant (544b).

(544) a. *ngganggin m-a-   kaga⟨h⟩ib*
        croton(IV) OBJ-3SG.A- break⟨IV.U⟩
        'S/he broke off croton twigs.'

     b. *isala   ø-a-   kagub*
        sitting.platform(III) NTRL-3SG.A- break:III.U
        'It was the platform that broke.'   [W19:0077]

Now, the question arises whether it makes sense to classify the verbs *saletok* 'hide' and *kagub* 'break' as labile. The term labile typically denotes verbs that appear in intransitive and transitive argument frames without any accompanying derivational marking. According to this description, English *break* is labile, but French *casser* 'break' is not, since it requires reflexive marking to be used intransitively (*se casser* 'break itself'). A reasonable observation would be that the middle indexing pattern seen in the (b)-sentences of (543–544) acts as a sort of derivational device (much like the French reflexive in *se casser*) and that therefore these verbs should not count as labile.[6]

For descriptive purposes, however, the exclusion of alternating verbs from the set of labile verbs appears unmotivated. Being invariant or alternating is a lexical property of verb lexemes (and hence largely arbitrary) and it is clearly not a productive pattern (see Chapter 10). A verb that is specified as alternating has a slot somewhere in its stem that indexes the patient-like participant, and this slot cannot be left empty. When such a verb is used intransitively, the S-argument will trigger indexing in the verb stem, as it is the only available argument. Thus, the middle indexing pattern on the intransitive member of some labile pairs follows from the fact that these verbs happen to belong

---

[6] For example, Nichols et al. (2004: 159) state that P-labile verbs ("ambitransitive verbs" in their terminology) in languages with both subject and object agreement will only have subject agreement when used intransitively, so Coastal Marind *saletok* 'hide' and *kagub* 'break' would not qualify as labile in this classification, but as having a derived intransitive version (a "reduced verb" in Nichols et al. 2004). In another much cited work on the same phenomenon, Haspelmath (1993), the intransitive versions only count as derived if they exhibit some additional marking distinguishing them from the transitive base verbs, which arguably is not the case with the relevant Coastal Marind verbs (since verb stems such as *saletok* and *kagub* index an argument in both their intransitive and transitive uses).

to the alternating portion of the verbal lexicon, and this indexing pattern is not some derivational mechanism for creating intransitive verbs from transitives ones – at least not synchronically. I conclude that alternating labile verbs such as *kagub* 'break' in (544) do not differ in lability from invariant labile verbs such as (the near-synonymous) *keway* 'break' in (541).

12.5.2 P-labile verbs and patientive intransitives

A second issue concerns whether or not the S-argument of the intransitive version of a labile verb is reflected in the Actor indexing prefixes (§9.2). Most alternating labile verbs behave like *saletok* and index the S-argument by means of an Actor prefix and verb stem alternation simultaneously (these belong to the so called 'middle' verbs, see §10.1.2), as in (545). In addition, it is only middle verbs that allow Imperative formation in the intransitive use, as seen with *saletok* in (543b) above.

(545)　anem　e=　　nd-a-　　　sal⟨e⟩tok-a　　　　　　　ehe　　　　bus　　　　　　　　ehe
　　　　man　　PROX=　LOC-3SG.A-　hide⟨3SG.U⟩-EXT　PROX:III　eucalyptus(III)　PROX:III
　　　　'Somebody is hiding here among the eucalyptus trees.'　　　　　　　　　　[M02:0526]

The indexing of the S-argument in the Actor prefix corresponds to the agentive semantics of the verb (since hiding oneself requires an instigating agent), while the simultaneous indexing of the S by means of the Undergoer alternation in the stem follows from the fact that the stem indexes the only available argument in the absence of an O-argument.

But at least some P-labile verbs lack agentive semantics in their intransitive use. These verbs follow a patientive indexing template (cf. §12.2.2) when they are used intransitively, meaning that the S-argument is indexed only in the verb stem, while the Actor prefix is invariant 3SG. The most common P-labile verb that is patientive in its intransitive use is *balen* (2|3pl stem *bahin*) 'finish'. The transitive use of this verb is shown in (546a), where it describes truck drivers herding villagers onto trucks until they have finished herding all. The intransitive use, which could be translated as 'become finished, run out, be none left', is in (546b), where the verb 'finish' displays the patientive indexing template with invariant 3SG.A along with a 1st person Undergoer stem *banin* 'finish us'.

(546) a. Some Kimaam Islanders were taken in trucks and transported to Merauke for a celebration.

mayay mbya Kimaam-anim m-a- y-ahik,
first all K.-people OBJ-3SG.A- 2|3PL.U-accompany

Kimaam-anim aaa, ka-n-ap- ba⟨h⟩in
K.-people until DIR-3PL.A-CT- finish⟨2|3PL.U⟩

'First they took the Kimaam people, all the Kimaam people until…they finished them.' [W18:0180–0181]

b. *inah ti ø-nan-d-e- huhu-n,*
two with NTRL-1.A-DUR-1PL- emerge.PLA-1.U

yahaa k-ø-e-p- ba⟨n⟩in
all.the.way.to DIR-3SG.A-1PL-CT- finish⟨1.U⟩

'We went out two by two, until none of us were left.'

Other P-labile verbs that have an intransitive variant with patientive indexing are *oleb* 'change', *ibayeb* 'make round; become round' and *walimayeb* 'bend; become bent, crooked'. Note that *walimayeb* has a slightly different meaning than the non-patientive verb *masetok*, which also means 'bend' as a transitive verb but 'lean forward' in its intransitive use. The agentive meaning 'lean forward' is reflected in the fact that *masetok* is middle marking and not patientive in its intransitive use.

Table 12.5 indicates whether a labile verb has alternating (indexing person/number of the Undergoer) or invariant stems, and the type of indexing template exhibited by the verb in its intransitive use. For verbs that are attested only with inanimate undergoers it is not possible to distinguish the middle and patientive patterns, since inanimates lack number and trigger 3sg Actor marking by default.

Tab. 12.5: P-labile verbs

Verb	Gloss	Alternating	Itr. indexing
tak	'clear, empty'	no	n/a
keway	'break, ruin'	no	n/a
kamak	'start'	no	n/a
kab	'open'	no	n/a
lalid	'close'	no	n/a
betok	'pile up'	yes	n/a
yuyam	'rock, shake'	yes	n/a
hyahyak	'split'	yes	n/a
ihwaluk	'dangle'	yes	n/a
luyad	'pour, spill'	yes	n/a
panggak	'unfold'	yes	n/a
kakak	'lose'	yes	n/a
kibib	'roll'	yes	middle
ibinggab	'gather'	yes	middle
hwayob	'hang'	yes	middle
masetok	'bend; lean forward'	yes	middle
saletok	'hide'	yes	middle
dahetok	'turn'	yes	middle
lawetok	'turn'	yes	middle
oleb	'change'	yes	patientive
ibayeb	'make round'	yes	patientive
walimayeb	'bend'	yes	patientive
balen	'finish'	yes	patientive
kagub	'break'	yes	patientive

13 Valence-changing constructions

This chapter describes constructions in which a verb is used with a different number of arguments compared to its standard use outside the construction. The five types of applicative constructions (marked by four prefixes on the verb) add an argument expressing an instrument or various types of patient-like participants to the clause, as described in §13.1.

The only major valence-reducing structure in Coastal Marind is the Reciprocal, described in §13.2.

There are no clear instances of grammaticalised causative or reflexive constructions in the language. §13.3 discusses some ways of expressing these concepts.

13.1 Applicatives

Coastal Marind has five applicative constructions, which are marked by applicative prefixes on the verb and introduce an additional argument into the clause. An overview of the semantics and morphosyntax of the different applicatives is given in §13.1.1. The object properties acquired by the applicative objects are described in §13.1.2, and indexing of the applicative object is treated in §13.1.3. After that, more detailed descriptions of the use of the five applicatives structures are given: the Instrumental (§13.1.4), the Comitative (§13.1.5), the Accompaniment (§13.1.6), the Allative (§13.1.7) and the Separative (§13.1.8). Note that benefactives, which are often introduced by applicatives across languages, are not involved in applicative formation in Coastal Marind. A benefactive participant can be expressed by using the Dative prefixes — see §9.3.2.

13.1.1 Overview of applicative constructions

A verb prefixed with an applicative prefix allows one more argument than the verb normally takes outside the applicative construction. I refer to the added argument as the applicative argument or applicative object. As will be shown below, the applicative argument shares some properties with standard O-arguments, with the exception of the Instrumental, whose applicative argument is more similar to S/A-arguments. This section briefly illustrates the use of each applicative construction, and the verb prefixes that mark them.

The Instrumental (§13.1.4) allows an instrument NP to appear without postpositional marking, typically in the slot immediately preceding the verb. The Instrumental verb is marked by a prefix *k-* before a vowel and *ka-* before a consonant other than /k/. Before /k/, the prefix is realised as *i-*. The prefix is part of the verb stem (and not the prefixal complex preceding the verb stem). The same prefix is also used to signal the Comitative applicative, so I use the gloss 'WITH' to capture the two meanings. Two simple sentences illustrating the use of the Instrumental are in (547). (547a) shows the base verb *wamuk* 'hit' and (547b) shows the derived verb *kwamuk* 'hit with'.

(547) a. nok   ø-no-   w-amuk
       1   NTRL-1.A-   3SG.U-hit
       'I hit him/her.'

   b. nok kalik   ø-no-   k-w-amuk
      1   throwing.stick   NTRL-1.A-   WITH-3SG.U-hit
      'I hit him/her with a throwing stick.'

The Comitative is typically used with motion verbs and then adds an argument expressing an item that is brought along (§13.1.5). (548a) illustrates the base verb *yet* 'be moving', and (548b) the derived verb *kayet* 'bring'. Although the Comitative is marked by the same prefix as the Instrumental (*k-* 'WITH'), the two constructions differ syntactically in that the the applicative argument in (547b), which expresses the instrument, triggers the use of the Neutral Orientation prefix on the verb, whereas the applicative argument in (548b), which expresses a comitative object, triggers the Object Orientation prefix *ma-* on the verb. These features are described further in §13.1.2.

(548) a. nok   ø-no-d-   yet
       1   NTRL-1.A-DUR-   be.moving
       'I went along.'

   b. nok mih ma-no-d-   ka-yet
      1   bow OBJ-1.A-DUR-   WITH-be.moving
      'I was bringing along a bow.'

The Accompaniment, marked by the prefix *e-* in the prefixal complex, has a similar range of uses as the Comitative, but is used mainly with animates as the applicative object, i.e. a person or animal who is brought along. (549a) illustrates the base verb *umuh* 'go (away)', and (549b) its use as a transitive verb meaning 'go away with s.b.' or 'take s.b. away' marked by the Accompaniment prefix *e-*.

(549) a. Alo   ø-a-   umuh
       A.   NTRL-3SG.A-   go:3SG.U
       'Alo went.'

   b. Alo nggat m-ø-e-   umuh
      A. dog   OBJ-3SG.A-ACPN-   go:3SG.U
      'Alo went with the dog(s)/took the dog(s) with him.'

The Allative, marked by the prefix *ind-*, adds an applicative object towards which some action is directed (§13.1.7). A typical use is when a motion event, such as that expressed by *ihon* 'run away' in (550a), has an animate participant as its goal, as in (550b).

(550) a. *Maria ø-a- ihon*
M. NTRL-3SG.A- run.away:3SG.U
'Maria ran away.'

b. *Maria ehway m-ø-in- ihon*
M. father:3 OBJ-3SG.A-ALL- run.away:3SG.U
'Maria ran towards her father.'

The mirror image of the Allative is the Separative, marked by the prefix *is-*, expressing that the agent moves away from the added participant. Compare (550) with (551).

(551) *Maria ehway m-ø-is- ihon*
M. father:3 OBJ-3SG.A-SEP- run.away:3SG.U
'Maria ran away from her father.'

13.1.2 Morphosyntactic properties of applicative arguments

This section investigates the treatment of applicative objects, more specifically how their morphosyntactic properties compare with those of the patient-like arguments of standard monotransitive verbs. Two properties are shared by the patient-like arguments of transitive verbs such as 'hit', 'break' or 'see'. The first is the ability to trigger person/number indexing by means of so-called Undergoer stem alternations, as described in §10.1. The second is the ability of a patient NP to trigger the use of the Object Orientation prefix *m-* when the NP is in the immediately pre-verbal position, as described in §11.1.3. Here I refer to these as *object properties*. Below I will show that applicatives objects do not pattern with standard O-arguments with respect to the first property (Undergoer indexing). (Indexing of applicative objects does occur, but in limited circumstances, and then only with the Dative prefixes, as shown in §13.1.3.) On the other hand, we will see that applicative objects do pattern like standard O-arguments in the use of the Object Orientation prefix (with the exception of the Instrumental applicative, which patterns with S/A-arguments).

Many verb stems index person, number or gender of a patient-like participant, but the participant of a derived applicative verb that is indexed by the Undergoer alternations is always the patient of the base verb. Unlike the O-arguments of monotransitive verbs, the applicative object never triggers Undergoer indexing. For example, the transitive verb *saletok* 'hide' in (552) indexes the patient *katal* 'money', and not the applicative object *Alo*, which is introduced by the Separative applicative.

(552) katal   mak-is-   sal⟨i⟩tuk   Alo
      money(IV) FUT:1.A-SEP- hide⟨IV.U⟩   A.
      'I will hide the money from Alo.'

Example (553) illustrates that the same principle holds for the Comitative applicative, and also that it applies to the large class of so-called Middle verbs. Recall that many motion verbs in Coastal Marind index their sole argument according to the Middle pattern, in which the Actor and Undergoer affixes co-index person/number of the agent (§10.1.2, §12.2.3). This indexing pattern is retained even when an applicative object is added, as shown by the Middle verb *kwamin* 'enter' in (553). The Undergoer affix (realised as an infix with this particular verb) indexes the S/A-participant, despite the introduction of the arguably more patient-like applicative object into the clause. The generalisation is that the Actor and Undergoer indexing exhibited by the base verb is retained when the verb enters an applicative structure.

(553) yoɣ   da   ah-   i-k⟨y⟩amin-em
      2PL   sago(III) IMP- WITH-⟨2|3PL.U⟩enter-PL.IMP
      'You (pl) take the sago inside!'   [W19:0437]

The same generalisation holds for the Allative applicative, as well as the Instrumental. Example (554) shows that the verb *wamuk* 'hit' indexes the patient by means of the Undergoer prefix on the stem, and not the instrument *kupa* 'stone club'. We will see below that the applicative argument introduced by the Instrumental actually patterns with S/A-arguments, rather than the O-argument, with regard to the Orientation prefixes on the verb, but example (554) allows us to verify that the applicative argument is not indexed in the Actor prefix either.

(554) ehe   kupa   e=   te-ka-no-   ka-y-amuk-e
      PROX:III   stone.club(III)   PROX:III=   GIV:III-PRS.NTRL-1.A- WITH-2SG.U-hit-IPFV
      'I'm going to hit you with this stone club.'   [D11:0016]

The observation that the applicative argument does not trigger Actor or Undergoer indexing extends to verbs that are suppletive for participant number. Several common verbs in Coastal Marind show stem suppletion according to the number of the absolutive argument (see §10.5). All of the intransitive suppletive verbs, e.g. 'come' (singular *man*, plural *nayam*), are common in applicative constructions, in which they occur with an applicative object. In this configuration, the verb still suppletes according to the number of the agent, i.e. the S-argument of the base verb, and not according to the added applicative object. The data in (555) and (556) illustrate this. The singular verb *man* is used in (555), and the plural *nayam* in (556), in accordance with the plural agent.

(555) ehe   basik menda-b-ø-e-   man
      PROX:I pig(II) PERF-ACT-3SG.A-ACPN- come
      'He already brought a pig.' [D05:0039]

(556) Vitalis a   yay Ambay sayam te-nda-n-e-   nayam
      V.   and uncle A.   wallaby GIV:III-LOC-3PL.A-ACPN- come.PL
      'Then Vitalis and uncle Ambay brought the wallaby.' [W11:0837]

Suppletion of an intransitive base verb in an applicative construction, as in the previous examples, is the only instance in the language in which suppletion according to participant number can be argued to follow not an absolutive pattern, but a nominative pattern, as the suppletion effectively is triggered by the A-argument of the derived applicative expression.[1] A minimal quadruplet showing all four combinations of singular and plural arguments is given in (557).

(557) a. nggat hyakod m-ø-e-   man-em
         dog   one   OBJ-3SG.A-ACPN- come-VEN
         'S/he's bringing one dog.'

      b. nggat inah m-ø-e-   man-em
         dog   two   OBJ-3SG.A-ACPN- come-VEN
         'S/he's bringing two dogs.'

      c. nggat hyakod ma-n-e-   nayam-em
         dog   one   OBJ-3PL.A-ACPN- come.PL-VEN
         'They're bringing one dog.'

      d. nggat inah ma-n-e-   nayam-em
         dog   one   OBJ-3PL.A-ACPN- come.PL-VEN
         'They're bringing two dogs.'

The examples in (556) and (557) also illustrate a rather subtle way in which the addition of an applicative object can affect participant indexing, viz. the use of the 3pl Actor prefix *n-*, instead of the default 3sg indexing that occurs with suppletive verbs outside applicative constructions. Among the applicatives, this phenomenon is restricted to the Accompaniment, Allative and Separative structures, but it also occurs with some non-applicative formations — see §9.2.2.2 for the full range of facts.

The second object property that will be assessed is the ability of an applicative argument to trigger the occurrence of the Object Orientation prefix *m-* when placed in

---

[1] Similar observations about verbal suppletion according to the base subject in derived applicatives have been made for Uto-Aztecan languages (e.g. Comrie 1982, Peterson 2007: 56), but if this pattern holds across languages more generally is unclear.

the immediately pre-verbal position. When a NP in the S/A-role is placed pre-verbally (e.g. because it is focused) the verb carries the Neutral Orientation prefix, *k-* (present tense) or *ø-* (past or future tense contexts), whereas a NP in the O-role typically corresponds to a verb marked with Object Orientation *m-*. (See Chapter 11 for an account of the Orientation system.) If the arguments introduced by the applicative structures were treated as the O-arguments of standard transitive verbs, we would expect them to trigger the Object prefix *m-* on the verb. This is in fact the case for four of the five applicatives (the Comitative, Accompaniment, Allative and Separative) but not for the fifth (the Instrumental). The relevant data were already presented in §13.1.1 above, but I will review the evidence in more detail here. Example (547b) showed that the argument introduced by the Instrumental co-occurs with a Neutral-marked verb, a property it shares with arguments in the S/A function. The same property is illustrated in the corpus examples (558) and (559).

(558) Comment about a piglet that was rooting the ground.
 tamuy anggip k-a- k-w-alaw-a
 food nose(IV) PRS.NTRL-3SG.A- WITH-3SG.U-search-EXT
 'It's looking for food with its snout.' [W13:0266]

(559) nahe ipe ehe kahos e= te-ø-d-an-
 ancestors:1 DIST:I/II.PL PROX:III betelnut(III) PROX:III= GIV:III-NTRL-DUR-3PL.A-
 ka-sasayi-ma
 WITH-work-PST.HAB
 'Our ancestors used to work using (i.e. while chewing) this (kind of) betelnut.' [W13:0129]

It is not surprising that the instrument argument lacks this object property, and instead shows similarities with A-arguments, since both argument types perform a causal role in bringing about events.[2] However, the applicative instrument NP lacks the other main characteristic of A-arguments, viz. the ability to trigger Actor person/number indexing, so its status falls somewhere inbetween a zero-marked adjunct (i.e. an adjunct without adpositional marking) and an argument proper.

13.1.3 Dative indexing of applicative objects

The standard uses of the Dative prefix series (indexing recipients, possessors of body parts, etc.) were described in §9.3. In the preceding section, we saw that unlike stan-

---

[2] Several instances of instrumental applicatives failing to show object properties are mentioned in Peterson's study of applicatives (2007: 10–12, 34, 53, 59).

dard O-arguments, applicative objects are not indexed by means of the Undergoer alternations in the verb stem. The use of the Dative prefixes to index applicative objects compensates for this, but it is restricted to participants introduced by the Accompaniment *e-*, Allative *ind-* and Separative *is-*, i.e. the applicatives that can introduce animate participants into the clause, and of these participants, only 1st person (singular or plural) and 2nd person singular are indexed. Table 13.1 shows the full set of Dative prefixes normally used, and the restricted set used for indexing applicative participants.

Tab. 13.1: Standard (left) and applicative (right) Dative indexing

	SG	PL		SG	PL
1	na-		1	na-	
2	a-	e-	2	a-	
3	o-		3		

Examples involving 3rd person applicative objects, and therefore lacking Dative indexing, were given in §13.1.1 and §13.1.2. Below are examples illustrating Dative indexing of 1st and 2nd person singular participants. Recall from §9.3.1 that the 1st person Dative prefix undergoes partial affixal metathesis (resulting in the discontinuous morph *n-...a-*) when used with prefixes from some of the adjacent position classes, which include the Allative and Separative prefixes. This is seen in (560) and (561), which illustrate the Allative and Separative with 1st person applicative objects. (562) shows the Allative with a 2sg applicative object.

(560) Speaker complaining that relatives rarely come visit him.

    mbya k-i-n-ind-a-   *y-um*
    NEG   PRS.NTRL-3PL>1-1.DAT-ALL-1.DAT-   2|3PL.U-go.PLA
    'They never come to me.'   [W13:0886]

(561) About extinct native fish species.

    menda-b-ø-n-is-a-y-   *ikebeh*
    PERF-ACT-3SG.A-1.DAT-SEP-1.DAT-1PL-   disappear:2|3PL.U
    'They have disappeared from us.'   [W13:0616]

(562) How travellers arriving in a new village would identify members of their own clan by listening for people's names being called.

epe   sapla-anem   a-p-ø-ind-a-   man-em   epe,
DIST:I travel-man(I) DEP-FUT-3SG.A-ALL-2SG.DAT-   come-VEN   DIST:III

a-me-ø-   gan   igih   epe
DEP-FUT-3SG.A-   hear name(I)   DIST:I

'when the stranger walks towards you, when he hears that name, [then he'll know]'   [W13:0300]

The absence of Dative indexing in the remaining person/number combinations is visible in Table 13.2, which gives a full paradigm of the Separative with the verb 'run away'.

Although 2pl, 3sg and 3pl applicative objects cannot be indexed by means of the Dative prefix series, those prefixes may still appear on an applicative-marked verb if they fill one of the functions of standard Dative indexing (§9.3). Compare first (560) and (562) above, which showed Dative indexing of the applicative object of verbs marked with Allative *ind-*, with (563), which shows the lack of Dative indexing when the applicative object ('that girl') is 3rd person. Consider now (564), which has a 3rd person applicative object ('water'), but also a recipient participant ('for him'). It is the presence of the recipient that is signalled by the 3sg Dative prefix *o-* on the verb, following the normal principles for Dative indexing. This is an important observation as it shows that the lack of indexing of 2pl, 3sg and 3pl applicative objects is a morphosyntactic feature of applicatives, and not due to some morphophonological process causing the relevant Dative prefixes to be deleted in the presence of the applicative prefixes.

(563) oy   Teo ah-in-   uma⟨y⟩ah,   upe   anum   upe
      2SG T.   IMP-ALL- go⟨2SG.U⟩   DIST:II   woman(II) DIST:II

'You Teo, go get her, that girl!'   [W06:0100]

(564) adaka   h-ind-o-   uma⟨y⟩ah
      water   IMP-ALL-3SG.DAT-   go⟨2SG.U⟩

'Go get water for him!'   [W05:0051]

13.1.4 Use of the Instrumental applicative (*k-* WITH)

This is the preferred method for adding an instrument to a clause, with the alternative, oblique expression using the postposition *en* 'with' (§6.1.6) being much less frequent in corpus data. The lack of object features, which sets the Instrumental argument apart from the other types of applicative objects, was discussed in §13.1.2. Another difference

Tab. 13.2: Paradigm of *ihon* 'run away' with Separative *is-* showing indexing of A (Actor prefixes) and applicative O (Dative prefixes for 1sg/pl and 2sg)

	1SG (DAT n-...-a-)	1PL (DAT n-...-a-)	2SG (DAT a-)	2PL (no indexing)	3SG, 3PL (no indexing)
1SG.A	–	–	oɣ m-ak-is-a- ihya(n)on 'I fled from you'	yoɣ m-ak-is- ihya(n)on 'I fled from you'	nggat m-ak-is- ihya(n)on 'I fled from the dog(s)'
1PL.A	–	–	oɣ m-ak-is-a-y- awan 'we fled from you'	yoɣ m-ak-is-e- awan 'we fled from you'	nggat m-ak-is-e- awan 'we fled from the dog(s)'
2SG.A	nok m-u-n-is-a- ihya(ɣ)on 'you fled from me'	nok m-u-n-is-a-y- ihya(ɣ)on 'you fled from us'	–	–	nggat m-ø-us- ihya(ɣ)on 'you fled from the dog(s)'
2PL.A	nok m-i-n-is-a- awan 'you fled from me'	nok m-i-n-is-a-y- awan 'you fled from us'	–	–	nggat m-ø-is- awan 'you fled from the dog(s)'
3SG.A	nok m-a-n-is-a- ihon 's/he fled from me'	nok m-a-n-is-a-y- ihon 's/he fled from us'	oɣ m-ø-is-a- ihon 's/he fled from you'	yoɣ m-ø-is- ihon 's/he fled from you'	nggat m-is- ihon 's/he fled from the dog(s)'
3PL.A	nok m-i-n-is-a- awan 'they fled from me'	nok m-i-n-is-a-y- awan 'they fled from us'	oɣ ma-n-is-a- awan 'they fled from you'	yoɣ m-an-is- awan 'they fled from you'	nggat ma-n-is- awan 'they fled from the dog(s)'

is that the instrument NP introduced by the Instrumental structure is always placed in the immediately pre-verbal position (i.e. the position associated with constituent focus), whereas the other applicative arguments enjoy more syntactic freedom. This automatic association with the focus position is shared with the class of pre-verbal adverbials described in §18.4. The pre-verbal placement was seen in examples (547b), (554) and (558–559) above, and additional corpus examples are in (565–567).

(565) About the traditional hand nets used for fishing.
    ipe   *ehe*   *kipa*   *te-ø-d-e-*   *ka-na-koh-a*
    DIST:I/II.PL PROX:III net   GIV:III-NTRL-DUR-3PL>1- WITH-1.U-feed-EXT
    'They fed us using these nets.'   [W13:0691]

(566) *tagu*   *ø-nak-e-*   *ka-nayam*
    foot(III) NTRL-1.A-1PL- WITH-come.PL
    'We came here by foot.'   [W16:0108]

(567) *ember*   *ø-mo-*   *ka-lesad*   *mayay*
    bucket(m)(III) NTRL-FUT:2SG.A- WITH-draw.water first
    'Draw water with the bucket first!'   [W06:0236]

The WITH-prefix *k-* (*ka-* before a vowel, and *i-* before /k/) which is used to derive Instrumental verb stems is also used to derive Comitative verbs (§13.1.5). Some of the morphosyntactic properties distinguishing the two constructions were mentioned in §13.1.1 and §13.1.2. Another difference between these structures is that the Instrumental can be used with intransitive verbs, as in (566), monotransitive verbs, as in (567), and ditransitive verbs, as in (565), whereas the Comitative is restricted to intransitive base verbs. Furthermore, the Instrumental allows the applicative arguments to belong to Gender IV, as in (558), whereas the Comitative is compatible only with applicative objects in Gender III (nether allows animates from Gender I and Gender II).

Like other arguments, the instrument NP is usually omitted if the referent is easily recoverable from the context. In (568), the instrument in the second clause is omitted, since it was already established in the preceding clause ('an old thing').

(568) About a plant that had been used to inflict an injury.
    ehe   *tanama-namakad*   *k-a-*   *Ø,*
    PROX:III old:III-thing(III)   PRS.NTRL-3SG.A- be.NPST
    anim   *mbya*   *k-enam-*   *ka-na-sak-e*
    people NEG   PRS.NTRL-RCPR- WITH-RCPR-hit.PLA-IPFV
    'This is an old thing, people don't fight each other with [it] anymore.'
                                                                              [W19:0272]

The choice between the applicative Instrumental and the oblique construal with the postposition *en* 'with' mainly depends on the form of the verb and the presence of other material in the pre-verbal position. Consider (569), which was uttered after (568) above. The speaker wanted to convey restrictive constituent focus on the patient ('only you'), and because this constituent occupies the pre-verbal slot, the instrument must be expressed using the postpositional, oblique variant.

(569) namaya oy s-an- ya-sak ehe namakad en ehe
now 2SG ONLY-3PL.A- 2SG.U-hit.PLA PROX:III thing(III) INSTR PROX:III
'Now only you got beaten with this kind of thing.' [W19:0273]

Means of transport are treated as instruments and can appear as pre-verbal NPs (570). The conflation of instruments and means of transport is only made in the applicative structure. In the oblique construal, they are marked by different postpositions: instruments by the instrumental/possessive *en*, as in (569), and means of transport by the comitative *ti* 'with' (571).

(570) ihe inah ihe hyakod yahun ø-a- ka-nayam-em
PROX:I/II.PL two PROX:I/II.PL one canoe NTRL-3SG.A- WITH-come.PL-VEN
'The other two, they were coming with one canoe' [W12:0316]

(571) kwemek, nggawil-yahun ti ø-a- awat-a-m patul
morning motorcycle with:I/II.PL NTRL-3SG.A- run.PL-EXT-VEN boy
'In the morning, the boys drove to us with motorbikes.' [W18:0156]

Unlike instruments proper, the more frequent method for expressing means of transport is by using the postpositional construal. This seems to be a statistical preference in most contexts, but corresponds to an absolute constraint in content questions: instruments can only be questioned using the applicative version (572a), while means of transport can only be questioned using the postpositional variant (572b).

(572) a. ta ø-h-o-b- i-kipalud?
what NTRL-ROG-2SG.A-ACT- WITH-tie:III.U
'What did you use to tie it?'

b. ta ti ø-h-o-b- man?
what with:I NTRL-ROG-2SG.A-ACT- come
'With what (means of transport) did you come?'

The Instrumental applicative is used with some manner expressions, as in (573–574). The expressions *alil* and *kamay* appear to be nouns, meaning approximately 'slow speed' and 'fast speed' respectively, so literal translations of these utterances would be 'I walked using slow/fast speed'.

Tab. 13.3: Some frequent Comitative verbs

Base verb		Comitative verb	
dahetok	'return'	ka-dhetok	'return with s.t.'
ihon	'run away'	k-ihon	'run away with s.t., steal s.t.'
hwis	'descend'	ka-hwis	'descend with s.t.'
hawa	'emerge'	ka-hawa	'emerge with s.t.'
kahek	'climb up'	i-kahek	'climb up with s.t.'
kwamin	'enter'	i-kwamin	'take s.t. inside'
man	'come (SG)'	ka-man	'one to bring s.t.'
naɣam	'come (PL)'	ka-naɣam	'several to bring s.t.'
oha	'go down to beach'	k-oha	'take s.t. down to beach'
umuh	'go away'	k-umuh	'take s.t. away'

(573) alil ø-no-d- ka-yet
slow NTRL-1.A-DUR- WITH-be.moving
'I walked slowly.' [W02:0032]

(574) nok kamay ø-no-d- k-umak-ti
1 fast NTRL-1.A-DUR- WITH-be.running-DUR
'I was running fast.' [W12:0062]

13.1.5 Use of the Comitative applicative (*k-* WITH)

The most common use of the Comitative is with motion verbs, with which it forms transitive 'bring' verbs. Some common examples are listed in Table 13.3. The comitative object (i.e. the item being brought etc.) is treated as an O-argument, and triggers the use of the Object Orientation prefix when it is placed in the pre-verbal slot, as discussed in §13.1.2. In (575), the noun phrase *ndom-tas ya* 'a really bad bag' expresses the comitative theme licensed by the WITH-prefix.

(575) From a hunting story. Some bananas later fell out through a hole in the bag.
nok keti en napet, Ambay ndom-tas ya ma-d-ø- ka-yet
1 APL POSS banana A. bad-bag(m) real OBJ-DUR-3SG.A- WITH-be.moving
'[For] our bananas, Ambay was bringing along a really bad bag.' [W11:0619]

The only non-motion verb that is attested in the Comitative construction is *hayad* 'play', giving *kahayad* 'play with' (e.g. bow and arrow, sand etc.). The Comitative is not used with transitive verbs.

The comitative object shows the same syntactic distribution as standard O-arguments. If the participant is recoverable from the context it is often left unexpressed, as in (576), in which the comitative object 'sago' is implicit. The comitative object can be placed in the pre-verbal slot, as in (575) above, or appear as a topic in the beginning of the clause (576), or elsewhere in the clause, e.g. clause-finally, as in (578), according to the information packaging requirements of the context.

(576) The speaker had been asked to bring sago.
     kwemek mano- k-uma⟨n⟩ah, mate
     morning FUT:1.A- WITH-go⟨1.U⟩ never.mind
     'I'll bring [it] in the morning, don't worry.'   [W10:0230]

(577) *epe   tamuy epe,   usus   nd-a-p-   ka-hu-h*
     DIST:III food(III) DIST:III afternoon LOC-3SG.A-CT- WITH-emerge-2|3PL.U
     'That food, in the afternoon they brought it home.'   [W19:0184]

(578) *hari Minggu epe,   namek es-Wambi   mak-a-p-   ka-hawa*
     Sunday(m)(III) DIST:III mate behind-Wambi NAFUT-3SG.A-CT- WITH-emerge:3SG.U
     wati
     kava(III)
     'On Sundays, some mate from Eastern Wambi would bring out kava (coming from the church service).'   [W13:0890]

The relatively unconstrained placement of the comitative theme contrasts with the behaviour of an instrument NP licensed by the WITH-prefix, which is placed in the pre-verbal slot. The comitative structure is also compatible with morphology that does not permit focused arguments, such as the Perfect *mend-* (579). This feature further distinguishes the Comitative from the Instrumental construction, as the pre-verbal instrument NP obligatorily triggers the use of the Neutral Orientation prefix on the verb.

(579) *kak Wobi da   menda-b-ø-   ka-man*
     aunt W. sago(III) PERF-ACT-3SG.A- WITH-come
     'Aunt Wobi already brought sago.'   [W10:0252]

The frequent combination of the WITH-prefix and the generic motion verb *yet* has given rise to a reduced portmanteau stem: the full form *ka-yet*, as in (575) above, is interchangeable with the shortened form *kat*, with exactly the same meaning. A corpus example:

(580) Same speaker and context as (579).

   kwemek da ma-d-ø-o- kat
   morning sago OBJ-DUR-3SG.A-3SG.DAT- be.moving:WITH

   'In the morning she brought the sago for her.'   [W10:0262]

Three position verbs have variants with slightly irregular WITH-stems, showing regressive vowel harmony instead of the standard *ka*-prefix: *mil* 'be sitting' > *kimil* 'be sitting with', *tel* 'be lying' > *ketel* 'be lying with', and *nin* 'lie/sleep repeatedly' > *kinin* 'lie/sleep repeatedly with'. These can be used to describe someone sitting etc. while holding the comitative object, or keeping it next to themselves, as in (581).

(581) Commenting on a picture showing someone selling vegetables.

   ehe isi e= k-at-ø-i- kimil-e, ubi,
   PROX:I other PROX:I= PRS.NTRL-PRSTV-3SG.A-RE- sit:WITH-IPFV cassava(m)(III)

   labu
   pumpkin(m)(III)

   'Here somebody else is sitting with cassava, and pumpkin.'   [D09:0126]

The main semantic restriction on the Comitative construction is that it only allows inanimate nouns as the applicative object, and, among inanimates, only nouns that fall into Gender III (most inanimate nouns are in Gender III, cf. Chapter 5). If the applicative object is a Gender IV item, the Accompaniment construction (marked by the prefix *e*-) must be used (see §13.1.6). The Accompaniment construction is also used with animate applicative objects, i.e. humans and animals that are brought along. It is a remarkable quirk of Coastal Marind grammar that Gender IV nouns are treated as if they were animates in all structures that distinguish between animates and inanimates. I discussed these facts in relation to the gender system in §5.3.2.2.

 Some idiomatic expressions are based on the Comitative construction, but lack the meaning 'bring' found in its productive uses. The noun *ukna* 'fear' appears in the Comitative construction with the meaning 'to Verb out of fear, because one is afraid', or more literally 'Verb with fear'. Examples are in (582–583). The construction in (584) also appears to be an instance of the Comitative applicative, although the derivation of the meaning 'take a bath' is less transparent. See also example (427) on p. 266.

(582) *ukna m-a- k-abun*
   fear OBJ-3SG.A- WITH-bark

   '[The dog] is barking out of fear.'

(583) The speaker, an older man, is complaining that hunters nowadays hide from the pig instead of attacking it.

ukna m-e- k-u-sl⟨i⟩tuk-e namaya lik
fear OBJ-2PL.A- WITH-PLA-hide⟨2|3PL.U⟩-IPFV now from:I/II.PL

'You hide out of fear, you young people (lit. from nowadays).' [W11:0812]

(584) udug ap-o- ka-y-in
bath PST.Q-2SG.A- WITH-2SG.U-become

'Did you take a bath?'

13.1.6 Use of the Accompaniment applicative e-

The Accompaniment prefix is used with intransitive verbs, mostly expressing motion, and adds one argument to the verb. The added participant — the accompanee — is a participant in the motion event, typically being brought along by the agent. Often this involves carrying the accompanee, as in (585–587), or some other type of physical manipulation, such as transporting the accompanee in a vehicle. An accompanee that is retrievable from the context is typically not given overt expression, as seen in (586–587).

(585) uhetagu dohu uhe, hyakod ma-n-e- nayam
like.this:II fish.sp(II) PROX:II one OBJ-3PL.A-ACPN- come.PL

'A fish (sp.) this size, they brought one [such fish].' [W11:0337]

(586) The speaker tells her husband to take away their infant son so she can work.

ah-e- hwil, nok da mano- yol
IMP-ACPN- walk 1 sago FUT:1.A- beat.sago

'You go away with him, I'm going to beat sago.' [W20:0130]

(587) About an injured man being carried home by other villagers.

mayay anem Poce ø-ø-e- umuh
first man P. NTRL-3SG.A-ACPN- go:3SG.U

'First it was [that] man Poce who brought him.' [W21:0254]

The accompanee must be either an animate (as in the previous examples) or an inanimate belonging to Gender IV, as shown with the noun *nggol* 'betel leaf' in (588) and *bing* 'sago leaf base' in (589). It is not possible for the added participant to be an inanimate in Gender III — such nouns are only compatible with the Comitative construction marked by the WITH-prefix *k-* (§13.1.5). For the importance of this remarkable patterning for the analysis of the gender system, see §5.3.2.2.

(588) *ahan   nggol   mend-o-y-   man?*
        2SG.EMPH betel.leaf(IV) PERF-2SG.A-ACPN- come
        'You yourself brought betel?'   [W11:0063]

(589) *Budoy yaba-bing   anep   epe   nda-bat-ø-e-   umuh*
        B.   big-leaf.base(IV) EMPH:III there   LOC-AFF-3SG.A-ACPN-   go:3SG.U

       Moyga epe
        M.(III) DIST:III
        'Budoy brought a big leaf base from there in Moyga.'   [W11:0990]

The Accompaniment prefix is common with position verbs such as 'sit', 'lie' etc., and then derives expressions meaning roughly 'sit together with' and so on.

(590) The speaker describes how he came across some birds in the bush.
       mboha   wanangga epe   nda-da-n-e-   wayamat-a
        magpie.goose   children   there LOC-DUR-3PL.A-ACPN-   stand.PL-EXT
        'Magpie geese were standing there with their chicks.'   [W11:1011]

(591) *payum   nanggah   epe   Waliwam wanangga*
        candlenut   tree.base(III)   DIST:III W.   children

       e=   nda-d-ø-e-p-   mil-ti
        PROX=   LOC-DUR-3SG.A-ACPN-CT-   be.sitting-DUR
        'Under the candlenut tree Waliwam was sitting with her children.'
                                                                            [W10:0585]

As seen earlier for motion verbs, position verbs also combine with inanimate accompanees belonging to Gender IV (but not Gender III). This is illustrated with the Gender IV noun *ebta* 'sago thatch' in (592). A more literal translation of this expression would be 'we sat down with sago thatch'.

(592) *yap   epe   ebta   k-ak-e-y-   haman*
        night(III) DIST:III sago.thatch(IV) DIR-1.A-1PL-ACPN- sit.PL
        'In the evening, we made roofing from sago thatch.'   [W20:0276]

An important semantic feature of the use of the preceding examples of the Accompaniment construction is that the accompanees in these examples are relatively passive compared to the agent. In (586) and (587), the accompanees are carried by the agents from one place to another, so they are part of the motion event only passively. In (590) and (591), the accompanees — the chicks and the children, respectively — are perhaps more actively participating in the sitting event, but there is still an asymmetry with the agents (their parents) who play a supervising role by keeping them seated. Contrast this with alternative ways of expressing co-participation with motion and position verbs, without the asymmetry in agentivity between the participants. In (593), a postpositional phrase headed by *ti* 'with' is used (see §9.6 for this construction). In (594), the participants are enumerated at the beginning of the clause and jointly function as the sole argument of the verb. These examples differ from the examples with the Accompaniment prefix by expressing a relative symmetry between the co-participants, who both participate actively in the events.

(593) *Tepes eham   Mbombo ti   ø-d-a-   awat-a*
      T.   husband:3 M.   with NTRL-DUR-3SG.A- run.PL-EXT
      'Tepes's husband went with Mbombo.' or 'Tepes's husband and Mbombo went.' [W22:0113]

(594) *nok nene   Sela epe nd-an-d-e-ka-p-   hamat-a mayay epe*
      1   grandma(m) S.   there LOC-1.A-DUR-1PL-PRI-CT- sit.PL-EXT front(III) DIST:III
      'Grandma Sela and I were sitting there in front [of the house]' [W11:0428]

The passive participation of the accompanee in events expressed by the Accompaniment construction holds in most contexts, except for one common use, in which this feature is rather subtle. This use can be called the *sociative causative* use (as in Shibatani and Pardeshi 2001: 96–103), and occurs mainly with verbs meaning 'run' and 'stand' (or rather, 'come to a standstill'). In the sociative causative use with 'run', the resulting expression does not usually mean 'run with X' (e.g. by carrying X while running) but rather 'make X run by running together with X', or, in almost all cases, 'chase X'. (595) illustrates this use. Similarly, with a verb meaning 'stand', the normal interpretation is not 'stand with X' (e.g. while holding X), but 'make X stand by standing together with X'. This use primarily occurs in hunting contexts, when the hunting dogs keep the game at bay and vocalise until the hunter arrives with bow and arrow, as in (596).

(595) *Petrus menda-b-ø-e-   umak-em   yaba-basik*
      P.   PERF-ACT-3SG.A-ACPN- be.running-VEN big-pig
      'Petrus chased a big pig hither.' [W11:0704]

(596) basik e=   nd-a-   ihon,   nama nggat anup a,   hekay-mamuy ya
      pig   PROX= LOC-3SG.A-   run:3SG.U   now dog   EMPH:II TOP clearing-savanna real
      ka-n-e-   wayaman
      DIR-3PL.A-ACPN-   stand.PL

'The pig took off, then the dogs, they stopped it right in the open savanna.'
[W03:0090–0091]

The sociative causative meaning has been described as an extension of applicatives in some languages (Guillaume and Rose 2010: 392–394), and it is discussed by Peterson (2007: 136–138) as a bridging context between causative and applicative markers. In Coastal Marind, this use seems to be restricted to verbs meaning 'run' and 'stand', and speakers rejected its use with verbs in other semantic domains (e.g. 'sing').

Finally, a separate use is attested with verbs meaning 'cry'. With these verbs, the added object expresses a participant that evokes the emotions that cause the agent to cry. Example (597) describes a meeting with a long lost relative, and the elicited example in (598) can refer to a dead or missing dog.

(597) aywa!   epe   k-a-na-y-   ihwin   mayay   epe
      EXCLAM there DIR-3SG.A-1.DAT-ACPN-   start.to.cry   front(III) DIST:III

'[He said:] "Oh my!", then he started to cry at me, there in front [of the house].'
[W10:0408–0409]

(598) nggat m-ak-e-   ihw-e
      dog   OBJ-1.A-ACPN-   be.crying-IPFV

'I'm crying over the dog.'

13.1.7 Use of the Allative applicative *ind-*

This applicative expresses motion towards the added object, usually with an added purposive meaning, i.e. because the agent intends to manipulate (acquire, inspect, attack, etc.) the object in some way. The Allative prefix *ind-* (*in-* if followed by no other prefixes within the prefixal complex) is commonly, but not exclusively, found with motion verbs. Examples (599–600) illustrate motion with the intent of acquiring the applicative objects.

(599) ebta   mak-ind-e-ka-   ayak
      sago.thatch   FUT:1.A-ALL-1PL-PRI-   go.inland

'We will go inland for sago thatch.'
[W20:0253]

(600) tangge nda-n-ind-ap- hu-h-a-m milah mih
arrow LOC-3PL.A-ALL-CT- emerge-2|3PL.U-EXT-VEN house bow
'Then they came back here to the house to get arrows, and bows.'
[W09:0070]

This use of the applicative with motion verbs corresponds closely to an oblique construal with the purposive postposition *awe* 'for' marking the desired entity (§6.1.9).

With an animate applicative object, the agent typically moves towards the object to meet with them or take them along (601), to attack them (602) or to interact with them in some other way (603).

(601) Oy-Onggat ay! nok a-n-ind-a- man-em
O. VOC 1 IMP-1.DAT-ALL-1.DAT- come-VEN
'Hey Oy-Onggat! Come here and get me!'
[W10:0656]

(602) From a hunting story: a pig attacking a hunter.
tanama Yan m-ø-um-in- umak-em
then Y. OBJ-3SG.A-FRUS-ALL- be.running-VEN
'Then it tried to run towards Yan.'
[W11:0584]

(603) Describing how a boy approached a travelling party, asking for food.
yap m-a-n-ind-a-y- lolaw-em
night OBJ-3SG.A-1.DAT-ALL-1.DAT-1PL- crawl:3SG.U-VEN
'At night he came sneaking towards us.'
[W10:0074]

The Allative adds a purposive component to verbs describing change of posture (604–605), and the applicative object then corresponds to the item that the agent is hoping to acquire through the change of posture.

(604) The speaker described how the congregation received communion during Catholic mass.
nok ap k-ak-ind-e-p- ilumun
1 also DIR-1.A-ALL-1PL-CT- kneel.down
'We also kneeled down for it.'
[W16:0049]

(605) Discussing one of the pictures in the Family Problems task.
yah kosi-patul ta ma-b-ø-ind-i- lalak-a ehe
but small-boy(I) what OBJ-ACT-3SG.A-ALL-RE- reach.up-EXT PROX:I
'But what is this little boy reaching up for?'
[D09:0119]

The Allative applicative is used with verbs that describe change in gaze orientation (e.g. *mikeh* 'look to the side', *wabayed* 'look to the back', *kayam* 'look up', *lokeh* 'peek'). The applicative object is the participant that the agent is trying to perceive: 'the sun' in (606) and 'them' in (607).

(606)   *katane   m-ø-ind-ap-   i-kayam-e*
        sun   OBJ-3SG.A-ALL-CT-   PLA-look.up-IPFV

        'He's looking up at the sun.'   [D09:0246]

(607)   The speaker was looking for his friends during a hunt.
        ye   m-ak-in-   luka⟨n⟩ah,
        INGRS   OBJ-1.A-ALL- peek⟨1.U⟩

        lapang   epe   ka-d-ø-   ka-nayat
        field(m)(III) DIST:III   DIR-DUR-3SG.A- INESS-be.moving.PL

        'I peeked out for them, they were walking along the fields.'   [W11:0637]

The Allative is also used to express purposeful action more generally. In this rather abstract use it seems to lack any applicative function, because no object-like participant is added. Consider (608). The verb *kagub* 'break' (*kagahib* with a Gender IV O-argument) is mostly used for items being broken by accident. In the example, taken from an account of sago processing, the speaker explains how she broke off twigs in order to braid a cradle for the sago washing trough to rest on. This purpose motivates the use of *ind-*.

(608)   Preparing the apparatus for sago processing.
        ihimi   ye   m-ak-in-   kaga⟨h⟩ib, kandi-ihimi
        sago.shoot(IV) INGRS   OBJ-1.A-ALL- break⟨IV.U⟩ unripe-sago.shoot

        'I started breaking off sago shoots, young sago shoots.'   [W20:0085]

The Allative has a variety of uses that can be considered lexicalised to some degree, and which have to be memorised by the learner. Some examples will be mentioned here in lieu of a complete listing. Most of these expressions involve some sort of metaphorical directedness towards the applicative object. For example, adding the Allative to the intransitive verb *mahid* 'become angry' expresses 'become angry at somebody' (609), with the applicative object corresponding to the person at whom one is angry.

(609)   *oy   m-ø-ind-a-   mahid*
        2SG   OBJ-3SG.A-ALL-2SG.DAT-   become.angry

        'S/he is angry at you.'

Other verbs that form more or less unpredictable pairs with the Allative are: *tanggiy* 'give orders' > 'order somebody', *hayad* 'play' > 'disturb, bother somebody', *weheb* 'be delayed, be away for a long time' > 'trick somebody', 'pound, strike (an inanimate object)' > 'insist, force somebody verbally'. One particularly frequent pair is found with the verb *kamak*, meaning 'try' with the Contessive prefix *ap-* (610a), but 'start' with the Allative (610b). This alternation is rather opaque as it seems to involve neither valence increase nor directionality.

(610) a. *sinik ah-ap- kamak-em!*
carry IMP-CT- try-PL.IMP
'Try to carry them!' [W19:0390]

b. *tis epe lek, yol k-ak-ind-e- kamak*
that's.it after.that pound.sago DIR-1.A-ALL-1PL- start
'That's it, after that we started pounding the sago.' [W20:0038]

13.1.8 Use of the Separative applicative *is-*

The basic meaning of the Separative applicative can be thought of as expressing motion away from the added participant, with other meanings being more or less transparent extensions of the basic motion meaning. Below an attempt at a classification of the uses is made, although some uses show overlap and could no doubt be classified differently.

(A) MOTION AWAY. This meaning is primarily found with motion verbs, and can involve e.g. an agent fleeing from (611), or leaving (612), the applicative object. The applicative object is indexed by the Dative prefixes in a subset of person/number combinations — see §13.1.3.

(611) About a woman who left the village many years ago, under dramatic circumstances.
eham m-ø-is- ihon
husband:3SG OBJ-3SG.A-SEP- run:3SG.U
'She fled from her husband.'

(612) *yasti oso-pig m-a-n-is-a-y- dahetok*
old.man start-daylight OBJ-3SG.A-1.DAT-SEP-1.DAT-1PL- return
'The old man went away from us in the early morning.' [W18:0089]

(B) DISAPPEARANCE. The Separative is used with verbs meaning 'disappear', 'get lost' and 'hide', with the added argument expressing the person from whom something disappears etc. Examples (613–615) illustrate this use. This use is closely related to the general 'motion away' meaning of the Separative. Example (613) could perhaps be subsumed under the more general motion use, but examples involving depleted resources, like (614), do not necessarily involve motion. A speaker also confirmed that the use of the Separative in (615) is possible even when the does agent not move away from the applicative object (e.g. sneaking up to somebody and hiding behind their back).

(613)   A hunting story. The speaker was asked where his friend had gone.
   ago   epe   isawa   ø-ø-n-is-a-   kotib
   QUOT   DIST:I   maybe   NTRL-3SG.A-1.DAT-SEP-1.DAT-   get.lost:3SG.U
   'I said: "Maybe he got lost from me".'   [W02:0072]

(614)   The speaker compares today's fishing with that of his youth.
   saley   mbya   k-a-   Ø,   menda-b-ø-n-is-a-y-
   shrimp   NEG   PRS.NTRL-3SG.A-   be.NPST   PERF-ACT-3SG.A-1.DAT-SEP-1.DAT-1PL-
   ikebeh
   disappear:2|3PL.U
   'There is no shrimp, they have disappeared on us.'   [W24:0075]

(615)   *yayam   ehetagol   epe   k-ø-is-   sal⟨e⟩tok   nggat*
   tree.sp(III)   like.this:III   DIST:III   DIR-3SG.A-SEP-   hide⟨3SG.U⟩   dog
   '[The pig] hid from the dogs by a *yayam* tree this size.'   [M02:0127]

(C) AVOIDANCE. In this use the agent performs some non-motion action in order to avoid the applicative object. The examples above only showed intransitive verbs with the Separative, but the observed utterance in (617) contains a transitive verb.

(616)   The speaker wanted her pet magpie goose to stand up in front of the camera.
   anim   m-ø-is-   ka-yali
   people   OBJ-3SG.A-SEP-   INESS-lie.down
   'It lay down because of/to avoid the humans.'   [W17:0006]

(617)   *nanggit   m-ak-is-   kalemed   wanugu*
   mosquito   OBJ-1.A-SEP-   wear   clothes
   'I put on clothes [to avoid getting bitten by] mosquitos.'

(D) PASSING OF TIME. It is very common to use *is-* with verbs describing the passing of time. The added applicative object is someone affected by the elapsing time, e.g. travellers during an excursion, trying to reach home before dark. In the following two examples, I add 'on us' and 'as we reached' to the English translations so that they better convey the Coastal Marind structure.

(618) Mbian   k-a-n-is-a-y-   hayaman   katane
      Mb.   DIR-3SG.A-1.DAT-SEP-1.DAT-1PL-   enter.water sun
      'By the Bian River the sun went down on us.'   [W18:0172]

(619) Walakem k-a-n-is-a-y-   ka-pig
      W.   DIR-3SG.A-1.DAT-SEP-1.DAT-1PL-   INESS-become.day
      'It dawned as we reached Walakem.'   [W02:0042]

(E) COVER. The Separative can be prefixed to verbs meaning 'put, place', giving expressions meaning 'cover'. The added participant seems to correspond to the item or surface being covered (I have no clear examples of the covered entity expressed overtly in the same clause, so it needs to be investigated whether this use really has applicative syntax). It is difficult to understand what this use of *is-* has to do with the meaning 'motion away', which I suggested is the basic meaning of the prefix. It is perhaps related to the use with the verb 'hide' in (615) above, since the act of hiding something often implies covering it.

(620) Describing the final stage of sago processing: baking the sago loaves.
      salaku   ye   m-ak-is-ap-   ibotok
      dry.sago.leaf(III) INGRS   OBJ-1.A-SEP-CT-   put.PLA:III.U
      'I covered [the sago loaves] with dry sago leaves.'   [W20:0082]

(621) Describing how a leaf oven was prepared.
      katal   ye   ma-d-n-is-ap-   lawawt-a
      stone(IV)   INGRS   OBJ-DUR-3PL.A-SEP-CT- put.PLA:IV.U-EXT
      'They started putting the stones on top [of the oven].'   [W18:0049]

(F) POUR ONTO. A verb describing the spilling or pouring of a substance can be prefixed with the Separative. This adds a participant onto which the substance is spilled/poured, as seen in (622–624). Again, this use appears unrelated to the 'motion away' meaning of the Separative prefix, especially since the substance being poured/spilled moves towards the added participant, not away from it. One could speculate that there is a relationship with the 'cover' use discussed above, since an item onto which something is spilled might end up covered in it (e.g. a liquid).

(622) Addressing some children:

    udug ah- i-hyaman-em,   mak-is-ap-   luyad-e
    bath   IMP- PLA-enter.water-PL.IMP FUT:1.A-SEP-CT- pour-IPFV

    'You bathe! I will pour [water] on you (pl).'   [W06:0003]

(623) Using coconut water to prepare a sago dish.

    anep   en   gel   epe,   epe ka-mus-ap-   kayob epe   ago,
    EMPH:III POSS sap(III) DIST:III there DIR-FUT:2SG.A-SEP-CT- squeeze there PRWD:III
    da
    sago(III)

    'Its water, you squeeze it on top of what's-it-called, the sago.'   [W21:0018]

(624) adaka ma-d-ø-is-ap-   luyad wati
       water OBJ-DUR-3SG.A-SEP-CT- pour   kava

       'S/he watered the kava plants.'

(G) STEPPING ON. There is another enigmatic use, typically with positional verbs (sit, lie, stand), with which the Separative *is-* indicates that the agent e.g. steps on (625) or lies down on (626) the added participant. This use does not have the meaning component 'motion away' — rather the opposite — but can perhaps be seen as an extension of the 'cover' meaning mentioned above.

(625) tagu k-a-n-is-a-p-   ka-lemed
       foot   DIR-3SG.A-1.DAT-SEP-1.DAT-CT- INESS-stand.PLA

       'He stepped on my foot.'   [W11:0935]

(626) agi   k-ak-is-e-p-   hok,   mingguy
       PRWD:I/II.PL DIR-1.A-SEP-1PL-CT- lie.down.PL maggot

       'We lay down on top of the what's-it-called, maggots.'   [W10:0069]

I have also observed this use when there was no actual physical contact involved — e.g. a person lying down close to where someone else is sitting — so it is perhaps sufficient that the agent encroaches on the personal space of the added participant. This could explain the use of *is-* in (627), which describes how some villagers were taken in a truck to another village. The owners of the truck stopped and let even more people climb up onto the crowded truck, invading the space previously occupied by the speaker.

(627) nok ye   m-i-n-is-a-y-p-   yuka⟨h⟩in
       1   INGRS OBJ-3PL>1-1.DAT-SEP-1.DAT-1PL-CT- put.inside.PLA⟨2|3PL.U⟩

       (lit.) 'They loaded [the new passengers] unto us.'   [W15:0163]

(H) REACHING BEYOND. The Separative prefix is sometimes used to express that some inanimate entity reaches beyond the added participant. This seems to be an extension of the 'motion away' use, although there is usually no motion involved in such contexts. For example, if the water in a swamp is so deep that one cannot reach the bottom with one's feet without putting the head under water, one can say:

(628) adaka k-a-n-is-a-p- w-a kaw-ay
water(III) DIR-3SG.A-1.DAT-SEP-1.DAT-CT- 3SG.U-AUX INESS-become:III.U
(lit.) 'The water is past/goes beyond me.'

It seems likely that the 'go beyond' use of the Separative is the source of the common idiomatic expression 'forget'. This construction consists of the noun *kambet* 'ear', invariant 3sg Actor marking, Separative *is-* and the verb *kaway*, which probably is the same form as in (628), although I gloss it as unanalysable 'forget'. If this etymology is correct, the original meaning of (629) was perhaps 'it went beyond my ear' = 'I forgot it'.

(629) kambet k-a-n-is-a-p- kaway
ear   DIR-3SG.A-1.DAT-SEP-1.DAT-CT- forget
'I forgot it.' [W10:0330]

Recall from §13.1.3 that applicative objects in some person/number combinations, such as 3rd person singular and plural, are not indexed by Dative prefixes on the verb. But these prefixes can appear on the verb if they perform one of the other functions of the Dative series, such as indexing the owner of a body part. The expression 'forget' involves the body part 'ear', so the Dative prefixes can be used in any person/number combination to index the owner of the ears (630). This is one of the rare instances in which the Separative combines with 3rd person Dative prefixes.

(630) The speaker complained that young people nowadays do not pay attention to advice from elders.

a-me-ø- atin epe, kambet mak-ø-is-o-p- kaway
[DEP-FUT-3SG.A- stand.up DIST:III] ear NAFUT-3SG.A-SEP-3SG.DAT-CT- forget
epe
DIST:III
'When he stands up, he will forget it.' [W13:0486]

(I) DISSOCIATED ACTION. I identify one use of the Separative that can be called 'dissociated action'. The agent performs some action without the participation of others, and usually in a different location. A clear example is in (631). A hunter is complaining about the behaviour of one of his dogs, who he claims kept sleeping while another dog was pursuing the game. The verb 'sleep' (literally 'be lying down') is prefixed with *is-*, which I interpret as signalling that this dog is doing something completely different, in another place.

(631) kudaya ø-d-a- asa, hyakod uhe ka-d-ø-is- w-a
 alone NTRL-DUR-3SG.A- bark one PROX:II DIR-DUR-3SG.A-SEP- 3SG.U-AUX
 tel
 be.lying

'She alone was barking, whereas this one was sleeping.' [M02:0328]

Another example of dissociated action is in (632), again from a hunting context. Here the first clause describes the hunting party, while the following clauses describe the speaker and his associates (all teenage boys) lagging behind, looking for bush food. The Separative is borne by the verbs describing the last two actions, which contrasts them with the hunters going first.

(632) ohan mayay ka-d-na- ayad-a-ti,
 hunt front DIR-DUR-3PL.A- lead.hunt-EXT-DUR

 es nd-ak-is-e- nayam-em,
 back LOC-1.A-SEP-1PL- come.PL-VEN

 alib-nggal s-an-d-is-e- ka-yahwiy
 palm.sp ONLY-1.A-DUR-SEP-1PL- INESS-eat

'They were leading the hunt in front, we were coming from the back, we were just eating palm shoots.' [W11:0964]

It is unclear whether the Separative has a valence increasing function in the disassociated action use, or if this should be considered a non-applicative use of the Separative.

13.2 The Reciprocal

Reciprocal situations ('each other') are expressed by adding the prefix *enam-* (glossed RCPR) to the prefixal complex (633). This prefix has no other functions other than marking reciprocity (it does not indicate reflexivity, for instance).

(633) About some former enemies.
 alil en ye m-enam- lay mayan
 slow with INGRS OBJ-RCPR- talk speech

'Slowly they started talking to each other.' [W22:0116]

With invariant verb stems, such as *lay* 'talk' in (633), no further changes affect the verb stem in the Reciprocal construction. If the verb is of the alternating type, as in (634), the Undergoer affix in the stem is replaced by an invariant affix of the shape /n/ (or /na/ to avoid a consonant cluster). (Recall from Chapter 10 that alternating verbs are those that index person/number of a patient-like participant, by means of prefixes, suffix or infixes, depending on inflectional subclass.)

(634)   epe   k-enam-   na-sak
        there DIR-RCPR- RCPR-hit.PLA
        'There they started fighting.' [W16:0077]

Confusingly, this means that the '*n*-stem' used in a reciprocal context is always identical to the 1st person Undergoer stem of the verb (which is also marked by /n/). There is no semantic link between 1st person and reciprocals, so I gloss the *n*-portion of the stem 'RCPR' in the latter case.[3]

A second observation about the shape of the verb stem is that if a verb lexeme has a Pluractional form, then this stem is selected in reciprocal contexts, i.e. reciprocal situations are always treated as involving multiple events. At least 20% of the verb lexemes in the language have special Pluractional stems, either derived by prefixing or expressed by unrelated, suppletive-like Pluractional verbs (see §16.1). An example of a suppletive-like Pluractional was seen in (634), in which *nasak* is the Reciprocal stem of the Pluractional verb *usak* 'hit several times, fight' (cf. the non-Pluractional *wamuk* 'hit once'). Verbs that lack a Pluractional form are unaffected by this, and occur in their base form in reciprocal contexts, e.g. *lay* 'talk' in (633) above.

The valence of a Reciprocal verb is reduced by one, so a standard monotransitive verb (e.g. 'hit') becomes formally intransitive. The valence reduction is reflected in the replacement of the Undergoer indexing by the Reciprocal marker in the verb stem, and also in the inability of the Reciprocal verb to occur with the Object Orientation prefix *m-* which is associated with standard O-arguments (§11.1.3). An NP referring to

---

[3] In Olsson (2017) I treated this as polyfunctionality of the 1st person stems, and glossed a stem such as *na-sak* as '1.U-hit.PLA' in both 1st person and reciprocal contexts. In this grammar, I choose the gloss RCPR in reciprocal contexts, to make such examples easier to parse. Languages that index the object on the verb typically need to fill this affix slot when a reciprocal verb is derived. Some languages solve this by affixing a default 3sg object marker to the reciprocal verb — this is the case in Yélî Dnye, Savosavo and Basque (Evans 2008). This is perhaps the explanation for the use of the 1.U affix in reciprocal verbs in Coastal Marind, but there is no other evidence that 1.U functions as an inflectional default in the language. Note, however, that the 1.U stem seems to be a default in the neighbouring Anim language Kuni (Edwards-Fumey 2005: 21), which could be evidence of a 1st person default, at least diachronically. See also Olsson (2017: 385, n. 3) for comments on the possible diachrony behind the RCPR/1.U conflation.

the reciprocants triggers the Neutral Orientation prefix on the verb when it is place immediately pre-verbally, as illustrated by the interrogative pronoun *ti* 'who' in (635).[4]

(635) ti   ø-b-enam-   na-sak?
       who:I/II.PL NTRL-ACT-RCPR-   RCPR-hit.PLA
       'Who fought each other?'

The quantifier *mbya*, combined with an emphatic pronoun (*nahan* 'ourselves' etc.), is sometimes used in reciprocal contexts. This expression is not a reciprocal pronoun (such as English *each other*) but seems to have a quantifying meaning, emphasising that all of the reciprocants are involved in the mutual action (and not just some of them).[5] Placed pre-verbally, the combination of *mbya* and an emphatic pronoun triggers the Neutral Orientation (636), and not the Object Orientation *m-*, which would have been expected it these expressions were reciprocal pronouns filling the 'object slot' of the verb.

(636) ye   ma-n-   yaway, anip   muy mbya anip
       INGRS OBJ-3PL.A- cut.up EMPH:I/II.PL meat all EMPH:I/II.PL

       ø-enam-   na-koh
       NTRL-RCPR-   RCPR-feed

       'They started cutting up [the pig], and they shared the meat amongst each other.'   [W18:0068]

The reciprocants can be expressed overtly, e.g. by simply listing them in the beginning of the clause (637). To express only a subset of the reciprocants, e.g. because the other of two reciprocants is contextually given, the inclusory construction with the postposition *ti* 'with' is used (cf. §9.6.1), as in (638–639).

(637) Ambay a   age   Meka epe   k-inam-um-   na-sak
       A.   PTCL PRWD:I M.   there DIR-RCPR-FRUS-   RCPR-hit.PLA
       'Ambay and what's-his-name, Meka, almost started to fight there.'
                                                                      [W01:0094]

---

4 A preposed O-argument can trigger the Object Orientation with a ditransitive Reciprocal verb, as the suppressed argument in such clauses is the one expressing the recipient rather than the O-argument. See (644b) and (645b) below for examples of this.

5 Cf. Drabbe (1955: 102), who seems to treat *mbya nahan* etc. (*mba nahan* in the Eastern dialect described in his grammar) as reciprocal pronouns.

(638) About a wallaby that was being hunted.

  Yan ti epe nda-d-enam- na-sak-a
  Y. with there LOC-DUR-RCPR- RCPR-hit.PLA-EXT

  '[The wallaby] and Yan were fighting there.'   [W11:0664]

(639) ta ti ka-b-inam-in- i-mahid-a?
   who with PRS.NTRL-ACT-RCPR-ALL- PLA-become.angry-EXT

  (lit.) 'With whom were they angry at each other?'

The remainder of this section describes the morphology of Reciprocal formation in more detail.

The occurrence of participant indexing is heavily restricted in Reciprocal verbs. Some of the limits on indexing, such as the replacement of Undergoer indexing by invariant *n*-stems, follow from the valence-reducing nature of the Reciprocal, while other limitations on indexing seem like rather arbitrary morphological quirks. I will first describe the effects on prefixes in the prefixal complex, then discuss the choice of stem forms.

Three indexing categories can normally be expressed in the prefixal complex of the verb, viz. Actor, Dative and Genitive indexing (see Chapter 9). In a verb marked with the Reciprocal prefix *enam-*, only Actor marking can occur, and then only in the 1st person (640). The elicited example in (641) shows that the 2pl Actor prefix *e-* (which normally occurs before the Past Durative *d-*) is omitted before Reciprocal *enam-*, and (633–634) showed the absence of 3pl Actor *n-*.[6]

(640) mbya k-ak-inam-e- na-koh-e
   NEG PRS.NTRL-1.A-RCPR-1PL- RCPR-feed-IPFV

  'We're not feeding each other anymore.'   [W13:0745]

(641) wis epe nda-d-enam- na-sak-a-ti yoy?
   yesterday there LOC-DUR-RCPR- RCPR-hit.PLA-EXT-DUR 2PL

  'Did you (pl) fight each other there yesterday?'

Note that the /e/ in *enam-* undergoes regular vowel gradation, giving *inam-*, in the antepenultimate syllable of the prefixal complex (§2.5.1), as in (640) above. Adding additional material, such as the Repetitive prefix *i-* in (642), results in /a/ being deleted due to antepretonic syncope (§2.4.2), giving the output form *inm-*.

---

[6] The only evidence for the omission of 2PL.A *e-* in Reciprocal forms comes from elicited data, as the corpus data contain no 2pl forms with another prefix (such as DUR *d-* or ACT *b-*) intervening before the Reciprocal *enam-*, which is necessary to block *e-* from being deleted before the /e/ of *enam-*. The deletion of 2PL.A in (641) is not predicted by the system of position classes, as shown by the forms with 1.A prefix, which also belongs to position class –13.

(642) kwemek epe k-ak-inm-i-e-   lay, ago "mate"
morning there DIR-1.A-RCPR-RE-1PL- talk QUOT never.mind
'In the morning we talked to each other again there, saying "Never mind".'
[W19:0251]

Examples (640) and (642) also show that the role-neutral 1pl *e-* (§9.5) is always added to 1st person Reciprocal forms since a reciprocal situation necessarily involves plural participants.

Dative and Genitive indexing is not used if the Reciprocal prefix is present. For example, the verb *lay* 'talk' normally indexes the recipient-like argument (the addressee) by means of the Dative prefixes, but this marking is omitted in reciprocal contexts such as (633).[7]

It was already mentioned that alternating verb stems use a special Reciprocal *n*-stem (identical to the 1st person Undergoer stem) in reciprocal contexts. This is a simplification, and the true generalisation can be described as follows. The Reciprocal affix on the stem is only used if the participant roles of the reciprocants (i.e. the participants acting mutually) includes a participant role that would be indexed by means of an Undergoer affix in the non-reciprocal use of the verb. If the Undergoer affix in the verb stem indexes a participant that is not part of the set of reciprocants, then that indexing is retained in the Reciprocal construction (instead of being replaced by an invariant Reciprocal *n*-stem). I will illustrate this with mono- and ditransitive verbs.

Consider first a monotransitive verb such as *idih* 'see', which indexes the more patient-like participant by means of Undergoer prefixes on the stem (643a). In the corresponding reciprocal situation, the reciprocants are the agent and patient participants, and because 'see' indexes the patient in the verb stem, the Reciprocal form *n-idih* is used in (643b).

(643) a. mend-ak-e- hy-adih
PERF-1.A-1PL- 2|3PL.U-see
'We already saw them.' [W13:0514]

b. men-b-enam- n-idih
PERF-ACT-RCPR- RCPR-see
'They already met (lit. saw) each other.' [W09:0040]

---

7 In the templatic model of the prefixal complex (Chapter 8) the Reciprocal prefix *enam-* is described as a multi-class prefix, covering the position classes –10 and –9. Accordingly, *enam-* is mutually incompatible with the 3rd person Actor prefixes (class –10) and the Genitive prefix series (–9), but it may be combine with prefixes from the surrounding classes (classes –11 and –8). The Dative prefixes are closer to the verb stem (position class –5), so their incompatibility with the Reciprocal must be stipulated independently of the position template.

Consider now a ditransitive verb such as *ikalen* 'send'. This verb is one of the standard ditransitive verbs (§12.4.2) and indexes the theme participant (i.e. the entity being given or transferred) by means of Undergoer affixes in the stem, and the recipient by means of Dative prefixes. Themes in ditransitives are often inanimate, and the Undergoer affixes then index the gender of this participant, as seen in (644a). In the reciprocal use of 'send', the reciprocants have the participant roles agent and recipient (i.e. the people who send something to each other). Because the Undergoer affixes indexes the theme role, which is not part of the set of reciprocants, the stem does not take the Reciprocal *n*-affix, and instead continues to index the gender of the theme in the reciprocal version in (644b).

(644) a. katal   m-ø-o-   ikla⟨h⟩in
money(IV)   OBJ-3SG.A-3SG.DAT-   send⟨IV.U⟩
'S/he sent him/her money.'

b. katal   m-enam-   ikla⟨h⟩in
money(IV)   OBJ-RCPR-   send⟨IV.U⟩
'They sent each other money.'

Another interpretation of (644) could be that Reciprocal *n*-stems are not used with ditransitive verbs. This generalisation is incorrect, as shown by ditransitive verbs that index the recipient-like participant, rather than the theme, by means of the Undergoer affixes. A small number of transfer verbs show this pattern, and index the recipient-like participant in the verb stem, while leaving the theme unindexed (this valence class was described in §12.4.1). One such verb is *koh* 'feed something to somebody' (645a). When this verb is used in the reciprocal construction, the Reciprocal stem form *na-koh* is used (645b), in accordance with the principle that the Reciprocal affix replaces an Undergoer affix that would index one of the reciprocant roles (here, the recipient role).

(645) a. sapi   adaka   m-a-   ya-koh-e
cow(m)   water   OBJ-3SG.A-   2|3PL.U-feed-IPFV
'S/he's giving water to the cows.'

b. yoy   nahwin   ihan   wati   m-enam-   na-koh
2PL   fathers:1   2PL.EMPH   kava   OBJ-RCPR-   RCPR-feed
'You men are sharing (lit. feeding each other) the kava.'   [W18:0264]

Actions directed at body parts are similar to transfer events in that they involve an inanimate theme (the body part) and two animate participants (the agent, and the owner of the body part). Verbs expressing such actions behave like the ditransitives exemplified by (644) above, and index the gender of the theme, i.e. the body part, by means of Undergoer affixes in the verb stem, and the owner of the body part by means of the Dative prefix series. Since the participant indexed in the Undergoer affixes is not one of the reciprocants, the Reciprocal *n*-affixes are not used in (646–647).

(646) nd-ak-inam-e- wa-hanid sangga
LOC-1.A-RCPR-1PL- III.U-grasp.PLA hand(III)
'Then we shook each other's hands.' [W15:0063]

(647) Discussing a conflict between the addressees.
ihe anggip anip mayay m-inam-is- kuha⟨h⟩ig-a
PROX:IV nose(IV) therefore:I/II.PL OBJ-RCPR-SEP- throw⟨IV.U⟩.PLA-EXT
'Because of this you are turning your faces (lit. throwing the noses) from each other.' [M05:0017]

The final type of verbs to consider are those that show the middle indexing pattern, i.e. those that use co-referential Actor and Undergoer affixes to index their agent-like participant (cf. §12.2.3, §12.3.2). The agent-like participant role is always one of the roles filled by the reciprocants, and since middle verbs (co-)index the agent by means of the Undergoer affixes, the Reciprocal *n*-stem is always used when middle verbs occur in reciprocal contexts. Examples (648) and (649) illustrate this with the middle verbs *walaw* 'search' and *ig* 'ask s.o. for s.t.' respectively.

(648) Kolum bapa Tayon mbam
K. father(m) T. louse

i= k-at-enam- ka-n-alaw-a
PROX:I/II.PL= PRS.NTRL-PRSTV-RCPR- INESS-RCPR-search-EXT
'Kolum and uncle Tayon are searching each other for lice.' [W11:0266]

(649) ip-inam-ap- n-ig-made
DIST:I/II.PL-RCPR-CT- RCPR-beg-PRS.HAB
'They habitually ask each other for things.'

The only exception to this pattern is the construction involving the Auxiliary *wa*, which is a middle verb (see §17.1), co-occurring with a lexical verb stem. In this periphrastic structure, the Auxiliary retains its middle indexing pattern, reflecting person/number of the agent-like participant, while the lexical verb stem exhibits the Reciprocal *n*-stem (650–651). (See §17.3.1 for the use of this common construction.)

(650) ka-d-enam- y-a na-sak
DIR-DUR-RCPR- 2|3PL.U-AUX RCPR-hit.PLA
'They fought each other.' [D06:0007]

(651) ka-d-inam-ap- y-a apna⟨n⟩awn-ma
DIR-DUR-RCPR-CT- 2|3PL.U-AUX visit⟨RCPR⟩-PST.HAB
'They used to visit each other.' [W13:0882]

13.3 Expressing reflexive and causative situations

There is no grammaticalised reflexive construction in Coastal Marind, i.e. there is no devoted structure for expressing that an agent performs on herself an action that usually is performed on others (as in 'Mary voted for herself'). There are, however, some types of expressions that can be interpreted as reflexives, although they cannot be considered grammaticalised.

First it should be noted that unlike some other Papuan languages (e.g. I'saka and Alamblak; Donohue and San Roque 2004: 76, Bruce 1984: 76), Coastal Marind does not allow participant indexing on the verb to be interpreted reflexively. The agent in (652) cannot be interpreted as co-referential with the patient.

(652) a- idih
3SG.A- see:3SG.U
'S/he$_i$ saw him/her$_j$.'
*'S/he$_i$ saw him-/herself$_i$.'

There is a large class of 'middle' verbs that always occur with co-referential Actor and Undergoer affixes, but these verbs never have reflexive meanings (§10.1.2).

The emphatic demonstratives (*anep* etc.; see §4.2.2) and the emphatic pronouns (*nahan* 'myself' etc.; see §4.1) can be used in reflexive contexts. Reflexivity is clearly not one of their major functions, and the only corpus example in which one of these items seem to fill an argument slot is (653). Emphatics expressing co-referential possession are more common, in both corpus (654a) and elicited (654b) data.

(653) nok nahan ma-no- lay-e, mayay-Wambi k-a- Ø nok
1 1.EMPH OBJ-1.A- talk-IPFV front-W. PRS.NTRL-3SG.A- be.NPST 1
'I'm talking about myself — I am from western Wambi.' [W13:0885]

(654) a. nd-ak-e- u-dhetok-a-m, nahan keti en tamuy k-ak-e- sasayi
LOC-1.A-1PL- PLA-return-EXT-VEN 1.EMPH APL POSS food DIR-1.A-1PL- work
'Then we returned, and we prepared our own food.' [W18:0241]

b. ahan en mayan ek-o- gat-a?
2SG.EMPH POSS speech PRS.Q:I-2SG.A- hear-EXT
(lit.) 'Can you hear your own speech?' (on the recording)

The limited use of the emphatic pronouns and demonstratives in reflexive function is compensated for by two strategies: omission of Dative prefixes in actions on one's own body part, and the use of nouns such as *wahani* 'body' to express self-directed actions. I will give examples of each of these strategies.

First, a body part in an O-argument role is usually interpreted as belonging to the participant filling the A-argument role if the verb lacks Dative indexing. Recall from §9.3.2 that the Dative prefix series is used to index owners of body parts in contexts such as 'I hit him on the hand' (In Coastal Marind: 'I 3SG.DAT-hit the hand'; see examples on p. 207). Such indexing is only used if the bodypart is attached to someone other than the agent, however. If the Dative indexing is removed ('I hit the hand') a reflexive reading is permitted ('I hit my hand', 'I hit myself on the hand'). This use is illustrated in the following examples:

(655) a. *ehe   yasti   sangga   s-a-   haniy*
         PROX:I old.man(I) hand(III) ONLY-3SG.A- bite:III.U
         'This old man$_i$ is just biting his$_i$ hand.'   [D09:0216]

   b. *sangga   parang   ø-no-   k-esad*
       hand(III) parang.knife(m)   NTRL-1.A-   WITH-cut:III.U
       'I cut my hand with a knife.'

Such reflexive readings only arise when permitted by the context. The following example also contains a body part (*pa* 'head') in the O-argument role and a verb form without Dative indexing, but in this context (an account of headhunting) it is obvious that the heads are not attached to the agent.

(656) *pa   sa-p-ø-ap-   ka-hawa*
       head ONLY-FUT-3SG.A-CT-   WITH-emerge:3SG.U
       '[The headhunter] would only bring back the heads.'   [D06:0027]

A related strategy is to use a noun referring to (a part of) the agent, such as *wahani* 'body', in the O-argument role, again without any Dative indexing. The expression 'We killed the bodies' in (657a) is interpreted as 'We killed our own bodies', i.e. 'We killed ourselves', while (657b), literally 'Hide the body!' means 'Hide yourself!'. One could imagine this type of expression developing into a grammaticalised reflexive construction; however, these are the only instances of reflexives with *wahani* 'body' that I have found in the corpus, so there is no indication that Coastal Marind is on the way to establishing any true reflexive structure.

(657) a. a-nka-h-e-   yahwiy epe   ahaaa, wahani pen   ya   k-ak-e-
         DEP-1.A-DEP-1PL- eat   DIST:III until   body(III) murder real DIR-1.A-1PL-
         u-sak
         III.U-hit.PLA
         'When we ate, we really ate ourselves to death (lit. killed our bodies).'
                                                                [D05:0049-0050]

   b. wahani ah-   hwagib!
      body(III) IMP- put.away:III.U
      'Hide yourself!'   [M02:0121]

Example (658) shows a similar strategy, with *abab-anem* 'reflection' as the O-argument. The speaker suggested that this can be used for seeing oneself in a mirror or a body of water, but there seem to be no extended uses beyond these contexts.

(658) nok abab-anem   mak-ap-   idih-e
      1   reflection-man FUT:1.A-CT-   see:3SG.U-IPFV
      'I'm going to look at myself.' (in the mirror)

For other Papuan languages without dedicated reflexive constructions, see e.g. Foley (1991: 287) on Yimas and Aikhenvald (2008b: 423) on Manambu.

Coastal Marind also lacks any grammaticalised means of expressing causation. My impression is that causal situations such as 'I made him write the letter' would be expressed by some circumlocution in Coastal Marind, e.g. 'I told him: "Write the letter!'". There is a causative use of the verb *kamin* 'make', but this is only used with adjectives, i.e. 'make something Adj.', as in

(659) nd-a-   kama⟨h⟩in   sasodeh
      LOC-3SG.A-   make⟨2|3PL.U⟩ cold
      'Then they made [the food] cool down.'   [W11:0177]

14 Tense and aspect

This chapter is divided into two main sections. §14.1 provides general information about the tense-aspect system. Some readers might prefer to skim through this section and instead focus on §14.2, which describes the tense-aspect affixes in detail.

There are various other grammatical resources that express notions related to tense and aspect, but whose main functions lie elsewhere. Information about these categories is found in other chapters. See e.g. the Neutral Orientation, whose allomorphs distinguish between present and non-present (§11.1.2); the Deictic prefixes, which are restricted to present time contexts (§15.4); and the pre-verbal adverbials, expressing negation and various aspectual notions (§18.4).

14.1 Overview of the tense-aspect system

The heart of the Coastal Marind tense-aspect system is the battery of affixes listed in Table 14.1. Most of the affixes are difficult to categorise according to any strict division between tense vs. aspect, because they are sensitive to distinctions associated with both of these domains. For example, the Past Durative *d-* (§14.2.1) is obligatory with all situations in the past (a tense distinction) that are presented as durative (an aspectual distinction). Others are more clearly aspectual in their nature, e.g. the Extended *-la* (§14.2.3) and the Continuative *anepand-* (§14.2.4), because they may occur in clauses with any kind of time reference (past, present, future).

Note that it is possible for a verb to occur without any of the tense-aspect affixes, in which case the tense value of the clause depends on the semantics of the verb (basically present tense for inherently durative verbs, and past for punctual verbs; §14.1.1).

The affixes in Table 14.1 occur in various morphological sites within the verb complex, so there is no dedicated 'tense-aspect slot'. Five categories are realised by prefixes within the prefixal complex (The Perfect *mend-*, Continuative *anepand-*, the two Futures, and Past Durative *d-*), two by affixes attaching directly to the verb stem (the Pluractional prefixes and the Extended suffix *-la*), while the remaining five categories are realised as suffixes in the outer slot after the stem. More information is given in the respective subsections below.

14.1.1 The basic ingressive–durative distinction

The semantic distinction between ingressive and durative is crucial for understanding how Coastal Marind speakers employ aspect-sensitive morphology. The distinction is also manifested in verbal lexicalisation patterns. These notions will be clarified before addressing the details.

14.1 Overview of the tense-aspect system

Tab. 14.1: Overview of tense-aspect morphology

Category	Form	Gloss	Main functions	Time frame
Perfect	*mend-*	PERF	Current relevance	n/a
Continuative	*anepand-*	CONT	'keep V-ing'	n/a
General Future	*ndame-* (etc.)	FUT	Prediction, intention, etc.	Future
Non-asserted Future	*mak-* (etc.)	NAFUT	Neg. future, apprehensive	Future
Past Durative	*d-*	DUR	All durative situations	Past
Pluractional	*e-, i-* (etc.)	PLA	Iteration, distributivity	n/a
Extended	*-la*	EXT	Resultative	n/a
Non-past Imperfective	*-e*	IPFV	On-going, habitual	Non-past
Past Durative	*-ti*	DUR	Optional with DUR *d-*	Past
Past Habitual	*-ma*	PST.HAB	'used to V'	Past
Present Habitual	*-made*	PRS.HAB	'usually V-s'	Present
Future Habitual	*-motok*	FUT.HAB	'will V habitually'	Future

An event such as running can be thought of as consisting of three parts: the onset or initial boundary (start to run, take off running), the ensuing activity phase (be running), and the endpoint or final boundary (stop running). We can refer to these three parts as the ingressive part, the durative part, and the completion of the event. The most central concept in discussions of aspect has been completion, because linguists traditionally described the major difference between verb forms in e.g. Ancient Greek, Slavic, and Romance languages as either implying completion (aorists or perfective forms) or not implying completion (imperfective forms).

In Coastal Marind the notion of completion is largely irrelevant for the description of the tense-aspect morphology. Instead the main distinction is between situations that are presented as ingressive (i.e. referring to their initial boundary or starting point) and situations that are presented as durative. One facet of this is visible in lexicalisation of actionality distinctions (or 'Aktionsart'): Coastal Marind almost completely lacks state-denoting verbs such as 'be hungry' or 'be round', but there is a large number of verbs denoting the onset of such states, e.g. *wahun* 'become hungry' and *ibayeb* 'become round'. The corresponding states are expressed by derived Extended forms (§14.2.3), e.g. *wahut-a* 'be hungry'. This pattern recurs with e.g. motion verbs, so there are verbs such as *tapeb* 'fly up, take off flying' but no verb simply meaning 'fly'. To refer to the durative part of such situations one uses the derived Extended form, e.g. *tapeb-a* 'be flying, be in flight'.

A second concomitant of the importance of the initial boundary of events is that Coastal Marind appears to lack any grammaticalised resources that imply the completion of an activity. I made many attempts to probe this by discussing sentences like (660) — taken either from texts, or, as here, from elicitation — with speakers, but I failed to identify any (affixal or non-affixal) material that narrows down the meaning of activities such as working, cooking, eating, etc. to include their final boundary. I suggest that telicity is not grammaticalised in Coastal Marind (cf. Smith's analysis of Navajo as lacking grammaticalised telicity; Smith 1997: 297).

(660) hyakod mandaw ma-no-d- sasayi-ti aha
 one month OBJ-1.A-DUR- work-DUR house

OK: 'I built the house in one month [and now it's finished].'
OK: 'I was working on the house for one month [but didn't finish].'

Not even head-tail linkage (de Vries 2005), a technique which is fairly common in narratives, carries any implication of completion in Coastal Marind. Consider the narrative excerpt in (661). Scraping of coconuts is first mentioned in line 1, then reiterated in line 2. The verbs are prefixed with the Directional Orientation *k-* and Locational Orientation *nd-*, which together are the hallmark of head-tail linkage (see §20.3). But the meaning of this structure is not 'We scraped coconuts. After we had scraped coconuts, we...'. Rather, it is 'We started scraping coconuts. We scraped coconuts [for a while], then we...'. The reiteration of the verb (the 'tail') does not signal completion, but describes the durative phase of the activity, whereas the first mention (the 'head') refers to the onset of the activity.

(661) 1. tis, kumbu k-am-bat-e- atug
 that's.it coconut DIR-1.A-AFF-1PL- scrape.coconuts
 'Then, we started scraping coconuts.'

 2. kumbu nd-an-d-e- atug aaa balen
 coconut(III) LOC-1.A-DUR-1PL- scrape.coconuts until finish:III.U
 'We scraped coconuts, until we finished all.' [W18:0017-0018]

Of course, speakers have the option to indicate completion by lexical means. In the previous example the speaker used the gesture-like 'preposition' *aaa* (which can be lengthened for rhetorical purposes) followed by the bare verb stem *balen* 'finish, become finished' to signal the completion of the coconut-scraping. Surprisingly perhaps, lexical expression of completion by means of the verb 'finish' is not used much in the narratives that I collected, with a total of about 50 attestations (20 of which were contributed in a single 19-minute recording by one speaker).

Another example is in (662). Again there is no marking indicating the endpoints of any of the durative situations ('we went', 'we ate'); they are only understood as having come to an end because of the intervening mentions of punctual, ingressive events ('started eating', 'lay down').

(662) 1. nd-an-d-e- nayat, tamuy k-ak-e- yahwiy
 LOC-1.A-DUR-1PL- be.moving.PL food DIR-1.A-1PL- eat
 'We went, and then we started eating.'

2. tamuy nd-an-d-e-   yahwiy, epe   k-ak-e-   hok
   food   LOC-1.A-DUR-1PL- eat   there DIR-1.A-1PL- lie.down.PL
   'We ate, and then we lay down.' [W15:0067-0068]

The centrality of the ingressive-durative distinction (as opposed to completion) has been described for other languages of the South New Guinea area, notably languages in the Yam family (Evans 2015a, Döhler 2016: 271, Carroll 2016: 179), and is foreshadowed by Drabbe's distinction between *momentaan* [punctual] and *duratief* [durative] verbs (Drabbe 1955: 31–37).

14.1.2 Temporal interpretation of verb forms

The indication of tense is somewhat more complicated in Coastal Marind than in, say, English, because there is no straightforward distinction between e.g. past and present forms of the verb. As seen in Table 14.1, however, there are several tense-aspect affixes that are sensitive to tense distinctions, e.g. the Past Durative *d-*, which only may occur in past time contexts. There is also a clear distinction between verbs marked by the Future prefixes and non-future forms, although the Future prefixes may refer to past events in some contexts (cf. §14.2.7.6). Below I will mention one factor that aides the temporal interpretation of clauses (§14.1.2.1) and one that adds further complication (§14.1.2.2).

14.1.2.1 The default temporal interpretation

The contrast between punctual (ingressive) and durative verbs is reflected in what can be called the 'default' temporal interpretation of Coastal Marind verb forms. An inherently durative verb (such as *yet* 'be moving') occurring as part of a verb complex without any of the tense-aspect morphology in Table 14.1 always describes a present situation, whereas a punctual verb (such as *hi* 'fall') in the same form is understood to refer to a past event:

(663) a. epe   k-a-   yet
         there DIR-3SG.A- be.moving
         'S/he is walking along there.'

     b. epe   k-a-   hi
         there DIR-3SG.A- fall:3SG.U
         'S/he fell there.' [W03:0135]

This behaviour corresponds to the well-known observation that stative verbs 'automatically' have present-time reference and non-stative ones past-time reference in many languages lacking obligatory tense marking (see e.g. Comrie 1976: 82, Dahl 1985: 177).

14.1.2.2 Current relevance interpretation of past punctual events

It is commonly the case that Coastal Marind speakers use forms that have a past punctual meaning to describe presently on-going states or activities. A frequently heard example is (664). I would often drive some villager on my motorcycle, and the person would utter this when we came to a segment of the road that had been destroyed by the elements. The verb *keway* 'break, become broken' is a punctual verb, and since the verb complex contains no durativising morphology, the expected meaning should be as in (i), 'The road broke'. Yet, speakers use this form to refer to a present state, as in (ii), 'The road is broken'. This is a potential problem for the statement in the preceding section, in which unmarked punctual verbs were said to be interpreted as referring to the past, and not to the present. (The Auxiliary construction is used here to indicate a thetic, 'all-new' statement, and does not interact with aspect or tense; see §17.1.)

(664) kay k-a- w-a keway
road DIR-3SG.A- 3SG.U-AUX break
i. 'The road broke.'
ii. 'The road is broken.'

I believe that the explanation for this is that Coastal Marind is relatively generous in allowing verb forms describing the onset of states and activities to be used to talk about a state or activity that is on-going at the time of reference. Discussion of the 'current relevance' of past events is familiar from studies of perfects (e.g. Dahl and Hedin 2000). It is clear that the encoded meaning of the previous example is (i), and that the state described in translation (ii) is not part of the encoded meaning, because it is impossible to combine the verb *keway* with adverbials implying a present state without adding durativising morphology. Thus, the stative predication 'The road is still broken' is expressed as in (665), with the Extended suffix *-la* (realised as *-a* after a consonant) deriving a stative expression 'be broken'.

(665) kay ndom k-a- keway-a
road still PRS.NTRL-3SG.A- break-EXT
'The road is still broken.'

It is not clear in what contexts the 'current relevance' uses of past punctual forms are possible, but it seems that they are especially frequent with verbs of destruction (like *keway*).

14.1.3 Remarks on the aspectual classification of verbs

A particularly impressive feat of Drabbe's grammar of the Eastern dialect of Coastal Marind is the detailed classification of verbs according to their combinability with tense-aspect affixes (1955: 31–37). Drabbe investigated e.g. whether a verb could combine with (using my terminology) the Past Durative *d-* and the Extended *-la*, and, based on these aspectual 'tests', he arrived at a taxonomy consisting of four aspectual verb classes. Approximately 200 verbs are listed according to their membership in the four classes, and it appears that Drabbe tested the classification on a total of ca. 700 verbs (taken from Geurtjens 1933). This accomplishment is especially awe-inspiring in that it predates the general interest in Vendlerian verb classifications among grammarians.

Although I do not wish to diminish the ingenuity of Drabbe's insight that Coastal Marind verbs need to be classified according to their aspectual potential, I am somewhat perplexed by the details of his classification. Of the four aspectual classes, it seems that Drabbe's 3rd class, consisting of punctual verbs that have a corresponding durative counterpart formed with the Extended suffix *-la*, is the most convincing grouping. My own description of the resultative use of this suffix (§14.2.3.1) is fully compatible with Drabbe's verb class.

My impression is that the three remaining classes suffer from a confusion of several issues. Drabbe's 1st class consists of verbs that supposedly are inherently punctual, and therefore are incompatible with affixes that signal durative situations (e.g. the Past Durative *d-* or the Extended *-la*). The 2nd class consists of inherently durative verbs, which always require the presence of some such affix (e.g. *d-* in the past). I largely agree with Drabbe that the verbs in class 1 are used to describe punctual events, and that most of them may not combine with e.g. Past Durative *d-*.[1] The 2nd, durative, class is more problematic. Its most convincing members are a handful of high-frequency verbs that exclusively express durative situations. The explanation for the inability of these verbs to express punctual situations is the existence of a corresponding set of verbs (assigned to class 1) that express the onset of these situations. The pairs are listed in Table 14.2.

None of the remaining verbs in Drabbe's 2nd class appear to be inherently durative according to my data. For example, the verb *yol* 'pound sago' commonly appears without the Past Durative *d-* in past time contexts in which the onset of the activity is referred to, i.e. 'start pounding sago'. Similarly, the verb *akam* 'drip' occurs in past time without *d-* if it describes a single drop falling (i.e. a punctual situation), as opposed to repeated dripping (a durative situation). The assignment to Drabbe's 4th class — composed of verbs that are compatible with both punctual and durative uses — seems more accurate, despite some spurious members.[2]

---

[1] For a few verbs it seems that Drabbe did not realise that they may combine with e.g. Past Durative *d-* to describe multiple events in the past (this is the case for *ikalen* 'send' and the plural verb *ewah* 'give birth to many'). The verb *bakatok* 'turn upside-down' is a clear error, and should have been assigned to class 3, along with other (caused) position verbs, since it appears with the Extended suffix to encode the state 'be upside-down'.

[2] For example, the verbs *kab* 'open' and *keway* 'break' should have been assigned to Drabbe's class 3 according to my data.

Tab. 14.2: Punctual-durative verb pairs

Punctual		Durative	
umuh	'take off, go'	yet	'be in movement'
ihon	'run away'	umak	'be running'
ambid	'sit down (sg)'	mil	'be sitting (sg)'
yali	'lie down (sg)'	tel	'be lying (sg)'
atin	'stand up'	itala	'be standing'
ihwin	'burst into tears'	ihw	'be crying'
win, ay	'become'	ola	'be'

I am not capable of offering a revised model of aspectual verb classification here, but I will give a brief outline of an approach that I believe is more appropriate for the Coastal Marind data.[3] According to this view, the following five classes capture the main interactions between the tense-aspect affixes described in §14.2 and the semantics of individual verbs. Most verbs would be assigned to the first two classes, and a smaller remainder to the last three.

- *Ingressive activity verbs.* When these verbs appear without any affixes signalling durative situation, they express the onset of an activity, e.g. *yol* 'pound sago, start to pound sago'. With affixes like the Past Durative *d-*, reference is made to the activity phase, i.e. 'was pounding sago, pounded sago (for a while)'.
- *Punctual-resultative verbs.* These verbs express the entry into a state or activity in their base form, and combine with the Extended *-la* to express the corresponding durative situation. Example: *saletok* 'hide', *saletok-a* 'be hidden'. See §14.2.3.1.
- *Durative-only verbs.* A small set of verbs that are incapable of expressing punctual events, e.g. *itala* 'be standing'; cf. Table 14.2.
- *Punctual-only verbs.* A small number of verbs that describe the entry into a state, but lack a corresponding Extended form, e.g. *kahwid* 'die'; in addition, the punctual verbs in Table 14.2.
- *Multiplicative verbs.* Verbs that describe a single semelfactive 'micro-event' if used without any durativising morphology, e.g. *akam* 'drip (once)', but a set of repeated events when affixes like Past Durative *d-* are present ('was dripping').

The most noteworthy feature of this taxonomy is that it lacks anything corresponding to Vendlerian accomplishments, in accordance with the emphasis that Coastal Marind puts on aspectual onsets — to the detriment of endpoints — as discussed in §14.1.1.

Finally, it should be pointed out that any attempt to construct a taxonomy of aspectual classes for Coastal Marind faces the same problem as Vendlerian classification does for any language, viz. the question of what kind of entities (stems, lexemes, uses

---

3 My inspiration for this classification is the aspectual model presented in Tatevosov (2002).

of lexemes, clauses...) should be classified (see e.g. Sasse 2002). It is clear that many verbs that at first sight appear to be straightforwardly assignable to some class have uses that match one of the other classes. For example, the high-frequency verb *ay* 'become' is clearly a punctual-only verb, since it describes an entry into a state and corresponds to the unrelated durative-only verb *ola* 'be' if reference is made to the state itself. However, there is one use of *ay*, in the expression 'become rain, start to rain', in which *ay* behaves like a standard ingressive activity verb, and appears with the Past Duratives *d-* and *-ti* to express the on-going situation 'be raining':

(666) ye   epe   nda-d-ø-i-   ay-ti
       rain(III) there LOC-DUR-3SG.A-RE-   become:III.U-DUR
       'It was raining there again.'   [W11:0429]

Further investigation will without doubt reveal many more similar cases, which complicates the task of aspectual classification.

14.2 Functions of tense-aspect affixes

In this section I provide descriptions of the affixes that were listed in Table 14.1.

14.2.1 The Past Duratives *d-* and *-ti*

The main marker of durative events in the past is the prefix *d-*. The suffix *-ti* seems to have exactly the same function as *d-* and is optionally added to forms containing the prefix *d-*. They are treated separately in the following subsections.

14.2.1.1 The Past Durative prefix *d-*

This prefix is obligatorily present when a past event is presented as having duration. It cannot be used if the event is conceived of as punctual.

The Past Durative is the sole member of position class –12 of the prefixal complex, and is deleted whenever it is immediately followed by a prefix starting with /b/. The following position class (class –11) contains four *b*-initial prefixes (see §15.3) which means that *d-* is often lost. A prefix sequence such as /mend-d-b-/ (PERF-DUR-ACT-) is realised in the Eastern variety (which lacks this deletion rule) as *mendadab-*, whereas the Western variety described in this grammar loses the *d-*, giving *mendab-*. I do not indicate the presence of a deleted *d-* in the morphemic analysis (e.g. by a zero) since it sometimes is difficult to determine whether the Durative has been deleted or whether the event is presented as punctual.

If one of the inherently durative verbs is used in a past time context, *d-* is present, as in the following examples. Such verbs lack the capability of expressing an event as instantaneous, so they cannot be used in past time contexts without *d-*.

(667) inahinah yanid m-an-d-e- na-hwala
 four day OBJ-1.A-DUR-1PL- 1.U-be
 'We stayed for four days.' [W23:0018]

(668) Kolka-puk mbya ø-d-e- nayat
 K.-bivouac NEG NTRL-DUR-2PL.A- be.moving.PL
 'You didn't go to the bivouac in Kolka.' [W11:0671]

(669) epe lay takah nda-d-ø- mil
 there side fire LOC-DUR-3SG.A- be.sitting
 'She was sitting on one side of the fire.' [W11:0354]

The Past Durative *d-* is also obligatory if any affix with a durativising function is present. For example, the Extended *-la* (realised as *-a* after consonant, with stem final *-n* realised as [-t]) converts the punctual verb *kamin* 'make' into the durative 'be making'.

(670) ipe anip senter ma-d-ø- kama⟨h⟩it-a waninggap
 DIST:I/II.PL EMPH:I/II.PL flashlight(m) OBJ-DUR-3SG.A- make⟨2|3PL.U⟩-EXT good
 'They were repairing (lit. making good) the flashlight.' [W11:0131]

The other durativising affixes with which *d-* obligatorily occurs are the Past Habitual *-ma* (§14.2.6.1) and the Continuative *anepand-* (§14.2.4). The Past Durative cannot be omitted if any of these affixes are present and the clause has past time reference.

For verbs that are compatible with both punctual and durative interpretations (without adding durativising affixes such as the Extended *-la*) the Durative *d-* signals that the durative interpretation is intended. An example is the verb *idih* 'see', which can have the punctual meaning 'catch sight of', or 'find', as in (671), or the durative meaning 'watch, look at', as in (672). (In the sense 'look at' the Contessive prefix is added; see §16.5.)

(671) Kaler ø-a- idih kana
 K. NTRL-3SG.A- see:III.U egg(III)
 'Kaler found the eggs.' [W11:0645]

(672) About a Westerner that the speaker had seen in Merauke, and tried to befriend.

  dehi ma-d-a-p- n-idih, mayan mbya ø-ø-na-   ayi
  hard OBJ-DUR-3SG.A-CT- 1.U-see speech NEG NTRL-3SG.A-1.DAT- say

  'He just looked straight at me, he didn't say anything.'

Verbs that describe instantaneous events such as 'jump' and 'blink' occur without *d-* when they refer to single events in the past. However, when such verbs are used to refer to several repetitions of the same punctual event, with each repetition involving the same participant(s), the Past Durative is used. The repetition of punctual events on a single occasion should not be confused with habituals, which describe longer periods that are characterised by events occurring habitually on multiple occasions — see §14.2.6.

(673) About a wallaby.

  ehetagol tinggi e= ka-d-a-p-   ikyalun,
  like.this high(m) PROX= DIR-DUR-3SG.A-CT- jump

  a-da-h-a-p-   ikyalun epe, walak anup
  DEP-DUR-DEP-3SG.A-CT- jump   DIST:III fast EMPH:II

  'It was jumping high like this, when it was jumping, very fast.' [W11:0703]

This use (which also occurs with the Non-Past Imperfective *-e* for present events) is only possible with events that are easily repeatable (e.g. jumping or blinking several times). Punctual, non-repeatable verbs such as *kahwid* 'die' never occur with the Past Durative.

  The use of *d-* is more complicated for punctual events that are distributed over several participants. It seems that forms without *d-* are preferred if the events occur in the same place and at approximately the same time, whereas events that are distributed over different locations and are separated by longer intervals of time usually trigger *d-*. Compare (674), which refers to two women falling to the ground when their sitting platform breaks, to (675), which refers to a wallaby and a pig that were shot by my village brother Ambai. The animals were shot during one hunting occasion, but clearly not at the same time (which would require a single arrow killing two animals), and presumably in two separate spots. Only the latter example uses the Past Durative *d-*, since the events are spread out in time and space.

(674) Repeated from (149).

  isala   ti   ø-ø-e-   hihi-n
  platform(III) with:I/II.PL NTRL-3SG.A-1PL- fall.PLA-1.U

  'We fell with the sitting platform.' [W19:0058]

(675) say   ka-d-ø-   hihi-h
       place DIR-DUR-3SG.A-   fall.PLA-2|3PL.U
       'They fell right in the spot [where they were shot].'   [W11:0769]

Another context in which punctual verbs may occur with the Past Durative *d-* is with mass noun participants. Verbs like *ikyalun* 'jump' and *hawa* 'emerge' are strictly punctual when they describe a single participant jumping once or coming out of a house, but can be presented as durative if they are used to describe events such as blood splashing or smoke coming out (cf. §3.1.3.3).

(676) Commenting on one of the pictures in the Family Problems task.
       ehe   do   ø-d-a-p-   ikyalun isawa
       PROX:III   blood(III) NTRL-DUR-3SG.A-CT- jump   maybe
       'Maybe this blood was splashing.'   [D09:0192]

(677) iwag   upe   nd-ø-um-   w-alaw   ehetago   a,
       woman   DIST:II LOC-3SG.A-FRUS-   3SG.U-open.eyes   like.this PTCL

       lak   a-d-ø-   hawa   epe
       [smoke(III) DEP-DUR-3SG.A-   emerge:3SG.U   DIST:III]
       'The woman looked and surprisingly there was smoke coming out.'
                                                                  [D01:0011]

14.2.1.2 The Past Durative suffix -ti

A verb prefixed with the Past Durative prefix *d-* may optionally be suffixed with *-ti*. This suffix, which I gloss DUR (the same gloss as the synonymous *d-*), belongs to the set of mutually incompatible outer suffixes (§8.5). These are 'outer' since they can attach after the Extended suffix *-la* (*-a* after a consonant), which then is 'inner' as it is suffixed directly to the verb stem:

(678) Kiwi nd-an-d-e-p-   ku-hamat-a-ti
       K.   LOC-1.A-DUR-1PL-CT-   INESS-sit.PL-EXT-DUR
       'We sat inside [the forest] in Kiwi.'   [W11:0787]

I have not found any context in which the presence of *-ti* is obligatory, or where it adds any meaning other than that already contributed by the prefix *d-*.[4] A rough estimate (based on searches with regular expressions) is that the suffix *-ti* is added to somewhere between 10%–15% of the durative forms in my corpus.

---

4 *Pace* Drabbe (1955: 40), who states that *-ti* signals a longer duration than *d-*. Drabbe also claims that three verbs obligatorily occur with *-ti* in the past. These are, in the original Eastern spelling: *mir* 'be

Below are two near-identical clauses from my corpus, spoken by two different speakers at different points in the same recording. There is no meaning difference that explains the use of *-ti* in (679b). Nor is there any difference between different idiolects: both of these two speakers (which are amply represented in my corpus) use past durative forms with and without *-ti*, as do other speakers in my data.

(679) a. *Yakobus mbya ø-d-a- yet*
Y. NEG NTRL-DUR-3SG.A- be.moving
'Yakobus didn't go.' [W11:0393]

b. *kaka Kadoy mbya ø-d-a- yet-ti*
elder.sib(m) K. NEG NTRL-DUR-3SG.A- be.moving-DUR
'Kadoi didn't go.' [W11:0103]

For another near-minimal sentence pair, compare (680) with (669) above.

(680) *epe nda-d-ø- ka-mil-ti*
there LOC-DUR-3SG.A- INESS-be.sitting-DUR
'[The pig] was sitting there.' [W03:0096]

The suffix *-ti* may occur in contexts in which the lexical verb stem is 'moved' out of its position after the verb complex, and placed in the pre-verbal position (i.e. immediately preceding the prefixal complex). The Auxiliary *wa* then obligatorily fills the former site of the stem. Like the other outer suffixes, *-ti* does not move along to the pre-verbal position but stays in the original site, now attached to the Auxiliary:

(681) *n-idih sa-d-ø- w-a-ti*
1.U-see ONLY-DUR-3SG.A- 3SG.U-AUX-DUR
'She was just watching me (not doing anything else).' [W10:0590]

A suffix *-ti* also participates in another stem-preposing construction, but apparently without any durative meaning — see §17.2.3.

14.2.2 The Non-Past Imperfective *-e, -et*

The Non-Past Imperfective *-e* (rarer variant: *-et*) expresses currently on-going events ('I am singing'), events that are about to happen ('I'm going to sing, about to sing')

---

sitting' (Western *mil*), *rik* 'become a river' (Western *lik*) and *amasin* 'be averse, disgusted (?)' (Dutch *vies zijn van*; unattested in my corpus). It is unclear why Drabbe was under this impression: past forms of *mil* without the suffix *-ti* are found later in Drabbe's grammar, e.g. on p. 134, and the verb *lik* 'become a river' is always used with the Extended suffix *-la* in past durative contexts in my own data (giving *lik-a* 'river to flow'), never with *-ti*.

and present habituals ('I usually sing'). It may also be used in forms with the Future prefixes, which is why I label it 'Non-Past' rather than 'Present'. The Non-Past Imperfective (henceforth, the Imperfective) differs from the Past Durative *d-* in its temporal meaning, but also in its aspectual semantics. For example, the Past Durative is obligatory with past states (and all other durative situations in the past), whereas *-e* never occurs with stative verbs formed with the Extended suffix *-la* or with some inherently durative verbs such as *yet* 'be moving' and *ola* 'be'.

The Imperfective is a member of the outer suffix class (§8.5) and attaches after the verb stem:

(682) *awe   ma-n-   yahwiy-e*
       fish   OBJ-3PL.A-   eat-IPFV

'They are eating fish.'

The Imperfective is the only outer suffix with the ability to occur attached to the non-past copula, although it seems completely optional in this context. In present and future time contexts the copula consists of the prefixal complex alone, without any following verb stem (indicated by 'Ø' in the segmentation), as explained in §17.4. When the Imperfective suffix is used with the copula it attaches directly after the prefixes of the prefixal complex:

(683) *Meka   epe   nd-a-   Ø-e?*
       M.   there LOC-3SG.A-   be.NPST-IPFV

'Is Meka there?' [W06:0139]

Alternatively, one can say *epe nda-et* or *epe nda*, with the same meaning.

Like the other outer suffixes the Imperfective does not participate in affixal pied-piping (see §8.5), so it 'stays behind' in cases where the lexical verb stem is moved to the pre-verbal position, and appears suffixed to the verb (hosted by the Auxiliary, which is obligatory in such constructions):

(684) Complaining about how the addressees were drawing water from the well.

  timba   ap   ndom-kuhig   k-e-   y-a-e
  bucket(III) also bad-throw.PLA:III.U PRS.NTRL-2PL.A- 2|3PL.U-AUX-IPFV

'You're throwing the bucket badly!' [W06:0229]

Semantically *-e* is compatible with various kinds of situations that overlap with the present. As stated above, it is used with presently on-going activities, as illustrated in these corpus examples:

(685) People were searching for a rope for drawing water.

isahih   ap   ipa-n-um-e-   y-alaw-e
children also DIST:I/II.PL-3PL.A-FRUS-2|3PL.DAT- 2|3PL.U-search-IPFV

'The children are also searching [for a rope] for you.'   [W06:0163]

(686) Describing a picture from the Family Problems picture task.

ihe   sopi   ma-n-   yi-e
PROX:I/II.PL alcohol(m)(III) OBJ-3PL.A- eat:III.U-IPFV

'Here they are drinking alcohol.'   [D09:0067]

The Imperfective *-e* may combine with verbs expressing momentaneous events such as 'fall', 'die' and 'start' to refer to the preliminal phase leading up to the event itself, i.e. 'be about to fall' or 'be falling' etc. Example (687) is from a recording featuring some children of different ages around a well. The speaker jokingly made a movement as if she were about to push a younger child over the edge and into the well, and made this exclamation.

(687) *a-   ika-hi-e!*
3SG.A- INESS-fall:3SG.U-IPFV

'She's falling into it!'   [W06:0058]

The 'preliminal' use is very common in 1st person contexts to express one's plans for the immediate future, as in the following example, uttered right after I turned on the camera:

(688) *namaya nak-ind-e-   kamak-e   mayan*
now   1.A-ALL-1PL- start-IPFV   speech

'Now we're going to start the story.'   [W15:0001]

Punctual verbs may also occur with the Imperfective *-e* if the punctual event occurs repeatedly. Cf. the use of *d-* for past repeated events, discussed in §14.2.1.

(689) *tabak   k-a-   n-alok-e*
hiccup   PRS.NTRL-3SG.A-   1.U-stab-IPFV

'I'm having hiccups.' (lit. 'hiccups are stabbing me')

(690) *ka-no-   n-a   taman-e   nok*
DIR-1.A- 1.U-AUX fire.arrow-IPFV 1

'I'm shooting arrows.'

The Imperfective *-e* competes with the Present Habitual suffix *-made* (§14.2.6.2) in the expression of habitually occurring events overlapping with the present. I am not aware of any semantic or distributional difference between these two alternatives in habitual contexts (although the Imperfective, of course, is potentially ambiguous between on-going and habitual readings with some verbs). Two examples of the use of *-e* in habitual contexts:

(691) epe ep-ak-e- anik-e epe
[there DIST:III-1.A-1PL- sit.PLA-IPFV DIST:III]
'there where we usually sit' [W11:0231]

(692) ndom-milah k-a- Ø, dino k-a- ay-e yap
bad-village(III) PRS.NTRL-3SG.A- be.NPST dark PRS.NTRL-3SG.A- become:III.U-IPFV night
'It's a bad village, it becomes really dark there at night.' [W19:0356]

Note that verbs used in habitual contexts appear in their Pluractional form (§16.1), if there is such a form for the given verb. In the two preceding examples, 'sit' is expressed by the Pluractional *anik* 'sit repeatedly' instead of the non-Pluractional *haman* 'many to sit down', whereas the verb *ay* 'become' (only used for inanimates in Gender III) lacks a separate Pluractional form.

14.2.3 The Extended *-la*

The Extended suffix is added to the verb stem to form a new stem with a stative or progressive meaning. The stative meaning arises if the base verb describes a change-of-state (e.g. 'be hungry' from a base verb 'become hungry'), and the progressive meaning if the base verb describes the entry into an activity (e.g. 'be running' from a base verb 'start to run'). This use is described in §14.2.3.1. Some other uses are mentioned in §14.2.3.2.

The suffix *-la* is formally and semantically related to the Participial suffix (§3.7.3), which has the shape *-la* in Gender I and III, while the Extended *-la* does not exhibit gender agreement. Also, the Extended (but not the Participial) is usually reduced to *-a* after consonant-final stems,[5] and only the Extended occurs suffixed to a verb stem used in a fully inflected verb complex (the Participial derives adjectives). They are semantically related since they both express resultative meanings, i.e. state-like situations following as the result of some previous dynamic event (Nedjalkov 1988).

---

5 I have recorded reduced and unreduced forms of *-la* after consonants, i.e. *keway-la* 'broken' as well as *keway-a*. The reduced forms are overwhelmingly more common in Wambi, so I have standardised the orthography to show consistent *-a* after consonants. Speakers were divided on this issue.

The Extended suffix is *-la* after a vowel (693a), and *-a* after all consonants (including the glides *w* and *y*) (693b). A stem-final *n* is changed to *t* before *-a* (693c).

(693)

		Base verb	Derived stem	
a.		oha	oha**la**	'be going down to water'
		usu	usu**la**	'be cooked'
b.		betok	betok**a**	'be piled up'
		masud	masud**a**	'be bent'
		kab	kab**a**	'be open'
		walaw	walaw**a**	'keep eyes open'
		luhay	luhay**a**	'be fast asleep'
c.		haman	hama**ta**	'many be sitting'
		gan	ga**ta**	'be listening'

I consider the Extended suffix to be more tightly bound to the stem than the outer suffixes (the inflectional suffixes discussed in §8.5) for three reasons. (i) The Extended suffix triggers a segmental change in the preceding stem, as just seen. None of the Outer suffixes trigger phonological changes in the stem. (ii) Whereas the outer suffixes are mutually exlusive, the Extended may occur between the stem and an outer suffix such as Past Durative *-ti* or Future Habitual *-motok* (§14.2.6.3). (iii) In constructions where the lexical verb stem is 'moved' to the pre-verbal position, the Extended suffix follows along and remains attached to the stem in its new position (694a). Such 'affixal pied-piping' does not occur with outer suffixes such as the Past Durative *-ti*, which remains within the verb complex even when the lexical stem is preposed (694b). For these reasons, the Extended is described as a derivational suffix forming a derived verb stem, and not as an outer suffix attaching after the stem.

(694) a. hamat-a s-an-d-e- na-hwala nok
sit.PL-EXT ONLY-1.A-DUR-1PL- 1.U-be 1
'We were just sitting.' [W16:0041]

b. sayam upe tel sa-d-ø- w-a-ti
wallaby(II) DIST:II be.lying ONLY-DUR-3SG.A- 3SG.U-AUX-DUR
'The wallaby was just lying.' [W12:0135]

14.2.3.1 Resultative use
In its most common use the Extended combines with a verb stem expressing entry into a state or activity to form a verb expressing the resulting durative situation. In the case of entry-into-state verbs this is often accompanied by a change in the valence potential

of the verb, so that a verb that is transitive, or allows both transitive and intransitive uses, only appears intransitively in the Extended form.

Consider the verb *hanituk*. In its base form this verb is used transitively to mean 'lean', i.e. 'cause something to assume a leaning position'. This use is seen in the imperative form in (695a), which can be used e.g. to ask someone to put down a bamboo pole or a bow that they are holding so that it leans against something. (I have not recorded any intransitive use of *hanituk* in its base form.) Contrast this with (695b), which describes a stative situation in which a bamboo pole is leaning. The clause in (695a) is transitive with the handled item as the O-argument, whereas (695b) is intransitive, with the leaning item being the S-argument.

(695) a. suba ah- hanituk!
bamboo IMP- lean
'Lean the bamboo!'

b. The addressee had asked for a bamboo pole:
ep-ø- hanituk-a
DIST:III-3SG.A- lean-EXT
(Pointing:) 'It's leaning over there.' [W06:0156]

The verb *ihon* 'run away, take off running' describes the onset of the activity 'run' in its base form (696a). To describe the on-going activity 'be running' the Extended is added after the stem (696b). (The Locational Orientation *nd-* signals motion away from a source, and the Directional Orientation *k-* describes motion along a path in these examples. See §11.1.4.1, §11.1.5.1),

(696) a. e= nd-a- ihon
PROX= LOC-3SG.A- run.away:3SG.U
'S/he ran from here.' [W03:0090]

b. e= k-a- ihot-a
PROX= DIR-3SG.A- run.away:3SG.U-EXT
'S/he is running along here.' [W11:1129]

We saw in the previous subsections that on-going activities are marked by means of the Past Durative *d-* (in the past) and the Non-Past Imperfective *-e* (in the present and future). Verbs such as *ihon* are an exception to this pattern since they add the Extended *-la* to describe activities. Verbs that behave like *ihon* express past activities by combining *d-* and *-la*, as in (678) above, and present activities by means of *-la* only (the Non-Past Imperfective *-e* may not be added after *-la*). One can generalise by saying that verbs such as *hanituk* 'lean' and *ihon* 'run away' are punctual-resultative: they describe the punctual onset of a durative situation, but lack the ability to express the durative phase resulting from the onset unless they are suffixed by means of *-la*.

Verb forms that express states with a subset of verbs and on-going activities with others are common across languages (e.g. Chafe 1980). In Coastal Marind this is not caused by some sort of polyfunctionality of the Extended suffix, but follows from the fact that verbs like *hanituk* 'lean' describe the entry into a state, whereas verbs like *ihon* 'run away' describe the entry into an activity.

Some other common punctual-resultative verbs are listed in Table 14.3. An attempt has been made to put more state-like verbs in the top part of the table, and more activity-like verbs in the bottom.

Tab. 14.3: Some Extended stems with resultative meaning

Base verb		Extended	
alam	'swell up'	*alam-a*	'be swollen'
ihwim	'become dark'	*ihwim-a*	'be dark'
isik	'become full' (after eating)	*isik-a*	'be full'
wahun	'become hungry'	*wahut-a*	'be hungry'
ipah	'become constipated'	*ipah-a*	'be constipated'
betok	'become pile (itr.), pile up (tr.)'	*betok-a*	'be piled up'
kab	'open (itr./tr.)'	*kab-a*	'be open'
lalid	'close (itr./tr.)'	*lalid-a*	'be closed'
masud	'bend (itr./tr.)'	*masud-a*	'be bent'
tak	'clear (tr.), become empty (itr.)'	*tak-a*	'be empty'
mbin	'flatten (tr.)'	*mbit-a*	'be flat'
kalemed	'put on (garment)'	*kalemed-a*	'be wearing'
samandak	'block off river'	*samandak-a*	'river be blocked'
lik	'become river'	*lik-a*	'river be flowing'
han	'put horizontal item'	*hat-a*	'horizontal item be lying'
hatuk	'cover'	*hatuk-a*	'be covering'
hok	'many lie down'	*hok-a*	'many be lying'
haman	'many sit down'	*hamat-a*	'many be sitting'
ilumun	'kneel down'	*ilumut-a*	'be kneeling down'
mikeh	'turn one's head'	*mikeh-a*	'keep one's head turned'
gan	'hear'	*gat-a*	'be hearing, listening'
saletok	'hide (itr./tr.)'	*saletok-a*	'be hidden/hiding (itr.)'
takin	'start to wait'	*takit-a*	'be waiting'
bik	'grasp vertical item'	*bik-a*	'be holding vertical item'
takad	'open one's mouth'	*takad-a*	'keep one's mouth open'
tapeb	'take off flying'	*tapeb-a*	'be flying'
esoh	'start to follow'	*esoh-a*	'be following'
uhwasig	'go up from water'	*uhwasig-a*	'be walking up from water'
ihon	'run away'	*ihot-a*	'be running'
awan	'many run away'	*awat-a*	'many be running'
kamin	'start making'	*kamit-a*	'be making'

Given the meaning of the base form of a verb it is often possible to predict whether it belongs to the group of verbs that express a present durative situation with *-e* or *-la*. Verbs that belong to the latter type are:
1. Putting verbs, e.g. *bakeh* 'put down vertically oriented item (e.g. a bottle)' > *bakeh-a* 'such item be standing'.
2. Other verbs describing a change-of-state of the S/O-argument, e.g. *alam* 'swell up' > *alam-a* 'be swollen' and *kab* 'open' > *kab-a* 'be open'.
3. Change-of-posture verbs such as *ilumun* 'kneel down' > *ilumut-a* 'be kneeling down'.
4. Body part actions, e.g. *walaw* 'open one's eyes' > *walaw-a* 'keep one's eyes open'.
5. Verbs of grasping and carrying, e.g. *ahwikeh* 'take on one's shoulders' > *ahwikeh-a* 'be carrying on one's shoulders'.
6. Motion verbs, e.g. *dahetok* 'return, turn around' > *dahetok-a* 'be returning, be on the way home'.

There are some non-motion activities that belong to this class, for unknown reasons. An example is the verb *kamin* 'start making', with the Extended form *kamit-a* 'be making'. Note also that *gan* 'hear' is in this class (*gat-a* 'be hearing, be listening') whereas *idih* 'see, look at' is a standard activity verb without an Extended form — despite being a perception verb just like *gan*.

Most other verbs that can express an activity in progress do so without *-la*, e.g. *yahwiy* 'eat', *usak* 'hit, fight', *sasayi* 'work', *mahay* 'dance', and so on.

A small group of frequent verbs turn out to lack Extended forms, despite describing e.g. the onset of motion (*umuh* 'go, take off') or entry into a position (*ambid* 'sit down'). The explanation for this aberrant behaviour is that there happen to exist underived durative verbs that have the same meaning as the expected Extended form of these verbs would have. The existence of these verbs blocks the creation of Extended verb forms to express the same meaning. For example, *ambid* lacks the Extended form *ambid-a 'be sitting', since there is a morphologically unrelated verb *mil* 'be sitting' with precisely that meaning. The full list of such pairs was given in Table 14.2. Several of the inherently durative verbs end in *-l* or *-la* which suggests that they are historically Extended forms whose base form has been lost, e.g. *itala* 'be standing' (< *ita ?).

Finally, it should be pointed out that the classification of verbs as allowing or not allowing suffixation with the Extended to refer to the associated durative situation is a simplification, and that it is the uses of verbs rather than the verbs themselves that should be classified. Some verbs that under normal circumstances do not combine with *-la* may do so when they are used with certain meanings. Verbs of hitting, for example, do not occur with *-la* to express e.g. the state of having been hit (this could be expressed with the Perfect *mend-*). However, there are extended uses of hitting verbs to describe bodily changes-of-state such as 'become hungry' (lit. 'hunger hit me' etc.) or 'become sick' ('sickness hit me'). Such uses readily permit the Extended *-la* to be added to the verb of hitting, in order to describe the resulting state.

(697) tik   k-a-   w-asib-a
     illness PRS.NTRL-3SG.A-   3SG.U-hit-EXT
     'S/he's suffering from illness.'

There are some Extended forms that may have both stative and progressive, activity-like meanings corresponding to different uses of the base verb. This is evident for verbs of putting, many of which are also used with the meaning 'grasp'. For example, *han* may be used to mean either 'put a horizontally oriented object' or 'grasp a horizontally oriented object'. In the former use the corresponding Extended form is used intransitively to describe the state 'be lying' (i.e. 'having been put'), as in (698). In the latter use the Extended form is transitive, and describes the activity of holding something in one's hand (699).

(698) Describing a new road.

   namaya aspal   ep-a-p-   hat-a   epe
   now   asphalt(m)(III) DIST:III-3SG.A-CT-   put:III.U-EXT   there
   'Now asphalt is lying there.'   [W10:0484]

(699) Referring to my video camera.

   epe   namakad   ep-o-   hat-a   epe,   igih   ta
   [DIST:III thing(III) DIST:III-2SG.A-   grasp:III.U-EXT   DIST:III]   name   what
   ka-ha-b-ø-   ø?
   PRS.NTRL-ROG-ACT-3SG.A-   be.NPST
   'That thing that you're holding, what is it called?'   [W11:0210]

There are also uses of Extended forms that do not correspond to any use of the same verb without the Extended suffix. Consider the form *hat-a* 'horizontal object be lying', used to describe a scar in (700). (Scars are classified as horizontally oriented items, as opposed to e.g. skin boils, which are vertically oriented and require the verb *bakeh*). There is no corresponding use of the dynamic base verb *han* 'put a horizontally oriented object' to describe e.g. how the scar came about, since scars are not 'put' on the body (this would be expressed with the verb *ay* 'become').

(700) Child showing an almost healed wound.

   e   sa-p-a-na-   hat-a
   scar(III) ONLY-FUT-3SG.A-1.DAT-   put:III.U-EXT
   'Only the scar will remain on me.'

14.2.3.2 Distributive–ambulative use

The Extended *-la* interacts with plurality and distributivity in ways that remain poorly understood. For some verbs there seems to be a preference to mark a presently ongoing activity by means of Non-Past Imperfective *-e* if the S/O argument is singular, and with *-la* if it is plural. In the past this corresponds to a verb marked with the Past Durative *d-* (in the singular), and a verb marked with both *d-* and the Extended *-la* in the plural (optionally the Past Durative suffix *-ti* can be added to both forms).

For example, a speaker with whom I discussed the difference between the forms *yi-e* (eat-IPFV) and *yi-la* (eat-EXT) suggested that the Imperfective variant is appropriate for describing a pig eating one tuber, whereas the variant with the Extended suffix is better for a pig eating a lots of tubers. Other speakers offered similar comments, although I have not been able to find any clear patterns in the data confirming that this is the relevant distinction. A confounding factor seems to be that the likelihood of speakers using the Extended *-la* with plural S/O arguments seems to be higher if the subject performs the action while moving around (eat one tuber, then move, then eat another, etc.), giving a distributive or ambulative meaning (see also §16.1.4.2 for similar uses of Pluractional forms).

The ambulative use is evident in data such as the following. Example (701) was given to me when I asked a speaker what his daughter was doing as she was walking around, bent over, in the vegetation on the upper beach. In (702) a speaker described how he was killing mosquitos inside his mosquito net, which I imagine involves killing them in different spots. In both examples the Extended *-la* is used, which contrasts with other uses of these and similar verbs in contexts involving no movement. In such contexts the verbs occur unsuffixed (in the past) or with Imperfective *-e* (in the present).

(701) nggalnggamil-nggol m-a-   kepad-a,   yanakeh nanggo
       creeper.sp-leaf(III)   OBJ-3SG.A- break.off:III.U-EXT cook   for
       'She's plucking creeper (sp.) leaves, for cooking.'

(702) nanggit   m-an-d-ap-   kw-i-sak-a
       mosquito OBJ-1.A-DUR-CT- INESS-2|3PL.U-hit.PLA-EXT
       'I was killing mosquitos.'   [W03:0039]

14.2.4 Continuative *anVpand-*

The Continuative prefix *anVpand-* (or *anVpanda-*, before a consonant) expresses that a situation continues longer than one could have expected, i.e. 'keep on Verb-ing' or 'stay Verb-ed'. As indicated by the notation V, the prefix is host to a gender marking vowel, which alternates according to the paradigm in Table 14.4.[6]

Tab. 14.4: Gender forms of the Continuative prefix

	SG	PL
I	anepand-	anipand-
II	anupand-	
III	anepand-	
IV	anipand-	

Almost all corpus attestations of the Continuative are with one-place predicates (in which the prefix agrees with the sole argument), so it is not known which argument triggers agreement with e.g. mono- and ditransitive verbs. Elicited data suggest that any argument of such verbs can act as the agreement controller of the *anepand-*, perhaps based on topicality or some other kind of prominence, but a much larger corpus will be needed to establish this.

The Continuative prefix appears with punctual verbs that have been converted into duratives by means of suffixation with the Extended -*(l)a*, as in (703–704), or with inherently durative verbs such as *nayat* in (705).

(703) Commenting on my video camera.

anepand-a- kab-a epe, ehe mayan
CONT:III-3SG.A- open-EXT DIST:III [PROX:III speech(III)

e-nak-e-p- lay-e epe k-a- kwamin-e
PROX:III-1.A-1PL-CT- tell-IPFV] there DIR-3SG.A- enter:III.U-IPFV

'It stays open, what we are saying now enters there.' [W11:0235]

(704) From an account of sago processing.

wanangga anipanda-d-ø- wayamat-a
children CONT:I/II.PL-DUR-3SG.A- stand.PL-EXT

'The children kept standing [by the washing troughs].' [W19:0192]

---

[6] The Continuative is perhaps diachronically related to the 3rd person emphatic demonstratives *anep* (§4.2), followed by the Locational Orientation prefix *nd-*. The emphatic demonstrative has the same exponents of gender as the Continuative prefix, although it is difficult to see any semantic connection between the two grams.

(705) *Balaw-Mit nanggo anipand-an-d-e- nayat*
B.-M. towards CONT:I/II.PL-1.A-DUR-1PL- be.moving.PL
'We kept walking towards Balaw-Mit.' [W02:0019]

Since the last two examples express durative situations in the past the Past Durative *d-* (§14.2.1) must be present.

The Continuative can combine with verbs that denote punctual events to express that the event keeps repeating, as in the following examples. Again, the verb stem must be followed by a durativising suffix such as the Non-Past Imperfective (§14.2.2) in (706) or the Extended (§14.2.3) in (707) for such readings to be possible.

(706) During a hunt.
pu-suba bangi anepand-a- w-alin-e
rifle sound.of.gun(III) CONT:III-3SG.A- III.U-call-IPFV
'The gun shots keep on sounding.' [M02:0623]

(707) About a man who was grinding his teeth.
manggat lili, lala anepanda-d-ø-o- w-it-a
tooth noise noise CONT:III-DUR-3SG.A-3SG.DAT- III.U-become-EXT
'His teeth kept making noises.' [W10:0151]

The only situation in which a verb prefixed with the Continuative and appearing in a past time context is not also prefixed with the Past Durative *d-* is if the verb stem is followed by the Venitive suffix *-em* 'hither'. (This aspectual peculiarity of the Venitive suffix is described in §16.7.)

(708) *Dadami-Mit mbya ø-nak-e- haman, anipand-ak-e- nayam-em*
D.-M. NEG NTRL-1.A-1PL- sit.PL CONT:I/II.PL-1.A-1PL- come.PL-VEN
'We didn't stop in Dadami-Mit, we kept on walking hither.' [W03:0150]

14.2.5 The Perfect *mend-*

14.2.5.1 Form of the Perfect

The Perfect *mend-* is a multi-class prefix (see §8.3.1), and occurs at the left edge of the prefixal complex. The prefix spans position classes –17 to –14, meaning that the Perfect is incompatible with e.g. the Orientation prefixes (Chapter 11) and the imperative and question-forming prefixes (Chapter 19). The shape *mend-* only occurs before a vowel-initial prefix. Before a consonant, the prefix is *menda-*, with epenthetic /a/, or, if the epenthetic vowel is lost due to Antepretonic Syncope (§2.4.2), *men-* (with /nd/ simplified to [n] in coda position; §2.1.1.1). Examples:

(709) "*muy mak-a-   og*" *ago,* "*ehe yaba-sayam menda-no- w-asib*"
      meat FUT:1.A-2SG.DAT- give QUOT here big-wallaby   PERF-1.A- 3SG.U-hit
      ' "I will give you meat", I said, "I have killed a big wallaby".' [W10:0424]

(710) *nok wanangga men-ba-n-ap-   kw-i-mahid*
      1   children PERF-ACT-3PL.A-CT-   INESS-PLA-become.angry
      'My children had already become angry.' [W19:0330]

The Perfect escapes Antepenultimate heightening of /e/ to *i*. This is seen in (710) above, in which the /e/ of of the Perfect prefix is in the penultimate syllable of the prefixal complex, but is unaffected by gradation (see further §2.5.1).[7]

14.2.5.2 Functions of the Perfect

The Perfect can generally be understood as signalling a previous change-of-state with consequences or relevance for the present. It is commonly used to express that one has performed some action, or is now in a state (tired, hungry, grown-up, etc.), that had not been attained before, and because of this, something will (or will not) happen now. In (709) above, the speaker had killed a wallaby, and because of that he could give the addressee some meat. In (711), Ambai-Iwag was telling her daughter, whom she was weaning, that she's already big, so she can't breastfeed anymore.

(711) *bub   mbya k-ak-ø-   yi-e,   amimil   menda-b-ø-   y-in*
      milk(III) NEG   PRS.NTRL-1.A-1PL- eat:III.U-IPFV grown.up PERF-ACT-3SG.A- 2SG.U-become

      oy
      2SG

      'No, we're not going to drink milk, you are already big.' [W13:0480]

---

[7] The failure to undergo Antepenultimate gradation suggests that *mend-* historically involves a word boundary. A likely origin would be an unknown particle **me* occurring before the Locational Orientation prefix *nd-*, which would explain the incompatibility of *mend-* with Orientation prefixes synchronically. In the closely related Bush Marind, the Perfect is expressed by the seemingly non-cognate prefixes *bed-* and *ah-* (depending on the village), suggesting a relatively recent grammaticalisation of the Perfect. Contrastive examples from my field notes:

(i) Coastal Marind, Wambi variety: *nu **mend**abap- nihwid* ⎫
     Bush Marind, Alatep variety: *nu **bed**ap- nehig*   ⎬ 'I am sleepy'
     Bush Marind, Domande variety: *nu **ah**ap- nehig*   ⎭

It is useful to contrast the meaning of the Perfect with that of the Extended *-la*, since both can express a stative situation, but with the difference that the Extended only asserts the state itself, without presupposing a change-of-state. Consider the sentences in (712). The utterance in (712a), which uses the Perfect, is the usual way of announcing during a meal that one has had enough food, that the others can finish the rest of the food, etc. The utterance in (712b) would not be used in this context. A typical context for (712b) is the following: I was sitting eating some sago when one of the boys in the family walked past. I asked if he would like to share the sago with me. He declined and uttered (712b).

(712) a. *tis ka,   men-b-a-na-p-   isik*
         that's.it PERF-ACT-3SG.A-1.DAT-CT- become.full
         'That's it, I'm full.'

   b. *k-a-na-p-   w-a   isik-a*
      DIR-3SG.A-1.DAT-CT- 3SG.U-AUX become.full-EXT
      'I'm full.'

The difference between (712a–b) is that for (712a), the change from the preceding state (not being full) is relevant for the present, because one can now do something that was not possible before (stop eating). For (712b) the change-of-state is irrelevant. What matters is that the speaker is presently full; whether there was a preceding state of not being full does not matter for the purpose of declining the sago. The change-of-state meaning of the Coastal Marind Perfect often translates as *already*, a feature that is familiar from other perfect-like markers, especially in languages of South-East Asia (Olsson 2013, Dahl and Wälchli 2016).

The meaning of the Perfect makes it especially frequent in contexts expressing change reached through accumulation of some property, e.g. 'become ripe' or 'become big':

(713) *napet-eho,   eho   menda-b-ø-am-   ay*
      banana.sp(III) ripe:III PERF-ACT-3SG.A-2SG.GEN- become:III.U
      'Your bananas, they're already ripe.'   [W11:0477]

(714) About a pig.

   papes-yaba   menda-b-ø-   w-in,   gomna
   small-big   PERF-ACT-3SG.A- 3SG.U-become tusk(III)

   menda-b-ø-o-   hawa
   PERF-ACT-3SG.A-3SG.DAT- emerge:III.U
   'It was already pretty big, its tusks had already come out.'   [W11:0526-0527]

The Perfect is not sensitive to the time reference of the clause, so it can be used to refer to a present situation (as in the preceding examples) or to a situation that held in the past:

(715) adaka ti   ø-d-a-   ola, adaka menda-b-ø-e-   daha⟨n⟩ip
      water with   NTRL-DUR-3SG.A- be:III.U water PERF-ACT-3SG.A-1PL- become.thirsty⟨1.U⟩
      'They were filled with water, and we were already thirsty [so we drank].'
      [W10:0105]

(716) yah namaya e=   ka-d-na-   hwetok ago, "anup Bakaluk
      but now   PROX-DIR-DUR-3PL.A- think   QUOT EMPH:II B.

      up-ø-   Ø-e",   padahal Bakaluk menda-b-ø-   umuh
      DIST:II-3SG.A- be.NPST-IPFV in.fact(m) B. PERF-ACT-3SG.A- go:3SG.U
      'Now they thought: "That must be Bakaluk", but in fact Bakaluk had already left.'
      [W11:0284]

The Perfect can combine with the Future prefixes to refer to a change-of-state that will have occurred in the future (717).

(717) The speaker was explaining the difference between *kanis* 'betelnut' and *kahos* 'chewed betelnut, betel mush'.

      ka-mo-   y-a   kababuy-a,   epe   kahos
      DIR-FUT:2SG.A- 2SG.U-AUX immerse.in.water-EXT DIST:III betel.mush(III)

      menda-me-b-ø-   ay
      PERF-FUT-ACT-3SG.A- become:III.U
      'You'll soak it (in your saliva), then it will already have become *kahos* ['betel mush'].'
      [W13:0445]

Most attestations of the Perfect followed by a Future prefix are in contexts describing habitual sequences of events, as in (718), which is a part of an explanation of how to cook in a leaf oven. Such clauses do not necessarily involve future time reference, because they may be used for habitual sequences that only took place in the past (e.g. headhunting) as well as presently occurring habits. See further §14.2.7.6 for the use of the Future to express habitually occurring sequences of events.

(718) imu   a-me-ø-   hawa   epe,
      smell(III) DEP-FUT-3SG.A-   emerge:III.U DIST:III

      menda-me-b-ø-   usu
      PERF-FUT-ACT-3SG.A- become.cooked:III.U
      'When the smell appears, it will already be cooked.'

An important difference between the Coastal Marind Perfect and the English *have V-ed* Perfect follows from the emphasis that Coastal Marind puts on the onset, or initial boundary, of activities. If a verb such as *atug* 'scrape coconuts' is marked with the Perfect, it does not mean 'X has already scraped coconuts' but rather 'X has already started scraping coconuts' or simply 'X is scraping coconuts'. A corpus example is in (719), from a story. The speaker is urging the addressee to join some villagers to help them scrape coconuts for a feast. The context makes it clear that the activity is still on-going, because later when the addressee joins them, they are still scraping.

(719) anim menda-b-na- atug kumbu
people PERF-ACT-3PL.A- scrape.coconuts coconut
'People are already scraping coconuts.' [W19:0012]

To make it explicit that the final boundary of an activity has been crossed, one can use the verb *balen* 'finish':

(720) mend-am-b-e-p- i-balen kumbu atug,
PERF-1.A-ACT-1PL-CT- PLA-finish:III.U coconut(III) scrape.coconuts

te-nd-a-p- hu-h ipe
GIV:III-LOC-3SG.A-CT- emerge-2|3PL.U DIST:I/II.PL

'We had already finished scraping the coconuts, that's when they arrived.'
[W19:0199]

The Perfect usually occurs in combination with the Actualis *b-*, which seems to contribute very little meaning to the combination — see §15.3.1.

14.2.5.3 A perfect-like use of participles

In §3.7.3 I discussed participles, i.e. adjectival forms derived from verbs by means of the suffix *-la/-lVk*.

There is some evidence suggesting that participles predicated by the copula have come to occupy a special niche within the tense-aspect system of Coastal Marind, similar perhaps to the so-called 'hot news' use of the English Perfect (as in *Bill has just arrived*; Comrie 1976: 60). The crucial difference between this use and the adjectival uses of participles is that the participle does not have a strictly resultative meaning here, but rather one of temporal recency, which makes it possible to use participles derived from verbs without a clear end-result (e.g. 'dance') in this construction.

The following observed example clarifies this. One evening outside my house in Wambi, I met one of the daughters in my host family, and I asked where she was coming from. Her answer used the participle *mahay-luk*, which surprised me, since I thought that this unfamiliar construction must mean something like 'I am danced'. Context made it clear, however, that she meant that she was returning from the dance celebration that was taking place in another part of the village, and that she had been dancing there before returning. Since the Participial suffixes -*la* and -*lVk* likely originated from the postposition *lek* 'from' (cf. §3.7.3), a good literal translation of this construction would perhaps be 'I am from dancing'.[8]

(721) mahay-luk ka-ø- Ø nok
 dance-PTCP:II PRS.NTRL-1.A- be.NPST 1
 'I (female) just danced.'

Another instance of the same use is in the following example, which was volunteered by a speaker when I asked for an example with the verb *alam* 'swell up'. The literal translation in this case would be 'we are from fighting'.

(722) wahani k-a-na-y- w-a alam-a, na-sak-lik
 body DIR-3SG.A-1.DAT-1PL- 3SG.U-AUX swell.up-EXT RCPR-fight-PTCP:I/II.PL
 k-ak-e- Ø nok
 PRS.NTRL-1.A-1PL- be.NPST 1
 'Our bodies are swollen, [because] we were fighting just now.'

14.2.6 The Habituals

Habituals "describe a situation which is characteristic of an extended period of time" (Comrie 1976: 27–28), a definition that covers most uses of the suffixes -*ma* and -*made*, which are used for such situations in the past and present respectively. These make a triad with the suffix -*motok*, which I tentatively label the Future Habitual, although as explained in the last subsection its function is less well understood than the functions of the other two. The three suffixes are members of the outer suffix group (§8.5).

14.2.6.1 Past Habitual -*ma*

The suffix -*ma* serves to express a habitual situation holding in the past. Since habituals always describe multiple events, the Pluractional form (§16.1) of the verb is typically used, if the verb has such a form. Corpus examples:

---

[8] This is reminiscent of the famous *be after*-Perfect of Irish English, with similar semantics.

(723) From a description of traditional *wati* [kava] agriculture.

epe mandin gogo, gogo
DIST:III long.ago sun.shade(III) sun.shade

ø-da-n- k-i-hwagib-ma
NTRL-DUR-3PL.A- WITH-PLA-put.away:III.U-PST.HAB

'In the old days [it was] a sun shade, they put the [kava] away using a sun shade.' (i.e. to protect the plants from sunshine) [W04:0134]

(724) From a story about Stork (*ndik*), the ancestor of the Ndikend clan.

nok amay epe, e= nda-d-a-p- huhu-ma,
1 ancestor(I) DIST:I PROX= LOC-DUR-3SG.A-CT- emerge.PLA:3SG.U-PST.HAB

epe nda-d-ø- lemed-ma, Ndalil
there LOC-DUR-3SG.A- stand.PLA-PST.HAB Nd.

'My ancestor, he used to travel down from here, and he used to land there, in Ndalil.' [D11:0001-0003]

(725) *yahun a-d-a-p- kw-anik-ma*
[canoe DEP-DUR-3SG.A-CT- INESS-sit.PLA-PST.HAB]

'(the boatsman,) the one who used to sit in the boat' [W10:0123]

Many verbs lack a Pluractional stem, and thus appear in their usual shape in habitual contexts. This is the case for *hus* 'cross river' in (726). Note also that the verb *ola* occurs without the Past Habitual suffix *-ma*. It appears that habitual marking is used only if the verb describes repeated events that characterise a period, not when it describes a stative situation lasting throughout a period.

(726) Describing a place near the village Urumb, where there is a bridge nowadays.

Palputi, mandin Palputi ø-d-a- ola,
P. long.ago P. NTRL-DUR-3SG.A- be:III.U

epe ka-d-na- hus-ma mandin
there DIR-DUR-3PL.A- cross.river-PST.HAB long.ago

'Palputi, in the old days it was [called] Palputi, they used to cross the river there in the old days.' [W10:0500-0501]

The distinction between past and present habituals is not found in the Eastern variety of Coastal Marind, which uses *-made* for both past and present (Drabbe 1955: passim).

14.2.6.2 Present Habitual *-made*

The suffix *-made* has the same habitual meaning as *-ma*, but is used when the period associated with the habitual activity overlaps with the present. It is unclear what the morphological relationship between -*ma* and -*made* is; there is no suffix *-*de*, so further segmentation of -*made* is not possible. It seems that -*made* is always interchangeable with the Non-Past Imperfective -*e*, which also may serve to express habituality, among various other meanings (§14.2.2).

As with the Past Habitual -*ma*, a verb suffixed with -*made* typically occurs in its Pluractional form (§16.1), if it has such a stem. This is seen in (727): the verbs 'go' and 'become' are expressed by the Pluractional forms *yum* 'go repeatedly (2|3PL.U)' and *enggat* 'become repeatedly (2|3PL.U)'. A few verbs can appear in habitual contexts in either their Pluractional or non-Pluractional form, without any known meaning difference. Compare 'hide' in (728), using the non-Pluractional stem *salituk*, with example (583) on p. 333, in which Pluractional *uslituk* appears.

(727) The speaker is complaining about two elderly women, who had been scared out of their wits when he and some other teenage boys played a prank on them in the village, at night. How come they are so afraid when they are in the village, he asks, yet they are not afraid to go far away looking for food.

yah dak   ip-ø-   y-um-made,
but fish.with.rod DIST:I/II.PL-3SG.A- 2|3PL.U-go.PLA-PRS.HAB

ukna mbya k-a-p-   e-nggat-made
fear NEG PRS.NTRL-3SG.A-CT- 2|3PL.U-become.PLA-PRS.HAB

'But when they go fishing, then they're never afraid.'   [W11:0255]

(728) An elderly man speculating about why young men spend so much time hunting in the bush, but rarely return with any meat.

ihus   m-e-   sal⟨i⟩tuk-made   deg   epe nd-ah-e-   ø
wives:2|3PL OBJ-2PL.A-   hide⟨2|3PL.U⟩-PRS.HAB forest [there LOC-DEP-2PL.A- be.NPST]

'You hide your mistresses in the forest, there where you are.' [W11:0816]

It was already pointed out above that verbs that lack a Pluractional counterpart appear in their standard form with -*made*. The verb *ay*, which is used with inanimates (of Gender III) to express 'become', has no Pluractional stem and may therefore appear freely in habitual contexts (729). Compare this with the verb *win* 'become', used for animates (and inanimates of Gender IV), whose Pluractional stem *enggat* was seen in (727) above.

(729) The addressee had opined that pig manure does not smell very bad, because pigs eat a lot of different things. The speaker replied sarcastically:

ee   yah yel ya ka-bat-ø-   ay-made
EXCLAM PTCL tasty real PRS.NTRL-AFF-3SG.A- become:III.U-PRS.HAB

'Oh yes, it usually becomes very tasty.'   [W11:0897]

14.2.6.3 Future Habitual *-motok*

The functions of the suffix *-motok* are less clear than those of the two preceding suffixes. The tentative labelling of it as a 'future habitual' is partly based on its formal and paradigmatic relatedness with the other habituals *-ma* and *-made*, but it also seems to have various non-habitual functions. The habitual use of *-motok* is clearest with verbs marked with one of the Future prefixes (§14.2.7). Consider first the data (730), which was volunteered to me while working on Dative indexing. The speaker's intuition about the contribution of *-motok* is given in (730b).

(730) a. *epe nda-p-o-   sasayi-e*
         there LOC-FUT:1.A-3SG.DAT- work-IPFV
         'I'm going to be working for him/her there.'

  b. *epe nda-p-o-   sasayi-motok*
     there LOC-FUT:1.A-3SG.DAT- work-FUT.HAB
     [Speaker's comment: "You work again and again, work for a long time."]

The following corpus example is also consistent with a future habitual analysis:

(731) A speaker joking (?) about what to do with my camera when I leave the field.
   nok   ka-mo-na-   yad⟨e⟩wn,   mano-   poto-motok   yah
   1   DIR-FUT:2SG.A-1.DAT- leave⟨III.U⟩ FUT:1.A- take.picture(m)-FUT.HAB PTCL
   'You should leave it for me, [then] I will be taking pictures.'   [W11:0216]

However, *-motok* also combines with inherently durative verbs such as *ola* 'be' (732) and *nayat* 'many be moving' (733) to express non-habitual, state-like situations in the future.[9] These examples do not use the Future prefixes. There are no corresponding uses of the Past and Present Habituals *-ma*/*-made*.

(732) Referring to a feast that was going to take place a couple of weeks later.
   epe   Bruno ndom   k-o-   ya-hwala-la-motok   ehe nde ehe
   DIST:III B.   still PRS.NTRL-2SG.A- 2SG.U-be-EXT-FUT.HAB   here at PROX:III
   'That [date], Bruno you are still going to be here.'   [W19:0446]

---

9 Drabbe considers the cognate suffix *-moto* in the Eastern variety of Coastal Marind to be a marker of durative proximate future, and contrasts its use with that of the Non-Past Imperfective *-e* (1955: 42–43). Drabbe claims that the Non-Past Imperfective *-e* combined with the verb 'tie' would be used for e.g. 'We're about to tie a knot' (this is what I call the preliminal phase use of the Imperfective, see §14.2.2), whereas the same verb with *-moto* would express e.g. 'We're going to tie a fence'. I believe this rigid emphasis on punctual/durative (or short/long duration) is something of an oversimplification. Drabbe also claims that *-moto* is used exclusively in the future, but there is a textual example of past use in one of his texts (p. 163).

(733) mesiwag   ay,   alil   k-ak-e-   ka-nayat-motok
       old.woman VOC   slow   PRS.NTRL-1.A-1PL- WITH-be.moving.PL-FUT.HAB
       'Auntie, we're going to be walking slowly.'   [W21:0252]

The suffix -*motok* is occasionally used in past time contexts in narratives, as in the next example. This use does not involve habituality (or durativity), so it is completely unclear what function -*motok* has in these structures.

(734) nd-a-   ka-timin-motok,   lampu epe   k-a-   kwagin
       LOC-3SG.A- INESS-wake.up-FUT.HAB lamp(III) there DIR-3SG.A- throw:III.U
       'Then he woke up, and threw the lamp over there.'   [W11:0092]

14.2.7 The Futures

Coastal Marind has two sets of Future prefixes, labelled the General Future (or simply Future, glossed FUT) and the Non-Asserted Future (glossed NAFUT). These labels are intended as rough mnemonic aids, and do not capture all of their uses. The main functions of the two categories can be summarised as follows:
- General Future
   i. Future events in general (predictions, intention, desire): 'I will/am going/want to Verb'
   ii. Future conditionals
- Non-Asserted Future
   i. Negated future 'I will not Verb'
   ii. Apprehensive 'I might Verb/lest that I Verb'

The Futures also occur in non-future contexts to describe sequences of habitually occurring events 'I would do X, then I would do Y'. This, and other functions are discussed in §14.2.7.3 to §14.2.7.6. Before that, the formal realisation of the Futures, which involves various complicated processes, is described in §14.2.7.1 and §14.2.7.2.

14.2.7.1 Form of the General Future

The General Future is described here as belonging to position class –13, along with the 1st and 2nd person Actor prefixes. An example supporting this assignment is provided in (735); an extra line has been added to show the phonemic representation of the affixes (separated by blanks for clarity). The General Future prefix *p*- undergoes Plosive Nasalisation (§2.5.2) before *b*-, surfacing as *m*-. It is preceded by the Interrogative prefix *h*- (of position class –14) and followed by the modal prefix *b*- (of class –11). The Future prefixes do not combine with Past Durative *d*- (of position class –12); I consider this incompatibility purely semantic, so it does not affect the assignment to position classes.

(735) ta   nda- ha- m-   b-   e-   sasayi
           /nd-   h-   p-   b-   e-/
     what LOC- ROG- FUT:1.A- ACT- 1PL- work
     'When are we going to work?'

(In this example the combination *ta* 'what' and the Locational Orientation *nd-* expresses 'what time' — see §19.3.2.3.)

The General Future prefixes that are used together with 1st and 2nd person Actors (i.e. the Actors that are indexed in position class –13) conflate future tense marking with Actor indexing (i.e., the prefixes are portmanteaux), whereas the expression of future tense combined with 3rd person Actor indexing (which is realised in position class –10) allows morphemic segmentation since the two categories are realised in separate position classes. The allomorphy of the General Future is more complicated than other inflectional prefixes, and shares some forms with the Non-Asserted Future (discussed in §14.2.7.2).

The allomorphs used with a 2nd person Actor are more straightforward than the 3rd and 1st person forms, and will be discussed first. I distinguish between the heavy and light allomorphs:

	Heavy form	Light form
2SG.A	ndamo-	-mo-
2PL.A	ndame-	-me-

The light form of the General Future is used after another prefix (736); elsewhere, the heavy form (augmented with the formative *nda-*) is used (737).

(736) emba   ka-mo-   i-lawewn
      side   DIR-FUT:2SG.A- PLA-put
      'You (sg) will put them on the side.'   [W06:0119]

(737) ndame-bat-   dahetok
      FUT:2PL.A-AFF- return
      'You (pl) will return home.'   [W09:0134]

When the General Future co-occurs with a 3rd person agent, its allomorphs do not vary according to number. Recall that 3rd person actors are indexed in position class –10 of the prefixal template, and because the Future prefixes and the 3rd person prefixes are realised in different prefix slots they have not coalesced into portmanteau prefixes.

Unlike the 2nd person forms, the allomorphs used with a 3rd person Actor vary according to the right-side context: forms ending in *me-* are used immediately before the right boundary of the prefixal complex (symbolised by means of '#'), or if only a prefix of the shape -C- intervenes (i.e. the 3PL.A prefix *n-* or the Actualis prefix *b-*); if any other prefix follows the General Future, allomorphs ending in *p-* are used.

	Context	Heavy form	Light form
(3SG/PL.A)	_#, _C#	ndame-	-me-
	elsewhere	ndap-	-p-

Corpus data illustrating the heavy forms of the General Future combined with 3rd person Actors are in (738–739); the light forms are found in examples (740–741).

(738) ndame-ø- kw-ambid
 FUT-3SG.A- INESS-sit
 '(The water) will settle.' [W06:0181]

(739) ndap-a-p- y-idih-e
 FUT-3SG.A-CT- 2SG.U-see-IPFV
 'He will watch you.' [W06:0069]

(740) ka-me-n- y-a y⟨u⟩nakeh-e
 DIR-FUT-3PL.A- 2|3PL.U-AUX cook⟨PLA⟩-IPFV
 'Then they will be cooking.' [W04:0033]

(741) a-p-ø-a- ayi
 [DEP-FUT-3SG.A-2SG.DAT- say]
 'if he says so to you' [D03:0013]

The allomorphs used in the 1st person display the same contextual sensitivity as the 3rd person forms. Note that the light forms are identical with allomorphs from the paradigms of the 2nd (*-mo-*) and 3rd (*-p-*) persons, while the heavy forms differ from the heavy forms seen above (which involved a formative *nda-*) but are identical to the common sequences of the Object Orientation prefix (*m-*) and the regular 1st person Actor prefixes (*no-* and *ak-*) — it is as if the General Future paradigm of the 1st person has been assembled by recycling parts of other paradigms:

	Context	heavy form	light form
1.A	_#, _C#	mano-	-mo-
	elsewhere	mak-	-p-

Corpus data illustrating the allomorphy are in (742–745). Note that plurality of a 1st person argument is indexed separately by the prefix *e-* (of position class –4, cf. §9.5), which means that the allomorphs in the upper row (*mano-* and *mo-*) never occur with a 1pl Actor.

(742) mano-   y-amuk
      FUT:1.A- 2SG.U-hit
      'I will kill you.'   [D11:0016]

(743) mak-e-   dahetok
      FUT:1.A-1PL- return
      'We will return.'   [W23:0030]

(744) e=   ka-mo-   asik
      PROX= DIR-FUT:1.A- hunt
      'I will hunt here.'   [W01:0053]

(745) epe   ka-p-e-   uma⟨n⟩ah
      there DIR-FUT:1.A-1PL-   go⟨1.U⟩
      'We will go there.'   [W03:0159]

All allomorphs of the General Future that end in plosives (e.g. 1st person *mak-*, 3rd person *ndap-*) undergo Plosive nasalisation (§2.5.2) before prefixes with initial *b-* (746–747).

(746) mam-bat-e-   uma⟨n⟩ah
      FUT:1.A-AFF-1PL-   go⟨1.U⟩
      '(Poor us,) we are leaving.'   [W03:0016]

(747) ndam-bat-ø-   kahwid
      FUT-AFF-3SG.A-   die:3SG.U
      'He will die (poor one).'

An example paradigm of the General Future with the verb *kab* 'open (e.g. a door)' in various morphological combinations is given in Table 14.5.

14.2.7.2 Form of the Non-Asserted Future

The Non-Asserted Future is best described as a multi-class prefix set, since its members are mutually exclusive with all prefixes in classes –16 to –12. The use of these prefixes (mainly expressing negated future) is described in §14.2.7.

The Non-Asserted Future prefixes partly look like simplified versions of the General Future counterparts:

Context	1	2SG	2PL	3
_#, _C#	*mano-*	*mo-*	*me-*	*me-*
elsewhere:	*mank-*	*mo-*	*me-*	*mak-*

The main differences with the General Future (as discussed in the previous subsection) are the absence of the formative *nda-* and the *p-*allomorphs, and the presence of a 1st person allomorph *mank-* and 3rd person allomorph *mak-*. The allomorphs of the top row are used when the Non-Asserted Future is followed by no other prefixes, or, in the case of 3rd person, when it is followed by 3PL.A *n-*.[10] The reason for the resemblance between the 3rd person *mak-*allomorphs and the General Future 1st person allomorph *mak-* is unknown.

The Non-Asserted Future also differs from the General Future in not having special allomorphs triggered by preceding prefixes. The only prefix that may be present before the Non-Asserted Future is the Given prefix of class –17, exemplified in (748).

(748) *ipe   ti-mak-an-o-p-   esak*
      DIST:I/II.PL GIV:I/II.PL-NAFUT-3PL.A-3SG.DAT-CT- break.off
      'Those were the ones who would break up [the soil].'   [W04:0061]

A paradigm with the verb *kab* 'open' is in Table 14.6.
The following subsections describe the functions of the two Futures.

14.2.7.3 General Future marking future events

The General Future prefixes mark various types of future situations: e.g. future conditionals/predictions (749), intentions (750), and ability (751).

(749) *bekay k-a-p-a-p-   y-alok,   ka-me-ø-   w-a   kahi⟨y⟩ad*
      [heart DIR-DEP-FUT-3SG.A-CT- 2SG.U-stab] DIR-FUT-3SG.A- 3SG.U-AUX die⟨2SG.U⟩
      'If [a cow] stabs you in the heart, you will die.'

(750) *nok e=   k-ak-e-   n-a   ayi, mano-   i-sak   yoy*
      1   PROX= DIR-1.A-2|3PL.DAT-   1.U-AUX say   FUT:1.A-   2|3PL.U-hit.PLA   2PL
      'I said like this to them: "I'm going to hit you".'   [W10:0210]

---

[10] The only other prefix of the shape C-, the Actualis prefix *b-*, is not attested with the Non-Asserted Future.

Tab. 14.5: The General Future.
a. Future/Actor marking; b. Future preceded by Dependent *a(h)*-; c. Future followed by 3sg Dative *o*-;
d. Future preceded by Dependent *a(h)*- and followed by 3sg Dative *o*-.
The prefix *e-/y-* in the 1pl column is described in §9.5.

	1SG	1PL	2SG	2PL	3SG	3PL
a.	*mano- kab* 'I will open'	*mak-e- kab* 'we will open'	*ndamo- kab* 'you will open'	*ndame- kab* 'you will open'	*ndame-ø- kab* 's/he will open'	*ndame-n- kab* 'they will open'
b.	*a-mo- kab* 'if I open'	*a-p-e- kab* 'if we open'	*a-mo- kab* 'if you open'	*a-me- kab* 'if you open'	*a-me-ø- kab* 'if s/he opens'	*a-me-n- kab* 'if they open'
c.	*mak-o- kab* 'I will open for him/her'	*mak-o-y- kab* 'we will open for him/her'	*ndam-o- kab* 'you will open for him/her'	*ndame-o- kab* 'you will open for him/her'	*ndap-ø-o- kab* 's/he will open for him/her'	*ndap-an-o- kab* 'they will open for him/her'
d.	*a-p-o- kab* 'if I open for him/her'	*a-p-o-y- kab* 'if we open for him/her'	*a-m-o- kab* 'if you open for him/her'	*a-me-o- kab* 'if you open for him/her'	*a-p-ø-o- kab* 'if s/he opens for him/her'	*a-p-an-o- kab* 'if they open for him/her'

Tab. 14.6: The Non-Asserted Future. With *mbya* 'NEG'.
a. Non-Asserted Future/Actor marking; b. Non-Asserted Future followed by 3sg Dative *o*-.
For 1pl *e-/y-*, see §9.5.

	1SG	1PL	2SG	2PL	3SG	3PL
a.	*mbya mano- kab* 'I will not open'	*mbya mank-e- kab* 'we will not open'	*mbya mo- kab* 'you will not open'	*mbya me- kab* 'you will not open'	*mbya me-ø- kab* 's/he will not open'	*mbya me-n- kab* 'they will not open'
b.	*mbya mank-o- kab* 'I will not open for him/her'	*mbya mank-o-y- kab* 'we will not open for him/her'	*mbya m-o- kab* 'you will not open for him/her'	*mbya me-o- kab* 'you will not open for him/her'	*mbya mak-ø-o- kab* 's/he will not open for him/her'	*mbya mak-an-o- kab* 'they will not open for him/her'

(751) The speaker was struggling to remember a term relating to traditional kava agriculture.

pu-igih	en	mak-e-	lu,	yah	malin-igih	m-ak-um-	hwetok
Indo.-name	INSTR	FUT:1.A-1PL-	call:III.U	but	Marind-name	OBJ-1.A-FRUS-	think

'We can call it by the Indonesian name, but I'm trying to think of the Marind name.' [W04:0121]

It is very common to use the 2nd person Actor forms of the General Future to formulate commands. Such commands are less direct than commands formed with the Imperative *ah-* (§19.1.1), and often sound more like a suggestion.

(752) The speaker invited some passers-by to join the recording session.

manemna	ndame-p-	lay,	e=	ka-me-	ku-haman
story	FUT:2PL.A-CT-	speak	PROX=	DIR-FUT:2PL.A-	INESS-sit.PL

'You should tell stories, you should sit down here.' [W18:0001]

The General Future can express desire, 'want to V'. Example (753) reports the speech of some villagers who had been inland for a few days. The context suggest that the clause expresses desire rather than intention, and in the next line another villager gives permission, saying 'Return to the beach!'. Other ways of rendering English *want* are indirect speech (§20.2.2), and the Frustrative (for thwarted desire, §15.2).

(753)
ado,	nok	hyuw	ya	k-a-	∅	nok	ehe,
alas	1	long.time	real	PRS.NTRL-3SG.A-	be.NPST	1	PROX

duh	mak-e-	idih-e
beach(III)	FUT:1.A-1PL-	see:III.U-IPFV

'Oh, we've been here for a really long time, we want to see the coast.' [W21:0246]

Note that the Non-Past Imperfective (§14.2.2), and not the General Future, is used to describe imminent future, as when an event is in its preliminary phase, i.e. about to happen.

14.2.7.4 Non-Asserted Future marking negated future

To express that something is not going to take place the standard negator *mbya* (§18.4.1) is used in combination with the Non-Asserted Future prefixes (754–755).

(754)
epe	mbya	me-ø-	man
DIST:I	NEG	NAFUT-3SG.A-	come

'He is not going to come.' [W19:0369]

(755) makan mbya mank-e- haman, nggat otih k-a- ∅
ground NEG NAFUT:1.A-1PL- sit.PL dog many PRS.NTRL-3SG.A- be.NPST

'We can't sit on the ground, there are [too] many dogs.' [W20:0211]

The only context in which a negated verb takes the General Future prefixes instead of the Non-Asserted Future is in negated future conditionals. The Non-Asserted Future does not occur in subordinate clauses.

14.2.7.5 Non-Asserted Future in apprehensional contexts

The other main use of the Non-Asserted Future is in what has been called apprehensional contexts (Dixon 1977, Lichtenberk 1995), i.e. clauses expressing some unpleasant or unwanted event that might happen unless steps are taken to avoid it. In (756) the speaker suggests letting the pig run to avoid getting killed by it.

(756) From a hunting story. The hunters encounter a large boar but decide not to pursue it.

yaba-basik k-a- ∅, mawta ka, mak-ø-e- n-asak
big-pig PRS.NTRL-3SG.A- be.NPST never.mind NAFUT-3SG.A-1PL- 1.U-hit.PLA

'It's a big pig, never mind it, it might kill us.' [W11:0988]

Such apprehensional clauses are often combined with some other clause indicating the kind of action that should be undertaken to avoid the unpleasant event, e.g. *make-umanah* 'Let's go' in (757). The apprehensional clause can be rendered in English as 'it might Verb', or, perhaps more idiomatically, 'so that X doesn't Verb' (more archaically: 'lest X Verb'). Note, however, that the apprehensional clause is a fully independent clause, and shows no signs of being subordinate to the preceding clause. It is also very common to hear apprehensional clauses with the interjection *way!* 'Watch out, careful!', as in (758).

(757) mak-e- uma⟨n⟩ah, katane me-ø- ay yap
FUT:1.A-1PL- go⟨1.U⟩ sun(III) NAFUT-3SG.A- become:III.U night

'Let's go, it might become dark.'
'Let's go, so that it doesn't become dark.' [W21:0110]

(758) way! me-ø- ya⟨y⟩ab!
EXCLAM NAFUT-3SG.A- slip⟨2SG.U⟩

'Careful! You might slip!'
'Careful! So that you don't slip!'

It seems that the Non-Asserted Future leaves it somewhat open whether the menacing event will happen or not, as captured by the word 'might' in the free translations. The pig in (756) above will perhaps kill the hunters, or maybe it won't — in any case it is not worth the risk. Speakers sometimes choose to present the unpleasant event as unavoidable by using the General Future instead, as in (759). The participants were looking for a bamboo pole for climbing down a well, in order to clean it.

(759) Reply to: "You can climb down without a bamboo pole."

  ane!   mbaymbay   k-a-   Ø,
  EXCLAM   unable   PRS.NTRL-3SG.A-   be.NPST

  hayaw   ka-p-ø-a-   kagub
  bone(III) DIR-FUT-3SG.A-2SG.DAT-   break:III.U

  'No way! It's impossible, you will break your bones.'   [W06:0197]

I end the discussion of future time reference with a short excerpt from a story illustrating both Future prefix series. The speaker recounts how she and another lady fell from a platform. An onlooker laughed at them instead of coming to their rescue. The quoted phrase in line 1 uses the General Future. In line 2 the speaker quotes herself using the Non-Asserted Future, which I interpret as an epistemically weaker version of the quote from the other lady (who used the General Future). The onlooker replies using the Non-Asserted Future — since the clause is negated — in line 3.

(760) 1. ka-p-ø-e-   w-a   yahwahwen   nok,
           DIR-FUT-3SG.A-1PL-   3SG.U-AUX   die.PLA:1.U 1

           men-m-b-ind-e-   mahid
           PERF-1.A-ACT-ALL-1PL-   become.angry

           ' "We're going to die", we scolded him.'

       2. mak-ø-e-   yahwahwen   ehe
           NAFUT-3SG.A-1PL-   die.PLA:1.U here

           '[I said:] "We might die here".'

       3. ah,   mbya   me-ø-   yahwahwih
           EXCLAM   NEG   NAFUT-3SG.A-   die.PLA:2|3PL.U

           '[He replied:] "Pfft, you're not going to die".'   [W19:0075]

14.2.7.6 Expressing habitually occurring sequences of events

In this use the Future prefixes (mainly those of the General Future) may occur in descriptions of series of events that used to take place in the past (e.g. headhunting), as well as sequences of events that still occur.

In the next example, I provide an excerpt from a discussion of traditional kava agriculture. A man would summon a group of men (relatives and/or clan members) to prepare the plantbed for him in exchange for kava and food. The speakers made clear in the beginning of the conversation that the description concerns past (*mandin* 'long ago') events, yet all steps in the description are expressed with Future prefixes, since they are presented as a repeatedly occurring set of actions. (Some repetitions and false starts have been omitted).

(761) 1. nda-pa-n-ap-   balen   wambad
       LOC-FUT-3PL.A-CT- finish:III.U make.plantbed
       'They would finish making the plantbed.'

2. nda-p-a-p-   hu-h,   milah [...]
   LOC-FUT-3SG.A-CT-   emerge-2|3PL.U village
   'Then they would return to the village'

3. wati   ka-me-n-   yi   usus   epe   [...]
   kava(III) DIR-FUT-3PL.A-   drink:III.U   afternoon DIST:III
   'In the afternoon they would drink kava.'

4. wati yi   nda-p-enam-   na-koh-a,   tis ka
   kava drink LOC-FUT-RCPR- RCPR-feed-EXT   that's.it
   'They would share the kava amongst each other, that's it.'

5. da   nda-p-enam-   na-koh-a
   sago LOC-FUT-RCPR- RCPR-feed-EXT
   'They would share the sago amongst each other.'

6. wambadla   menda-me-b-ø-   ay
   plant.bed(III) PERF-FUT-ACT-3SG.A-   become:III.U
   'The plant bed would already be finished.'

7. menda-m-ba-n-o-   wambad   epe
   PERF-FUT-ACT-3PL.A-3SG.DAT- make.plantbed DIST:III
   'They would already have made the plantbed for him.'   [W04:0069-0080]

This use of Future prefixes is also typical of procedural texts, in which it combines either with 1st or 3rd person ('we/they do like this, then we/they...') or 2nd person (as instructions 'you should do like this, then...').

Statements about habitual sequences are often similar to the apodosis in future conditionals: compare *Whenever I hunt, I'll kill a deer* to *If I hunt, I'll kill a deer*. In example (762) the speaker argues that meat fills you up better than other foods. He makes clear that he is referring to a habitual situation by using the Present Habitual -*made* in the first clause. The use of the General Future in the second clause can probably be seen either as expressing a habitually occurring event, or as the apodosis of an implicit conditional (if you eat meat, it will make you full).

(762) muy ti   epe   k-a-   w-a   ay-made,
       meat with DIST:III DIR-3SG.A- 3SG.U-AUX become:III.U-PRS.HAB

       anep   ka-p-ø-a-p-   w-a   isik,   ay tete?
       EMPH:III DIR-FUT-3SG.A-2SG.DAT-CT- 3SG.U-AUX become.full Q grandpa(m)

       'With meat it's usually like that, it really makes you full, right grandpa?'
       [W11:0923]

The use of grams that also express futurity or irrealis to mark habitually occurring sequences is not uncommon cross-linguistically (e.g. the Kayardild Potential suffix, which may mark "repeated actions in the past", Evans 1995: 260; or the Manam Definite Irrealis, Lichtenberk 1983: 189). There is an unfortunate tendency in the literature (e.g. Bybee et al. 1994: 157–158, Cristofaro 2004) to conflate the expression of such sequences with habituals proper, i.e. stative-like descriptions of a habit as characterising a whole period. Languages like Coastal Marind, which distinguish state-like habituals (marked by the Habitual suffixes described in §14.2.6) from habitually occurring sequences of events, show that it is useful to separate the two types of contexts.

The use of future/irrealis forms for habitual sequences seems to be common in the South New Guinea area and has been documented for e.g. Yam languages spoken to the east of Marind (Döhler 2016: 305, Carroll 2016: 177).

15 Mood, attitude and engagement

This chapter brings together descriptions of a range of verb forms with functions that concern the realisation of events, the speaker's attitude towards the statement, and the attentional or epistemic state of the addressee.

§15.1 is a brief description of the only unambiguously modal affix in the language, the Counterfactual suffix *-um*.

A prefix of the same shape, the Frustrative *um-*, has various meanings that relate to the non-realisation of an event (§15.2).

§15.3 describes a number of Speaker Attitude prefixes that occur in the same prefixal slot, and express stance-like meanings.

§15.4 describes the Deictic verb forms (called 'the Absconditive' in Olsson 2019a), which have an engagement function, viz. that of signalling that the addressee's focus of attention is not on the state-of-affairs described by the verb, and that the addressee should realign their attention to achieve joint attention with the speaker. The general term engagement is taken from Evans et al. (2018b), who define it as the "grammaticalised means for encoding the relative mental directedness of speaker and addressee towards an entity or state of affairs". Verb forms with clear engagement semantics have only been described for a few languages, so this is one of the most interesting features of Coastal Marind verb inflection.

15.1 The Counterfactual *-um*

The suffix *-um* (a member of the outer suffix class; see §8.5) has two rather different uses: it marks counterfactuals and continuative imperatives ('keep on Verb-ing!'). The counterfactual use is found in conditional sentences describing past, unrealised states-of-affairs (cf. §20.1.2.3). The suffix *-um* is added to the verb of the then-clause, as in (763), or simultaneously to both the if-clause and the then-clause, as in example (764), or example (191) on p. 141.

(763) I had met a villager who just came back from a successful hunt. Another speaker later wondered why I hadn't asked the hunter for some meat.

ah-ø-o- kabed, menda-b-ø-a- og-um
[DEP-2SG.A-3SG.DAT- ask] PERF-ACT-3SG.A-2SG.DAT- give-CTFT

'If you had asked him [for meat], he would have given to you.'

(764)   a-no-   idih-um   oso   nde,   upe   k-ak-ap-   n-a
        [DEP-1.A- see:3SG.U-CTFT   beginning   at   ]   DIST:II DIR-1.A-CT- 1.U-AUX
        ah⟨e⟩b-um
        pass⟨3SG.U⟩-CTFT

'If I had seen it [the wallaby] before, then I would have gone past it (and blocked its path).' [W12:0233]

The Counterfactual can be used without a corresponding conditional clause if the condition can be understood from the context. In (765), taken from discussion of the traditional fishing nets that the old-timers used to make from coconut fibers, the implicit condition can be understood as 'If you had been alive back then, ...'.

(765)   mend-o-   idih-um,   mbya   k-a-   kama⟨h⟩in-e   namaya
        PERF-2SG.A- see:III.U-CTFT   NEG   PRS.NTRL-3SG.A-   make⟨2|3PL.U⟩-IPFV   now

'You would have seen [the nets], nowadays they don't make them anymore.' [W13:0704]

A particularly complex corpus example containing several counterfactual clauses is in (766). The speaker was recounting how she and another lady fell from a platform along with several large trays filled with sago, during the preparations of a feast meal. In the following counterfactual scenario she details what would have happened if the sago had spilled out of the trays. All of the four verb forms in this excerpt are marked with the Counterfactual -*um*.

(766) 1. epe   da   ah-ø-   luyad-um,
           [DIST:III sago(III) DEP-3SG.A- spill:III.U-CTFT]

           ndom-n-in   s-ø-e-   w-a-um
           bad-1.U-become   ONLY-3SG.A-1PL-   3SG.U-AUX-CTFT

           'If that sago had spilled, then it would only have been bad for us.'

       2. sep   anep   ndom-ay   epe   k-a-   w-a-um
           leaf.oven(III) EMPH:III bad-become:III.U   DIST:III   DIR-3SG.A-   3SG.U-AUX-CTFT

           'Then the cooking (lit. leaf oven) would have been bad.'

       3. sep   isawa   mbya   ø-nak-e-   og-um,   ayok
           leaf.oven   maybe   NEG   NTRL-1.A-1PL-   do-CTFT   prepare.leaf.oven

           'The leaf oven, maybe we would not have done it, [I mean] prepare it.' [W19:0059]

The preceding example contains two instances of verb stems that are 'fronted' to a position before the verb complex (*nin* and *ay*, both compounded with *ndom* 'bad') while the Auxiliary fills the slot in the verb complex vacated by the verb stem (see §17.2 for more information about these structures). In such constructions *-um* behaves like the other outer suffixes, and retains its place within the verb complex, now attached to the Auxiliary. It does not move along with the fronted verb stem. Cf. also example (694b) on p. 369.

In its second use, *-um* may be added to a standard imperative form (containing the Imperative prefix *ah-*), as in (767–768), to urge the addressee to continue doing an action that was already initiated. It may also combine with the Hortative *mat-* (769) or the Jussive *anam-*, as in example (1023b), p. 502. There is no corresponding use with the Prohibitive forms (§19.1.4).

(767) ah-   yet-um!
      IMP-   be.moving-CTFT
      'Keep on going!'

(768) ah-   yahwiy-um!   yahyahy   ndame-ø-   ay
      IMP-   eat-CTFT   soft:III FUT-3SG.A-   become:III.U
      'Keep chewing! [The meat] will become soft.'

(769) da   idih   mat-ind-i-e-p-   nayat-um
      sago(III) see:III.U   HORT-ALL-RE-1PL-CT-   be.moving.PL-CTFT
      'Let's keep going, and have a look at the sago.'   [W23:0042]

There are various restrictions on the use of *-um* in commands. First, the suffix may only be added to verbs that express durative events, so punctual verbs such as *umuh* 'go, take off' do not combine with *-um* to express commands. (This constraint does not apply in the counterfactual uses of *-um*.)

Second, the suffix *-um* may only be used with the Imperative *ah-* if the addressee is singular. Imperatives directed to several addressees take the Plural Imperative suffix *-em* (§19.1.1), which also belongs to the class of outer suffixes. At most one outer suffix may be added after the verb stem, so combinations such as **nayat-um-em* (be.moving.PL-CTFT-PL.IMP) are excluded.

It is likely that the counterfactual use and imperative use of *-um* are diachronically related, because similar patterns of polyfunctionality (between irrealis forms and continuative imperatives) have been noted for several western Pama-Nyungan languages in Australia (Dixon 2002a: 214, McGregor 2013: 121).

Another interesting diachronic observation concerns the relationship between the Counterfactual suffix *-um* and the Frustrative prefix *um-* (§15.2). In the Eastern dialect of Coastal Marind, as described by Drabbe, there is only a single prefix *um-*, which functions both as a marker of counterfactuality and a frustrative (Drabbe 1955: 129–130). It is common across languages to find markers that code both frustratives and counterfactuals (Kroeger 2017, Overall 2017).

15.2 The Frustrative *um-*

The Frustrative prefix serves to express that the expected outcome of an event was going to materialise, but did not, because something else happened instead. It is the only member of position class –8 (cf. Chapter 8). There are no known co-occurrence restrictions on the Frustrative with other prefixes of the prefixal complex.

I distinguish the following uses: (A) failed attempt, (B) unfulfilled intention, (C) action performed in vain, (D) action performed with unexpected consequences, and (E) narrowly averted events in general. These are illustrated with examples below. Where possible, I have chosen examples in which the intervening event (preventing the realisation of the Frustrative-marked action) is given explicit mention, which makes interpretation easier for the reader.

(A) Failed attempt. The verb marked by *um-* describes an action that the agent attempted unsuccessfully:

(770) The speaker was making roofing from sago thatch (*ebta*, Gender IV).

ba⟨h⟩in   k-ak-um-ind-e-   ka-n-in,
finish⟨IV.U⟩ DIR-1.A-FRUS-ALL-1PL- WITH-1.U-become

nu   menda-b-ø-e-p-   n-ihwid
sleep PERF-ACT-3SG.A-1PL-CT-   1.U-become.sleepy

'We were trying to finish, [but] we were already [too] sleepy.'   [W20:0284]

(771) tis,   nama ago   ma-d-ø-um-   wayamat-a,
that's.it now   PRWD:III OBJ-DUR-3SG.A-FRUS- stand.PL-EXT

ipe   wati menda-b-ø-e-p-   mabuk
DIST:I/II.PL   kava PERF-ACT-3SG.A-2|3PL.DAT-CT- drunk(m)

'That's it, now they were trying to keep standing up, [but] they were already drunk from the kava.'   [W21:0051]

(B) Unfulfilled intention. The *um-*marked verb describes an action that the agent intended to perform, but something else intervened before the action was attempted:

(772) mayay e=   k-ak-um-e-   uma⟨n⟩ah Ulolya, [...]
first   PROX= DIR-1.A-FRUS-1PL-   go⟨1.U⟩   U.

ago nok a   mak-e-   uma⟨n⟩ah-e Buy
QUOT 1   PTCL FUT:1.A-1PL-   go⟨1.U⟩-IPFV B.

'First we were going to go to Ulolya, [but the others] said: "We are going to Buy".'   [W08:0004-0007]

(773) nok ø-nak-um-ap- dahuy, yah mawta ka
　　　 1   NTRL-1.A-FRUS-CT- ask.to.bring but never.mind

'I was going to ask him to get me something, but [I thought:] never mind.'

[W22:0031]

(C) Action performed in vain. The Frustrative signals that the agent managed to perform the action, but the intended outcomes did not occur. This use is especially frequent with the verb *walaw* 'search', i.e. 'search for without finding', as in (774). Note also the use in (776), in which *um-* is prefixed to *ayi* 'say', since the act of saying did not have the expected result.

(774) nda-d-ø-um- y-alaw-a,
　　　 LOC-DUR-3SG.A-FRUS- 2|3PL.U-search-EXT

　　　 rusa wahani mbya ø-n-o- idih
　　　 deer body(III) NEG NTRL-3PL.A-3SG.DAT- see:III.U

'Then they searched for deer, [but] they didn't see a single one.' [W02:0149]

(775) ehetagol ah-ø-um- deh, padahal mbya ø-a- deh,
　　　 like.this:III DEP-3SG.A-FRUS- shoot:3SG.U in.fact(m) NEG NTRL-3SG.A- shoot:3SG.U

　　　 emba k-ø-is-ap- og
　　　 side DIR-3SG.A-SEP-CT- do

'When he shot like this, in fact he didn't shoot it, he shot at the side.'

[W11:1149]

(776) "mak-e- lemeh", koyhi-anem ø-ø-um- ayi, "mbya ka, oy
　　　 FUT:1.A-1PL- catch.PLA:2|3PL.U white-man NTRL-3SG.A-FRUS- say NEG 2SG

　　　 dalo me-ø- y-in, adeh m-o- ø ay"
　　　 mud NAFUT-3SG.A- 2SG.U-become RLQ OBJ-2SG.A- be.NPST Q

'"Let's go catch [fish]", Bruno said [like that], [I said:] "No, you'll get covered in mud, you stay here, ok".'

[W08:0028]

(D) Unintended consequences. In this use, the action is performed successfully, but eventually leads to some other, typically unfavourable, event. I illustrate this use with the following two examples. In (777) the verb *bug* 'cut up animal in order to disembowel it' is marked with the Frustrative in the first clause since the action unexpectedly led to the agent being sprayed with fecal matter, as described in the subsequent clauses. Example (778) sets the scene for a description of a prank that a neighbouring boy played on a couple of elderly women. The women were resting by the fire at night when the boy suddenly jumped up with bow and arrow, as if to attack them. In this sentence, the verb *tel* 'be lying' is marked by the Frustrative *um-*, since it lead to the elderly lady being subject to the boy's prank.

(777) Vitalis ø-ø-um-o-p-   bug,
      V.   NTRL-3SG.A-FRUS-3SG.DAT-CT- cut.up.animal

      na   k-ø-o-   w-a   isug,
      faeces(III) DIR-3SG.A-3SG.DAT- 3SG.U-AUX cut:III.U

      Vitalis na   ti   ø-d-a-p-   tel,
      V.   faeces with:I NTRL-DUR-3SG.A-CT- be.lying

      na   k-ø-o-   w-a   taman
      faeces DIR-3SG.A-3SG.DAT- 3SG.U-AUX shoot

      'Vitalis cut it up, he cut up its gut (lit. faeces), then Vitalis was lying covered in faeces, the faeces sprayed up on him.' [W11:0889]

(778) tanama Walmeleng a,   takah nda-d-ø-um-ap-   tel-ti
      then   W.   PTCL fire   LOC-DUR-3SG.A-FRUS-CT- be.lying-DUR
      'Then Walmeleng, she was sleeping by the fire.' [W11:0256]

(E) Narrowly averted events, 'almost V-ed'. This use differs from the previous ones as there is no conscious effort to bring about the event. It is illustrated below in a corpus example (779) and two observed utterances. Example (780) was uttered by Pau Yolmend, who had rushed out of the house after eating a tuber that was left from last day's dinner — it had apparently gone bad. In example (781) Pau's cousin Yakobus described how he and I almost fell with my motorcycle while driving on the beach.

(779) k-ak-um-e-p-   n-a   ihe⟨hy⟩ab
      DIR-1.A-FRUS-1PL-CT- 1.U-AUX pass⟨2|3PL.U⟩
      'We almost went past them.' [W10:0320]

(780) nak-um-   yod
      1.A-FRUS- throw.up
      'I almost threw up.'

(781) e=   k-ø-um-e-   hihi-n
      PROX= DIR-3SG.A-FRUS-1PL- fall.PLA-1.U
      'We almost fell there.'

This use of the Frustrative is also common with a verb preceded by the aspectual particle *oso* 'start, beginning', as described in §18.4.3. The resulting construction has the meaning 'was just about to V, but didn't'. I admit that it is difficult to tell how this meaning differs from 'almost V'. My impression is that the structure with *oso* and *um-* is preferred with agentive actions, perhaps to cancel readings such as 'in vain', whereas *um-* alone is sufficient with less agentive actions such as 'vomit', since the presence of the Frustrative with such verbs is unlikely to invite the 'in vain'-reading (one rarely throws up 'in vain').

There are some other uses of the Frustrative that are difficult to fit into any of the five functions listed above. For example, *um-* may appear with verbs meaning 'say', 'guess' etc. to express 'wrongly', as in (782).

(782)   *kihwa   k-ak-um-o-p-   kayub,* [...],
        saratoga DIR-1.A-FRUS-3SG.DAT-CT- guess

   mbya k-a-   Ø,   ago kalambu k-a-   Ø
   NEG   PRS.NTRL-3SG.A- be.NPST QUOT mullet   PRS.NTRL-3SG.A- be.NPST

   'I wrongly guessed it was a saratoga fish [...], [then I realised:] "No, it's a mullet".'   [W23:0027-0029]

Note also the use of *um-* in some constructions expressing surprising developments in narratives: see §15.3.2.1.

Interaction between the Frustrative and other grammatical categories is an interesting topic that remains largely unexplored. I end with an example of Frustrative *um-* occurring in a negated clause (783). The speaker makes an apology after being corrected by one of the other participants in the conversation. It seems most likely that this is the 'unintended consequence' use of the Frustrative, which clearly is outside the scope of negation, i.e. roughly 'I'm not thinking, which had the consequence that I misspoke'.

(783) *o   ahak, mbya k-ak-um-ap-   hwetok*
       oh yes   NEG   PRS.NTRL-1.A-FRUS-CT-   think
       'Oh right, I'm not thinking/not paying attention.'   [W11:0280]

15.3 Speaker attitude prefixes

In this section I describe the Actualis *b-* (§15.3.1), the Mirative *bam-* (§15.3.2), the Affectionate *bat-* (§15.3.3), the Self-interrogative *bah-* (§15.3.4), and the Presentative *hat-* (§15.3.5).

I treat these five prefixes together, since they belong to a single slot in the morphotactic template (position class –11), and since all of them have meanings that reflect the stance or attitude of the speaker to what is being said.

The five prefixes share two phonological similarities: the segment /b/ reoccurs in *b-*, *bah-*, *bam-* and *bat-*, and the sequence /at/ appears in both *bat-* and *hat-*. This is perhaps the result of concatenation of what once were independent affixes; synchronically, however, no further segmentation is possible.

A noteworthy property of the prefixes in this class is that they do not occur preceded by the Past Durative *d-*, despite the fact that *d-* belongs to the preceding position class. The reason for this is mainly phonological: the Western variety of Coastal Marind deletes /d/ before /b/ (cf. §2.5.3), so *d-* cannot surface before the *b*-initial prefixes *b-*, *bah-*, *bam-* and *bat-* (this phonological rule does not apply in the Eastern variety described in Geurtjens 1933 and Drabbe 1955). The Presentative *hat-* (§15.3.5) is used in clauses with present time reference and is therefore not attested with the Durative *d-*, which only occurs in past time context.

15.3.1 The Actualis *b-*

The basic function of the Actualis *b-* seems to be to emphasise the truth value of the proposition, that something indeed happened, as discussed in (§15.3.1.1). This use is very rare in the corpus, and most other attestations are in two more or less idiomatic combinations with other prefixes. The first is content questions, in which the Actualis (along with the Interrogative *h-*) is obligatory and does not contribute any additional meaning (§15.3.1.2). The second is with the Perfect *mend-*, with which the Actualis is optional, but extremely frequent, although it seems to add very little meaning (§15.3.1.3).

15.3.1.1 Basic function

In its use outside forms with the Perfect *mend-* and content question, the Actualis prefix seems to have a range of modal functions, that are difficult to delineate, but probably involve an emphasis on the actuality or truth-value of the proposition. Speakers sometimes render the contribution of *b-* as Malay *memang* 'indeed', and a verb marked with *b-* cannot be modified by *isawa* 'maybe'. According to Drabbe (1955: 125), *b-* is used when one "wants to assert something with certainty or emphasis".[1] This use of the prefix is very rare in my corpus, with only 13 attestations so far, which makes it difficult to narrow down the pragmatics and semantics of its use. Some corpus data illustrating the use of *b-* will be discussed here.

Consider first (784–785). The speaker describes how he and some other hunters feasted on a pig. In the context of eating, the expression 'kill oneself' (literally 'kill one's body') in (784) refers to eating a very large amount of food, i.e. 'gorge oneself' or 'eat like a horse'. This is the second time the speaker repeats this expression — cf. example (657) on p. 353 for the first mention — but now he adds the prefix *b-*, which I interpret as a way of adding force to the hyperbolic expression (*we really gorged ourselves — I really mean it!*).

---

[1] "*De modus-wijzer b-* [...] *drukt uit dat men iets met beslistheid of nadrukkelijk wil beweren*". Unfortunately, Drabbe muddies the waters by stating that the Presentative *hat-* (§15.3.5) has the same meaning as *b-*, which is not the case.

(784) pen   ya   k-am-b-e-   u-sak   wahani
     murder real DIR-1.A-ACT-1PL- III.U-hit.PLA body(III)
     '[Indeed] we really ate ourselves to death.'   [D05:0053]

The hyperbolic mode of expression continues in the next utterance by the same speaker, again using the Actualis prefix:

(785) upe   anup   hyakod ya   m-am-b-e-   aheb   basik   upe
     DIST:II   EMPH:II   one   real OBJ-1.A-ACT-1PL- eat:3SG.U pig(II) DIST:II
     '[Indeed] we ate that one entire pig.'   [D05:0054]

The speaker with whom I translated this text conveyed this emphasis by means of Malay *memang*, approximately 'indeed', which I have added within brackets.

The next example comes from a discussion after a hunting expedition. The speaker, Libo, is scolding one of the other hunters, Edison, who shot at a deer with a small bamboo arrow instead of one of the large metal arrows that Libo had given him. The shot failed to kill the deer, and it ran away with the arrow sticking out of its skin. Edison should have been able to kill the deer, according to Libo, because the dogs had chased it close to where the Edison was standing guard. Edison defends himself, saying he got confused when the deer was running towards him. But Libo states bluntly:

(786) anup   o-b-   haletok
     EMPH:II   2SG.A-ACT-   miss
     'You missed the shot.'   [M02:0557]

A couple of lines later, Libo clarifies:

(787) anup   ugu   m-o-b-o-   deh
     EMPH:II skin(III)   OBJ-2SG.A-ACT-3SG.DAT- shoot:III.U
     '[In fact] you shot it in the skin.'   [M02:0560]

In this context, Libo probably uses the Actualis to emphasise that his account of the events ('you could have killed it, but you missed the shot, you shot its skin') is the correct one, no matter what Edison claims. Note that the emphatic demonstrative *anup* appears in a discourse particle-like function in (785–787), apparently reinforcing the meaning of the Actualis.

Several instances of the Actualis are with negated verbs, and then its meaning seems to be slightly different from the affirmative examples above. All of the corpus examples involve some event that was expected or hoped for, and when it finally does not happen, the verb describing the non-occurring event is marked with the Actualis.

In (788), a truck driver had been asked by the speaker to bring a group of villagers back to Wambi from another village. He replies that he will only do this on condition that they supply him with palm wine. The villagers had no wine, so the driver refused to take them. The speaker marks the verb form in 'He didn't take them' with *b-*:

(788) 1. sageru   me-na-   og, yah mano- y-ahik
         palm.wine(m) FUT:2PL.A-1.DAT-   give PTCL FUT:1.A- 2|3PL.U-accompany

      2. mbya ø-b-a-   y-ahik,
         NEG NTRL-ACT-3SG.A- 2|3PL.U-accompany

         sageru   mbya ø-d-a-namb-e-   ola-la
         palm.wine(III) NEG NTRL-DUR-3SG.A-1.GEN-1PL- be:III.U-EXT

      1. '"[The driver said:] You're going to give me palm wine, and then I will drive them [home]".'
      2. 'He didn't drive them, [because] we didn't have any palm wine.'
                                                                   [W11:0247-0248]

A similar example is in (789). The speaker recalled how she and some other villagers were just about to return home to Wambi from another village, when news reached them that a relative had passed away in Nasem, a village outside the district capital Merauke. They changed their plans, and did not return to Wambi, which the speaker marks with the Actualis prefix.

(789) tis ka,   nok mbya ø-nam-b-e-   dahetok
      that's.it 1   NEG NTRL-1.A-ACT-1PL-   return
      'That's it, we didn't return [we went to Nasem instead].'   [W19:0257]

15.3.1.2 In content questions

Content questions (§19.3) are formed by placing an interrogative phrase ('who', 'where' etc.) in the pre-verbal syntactic slot, and adding the Interrogative prefix *h-* (ROG) to the prefixal complex, followed by the Actualis *b-*. The prefix sequence *h-...b-* has as its only function that of signalling that the verb is used in a content question — a typological oddity since the presence of an interrogative pronoun (perhaps combined with intonation) is sufficient in most languages to mark an utterance as a content question.

It is not possible to assign a meaning to *b-* when it appears as a part of content questions. It is not a completely fossilised part of such structures, however, because *b-* may be replaced by the Affectionate *bat-* (790b), which is one of the other 'speaker attitude' prefixes occurring in position class –11 (see §15.3.3).

(790) a. en   nda-h-o-b-   man?
        where   LOC-ROG-2SG.A-ACT-   come
        'Where are you coming from?'   [W11:0058]

     b. en   nda-h-o-bat-   man?
        where   LOC-ROG-2SG.A-AFF-   come
        'Where are you coming from[, poor one]?'

15.3.1.3 With the Perfect *mend-*

The Perfect prefix *mend-* (§14.2.5) collocates strongly with the Actualis *b-*. The combination of these two prefixes is seen in the second line of the dialogue in (791), and in many other examples in this grammar.

(791) 1. yah   loyang   apa-bt-e-o-   ka-dhetok?
         but   bowl(m)   PST.Q-AFF-2PL.A-3SG.DAT-   WITH-return

      2. mend-am-b-o-   ka-dhetok, yah nu   ndom ø-d-a-   tel
         PERF-1.A-ACT-3SG.DAT-   WITH-return but sleep still NTRL-DUR-3SG.A- be.lying

         1. 'So did you return the bowl to her?'
         2. 'I already returned it to her, but she was still sleeping.'   [W13:0475–0476]

The corpus count reported in Olsson (2017: 458) found that 80% of the occurrences of the Perfect were in combination with the Actualis *b-*. The meaning contribution of the Actualis in Perfect verb forms is extremely subtle, but could be seen as de-emphasising the change-of-state meaning of the Perfect. This can be seen in the minority of cases in which the Perfect is used without the Actualis, as explained below.

   The main pattern is that the Actualis is omitted if the Perfect is used with a durative verb form, i.e. inherently durative verbs such as *ola* 'be' or verbs derived with the Extended *-a* (§14.2.3). An illustration of this pattern is in (792). The first verb describes a punctual event, *ay* 'become', and uses the standard combination of the Perfect *mend-* and the Actualis *b-*. The verb in the second clause is *ola* 'be', and the Actualis is omitted with this durative verb, just like it is with almost all other Perfect-marked durative verbs in the corpus. The reason for this distribution seems to be that the Actualis emphasises the change-of-state leading to a new situation (*become night*) in the first clause, while its absence in the second clause shows that the new situation (*the moon was out*) was already on-going at reference time.

(792) yap   menda-b-ø-   ay,   mandaw   menda-d-ø-   ola
      night(III) PERF-ACT-3SG.A-   become:III.U   moon(III) PERF-DUR-3SG.A-   be:III.U
      'It had already become night, the moon was already out.'   [W15:0171]

The second context in which the Actualis is omitted is when the word *mandin* 'long ago' combines with a Perfect-marked verb to express an event that took place earlier than expected (793). This use occurs with both durative and punctual verbs.

(793) A hunting story. A hunter thought he had hit a deer, because he spotted an arrow sticking out of its skin as it fled, but it turned out to be an old injury.

anim   mandin   menda-n-   deh
people long.ago PERF-3PL.A- shoot:3SG.U

'[In fact] somebody had already shot it before.'   [W11:1154]

Again, the omission of the Actualis seems to correspond to the lack of a new change-of-state, since the emphasis is on an 'old' change-of-state (*become shot*) that continues into reference time.[2]

Note finally that the Actualis prefix, in combination with the Perfect, clearly lacks the meaning of certainty or actuality that it expresses in its basic use (as discussed in §15.3.1.1). For example, verbs prefixed with Perfect *mend-* and *b-* are free to co-occur with the adverb *isawa* 'maybe':

(794) *napet   menda-b-ø-   usu   isawa*
banana(III) PERF-ACT-3SG.U- become.ripe:III.U maybe

'Maybe the bananas have become ripe.'   [W11:0127]

15.3.2 The Mirative *bam-*

This prefix is used to signal that the state-of-affairs described by the verb is surprising to the speaker or represents a sudden, unexpected discovery. I label it Mirative in line with DeLancey (1997) and many other descriptions of categories expressing surprise. I have only observed the Mirative *bam-* used to express surprise or sudden discoveries on the part of the speaker. To signal that a development in a narrative is surprising for the characters inside the story, other strategies are used (§15.3.2.1). The Coastal Marind Mirative is restricted to the 'here and now': although it can be occur in contexts with both past and present time reference, the Mirative always signals that the speaker experiences surprise at the moment of speech. This means that the Mirative *bam-* is frequent in face-to-face conversation, but rare in narratives, where it is largely restricted to the reported speech of the characters in the narrative.

---

[2] See also Olsson (2017: 458) for some comments on the difficulty of determining the meaning of the Actualis.

Below some examples are given, from the corpus and from observed usage, to illustrate the meaning conveyed by the Mirative.

The first example is from an account of a trip to the provincial capital Merauke. The narrator and his family had arrived at the Domande village at night, and went to sleep in the outskirts of the village. Their arrival was noticed by the villagers, and in the morning a woman comes with food for the them. She discovers that one of the visitors (the narrator) is a relative of hers. The sense of surprise is expressed by the Mirative:

(795) o,   yoy ø-e-bam-   nayam   yap
       oh   2PL NTRL-2PL.A-MIR-   come.PL night

'Oh, it was you who came at night.' [W10:0261]

This examples illustrates the point about the Mirative always expressing surprise in the moment of speech. Although the verb describes a past event ('you came at night'), it is now that the speaker discovers the identity of the visitors that she is surprised.

The second example comes from an interaction taking place in the kitchen of my host family's house in Wambi. This day, there had been a standing joke about Kolum, one of the teenage boys that usually loiters around the house, who had been carrying around a toy boat made from sago stalk (*gis*). When Kolum appeared in the doorway, Paulus Yolmend, the father in the family, exclaimed, feigning surprise:

(796) ee   slup-k-um-anem   ka-bam-ø-   ø-e
       EXCLAM motorboat(m)-WITH-go.PLA:3SG.U-man   PRS.NTRL-MIR-3SG.A-   be.NPST-IPFV

'Oh my! It's the motorboat helmsman!' [W11:0068]

The following example was overheard. The mother in my host family was sitting by my house with a saucepan containing some food next to her. She asked a young girl to go get a lid for the saucepan in the kitchen nextdoor. The girl returns with a lid, tries to put it on top of the saucepan, but finds that it does not fit. She announced the discovery using the Mirative *bam-* and returned to the kitchen to look for another lid.

(797) mbya ka-bam-ø-   ø
       NEG   PRS.NTRL-MIR-3SG.A-   be.NPST

'It's not [this one].'

The final example is from a story. In this excerpt the protagonist of the story had encountered a man, Sigawle, with whom he chewed betelnut before taking leave. However, Sigawle follows in the tracks of the protagonist, and manages to pass him. The protagonist, unaware of this, reacts with surprise when he sees Sigawle sitting in wait for him:

(798) ee   ehe   Sigawle ka-bam-ø-i-ap-   mil-e   ehe
       EXCLAM PROX:I   S.   PRS.NTRL-MIR-3SG.A-RE-CT-   be.sitting-IPFV   PROX:I
       'Oh! Sigawle is sitting here again!'   [D01:0087]

15.3.2.1 Expressing surprise in narratives

Surprising developments in a narrative are expressed by means of a biclausal structure, consisting of an initial clause containing an idiomatic sequence of independent and affixal elements which together serve to express surprise, and a second clause describing the surprising event itself. The verb of the first clause is built with the Locational Orientation prefix *nd-*, the relevant Actor prefix (reflecting the participant experiencing the surprise), the Frustrative *um-*, and a verb stem, usually *og* 'do' or a motion verb. To the predicate is often added either the word *ago* (the Gender III form of the 'pro-word' *ago*, see §4.4) or a property demonstrative (§4.2.3) such as *ehetago* 'like this'.

The following three corpus examples show three different instantiations of this construction. It is unclear how the initial clauses are best translated into English. In the corpus I have oscillated between renderings such as 'Suddenly, X happened', 'We were surprised to see X happen', and so on. Below I retain whatever translation I used during transcription:

(799) The speaker encountered a man while walking along the beach late one afternoon.

nd-ak-um-e-   og   a,
LOC-1.A-FRUS-1PL-   do   PTCL

Sukegel lek   anem   ka-d-ø-   w-a   ola
S.   from:I   man(I)   DIR-DUR-3SG.A-   3SG.U-AUX   be:3SG.U

'Unexpectedly, there was a man from Sukegel.'   [W18:0145]

(800) This is the reported reaction of the man in (799).

ehetagol   nd-ø-um-   og,
like.this:III   LOC-3SG.A-FRUS-   do

ane!   an   ke   i=   k-at-ø-   nayam
EXCLAM   mother   APL   PROX:I/II.PL=   PRS.NTRL-PRSTV-3SG.A-   come.PL

'He was surprised and said, "Oh! Mother and the others are coming".'
                                                                                [W18:0147]

(801) bapa   Mili ago   nda-d-ø-um-   yet,
      father(m) M. PRWD:III LOC-DUR-3SG.A-FRUS-   be.moving

      na   jari-jari   k-a-   huhu
      faeces(III) fingers(m)   DIR-3SG.A-   emerge.PLA:III.U

      'Unexpectedly, Uncle Mili shat all over his fingers.'   [W11:0926]

The combination of words and and affixes is non-compositional, and I cannot explain how this particular structure came to be conventionalised in the expression of narrated surprise.[3]

15.3.3 The Affectionate *bat-*

By using this prefix the speakers express that they regard the participants in the predicated event with pity, solidarity, or affection in general. When asked about some sentence in which the Affectionate is used, speakers explain its presence using the Malay verb *sayang* 'to pity, feel sorry for' (also used as a noun 'darling, poor one'), as in *kita sayang dia* 'we pity/feel sorry for him/her'. I add 'poor one' (within brackets) to the translations below in an attempt to convey this. This translation should not be taken too literally, because the prefix does not convey sadness. Rather, the effect of *bat-* is mainly to provide an affectionate or empathetic nuance to the utterance. Its frequent use could perhaps be likened to the use to e.g. diminutive forms of personal names in Slavic languages.

A typical example is (802). Here *bat-* appears twice. Both instances are in copula clauses, so there are no lexical verb stems present. In a story, a woman meets a long-lost brother for the first time in many years:

(802) ane   mame   namek   ka-bat-ø-   ø-e,
      EXCLAM EXCLAM   clanmate   PRS.NTRL-AFF-3SG.A-   be.NPST-IPFV

      mayay-anem   ka-bat-ø-   ø
      front-man   PRS.NTRL-AFF-3SG.A-   be.NPST

      'Oh my! It's my brother, it's my elder brother[, poor one]!'   [W10:0259]

It is also very common to add the Affectionate *bat-* to commands, which lends them a gentler quality:

---

[3] Local Malay (but not the standard Indonesian language) also uses a biclausal structure in these contexts, with the first clause being either *X lihat begini* 'X looked like this' or *X jalan begini* 'X went like this'. Thus, the Malay translation that I got for example (800) was *Dia lihat begini, "Ya! Mama dorang ada datang ini!"*, literally 'He looked like this, "Woah! Mother and the others are coming here!"'.

(803) *a-bat-   man!*
      IMP-AFF- come
      'Come here[, poor one]!'   [W11:0206]

It is difficult to generalise about the referents that typically occur as arguments in *bat*-marked clauses. Utterances about children are natural targets for *bat*-prefixation, especially if the children are portrayed as small or helpless in some way (804–805). It is also no surprise that *bat-* is used in reference to a recently deceased relative (806).

(804) *noy-anem   ndom   ø-d-a-   ola,*
      young-man   still NTRL-DUR-3SG.A-   be:3SG.U

      wanangga   isahih   ndom   ø-bat-ø-om-   ya-hwala
      children   small.PL   still   NTRL-AFF-3SG.A-3SG.GEN-   2|3.U-be
      'He was still a young man, his children were still small[, poor ones].'
                                                                         [W10:0026]

(805) *kadam   ti   ø-bat-ø-   ola,   patul ehe,   Sil*
      clubfoot with:I   NTRL-AFF-3SG.A-   be:3SG.U boy   PROX:I S.
      'He had a clubfoot[, poor one], this boy, Sil.'   [W10:0641-0642]

(806) *nahan namek   a-bat-ø-   o-nggat   yawal,   Nasem epe*
      1.EMPH clanmate DEP-AFF-3SG.A- 3SG.U-become.PLA   deceased N.   there
      'our own [poor] brother who passed away, there in Nasem'   [W19:0253-0254]

But many uses of the Affectionate *bat-* involve referents that one would not normally think of as deserving of pity or empathy. For example, while walking along the beach away from the village I have observed speakers exclaim 'Oh there *bat*-are coconut palms there', pointing to some trees in the distance. It is not clear to me whether such occurrences of the Affectionate are motivated by the fact that the coconut is a totemic plant, or whether one feels affection towards it for its general usefulness, or perhaps because a coconut grove is a sign of human presence.

The use of *bat-* in reference to coconuts is also observed when the coconut is represented in a drawing or photograph. The following utterance was made in reaction to one of the drawings in the Family Problems picture task, in which some palms are visible in the background.

(807) *aywa   onggat   ka-bat-ø-   ehay-a   ehe*
      EXCLAM   coconut(III)   PRS.NTRL-AFF-3SG.A-   stand.PLA-EXT   PROX:III
      'Oh my, there are coconut trees standing here.'   [D09:0247]

In fact the Affectionate is especially common when speakers make comments about people visible in photographs or in my video recordings. In example (808) I was recording some teenagers cleaning a well. A passer-by looked over my shoulder and saw the image of the teenagers on the monitor of the camera. He comments on this using *bat-*. My impression is that the affection one feels for people is intensified when seeing them in pictures, possibly because of the tiny size of people in most graphic representations.

(808) nok   mat-i-ap-   hyadih, tepta   epe   nda-bat-na-   lesad
       1   HORT-RE-CT- see:2|3PL.U EXCLAM there LOC-AFF-3PL.A- draw.water
       'Let me see them, holy cow, there they are drawing water[, poor ones].'
       [W06:0150]

Verbal categories that are similar to the Affectionate *bat-* have been reported for other languages. In the same geographic area, Suki (a language of the Gogodala-Suki family spoken across the border in Papua New Guinea) has a verb suffix *-dr* which van Tongeren (2015) labels the SORRY-morpheme, usually translated as "poor X". Further away, Ngalakan (a Gunwinyguan language of Northern Australia) has a "compassion prefix" *wirli-* with the meaning "poor thing" (Merlan 1983: 66), and Cup'ik (a dialect of Central Alaskan Yup'ik) has an affix *-rurlur-* which can be applied to either nouns or verbs with the meanings 'poor dear Noun' and 'poor dear (subject) Verbs' respectively (Woodbury 1998: 241).

15.3.4 The Self-interrogative *bah-*

This prefix almost always occurs in the same interrogative structure that is used to form content questions (with a question word/interrogative phrase in the pre-verbal position; §19.3), but without the prefix sequence *h-...b-* (i.e. the Interrogative *h-* and the Actualis *b-*). The use of *bah-* signals that the question should not be interpreted as seeking information from the hearer, but rather conveying that the speaker lacks the relevant information and does not expect to get access to it. A Coastal Marind question of the form "What *bah-*is that?" could be translated into English as 'What on earth could that be' or 'I wonder what that is'.[4]

---

[4] I am not aware of much research on this type of question. Obenauer (2004), in a study of an Italian dialect, labels questions of this type "can't find the value"-questions, signalling that the speaker has exhausted the possible values without finding an appropriate answer. A vaguely similar morpheme is found in Ngiyambaa (a Pama-Nyungan language of Australia), which has an 'Ignorative' marker *-ga:* that attaches to question words, converting them to non-questions in a way similar to Coastal Marind *bah-* (Donaldson 1980, Mushin 1995). An earlier version of this grammar used the label 'Ignorative' also for the Coastal Marind prefix, but a reviewer pointed out that this term is better reserved for question words and indefinite pronouns, and suggested the label 'Self-interrogative' instead.

Such (non-)questions are used when one does not expect an answer from the addressee, or when one directs the question at oneself. The following textual example shows such a self-directed question. In the story, a Wambi villager is walking in the dark towards a house in a neighbouring village. The owner of the house sees the approaching man and delivers the following soliloquy:

(809) *Wambi-age k-a-   man-em ehe,*
       W.-PRWD:I   PRS.NTRL-3SG.A- come-VEN PROX:I

       anem ta   ka-bah-ø-   man-em
       man   who:I PRS.NTRL-SLF.INT-3SG.A-   come-VEN

       'A Wambi villager is coming here, what man could that be coming.'
       [W10:0406]

A *bah*-marked question is also an evasive and perhaps politer way to express that one does not have the answer to a previous (information-seeking) question. Variations on the following mini-dialogue often occured in Wambi. I would ask for the name of some item for my lexical file, as in (810.1), whereupon the speaker would provide a non-reply as in (810.2):

(810) 1. *ehe   namakad,   ta   ka-ha-b-ø-   ø?*
           PROX:III thing(III) what:III PRS.NTRL-ROG-ACT-3SG.A-   be.NPST
           'What is this thing?'

       2. *ta   ka-bah-ø-   ø*
           what:III   PRS.NTRL-SLF.INT-3SG.A-   be.NPST
           'What on earth could that be.'

The Self-interrogative *bah-* also appears in contexts that are similar to indirect questions in English grammar. In (811) the *bah*-marked verb appears after a clause with the expression *mbaymbay* 'don't know, unable'. I provide two translations: one literal with two independent clauses, and one more idiomatic with an embedded question.

(811) *ehe   kemlay   ehe   mbaymbay   ka-ø-   ø   nok,*
       PROX:I   nephew(I)   PROX:I   not.knowing   PRS.NTRL-1.A-   be.NPST   1

       ta   ti   ø-bah-ø-   awat-a
       who   with   NTRL-SLF.INT-3SG.A-   run.PL-EXT

       'As for my nephew here, I don't know, who on earth did he go with?'
       'I don't know who my nephew went with.'   [W22:0114]

There is also a use of the Self-interrogative which has a similar meaning to English exclamative *wh*-constructions (e.g. *What an idiot he is!*). In the following example the interrogative phrase is *untagul ukna-anum*, literally 'what kind of coward'. The speaker with whom I transcribed this text rendered this sentence in Malay as *Nene Mia ini tukang takut sekali* 'Grandma Mia is a real coward', but I believe that my English translation reflects more closely both the form and the meaning of the Coastal Marind original.

(812) nene   Mia untagul ukna-anum   ka-bah-ø-   ø
      grandma(m) Mia how:II   fear-woman(II)   PRS.NTRL-SLF.INT-3SG.A- be.NPST
      'Grandma Mia, what a coward she is!'   [W11:0356]

The use of the Self-interrogative is very rare outside interrogative constructions (with an interrogative pronoun, as in all the preceding examples), and only a couple of examples have been recorded. In the following example the copula clause *Kapio kabah* expresses something like 'perhaps it's Kapio?' or 'could it be Kapio?'. Again, although I use a question mark in the translation, there is no sign that the expression is information-seeking.

(813) tak   epe   nd-a-   ø,   Kapio ka-bah-ø-   ø,
      source there LOC-3SG.A-   be.NPST   K.   PRS.NTRL-SLF.INT-3SG.A- be.NPST

      mbaymbay ka-ø-   ø   nok tak   epe
      not.know PRS.NTRL-1.A- be.NPST   1   source(III) DIST:III
      'A source is there — could it be Kapio? I don't know [the name] of that source.'
                                                                                    [W15:0115]

The Self-interrogative may also occur in what is formally a yes/no-question, formed with the polar question prefix *ap-* (*apa-* before consonant). All attestations of this use were volunteered to me during elicitation, so this use of *bah-* is unattested in the corpus. The *bah*-marked verb occurs as part of a command, roughly 'check if P or not P':

(814) kin h-ind-i-ap-   ka⟨y⟩amit-a-m,
      eye IMP-ALL-RE-CT-   (2SG.U)enter-EXT-VEN

      patul   epe   nu   apa-bah-ø-   yali
      boy(I) DIST:I sleep PST.Q-SLF.INT-3SG.A-   lie.down
      'Please go in and see whether the boy is sleeping.'

Apparently the use of *bah-* extends outside the content question-construction, but more corpus attestations are needed before this can be explored further.

15.3.5 The Presentative *hat-*

All attestations of the prefix *hat-* are as a part of the Presentational construction, so the reader is also advised to consult §18.6.[5] The Presentational construction only occurs in present time contexts, so *hat-* is also restricted to verb forms describing present situations (although see below for an exception). The prefix serves to express that the state-of-affairs described by the verb can be seen (or perceived) by everyone, because it is in plain sight, right in front of the participants, or obvious in some other way. It occurs in the type of contexts in which the Presentational construction is used, e.g. with motion verbs ('There's an X coming') or position verbs ('There's an X sitting there') etc.

I provide a still from a video recording in Figure 15.1 showing a typical use of the Presentative *hat-*. The two boys in this interaction were engaged in cleaning the well in front of them. The addressee (indicated by 'Addr.' in the image) had asked for a bamboo pole (*ndakla*, Gender III), and the speaker ('Spkr.') points to a location (off camera) and replies that the bamboo is there. The bamboo is located in the direction they are both looking, in plain sight, which justifies the use of the Presentative. The fully glossed version is given below.

(815) onggat mit e= k-at-ø- hanituk-a
coconut at PROX:III= PRS.NTRL-PRSTV-3SG.A- lean-EXT
'It's leaning there by the coconut tree.' [W06:0195]

The /h/ in *hat-* can only surface if the sequence *hat-* makes up the final syllable of the Prefixal complex, as in

(816) rusa u= ka-hat-ø- man
deer(m)(II) PROX:II- PRS.NTRL-PRSTV-3SG.A- come
'There's a deer coming.' [W10:0135]

However, the /h/ is usually elided even in the final syllable, so that the form above is pronounced *rusa ukat-man* instead of *rusa ukahat-man*, at least in casual speech. In all other positions, the prefix is invariably *at-*:

(817) i= k-at-a-p- hu-h-a-m
PROX:I/II.PL= PRS.NTRL-PRSTV-3SG.A-CT- emerge-2|3PL.U-EXT-VEN
'Here they are, they're returning home.' [W19:0196]

---

[5] This is a major difference between my description of Coastal Marind and Drabbe's (1955) grammar of the Eastern dialect. Drabbe (pp. 126–127) lists a range of forms with past and future time reference. None of these forms are attested in my data. According to Drabbe, *hat-* means 'decidedly' [*beslist*] or 'really, actually' [*werkelijk*]. This gloss does not fit with my observation and I find no support for it in the texts collected by Drabbe.

Fig. 15.1: Use of the Presentative *hat-* in example (815): the speaker is pointing to a bamboo pole (off camera, to the right)

(The verb *hawa* 'emerge' has the idiomatic meaning 'return home' when prefixed with the Contessive *ap-*.)

The basic meaning of *hat-*, 'in plain sight' or 'obvious to everyone', is evident in contexts where speaker and addressee interact face-to-face within a delimited space, and share the visual access to the referent. But I have also recorded instances in which *hat-* is used without any shared visual access to the relevant state-of-affairs.

Consider the following corpus example, in which Yustina, the mother in my host family in Wambi, addressed me from the other room to remind me about a bunch of bananas that had been donated to me by a villager. The speaker was probably worried that someone might steal bananas from me, or that they were going to go bad unless I ate them. I could not see the bananas, since the kitchen (where I was sitting) is separated from the adjacent room by a bamboo wall (and I was sitting with my back against this wall).

(818) Bruno napet-eho   e=   k-at-ø-am-   ka-hwayob-a
       B.   banana.sp(III) PROX:III= PRS.NTRL-PRSTV-3SG.A-2SG.GEN- INESS-hang:III.U-EXT
       'Bruno, your bananas are hanging in here.'   [W11:0473]

My hypothesis about such uses is that the speaker wants to communicate that the referent is in the open, and potentially available for the addressee to view at a later point in time. The bananas, which were hanging from a crossbeam in the ceiling, are also plain for everybody else to see, which could be of relevance if the worry is that they will be stolen unless I stash them away.

Compare with the use of the Deictic prefix series, which is used as an invitation to the hearer to realign her attention to some referent that is outside her current focus (§15.4). According to my understanding, the Deictic prefix is not used here since the speaker is not asking me to get up, move to the doorway, and direct my attention to the bananas — she only informs me that the bananas are there, plainly visible, and will remain so until I take care of them.

The prefix *hat-* is not only used with referents or state-of-affairs that are visually evident, but also when it is the sound of an event or the noise made by the referent that can be clearly perceived. Example (819) can be said if one hears a motorcycle approaching in the distance; the motorcycle does not have to be visible for *hat-* to be used. The utterance in (820) was said as an explanation for the noises that were coming from a bag with newly caught fish that the speaker was holding. The fish itself was not visible to either the speaker or me. (The use of the Auxiliary *wa* to express animal vocalisations is described in §17.1.2.1.)

(819) motor   epe   te-k-at-ø-   w-alin-em
       motorcycle(m)(III) DIST:III GIV:III-PRS.NTRL-PRSTV-3SG.A- III.U-call-VEN
       (lit.) 'There's a motorcycle making noise hither.'

(820) banggabang u=   ka-hat-ø-   w-a
       pufferfish(II) PROX:II= PRS.NTRL-PRSTV-3SG.A- 3SG.U-AUX
       'There's a pufferfish making noise.'

There is a single example of *hat-* (out of a total of ca. 50 corpus attestations) in a past time context. The speaker was describing the search for a person who was separated from the rest of the group during a hunt. In the account of these events, one of the protagonists sees tracks in the grass and says

(821) e=   k-at-ø-   toman,   kwemek epe
       PROX= DIR-PRSTV-3SG.A- descend.to.swamp morning DIST:III
       'Here's where he went down, in the morning.'   [W02:0081]

which clearly has past time reference, as indicated by the context (the person had disappeared in the morning) and the explicit use of the time adverbial 'in the morning'.[6] Interestingly, the reason *hat-* is used must be the presence of tracks in the grass, which

---

[6] In this example, the *k-* prefix must be the Directional Orientation, which is used to signal location with punctual events (§11.1.4.1). The preceding clitic must be the reduced version of the adverb *ehe* 'here', rather than the gender clitic of the Presentational construction. The prefix *k-* is identical to the allomorph of the Neutral orientation used in present time contexts, but it is not possible to interpret this clause as having present time reference ('here he is going down').

are plainly visible at the (narrated) moment of speech. A possible interpretation of this is that *hat-* may be used about past events as long as they are inferred from presently available evidence (i.e. basically an evidential use). This is an interesting possibility that needs to be explored in future work on Coastal Marind.

15.4 Engagement marking: The Deictic prefixes

The Deictic prefix series (Proximal *eh-* and Distal *ep-*) has two main uses: verbs carrying these prefixes are used to talk about current states-of-affairs that are outside the addressee's focus of attention, as discussed in this section, and they are used to form present tense dependent clauses, as discussed in §20.1.1.2. The formal properties of the Deictic series are addressed before the description of its function in main clauses (§15.4.2).

15.4.1 Shape of the Deictic prefixes

The Deictic verb prefix consists of the substring *V-* marking gender agreement, followed by either *h-*, marking proximal deixis, or *p-*, marking distal deixis. I consider the variant with *p-* to be the unmarked choice, so only the Proximal *h-* is labelled in the morphemic analysis ('PROX'). The combinations of gender vowels with *h-/p-* are shown in Table 15.1. Compare the Proximal and Distal demonstratives *ehe* 'this, here' and *epe* 'that, there' (§4.2), from which the Deictic forms are probably somehow derived.

Tab. 15.1: The Deictic verb prefixes

	PROX SG	PROX PL	DIST SG	DIST PL
I	eh-	ih-	ep-	ip-
II	uh-		up-	
III	eh-		ep-	
IV	ih-		ip-	

Since the gender marking vowel and the Proximal/Distal segments never occur separated, the combination is best thought of as a compound affix, and not as two separate prefixes occupying separate position classes. The gender vowel is not separated from the deictic component in the interlinear glossing, so the sequence is treated as a unit, e.g. *up-* 'DIST:II' or *ih-* 'PROX:I/II.PL'.

Any argument in the clause may act as the controller of gender agreement in the Deictic prefix. For example, S-arguments are controllers in examples (822–824) below; a recipient-like argument in (825), further below; a transitive O-argument in (1082) on p. 530; and a transitive A-argument was seen in (1a) on p. 2. The choice of agreement trigger in clauses with multiple arguments (with different genders) is probably related to relative prominence or topichood, as has been noted for other languages with similarly 'trigger-happy' agreement targets (Comrie 2003).

The Deictic spans position classes –17 to –14. It can be followed by the 1st or 2nd person Actor prefixes of class –13, e.g. 1st person *no-* (although it is incompatible with the Future of the same class).

(822)   *epa-no-   man-em!*
        DIST:I-1.A-   come-VEN
        'I'm coming!'

As the preceding example shows, the vowel *e-* (here marking the singular of Gender I) escapes antepenultimate raising to [i] (§2.5.1), despite being in the third syllable from the right edge of the prefixal complex. The preservation of *e* always happens when the vowel is the exponence of gender (e.g. in the Present Polar Question prefix *ek-*, §19.2.1).

15.4.2 Realignment of attention

This is the most prominent use of the Deictic prefixes in face-to-face conversation. In brief, a verb form marked with the Deictic series is used to make a statement about a current state-of-affairs that is outside the addressee's focus of attention, usually with the implied meaning that the Addressee should shift his or her attention to the state-of-affairs in question, thereby aligning it with the attention of the speaker. This attention-realigning function is discussed at length in Olsson (2019a), in which the label 'Absconditive' (from Latin *absconditus* 'hidden') was used to capture the fact that the state-of-affairs is in some way hidden from the addressee. I opt for the label 'Deictic' in this grammar as it is easier to reconcile with both the main clause use described here and the unrelated use in subordinate clauses described in §20.1.1.2.

I will clarify the attention-realigning function of the Deictic prefixes by discussing some examples. Consider first the scene in Figure 15.2, which shows a still from a video recording of some teenagers cleaning out the well outside my house in Wambi. Dula, the boy in the left periphery of the image (marked by 'Spkr.'), sees someone approaching (from the right, off camera) carrying two large buckets. He addresses Pau and Yakoba, the boy and the girl who are busy drawing water from the well (both marked 'Addr.'), with the utterance given in glossed form in (823). (Teo, the younger boy standing with his back against the camera, does not seem to be intended as an addressee of Dula's utterance.)

420 — 15 Mood, attitude and engagement

Fig. 15.2: Use of the Deictic verb prefix in example (823): the speaker sees someone approaching from the right, off camera

(823) ep-ø-   man-em,   dua   ya   m-a-   ka-man
       DIST:I-3SG.A- come-VEN two(m) real OBJ-3SG.A- WITH-come
       'There he's coming, he's bringing two.'   [W06:0103]

The use of the Distal prefix *ep-* (agreeing in Gender I, since the subject is a male person) in the first clause of the utterance is motivated by the fact that the two addressees are focusing their attention on the well, away from the referent that Dula wants to bring to their attention. After hearing Dula's statement, the addressees turn around and look at the approaching person. They realign their focus of attention with that of Dula, meaning that the interactional goal implied by his use of the Deictic prefix is achieved.

Another occurrence of the Deictic prefix series, from the same video recording, is illustrated in Figure 15.3. The speaker Teo (ca. 7 years old; marked 'Spr') has just been told to go away from the well by Pau, who is drawing water. Pau wants Teo and his younger sister Susana (visible behind Teo) to take off their shirts so that Pau can pour water on the children. Teo is not interested in showering, so he refuses and attempts to deflect Pau's attention from this by pointing out that there is a little fish swimming around inside the well (or so he imagines). Teo's utterance, given in (824), uses the Distal prefix since he wants Pau to shift his attention away from him and his sister, and look at the fish in the well.

Fig. 15.3: Another use of the Deictic verb prefix, in example (824): the speaker sees a fish in the well

(824) mbya ka, ade! kosi-awe   up-ø-   kw-ayit-a
      no   EXCLAM small-fish(II) DIST:II-3SG.A- INESS-run.around:3SG.U-EXT
      'No, wait! There's a little fish swimming around inside.' [W06:0006]

The Deictic series may also be used to redirect attention in a more abstract sense, as when one corrects some erroneous assumption made by the addressee. This is how I interpret the use of the Distal Deictic in (825), which was observed in the following situation. I was sitting with an elderly woman who was talking to me in Marind. During a pause in the conversation, my adoptive brother-in-law walked by, and must have assumed that we had been sitting in silence, because he said to the lady 'You should talk to him in Marind, so that he learns'. The lady replied as in (825). The function of the Distal Deictic prefix in this utterance is clearly not to redirect the addressee's attention to some physical state-of-affairs (unlike the previously discussed examples), but rather to shift his attention away from the erroneous assumption that he had made ('She is not talking to him') to the actual situation.

(825) ep-ak-o-   lay-e!
      DIST:I-1.A-3SG.DAT-   talk-IPFV
      'I *am* talking to him!'

Note that (825) features the Distal *p*-version of the Deictic series, yet the state-of-affairs that it points to is not distant from either of the participants. It is because of uses like this that I consider the Distal variant to be unmarked: it does not seem to contribute much of a deictic specification. This contrasts with the Proximal Deictic series, which always indicates that the state-of-affairs is 'here' with respect to the speaker. Most attestations are in copula clauses (§17.4), in which the speaker draws the attention of the addressee to some item, e.g. one that the speaker is holding:

(826) muy   eh-ø-am-   Ø
      meat(III) PROX:III-3SG.A-2SG.GEN- be.NPST
      'Here you go, here's your meat.'   [W12:0343]

The suggestion that the Distal verb prefix provides little information about deixis corresponds to the observation that the Distal demonstrative *epe* seems to be relatively vague in its specification for distance (see §4.2.1).

The attention-realigning function of the Deictic prefices is essentially the opposite of that of the Presentative prefix *hat-*, which signals that a state-of-affairs is in plain sight (see §15.3.5).

16 Distribution of events in time and space

This chapter groups together a number of verbal categories that describe how events are distributed in time and space. The first three sections discuss categories that have vaguely aspect-like meanings: §16.1 describes the use of Pluractional forms, §16.2 describes the Repetitive *i-* and §16.3 describes the Prioritive *ka-*. The remaining sections concern distribution in space: §16.4 describes the Remote *an-*, §16.5 the Contessive *ap-*, §16.6 the Inessive *kw-*, and §16.7 the Venitive suffix *-em*.

16.1 Pluractionality

16.1.1 General remarks

The Pluractional[1] form of a verb serves to express multiple events, i.e. that an action is distributed over time (occurring several times in succession/habitually) or distributed in space (occurring in different places). There is frequently interaction with participant number, so that a Pluractional form must be used with a plural S/O participant, or because the action is performed individually rather than collectively.

Consider the verb 'carry on one's shoulders', which uses the stem *ahwikeh* with a 3sg Undergoer (e.g. an animal being carried) or an inanimate Undergoer from Gender III, such as one or several bamboo poles. As seen in (827), however, the Pluractional stem *lahwikeh* (formed with a prefix *l-*) must be used if the act is distributed over time, as indicated by the word 'repeatedly' in the translations of (827b); it is also used if multiple participants carry one or several poles each, as indicated by 'individually' in translation (ii) of example (827b) (alternatively, this could be considered distribution over space, since each person carries in a different spot).

(827) a. *ahwikeh*
  i. one person carry bamboo pole(s) once
  ii. several people (collectively) carry one bamboo pole once

 b. *lahwikeh*
  i. one person carry bamboo pole(s) repeatedly
  ii. several people (individually) carry bamboo poles once/repeatedly
  iii. several people (collectively) carry one bamboo pole repeatedly

---

[1] Terminology introduced by Newman (1990). Pluractionality is prominent in many of the languages spoken in the South New Guinea area, e.g. Marori (Arka 2012) and the languages of the Yam family (Carroll 2016: 246–258, Lee 2016, inter alia).

Pluractional marking, which expresses plurality of events, must be distinguished from person indexing in the verb stem, which marks person/number of animates (and gender for inanimates) — see Chapter 10. Number indexing and pluractionality are orthogonal categories and verb stems may be marked simultaneously according to both. Thus, the 2|3PL.U stem *ahwikah* is used for several animals (e.g. a bag full of shrimp) being carried by one person, whereas its Pluractional form *lahwikah* would be used for several people carrying several animals independently, and so on.

Pluractional marking is only relevant for a subset of Coastal Marind verbs. I have identified ca. 120 verbs for which corresponding Pluractional stems exist (20% of known verbs), derived by means of prefixes *l-*, *e-*, *i-*, *o-*, *u-*. The distribution of these prefixes is somewhat complicated and shows various irregularities (such as being realised as infixes for a small number of verbs); the details are given in §16.1.2. A small number of verbs are considered inherently Pluractional, as discussed in §16.1.3. Of the remaining 500-odd verbs in my lexical file there are probably some for which I failed to identify the Pluractional form, so the actual proportion of verbs with a Pluractional counterpart is perhaps closer to 25–30%.

The semantics of Pluractional forms are addressed in §16.1.4.

16.1.2 The Pluractional prefix

Here I describe the form of the Pluractional stems. Verbs that can form a Pluractional stem (around 20–30% of all verbs) do so by means of a prefix. The prefix *l-* is the default prefix with vowel-initial stems (828).

(828)

Base verb	Derived stem	
ahwikeh	lahwikeh	'many carry on shoulders'[2]
ahwasiy	lahwasiy	'suck repeatedly'
asik	lasik	'hunt repeatedly'
ehwes	lehwes	'pile up lots'
esad	lesad	'cut in pieces'
isik	lisik	'many become full'
isiy	lisiy	'bite repeatedly'

Most consonant-initial verbs use the prefix /e-/, realised as *e-* in monosyllabic stems, and *i-* in polysyllabic stems (829), as predicted by the rules of vowel gradation (§2.5.1).

---

[2] It is impossible to convey the full semantic range of a Pluractional stem in a gloss; the glosses given are rough approximations chosen for quotability rather than precision.

(829) bay   ebay   'finish (food) repeatedly'
       gan   egan   'hear repeatedly'
       yad   eyad   'flash light repeatedly'
       bahin   ibahin   'finish (2|3PL.U) repeatedly'
       haniy   ihaniy   'bite several spots'
       hwayik   ihwayik   'many get hooked'
       kababuy ikbabuy   'many sink'
       kahod   ikahod   'bend head down repeatedly'
       lawetok ilwetok   'turn around repeatedly'
       mahid   imahid   'many get angry'

Verbs beginning with one of the coronal obstruents /d t s/ use the prefix /o-/, which is realised as o- if the stem is monosyllabic but undergoes gradation (§2.5.1) to u- if it has two or more syllables (830).

(830) tad   otad   'cause to burn many'
       tak   otak   'many become empty'
       dahetok   udhetok   'go back and forth repeatedly'
       saletok   usletok   'hide in several spots'
       samandak usmandak 'block off (river) repeatedly'
       taheb   utaheb   'fill several'
       tamak   utamak   'many float'
       timin   utimin   'many wake up'

This rule only targets obstruents, because verb roots beginning with the coronal non-obstruent /l/ do not occur with the o- and u- prefixes, as seen for the verb i-lwetok 'turn around repeatedly' given earlier. This formulation also predicts that the rule does not affect verbs with initial non-obstruents /n-/ and /nd-/, but this is impossible to evaluate as there are no such verb roots among the verbs that take Pluractional prefixes.[3]

An exception to the observation that stems with an initial coronal obstruent take the prefix /o-/ in the Pluractional is a small group of such verbs that have the vowel u in their final syllable. The prefix /o-/ (most likely an innovation) has not spread to these verbs, which have prefixed i- in the Pluractional forms just like other consonant-initial stems (this is an allomorph of /e-/, although I am not aware of any monosyllabic verb stems with an initial coronal obstruent and the vowel u where it would surface as e-).

---

[3] In fact, the only verb roots with initial /n-/ found so far in the language are nahek 'stay awake throughout the night', the suppletive plural stem nayat 'many be moving' and the Pluractional stem nin 'lie down repeatedly'. There are no verbs with initial /nd-/. I am not aware of the explanation for the absence of these sounds in the beginning of verb roots (they are not uncommon in nouns).

(831) | dahuy | idahuy | 'hold s.b. back repeatedly'
| sakud | isakud | 'fasten tight-fitting objects (III)'
| sakituk | iskituk | 'fasten tight-fitting objects (IV)'
| tahuk | itahuk | 'stick many to surface'
| tahun | itahun | 'clean s.b.'s bottom repeatedly'
| takun | itakun | 'make roof repeatedly'
| talun | italun | 'push repeatedly'

A remarkable fact about the alternation between the allomorphs of the Pluractional prefix is that their shape is triggered by the shape of the 3sg stems of the verb: if a stem has a Pluractional form with a prefixed *u-* in 3sg, it retains the *u-* throughout the stem paradigm, even in forms that have a final syllable with the vowel /u/. Thus, the 3sg Pluractional of *saletok* 'hide' is *usletok*, while the 2|3pl stem *salituk* has the Pluractional stem *uslituk*, and not **islituk*. Conversely, the Pluractional of *tahuk* 'stick to a surface' uses the prefix *i-* even in forms without syllable-final /u/, e.g. the stem *tahyohyab* 'stick item of Gender IV to a surface', which has the Pluractional stem *ithyohyab*.

A small group of monosyllabic verbs with initial /b/ fail to take the expected prefix *e-* (cf. *ebay* 'finish food/drink'), for no clear reason (832).

(832) | bad | obad | 'dig wells'
| bak | obak | 'perforate in several spots'
| bewn | obewn | 'lean forward repeatedly'
| bug | **u**bug | 'cut open animals'

Another group of verbs take the prefix *l-* found with vowel-initial stems, but show various idiosyncrasies, either in the prefixed material or elsewhere in the stem.

(833) | hwis | **l**ohwis | 'many descend'
| lik | **l**alik | 'rivers to flow'
| masud | **l**imasud | 'fold repeatedly'
| akam | **l**alakam | 'drip in several spots'
| ahuy | **l**ahum | 'many carry strapped to head'
| ahus | **l**ahos | 'pull out many'

Two small groups of verbs form the Pluractional stem with an infixed vowel after the first consonant, which in the first group is always *k-* (834).

(834) | kasid | k**i**sid | 'tie many'
| kadahib | k**i**dahib | 'embrace repeatedly'
| kahaleb | k**i**haleb | 'lose grip, drop repeatedly'
| kandakib | k**i**ndakib | 'pull repeatedly'
| kahwab | k**o**hab | 'remove tight-fitting objects'
| katab | k**o**tab | 'pluck many'

It is not clear why these have an infixed vowel or what determines its quality (it is sometimes *i*, sometimes *o*). Other verbs starting with *k-* take the expected prefix, e.g. *ikayam* 'look up'. The second group has stems starting with *y-* (835).

(835) yadak   yedak   'hit repeatedly'
       yadan   yedan   'get blisters'
       yadewn   yedewn   'leave (tr.) repeatedly'
       yadaman   yidaman   'sky become red all over'
       yadetok   yudetok   'pierce body part repeatedly'
       yanetok   yunetok   'many carry'
       yanakeh   yunakeh   'cook (repeatedly?)'

Again, it is not clear why these have an infixed vowel or what determines its quality (apparently /e-/ in the first four verbs above, but *u* in others).

Three disyllabic verbs starting in /ɣ-/ do not exhibit infixation, but employ the prefix *ya-* (836).

(836) yakeh   yayakeh   'lie down on one's back'
       yaneb   yayaneb   'carry s.b. on one's hip'
       yoman   yayoman   'approach'

Three common verbs, *hawa* 'emerge', *hi* '(animate) fall' and *hay* 'inanimate fall', express the Pluractional by means of a unique pattern of reduplication of material from the initial syllable. The first two verbs belong to the small class of verbs that index the Undergoer by means of suffixes (cf. §10.3.3); below forms for 3rd and 1st person Undergoers are given. None of the other lexemes belonging to this inflectional class show this pattern of reduplication.

(837) hawa   huhu   'emerge repeatedly (3SG.U)'
       hun   huhun   'emerge repeatedly (1.U)'
       hi   hihi   'fall repeatedly (3SG.U)'
       hin   hihin   'fall repeatedly (1.U)'
       hay   hehay   'fall repeatedly (inanimate)'

There are ca. 20 verbs that lack Pluractional forms, but for which there exist unrelated verbs with a corresponding Pluractional meaning. Such pairings are described in §16.1.3.

16.1.3 Inherently Pluractional verbs

Ca. 20 verbs have inherently pluractional semantics, e.g. *anik* 'sit down on several occasions'. This verb covers the range of meanings that a Pluractional form of *ambid* 'sit down' would have, and therefore blocks the prefixal derivation of a stem *l-ambid, resulting in a suppletion-like relationship between lexemes such as 'sit down' and 'sit down on several occasions'. Again, pluractionality must be kept separate from number indexing: *ambid* has a suppletive plural stem *haman*, which is used for more than one person sitting down. This stem is not Pluractional, because it may only be used about several people sitting down on one occasion. If several people sit down on different occasions, the Pluractional *anik* is used (*anik* does not distinguish the number of the subject).

Certain verbs lack stems used for plural S/O arguments, and one must instead employ the corresponding Pluractional verb. This seems to be the case especially when the action is such that plural S/O participants are unlikely to act/be acted upon collectively. For example, *kahek* 'climb' is only used with a singular subject, and the Pluractional verb *kapet* must be used with a plural subject, even if the climbing occurs on a single occasion and in one place. One could speculate that the Pluractional form has ousted the standard form in plural-subject contexts because climbing typically is performed individually. If several people climb in one tree, they do so in different spots, hanging on to different branches, which matches the semantics of Pluractional forms.

I list all verbs that correspond to distinct Pluractional verbs in Table 16.1. The table also indicates which of these verbs have stems that are suppletive in the plural. Number-suppletion is restricted to non-Pluractional verbs. The table is divided into two pairs of columns. The rightmost two columns, labelled 'Multiple events', show the verbs that would be used in contexts that normally trigger Pluractional forms, i.e. actions distributed in time/space (cf. §16.1.1). The left two columns, labelled 'One event', show verbs that are used in contexts in which those conditions are not met. As seen in the lower part of the table, several Pluractional verbs have intruded into the left half, and are used whenever plural S/O arguments are used, even if there is no distribution in space or over several occasions. I still consider such verbs inherently Pluractional, so *kapet* is glossed 'climb.PLA' regardless of whether it is used to mean 'one person climb on several occasions' or 'several people climb on one occasion'.

Interestingly, there are few clear examples of Pluractional forms derived by prefixes that have become obligatory whenever the S/O argument is plural. The only clear case is *hayaman* 'enter water', since its Pluractional stem *ihyaman* (not in the table) has to be used if several people enter water. For some other verbs there is a strong preference for the Pluractional to be used with plural participants, but it is not exceptionless. For example, *hwis* 'go down' normally occurs in its Pluractional form *lohwis* with a plural subject, but the simplex form *hwis* seems to be acceptable if the participants form a unitary group (e.g. travelling in a vehicle).

Tab. 16.1: Verbal meanings expressed by inherently Pluractional verbs (right side of the dividing line). Stems that are suppletive for plural participant number are indicated by boldface.

	One event		Multiple events	
Gloss	SG S/O	PL S/O	SG S/O	PL S/O
'item be standing'	itala	itala	ehaya	ehaya
'grasp vertical item'	bik	bituk	loban	lobah
'plant'	yaɣahwig	yaɣahwig	yayoh	yayoh
'become'	win	in	onggat	enggat
'throw'	kwegen	kugahin	kuhig	kuhahig
'go, leave'	umuh	umah	um	yum
'come'	man	**nayam**	um	yum
'be moving'	yet	**nayat**	um	yum
'sit down'	ambid	**haman**	anik	anik
'stand up'	atin	**wayaman**	lemed	lemed
'lie down'	yali	**hok**	nin	nin
'run away'	ihon	**awan**	bamet	bamet
'climb'	kahek	kapet	kapet	kapet
'cry'	ihw	lihwanak	lihwanak	lihwanak
'shoot'	deh	yas	was	yas
'put horizontal item'	han	ibutuk	ibotok	ibutuk
'grasp horizontal item'	han	yahanid	wahanid	yahanid
'put vertical items'	bakeh	ilawewn	ilawewn	ilawewn
'plant coconut'	bakeh	yok	yok	yok
'catch'	yakeh	lemeh	lemem	lemeh
'hit'	wamuk/wasib	isak	usak	isak
'put inside'	kahekon	yukahin	yokun	yukahin
'give birth to'	kaguh	ewah	ewah	ewah

16.1.4 Functions of Pluractional forms

The Pluractional is semantically heterogeneous. Just as the formation (and existence) of a Pluractional form for a given verb typically is more or less unpredictable, it seems that the semantics of Pluractional forms vary from verb to verb. For certain verbs the Pluractional seems largely optional in contexts referring to plural events, whereas other verbs obligatorily appear in their Pluractional form whenever the described action is distributed in time or space. For some verbs, distribution in space appears to be more relevant that distribution in time, and vice versa. Despite spending considerable time in the field attempting to systematise these differences, I was not able to arrive at any comprehensive taxonomy, so this will be left for future investigation. Below I present a selection of uses that are typical for some, but probably not all, Pluractional forms.

16.1.4.1 Distribution over time

See §14.2.6 for the use of Pluractionals in habitual contexts. Pluractional forms are also used with expressions of exact cardinality ('*n* times', usually expressed by a numeral plus *se* or the prefix *s-*, both meaning 'only'). In this respect Coastal Marind differs from many other languages in which pluractionals may not be used if the number of events is made explicit (Hofherr and Laca 2012: 16).

(838) a. *hyakod sa-mo-   w-asib!*
       one   ONLY-FUT:2SG.A- 3SG.U-hit
       'Hit him/her once!'

   b. *inah sa-mo-   u-sak*
      two   ONLY-FUT:2SG.A- 3SG.U-hit.PLA
      'Hit him/her twice!'

Pluractional forms are used in contexts describing general ability or potential, as in the following examples. See also example (759.1) above.

(839) *mbya k-a-   ewah-e*
      NEG   PRS.NTRL-3SG.A-   give.birth.PLA-IPFV
      'She is sterile/can't give birth.'

(840) *kambet menda-b-ø-   lissa⟨n⟩ab,   mbya ka-no-   e-gan-e*
      ear   PERF-ACT-3SG.A- become.deaf⟨1.U⟩ NEG   PRS.NTRL-1.A-   PLA-hear-IPFV
      'I've become deaf, I can't hear.'

Verbs describing events that typically consist of multiple identical microevents performed in succession and involving the same participants ('multiplicative' actions in Xrakovskij 1997) do not use Pluractional forms to express this. For example, the verbs *atuk* 'flap wings', *yoseh* 'wallaby to jump', *mamud* 'grind' and *alak* 'chop off bark' lack separate Pluractional stems, and employ standard durativising morphology such as the Past Durative *d-* or Non-Past Imperfective *-e* to express 'be flapping one's wings' and so on. The verb *akam* 'drip' has a Pluractional stem *lalakam* but uses it for distribution in space, i.e. 'dripping in several places', as when a ceiling is leaking in several spots. Other verbs require the Pluractional to express multiplicative actions, e.g. *e-yad* 'PLA-uncover' in the sense 'keep flashing a flashlight', or *y⟨e⟩dak* 'thump repeatedly' (from *yadak* 'thump once'), as in:

(841) A hunter describing how he attracted a wallaby by imitating mating behaviour.
      nama k-ak-o-   n-a   y⟨e⟩dak: gu, gu, gu
      now   DIR-1.A-3SG.DAT- 1.U-AUX ⟨PLA⟩thump
      'Now I started thumping the ground at it: bang, bang, bang.' [W12:0194-0195]

Another prefix whose meaning involves more than one event is the Repetitive *i-* 'again' (§16.2). The difference is that the use of *i-* presupposes rather than asserts multiple events, so I do not consider *i-* to be a pluractional marker. The use of the Repetitive does not require the verb to be in the Pluractional form, as seen in the following example, because *hi* here refers to a single falling event (although a previous falling event is presupposed).

(842) *Yaba-Takah epe k-ø-i-   hi   muy ti*
      Y.-B.   there DIR-3SG.A-RE- fall:3SG.U meat with
      'There Yaba-Takah fell again with the meat.'   [W03:0138]

The Repetitive may combine with a Pluractional verb (such as *hihi* 'fall.PLA') to describe e.g. a person falling several times after having fallen on a previous occasion.

Recall also that Pluractional forms are used in the formation of some nominal forms suggesting plurality of events: in compounds such as *onggat-kapet* 'climbing of coconut palms' (< *kapet* 'climb.PLA'; §3.6.1.5), and in deverbal instrument nouns such as *kehway* 'paddle' (< *e-hway* 'PLA-paddle'; §3.7.2).

16.1.4.2 Distribution over space

The following examples illustrate events in single vs. multiple locations with the verb 'fill'. In (843) reference is made to a single location (a church) being filled up with people, so the non-Pluractional form 2|3PL.U *tahab* is used. In (844) several boxes are filled up with sago, hence the use of Pluractional *utaheb* (as well as the Past Durative *d-*).

(843) *gereja   ah-ø-   kyamin   ehetago Makaling, k-a-p-   w-a*
      church(m) DEP-3SG.A- enter:2|3PL.U like.this M.   DIR-3SG.A-CT- 3SG.U-AUX
      tahab
      fill:2|3PL.U
      'When they entered the church in Makaling, they filled it up.'
                                                                      [W16:0034-0035]

(844) *da   karton ka-d-e-na-y-   yokun,*
      sago(III) box(m) DIR-DUR-3PL>1-1.DAT-1PL- put.inside.PLA:III.U
      ka-d-a-p-   w-a   u-tah⟨e⟩b, [...]
      DIR-DUR-3SG.A-CT- 3SG.U-AUX PLA-fill⟨III.U⟩
      'They put sago in boxes for us, it filled up [the boxes]. [...]' [W15:0083]

Some verbs can appear in the Pluractional form to express that the action is performed while moving around, i.e. an ambulative use (Dressler 1968). Consider the inherently

Pluractional verb *loban*, which usually is used in the sense 'grasp several vertically oriented items' (e.g. two bottles; the corresponding non-Pluractional verb is *bik*). In the following overheard example, however, the verb is used about a single camera bag that I had asked a boy to carry while I was taking photographs. The friend who asked what he was carrying used the Pluractional verb despite there being only one carried item, since the boy was carrying it while walking around.

(845) ta   ma-h-o-b-   loban-e?
      what   OBJ-ROG-2SG.A-ACT-   grasp.PLA:III.U-IPFV
      'What are you carrying around?'

16.1.4.3 Distribution over participants

Pluractional forms are used in various contexts that imply a plurality of events because the action is distributed over several participants. For example, Pluractional verbs are used with distributive numeral expressions, as illustrated by the elicited data in (846). Example (846a) describes a single event of giving (literally: putting), so the non-Pluractional *hahin* is used. In (846b), one gift is distributed to each recipient. Each giving-event involves a single gift given to a single recipient, but since this implies multiple giving events, the situation as a whole must be expressed by means of the Pluractional verb *ibutuk*.

(846) a. dadami   kyasom hyakod m-ak-e-   hahin
          betel.pepper(IV) girl   one   OBJ-1.A-2|3PL.DAT-   put:IV.U
          'I gave the girls one betel pepper.' (to share)

      b. dadami   hyakod ti   m-ak-e-   ibutuk
          betel.pepper(IV) one   with OBJ-1.A-2|3PL.DAT-   put.PLA:IV.U
          'I gave them one betel pepper each.'

The same situation obtains in reciprocal contexts (847). Since 'give each other' implies at least two different acts of giving, the Pluractional form of the verb (if there is such a form) is used, as in (847b). A corpus example is in (848). See also §13.2.

(847) a. katal   m-ak-o-   hahin
          money(IV) OBJ-1.A-3SG.DAT- put:IV.U
          'I gave him/her money.'

      b. katal   m-enam-   ibutuk-a
          money(IV) OBJ-RCPR-   put.PLA:IV.U-EXT
          'They are giving each other money.'

(848) epe   k-inam-i-   y⟨i⟩da⟨n⟩awn
       there DIR-RCPR-RE-   ⟨PLA⟩leave⟨RCPR⟩

'There they left each other again.'   [D03:0106]

It is sometimes impossible to distinguish distribution over participants from distribution in space. Consider the corpus data in (849). The speaker described how she and other villagers were about to return home after a gathering. When transcribing this text, I was initially confused by the Pluractional form *huhun* in line 1, followed by the non-Pluractional version *hun* in line 2. The speaker with whom I was working explained that in line 1, the speaker is referring to all the different villagers who were about to return to their respective houses. The Pluractional is used since each group of participants is going to a different place. In line 2, the speaker refers to herself and her family, who returned to the house where I recorded her. A single group of participants went to one place, hence the non-Pluractional form *hun*.

(849) 1. nok   ka-p-e-p-   n-a   huhu-n
          1   DIR-FUT:1.A-1PL-CT-   1.U-AUX   emerge.PLA-1.U

      'Each of us were going to go home.'

      2. nok   k-ak-e-p-   n-a   hu-n
          1   DIR-1.A-1PL-CT-   1.U-AUX   emerge-1.U

      'We went home.'   [W16:0065-0066]

16.2 The Repetitive *i-*

This prefix has the same meanings as English *again*, i.e. 'for a second time' (repetitive use) and 'back to the previous situation' (restitutive use; see e.g. Kamp and Rossdeutscher 1994). Positionally it belongs to position class −6 of the prefixal complex. It is the sole member of this position class, so it can co-occur with any other prefixes. To keep the interlinear glosses short, I gloss it 'RE' (like the English prefix *re-* in *reconsider* or *re-start*).

In its most common use, the addition of *i-* to a verb signals repetition, i.e. that the event takes place for a second (or third, or *n*-th) time:

(850) The speaker described how the sago beating equipment was taken care of after a sago pounding session.

> aphan ago, adeh m-a-p- l-ehwek-a,
> washing.trough(III) QUOT RLQ OBJ-3SG.A-CT- PLA-put.in.bifurcation:III.U-EXT
>
> yapap mak-i-e- yol
> tomorrow FUT:1.A-RE-1PL- pound.sago
>
> '[About the] washing trough, I said: "Let it be, tomorrow we will pound sago again".' [W20:0074]

The prefix is more rarely attested in the restitutive use. A corpus example is in (851). The preceding context describes how the participants got a lift from a neighbouring village with a truck driver. The driver let the passengers alight as they reached Awidab, the easternmost part of Wambi. This is the first time the participants alight from the truck, so the prefix *i-* does not signal 'for the second time', rather it expresses a return to a previous state, i.e. the state of being outside the truck.

(851) *Awidab, anep kay masuk ya k-ø-i-e- luya⟨n⟩ab*
A. EMPH:III road enter(m) real DIR-3SG.A-RE-1PL- pour⟨1.U⟩
'In Awidab, he dropped (lit. poured) us off again by the road that goes in.' [W19:0422]

An elicited example showing the restitutive use is in (852). In the second clause the addressee is urged to return the door to its previous state of being closed. In Malay this would correspond to the unambiguous *tutup kembali* (lit.) 'close return', whereas the Coastal Marind and English equivalents are ambiguous between the repetitive and restitutive readings.

(852) *kay ah- kab! ah-i- lalid!*
door IMP- open IMP-RE- close
'Open the door! Close it again!'

Another corpus example illustrating the restitutive use is in (853). Note that the verb in the first clause is marked with the Prioritive *ka-*. This prefix presents something of a mirror image of *i-*, since it presupposes a following event, whereas *i-* presupposes a preceding event (cf. §16.3).

(853) Complaining about a small child playing in the kitchen as others were cooking.
mayay mend-a-ka- kwamin, ehe tanama e= k-ø-i- hawa
first PERF-3SG.A-PRI- enter:3SG.U here again PROX= DIR-3SG.A-RE- emerge:3SG.U
'First she went in, then she went out again.' [W11:0348]

As seen in (853), Coastal Marind has a second expression meaning 'again', viz. the adverb *tanama* (§18.4.6). This adverb seems to be preferred over *i-* in certain contexts, notably with motion verbs to express the restitutive 'back to the previous place' (e.g. 'they went back again'). In other contexts the two markers are freely interchangeable, and they frequently co-occur within the same clause, as in (854). This reinforcement does not affect the meaning 'again'.

(854) *yamu-yanakeh   tanama   ka-n-i-   y-a,   mayay-milah epe*
       mourning.feast-cook again   DIR-3PL.A-RE-   2|3PL.U-AUX front-village   DIST:III

   'They prepared a *yamu* feast again, in the western part of the village.'
   [W19:0229]

Cf. Wälchli (2006) on 'light' and 'heavy' *again*-expressions.

16.3 The Prioritive *ka-*

In its main use the Prioritive *ka-* expresses a preceding event (§16.3.1). Less frequently it appears with a similative meaning (§16.3.2). The Prioritive is assigned to position class –2 in the templatic system presented in Chapter 8, i.e. the next-to-last position class. There seem to be no co-occurrence restrictions on the Prioritive, so it can be combined with any other prefix of the prefixal complex, except for the Remote prefix *an-*, which is the other member of position class –2.

16.3.1 Expressing a preceding event

In this use, *ka-* serves to express 'first', as in 'do something before doing something else'. This presupposes some other event that follows the event expressed by the verb marked by Prioritive *ka-*. (Cf. *i-* 'again', which presupposes a preceding event; §16.2.) A corpus example:

(855) Describing events that led up to an encounter with a wild boar.

   nd-ak-e-ka-   k-ihyaman   bus-yah   epe,
   LOC-1.A-1PL-PRI-   INESS-enter.water   eucalyptus-grove(III)   DIST:III

   tanama   ø-nak-um-e-p-   lesad   lay   nanggo
   then   NTRL-1.A-FRUS-1PL-CT-   cross.water   side   for

   'First we entered the water by the eucalyptus grove, then we were crossing to the other side.'
   [W11:0517]

The following example contains three occurrences of the Prioritive prefix. The first two express that the unprocessed sago pith will remain temporarily in its place before the speaker starts to process it; I translate this as 'for now' rather than 'first' to make the English more idiomatic. The second clause features the copula clause *adeh maka* 'let it remain first', consisting of the Relinquitive particle *adeh* followed by the present tense copula marked with the Prioritive prefix.

(856)   *da*   *epe*   *nda-d-a-ka-*   *ola,*   *ago*   *adeh*   *m-a-ka-*   Ø,
        sago(III)   there   LOC-DUR-3SG.A-PRI-   be:III.U   QUOT   RLQ   OBJ-3SG.A-PRI-   be.NPST

        tamuy   *mata-ka-*   *yahwiy*
        food   HORT-PRI-   eat

        'The sago stayed there for now, [I thought:] "Let it be for now, I'm going to eat first".'   [W20:0145]

The Prioritive is very frequent in commands and hortatives, as in (857). In such contexts the presupposition of a following event is usually backgrounded, and the function of the Prioritive is primarily as a way of making the command sound less imposing. For example, the addressees in (858) were not — as far as I can tell — planning to engage in some other activity that the speaker wanted them to postpone (teenage boys sitting idly in the kitchen). The speaker tells them to speak up, since I am recording the interaction, and she uses the Prioritive to soften the command ('Please'). The same use is in (859), which is a standard formulation used before taking leave.

(857)   *ah-*   *man*   *oy,*   *mak-e-ka-*   *yahwiy*   *tamuy*
        IMP-   come   2SG   FUT:1.A-1PL-PRI-   eat   food

        'Come here, let's eat first!'   [W20:0297]

(858)   *mayan*   *ha-ka-*   *ka-lay-em!*
        speech   IMP-PRI-   INESS-talk-PL.IMP

        'Please speak, you all!'   [W11:0364]

(859)   *nok*   *mat-e-ka-*   *uma⟨n⟩ah*
        1   HORT-1PL-PRI-   go⟨1.U⟩

        'We'll excuse ourselves, if you don't mind.' (lit. 'Let us go first')   [W11:0275]

For an extra layer of politeness, the Prioritive can be combined with the Contessive (§16.5), as in the following two examples. This combination can also be used in polar questions, to make them less intrusive (861).

(860)   In a story, a priest talks sense into some drunk men.

        yoy   *mabuk-anim*   *ha-ka-p-*   *haman-em*
        2PL   drunk(m)-people   IMP-PRI-CT-   sit.PL-PL.IMP

        'You drunkards, please have a seat.'   [W15:0132]

(861) *Meka ap-e-ka-p-   idih?*
      M.   PST.Q-2PL.A-PRI-CT- see:3SG.U
      'Excuse me, have you seen Meka?'   [W06:0138]

16.3.2 Similative use

In this use the *ka*-marked verb is preceded by a noun phrase in a similative role, with the meaning 'Verb like an NP' or 'as if Verb-ing an NP'. The following examples clarify this. Example (862) is taken from the Family Pictures task: the speaker looks at a drawing in which a small child is sitting on its mother's hip, holding on to her. The noun *pakapak* provides a participant-oriented specification: the child is clinging on to the mother as if it were a frog.

(862) *nalakam pakapak k-ø-o-ka-p-   tahob-a*
      child   frog   PRS.NTRL-3SG.A-3SG.DAT-PRI-CT- cling.on.to:3SG.U-EXT
      'The child is clinging on to her like a frog.'   [D09:0219]

The next example is from a discussion about the best way to climb down a well to clean it. One participant suggested using a bamboo pole into which steps could be carved. In order to climb out of the well the addressee would be able to climb up the pole just like one climbs up a coconut palm:

(863) *tanama onggat ma-mo-ka-   kahek-a-m*
      then   coconut OBJ-FUT:2SG.A-PRI- climb-EXT-VEN
      'Then you will climb up hither as [if climbing] a coconut palm.' [W06:0222]

Note that the use of Orientation prefixes with these verbs shows that the nouns preceding the verb group are participant-oriented, rather than functioning as manner adverbials. In (862) the Neutral Orientation *k-* is used since *pakapak* 'frog' describes the S-argument *nalakam* 'child', whereas the Object Orientation *m-* is used in (863) since it describes the O-argument of the verb *kahek* 'climb something' (see also §18.5).

It is not clear how the similative use of *ka-* relates to its more common temporal use ('first').[4] Drabbe (1955: 124) also noted the similative use of *ka-*, and provides very similar examples of it, from the Eastern variety described in his grammar. The marking of a similative role on the verb instead of on the noun itself (as in English, which marks the similative role by means of the preposition *like*) is typologically interesting. To my

---

[4] Interestingly, the use of a similative morpheme as a marker of anteriority in clause combining is described for the Cushitic language Kambaata by Treis (2017).

16.4 The Remote *an-*

This is probably the most poorly understood prefix in the prefixal complex, because it is only sparsely attested in corpus data. Attestations are mostly with motion verbs, and the only function of the prefix appears to be to express direction towards some distant goal. In its occurrences in the corpus the Remote always appears as part of the Predicated Manner construction (§17.3.2), which consists of the Auxiliary followed by a lexical verb stem, and a demonstrative preceding the prefixal complex. When the Remote is used, the demonstrative element may only be *e=*, i.e the reduced proclitic form of the Proximal *ehe*, as in (864). The speaker typically indicates the direction by means of a gesture.

(864) e=   k-ø-an-   w-a   ihon   yahun a
      PROX= DIR-3SG.A-REM- 3SG.U-AUX run.away:3SG.U canoe PTCL
      'The truck drove away to over there.'   [W19:0410]

The clitic *e=* is a fixed part of the structure in which the Remote *an-* occurs and does not seem to provide any distance specification with regards to the goal of the motion event. A deictically used demonstrative may be added elsewhere in the same clause, but then the demonstrative must be the Remote demonstrative *ehan*, as in (865). Speakers claimed that neither the Distal *epe* nor (the full form of) the Proximal *ehe* may co-occur with the Remote prefix *an-*.

(865) nggol   e=   ka-d-ø-an-   w-a   ola   emba   ehan
      top.of.tree(III) PROX= DIR-DUR-3SG.A-REM- 3SG.U-AUX be:III.U side   over.there
      'The top [of the fallen tree] was in that direction over there.'   [M02:0366]

Elicited data shows that the Remote prefix has the same morphotactic distribution as the Prioritive *ka-* (§16.3), with which it is mutually exclusive. Therefore both of these prefixes are assigned to position class −2, the second rightmost class before the Contessive prefix *ap-*.

16.5 The Contessive *ap-*

The Contessive prefix is very common, particularly with verbs of position, putting and motion, with which the Contessive expresses placement or movement on a surface off of the ground (§16.5.1).⁵ The Contessive also has minimising or attenuative uses (§16.5.2). Most uses, however, seem to be lexicalised and need to be memorised for each lexeme (§16.5.3).

The Contessive is the sole member of the rightmost position class (class –1), which means that it is never followed by other prefixes of the prefixal complex.

16.5.1 Marking contact with surface/off of the ground

This use of the Contessive is the easiest to understand, and it appears to be completely systematic with position verbs (e.g. *ambid* 'sit down', *mil* 'be sitting down', *yali* 'lie down'), verbs of putting (e.g. *han* 'put, grasp horizontally oriented object', *bakeh* 'put vertically oriented object', *eyawn* 'put down what one is carrying') and motion verbs, at least those describing motion on land (*man* 'come', *yet* 'be moving', *umak* 'be running', *ayin* 'run around' etc.). The same distinction can also be made with some other verbs (e.g. *iyalak* 'sweep'), but I have not figured out if there is any pattern predicting whether a verb permits the use of the Contessive to signal that the action is carried out on a surface off of the ground.

The Contessive is obligatory if an entity is positioned on top of a surface such as a chair, table, sitting platform, the roof of a house, a tree top, and so on. It is never used for an entity that is positioned or moves directly on the ground. However, the Contessive is also always used when the surface is the part of the beach that is exposed to water (below the vegetation limit), as well as the surface of the enormous mudflat that is exposed during low tide. Apparently, this part of the beach does not count as 'on the ground'. The sand dune just above the beach, on top of which houses are built in Wambi, behaves like the rest of the ground, and is not associated with use of the Contessive. I am not sure of the reason for this; perhaps it is related to the fact that the sand on the wet beach has a relatively solid surface, while the soft, dry sand on the dune is less firm and more irregular, i.e. less of a surface. With motion verbs the use of the Contessive typically expresses movement on the beach (since one rarely walks on top of e.g. a table).

In the following I illustrate the use of the Contessive *ap-* with contrastive examples from the corpus.

In (866a) a wallaby sits down on the ground, so the verb *ambid* 'sit down' is not prefixed with the Contessive (nor is the verb *kalim* 'defecate'). In (866b) the speaker sits on a motorcycle. Since this is a surface off of the ground the Contessive must be used.⁶

---

5 The label 'contessive' is used in descriptions of some languages of the Caucasus to denote a nominal case signalling contact with a surface, e.g. Khalilova 2009: 83.
6 As in this example, the 3sg Dative prefix *o-* is often used with a sitting verb in the sense 'sit on a motorcycle', for unknown reasons.

(866) a. upe   sayam   nama nok na   a-no-d-   kalim   epe,
         DIST:II wallaby(II) now 1   faeces DEP-1.A-DUR- defecate DIST:III

         epe   k-a-   ambid
         there DIR-3SG.A-   sit.down

         'The wallaby, where I had been pooping, there it sat down.' [W11:0949]

    b.   nd-ak-e-   nayam   motor   nd-ak-o-p-   ambid
         LOC-1.A-1PL- come.PL motorcycle(m) LOC-1.A-3SG.DAT-CT- sit.down

         'Then we came back and I got on the motorbike.' [W02:0203]

Example (867a) describes how the participants camped outside the new church during its inauguration, because there were too many people inside. The absence of the Contessive shows that they lie down on the ground. In (867b) the participants lie down on an *isala*, a simple sitting platform made of planks. This is a surface off of the ground, so the verb must be prefixed with the Contessive.

(867) a. nok bak   k-am-bat-e-   hok
         1   outside   DIR-1.A-AFF-1PL-   lie.down.PL

         'We lay down outside.' [W16:0037]

    b.   nok Yamay-Pale isala   k-am-bat-e-p-   hok
         1   Y.-P.   platform DIR-1.A-AFF-1PL-CT-   lie.down.PL

         'In Yamay-Pale we lay down on a platform.' [W10:0526]

Example (868a) describes a wild boar in its nest. Boars build their nests directly on the ground, so the Contessive is not used. The following examples show uses of the Contessive: in (868b) it is used since the sitting occurs in a tree, and in (868c) because it is on the beach, which counts as off of the ground for the purposes of the Contessive.

(868) a. ala   nda-d-ø-   ka-mil
         nest LOC-DUR-3SG.A- INESS-be.sitting

         '[The pig] was sitting in its nest.' [W11:0463]

    b.   de   k-ø-is-   kahek, lahwalah nda-d-ø-is-ap-   mil
         tree DIR-3SG.A-SEP- climp   on.top   LOC-DUR-3SG.A-SEP-CT- be.sitting

         'He climbed up the tree, and was sitting on top.' [W11:0586]

    c.   onos   Babu, duh   nda-d-a-p-   mil
         cousin B.   beach LOC-DUR-3SG.A-CT-   be.sitting

         'My cousin Babu, he was sitting on the beach.' [W10:0459]

In (869a) the verb *han* 'put' is used to describe how a truck is parked next to a river (the Contessive would have been used if it had been parked on the beach). In (869b) a package of sago is placed on top of somebody's outstretched hands. This is a surface off of the ground, so the Contessive is used.

(869) a. lay   Mbian   epe   ka-n-   han   mobil
side   Mb.   there   DIR-3PL.A- put:III.U car(m)(III)
'They parked the truck there on the side of the Bian river.'   [W10:0156]

b. Handing over sago during a ritual.

da   epe   sangga   lahwalah e=   ka-p-e-p-   han
sago(III) DIST:III hand   on.top   PROX:III= DIR-FUT:1.A-1PL-CT- put:III.U
'We put the sago on top of the hands.'   [W21:0048]

The following example also illustrates the 'beach' use of the Contessive, in the first clause with *mil* 'be sitting', and in the second clause with the motion verb *man* 'come':

(870) Two lines from a popular Marind song (modified).[7]

duh   nd-an-d-ap-   mil
beach LOC-1.A-DUR-CT- be.sitting

anum   wayuklu   duh   k-a-p-   man-em
woman girl   beach DIR-3SG.A-CT- come-VEN

'I was sitting on the beach. A young woman came walking along the beach.'

16.5.2 Attenuative use

In some contexts the Contessive can have a minimising effect, weakening the effects of the action described by the verb somewhat. The minimal pairs in the next examples are elicited, but were checked with two different speakers. It is not known to what degree this function is productive, and whether it can be extended to e.g. all verbs of hitting.

---

[7] When this song is performed, the shape of the verb in the first line is usually *ndakadap-mil*, in which the final /k/ of the 1.A prefix *ak-* has escaped Plosive Nasalisation to [n]. This means that the prefixal complex has the same shape (*ndakadap-*) as in the Eastern Dialect, in which Plosive Nasalisation does not occur. Since the Eastern variant *ndakadap-* has three syllables it fits better with the melody than two-syllable *ndandap-*. The stem, however, is clearly the Western variant *mil* (Eastern is *mir*). Mixing the dialects makes the song sound better, speakers told me.

(871) a. pa   e=   k-a-   w-asib
        head(III) PROX:III= DIR-3SG.A- III.U-hit
        'S/he hit/punched the head.'

   b. pa   e=   k-a-p-   w-asib
      head(III) PROX:III= DIR-3SG.A-CT- III.U-hit
      'S/he hit lightly on the head.' (just playing, tapping not so hard)

(872) a. tagu   k-a-na-   w-a   alam-a
        foot(III) DIR-3SG.A-1.DAT- 3SG.U-AUX become.swollen:III.U-EXT
        'My foot is swollen.'

   b. tagu   k-a-na-p-   w-a   alam-a
      foot(III) DIR-3SG.A-1.DAT-CT- 3SG.U-AUX become.swollen:III.U-EXT
      'My foot is a little swollen.'

The Contessive is frequently used together with the Prioritive *ka*-prefix (§16.3) in order to soften a request or command. This is another attenuative use, and does not involve contact with a surface off of the ground. For example, in (874) the addressee was asked to move a pile of firewood to a dry spot on the ground below the overhanging eaves of the roof, as it was starting to rain.

(873) roko   ek-o-ka-p-   ka-y-um?
      tobacco(m) PRS.Q:I-2SG.A-PRI-CT- WITH-2SG.U-go.PLA
      'Are you bringing tobacco?'   [W02:0111]

(874) pindopo   epe ka-mo-ka-p-   ibotok!
      eaves.of.roof(m) there DIR-FUT:2SG.A-PRI-CT- put.PLA:III.U
      'Put [the firewood] there under the eaves!'   [W11:0592]

Other examples of this use were given at the end of §16.3.

In another frequent prefix combination, the Contessive combines with the prefix *i-* 'again' (§16.2) in order to soften a command, a request, or a suggestion (typically one involving the addressee). The meaning of the resulting prefix sequence *i-...ap-* is non-compositional, because it does not involve the meaning 'again' or 'in contact with a surface' — it only makes the command sound less harsh. Speakers translate these forms using the Malay word *coba* 'try', which is used in Malay with a similar function. Two corpus examples are in (875–876).

(875) h-i-ap-   sinik-em!
      IMP-RE-CT-   carry-PL.IMP
      'Please carry!'   [W19:0392]

Tab. 16.2: Some verb pairs differing in the presence of Contessive *ap-*

Verb	Without *ap-*	With *ap-*
hawa	'emerge, come out, appear'	'arrive at coast/village from inland'
lay	'talk to s.b.; speak [a language]'	'chat; tell a story'
yanid	'push (an inanimate)'	'pick s.b. up (Malay *jemput*)'
anetok	'divide, distribute'	'remove from fire'
kamem	'suffice'	'suffice for s.b.'
oleb	'change'	'exchange, sell'
dahuy	'prevent s.b. from leaving'	'order s.t. from s.b.'
yuyeh	'shake, shudder'	'become startled'
lesad	'cut in pieces; draw water'	'cross river'

(876) usus   mak-i-ap-   uma⟨n⟩ah asik,
      afternoon FUT:1.A-RE-CT- go⟨1.U⟩   hunt

      e=   nda-p-i-ap-   kw-asik-a   ehe   ehe
      PROX= LOC-FUT:1.A-RE-CT-   INESS-hunt-EXT PROX PROX

'In the afternoon I will hunt, I will hunt here.'   [W02:0118]

16.5.3 Lexicalised uses of the Contessive

Many verbs always occur with the Contessive *ap-*, and lack a corresponding use without this prefix, as far as I have been able to establish. Such verbs have to be listed with this information in the dictionary, and be memorised by the learner. Some examples: *balen* 'finish', *bay* 'finish food/drink', *hayan* 'become silent, wind stop blowing', *kamaneb* 'leave (food) for s.b.', *kamob* 'get intoxicated from betel', *taheb* 'fill', *wig* 'beg s.b. for s.t.', *nu wihid* 'become tired'.

There are also verbs that have a different meaning when the Contessive is present, seemingly without following any clear pattern. I consider such pairs to correspond to two separate lexemes: one with the Contessive, and one without it. For example, *aheb* means 'eat' without the Contessive, but 'pass' with the Contessive. It is difficult to find any connection between these two meanings, and the two uses are clearly different lexemes, because 'eat' has a suppletive stem with a plural object (*hi* 'eat many') whereas 'pass' has a non-suppletive 2|3PL.U stem (*ihehab* 'pass you all/them'). Table 16.2 lists a few common pairs.

16.6 The Inessive

The Inessive ('INESS' in the glosses) can be prefixed to many verb stems to derive verbs meaning 'to V inside/within a confined space'. For example, the verb *ambid* 'sit' is used for sitting outdoors, whereas its Inessive form *kwambid* 'sit inside' is used for sitting indoors. When glossing Inessive stems I simply add the word 'inside' to the standard gloss, although it will be shown in §16.6.2 that the meaning of the Inessive is somewhat more complicated in reality.

16.6.1 Form of the Inessive

Before the non-back vowels /i e a/ the prefix *kw-* is used (877).

(877)
Base verb	**Derived stem**	
asa	**kw**asa	'bark inside'
akam	**kw**akam	'drip inside'
eyak	**kw**eyak	'untie inside'
ehwek	**kw**ehwek	'get stuck inside'
ihon	**kw**ihon	'run away inside'
isak	**kw**isak	'hit inside (2|3PL.U)'

The allomorph *k-* occurs before back vowels /u o/ and glides /j w/ (878).

(878)
omos	**k**omos	'spread out inside'
umak	**k**umak	'run inside'
yayahwig	**k**yayahwig	'plant inside'
yalin	**k**yalin	'call inside (2|3PL.U)'
walaw	**k**walaw	'search inside'
walok	**k**walok	'stab inside'

Before consonant-initial stems, *k-* is used, with epenthetic *a* giving *ka-* (879).

(879)
bakeh	**ka**bakeh	'put inside'
dahetok	**ka**dhetok	'turn opposite direction inside'
yoseh	**ka**yoseh	'jump along inside'
halay	**ka**halay	'become clear inside'
hok	**ka**hok	'many lie down inside'
lolaw	**ka**lolaw	'crawl inside'
mil	**ka**mil	'be sitting inside'
nayat	**ka**nayat	'many go inside'
tel	**ka**tel	'be lying down inside'
hwayob	**ka**hwayob	'hang inside'

16.6 The Inessive

The exception is consonant-initial stems on *k*-, which form the Inessive with *i*- (880).

(880)   kababuy   ikbabuy   'immerse oneself in water inside'
        kahek   ikahek   'climb inside'
        kakok   ikakok   'hang on back inside'
        kipalud   ikipalud   'tie inside'

With monosyllabic stems beginning with a (non-back) vowel, the Inessive is *kaw*- (881).

(881)   ay   kaway   'become inside'
        eg   kaweg   'dig inside'
        in   kawin   'make sound inside (2|3PL.U)'

This follows from the fact that initial clusters containing a glide (CGV) are avoided in closed syllables (*CGVC) (see §2.2), excluding forms such as *kway, *kweg and *kwin. In trisyllabic stems beinning with a closed syllable *iC*, the usual allomorph *kw*- is replaced by *k*- for the same reason (882).

(882)   ibkatok   kibkatok   'turn many upside down inside'
        ihyaman   kihyaman   'many enter water inside'

The sequence *kwa*- is also avoided in the antepretonic syllable, disallowing words of the shape *kwa.σ.σ. In trisyllabic bases with a first syllable consisting of *a*- or *wa*-, this syllable is deleted and replaced by *ku*- (883).

(883)   ahwasah   kuhwasah   'pull out inside (IV)'
        ahwasiy   kuhwasiy   'suck inside'
        alalay   kulalay   'become dry inside'
        ayanin   kuyanin   'run around inside (1.U)'
        wahanid   kuhanid   'gather inside'
        wayaman   kuyaman   'many stand inside'

There is no corresponding restriction against words of the shape *kwi*.σ.σ, so e.g. trisyllabic *iyalak* 'sweep, gather garbage' has the predicted Inessive *kwiyalak*.

Three exceptional verbs form the Inessive stem by means of the prefix *ik(a)*- (884).

(884)   hi   ikahi   'animate fall inside'
        hay   ikahay   'inanimate fall inside'
        bay   ikabay   'finish food/drink inside'

These are all monosyllabic, but note that the prefix *ik(a)-* occurs even when the base is a disyllabic form of the same lexeme, so the Pluractional stem of 'inanimate fall', *hehay*, has a corresponding Inessive stem **ikhehay**.

Note finally the verb *kwamin* 'enter' (1.U *kanamin*) which must be an historical Inessive stem, but which lacks a base stem *wamin synchronically.

The Pluractional prefixes can co-occur with the Inessive described in the following section. The Pluractional then occurs closest to the stem, inside the Inessive prefix (cf. §8.4).

(885)   a.   *k-i-hnituk*
             INESS-PLA-lean
             'many (things) to lean inside'

        b.   *k-u-timin*
             INESS-PLA-wake.up
             'many to wake up inside'

16.6.2 Use of the Inessive

The following corpus examples illustrate the use of Inessive verb stems. In example (886), both the speaker and the addressee (her daughter, ca. 2 years old) were inside my house, so the Inessive form *kwambid* is used. (The speaker also uses the Contessive *ap-* since she is asking the daughter to sit on top of her lap; see §16.5). In (887) the Inessive is used since the act of carrying takes place inside the forest.

(886)   *oɣ   Susana   ah-ap-   kw-ambid*
        2SG   S.   IMP-CT-   INESS-sit.down
        'Sit down Susana!'   [W09:0002]

(887)   *deg   k-ak-e-   ka-l-hwik⟨e⟩h-a-m   napet-nen*
        forest   DIR-1.A-1PL-   INESS-PLA-carry⟨III.U⟩-EXT-VEN   banana-shoot(III)
        'We carried the banana shoots through the forest.'   [W11:0978]

The general meaning of the Inessive — 'to Verb inside a confined space' — appears straightforward at first sight, but its use is complicated by (i) the question of what exactly constitutes a confined space, and (ii) the fact that verbs differ as to how sensitive they are to this distinction. I will first consider some contexts that call for Inessive forms (listed as A–D below), before commenting on differences between verb types.

(A) Inside houses and huts. Actions inside bivouacs (*puk*) do not trigger the use of the Inessive. Bivouacs are usually simple structures consisting of poles stuck in the ground with tarpaulin or dry leaves as a protection against rain and wind, so they are less confined than the houses in the village.

(B) Inside containers such as bags, boxes. The Inessive stem *ikabay* (from *bay* 'finish food/drink') is used for finishing drinking from a glass. The Inessive stem *kawa* of the Auxiliary (3SG.U form *wa*) can be used for a chick chirping inside an egg (cf. §17.1.2.1), as in the following elicited example:

(888) ayam   k-a-   ka-w-a
      chicken(m) DIR-3SG.A-   INESS-3SG.U-AUX
      'A chicken is chirping inside the egg.'

(C) Inside the body:

(889) yandam yoyo   k-a-na-   ka-w-it-a
      stomach bubbling.noise DIR-3SG.A-1.DAT- INESS-III.U-become-EXT
      'My stomach is rumbling.'

(D) Inside certain kinds of terrain. Within the landscape, the spaces that most consistently trigger the Inessive are forest (but not e.g. a coconut grove), water (as long as the agent is partly immersed, e.g. wading through water — but not sitting in a canoe on water), the vast mudflat that is revealed during low tide (but not the dry beach; cf. the Contessive, which makes the same distinction: §16.5.1), patches with tall grass, and swamps (both during dry season and when filled with water).

The usage with events taking place in the savanna (*mamuy*) is unclear to me: the Inessive is sometimes used, sometimes not. Some parts of the savanna are perhaps considered more confined than others (e.g. parts with tall grass?).

In addition to the dry beach, some parts of the landscape that never trigger the Inessive are: roads and paths, sand ridges (*pale*), clearings in the forest (*hekay*).

The following example illustrates how the use of the Inessive depends on features of the landscape. The speaker recounts how she buried betelnut during an expedition, in order to retrieve it on the return journey. The speaker with whom I transcribed this story explained that the Inessive is used in the second clause, because Almung is a swamp. (I have no further information on the landscape in Kalakal-Ugu.)

(890) ma   mayay Kalakal-Ugu k-an-d-ap-   ugaman
      PTCL first K.-U.   DIR-1.A-DUR-CT- bury:III.U

      tanama Almung ka-no-d-   k-ugaman
      then   A.   DIR-1.A-DUR- INESS-bury:III.U
      'Um, first I buried betelnut in Kalakal-Ugu, then I buried in Almung.'
      [W21:0138]

Finally, there are lexical differences between different verbs. Many verbs lack an Inessive stem. Some verbs lack an Inessive stem because their semantics are not compatible with 'inside' (e.g. *hawa* 'emerge'), or because they are originally Inessive verbs whose non-Inessive form no longer exists (e.g. *kwamin* 'enter'; there is no *wamin*. Cf. remark in §10.3.1). For other verbs it is unclear how to explain the lack of an Inessive form. For example, there is Inessive *kagan* 'hear inside' (< *gan* 'hear'), but I have failed to get **kwidih* 'see inside' (*idih* 'see').

Verbs also differ in how systematically their Inessive form is used. With verbs of position ('sit', 'stand', etc.) and putting the Inessive is obligatory when the action occurs indoors (in the forest, etc.) — it is simply wrong to use *ambid* 'sit' (instead of *kwambid* 'sit inside') if the action occurs indoors — whereas for a verb such as *lay* 'talk' the use of the Inessive in the same context seems completely optional. I will leave a more detailed investigation of these issues for the future.

16.7 The Venitive *-em*

The suffix *-em* expresses direction towards the deictic centre, i.e. 'hither'. In the narration of events, the deictic centre can be either the narrator or the focal participant of the narrated action, and the usage of the Venitive often switches back and forth between the two centres during the narration. The Venitive is mostly used with motion verbs, both those that involve a trajectory, such as *umak* 'be running', *dahetok* 'return', and those that primarily describe a manner, such as *lolaw* 'crawl', *deh* 'limp' in (891–892).[8]

(891) kay   k-a-p-   dah-em, kaw tu   ø-a-   man
       road DIR-3SG.A-CT-   limp-VEN stick with:II NTRL-3SG.A-   come
       'She limped hither along the road, she came with a stick.'   [W19:0270]

---

[8] This simple system of venitive marking on the verb is found across the Anim family, from Yaqay in the west to Ipiko in the east, and was most likely a feature of proto-Anim. Similar systems are also found in other families of Southern New Guinea, such as the neighbouring languages Ngkolmpu (Yam; Carroll 2016: 198), and Yelmek (Bulaka River; Gregor 2020), but also as far to the east as Idi (Pahoturi River; Evans et al. 2018a: 702). Some of the Yam languages contrast venitive and andative ('away') directional affixes (Nen and Komnzo; Evans 2015a, Döhler 2016: 263). Simple, one- or two-term directional systems is probably one of the few obvious candidates for areal features of the region. The flat landscape, with its slow meandering rivers, has probably not favoured the development of more complex directional systems ('uphill', 'downhill', 'downriver' etc.), as found in some other Papuan languages.

(892) ehe   nak   k-a-   Ø   ehe,
       PROX:III vine(III) PRS.NTRL-3SG.A-   be.NPST   PROX:III

   eh-ø-   lolaw-em   ehe nanggol ehe
   [PROX:III-3SG.A- crawl:III.U-VEN   here towards PROX:III]

   'This is a vine, this one that's creeping towards here.'   [W13:0183]

The most common host of the Venitive is the verb *man* 'come'. With this verb the suffix is entirely optional, and redundant, since the notion 'come' already implies motion towards the deictic centre.

Many verbs in Coastal Marind, and most motion verbs, denote the inception of movement in their base form, e.g. *tapeb* 'start flying, take off flying'. To express the ensuing action, a durative stem is derived by adding the Extended suffix *-(l)a* (*tapeb-a* 'be flying, be in flight'; see §14.2.4). The Venitive is only used with the Extended form of such verbs, and then has the shape *-m* (*tapeb-a-m* 'be flying hither'). Indeed, most Venitive attestations in the corpus follow the Extended suffix, as in (893).

(893) ipe   sawanggi-anim   k-a-   Ø,   lay
       DIST:I/II.PL   evil.spirit(m)-people   PRS.NTRL-3SG.A- be.NPST   side

   e=   ka-n-   i-hyamat-a-m
   PROX=   PRS.NTRL-3PL.A-   PLA-enter.water-EXT-VEN

   'Those are evil spirits, they're coming in the water on this side.'   [W12:0296]

The overwhelming majority of corpus attestations of the Venitive are with motion verbs. But the suffix may also be used with non-motion verbs, meaning that the action described by the verb was performed while moving towards the deictic centre. In (894), the speaker described how he was sitting on a motorcycle, returning from a hunting trip. The non-motion verbs *mil* 'be sitting' and *kahod* 'duck, bend head down' are suffixed with the Venitive, resulting in the literal meanings 'be sitting while moving hither' and *kahodam* 'be ducking while moving hither'. The speaker in (894) uses the Venitive with *yi* to refer to some sago that she and her companions had eaten on the way back to the village.

(894) motor   lahwalah   a-nka-h-ap-   mil-em,
       [motorcycle(m) on.top   DEP-1.A-DEP-CT-   be.sitting-VEN]

   ka-no-   n-a   kahod-a-m
   DIR-1.A- 1.U-AUX   duck-EXT-VEN

   'While I was sitting on the motorbike, I was bending my head down.'
                                                                       [W02:0181]

(895) anep   in-kay   a-nka-h-e-   yi-la-m   epe,   epe
       [EMPH:III middle-road DEP-1.A-DEP-1PL- eat:III.U-EXT-VEN DIST:III] DIST:III
       te-ø-nak-e-   ka-hok
       GIV:III-NTRL-1.A-1PL-   WITH-lie.down.PL

'[The food] that we had eaten coming here, we went to sleep with (i.e. having eaten) just that.' [W21:0308]

With the perception verbs *idih* 'see' and *gan* 'hear', the Venitive is sometimes used to signal that the perceived stimulus is directed towards the perceiver, as in (896), or even moving towards the perceiver, as in (897). This is an interesting contrast to the more common uses of the Venitive, which usually imply that the agent-like participant of the Venitive-marked verb is moving. It is clear that the agent in (897), Yan, is not moving at all, as he is sitting perched in a tree, so the Venitive signals that the O-argument of *idih* 'see' (the pig) is moving towards him.

(896) yah ipe   mayan esol   ka-n-ap-   gat-a-m,   mesiwag   ah-ø-
       but DIST:I/II.PL speech noise DIR-3PL-A-CT- hear-EXT-VEN   [old.woman DEP-3SG.A-
       w-alit-a-m
       3SG.U-call-EXT-VEN]

'But then they heard the screaming, when my wife was calling out towards them.' [W10:0657]

(897) Yan nd-a-p-   idih-a-m,   anwaya k-a-   w-a   w-in
       Y.   LOC-3SG.A-CT-   see:3SG.A-EXT-VEN   close   DIR-3SG.A- 3SG.U-AUX 3SG.U-become

'Yan saw [the pig] coming towards him, it was already close.' [W11:0586]

Beyond verbs of perception, the Venitive can also refer to motion of the O-argument with some verbs of putting. In (898), which was overheard, the speaker said that her son in Merauke was going to send something to the village by boat. Her son was not going in the boat himself, so she used the Venitive to express that the sent item would come towards her as a result of being put in the boat. This use has not been attested in the recorded corpus.

(898) ndame-ø-   kahakut-a-m
       FUT-3SG.A-   put.inside:III.U-EXT-VEN

(lit.) 'He will put it in [the boat] hither.'

Because the Venitive is predominantly found with verbs that already encode motion, it should be regarded as a directional marker, and not a marker of associated motion (as described by Koch 1984 and Wilkins 1991). The main counterexamples are the uses seen in (894–898), in which the Venitive does in fact add a motion component to non-motion verbs. Such association motion-like uses have been noted for directional markers in some other languages (Guillaume 2016: 89).

The Venitive is mutually exclusive with all inflectional suffixes that attach after the verb stem, such as the Counterfactual *-um*, the Habitual suffixes, and the (homophonous) Plural Imperative *-em*. In constructions in which the verb stem appears in the pre-verbal position, the Venitive (like the other inflectional suffixes) remains within the verb complex, attached to the Auxiliary which replaces the lexical stem (899). This Auxiliary construction is described in §17.2.1.

(899) kosay-naɣam   k-ak-e-   n-a-em
      difficult-come.PL DIR-1.A-1PL- 1.U-AUX-VEN
      'We came here with difficulty.'
      (lit. 'We difficult-coming did-hither')   [W21:0277]

Verbs suffixed with the Venitive exhibit an important morphological peculiarity. When a Venitive-marked verb has past tense reference, the Past Durative prefix *d-* (§14.2.1), which normally is obligatory with verbs that express durative situations, is omitted. Consider (894) above, in which the Venitive is added to the inherently durative verb *mil* 'be sitting' and to verb suffixed with the Extended, *kahod-a* 'be bending head down'. The context makes it clear that the two clauses describe durative events: the speaker had been travelling through the bush on the back of a motorcycle, continuously bowing his head down to avoid getting hit by the vegetation. This shows that the omission of the Past Durative *d-* is a purely morphological fact, and does not affect the aspectual semantics of these verbs, which still express durative, not punctual, events. This is also confirmed by the fact that verbs suffixed with the Venitive occur in forms with present time reference, as in (892–893) above, and (900) below. Punctual verbs cannot be used in present tense contexts, so this is evidence that the Venitive is not a punctualising suffix, despite the absence of the Durative *d-* in past contexts.

(900) u=   k-at-ø-   w-alit-a-m
      PROX:II= PRS.NTRL-PRSTV-3SG.A- 3SG.U-call-EXT-VEN
      'Here she comes screaming.'   [W10:0660]

17 The Auxiliary, copula clauses and light verbs

The first three sections of this chapter provide general information about the most frequent verb in Coastal Marind, the Auxiliary (§17.1, §17.2 and §17.3). The fourth section describes copula clauses, which differ from other clauses in the language in that the verb complex may lack a verb stem (§17.4). The last section describes four common verbs that I call 'light verbs' (§17.5).

17.1 Form and function of the Auxiliary *wa*

I distinguish the lexical uses of the Auxiliary (§17.1.2), in which it functions as a standard verb (albeit wihout any clear semantic content), from its grammatical uses (§17.2, §17.3), in which it forms a periphrastic expression together with a lexical verb stem (similar to *be* in the English Progressive *be Verb-ing*).

17.1.1 Form of the Auxiliary

Morphologically, the Auxiliary is a verb that belongs to the prefixing stem class (§10.3.1). Its full stem paradigm is

	SG	PL
1	*n-a*	*y-a*
2	*y-a*	*y-a*
3	*w-a*	*y-a*

Like any verb, the Auxiliary forms the verb complex of a clause together with the preceding prefixal complex. In its lexical uses, the Auxiliary occurs without any other verb stem (§17.1.2). In the grammatical uses of the Auxiliary, the lexical verb stem occurs either before the verb complex (§17.2), or immediately following it (§17.3), depending on the construction. The lexical verb stem in these structures appears bare, i.e. not preceded by any of the prefixes belonging in the prefixal complex. The lack of inflectional prefixes makes it similar to an infinitive in English (e.g. *will run*, not **will runs*), but note that the stem itself may display the full range of (stem-deriving) modifications described in §8.4.

The person-indexing exhibited by the stem of the Auxiliary follows the same principle as the so-called middle verbs (§10.1.2), meaning that the prefixed person marker on the stem reflects, or copies, the person/number features of the Actor. I illustrate this in (901) using structures with a postposed lexical verb stem, viz. the Thetic Predication construction, but the same indexing patterns recur in all grammatical uses of the Auxiliary. (The meaning of this construction is discussed in §17.3.1; here the only concern is the morphological facts.)

(901) a. ka-no- n-a yol
DIR-1.A- 1.U-AUX beat.sago
'I beat sago.'

b. k-o- y-a yol
DIR-2SG.A- 2SG.U-AUX beat.sago
'You beat sago.'

The only effect that the use of the Auxiliary has on the shape of the prefixal complex is that the Orientation prefixes follow special rules in certain constructions involving the Auxiliary. For example, the structures with a postposed lexical verb stem described in §17.3 require the presence of the Directional Orientation *k-* (cf. §11.1 for the usual functions of the Orientation prefixes).

All other prefixes (e.g. person indexing) occur just like they would do if the Auxiliary were not present. This includes prefixes that are a fixed part of the morphological template of a verb. For example, the verb *balen* is always prefixed with the Contessive prefix *ap-* (cf. §16.5.3), so if *balen* is used in a periphrastic structure with the Auxiliary, the Auxiliary will be prefixed with the Contessive. One could say the prefixal complex that precedes the Auxiliary 'inherits' whatever set of prefixes is required by the lexical verb.

A consequence of the fact that the stem of the Auxiliary simply appears in the person/number of the Actor, without having any effect on the indexing in the prefixal complex, is that none of the various quirks that affect person indexing in Coastal Marind interact with the Auxiliary. I will illustrate this with middle verbs.

Recall from §9.2.2.2 that middle verbs exhibit invariant singular person indexing in the 3rd person: the Actor prefix is 3sg even when the Actor is plural. Compare the Actor indexing of the non-middle *ayak* 'go inland' (902a) with that of the middle verb *umuh* 'go, take off' (902b).

(902) a. tanama ka-n- ayak
again DIR-3PL.A- go.inland
'They went inland again.' [W21:0170]

b. tanama k-a- umah
again DIR-3SG.A- go:2|3PL.U
'They left again.' [W21:0221]

Since the Auxiliary behaves like a middle verb in that its stem indexes the person/number of the Actor, one could expect that it too would trigger invariant 3SG.A marking with a 3rd plural subject. This is not the case, as (903) shows, because the Actor indexing of the prefixal complex simply follows the pattern associated with the lexical verb. In (903a), indexing is realised by 3PL.A since 'go inland' is a non-middle, and in (903b) it is 3SG.A since 'go' is a middle verb.¹

(903) a. ka-n- y-a ayak
DIR-3PL.A- 2|3PL.U-AUX go.inland
'They went inland.' [W18:0102]

b. k-a- y-a umah
DIR-3SG.A- 2|3PL.U-AUX go:2|3PL.U
'They left.' [W11:0186]

It is as if the Auxiliary were plugged into the verb complex at a stage after all of the complicating interactions of Coastal Marind person indexing had been resolved. Therefore, the middle indexing pattern of the Auxiliary does not affect the Actor indexing in the prefixal complex in (903a).

There is, however, a single situation in which the person indexing on the Auxiliary is affected by the presence of a prefix within the prefixal complex, viz. the 3pl>1 constellation discussed in §9.2.2.3. Whenever a 3rd person plural Actor acts on a 1st person, a special divalent Actor prefix *e-* is used. For some reason, the Auxiliary appears in the 3SG.U form *wa* in this context instead of the usual 2|3PL.U stem *ya*. Compare (904a) below, in which the Auxiliary copies the plural feature from Actor indexing (according to the normal rules outlined above), with the 3pl>1 constellation in (904b), in which the 3SG.U form *wa* is used, despite the 3pl subject.

(904) a. k-an- y-a yed⟨e⟩b
DIR-3PL.A- 2|3PL.U-AUX hit⟨3SG.U⟩
'They hit him/her.'

b. k-e- w-a yida⟨n⟩ab
DIR-3PL>1- 3SG.U-AUX hit⟨1.U⟩
'They hit me.'

The following corpus example shows the same phenomenon. (Here, the 1pl prefix *e-* is deleted since it occurs after another prefix of the shape *e-*).

---

1 Drabbe (1955: 93) claims for the Eastern dialect of Coastal Marind that the Auxiliary agrees with the O-argument when it is used with a transitive lexical verb and the O-argument is animate. It seems that this rule is meant to apply in contexts where the verb stem is preposed. Unfortunately, I have not found any examples supporting this in the texts collected in the back of Drabbe's grammar. There is no such rule in the Western dialect described here.

(905) ihe   anim a,   k-e-ø-p-   w-a   n-idih-em nok
      PROX:I/II.PL people PTCL DIR-3PL>1-1PL-CT- 3SG.U-AUX   1.U-see-VEN 1
      'These people, they are watching us.'   [W10:0304]

17.1.2 Lexical uses

The Auxiliary appears in various combinations in which the predicated element is not a verb stem — as in the other, more grammaticalised, constructions in this chapter — but e.g. an ideophone or a noun. Some of these combinations appear to be productive constructions that can combine with various lexical items according to some predictable semantic principle (§17.1.2.1, §17.1.2.2), whereas others are unpredictable idioms that must be fully specified in the dictionary (§17.1.2.3). It seems that the Auxiliary is interchangeable with the light verb *win* 'become' in these constructions, without any perceivable meaning difference.

17.1.2.1 Characteristic vocalisation

In this interesting use the Auxiliary occurs with a subject referring to an animal to express that it is making the vocalisation that is characteristic for that animal. I have only observed this use for smaller animals (e.g. birds and frogs) never for larger animals like deer or pigs. For dogs, *abun* 'bark' would be used.

(906) salaw   k-a-   y-a
      friarbird DIR-3SG.A-   2|3PL.U-AUX
      'The friarbirds are singing/making their call.'

Note that in this and other lexical uses the Auxiliary behaves like a standard middle verb and triggers invariant 3sg Actor marking with a 3rd person plural S/A-arguments (§9.2.2.2). This does not happen in the grammatical uses of the Auxiliary, as explained above.

Syntactically, the Auxiliary functions as a standard lexical verb in this context, and may for example occur in the Thetic Predication construction (described in §17.3.1). In this construction the Auxiliary — in its grammatical use — is placed between the prefixal complex and the verb stem. In (907) this means that there will be two consecutive occurrences of the Auxiliary, the first licensed by the Thetic Auxiliary construction (signalling an 'all-new' or 'out-of-the-blue' utterance), and the second being the Auxiliary in its lexical use expressing the chirping sound of the pufferfish.

(907) This example was offered as an alternative way of expressing (820).

banggabang k-a-na-y-p- w-a w-a
pufferfish DIR-3SG.A-1.DAT-1PL-CT- 3SG.U-AUX 3SG.U-AUX
'The pufferfish is making noise at us.'

17.1.2.2 Emission of sound

In this use the Auxiliary predicates a sound that the subject is doing, typically referred to by an ideophone such as *tataya* 'munching/smacking sounds from eating' (908). The same use is also attested with a linguistic expression in its 'mention' usage, as with *ahak* 'yes' in (909).[2]

(908) *tataya tamohat- y-a!*
IDEO PROH:2SG.A- 2SG.U-AUX
'Don't make *tataya* [i.e. chewing noise while eating]!'

(909) The speaker tells about a conversation she had had earlier.

yah nok "ahak" s-an-d-omb-ap- n-a
but 1 yes ONLY-1.A-DUR-3SG.GEN-CT- 1.U-AUX
'I just kept saying "yes".' [M05:0062]

17.1.2.3 Other idiomatic uses

Examples of verb idioms in which the Auxiliary *wa* is used as the predicating element are *bekay wa* 'catch one's breath' (< *bekay* 'heart'; in this idiom the Contessive prefix *ap-* always occurs) and *nggem wa* 'paint one's face with white clay' (< *nggem* 'k.o. white clay'), as when women mourn a deceased relative.[3]

(910) *bekay epe nd-an-d-e-p- n-a*
heart there LOC-1.A-DUR-1PL-CT- 1.U-AUX
'We caught our breath there.' [W08:0049]

---

2 It is not clear what the function of the 3sg Genitive prefix *omb-* is in this example. It is possibly the causal use discussed in §9.4.2, i.e. 'I kept saying "yes" because of him', referring to the person with whom she was having the conversation.

3 These idioms belong either to the middle intransitive valence class (§12.2.3) or the middle transitive class (§12.3.2), depending on the argument status of the co-nominal *bekay/nggem*, which remains unclear.

(911) amimil   Doyo, e=   nda-bat-ø-   w-a   nggem
      grown.up D.   PROX= LOC-AFF-3SG.A- 3SG.U-AUX white.clay
      'Elder sister Doyo, she is painting her face with white clay here.'   [W10:0435]

17.2 The Auxiliary predicating a preposed verb stem

In this construction the verb stem appears before the Auxiliary. Preposed, a verb stem functions nominally, heading a noun phrase, which allows it to appear with nominal modifiers such as *ya* 'real, very' or *mbya* 'all, completely' (913).[4] These modifiers are only used adnominally (not adverbially), so in order to use them for describing an event the verb stem has to be 'converted' into a nominal by moving it out of its normal position inside the verb complex. I add brackets around the nominal phrases in these two examples.

(912) [haman ya]_{NP} ka-me-   y-a!
      sit.PL   real   DIR-FUT:2PL.A- 2|3PL.U-AUX
      'You (pl) sit properly!'

(913) Commenting on bad luck during hunt.
      awe   [mbya keway]_{NP} mend-am-b-e-   n-a
      game   all   destroy   PERF-1.A-ACT-1PL- 1.U-AUX
      'We already ruined the animals completely.' (i.e. scared them away)
                                                                     [W02:0157]

To simplify the parsing of these sentences one can imagine that the Auxiliary means 'do', so that (912) can be translated 'Do real sitting!' etc.

The most common type of modification of a preposed verb stem is compounding, described in §17.2.1. A second consequence of preposing a verb stem is that it can be assigned constituent focus, which is associated with the pre-verbal slot (Chapter 11). This possibility is primarily used to express 'only'-focus, i.e. 'only Verb', as discussed in §17.2.2. Another construction, with an element -*ti* added to the preposed verb stem, is described in (§17.2.3).

17.2.1 Predication of verb compounds

Compounds headed by a verb stem that are predicated by the Auxiliary usually have a nominal first member (typically an adjective) that provides some kind of adverbial

---
4 Positioned before the inflected verb, *mbya* expresses negation; see §18.4.1.

specification. A straightforward example from the corpus is in (914), in which the Pluractional verb stem *isak* is compounded with *yaba* 'big'. Using pseudo-English we could render this more literally as 'They did big-beating on them'.

(914) yaba-i-sak   ka-n-   y-a
       big-2|3PL.U-fight DIR-3PL.A-   2|3PL.U-AUX
       'They beat them up big-time.'   [W09:0105]

Some of the most common first members in this structure are *mayay* 'first' and *ndom* 'bad'. The two following examples illustrate the use of compounds with *mayay*. The meaning difference between these examples and other expressions meaning 'first', viz. the word *mayay* used as an independent adverbial and the Prioritive prefix *ka-* (§16.3) appears to be rather subtle.

(915) About the preparations for a feast.
       nok mayay-atug   ø-nak-e-   n-a   kumbu
       1   first-scrape   NTRL-1.A-1PL-   1.U-AUX   coconut
       'We scraped coconuts beforehand.'   [W19:0198]

(916) From a hunting story.
       basik a,   mayay-ka-hawa   ø-ø-n-is-a-y-   w-a
       pig   PTCL first-INESS-emerge:3SG.U   NTRL-3SG.A-1.DAT-SEP-1.DAT-1PL-   3SG.U-AUX
       'A pig, it went out first [running] away from us'   [W11:0495]

The following examples show *ndom* 'bad' compounded to the verb stem. Such compounds are the only way to use *ndom* in the adverbial sense 'badly' or 'wrongly'.[5]

(917) The speaker had accused a neighbour of steeling some kava from him.
       namakad   ndom-k-u-hanid   epe   te-k-a-nam-   w-a-e
       thing(III) bad-INESS-III.U-take.PLA DIST:III GIV:III-PRS.NTRL-3SG.A-1.GEN-   3SG.U-AUX-IPFV
       'He takes my things badly (i.e., without asking)'   [W05:0007]

(918) During the telling of a story, the speaker hesitated and asked a co-narrator to help her remember the names of some of the participants.
       ndom-hyamin mano-   n-a
       bad-call:2|3PL.U NAFUT:1.A- 1.U-AUX
       'I might say [their] names wrong.'   [W19:0114]

---

5 There is an independent adverb with the shape *ndom*, viz. the homophonous *ndom* 'still' (§18.4.2) or 'also' (§6.3.1), so one could speculate that *ndom* 'bad' needs to be compounded with the verb stem in its adverbial use in order to avoid ambiguity with 'still'/'also'.

Compounds headed by verb stems are also common outside the construction with the Auxiliary (see §3.6.1.5).

17.2.2 Restrictive focus on verb stems: 'only/just Verb'

Recall that the preferred way of expressing 'only' in Coastal Marind is by means of the Restrictive Orientation prefix *s-*, which has scope over the constituent placed in the syntactic slot immediately preceding the verb (see §11.1.6). This slot is associated with the expression of focus, so an expression must be placed in this position in order for it to be interpreted as in-focus. To express the meaning 'only Verb' or 'just Verb' (i.e. 'do nothing but Verb'), with the verb in the scope of *s-*, the verb stem has to be placed in the pre-verbal position. The Auxiliary, attached after the prefixal complex, is used to predicate the preposed verb stem.

These expressions are common in the corpus, with about 85 attestations. Some examples:

(919)   hok   s-ak-e-   n-a
        lie.down.PL ONLY-1.A-1PL-   1.U-AUX
        'We just lay down/went to sleep.'   [W21:0231]

(920)   nok idih   s-an-d-e-p-   n-a-ti
        1   see:3SG.U ONLY-1.A-DUR-1PL-CT-   1.U-AUX-DUR
        'We were just watching him.'   [W03:0045]

(921)   yambeyay,   nayat   s-an-d-e-   n-a   epetagol   epe
        slippery   be.moving.PL   ONLY-1.A-DUR-1PL- 1.U-AUX like.that:III DIST:III
        '[It was] slippery, we just went like that.'   [W03:0061]

(922)   ikyalun   sa-me-p-   y-a!
        jump   ONLY-FUT:2PL.A-CT-   2|3PL.U-AUX
        'You just jump down!'   [W06:0191]

Unlike the English word 'just', the Coastal Marind combination of a verb stem and *s-* cannot be used to convey the temporal meaning 'just Verb-ed, Verb-ed just now', i.e. the signalling of a zero interval between the moment of reference and the preceding event. For the temporal 'just', Coastal Marind uses the word *namaya* 'now' or the construction with *oso* 'start' described in §18.4.3.

17.2.3 The Verb-*ti*–Auxiliary construction

In this structure an element -*ti* appears suffixed to the stem, which is placed in the pre-verbal position. The verb always carries the Neutral prefix ø-.

(923) bes   kw-ehwek-ti   ø-n-e-   y-a
      beating.stick(III) INESS-pile.up:III.U-TI NTRL-3PL.A-3PL.DAT- 2|3PL.U-AUX
      'They handed over the beating sticks to them.'   [W18:0060]

This construction is restricted to narrative contexts, and is used to describe punctual events (including the onset of an activity; cf. §14.1.1) in the storyline. The same structure can be used to describe a durative event if the Auxiliary is replaced by the verb *ola* 'be', as exemplified in §17.5 below.

The Verb-*ti*–Auxiliary structure appears to be similar to the construction with a postposed verb stem discussed in §17.3.1 in that it reports an event without presenting any constituent as being particularly prominent/within focus. In my corpus it is rare, and most attestations come from two narratives recorded by a single speaker, an elderly woman, although it seems that members of all generations understand and can produce the construction.

The function of -*ti* in this construction is not known. It is unclear whether this -*ti* is related to the Past Durative suffix -*ti* (§14.2.1.2), especially since the construction has punctual semantics, and since outer suffixes such as -*ti* are normally not allowed to appear on a dislocated verb stem. One possibility is that the verbal suffix -*ti* developed from the comitative postposition *ti* 'with'. In such a scenario the comitative postposition attached to a nominally used verb stem, just like the postposition *lek* seems to be the source of the Participial suffix -*la* (§3.7.3). One could speculate that this somehow led to -*ti* being associated with past tense semantics, and that it spread from the auxiliary construction into past durative contexts (cf. McGregor 2003 for comitative case developing into progressive markers in some Australian languages). I gloss -*ti* as 'TI' in this section in order not to anticipate its proper analysis.

Below are two more corpus examples.

(924) nd-a-   y-um-a-m,   wati   yi-ti   ø-na-   y-a
      LOC-3SG.A- 2|3PL.U-go.PLA-EXT-VEN kava(III) drink:III.U-TI NTRL-3PL.A- 2|3PL.U-AUX
      'Then they came forward, and started drinking the kava.'   [W18:0057]

(925) muy   han-ti   ø-ø-o-p-   w-a,
      meat(III) put:III.U-TI   NTRL-3SG.A-3SG.DAT-CT- 3SG.U-AUX

      "ah- uma⟨y⟩ah oy,   usus   menda-b-ø-   ay"
      IMP- go⟨2SG.U⟩ 2SG afternoon(III) PERF-ACT-3SG.A-   become:III.U
      'He put the meat [on the horse], [and I said,] "Go now, it's already afternoon".'
                                                                   [D05:0108]

The rarity of this construction in my corpus is a striking difference between my data and the texts collected in Drabbe (1955), in which the Verb-*ti* construction is frequent (although Drabbe does not mention it in his treatment of the grammar). This could be a dialect difference, since Drabbe's texts represent the Eastern variety of Coastal Marind, or it could be a sign that the popularity of the construction has waned in the almost 70 years since Drabbe's data were collected.

17.3 The Auxiliary predicating a postposed verb stem

There are two important structures in which the verb stem appears after the Auxiliary: the Thetic Predication construction (§17.3.1) and the Predicated Manner construction (§17.3.2).

An important structural difference between these and structures with a preposed verb stem is that the verb stem forms a tight unit together with the prefixal complex and the intervening Auxiliary, as shown by the fact that nothing may intervene between the Auxiliary and the following verb stem. There are no signs of the verb stem having any sort of nominal function, and it may occur suffixed with outer suffixes (§8.5) just like when it is directly attached to the prefixal complex.

17.3.1 The Thetic Predication construction

This construction is used to make statements in which no particular constituent is presented as being in focus, i.e. statements that the speaker presents as containing 'all-new' information, with all parts being equally important and informative. According to my understanding the use of this structure is similar to the function of what has been called "event-reporting" (Lambrecht 1994: 124) or "thetic" (Kuroda 1972, Sasse 1987) sentences. Its structure, from left to right, is

i. The prefixal complex, with Directional Orientation *k-* (§11.1.4) as the only fixed member.
ii. The Auxiliary.
iii. A lexical verb stem.

This is schematised in Figure 17.1. Other constituents are placed before and/or after the verb complex.

| *k-*...- | AUXILIARY | VERB STEM |

Fig. 17.1: The Thetic Predication construction

The function of this construction is easiest to appreciate once a basic grasp of Coastal Marind information packaging has been acquired. The pervasive impact of information structure on the architecture of the clause and the verb was discussed in Chapter 11. In short, it was argued there that Coastal Marind restricts the placement of a focused constituent to the syntactic slot immediately preceding the verb complex, and indicates the role of this constituent (S/A-argument, O-argument, etc.) by means of morphological focus marking on the verb, realised by the 'Orientation prefixes' (§11.1).

The types of expressions that are placed in the pre-verbal slot are e.g. question words and constituents under contrastive focus. There are also cases in which the pre-verbal constituent is not focused, but rather packaged together with the verb because the two form a unit. This is the case in topic-comment structures (§11.2.2), in which the constituent in the pre-verbal position forms the main part of the comment, along with the verb. Clauses with a constituent placed in the pre-verbal position (because it is focused or part of the comment) always have a standard verb unit consisting of the prefixal complex combined with a lexical verb stem.

By contrast, most forms of the verb complex containing only the set of prefixes and a verb stem are not appropriate in contexts where equal attention is given to all parts of the proposition, as in the answer to the question "What happened?". In fact, the speaker with whom I discussed (926a) struggled to think of any context to use this form, although this combination of a person prefix and a stem is impeccable from a morphological point of view. The idiomatic way to answer this question is by means of the Thetic Auxiliary construction, as in (926b).

(926) 'What happened?'

    a. ?*no-* *oyad*
        1.A- yawn
        'I yawned.'

    b. *ka-no-* *n-a*   *oyad*
        DIR-1.A- 1.U-AUX yawn
        'I yawned.'

The structure in (926b) is also used in 'out-of-the-blue' contexts. When eliciting e.g. person forms I would ask the speaker to translate 'I yawned' (or whatever verb I was investigating) from Malay, and invariably get replies as in (926b), using the Auxiliary.

The Thetic Auxiliary construction is not used to answer content questions asking about information about some participant ('Who Verbed?') or circumstance ('When did you Verb?'), since answers to such question contain a constituent that provides the crucial information that is being requested, and therefore occurs in the pre-verbal position. Thus, (927a) below is an appropriate answer to 'Who yawned?' whereas (927b) is not.

(927) 'Who yawned?'

    a. nok ø-no-   oyad
        1   NTRL-1.A- yawn

    'It was I who yawned.'

    b. #nok ka-no- n-a   oyad
        1   DIR-1.A- 1.U-AUX yawn

    'I yawned.'

The utterance in (927b) — the same as in (926b), with *nok* 'I' added — is structurally flawless, and could be used as an anwer to 'What happened?', but is pragmatically odd in contexts that require focus to be placed on *nok*.

In addition to these basic information packaging constraints on the use of the construction, there are various grammatical factors that restrict its use.

First, recall from Chapter 11 that certain expressions are grammatically associated with focus, meaning that they only appear in the pre-verbal position, and with a certain Orientation prefix that must be specified for this particular expression. Examples are the negator *mbya*, which triggers the use of the Neutral Orientation prefix (§11.1.2.5), or aspectual particles such as Ingressive *ye* (§11.1.3.5, §18.4.4), which invariably occurs with the Object Orientation prefix *m-*. The Thetic Auxiliary construction may not combine with these adverbials, presumably because the function of the structure is to "remove" the possibility of focus from the clause.

Second, there are several prefixes belonging to the prefixal complex that are similar to the Thetic Auxiliary construction in that they do not allow the expression of a focused constituent in the pre-verbal position, and block the occurrence of Orientation prefixes (see §11.3.1). These prefixes do not occur in the Thetic Auxiliary construction. Among the prefixes are command-forming prefixes such as the Imperative *ah-*, the polar question prefixes *ap-* and *Vk-*, the Perfect *mend-* and the Deictic prefix series *ep-* etc. Such prefixes are excluded from contexts that require a constituent to be within focus, e.g. content question. I assume that since clauses with these prefixes are already 'focus-less', there is no reason for them to combine with the Auxiliary in a structure whose primary function is to suppress focus.

The Thetic Auxiliary construction is very common in the corpus, with approximately 600 occurrences out of a total of ca. 8200 inflected verbs (i.e. 7%; I exclude the present tense copula from the count since it does not contain a verb stem). Below I discuss some representative corpus examples.

In the narrative excerpt in (928) the speaker has introduced a woman who went to the aid post. The first sentence is a copula clause ('Her child was sick'). Copula clauses always have a topic-comment articulation, with the copula complement in the pre-verbal position (§17.4), and do not occur in the Thetic Predication construction. In the second clause the speaker explains what was wrong with the child, as if answering an implicit question 'What was the matter?'.[6] This is a typical case of a thetic statement, so the construction with the Auxiliary is used.

(928) Repeated from (368) and (370).

    1. nalakam elel ø-d-ø-om-　　　　　　ola
        child　　sick　NTRL-DUR-3SG.A-3SG.GEN-　be:3SG.U

    2. yandam k-ø-omb-o-　　　　　　　w-a　　　yadan
        stomach　DIR-3SG.A-3SG.GEN-3SG.DAT-　3SG.U-AUX　get.swollen

    1. 'Her child was sick.'
    2. 'His stomach was swollen.'　　　　　　　　　　　　　　　　[W09:0011-0012]

The next example is from an account of how a man was injured during an expedition and had to be carried back to the village. The narrator quotes stupefied onlookers who are wondering how the party is going to manage with all their belongings and an injured man. The first clause appears to be a standard topic-comment structure '[As for] these [people], will they carry the man?'. The second clause contains the verb *sinik* 'carry things', which appears without any overt arguments, so there is no other constituents in this clause that can be cast as in-focus. Rather, focus is on the event as a whole, i.e. 'do thing-carrying', corresponding to the use of the Thetic Predication construction.

(929) 1. ihe　　　　anem　ka-me-n-　　l-ambatok　　　　　　　ay,
        PROX:I/II.PL　man　DIR-FUT-3PL.A-　PLA-carry.on.shoulders:3SG.U　Q

    2. ka-me-n-　　　y-a　　　　sinik?
        DIR-FUT-3PL.A-　2|3PL.U-AUX　carry.things

    1. 'Will these [people] carry the person,
    2. '[or] will they carry the things?'　　　　　　　　　　　　　　　　[W21:0241]

The construction described in the next section is formally similar to the Thetic Predication structure, and could perhaps be seen as a variant of it.

17.3.2 The Predicated Manner construction

The Auxiliary construction described here is used to express the manner in which some action is carried out, i.e. 'Verb like this/that' or 'Verb in this/that way', as when answering a question 'How did X Verb?'. The construction is made up of four elements, listed from left to right:

---

6 Cf. Lambrecht's (1994: 137) discussion of an exactly parallel example.

i. The Distal demonstrative *epe* or the Proximal clitic *e=* (the reduced form of the Proximal demonstrative *ehe*) in the pre-verbal position.
ii. The Directional Orientation prefix *k-* in the prefixal complex (followed by other prefixes, as required by the context).
iii. The Auxiliary.
iv. A lexical verb stem.

The demonstrative element is always in the default Gender III form in this construction, so I gloss it DIST or PROX without indication of gender. The structure can be schematised as in Figure 17.2. Note that the only formal difference between this construction and the structure discussed in §17.3.1 is the presence of the preposed demonstrative element.

| *e=/epe* | *k-...-* | AUXILIARY | VERB STEM |

Fig. 17.2: The Predicated Manner construction

This construction is non-compositional: there is no sub-part of the construction that provides the meaning 'like' as in English 'like this/that'. Below are two simple examples with the lexical verb *og* 'do', and a 3sg and 1sg subject respectively.

(930) a. *epe k-a-   w-a   og*
         DIST DIR-3SG.A- 3SG.U-AUX do
         'S/he did like that.'

    b. *epe ka-no- n-a   og*
         DIST DIR-1.A- 1.U-AUX do
         'I did like that.'

The basic function of the Predicated Manner Construction is to refer to an action that the speaker is mimicking, or to refer to the manner in which some contextually given action is performed. A corpus example of the mimicking use is in (931).

(931) The speaker shows an action using her hands.
      ehe e=   k-o-d-   y-a   og ay?
      PROX PROX= DIR-2SG.A-DUR- 2SG.U-AUX   do Q
      'You were doing like this, right?'   [W06:0123]

The construction may also be used to refer to some more abstract state-of-affairs, such as the contents of a stretch of discourse (932).

(932) In a story, a person informs someone that their relative in another village has died. The person ends like so:

e=	k-a-	w-a	ay	mayan
PROX=	DIR-3SG.A-	3SG.U-AUX	become:III.U	speech(III)

'That's how the message is.' [W19:0255]

The discourse-referring function is often used in narrative to introduce direct speech or thought, i.e. 's/he said like this: "..."'. The quotative marker *ago* (§20.2) is often present, which might seem redundant since it also has function of signalling a shift to reported discourse.

(933) e=   ka-n-e-   y-a   aɣi, ago   "na   m-an-d-e-
      PROX DIR-3PL.A-2|3PL.DAT- 2|3PL.U-AUX say   QUOT faeces OBJ-1.A-DUR-1PL-
      ka-nayat"
      WITH-be.moving.PL

'They said like this to them: "We went to defecate".' [W09:0047]

The meaning of the Predicated Manner construction overlaps partly with that of the property demonstratives *epetago* 'like this' etc. (§4.2.3), which sometimes (albeit more rarely) are used to point to manner. In their other uses they are distinct. For example, the Predicated Manner construction may not be used to express amount or extent indicated by showing on/with a body part ('The water was deep like this' — showing with the hand on one's leg), which is one of the functions of the *tago*-series.

The Predicated Manner construction corresponds to a special type of content question. Unlike all other information questions in Coastal Marind, manner questions do not contain an interrogative pronoun, so there is no word meaning 'how'. Instead the Auxiliary is used, like in the Predicated Manner construction, but without a preceding demonstrative and with the Directional prefix *k-* replaced by the Locational *nd-*. The prefixal complex also contains the usual prefix sequence *h-...b-* (ROG-...ACT-), which is used to mark all context questions in Coastal Marind. See §19.3.2.5 for examples.

The expression of manner by means of a semantically opaque auxiliary construction is most likely a cross-linguistic rarissimum. Deictic expressions referring specifically to manner have not been subject to as much research as standard demonstratives (cf. Diessel 1999: 74), but this is likely an area of interesting cross-linguistic differences. For example, Dixon (2003: 72, 101) discusses 'verbal demonstratives', by which he means verbs with the deictic meaning 'to do like this/that', based on data from Fijian and Dyirbal. Also, McGregor (2017) discusses a set of remarkable manner-indicating structures in Shua (a Khoe-Kwadi language of Botswana) that are somewhat similar to the Coastal Marind Predicated Manner construction in that they are also clause-level constructions. However, I am not aware of any reports of manner-indicating auxiliary constructions similar to the Coastal Marind structure in the literature.

17.4 The copula and copula clauses

17.4.1 Morphology of the copula

The copula verb *ola* 'be' differs from all other verbs in that it has a zero stem in the non-past. The zero version of the copula, which is used in present and future tense contexts, is represented by Ø and glossed as 'be.NPST' in the examples in this grammar. Compare the past tense copula clause in (934) with the copulas in present (935) and future (936) tense contexts. Note that even when the verb stem is zero, the inflectional prefixes of the prefixal complex are retained (935–936), attaching, as it were, to the zero stem.

(934) About fishing in the old days.
       akada   mbya   ø-d-a-   ola
       fish.hook(III) NEG   NTRL-DUR-3SG.A-   be:III.U
       'There were no fish hooks.'   [W13:0553]

(935) koy   epe   yalet   k-a-   Ø
       slaked.lime(III) DIST:III mean   PRS.NTRL-3SG.A-   be.NPST
       'That lime powder is strong.' (i.e. it burns your mouth)   [W13:0096]

(936) yapap   e=   nda-mo-   Ø   nok
       tomorrow   PROX=   LOC-FUT:1.A-   be.NPST 1
       'Tomorrow, I will be here.'   [W19:0443]

Zero copulas that are restricted to the present tense are well-known from Russian and other languages (see e.g. Stassen 1997: 64), but the retention of the cluster of inflectional affixes in the absence of an overt stem is, of course, a peculiarity of Coastal Marind morphosyntax.[7]

Morphologically, the (non-zero) copula *ola* is an alternating verb belonging to the prefixing inflectional class (§10.3.1). The indexing patterned exhibited by *ola* in copula clauses is the so-called middle pattern (§10.1.2), with co-referential Actor and Undergoer marking. A paradigm of person/number forms of the copula, in its past and present tense versions, is given in Table 17.1. Like other middle verbs, Actor indexing in the copula uses an invariant 3sg Actor prefix *a-*, so the 3PL.A prefix *n-* never occurs with the copula. This pattern is also found with the non-past zero copula, as if the 'deleted' verb stem were a middle verb. Thus, the copula in the present is *k-a* for both singular and plural 3rd person subjects, never *ka-n*.

---

[7] The Western dialect described here differs from the Eastern dialect in that copula clauses in the Eastern dialect lack a verb stem in all tenses (see Drabbe 1955: 58–62).

Tab. 17.1: The copula

	Past tense				Present tense			
	SG		PL		SG		PL	
1	ø-no-d- NTRL-1.A-DUR- 'I was'	na-hwala 1.U-be	ø-nan-d-e- NTRL-1.A-DUR-1PL- 'we were'	na-hwala 1.U-be	ka-no- PRS.NTRL-1.A- 'I am'	ø be.NPST	k-ak-e- PRS.NTRL-1.A-1PL 'we are'	ø be.NPST
2	ø-d-o- NTRL-DUR-2SG.A- 'you were'	ya-hwala 2SG.U-be	ø-d-e- NTRL-DUR-2PL.A- 'you were'	ya-hwala 2|3PL.U-be	k-o- PRS.NTRL-2SG.A- 'you are'	ø be.NPST	k-e- PRS.NTRL-2PL.A- 'you are'	ø be.NPST
3	ø-d-a- NTRL-DUR-3SG.A- 's/he was'[a]	ola be:3SG.U	ø-d-a- NTRL-DUR-3SG.A- 'they were'[b]	ya-hwala 2|3PL.U-be	k-a- PRS.NTRL-3SG.A- 's/he is, they are'[a,b]	ø be.NPST		

[a] Also used with (singular or plural) inanimates in Gender III.
[b] Also used with (singular or plural) inanimates in Gender IV.

The copula also occurs with the Dative and Genitive series of participant indexing, as shown in §17.4.4 below. Beyond participant indexing, the inflectional possibilities of the copula show various limitations compared to lexical verbs, the most important of which will be listed here.

Of the Orientation prefixes (Chapter 11), which mark the role of the immediately pre-verbal constituent, the copula occurs with the Neutral Orientation in nominal and adjectival predication (§17.4.2), and the Locational *nd-* in locative predication (§17.4.3). The Directional *k-* is not used with the copula. The valence of the copula does not license an O-argument, so the Object Orientation *m-* does not occur, except when the copula is preceded by one of the adverbial expressions that trigger the Object Orientation, such as *anep mayay* 'therefore' (937), or the Relinquitive imperative *adeh* (938) (see also §11.1.3.5).

(937) About children in other villages increasingly speaking Malay.

yah anip mayay   m-a-   Ø   namaya ehetagol   ehe
but therefore:I/II.PL OBJ-3SG.A- be.NPST now like.this:III PROX:III

'But because of them it is like this now.'   [W13:0019]

(938) What to do after the leaf oven has been lit.

adeh m-a-   Ø,   kosi   ndamo-p-   mil-e
RLQ   OBJ-3SG.A- be.NPST small FUT:2SG.A-CT- be.sitting-IPFV

'Let it be, then you sit [and wait] a little while.'   [D04:0085–0086]

The Restrictive Orientation *s-* can be prefixed to the copula to express 'it is only X, only X exists, etc.' (939).

(939) About native fish being replaced by intrusive species.

namaya kati   mbya   k-a-   Ø,
now   fish.sp NEG   PRS.NTRL-3SG.A- be.NPST

betik   s-a-   Ø   otih
fish.sp(m)   ONLY-3SG.A- be.NPST many

'Now there's no more *kati* fish, only the climbing perch are numerous.'
[W13:0551]

With the exception of the Relinquitive construction illustrated in (938) above, none of the command-forming prefixes (§19.1) occur with the copula, nor do the valence changing prefixes described in Chapter 13.

Of the suffixes that attach after the verb stem (§8.5), the Non-past Imperfective *-e* or *-et* is often added to the non-past copula (940). This usage appears to be completely optional and has no discernible effect on the meaning of the clause.

(940) ihe   sayam   a,   mbya k-a-   ∅-et   ihe
      PROX:I/II.PL wallaby PTCL NEG   PRS.NTRL-3SG.A- be.NPST-IPFV PROX:I/II.PL
      'The wallabies, they're not here.'   [W12:0118]

Unlike other inherently durative verbs, *ola* allows suffixation with the Extended *-la*, and speakers employ this combination quite frequently, often with the optional Past Durative suffix *-ti* added at the end, as seen twice in (941). The Extended suffix normally derives durative verbs from punctual ones (§14.2.3), and it does not seem to add any meaning to the copula, which is already durative.

(941) kamanday-anim mbya ya   ∅-d-a-   ya-hwala-la-ti,   Yan kudaya
      guard-people   NEG   very NTRL-DUR-3SG.A-   2|3PL.U-be-EXT-DUR   Y. alone
      ∅-d-a-   ola-la-ti
      NTRL-DUR-3SG.A-   be:3SG.U-EXT-DUR
      'There were no guards (during the hunt) at all, Yan was alone.'   [W11:0732]

One elderly speaker deplored the addition of *-la* to the copula as incorrect, claiming that it is a recent fashion, but it is amply attested in my corpus, and was documented for the Eastern dialect already by Drabbe (1955: 86). Cf. also the use of the Future Habitual suffix *-motok* with the copula, shown in (732) on p. 384.

17.4.2 Nominal and adjectival predication

Copula clauses are used in e.g. adjectival (942) and nominal predication (943).

(942) lemed   kosay   ya   k-a-   ∅
      stand.up.PLA difficult very PRS.NTRL-3SG.A-   be.NPST
      'Standing up is really difficult.' (due to a sore knee)   [W11:0406]

(943) uhe   nikna   uhe   wayuklu   ∅-d-a-   ola
      PROX:II   son's.wife(II) PROX:II   young.girl NTRL-DUR-3SG.A-   be:3SG.A
      '[At that time] my daughter-in-law here was a young girl.'   [W11:0045]

Copula clauses follow the word order pattern of topic-comment sentences (§11.2.2) with the predicative expression (or copula complement) placed in the position immediately preceding the verb complex (with which it forms the comment). The referential expression (the topic) can be placed either before, as in (943) above, or, less commonly, after the comment (944). The topic is often omitted if it is retrievable from the context, as in (942a) above. The verb is marked with the Neutral Orientation prefix in nominal and adjectival predication (§11.1.2).

(944) Papu ø-d-a- ola igih
P. NTRL-DUR-3SG.A- be:3SG.U name
'His name was Papu.' [D08:0077]

In present tense copula clauses with a 1st or 2nd person subject there is a strong preference to add a corresponding pronoun immediately following the copula. Thus, the question 'Who's there?' can be answered either by (945a) or by the much more common (945b). See also Drabbe (1955: 58) for the same situation in the Eastern dialect.

(945) a. nok k-ak-e- Ø
1 PRS.NTRL-1.A-1PL- be.NPST
'It's us.' [W03:0044]

b. nok k-ak-e- Ø nok
1 PRS.NTRL-1.A-1PL- be.NPST 1
'It's us.' [W03:0045]

The copula can predicate pure existence, i.e. without any locational specification, as in (946) and (947).

(946) Elicited, answering 'Were we born at that time?'.
mend-an-d-e- na-hwala
PERF-1.A-DUR-1PL- 1.U-be
'[Yes,] we already existed.'

(947) A speaker assessing the future of the Marind language.
mbya me-ø- Ø
NEG NAFUT-3SG.A- be.NPST
'It won't exist.' [W13:0460]

Note finally that the copula forms an idiomatic expression with *bekay* 'heart' meaning 'to like':

(948) nok bekay mbya k-a- Ø ehetago weheb ehe
1 heart NEG PRS.NTRL-3SG.A- be.NPST like.this:III wait PROX:III
'I don't like waiting this long.' (lit. 'this kind of waiting') [W19:0318]

17.4.3 Locative predication

To predicate the location of some entity, as in (949–951), the Locational Orientation *nd-* (§11.1.5) is prefixed to the copula, and the locative expression is placed in the immediately pre-verbal position, i.e. the position of focused elements. As in its other uses, the copula has the stem *ola* in past tense contexts (949), while in the present and future the stem has zero expression (950–951).

(949) yoy emba nd-e-d- ya-hwala
 2PL side LOC-2PL.A-DUR- 2|3PL.U-be
 'You were somewhere else (lit. on the side).' [W11:0815]

(950) About fish that used to be found in coastal waters.
 aliki nd-a- ø ipe namaya
 river LOC-3SG.A- be.NPST DIST:I/II.PL now
 'They are in the rivers nowadays.' [W13:0614]

(951) milah nda-p-e- ø nok yapap
 village LOC-FUT:1.A-1PL- be.NPST 1 tomorrow
 'We will be at home tomorrow.' [W20:0183]

If the location cannot be expressed in the pre-verbal slot — e.g. because this slot is occupied by one of the pre-verbal adverbials (§18.4), such as the negator *mbya* in (952) — it has to be placed elsewhere in the clause, and given oblique expression with the locational postposition *nde* (§6.1.8).

(952) jam 4 ehe nde mbya ø-nan-d-e- na-hwala
 four.o'clock(m) here at NEG NTRL-1.A-DUR-1PL- 1.U-be
 'At four o'clock we weren't here anymore.' [W15:0095]

Standard locative clauses like those in (949–951) are suitable answers to 'where' questions. If the asked-for entity is visible to the speakers, e.g. if the other speaker points to it or hands it over, the reply uses the Presentational structure described in §18.6 instead of the Locational *nd-*, as witnessed by the mini-dialogue in (953).

(953) 1. isi en nda-ha-b-ø- ø?
 other where:III LOC-ROG-ACT-3SG.A- be.NPST
 (Asking for a knife:) 'Where's the other one?'

 a. isi e= ka-hat-ø- ø ehe
 other PROX:III= PRS.NTRL-PRSTV-3SG.A- be.NPST PROX:III
 (Handing it over:) 'The other one is here.' [W11:0123–0125]

The copula is the general option for predicating location, but speakers often opt for more specific positional verbs, most of which are derived from dynamic placement verbs with the Extended -*la* (§14.2.3). This is the case e.g. when the position is relevant for locating the entity, and also when talking about the location of landmarks, as in (954).

(954) epe   nd-a-   hat-a   bob,   da-bak   epe
      there   LOC-3SG.A-   put:III.U-EXT   swamp(III),   sago-grove(III)   DIST:III
      'There was a swamp there, by the sago grove.'   [W10:0572]

17.4.4 Predicative possession: *to have*

To express 'X has NP' the copula is used, with the possessor indexed in the prefixal complex by means of the Genitive prefix series (§9.4). This is basically an existential clause, i.e. 'NP exists to X'.

(955) tamuy   mbya   ø-d-a-namb-e-   ola
      food(III)   NEG   NTRL-DUR-3SG.A-1.GEN-1PL-   be:III.U
      'We didn't have any food.'   [W10:0105]

A characteristic of predicative possession is that speakers almost always use the Deictic prefix series to speak about present possession (956), unless the possessed item is in sight at the time of speech, or in contexts that do not allow the Deictic verb prefixes, e.g. negated clauses (957). See §15.4 for information about the Deictic prefixes.

(956) katal   ti   anem   k-a-   Ø,   katal   ip-ø-omb-
      money   with:I   man(I)   PRS.NTRL-3SG.A-   be.NPST   money(IV)   DIST:IV-3SG.A-3SG.GEN-
      Ø-e
      be.NPST-IPFV
      'He is a rich man, he has money.'   [W11:0419]

(957) mbya   k-a-namb-   Ø-e   kanis
      NEG   PRS.NTRL-3SG.A-1.GEN-   be.NPST-IPFV   betelnut
      'I don't have any betelnut.'   [W20:0050]

If the possessed item is a body part (958–959), the Dative prefix series are used, in accordance with the principles described in §9.3.

(958) isawa kambet sam k-ø-e-   Ø
      maybe ear   big PRS.NTRL-3SG.A-2|3PL.DAT- be.NPST
      'Maybe they have big ears.'

(959) an   Koway upe   nay   sam ø-d-ø-o-   ola
      mother K.   DIST:II voice(III) big NTRL-DUR-3SG.A-3SG.DAT- be:III.U
      'Auntie Koway had a powerful voice.'   [W13:0733]

17.4.5 Copula marking topics

The 3rd person present form of the copula (i.e. *k-a*) is often used to announce a topic in the beginning of an utterance. This is one of several strategies for indicating topics (see §18.3.3), and it seems to be especially common when the topic is a list of referents: 'As for X, Y and Z, …'. Strangely, this use of the present form *ka* also occurs in past time contexts, as in (960), so it is perhaps better to consider *ka* an unanalysable particle.

(960) nama uhe   yay-sah   k-a-   Ø,   yay   k-a-   Ø,
      now   PROX:II uncle-wife(II)   PRS.NTRL-3SG.A- be.NPST uncle PRS.NTRL-3SG.A- be.NPST
      menda-b-ø-   umah
      PERF-ACT-3SG.A- go:2|3PL.U
      'Now, the aunt, and the uncle, they had already left.'   [W19:0312]

17.5 Light verbs

The four verbs *ola*, *win*, *ay*, and *onggat* occur in a wide range of contexts. It is often difficult to determine what the meaning of these verbs is, because their meaning shifts according to the expression or construction in which they appear. In this sense they are semantically 'light' (see Butt 2010 for the use of the term). Judging from their most frequent uses, I have decided to gloss *ola* as 'be'; *win* and *ay* as 'become'; and *onggat* as 'become.PLA' (i.e. Pluractional). The detailed description of these verbs in the Eastern Dialect is one of the highlights of Drabbe's grammar (1955: 85–102). Here I will provide a brief overview of their various uses.

17.5.1 *ola* 'be'

The use of *ola* 'be' as a copula verb in past tense contexts was described in §17.4. There are various verb idioms with *ola* as a fixed part. Examples: with *kambet* 'ear' and the Contessive prefix *ap-* in an idiom meaning 'remember' (961); with the noun *mombali* 'lie' in an idiom meaning 'to lie'. Both idioms are middle indexing (§10.1.2).

(961) kambet ndom k-ak-ap- na-hwala
 ear still PRS.NTRL-1.A-CT- 1.U-be
 'I still remember it.'

(962) mombali ma-d-ø- ya-hwala
 lie OBJ-DUR-3SG.A- 2|3PL.U-be
 'They were lying.' [W10:0198]

The verb *ola* occurs in periphrastic constructions with a lexical verb stem placed before the verb complex. These structures correspond to the constructions with a preposed verb stem predicated by the Auxiliary described in §17.2, but emphasise the duration of the event. This use is most frequent with the Restrictive Orientation prefix *s-* scoping over the preposed verb stem, expressing 'only be V-ing, only remain V-ing'. Compare the construction with the Auxiliary in (963a) with the corresponding durative version in (963b). In the latter the preposed verb stem is in its Extended form (*hamata* 'many be sitting'), predicated by the 'be' verb.

(963) a. haman s-ak-e- n-a
 sit.PL ONLY-1.A-1PL- 1.U-AUX
 'We just sat down.' [W11:0330]

 b. hamat-a s-an-d-e- na-hwala
 sit.PL-EXT ONLY-1.A-DUR-1PL- 1.U-be
 'We just remained sitting.' [W21:0202]

Another corpus example is in (964). The speaker, Yohanes, was making a fire on the ground and asked his niece Biliwag (ca. 7 years old) to fetch tongs for stirring the fire. Biliwag declined, suggesting that he could use his hands. A literal translation of (964.2) would be something like 'You should just remain hand-turning it'.

(964) 1. Biliwag ago kahil mbya k-a-namb- ø-e
 B. PRWD:III tongs(IV) NEG PRS.NTRL-3SG.A-1.GEN- be.NPST-IPFV

> 2. *sangga en i-lw⟨e⟩tok sa-mo-ka-p- ya-hwala*
> hand INSTR PLA-turn⟨III.U⟩ ONLY-FUT:2SG.A-PRI-CT- 2SG.U-be
>
> 1. (Yohanes:) 'Biliwag, I don't have any what's-it-called, tongs.' (i.e., you go get the tongs for me)
> 2. (Biliwag:) 'You can just turn [the fire] with your hands.' [W05:0049]

It seems that *ola* is used to form a durative version of the poorly understood Verb-*ti*–Auxiliary construction (§17.2.3), as in the next example.

(965) *muy ibotok-a-ti ø-da-n-ap- ya-hwala*
meat(III) put.PLA:III.U-EXT-TI NTRL-DUR-3PL.A-CT- 2|3PL.U-be
'They spread out the pieces of meat [on top of the sago].' [W19:0105]

17.5.2 *win* and *ay* 'become'

These verbs frequently express a change-of-state: *win* if the participant that undergoes the change is animate, or an inanimate of Gender IV, and *ay* if it is an inanimate of Gender III. The noun or adjective that expresses the result of the change occurs in the pre-verbal position and triggers the use of the Directional prefix *k-*. The person or gender features of this expression are not reflected in the indexing on the verb, which follows the patientive pattern (§12.2.2).

(966) From a story.

namaya iwag ihe, dul lek yubyala k-a- in
now woman PROX:I/II.PL shame from Syzygium.sp DIR-3SG.A- become:2|3PL.U

'Now these women, because of the shame, they turned into rose apple trees.' [D01:0243]

There are various verb idioms involving the 'become' verbs. For example, *win* combined with *yandam* 'stomach' is an idiom 'become pregnant' (967). Other idioms with nominals and *win/ay* are *mayay win* 'realise' (*mayay* 'able, knowing'), *abna win* 'steal' (*abna* 'theft'), and life stage expressions such as *SMP win* 'start junior high school' (children in Indonesia start SMP, or *sekolah menengah pertama*, around the age of 12).

(967) From a story.

kwemek	ah-ø-	pig	ehetago,
morning	DEP-3SG.A-	become.bright	like.this

yandam	menda-b-ø-	in
stomach	PERF-ACT-3SG.A-	become:2|3PL.U

'When it became morning, unexpectedly, they were already pregnant.'

[D11:0042]

These verbs are also used to express 'be born' or 'come alive', as in examples (1001) on p. 492 and (969a) further below; or to express that the subject has reached a location:

(968)
etob	yey	mit	menda-b-ø-	ay
tide(III)	land	at	PERF-ACT-3SG.A-	become:III.U

'The tide was already close to land.'

[W10:0295]

17.5.3 *onggat* 'become.PLA'

This verb is primarily the Pluractional counterpart of *win* 'become' (*ay*, used for inanimates in Gender III, does not have any Pluractional equivalent), and means roughly 'become multiple times'; see §16.1 for general information about pluractionality. In (969a) *nin* (the 1st person form of *win*) is used to refer to the birth of the speaker, a single event. In (969b), the speaker refers to the births of himself and all his paternal ancestors in the *Ndiken* (Stork) clan, i.e. events taking place at multiple occasions, which means that the Pluractional verb must be used. (Multiple births that take place on a single occasion, as when a woman gives birth to twins, are referred to by means of the non-Pluractional verb *win*.)

(969) a.
nok	Bamay	e=	k-a-	n-in	Duhmilah	ehe
1	B.	PROX=	DIR-3SG.A-	1.U-become	D.	here

'I, Bamay, was born here in Duhmilah.'

[D11:0073]

b.
nok	e=	k-ø-e-	na-nggat
1	PROX=	DIR-3SG.A-1PL-	1.U-become.PLA

'We were born here.'

[D08:0146]

Verb idioms involving *win* 'become' also express multiple or habitual occurrences by means of *onggat*, so *abna win* 'steal' corresponds to *abna onggat* 'steal on several occasions' etc.

In addition, there are various verbal idioms that involve *onggat* regardless of not describing multiple events. Examples are *alil onggat* 'do carefully, properly; finish (tr.)'

(*alil* means 'slow' outside this idiom) and *hi onggat* 'perform sing-sing' (*hi* 'song'), both of which index their S/A-arguments according to the middle template; and *elel onggat* 'become sick' (*elel* 'sick') and *yawal onggat* 'pass away' (*yawal* has no use outside this idiom, but I gloss it 'deceased' for clarity, as in ex. 806 on p. 411), both of which exhibit patientive indexing.

18 Basic clausal syntax

This chapter describes the building blocks of clausal syntax. Criteria for argumenthood are discussed in §18.1. The obligatory kernel of the clause is the verb complex, and such minimal sentences are described in §18.2.

Constituent order of the clause is free, but there is a clear statistical preference for placing the verb after its arguments (§18.3.1). Coastal Marind is a prime example of a so-called 'discourse configurational language', in which the syntactic organisation of the clause is not based on syntactic or semantic roles (subject, object, agent, etc.) but on discourse functions such as topic and focus. The discourse functions of arguments usually have consequences for the shape of the verb, most importantly in the choice of a so-called Orientation prefix marking the role of the focused constituent. This means that it is often impossible to tease apart syntax from morphology. The morphosyntax of focus was dealt with in Chapter 11, so in §18.3.2 of this chapter I will summarise some of that information and put it in a broader syntactic context, along with brief discussion of topics §18.3.3.

In §18.4 I describe a class of adverbial expressions that have a fixed position before the verb complex. Secondary predicates are discussed in §18.5. The final section is a brief description of the Presentational construction (§18.6).

18.1 Grammatical relations

Linguists often distinguish between arguments and adjuncts in language description. Intuitively, arguments realise verb-specific roles (e.g. the direct object of 'eat' expressing the eaten item) whereas adjuncts serve to express props and circumstantials that are not tied to any specific verb meaning (e.g. 'in the house'). This semantic distinction often has language-particular grammatical reflexes. For example, the arguments expressing core participants may appear in certain syntactic positions (e.g. next to the verb), be obligatory, appear as bare NPs (without adpositional marking), trigger person/number indexing, and have the ability to participate in passives or relativisation constructions. Adjuncts may lack some or all of these properties, in accordance with their status as more peripheral to the described event. (See e.g. Creissels 2014a for a critical assessment of the argument/adjunct notions.)

Most such diagnostics fail to provide support for an argument/adjunct distinction in Coastal Marind. No restrictions on the ordering of core vs. peripheral elements of the clause have been found; bare NPs are common even in the expression of many adverbial notions; no passive exists; and relative clauses are adjoined at the clause level, standing in a paratactic relationship to the modified noun (§20.1). NPs are not obligatory, even when they express participants that are central to the event, as in (970), in which none of the three participants indexed on the verb are realised by NPs.

One could probably argue that NPs are only added to utterances when their referents are not recoverable from the context, and that under 'normal' circumstances they are left out.

(970) Previous utterance, addressing nurses at the aid post: "Auntie Siana's child is sick."

ndame-om-   idih
FUT:2PL.A$_i$-3SG.GEN$_j$- see:3SG.U$_k$

'You$_i$ should have a look at her$_j$ [child$_k$]' [W09:0024]

Since none of these criteria can be used to distinguish arguments from adjuncts we are left with participant indexing and gender agreement in the verb, which I would suggest are the only phenomena that motivate a distinction between arguments (which have the ability to trigger indexing and agreement) and adjuncts (which don't). Consider example (971), in which the benefactive participant ('for us') is construed as an adjunct (in this case expressed with the postposition *nanggo*). As it is an adjunct, there is no indexing of the 1pl participant on the verb; notably, the role-neutral 1pl prefix *e-* (used whenever a 1pl participant is an argument; see §9.5) is absent. Instead, plurality of the 1st person pronoun *nok* is encoded in the NP by means of the Associative Plural *ke*. The addition of *ke* is a common strategy when *nok* 'I/we' is used as an adjunct, since the number reference of the first person participant can only be disambiguated by indexing when *nok* functions as an argument.

(971) A line from a popular Christian song.

nok ke nanggo ma-me-ø-   man-em
1   APL for   OBJ-FUT-3SG.A- come-VEN

'He will come for us.'

Compare this to (972), in which the benefactive participant is construed as an argument, and therefore receives full indexing within the verb complex in no less than three sites: the 3PL>1 ('3pl acting on 1st person') prefix *e-* (§9.2.2.3), the Dative prefix *na-* (§9.3), and the role-neutral 1pl prefix *e-* (realised as a glide *y-* in coda position). Note that the pronoun *nok* appears without the Associative Plural *ke*, since plurality is marked by the 1pl prefix (the other two prefixes, 3PL>1 *e-* and 1.DAT *na-* do not signal number of the 1st person participant).

(972) During inauguration of a new church, there was not room for everybody inside.

nok tenda-aha   bak   ka-d-e-na-y-p-   yak
1   tent(m)-house outside DIR-DUR-3PL>1-1.DAT-1PL-CT- pitch

'They pitched a tent for us outside.' [W15:0078]

The participants used to define valence classes in Chapter 12 are expressed by arguments according to the indexing/agreement criterion. The only exceptions are frozen nominals such as *emel* 'hunger' in idioms such as *emel wahun* 'become hungry' (§12.3.5), which correspond to fixed 3sg indexing in the verb, but then it probably makes sense to consider such frozen elements as less typical arguments.

The broad grammatical relations 'subject' and 'object' do not play any role in this grammar. Participant indexing on verbs must be described with reference to more fine-grained notions (e.g. the S participant of a patientive verb being indexed by means of Undergoer affixes, §12.2.2) and often with reference to quite verb-specific patterns (e.g. the O-argument of *kalalid* 'invite' being indexed by the Dative prefix series, §12.3.3).

The groupings of participant roles that are reflected in the Verb Orientation prefixes (Chapter 11) are more akin to traditional grammatical relations. One could use this evidence to posit subjects (grouping S/A arguments, and triggering the Neutral Orientation prefix, §11.1.2), direct objects (O arguments, triggering the Object Orientation prefix, §11.1.3) and indirect objects (recipients, triggering the Directional Orientation prefix, §11.1.4) as fundamental grammatical relations in Coastal Marind. But these groupings show no clear correspondences with other phenomena in the language (such as word order, control of anaphora, valence-changing or clause-combining constructions), so it does not seem that positing these categories would have any descriptive benefits.

18.2 The minimal sentence

A verb is sufficient — and necessary — to make up a complete sentence in Coastal Marind. The verb complex consists of two units: the Prefixal complex, which is a cluster of inflection-like prefixes, followed by a verb stem (Chapter 8). These two units are two separate phonological words, but together they make up a single grammatical unit. No other constituents may intervene between the Prefixal complex and the stem. Some examples:

(973) *mak-e-na-*   *haniy*
     NAFUT-3PL>1-1.DAT- bite
     'They might bite me.' (so I better flee)   [W03:0097]

(974) *ap-e-*   *hwehway?*
     PST.Q-2PL.A- put.in.order
     'Are you ready/prepared?'   [W19:0371]

One particular clause type lacks a verb stem, so that an entire utterance can consist of a string of affixes alone: non-past tense copula clauses. In this grammar, such clauses are glossed as if they contained a verb stem without phonological content, i.e. a zero verb stem. Copula clauses consisting only of a zero stem surrounded by inflectional affixes are mostly used in existential contexts, as in the answer in the typical exchange in (975).

(975) 1. *tamuɣ ek-ø-   ø-e?*
food(III) PRS.Q:III-3SG.A- be.NPST-IPFV
'Is there any food?'

2. *ep-ø-   ø-e*
DIST:III-3SG.A- be.NPST-IPFV
'[Yes,] there is.'

Copula clauses are discussed in §17.4.

18.3 Constituent order

18.3.1 Arguments

The ordering of the constituents in the clause is relatively free, and all logically possible orderings of a verb and its arguments are attested. Constituent order is primarily constrained by information structure: the leftmost, extraclausal position hosts topicalised constituents (§18.3.3), and the immediately pre-verbal position hosts focused constituents (§11.2.1).

Despite the overall syntactic freedom, there is a clear statistical preference for placing any overt arguments before the verb. Table 18.1 shows the orders of the verb and its arguments in a sample of three texts.[1] The orders in which the verb is placed after its arguments (i.e. AOV, OAV, OV, AV, SV) make up 85% of the sampled clauses. In monotransitive clauses with both A and O expressed overtly, 64% have the order AOV. This shows that Coastal Marind can be described as a mildly verb-final language.

18.3.2 Focused constituents

The syntactic slot that is most intimately connected with the verb is the position immediately preceding the verb complex (referred to as the pre-verbal position). This is the

---

[1] The three texts are W12, W18 and W20, all of which are narratives, told by a man in his 60s, a woman in her 60s and a woman in her 30s, respectively. The text count is restricted to intransitive and monotransitive verbs with at least one overt argument, expressed either by a lexical NP or an independent pronoun. It excludes copula clauses and ditransitive verbs, and the large number of clauses with no overt arguments at all.

Tab. 18.1: Constituent order in a sample of three texts

	Text 1	Text 2	Text 3	Total	%
Monotransitive verbs: two overt arguments					
AOV	14	7	14	35	64%
AVO	3	2	4	9	16%
OVA	5	0	4	9	16%
OAV	1	0	0	1	2%
VAO	0	1	0	1	2%
VOA	0	0	0	0	0%
Total:				55	
Monotransitive verbs: one overt argument					
OV	80	48	119	247	78%
VO	12	10	10	32	10%
AV	8	7	16	31	10%
VA	2	4	2	8	3%
Total:				318	
Intransitive verbs: one overt argument					
SV	70	63	35	168	87%
VS	10	8	7	25	13%
Total:				193	

site of e.g. a focused constituent (such as the question word in a content question). The discourse function of the material in the pre-verbal position was discussed in §11.2, so I will only reiterate the main points here.

Consider example (976) below. Several fundamental principles of constituent order are at work in this exchange. In the first turn, the speaker pointed to a man (sitting with his family) in one of the drawings in the Family Problems picture task, and asked a content question. Interrogative phrases (here *ta* 'what') are always considered in focus in content questions so *ta* therefore occupies the pre-verbal position. The man to which the speaker is pointing clearly constitutes the topic of the question, so the demonstrative *ehe* 'this one' is realised clause-initially, like most topics.

Since the topic is already established it is not repeated in the reply (line 2). This clause is best described as a comment, providing information about the (implicit) topic. Comment structures usually involve a verb preceded by a constituent in the pre-verbal position. In a monotransitive clause it is often the O-argument that occupies the pre-verbal position, as in this example, where the O-argument *mayan* 'speech' (in a phrasal expression 'tell speech', i.e. 'talk, chat') is placed before the verb. The pre-verbal constituent is usually not in focus in such contexts. Rather, the reason for this constituent being placed in the slot preceding the verb is that this piece of information together with the verb make up the most important part of the comment.

(976) 1. ehe   ta   ma-b-ø-ind-e-p-   k-umat-a?
       PROX:I what OBJ-ACT-3SG.A-ALL-2|3PL.DAT-CT- INESS-show-EXT
       'This one, what is he teaching them?'

   2. mayan m-ø-e-p-   ka-lay-a
      speech OBJ-3SG.A-2|3PL.DAT-CT- INESS-tell-EXT
      'He is talking to them.'   [D09:0234]

The roles of the constituents placed in the pre-verbal position are signalled by means of the Orientation prefixes. In (976) the Object Orientation *m-* (§11.1.3.1) marks the pre-verbal constituents *ta* 'what' and *mayan* 'speech' as O-arguments of their clauses.

Consider also the performance error in (977). The speaker intends to say 'the dogs are barking at a pig', but switches the positions of the arguments. The sentence in line 1 can only have the — however unlikely — interpretation that *nggat* 'dog(s)' is the O-argument, since it is placed immediately before a verb bearing the Object Orientation prefix *m-*.

(977) 1. basik ihe   nggat ma-n-   asa-e,
       pig   PROX:I/II.PL dog   OBJ-3PL.A- bark-IPFV
       'The pigs are barking at a dog,'

   2. ee!   nggat ihe   basik ma-n-   asa-e
      EXCLAM dog   PROX:I/II.PL pig   OBJ-3PL.A- bark-IPFV
      '...Eh!, [I mean:], the dogs are barking at a pig.'   [M02:0309]

If the A-argument of a transitive clause is in focus, it will be placed in the pre-verbal position, and the verb prefixed by means of the Neutral Orientation prefix (realised as zero in non-present contexts). In (978) the A-argument, realised by the 2sg pronoun *oy*, is given focal prominence and occupies the pre-verbal position. The O-argument *kipa* 'net' is in the more peripheral topic position. The same articulation is found in (979), with the emphatic 1st person pronoun *nahan* expressing the focused A-argument.

(978) From an account about a recent event: the police accuse a villager of having sold a stolen net.
       kipa   oy   ø-o-p-   ol⟨e⟩b
       net(III) 2SG NTRL-2SG.A-CT- sell⟨III.U⟩
       'It was *you* who sold the net.'   [W22:0108]

(979) From a story in which the protagonists quarrel over some land.
       ehe   say   nahan ø-no-   yak⟨e⟩h   mayay ehe
       PROX:III place(III) 1.EMPH NTRL-1.A- catch⟨III.U⟩ first PROX:III
       'It was *I* who claimed this place first.'   [D01:0059]

Speakers adhere to the pre-verbal placement of focused arguments even when they have trouble retrieving the proper lexical item. If this is the case, the pro-word *ago* is used as a place-holder 'what's-it-called' in the position corresponding to the focused constituent, and the right lexical item can then be filled in at the end of the utterance.

(980) The speaker and other villagers travelled in a truck on a dirt road.

nanih ago ø-d-ø-e- yayo⟨n⟩ab-a gumna
face PRWD:III NTRL-DUR-3SG.A-1PL- cover⟨1.U⟩-EXT dust(III)

'Our faces were covered by what's-it-called…dust.' [W15:0028]

The preceding discussion should have made it clear that it makes little sense to classify Coastal Marind using labels from traditional whole-language typology such as 'AOV' or 'OAV' (or 'SOV' etc.). These fail to capture the key role that information-packaging plays in Coastal Marind clausal syntax. In a monotransitive clause with two overt arguments the A or the O will be placed in the pre-verbal slot depending on the whether the A-argument is in focus (giving OAV or AVO) or cast as a topic (AOV or OVA). The two options correspond to different morphological Orientation marking on the verb, as discussed at length in Chapter 11.

Certain forms of the verb are incompatible with the Orientation prefixes, and clauses in which such verb forms occur lack the ability to place focus on a constituent. The prefixes that are incompatible with focus were listed in §11.3.1. Constituent focus is also absent in the common Thetic Predication construction (§17.3.1), whose function is to give prominence to the entire clause instead of focusing on any specific constituent. Constituent order in these clause types appears to be largely free, and I am not aware of any particular ordering preferences, beyond the general tendency for placing the verb towards the end of the clause.

18.3.3 Topics

It is common to start an utterance by naming some entity — the topic — about which the following discourse provides information. As Hockett famously put it, "the speaker announces a topic and then says something about it" (Hockett 1958: 201). A topic may be pronounced under a separate intonation contour, and with a pause distinguishing it the from the rest of the utterance, or be completely integrated within the intonation contour of the following material. If a topic is new, important, and stands in contrast to other potential topics, it is usually given more intonational prominence. It may also be marked either by the particle *a* or by a demonstrative.

The following examples show the use of *a* marking the topic. Example (981) is reported dialogue from a story, about how a man who was injured during a trip inland had to be carried back to the village. In the story, someone asks the returning travellers what has happened. In the response, *Mbakos* is announced as the topic, about which the following material — the comment — gives information.

(981) a. aw,   yoy nda-ha-b-ø-   y-a   in?
           EXCLAM 2PL LOC-ROG-ACT-3SG.A-   2|3PL.U-AUX   become:2|3PL.U
           'Hey, what happened to you?'

       b. Mbakos a,   awe-upen   ø-a-   w-alok
           Mb.   PTCL fish-fin   NTRL-3SG.A-   3SG.U-stab
           'Mbakos, the fin of a fish stung him.'   [W21:0205–0206]

The next example is also from a narrative. The speaker talks about how he arrived at a relative's place in another village. A new participant, 'the boy', is here introduced for the first time, in the form of a topic followed by the particle *a*. The speaker goes on to talk about this boy in the following 7 turns, before talking about other things.

(982) patul a,   imimil-patul   menda-b-ø-om-   w-in,
       boy   PTCL grown.up-boy   PERF-ACT-3SG.A-3SG.GEN-   3SG.U-become

       elel   ø-d-ø-om-   ola
       sick   NTRL-DUR-3SG.A-3SG.GEN-   be:3SG.U
       'The boy, her boy had already become big, he was sick.'   [W10:0017]

The topic is often followed by a demonstrative, used in some of the deictic functions described in §7.2.3. In (983) 'the fish' points back to fish that had been mentioned earlier in the discourse. In (984) a plant is introduced, and it is stated that it was used in black magic. This is presumably a recognitional use, signalling that the speakers should use their general knowledge to pin down the class of referents.

(983) awe ipe,   kilub pe
       fish DIST:I/II.PL catfish intestines(III)

       ye   m-ak-e-y-   ka-l-ahos
       INGRS   OBJ-1.A-2|3PL.DAT-1PL- INESS-PLA-pull.out:III.U
       'As for the fish, we cleaned out the intestines of the catfish.'   [W20:0201]

(984) manenggop-nak epe,   epe   te-ø-d-a-   i-kipas⟨e⟩b
       plant.sp(III)   DIST:III DIST:III GIV:III-NTRL-DUR-3SG.A- WITH-whip⟨3SG.U⟩
       'That *manenggop-nak* plant, that's what he hit her with.'   [W19:0267]

Another type of topic that typically is followed by a demonstrative is conditional clauses, as in (985); cf. Haiman (1978) for the topichood of conditionals. Demonstratives always appear in their default Gender III form *epe* in this use.

(985) anim   a-p-e-   ya-koh   kopi   epe,
       [people DEP-FUT:1.A-1PL- 2|3PL.U-feed coffee(m) DIST]

   gula   mbya k-a-   Ø
   sugar(m) NEG   PRS.NTRL-3SG.A-   be.NPST

   'If we are going to give people coffee, there is no sugar.' (so we need to buy some) [W22:0074]

This example is an instance of what is known in the literature as a "biscuit conditional"; see e.g. (211) on p. 150 for a non-biscuit conditional.

In fact, there is no requirement that the topic noun phrase must correspond to some argument position, semantic role, etc., in the clause that follows the topic. It is not uncommon to hear a topic announced at the beginning of an utterance that has no direct relationship to the following verb. For example, the sentence-initial topic in (986) is *sep* 'leaf oven'. The information added about this topic is literally 'they didn't bring any'. From the preceding discourse it is clear that the speaker is referring to an insufficient amount of fish that had been brought, and that this fish was supposed to have been cooked in the leaf oven. There are no overt clues as to the relationship of the comment to the topic in this example, but any hearer with the right contextual and cultural knowledge will be able to compute how the information in the comment is of relevance to the topic.

(986) Previous utterance: "They only brought a little fish."

   sep   mbya ø-n-e-   nayam
   leaf.oven   NEG   NTRL-3PL.A-ACPN-   come.PL

   'The leaf oven, they didn't bring any [fish] for [cooking in it] .' [W21:0214]

See (575) on p. 330 for another good example of a topic in an indirect relationship to the comment.

Note finally that it is important to distinguish the syntactic position of the topic, a peripheral position of the clause, from the slot immediately preceding the verb complex. This position hosts a constituent that is in focus, or that makes up the comment together with the verb complex, and interacts with the Orientation marking on the verb — see §11.2.2.

18.4 Pre-verbal adverbials

The expressions discussed here appear in the syntactic slot immediately preceding the verb complex. Their meanings mostly relate to temporal-aspectual notions, but also include negation (*mbya*, §18.4.1) and reason (*anep mayay*, §18.4.5).

Each of the pre-verbal adverbials described below triggers one of the Orientation prefixes on the verb (Chapter 11), but it is difficult to find any (synchronic) explanation for these combinations, and the learner must simply memorise which adverbial triggers which Orientation prefix.

One additional pre-verbal adverbial, the Relinquitive imperative *adeh*, is described in the section on commands (§19.1.5).

18.4.1 *mbya* ø- Negation

Negation is realised by means of the word *mbya* placed before the verb complex: compare the sentences in the (a)-examples below with their negated counterparts in (b). The verb is always marked with the Neutral Orientation prefix (ø- in non-present time contexts, *k-* in present; §11.1.2). The Neutral Orientation prefix is used even when the affirmative counterpart would use another Orientation prefix. For example, the verb in (988a) has the Object Orientation prefix *m-* because the pre-verbal constituent is the object, but must be replaced by the Neutral Orientation under negation (988b).

(987) a. Maria ø-a- man
M. NTRL-3SG.A- come
'Maria came.'

b. Maria mbya ø-a- man
M. NEG NTRL-3SG.A- come
'Maria didn't come.'

(988) a. Onggat-Iwag da m-a- ka-man
O. sago OBJ-3SG.A- WITH-come
'Onggat-Iwag brought sago.' [Elicited based on (b)]

b. Onggat-Iwag da mbya ø-a- ka-man
O. sago NEG NTRL-3SG.A- WITH-come
'Onggat-Iwag didn't bring any sago.' [W10:0229]

The obligatory use of the Neutral Orientation with the negator *mbya* means that prefixes that are incompatible with the Neutral Orientation prefix are also incompatible with negation. Common prefixes that are mutually exclusive with the Orientation prefixes, and therefore do not occur in negated clauses, include the Perfect *mend-* (§14.2.5), the polar question markers *ap-* and *Vk-* (§19.2), the Deictic prefix series (§15.4) and the Imperative (§19.1.1). Negated commands are expressed by dedicated prohibitive forms, described in §19.1.4. Note also that the standard Future prefixes are not used in negated clauses, where they are replaced by the so-called Non-Asserted Future forms (§14.2.7.4), as shown in (989).

(989) a. mak-a-y-p-   esoh nok
         FUT:1.A-2SG.DAT-1PL-CT- follow 1

      'We will follow you.'   [Elicited based on (b)]

   b. mbya mank-a-y-p-   esoh nok, ndom-anem k-o-
      NEG NAFUT:1.A-2SG.DAT-1PL-CT- follow 1   bad-man   PRS.NTRL-2SG.A-
      ø   oy
      be.NPST 2SG

      'We are not going to follow you. You are a bad man.'   [D01:0214]

Coastal Marind lacks alternative strategies for expressing constituent negation. Placing *mbya* before a nominal does not negate the nominal, but has the maximalising meanings 'all, completely' or 'every': cf. *mbya patul* 'all boys' (as in 'they were all boys/only boys') and *mbya yanid* 'every day'. To restrict the scope of negation to a certain constituent, a standard negated clause such as the one in (987) is used, in which the negated constituent is placed before *mbya* and given prosodic prominence: *María mbya a-man* 'MARIA didn't come (it was Bill who did)'.

It is surprising that *mbya* has almost opposite meanings with verbs ('not V') and with nominals ('all, completely N'). The diachronic explanation for this situation is that the negator *mbya* was originally a maximising particle 'all', which combined with a verb marked by a negative prefix, to mean 'not Verb *at all*'. The negative prefix was lost in Coastal Marind (although it survives as the sequence *ta-* in the Prohibitive prefix series, §19.1.4), and *mbya* gained the status as negator (cf. Olsson 2017: 524, Dahl 1979).

18.4.2 *ndom* ø- 'still'

This is the only 'phasal' adverbial in Coastal Marind, i.e. there are no other expressions corresponding to 'already', 'no longer' or 'not yet' (cf. van der Auwera 1998). The following verb is marked with the Neutral Orientation, which is ø- in non-present contexts (990), and *k-* with present time reference.

(990) usus   mbya ø-a-   ay,   yanid ndom ø-d-a-   ola
      afternoon(III) NEG NTRL-3SG.A- become:III.U day   still NTRL-DUR-3SG.A- be:III.U
      katane
      sun(III)

      'It had not become afternoon, it was still noon.'   [W19:0193]

The origin of *ndom* is unknown, so it is not clear whether its strict pre-verbal placement has anything to do with being in focus. There is a homophonous additive focus particle *ndom* 'too', apparently restricted to comitative motion contexts ('bring someone too'; §6.3.1).

18.4.3 *oso m-* 'just about to V, just V-ed'

This word is also a noun meaning 'start, beginning'. It is used before a verb (always marked with the Object Orientation prefix *m-*) as a temporal/aspectual particle 'just about to V' (991) or 'had just V-ed' (992). In the former use it is typically used to indicate that some event was interrupted by another just before its culmination.

(991) yahun luk   oso m-ak-ap-   hwis   epe
      canoe from:II start OBJ-1.A-CT- descend there
      'I was just about to step down from the truck[, when X said...]' [W19:0428]

(992) Henki oso m-a-   kisa   agu,   Apliw   uhe
      H.   start OBJ-3SG.A- grab:3SG.U PRWD:II A.   PROX:II
      'Henki had just married what's-her-name, Apliw.' [W10:0520]

If the intervening event means that the attempted action fails, the Frustrative prefix *um-* (§15.2) is added:

(993) oso m-ø-um-   toman   kala   nanggo,
      start OBJ-3SG.A-FRUS-   descend.to.swamp depression   towards
      dalo te-nd-a-   kuhas⟨e⟩b
      mud GIV:III-LOC-3SG.A-   get.stuck⟨3SG.U⟩
      'He was about to enter the swamp, and that's when he got stuck in the mud.' [W08:0030]

(994) The context following this line describes how the participants pitched a tent to protect them from the rain.
      oso m-ak-um-e-   hok   epe,   ye te-nd-a-   yanid-a-m
      start OBJ-1.A-FRUS-1PL-   lie.down.PL DIST:III rain GIV:III-LOC-3SG.A- push-EXT-VEN
      'We were just about to sleep, that's when the rain started.' [W11:0828]

Compare Kuteva's (1998) investigation of constructions meaning 'was on the verge of V-ing, but didn't V', which she labels avertive constructions.

18.4.4 Ingressive *ye m-* 'start to V'

This marker (and its variant *yiti*) is extremely common, with 330 attestations in the corpus. It is used with past tense verbs to emphasise the beginning of the action depicted by the verb, i.e. 'started to'. The verb invariably carries the Object Orientation prefix *m-* in this construction. My description of this as an Ingressive marker is based on the translation 'start to V', which is invariably given by speakers (Malay *mulai* + V). Indeed, a translation with English 'start' often seems appropriate:

(995) *nama nd-a-   umak-em   a,   k-a-p-   han,*
      now LOC-3SG.A- be.running-VEN PTCL DIR-3SG.A-CT- put:III.U

   nok ye   m-ak-e-   yokun   namakad
   1   INGRS OBJ-1.A-1PL- put.inside.PLA:III.U thing(III)

   'Then the truck was coming, it stopped, and we started loading the things.'
                                                                    [W19:0031]

However, it is often completely unclear how 'start' fits into the sentence, as when the verb preceded by *ye* unambiguously marks the entry of a state or process even without *ye*. This is the case in (996), since the verb *atin* 'stand up, come to a standstill' denotes a punctual action (the 'beginning' of being in a standing position).

(996) *Lukas ye   m-a-   atin,   "Yawim, aw!"*
      L.   INGRS OBJ-3SG.A- stand.up Y.   EXCLAM
   'Lukas stood up, [and said:] "Hey, Yawim!".'   [W10:0635]

It is not easy to understand what contribution 'begin' could make in this context, yet, the speaker with whom I translated this text provided a Malay translation with *mulai berdiri* 'start to stand', which sounds as odd in Malay as it does in English (given this context), so it looks like a Marind calque. It is likely that *ye* in addition to the ingressive meaning has some other, not yet understood, meaning, but that speakers generalise Malay *mulai* 'start' to cover all of these uses.

18.4.5 *anep mayay m-* 'therefore'

This expression consists of a non-compositional combination of the emphatic demonstrative *anep* and the ability noun *mayay* 'can, knows etc.' (§4.2.2), followed by a verb marked with the Object Orientation *m-*. The meaning 'therefore' or 'because of that' refers to something in the preceding discourse, usually something mentioned in the preceding clause, as in (997).

(997) *namaya anep   milah   ago   ø-ø-na-   awiy,*
      now   EMPH:III village(III) PRWD NTRL-3SG.A-1.DAT- hurt

   anep mayay ma-no-   dahetok
   therefore:I OBJ-1.A- return

   'Then I was feeling homesick, and because of that I returned.'   [D03:0051]

When the emphatic *anep* is part of this complex adverbial, it shows agreement with the most topical argument of its clause. In (997), this is the subject of the clause (the male speaker, hence Gender I); in (998), the controller appears to be the Gender III noun *wahani* 'body'; and in (999) the plural subject 'they'.

(998) About how the old-timers used to eat bush foods.

wahani dehi anep mayay ma-d-ø-e- *ola,* *epe* *tamuy lek*
body(III) hard therefore:III OBJ-DUR-3SG.A-2|3PL.DAT- be:III.U DIST:III food(III) from

epe
DIST:III

'Therefore, their bodies were strong, because of that food.' [W13:0152]

(999) About how young people don't listen to the advice of elders anymore.

namakad anip mayay *ma-n-* *keway-a*
thing(III) therefore:I/II.PL OBJ-3PL.A- break-EXT

'Because of that, they keep ruining things.' [W13:0380]

18.4.6 *tanama k-* 'again'

This form, which is identical to the Gender III form of the adjective *tanama* 'old', usually appears in the pre-verbal slot, with the verb marked by the Directional prefix *k-*. It seems likely that this structure originally meant something like 'back to the old [place]' (cf. the section on the Directional *k-*: §11.1.4.5). It is most common with motion verbs:

(1000) *tanama ka-n-* *dahetok*
again DIR-3PL.A- return

'They returned/went home again.' [W09:0015]

With non-motion verbs *tanama* gives restitutive ('back to the previous situation'), as in (1001), as well as repetitive readings ('for a second time'), as in (1002). There is a tendency to add the inflectional repetitive prefix *i-* (also with the meaning 'again') to the verb in these contexts, as is done in these two examples.

(1001) About the ailing hibiscus tree outside my house.

kiwal lek k-ø-um- *w-a* *kahwid,*
wind from DIR-3SG.A-FRUS- 3SG.U-AUX die:III.U

yah tanama k-ø-i- *ay*
but again DIR-3SG.A-RE- become:III.U

'[The tree] almost died from the wind, but then it lived again.'

(1002) usus   basik tanama k-i-n-i-a-y-   w-asib
        afternoon pig   again   DIR-3PL>1-1.DAT-RE-1.DAT-1PL-   3SG.U-hit
        'In the afternoon they killed a pig for us again.'   [W18:0269]

The positioning of *tanama* is less strict than for the other pre-verbal adverbials, and it is also possible to place it in other positions of the clause.

18.4.7 *lun k-* 'without hesitation, straight away'

This marker always co-occurs with the Directional Orientation prefix *k-* on the verb, and means something similar to 'without hesitation', 'straight away' or 'directly'. Speakers mostly translate it with Malay *langsung* which has this meaning, although one speaker, when asked, pointed out that there is some difference between *lun* and Malay *langsung* although he could not identify it more precisely.

(1003) anep   tamuy   alilala   ø-d-a-   ola,
        EMPH:III   food(III) ready   NTRL-DUR-3SG.A-   be:III.U

        lun   k-an-d-e-   nayat   epe,   tamuy   k-ak-e-   yahwiy
        straight.away   DIR-1.A-DUR-1PL-   be.moving.PL   DIST:III food   DIR-1.A-1PL-   eat
        'The food was done, we went directly, then we started eating.'
                                                                                        [W16:0023-0024]

18.4.8 *hindun s-* 'keep on V-ing'

The Restrictive *s-* (§11.1.6) occurs with *hindun* 'forever, for good', resulting in the continuative meaning 'keep on V-ing', as in

(1004) hindun   sa-p-e-   nayat
        long.time   ONLY-FUT:1.A-1PL-   be.moving.PL
        'We are going to keep on going.'   [W07:0021]

18.5 Secondary predication

This section concerns the function of expressions like *ihwla* 'crying' in (1005) and *amamun* 'whole' in (1006). The construction that these expressions instantiate shares a number of semantic and morphosyntactic properties that distinguish it from standard adverbial-like expressions in Coastal Marind. Some of these properties are similar to those of English *raw* in *I ate the fish raw*, i.e. the types of expressions called 'depictive attributes' (Halliday 1967a: 63) or, more generally, 'secondary predicates'. This section draws on the studies in Schultze-Berndt and Himmelmann 2004 and Himmelmann and Schultze-Berndt 2005.

(1005) ihw-la   ø-no-d-   yet
        be.crying-PTCP:I   NTRL-1.A-DUR- be.moving
        'I [male] was walking along crying.'

(1006) amamun m-a-   kusatok
        whole   OBJ-3SG.A- swallow
        'S/he swallowed it whole.'

The main properties that characterise secondary predicates in Coastal Marind are:
i. A secondary predicate conveys information about one of the participants (the controlling argument) in the event. Typically, it expresses a state or an activity that holds at the reference time of the main predicate of the clause.
ii. The secondary predicate, if it is headed by a target capable of gender agreement, agrees in gender with the controlling argument.
iii. A secondary predicate placed in the pre-verbal slot triggers the use of the Orientation prefix corresponding to the role of the controlling argument.
iv. The secondary predicate is not referential, and does not realise an argument.

Criterion (i) differentiates secondary predicates from standard adverbials, which add information about the event expressed by the verb or clause as a whole, rather than about a participant. The expressions *ihwla* 'crying' and *amamun* 'whole' in the preceding examples describe the respective participants (the walking person/the eaten item), not a special type of walking/eating event. Compare this to adverbials meaning 'to school' or 'fast' which would describe the event rather than the participants. Secondary predicates describing states are formed with adjectives (e.g. *amamun* 'whole') or nouns (giving e.g. similative meanings, see below). Participles (§3.7.3) describe either a state or — like *ihwla* in (1005) — an activity, depending on the semantics of the base verb.

Criterion (ii) was illustrated by the agreeing participle *ihwla* in (1005) above. Another illustration is provided by the agreeing postposition *lek* in (1007), which forms a secondary predicate with the action noun *walak* 'speed, fast running'. In (a), the secondary predicate describes the A-argument of the verb 'see', i.e. 'I', and agrees in Gender I (whose members are male humans). This clause does not indicate the gender of the O-argument of 'see'. In (b), the same expression is used to describe the O-

18.5 Secondary predication

argument. Gender agreement is with Gender II, so the controlling argument is either an animal or a female human (see Chapter 5).

(1007) a. walak lek ø-no- idih
running from:I NTRL-1.A- see:3SG.U
'I [male] saw him/her/it running (=while I was running).'

b. walak luk ma-no- idih
running from:II OBJ-1.A- see:3SG.U
'I saw her/it running (=while she/it was running).'

Criterion (iii) explains how we are able to determine that *walak lek* in (1007a) describes the A-argument, while *walak luk* in (b) describes the O-argument. The main predicate in (a) bears the Neutral Orientation prefix (realised as ø- in past time contexts; §11.1.2), which signals that the constituent in the pre-verbal syntactic slot corresponds to the S/A-argument. In (b) the Object Orientation prefix *m-* (§11.1.3) indicates that the constituent corresponds to the O-argument. (I have no data on secondary predicates describing participants in roles other than S, A and O, e.g. recipients.)

Criterion (iv) distinguishes secondary predicates from arguments. Secondary predicates describe arguments, and do not realise them. Since secondary predicates are not referential they never appear determined by demonstratives. This also explains why secondary predicates seemingly may cause mismatches in the person indexing. Consider the expression *mbya yaba-anim*, roughly 'all big people' or 'only big people' in (1008). If this expression realised the subject of the clause, we would expect the verb to show person indexing according to 3rd person plural, and the translation to be 'They were all big people…'. In fact, this expression describes the subject argument 'we' as consisting of plus-size people. The secondary predicate does not realise the argument, and does not interact with the person indexing in the verb.

(1008) Explaining why a platform broke.
mbya yaba-anim ø-nan-d-e-p- hamat-a isala
all big-people NTRL-1.A-DUR-1PL–CT- sit.PL-EXT platform
'All of us were big people sitting on the platform.' [W19:0091]

The preceding examples showed secondary predicates describing activities, as in (1005), and physical states (1006). It is also common for secondary predicates to have proprietive or comitative meaning ('having X, with X'), expressed by the postposition *ti*, or privative meaning ('lacking X, without X'), expressed by the postposition *ni*.

The following example illustrates a secondary predicate with *ni* 'without'. The verb 'run around' functions as a transitive verb 'run around with, bring along' due to the presence of the Accompaniment prefix *e-*. The secondary predicate *baju ne* 'shirtless, without a shirt' describes the O-argument *nalakam* 'child' (here, a boy) as indicated by the use of the Object Orientation prefix *m-* on the verb, and the Gender I form of the postposition *ni*. The same secondary predicate used to describe the A-argument (the parents bringing the boy along) would have triggered the Neutral Orientation prefix, and the plural form *ni* 'without:I/II.PL', since they A-argument 'they' is plural.

(1009) Describing a picture from the Family Problems picture task.
   nalakam baju ne ma-n-e- aya⟨h⟩it-a
   child shirt(m) without:I OBJ-3PL.A-ACPN- run.around⟨2|3PL.U⟩-EXT
   'They are bringing along the [male] child without a shirt.' [D09:0238]

See §6.1.2 for basic examples of *ti* forming secondary predicates with a proprietive or comitative meaning. Here I note that there are various idiomatic secondary predicates headed by *ti*. For example, it can form a secondary predicate expressing sound emission, as in (1010). In (1011) the expression *kin ti*, lit. 'with eyes' (something like 'be all eyes', i.e. be fully awake and alert) first appears predicated by the copula (I treat copula clauses as separate from secondary predication, see §17.4) and then as a secondary predicate describing the O-argument of the verb 'return with' (again, this is a verb that has been transitivised by the Accompaniment prefix *e-*).

(1010) From a hunting story: making noise while chasing a pig.
   kuku ti ø-nan-d-e- nayat
   IDEO with:I/II.PL NTRL-1.A-DUR-1PL- be.moving.PL
   'We went [while screaming] "kuku".' [W11:0553]

(1011) The speaker had asked her husband to take their toddler for a walk, in the hope that the toddler would fall asleep.
   anep kin ti ø-d-a- ola, kin ti m-ø-e- dahetok
   EMPH:I eye with:I NTRL-DUR-3SG.A- be:3SG.U eye with:I OBJ-3SG.A-ACPN- return
   'He was all eyes, [my husband] brought him back with eyes wide open.'
                 [W20:0136-0137]

Another common function of secondary predicates is to quantify one of the arguments, e.g. by means of a numeral (1012) or an adjective such as *sam* 'big', which can have the meaning 'much, lots of' in this context' (1013).

(1012) *mandin a, amay uhe, inah ø-nam-bat-e- asik-a-ti*
   long.ago PTCL ancestor PROX:II two NTRL-1.A-AFF-1PL- hunt-EXT-DUR
   'Long ago, [with] this old lady, the two of us went hunting.' [W12:0004]

(1013) muy sam   m-ak-e-p-   ka-hu-n
        meat big OBJ-1.A-1PL-CT- WITH-emerge-1.U
        'We brought home lots of meat.'   [W11:1113]

The secondary predicate may also be a plain noun and be interpreted as a similative 'like X'. The main verb is often marked with the Prioritive *ka-* as described in §16.3.2, but the same interpretation is sometimes possible without any special marking on the verb. The clearest corpus example of this comes from a speaker of the dialect spoken in Makaling, a village to the east of Wambi. However, a speaker of the Wambi dialect with whom I discussed this sentence assured me that the same phrasing would be used in the Wambi variety as well. The noun *kyasom* 'girl' describes the subject of the sentence, i.e. the group of men to which it is addressed. (Cf. Creissels 2014b: 619 on zero-marked 'functive' phrases.)

(1014) The addressee and his party had met a pig in the forest, but had nothing to shoot it with. The speaker comments on their failure:

        kyasom ø-e-d-   nayat
        girl   NTRL-2PL.A-DUR-   be.moving.PL
        'You went like girls.' (i.e. without bringing bow and arrow)   [M01:0064]

18.6 The Presentational construction

The Presentational construction is used to point to a referent that is in a position described by the verb (sitting, lying, ...), or that is engaged in an activity described by the verb (sleeping, approaching, ...). The construction is restricted to referring to present situations, so it is not used about past or future events, nor can the verb be punctual (since punctual events never overlap with the present). The restriction to the here-and-now means that the Presentational construction is very common in face-to-face conversation, whereas the only occurrences in narrative discourse are in reported speech attributed to the characters within the narrative.

The structure can be diagrammed as in Figure 18.1.

| (N) | DEMONSTRATIVE | (te-)k-....-hat-...- | VERB STEM | (-e/-la) |

Fig. 18.1: The Presentational construction

From left to right, the components are:

i. Optionally, a noun or noun phrase naming the participant that one is pointing out.
ii. A demonstrative element: either the Distal *Vpe* or the Proximal clitic *V=*. The demonstrative agrees in gender/number with the participant that one is pointing out.
iii. In the prefixal complex the present allomorph *k-* (*ka-* before consonant) of the Neutral Orientation always appears, usually preceded by the Given prefix *te-* (cited in its Gender III shape, with *tu-* in Gender II and *ti-* in Gender IV and with animate plurals; the agreement follows the gender on the demonstrative).
iv. The Presentative prefix *hat-* (§15.3.5) is almost always added to the prefixal complex.
v. A verb stem, either inherently durative (e.g. *mil* 'be sitting') or an activity verb (e.g. *yi* 'eat') suffixed with the Non-Past Imperfective *-e* or the Extended *-la*.

Motion verbs meaning 'come' or suffixed with the Venitive *-em* (§16.7) are also common in the construction, as illustrated in (1015) below.

Clauses with this structure can often be translated by English *There is a Noun Verbing*, and have a function similar to French *voilà* and *voici*. There is some variation in the realisation of the construction, primarily omission of the Given prefix, as in (b), and/or the Presentative prefix (c). These omissions do not cause any differences in meaning.

(1015) a. *anim ipe ti-ka-hat-ø- nayam*
people DIST:I/II.PL GIV:I/II.PL-PRS.NTRL-PRSTV-3SG.A- come.PL
'There's people coming.' [W12:0320]

b. *anim i= k-at-ø- nayam*
people PROX:I/II.PL= PRS.NTRL-PRSTV-3SG.A- come.PL
'There's people coming here.' [W10:0305]

c. *amay keti ipe ti-k-a- nayam*
ancestor APL DIST:I/II.PL GIV:I/II.PL-PRS.NTRL-3SG.A- come.PL
'Grandpa and the others are coming.' [W21:0174]

The next example contains two instances of the construction, with a position and an activity verb respectively.

(1016) *sayam u= tu-k-at-a-p- mil-e,*
wallaby(II) PROX:II= GIV:II-PRS.NTRL-PRSTV-3SG.A-CT- be.sitting-IPFV
u= k-at-a-p- yi-la
PROX:II PRS.NTRL-PRSTV-3SG.A-CT- eat-EXT
'There's a wallaby sitting there, there it is eating.' [W12:0129]

The status of the demonstrative element preceding the verb complex is somewhat ambiguous. It does not function as a determiner of the preceding noun, because the noun usually refers to a new, indefinite participant, and such nouns are usually not determined by demonstratives. It does not function as a locative adverbial 'here'/'there' either, because such adverbials do not agree in gender. Rather it seems that the demonstrative element combines features of both. This unique behaviour is only found in the Presentational construction.

Almost all corpus attestations of the Presentational construction are with intransitive verbs, or transitive verbs used in an intransitive frame, like *yi* 'eat' in the second clause of (1016) above. In all attestations in transitive clauses it is clearly the A-argument that is given prominence, as in example (648) on p. 350. Thus, agreement on the demonstrative element is with the S/A-argument of the clause.

It seems, however, to be possible to find contexts in which the demonstrative element agrees with a participant that is not an S/A-argument. I have only observed this in clauses in which a body part is the S-argument, but in which the owner of the body part arguably is more important or topical, as in the second clause of (1017). The first clause is a copula clause, without any verb stem (cf. §17.4). In the second clause *utup* 'lip(s)' is the S-argument of the verb *alam* 'become swollen', and the owner of the body part is indexed in the verb by means of the Dative prefix *e-*. The preposed demonstrative *i=* clearly agrees with the owner, and not with the body part, which would have triggered the Gender III form *e=*.

(1017) About some boys that had been beaten up.

    ihe   patul   i=   ti-k-a-   Ø,
    PROX:I/II.PL   boy   PROX:I/II.PL=   GIV:I/II.PL-PRS.NTRL-3SG.A-   be.NPST

    utup   i=   k-at-ø-e-   alam-a
    lip(III)   PROX:I/II.PL=   PRS.NTRL-PRSTV-3SG.A-2|3PL.DAT-   become.swollen:III.U-EXT

    'Here are the boys, here are their swollen lips.'   [W18:0198]

19 Non-declarative speech acts

This chapter describes commands (§19.1), polar questions (§19.2) and content questions (§19.3).

19.1 Commands

This section describes the following types of expressions: commands with the Imperative *ah-* ('Verb!'; §19.1.1), the Jussive *anam-* ('Make him/her Verb!'; §19.1.2), the Hortative ('Let me Verb!'; §19.1.3), the Prohibitive series ('Don't Verb!'; §19.1.4) and the Relinquitive *adeh* ('Leave it Verbing, let it remain Verbing'; §19.1.5).

19.1.1 Singular and plural imperatives

The Imperative prefix appears on the left edge of the prefixal complex. In the templatic model (Chapter 8) it is a multi-class prefix, incompatible with all prefixes belonging to position classes –17 to –12. Examples:

(1018) a. *ah- yi!*
         IMP- eat
         'Eat!' [W11:0479]

   b. *a-bat- man!*
       IMP-AFF- come
       'Come here!' [W11:0206]

   c. *ah-ap- ambid!*
       IMP-CT- sit.down
       'Sit down!' [W02:0166]

The leftmost prefix with which the Imperative occurs is the Affectionate *bat-*, of class –11, as in (1018b). (The *bat*-prefix softens a command). Note the pre-consonantal loss of /h/ (§2.5.4) in (1018b). /h/ is unaffected when *ah-* appears as the sole prefix, as in (1018a), or before a vowel-initial prefix, as in (1018c).

If the addressee of the command is plural, the Plural Imperative suffix *-em* is added:

(1019) a. *yoɣ da ah- i-k⟨y⟩amin-em*
         2PL sago IMP- WITH-⟨2|3PL.U⟩enter-PL.IMP
         'Bring the sago inside, you all!' [W19:0437]

b. *ah- wayaman-em!*
   IMP- stand.PL-PL.IMP
   'Stand up!' [W18:0189]

The Plural Imperative suffix is optional with a single verb, 'come', which has the suppletive plural stem *nayam*. Both variants *ah-nayam!* and *ah-nayamem!* 'you all come!' are common and have the same meaning. Other suppletive verbs, such as *wayaman* 'many stand' in (1019b) above, are obligatorily suffixed with *-em* if the addressee is plural.

The suffix *-em* is only used together with the Imperative *ah-*, and does not occur in any of the other command types described in the following subsections. Note also that *-em* is homophonous with the Venitive suffix *-em* (§16.7).

19.1.2 The Jussive *anam-*

The prefix *anam-* is a 3rd person imperative, most frequently used to tell the addressee to make someone else perform the action described by the verb. Jussive forms can often be translated as 'make X Verb!' or 'tell X to verb!'. Some examples are in (1020). The standard 3rd person Actor prefixes are added after the Jussive prefix.

(1020) a. *anam-ø- man*
         JUS-3SG.A- come
         'Make him/her come!'

      b. *isahih anam-na- kapet*
         children JUS-3PL.A- climb.PLA
         'Tell the children to climb up!' [W19:0303]

      c. *ipe anim ipe anam-ø- nayam-em*
         DIST:I/II.PL people DIST:I/II.PL JUS-3SG.A- come.PL-VEN
         'Make those people come here.' [W09:0117]

Sometimes the most idiomatic translation of a Jussive form uses a completely different verb, e.g. a transitive verb where Coastal Marind has an intransitive verb, as in (1021a). See also example (522) on p. 300.

(1021) a. *lampu anam-ø- aluy*
         lamp(m) JUS-3SG.A- flame.up
         'Turn the light on!' (lit. 'Make the lamp flame up!')

b. From a song.

(1021) *hyakod bekay anm-a-na-y- ay*
one heart(III) JUS-3SG.A-1.DAT-1PL- become:III.U
'Let us unite!' (lit. 'Cause our hearts to become one!')

Note that the second /a/ in *anam-* is syncopated in (1021b) due to Antepretonic Syncope (§2.4.2).

So-called patientive verbs (e.g. 'fall') index the sole participant by means of Undergoer prefixes on the verb stem, whereas the Actor prefix is invariable 3sg (§9.2.2.1). The Jussive is used to form a command directed at the sole argument of such verbs; it is impossible to use the Imperative *ah-* in this context. The expression *silaline win* 'become quiet' exhibits patientive indexing; a literal translation of (1022) would be 'Make it silence you!'.

(1022) *silaline anam-ø- y-in!*
quiet JUS-3SG.A- 2SG.U-become
'Be quiet!'

The combinatorics of *anam-* differ from those of the Imperative prefix *ah-*, so I prefer to describe the two prefixes as separate categories rather than a single imperative paradigm with different person forms. The Imperative *ah-* is a multi-class prefix and may not be preceded by any other prefixes in the prefixal complex. The Jussive, on the other hand, can be preceded by e.g. the Orientation prefixes of position class −16 such as Restrictive *s-* or Directional *k-* (1023). Unlike the Imperative *ah-*, the Jussive may be used with the Auxiliary *wa*, e.g. in the Auxiliary construction with a preposed verb stem, as in (1023b) (see §17.2.2 for this construction), and in the Thetic Predication construction (§17.3.1).

(1023) a. *in k-anam-a-p- ika-hay!*
middle DIR-JUS-3SG.A-CT- INESS-fall:III.U
'Fill half of the bottle!' (lit. 'Make it fall to the middle')

b. *timte-o- lay-e yoy, lay s-anam-ø- w-a-um*
PROH:2PL.A-3SG.DAT- talk-IPFV 2PL talk ONLY-JUS-3SG.A- 3SG.U-AUX-CTFT
'Don't talk to him, just let him keep talking!' [D13:0004]

c. *k-anam-ø- w-a ye⟨y⟩ab!*
DIR-JUS-3SG.A- 3SG.U-AUX slip⟨2SG.U⟩
'Slide down!' [W06:0202]

Note that the verb *yey* 'slip, slide' in (1023c) is patientive, like 'become quiet' in (1022) above, so the Jussive is added to express an imperative with this verb.

The exact position of the Jussive in the prefixal template (see Figure 8.1 on p. 177) is somewhat uncertain. I tentatively assign the prefix to position class –14 based on elicited data, but more work is needed on the morphotactic properties of *anam-*.

19.1.3 The Hortative *mat-*

The prefix *mat-* (*mata-* before a consonant) is primarily used to urge the addressee(s) to let the speaker perform the action expressed by the verb, as in (1024). The Prioritive *ka-* is often added to make the appeal sound less intrusive. Often forms with *mat-* are used as a polite way of announcing one's plans. Example (1024b) was uttered as the speaker stood up and left the conversation that was being recorded. The speaker was not expecting any explicit permission from the addressees, but it would be impolite to just get up and leave without any signal.

(1024) a. Addressing a child.

      oy   Mikaela ah- man   ago,   mata-ka-   yana⟨y⟩ab
      2SG M.   IMP- come PRWD HORT-PRI- carry.on.hip⟨2SG.U⟩

      'Come here Mikaela, let me carry you.'   [W11:0384]

b. *nok   mata-ka-   kw-atin*
   1   JUS-PRI-   INESS-stand.up

   'Let me stand up.'   [W11:0365]

With the role-neutral 1pl prefix *e-* present, *mat-* usually expresses an appeal to the addressee to join the speaker in the action:

(1025) *nggol   mat-e-   kap⟨i⟩tuk*
      betel.leaf(IV) HORT-1PL- break.off⟨IV.U⟩

      'Let's pluck betel leaves.'   [W21:0298]

Almost all examples of 1pl Hortatives have an 'inclusive' meaning (including the addressee in the action), but 1pl Hortatives may also be used to ask the addressee to allow an action to be performed by a group that includes the speaker but excludes the addressee, as in the following example.

(1026) *yoy   adeh m-e-   Ø   yoy, nok mat-e-ka-   toman*
      2PL   RLQ   OBJ-2|3PL.A- be.NPST 2PL   1   HORT-1PL-PRI- descend.to.swamp

      'You stay here, we will go down to the swamp.'   [W03:0075]

The Hortative is occasionally used as an appeal to inaction, i.e. to ask the addressee to let someone perform an action without being disturbed (1027a), or to let an item be

(1027b). These functions are more commonly expressed by means of the Relinquitive particle *adeh* (see §19.1.5).

(1027) a. Telling some stalkers off.

ihe	*iwag*	*mat-namb-e-*	*nayat,*
PROX:I/II.PL	woman	HORT-1.GEN-1PL-	be.moving.PL

nahan	*ke*	*en*	*iwag*	*k-a-*	*Ø*
1.EMPH	APL	POSS	woman	PRS.NTRL-3SG.A-	be.NPST

'Let our women keep walking, they are our women' [W10:0212]

b. Referring to chopped-off pieces of *dapa* (III) 'sago bark'.

mat-	*ibotok-a*
HORT-	put.PLA:III.U-EXT

'Let them lie there.' [W20:0128]

The Hortative prefix is similar to the Imperative in its distribution and appears leftmost in the prefixal complex, never preceded by other prefixes.[1] Hortative *mat-* is not attested with any prefixes from classes –17 through –11, so I describe it as a multi-class prefix spanning those positions. The leftmost prefix with which it occurs is the Reciprocal, itself a multi-class item filling positions –10 and –9:

(1028) *mat-enam- na-sak-e*
HORT-RCPR- RCPR-hit-IPFV
'Let them fight each other.'

19.1.4 The Prohibitive series: *tamohat-* etc.

The Prohibitive prefix series serves to express negative commands, i.e. 'Don't Verb!'.

(1029) | *awe* | *tamohat-* | *ah⟨e⟩b!* | *imu* | *tu* | *k-a-* | *Ø* |
|---|---|---|---|---|---|---|
| fish(II) | PROH:2SG.A- | eat⟨3SG.U⟩ | smell | with:II | PRS.NTRL-3SG.A- | be.NPST |

'Don't eat the fish! It's rotten.'

The Prohibitive prefix series derives from originally transparent combinations of prefixes that have been fossilised as units, and various phonological irregularities have

---

[1] Drabbe (1955: 131) gives one example from the Eastern variety of Coastal Marind of *mat-* preceded by the Given prefix of position class –17. This combination does not occur in the Western variety described here.

been introduced in this process. I will first introduce the 'basic' forms and explain their origin, which will be of help in understanding the alternations affecting this series. The Prohibitive spans position classes –17 to –11, except that the sequence *hat* in *tamohat-* may be replaced by the Affectionate *bat-* of position class –11, as explained below. The Prohibitive may not be preceded by other prefixes.

Table 19.1 gives the paradigm according to person/number of the potential Actor of the verb. The 3rd person forms mean 'Don't let him/her/them do it!'.

Tab. 19.1: The Prohibitive 'Don't do it!' etc.

	SG	PL
2	tamohat- og!	tamehat- og!
3	tapahat-ø- og!	tapahat-na- og!

These forms are partly decomposable. We can identify *hat-* as the prefix discussed in §15.3.5, while the preceding *mo-*, *me-* and *p-* are the Future prefixes for 2sg, 2pl, and 3rd person respectively. The usual 3pl Actor prefix *n-* (or *na-*) distinguishes 3pl Prohibitive from the 3sg form. What about the initial *ta*-sequence? Since these forms express a negative command, a guess would be that this is a remnant of an old negative prefix that has disappeared from the rest of the language. This hypothesis is confirmed by comparative data: the related language spoken at the Upper Bian, Bian Marind, is more conservative in this respect and retains the cognate prefix *tea-* as its standard negator (cf. discussion in §18.4.1). Thus, for all persons the same straightforward scenario can be posited, here illustrated for 2sg:

(1030) Reconstruction of the Prohibitive
  **ta-mo-hat-*   og > *tamohat-*   og
  NEG-FUT:2SG.A-PRSTV- do   PROH:2SG.A- do

which in turn has been subject to further changes resulting in partly interchangeable variants, as explained below.

Before turning to allomorphy, it should be noted that the sequence *hat* in *tamohat-* etc. can be replaced by the Affectionate prefix *bat-* (§15.3.3) as in

(1031) *sapi*   *tamobat-*   *w-asib!*
  cow(m) PROH:2SG.A:AFF- 3SG.U-hit
  'Don't hit that poor cow!'

which shows that the forms are still partly decomposable. However, *hat-* does not contribute to the meaning of the Prohibitive in any detectable way, so the long forms *tamohat* etc. will not be segmented in the interlinear glosses.

The allomorphic variations are as follows. If a vowel-initial prefix is added after *tamohat-* etc., two changes occur. For 2sg, the sequence *-amo-* is metathesised producing /tomahat-/. The /o/ in this form undergoes vowel gradation to [u] (§2.5.1), giving *tumahat-*. However, the /h/ is subject to intravocalic /h/-deletion (§2.5.4.2), giving the actual form *tumat-*. The 2pl forms show corresponding metathesis of /ame/ to *-ima-* (via gradation of /e/ to [i]), giving *timat-*. The 3rd person forms are only affected by /h/-deletion, as seen in the paradigm in Table 19.2.

Tab. 19.2: The Prohibitive + *ap-* 'ст': 'Don't talk!' etc.

	SG	PL
2	*tumat-ap- lay!* 'don't talk!'	*timat-ap- lay!* 'don't talk!'
3	*tapat-ap- lay!* 'don't let him/her talk!'	*tapt-an-ap- lay!* 'don't let them talk!'

If addition of morphological material results in two syllables following the Prohibitive prefixes, the final /a/ in *tumat-* etc. will be elided in accordance with Antepretonic Syncope (§2.4.2), giving *tumt-*, *tapt-* etc. Examples with the Reciprocal *enam-*:

(1032) a. *timt-enam-   na-sak!*
            PROH:2PL.A-RCPR- RCPR-fight
            'Don't fight each other!'

        b. *tapt-enam- na-sak!*
            PROH-RCPR-   RCPR-fight
            'Don't let them fight each other!'

(The 2nd and 3rd person Actor prefixes are always replaced by the Reciprocal *enam-*, as described in §13.2.)

The only consonant-initial prefixes that may follow the Prohibitive are the 1st person Dative (*na-*) and Genitive (*namb-*) prefixes. Intervening between the Prohibitive and these prefixes we do not find epenthetic /a/ as expected, but a vowel corresponding to the Actor prefix: /o/ for 2sg Prohibitives, and /e/ for 2pl (affected by vowel gradation to *u* and *i* as described in §2.5.1). I refer to these vowels as 'intrusive' 2nd person Actor prefixes, since they intrude without being licensed by the position class schema.

(1033) *timt-i-n-ind-a-y-   hayad-a*
        PROH:2PL.A-2PL.A-1.DAT-ALL-1.DAT-1PL- disturb-EXT
        'Don't disturb us!'

Tab. 19.3: The Prohibitive + Genitive: 'Don't listen to X['s voice]!'

	2SG.A		2PL.A	
	GEN SG	GEN PL	GEN SG	GEN PL
1	tumt-o-nam- gat-a	tumt-u-namb-e- gat-a	timt-e-nam- gat-a	timt-i-namb-e- gat-a
	'Don't listen to me!'	'…to us!'	'…to me!'	'…to us!'
3	tumat-om- gat-a	tumat-em- gat-a	timt-e-om- gat-a	timat-em- gat-a
	'Don't listen to him/her!'	'…to them!'	'…to him/her!'	'…to them!'

A 2pl Actor intrusive *e-* also occurs before the vowel-initial prefix *o-* '3SG.DAT' and *omb-* '3SG.GEN'. Since an /o/ following an /e/ always syllabifies separately, usually preceded by an epenthetic glide [j] in casual speech, it effectively behaves as if it were a consonant-initial sequence.

(1034) timt-e-o-   lay-e
        PROH:2PL.A-2PL.A-3SG.DAT- talk-IPFV
        'Don't talk to him!'   [M01:0004]

The reason why the 'intrusive' Actor prefixes are present in these forms is probably related to the preferred placement of heavy syllables described in §2.2.1. Note that forms such as *timteo-* (with the Actor marker *e-* intruding before *o-*) syllabify as [tim.te.'jo], which is one of the preferred patterns (CVC.CV.ó) described in §2.4.2. It is not known why the standard epenthetic /a/ is not used, however.

The alternations are visible in the paradigm in Table 19.3.

19.1.5 The Relinquitive *adeh*

The word *adeh* occurs before the Object Orientation prefix *m-* and forms a command urging the addressee to inaction, i.e. to let the situation expressed by the verb continue without interference (1035). Morphosyntactically, this particle patterns with the class of pre-verbal adverbials (§18.4), but it is discussed here because of its command-forming function.

(1035) Referring to the left-overs from a feast.
        ihwatok   epe   adeh   m-a-   ibotok-a,
        remains(III) DIST:III   RLQ   OBJ-3SG.A-   put.PLA:III.U-EXT

        anim   ipe   es   nda-me-n-   sasayi
        people   DIST:I/II.PL   back   LOC-FUT-3PL.A-   work

        'Let the left-overs remain lying, people will take care of them later.'
                                                               [W18:0277]

The most common use of the Relinquitive is in a copula clause expressing that the subject should remain in place. With a 3rd person subject the meaning is 'let it be' etc. With a 1st person subject, 'let's stay here', as in (1036). With a 2nd person subject, the meaning is 'you stay here' as in (1037). Recall from §17.4 that the copula in non-past contexts consists of the prefixal complex followed by a zero verb stem.

(1036) adeh m-ak-e-ka-   Ø   nok, yamu   ka-p-o-y-p-
       RLQ OBJ-1.A-1PL-PRI- be.NPST 1   mourning.feast DIR-FUT:1.A-3SG.DAT-1PL-CT-
       takin
       wait
       'Let's stay here for now, we will wait for the mourning feast.'   [W20:0233]

(1037) adeh m-e-   Ø   yoy
       RLQ OBJ-2PL.A- be.NPST 2PL
       'You stay here.' (don't come with me)   [W03:0013]

I have no information on the origin or meaning of *adeh*. The word is not attested in other functions.

19.2 Polar questions

There are three strategies for forming polar questions: the Present Polar Question prefix *Vk-* (§19.2.1), the Past Polar Question prefix *ap-* (§19.2.2) and the sentence-final particle *ay* (§19.2.3). Polar questions can be answered with *ahak* 'yes' or *mbya ka* 'no'. It is also common to reply by giving a full affirmative sentence, as shown in examples (1041) and (1044) below.

19.2.1 Present Polar Question *Vk-*

The Present Polar Question (glossed PRS.Q) is used to form yes/no-question about states or activities (1038a) or habitual situations (1038b) overlapping with the present. The prefix is made up of two substrings: a vowel showing gender agreement, and the segment *-k-*. Like other compound affixes I do not segment the substrings in the morphemic analysis.

(1038) a. rusa   ik-o-   hyadih-e   ihe?
           deer(m) PRS.Q:I/II.PL-2SG.A- see:2|3PL.U-IPFV PROX:I/II.PL
           'Do you see the deer?'   [W12:0043]

b. *sopi*   *ek-o-*   *yi-e?*
palm.liquor(m)(III)   PRS.Q:III-2SG.A-   drink:III.U-IPFV
'Do you drink *sopi*?'

One of the most frequent uses of *Vk-* is in copula clauses, to ask about existence or possession (1039). The present tense copula consists of the prefixal complex alone, followed by a 'zero' verb stem (see §17.4).

(1039)   *ngganggin e=*   *ka-ø- n-a*   *ikla⟨h⟩in, ik-ø-emb-*   *ø-e?*
        croton(IV)   PROX= DIR-1.A- 1.U-AUX   send⟨IV.U⟩ PRS.Q:IV-3SG.A-2|3PL.GEN- be.NPST-IPFV
        'I sent croton leaves here, do you have them?'   [W18:0250]

Another example:

(1040)   From a story, in which the speaker meets his sister for the first time in several years.

        nok ta   *ka-h-am-*   *ø*   *nok? ek-o-*   *n-idih-e?*
        1   who:I   PRS.NTRL-ROG-1.A:ACT- be.NPST 1   PRS.Q:I-2SG.A- 1.U-see-IPFV

        mayay ek-o-   *ø*   *oy?*
        able   PRS.Q:I-2SG.A- be.NPST 2SG
        'Who am I? Can you see me? Do you recognise [me]?'   [W10:0599]

19.2.2 Past polar question *ap-*

The prefix *ap-* is used to form yes/no-questions with past time reference. Like other forms with past reference, such questions refer to a punctual event without the Past Durative prefix *d-* (1041), and to a durative event when *d-* is present (1042).

(1041)   Discussing a hunt.

      1.   *ap-e-*   *w-amuk?*
          PST.Q-2PL.A- 3SG.U-hit
          'Did you kill it?'

      2.   *mbya ø-nak-e-*   *w-amuk*
          NEG   NTRL-1.A-1PL- 3SG.U-hit
          'We didn't kill it.'   [W11:0464-0465]

(1042) The speaker was trying to remember who went on an excursion to Alatep.

oy ap-o-d- yet Alatep?
2SG PST.Q-2SG.A-DUR- be.moving A.

'Did you go to Alatep?' [W11:0096]

Speakers often use forms referring to the onset of a past event to talk about some presently on-going activity or current state (§14.1.2.2). The question in (1043) is from a story in which the speaker and his companion hear splashing noises in the swamp, and try to see if it is humans or malevolent spirits that are causing them. Since the verb is a past non-durative form, a more literal translation would be 'Did you catch sight of anyone?'. Cf. (1038a) above.

(1043) *anim ap-o- hyadih?*
people PST.Q-2SG.A- see:2|3PL.U

'Do you see anyone?' [W12:0330]

19.2.3 Sentence final *ay*

As mentioned in §6.3.2, the particle *ay* can be used to signal that the speaker wants the addressee to confirm or reject the statement preceding the particle. There are several differences between questions formed with utterance-final *ay* and the prefixed Polar question markers *ap-* and *Vk-* described above. For example, only the strategy with *ay* can be used to form a yes/no question about the future, as in (1044), since the Future prefixes are incompatible with the Polar question prefixes.

(1044) Reported dialogue from a story.

    a. *ndamo- yi ay?*
        FUT:2SG.A- eat Q

    'Are you going to eat?'

    b. *mano- yahwiy, emel ø-a- n-ahun nok*
        FUT:1.A- eat hunger NTRL-3SG.A- 1.U-become.hungry 1

    'Yes I am, I am hungry.' [W10:0076]

A question formed with *ay* is also the only option when the question introduces a referent from a set of possible referents, and asks the addressee if this alternative is the correct one. The question in (1045) picks one of the members of the set {*amnanggib-basik* 'boar', *sah-basik* 'sow'} and asks for confirmation. Constituents that present such alternatives are always placed in the pre-verbal position (since they are within focus), and the verb is always prefixed with one of the Orientation prefixes described in Chapter 11. These prefixes are incompatible with the Polar question prefixes, so the question must be formed with *ay* instead.

(1045) amnanggib-basik ø-d-a- ola ay?
married.man-pig NTRL-DUR-3SG.A- be:3SG.U Q
'It was a boar, right?' [W11:0579]

The same principle is at work in the following conversational excerpt. The speaker in line 1 wants to know whether Muli is the right alternative, so this constituent is placed before the verb complex, and the statement is made into a question by adding *ay*.

(1046) 1. oy Muli nd-o- ihya⟨y⟩on namaya ay?
2SG M. LOC-2SG.A- run⟨2SG.U⟩ now Q

2. Wewung nd-ak-e- nayam, Wewung nda-no- man
W. LOC-1.A-1PL- come.PL W. LOC-1.A- come

3. o Wewung nd-o- man
EXCLAM W. LOC-2SG.A- come

1. (A:) 'You drove from Muli now, is it?'
2. (B:) 'We came from Wewung...I came from Wewung.'
3. (A:) 'Oh, you came from Wewung.' [W11:0057-0060]

19.3 Content questions

This section describes content questions, i.e. questions containing interrogative phrases such as 'where?' or 'what boy?'. A related expression type, 'Self-interrogatives', a kind of rhetorical question, was mentioned in §15.3.4; some more illustrations will be given in §19.3.3 below. Both structures place the interrogative element in the syntactic slot immediately preceding the verb complex, which can be described as the focus position in Coastal Marind (see further Chapter 11, especially §11.2).

19.3.1 Morphology of content questions

The prefixal complex in a content question contains the prefix sequence *h-...b-* (*ha-* before a consonant). An example:

(1047) patul ehe   namaya ta   ka-ha-b-ø-e-   umuh-e   ehe
        boy(I) PROX:I now   who   PRS.NTRL-ROG-ACT-3SG.A-ACPN-   go:3SG.U-IPFV PROX:I
        a,   Mbelom-Takah-Ahap-Kasip
        PTCL   M.

'This boy, who can bring him now, to Mbelom-Takah-Ahap-Kasip?'"

[W21:0272]

I label the prefix *h-* 'Interrogative' (ROG); it has no other use outside content question constructions. I identify the prefix *b-* as the Actualis prefix of position class −11 (§15.3.1). As pointed out in §15.3.1.2, it is not possible to say what meaning is expressed by *b-* in content questions, so I treat it as a fossilised component of this structure along with *h-*. Note, however, that *b-* may be replaced by the Affectionate prefix *bat-*, as in example (790) on p. 406.

I assign *h-* to position class −14. The prefix must be distinguished from the Dependent *ah-* (of class −15), with which it is mutually exclusive. The Dependent *ah-* is used in subordinate clauses, and unlike the Interrogative it is positionally unstable (cf. §8.3.2).[2]

Since the syntax of content questions dictates that the immediately pre-verbal position in a content question be filled by an interrogative phrase (e.g. *ta* 'who/what'), the verb always carries an appropriate Orientation prefix of position class −16, which marks the role of the interrogative phrase in the clause (see §11.1). The question in (1047) above uses the Neutral Orientation prefix since the preceding interrogative phrase corresponds to the S/A role. The next example has the Locational Orientation *nd-* since the question asks for a source of movement.

(1048) en   nda-ha-b-ø-   nayam-em?
        where LOC-ROG-ACT-3SG.A-   come.PL-VEN

'From where are they coming?'

---

[2] It is clear from comparative data that the Interrogative *h-* is historically distinct from the Dependent *ah-*. In the Eastern variety of Coastal Marind, the Dependent is also *ah-*, but the Interrogative is *s-* (see Drabbe 1955: 113–121). This is surprising since Western *h* and Eastern *s* do not form any regular sound correspondence (the expected forms would be *s-* in both varieties). The related language spoken in Sanggase, Bush Marind, patterns with Western Coastal Marind in the use of a prefix *h-* in content question, but differs from both varieties of Coastal Marind in the absence of any prefix *b-* in these forms. This is seen in the following (tentatively glossed) example.

(i) Bush Marind (Sanggase variety)
     te   h-ø-deh-me   oy   uhe?
     who:I   ROG-3SG.A-shoot:3SG.U-ASPECT wallaby(II)   PROX:II
     'Who shot this wallaby?' [Alatep fieldnotes, 2015]

The 1st and 2nd person Agent prefixes occur between the *h-* and the *b-* since they belong to the intervening position, class –13. The 1.A allomorph *ak-* (§9.2.1.1) undergoes Plosive Nasalisation before *b-*, and therefore always appears as *am-* in content questions.

(1049) ta   ma-h-am-b-e-   og?
        what   OBJ-ROG-1.A-ACT-1PL- do
        'What did we do?'

The corresponding verb forms with 2nd person Agent prefixes *o-* (2sg) and *e-* (2pl) — at least as pronounced in deliberately slow, elicited speech — are given below:

(1050) a. ta   ma-h-o-b-   og?
           what   OBJ-ROG-2SG.A-ACT-   do
           'What did you (sg) do?'

       b. ta   ma-h-e-b-   og?
           what   OBJ-ROG-2PL.A-ACT-   do
           'What did you (pl) do?'

In casual speech, the 2nd person forms have the following morphological peculiarity. The /a/ placed between the Focus marker and *h-* is typically assimilated to the following Agent prefix, so instead of the expected forms *mahob-* and *maheb-* (as in ex. 1050) we find the forms *mohob-* and *meheb-* (1051):

(1051) a. ta mo-h-o-b- og?
           'What did you (sg) do?'

       b. ta me-h-e-b- og?
           'What did you (pl) do?'

The assimilated variants in (1051) are by far the most commonly heard options; the options in (1050) seem to occur in deliberately slow speech only. This phonological idiosyncrasy affecting the 2sg and 2pl forms suggests that the prefix sequences *mohob-* etc. are completely lexicalised, so that it is no longer meaningful to disassemble them into morphological components. In order to simplify the interlinear glossing I have chosen to write all content questions in this grammar according to the more conservative variant in (1050).

The Interrogative *h-* undergoes phonologically conditioned deletion in two contexts: (i) it is always lost word-initially; (ii) it is optionally (but almost always) omitted if it occurs in any syllable other than the final syllable of the prefixal complex. Situation (i) only occurs in past-tense questions with an interrogative phrase in the S/A-role, since the Neutral Orientation prefix used with S/A-arguments in past tense has the shape ø- (i.e. zero, see §11.1.2). The loss of /h/ avoids formation of an illegal cluster *[hb] (epenthetic *a* is usually not inserted to rescue /h/ from cluster formation outside of the tonic syllable, see §2.5.4):

(1052) ta   ø-b-a-   deh?
        who   NTRL-ACT-3SG.A-   shoot:3SG.U

'Who shot it?'   [W11:1075]

If additional prefixes follow the *h-...b-* sequence, *h-* is practically always lost in casual speech, as in (1053). No ambiguity arises from the deletion of /h/ since the construction is redundantly marked (in addition to *h-* and *b-* by the question word *ta*).

(1053) ta   m-o-b-ap-   ol⟨e⟩b?
        what   OBJ-2SG.A-ACT-CT-   exchange⟨III.U⟩

'What did you (sg) exchange?'

Speakers often drop *h-* even when it occurs in the final syllable of the prefixal complex, at least in fast, casual speech. As a consequence, the question *ta mohob-og?* in (1051) has the shortened variant *ta mob-og?*. It seems that the *h*-prefix is on its way to becoming optional, so whenever it is absent in an example I omit it from the interlinear gloss, rather than re-instating it by means as a zero placeholder ø-.

The use of dedicated verb morphology (the sequence *h-...b-*) in content questions is a typological rarity. It is common across languages to use interrogative morphology in polar questions (e.g. Finnish interrogative suffix *-ko/-kö* or the Latin enclitic *-ne*) but employing a separate verb form for content questions appears to be rare, presumably since the presence of a question word makes the use of additional morphology redundant.[3]

19.3.2 Types of content questions

The three interrogative pronouns in Coastal Marind were presented in §4.3; they are: *ta* 'who, what', *en* 'where, which', *entago* (or *entagol*) 'what kind, how many'. This is a small inventory by cross-linguistic standards, although not exceptionally so (cf. Diessel 2003: 640–643). The inventory of semantic categories that are distinguished in content question is actually larger than the set of interrogative pronouns, since the prefixes making up the system of Verb Orientation (Chapter 11) add some further distinctions. The types of content questions are listed in Table 19.4; examples are given in the subsections below.

---

[3] See however the Interrogative suffix *-wa* in Kashaya (a Pomoan language of California), which seems to mark content questions, just like its Coastal Marind counterpart (Oswalt 1961: 286).

Tab. 19.4: Semantic categories in content questions

Interrogative expression	Orientation prefix	Category
ta	NTRL/OBJ/DIR	Person/thing: who/what
en	DIR	Place: towards where
en	LOC	Place: at, from where
ta	LOC	Time: when
en	NTRL/OBJ/DIR	Selection: which
entago	NTRL/OBJ/DIR	Property/amount: what kind/how many

A structurally distinct question type expresses manner ('how?'), and does not contain any interrogative pronoun (§19.3.2.5).

19.3.2.1 Person/thing: who/what?

Examples of questions with the interrogative pronoun *ta* were already given in the preceding pages. Further examples are in (1054). The Orientation prefix at the beginning of the prefixal complex signals the role of the interrogative phrase: the Neutral Orientation for an S/A-argument, which is realised as zero in past time contexts, as in (1054a), and as *k-* in non-past contexts, as in (1054b); Object Orientation for the O-argument in (1054c) and (1054d), and the Directional Orientation flagging the recipient argument in (1054e); for more information about the Orientation prefixes, see §11.1. Example (1054d) shows that an interrogative pronoun may be used adnominally, as in *ta mayan* (lit.) 'what speech'.

(1054) a. ta   ø-b-a-   ayi?
           who:I NTRL-ACT-3SG.A- say
           'Who said it?'   [W11:0881]

   b. ti   ka-b-e-na-ø-y-   hus-e?   katane usus
       who:I/II.PL PRS.NTRL-ACT-3PL>1-1.DAT-1PL-ACPN- cross.river-IPFV sun(III) afternoon
       menda-b-ø-   ay
       PERF-ACT-3SG.A- become:III.U
       'Who is going to take us across the river? It's already afternoon.'
                                                                              [W10:0122]

   c. ta   ma-h-o-b-   y-alit-a?
       who:I OBJ-ROG-2SG.A-ACT- 2SG.U-call-EXT
       'Who are you calling for?'   [W06:0168]

   d. ta   mayan   ma-b-a-p-   lay-a-ti?
       what:III speech(III) OBJ-ACT-3SG.A-CT- tell-EXT-DUR
       'What was he talking about?'   [W11:0031]

e. ta   ka-mo-b-o-   ikalen?
   who:I DIR-FUT:2SG.A-ACT-3SG.DAT-   send:III.U
   'To whom are you going to send it?'

Further distinctions are made with postpositional phrases such as *ta lek* 'because of what' (lit. 'from what') in (1055a) or *ta ti* 'with whom' in (1055b). There are special principles governing the use of the Orientation prefixes with such expressions; for these two examples see §11.1.3.5 and §11.1.2.4 respectively.

(1055) a. ta   lek   ma-ha-b-na-   u-sak?
          what from   OBJ-ROG-ACT-3PL.A-   3SG.U-hit.PLA
          'Why did they beat him up?'   [D09:0190]

       b. ta   ti   ø-b-a-   nayam?
          who   with:I/II.PL   NTRL-ACT-3SG.A-   come.PL
          'With whom did he come?'   [W11:0168]

Possession ('whose') is questioned either by means of an interrogative phrase with the Possessive postposition *en*, as in (1056a), or by using Genitive indexing (§9.4) on the verb, as in (1056b).

(1056) a. ta   en   ka-ha-b-ø-   ø   yaba-ember?
          who:I   POSS   PRS.NTRL-ROG-ACT-3SG.A-   be.NPST   big-bucket(m)
          'Whose is this big bucket?'   [W06:0132]

       b. oy   ta   k-o-b-omb-o-p-   mil-em
          2SG   who:I   DIR-2SG.A-ACT-3SG.GEN-3SG.DAT-CT-   be.sitting-VEN

          nggawil-yahun   epe?
          motor.cycle(III) DIST:III
          'Whose motorcycle did you sit on coming here?'   [D07:0061]

The latter example could be given the more literal paraphrase 'To whom did you sit on his motorcycle?'.[4] For the copula structure in (1056a), see §17.4.

19.3.2.2 Place/selection: where/which?

Questions about direction towards a location trigger the use of the Directional Orientation *k-*, as in (1057a–b). The Directional is also used in questions about the location of punctual events in general (1057c). The question word *Vn* 'where, which' does not

---

[4] The 3sg Dative prefix is often used with sitting verbs to describe sitting on a motorcycle.

show agreement in this context since it is used adverbially, so it appears in its default Gender III form *en*.

(1057) a. *kipa   en   ka-h-e-b-   kwagin?*
net(III) where DIR-ROG-2PL.A-ACT- throw:III.U
'Where did you throw the net?'

b. *en   ka-ha-m-b-e-   hok?*
where DIR-ROG-FUT:1.A-ACT-1PL- lie.down.PL
'Where shall we lie down [to sleep]?' [W16:0012]

c. *en   ka-b-a-n-is-a-y-   ihwim?*
where DIR-ACT-3SG.A-1.DAT-SEP-1.DAT-1PL- become.dark
'Where did it get dark on us?' [W11:0443]

(For the use of the Separative in 1057c above, see §13.1.8).

The Locational Orientation *nd-* is used in questions about motion away from a source (1058a) or static location (1058b).

(1058) a. *Rovina en   nda-h-o-b-   man?*
R.   where LOC-ROG-2SG.A-ACT- come
'Rovina, where are you coming from?' [W09:0048]

b. *en   nda-ha-b-ø-   hamat-a?*
where LOC-ROG-ACT-3SG.A- sit.PL-EXT
'Where are they sitting?'

Surprisingly, the question word 'where' occasionally shows gender agreement with the subject in questions about static location, as in the copula clause in (1059). This rare type of adverbial agreement seems to be completely optional, but is not uncommon in this context. According to speakers such agreement can only occur in present-tense contexts.

(1059) *wanangga in   nda-ha-b-ø-   ø-e?*
children   where:I/II.PL   LOC-ROG-ACT-3SG.A- be.NPST-IPFV
'Where are the children?' [W19:0023]

Used adnominally, *Vn* means 'which'. In this use it always agrees in gender with the head noun, e.g. *un nggat?* 'which dog?' (Gender II), *en aliki?* 'which river' (Gender III). A remarkable exception occurs when the interrogative phrase is embedded under the agreeing postposition *lVk* 'from' (i.e. 'from which N'). In this context the interrogative pronoun copies whatever agreement is exhibited by the postposition. In the following example, *lek* agrees with the subject *yoɣ* 'you (pl)', so the plural agreement percolates down to *Vn* 'which' as well.

(1060) in   milah   lik   ka-h-e-b-   Ø   yoɣ?
which:I/II.PL village(III) from:I/II.PL PRS.NTRL-ROG-2PL.A-ACT- be.NPST 2PL
'From which village are you?'

19.3.2.3 Time: when?

Time expressions (e.g. dates) combine with the Locational orientation on the verb, as described in §11.1.5.2. The corresponding content questions are formed by placing *ta* 'what' or a phrase such as *ta katane* 'what time' (lit. 'what sun') or *ta yanid* 'what day' before the verb complex. Examples:

(1061) a. *muy*   *ta*   *nda-ha-b-ø-*   *y-alaw*   *ehe?*
meat(III) what LOC-ROG-ACT-3SG.A- 2|3PL.U-search PROX:III
'When did they go looking for meat?' [W11:0166]

b. *ta*   *yanid nda-m-b-e-p-*   *hu-n?*
what day LOC-FUT:1.A-ACT-1PL-CT- emerge-1.U
'What day shall we go home?' [W23:0033]

19.3.2.4 Property/amount: what kind/how many?

The interrogative pronoun *entago* (or *entagol*, with the same meaning) is used to ask about property, i.e. 'what kind', and amount, 'how many, how much'. I gloss the interrogative pronoun 'how'. It is not clear whether there are any syntactic differences that distinguish the two meanings. During elicitation, one speaker claimed that if the interrogative pronoun is separated from the noun, as in (1062a), the reading 'how many' is more likely, whereas a continuous noun phrase such as *intagi awe* in (1062b) would be understood as meaning 'what kind'.

(1062) a. *intagi*   *m-o-b-ap-*   *olab*   *awe?*
how:I/II.PL OBJ-2SG.A-ACT-CT- buy:2|3PL.U fish(II)
'How many fish did you buy?'

b. *intagi*   *awe*   *m-o-b-ap-*   *olab?*
how:I/II.PL fish(II) OBJ-2SG.A-ACT-CT- buy:2|3PL.U
'What kinds of fish did you buy?'

According to the speaker this seems to be a preference rather than a rule, so the translations above can be swapped. There is not sufficient corpus data to evaluate these intuitions, unfortunately.

Below are some more examples of the 'how many' use.

(1063) a. *elel entago mandaw ma-ha-b-ø- y-ahwala?*
sick how:III moon(III) OBJ-ROG-ACT-3SG.A- 2SG.U-be

'How many months were you sick?'

b. *intagi ø-nam-b-e- nayat?*
how:I/II.PL NTRL-1.A-ACT-1PL- be.moving.PL

'How many of us went?' [W11:0381]

19.3.2.5 Manner questions

Manner questions ('How did you Verb' etc.) are formed using a special Auxiliary construction; this is the interrogative equivalent of the Predicated Manner construction described in §17.3.2. The verb is formed using the Locational Orientation prefix *nd-* (without any preceding interrogative phrase), the usual *h-...b-* sequence, the Auxiliary, and a following lexical verb. The Auxiliary is a middle verb and alternates by copying the person/number of the Actor argument, as described in §17.1.

Here is a question-answer pair illustrating a manner question (1064.1) as well as the affirmative Predicated Manner construction (1064.2):

(1064) 1. *nda-ha-b-ø- w-a hi-y?*
LOC-ROG-ACT-3SG.A- 3SG.U-AUX fall-2SG.U

'How did you fall?'

2. *e= k-a- w-a hi-n*
PROX= DIR-3SG.A- 3SG.U-AUX fall-1.U

'I fell like this.' (showing)

Manner questions have a rather broad range of uses. In addition to expressing manner, the same structure is used to ask 'What happened to X', as in (1065a) (lit. 'How did X become?'), and in metalinguistic questions such as 'How do you say "X"?', as in (1065b), or 'What did X say?', as in (1065c).

(1065) a. A line from a popular song.

nok ø-nak-um-o- kabed, nda-ha-b-ø- w-a y-in
1 ø-1.A-FRUS-3SG.DAT- ask LOC-ROG-ACT-3SG.A- 3SG.U-AUX 2SG.U-become

'I asked her: "What happened to you?"'

b. The speaker was trying to think of a Coastal Marind term to use in the recording.

nda-ha-m-b-e- n-a lu-e ehe, jeriken ehe
LOC-ROG-FUT:1.A-ACT-1PL- 1.U-AUX call:III.U-IPFV PROX:III jerrycan(m)(III) PROX:III
'What shall we call them, these jerrycans?' [W19:0289]

c. nda-b-ø-a- w-a ayi, waninggap k-a- ø
LOC-ACT-3SG.A-2SG.DAT- 3SG.U-AUX say good PRS.NTRL-3SG.A- be.NPST
ay?
Q
'What did he say to you? It's good right?' [W11:0224]

19.3.3 Self-interrogative questions

The structure used for content questions — with an interrogative phrase in the preverbal position — is also used to form 'self-interrogatives' marked by the prefix *bah-*, i.e. questions that express one's ignorance without being truly information-seeking (something like 'Who could have Verb-ed?', 'Who on earth Verb-ed?' etc.). General information about the meaning of these forms was given in §15.3.4.

Below I provide examples showing the Self-interrogative structure with some of the semantic categories that were described above for standard content questions. Place:

(1066) nd-an-d-e- nayat eee ago,
LOC-1.A-DUR-1PL- be.moving.PL all.the.way.to PRWD:III

en nd-am-bah-e- hamat-a-ti
where LOC-1.A-SLF.INT-1PL- sit.PL-EXT-DUR
'We went to um, where was it that we were sitting...' [W11:0777]

(1067) From a hunting story: the reported thoughts of a wallaby.
namuk un nda-bah-ø- ø-e sayam uhe?
clanmate:II where:II LOC-SLF.INT-3SG.A- be.NPST-IPFV wallaby(II) PROX:II
'Where on earth could my wallaby mate be?' [W12:0199]

Time:

(1068) ta   nda-m-bah-ø-   u-hwasig   duh   luk?
       what   LOC-FUT-SLF.INT-3SG.A-   3SG.U-go.up.from.water   beach from:II

'Who knows when she will come up from the beach.'

Manner:

(1069) anum   k-a-   w-a   w-alit-a-m,
       woman   PRS.NTRL-3SG.A-   3SG.U-AUX   3SG.U-call-EXT-VEN

       nda-bah-ø-   w-a   w-in
       LOC-SLF.INT-3SG.A-   3SG.U-AUX   3SG.U-become

'Some woman is screaming, what could have happened to her?'   [W10:0657]

20 Combinations of clauses

This chapter describes the multi-functional subordinate clause construction (§20.1), reported speech and extended uses thereof (§20.2) and a simple structure for expressing sequences of events in narratives (§20.3).

20.1 Subordinate clauses

While much of Coastal Marind morphosyntax is permeated by minute, and often largely redundant, attention to grammatical details, the domain of subordination offers the opposite picture, one of relative simplicity and underspecification. There is a single generalised subordinate clause type, which occurs at the periphery of a main clause rather than embedded within it, and the interpretation of the semantic relationship holding between this clause and the main clause is constrained mainly by contextual clues. This construction is very similar to what was called adjoined relative clauses in a famous paper (Hale 1976). Although widespread in Australian Aboriginal languages, this subordinate clause type has, to my knowledge, not been identified for any other Papuan language.[1]

20.1.1 Morphosyntax of subordinate clauses

This section describes two types of prefixes that mark subordinate verbs, the Dependent *ah-* (§20.1.1.1) and the Deictic prefix series (§20.1.1.2). Other than the restriction of the Deictic prefix series to the present tense, none of these subordinate verb forms show any inflectional limitations (such as reduced tense marking or participant indexing) that would suggest non-finite or nominalised status, so they are best described as full-fledged finite verbs.

Subordinate clauses are often followed by a final demonstrative (§20.1.1.3). The syntactic position of the subordinate clause is always at the periphery of the main clause, and there is often a prosodic break between the subordinate clause and the main clause (§20.1.1.4). These three properties are shared with topicalised con-

---

[1] Relative clauses in the neighbouring Yam languages Komnzo (Döhler 2016: 325) and Ngkolmpu (Carroll 2016: 318) have been described as being of the adjoined type, but since they are explicitly marked for their role in the matrix clause, and lack the temporal adverbial interpretation, the relative clauses in these languages do not match Hale's definition of adjoined clauses. The use of relative pronouns actually make the Yam clauses more similar to relative clauses in European languages (Siegel 2019). Jendraschek (2009: 140) uses the term for medial switch-reference clauses in Iatmul, noting that his use of the label differs from that of Hale.

stituents, and suggest that subordinate clauses are not embedded within the main clause, but should be analysed as extra-clausal, topic-like constituents.

The boundaries of subordinate clauses are delineated by means of square brackets in the gloss line of examples throughout this grammar. To make parsing easier for the reader, the part of the free translation that corresponds to the subordinate clause has been underlined throughout this section.

20.1.1.1 The Dependent *ah-*

The Dependent prefix is realised as *a-* before consonants. Under some circumstances the *h*-segment can avoid deletion by floating rightwards, and forming the onset of the final syllable of the prefixal complex, as described in §8.3.2.2.

The dependent *ah-* is used to mark the verb in subordinate clauses with past and future time reference, as in (1070–1071). If the clause has present time reference, the Deictic prefixes (§20.1.1.2 below) are used instead.

(1070) ah-ø-   dahetok-a-m epe,   hyakod   s-a-   yali   ehe
        [DEP-3SG.A- return-EXT-VEN DIST:III] one   ONLY-3SG.A- lie.down   PROX
        'When he returned here, he slept here only one night.'   [W22:0024]

(1071) yah namaya   a-m-o-   ayi,   malayu-mayan
        but now   [DEP-FUT:2SG.A-3SG.DAT- say] Malay-language

        ø-m-o-   k-ayi
        NTRL-FUT:2SG.A-3SG.DAT-   WITH-say

        'But now when/if you say something to her, you should say it in Indonesian.'
                                                                                [W13:0410]

There is one exceptional case in which the Dependent *ah-* is always used instead of the Deictic prefixes, even when the clause has present tense reference. This occurs when the subordinate clause has a focused constituent in the pre-verbal position, and therefore requires one of the Orientation prefixes to be present on the verb (Chapter 11). The Deictic prefixes are mutually incompatible with a range of other prefixes belonging to the leftmost end of the prefixal complex, as predicted by the morphotactic principles in §8.3, whereas the Dependent prefix can be preceded by Orientation prefixes, such as the Locational *nd-* in (1072).

(1072) patale   Yambuti nd-ah-ø-om-   hat-a,
        [grave(III) Buti   LOC-DEP-3SG.A-3SG.GEN-   put:III.U-EXT]

        yah igih u=   k-ak-e-p-   han   namaya
        but name PROX:II=   DIR-1.A-1PL-CT-   put:3SG.U   now

        'The one whose grave is in Buti, we gave her name to this [girl] now.'
                                                                          [W14:0005–0006]

The Dependent *ah-* is superficially similar to the Imperative *ah-* (§19.1.1), but the two prefixes belong to different position classes, and the Imperative does not exhibit *h*-floating. There is perhaps a diachronic relationship between these prefixes, and imperative verb forms are used to mark conditionals in some non-Anim languages in the area, e.g. Aghu (Greater Awyu; van den Heuvel 2016: 337) and Komnzo (Yam; Döhler 2016: 387).

20.1.1.2 The Proximal *eh-* and Distal *ep-*

The Proximal prefix series *eh-* etc. and the Distal series *ep-* (or, the Deictic prefixes for short) are identical to the corresponding demonstratives, i.e. *ehe* 'this' and *epe* 'that' (§4.2), minus the final /e/. Diachronically, these verb prefixes are most likely the result of incorporation of the independent demonstratives into the prefixal complex. Synchronically, the Deictic prefixes are polyfunctional, with two separate uses: one in independent main clauses, in which they have the attentional meaning described in §15.4, and another as markers of present tense subordinate verbs, as described here.

The shape of the Proximal and Distal prefix series was described in §15.4.1. The prefixes attach at the leftmost end of the verb and may not be preceded by any other prefixes. The Proximal *eh-* series is used when the situation or referent described by the subordinate clause is presented as being in the proximity of the deictic origo (1073), and the Distal *ep-*series when it is presented as distant (1074). Of course, the boundaries of deictic categories are quite flexible, and do not correspond to absolute distance: in (1073) the Proximal refers to plantations that are located in the swamps a 15 minute walk north of the village, while in (1074) the Distal refers to the camera that I was holding, across the room from the speaker.

(1073) *tis ka, nahe de-ito ø-da-n- k-wambad-ma,*
that's.it ancestors:1 wood-spade NTRL-DUR-3PL.A- WITH-make.plantbed-PST.HAB

topa eh-ø- ibotok-a ehe
[plant.bed(III) PROX:III-3SG.A- put.PLA:III.U-EXT PROX:III]

'That's it, our ancestors prepared them with wooden spades, <u>the plant beds that are here</u>.' [W13:0135]

(1074) *epe namakad ep-o- hat-a epe,*
[DIST:III thing(III) DIST:III-2SG.A- grasp:III.U-EXT DIST:III]

igih ta ka-ha-b-ø- Ø?
name what PRS.NTRL-ROG-ACT-3SG.A- be.NPST

'<u>The thing that you're holding</u>, what's it called?' [W11:0210]

Like the demonstratives, the Deictic verb prefixes exhibit gender agreement: *eh-/ep-* (I and III), *uh-/up-* (II), and *ih-/ip-* (IV and I/II.PL) — cf. Table 15.1 on p. 418. The vast majority of corpus examples show agreement with the S-argument, if the subordinate clause is intransitive, as in (1073), or the O-argument if it is transitive, as in (1074). However, the proper generalisation seems to be that agreement follows topicality or aboutness, rather than a strict absolutive pivot. The crucial evidence comes from transitive subordinate clauses in which the A-argument is more topical than the O-argument. In (1075), the subordinate clause refers to its A-argument (co-referential with the preposed topic, 'those people') rather than the O-argument *yahun* 'canoe, boat', and the Distal verb prefix therefore agrees with the A, and not the O.

(1075) *anim   ipe   anip   a,   yahun   ip-na-   hanil-a,*
        people   DIST:I/II.PL   EMPH:I/II.PL   PTCL   [canoe(III) DIST:I/II.PL-3PL.A-   hold-EXT]

anggay-anim   ndame-ø-   nayam
feast-people   FUT-3SG.A-   come.PL

'Those people, <u>those who take care of (lit. hold) the boats</u>, the feast organisers will come.' [W15:0112]

An alternative analysis of the data in (1073–1075) would be that the subordinate clauses are relative clauses, and that gender agreement is according to the gender of the relativised argument. This analysis is compatible with the examples above, and would be a counterargument against my claim that subordinate clauses in Coastal Marind are adjoined clauses whose function as relative or adverbial clauses is unspecified. But this analysis runs into problems when confronted with data such as that in (1076). Here, the subordinate clause can only be interpreted as a locational adverbial – it is clearly not a relative clause providing specifications about any of the participants in the main clause, but the Proximal prefix still shows gender agreement. Another good example of agreement in a subordinate clause that cannot be interpreted as a relative clause is (178) on p. 136 (in that case with a transitive A-argument).

(1076) *nama   i-nak-e-   hamat-a ehe,   Ihil-Otih*
        [now   PROX:I/II.PL-1.A-1PL-   sit.PL-EXT PROX:III] I.-O.

m-ak-e-   hamat-a milah,   milah-igih   Ihil-Otih   k-a-   ø
OBJ-1.A-1PL-   sit.PL-EXT village village-name I.-O.   PRS.NTRL-3SG.A-   be.NPST

'<u>Where we are sitting now</u>, we are sitting in the Ihil-Otih hamlet, the place-name is Ihil-Otih.' [D08:0005]

Note the deletion of the *h*-segment of the Proximal before a consonant (§2.5.4).

20.1.1.3 Final demonstratives

Subordinate clauses often end in a demonstrative, as seen above in examples (1070), (1073–1074) and (1076). The placement of the demonstrative suggests that it takes the whole subordinate clause in its scope. If the clause has a an adverbial interpretation (specifying a time, place or condition for the main clause), as in (1077), the demonstrative occurs in its Gender III form *ehe* (PROX) or *epe* (DIST). Gender III contains all location-denoting and temporal nouns in the language, and it is also the default form that agreeing targets take in non-agreeing contexts.

(1077) yoy a-me-   hu-h   sakola   lik   epe,
       [2PL DEP-FUT:2PL.A- emerge-2|3PL.U school(m) from:I/II.PL DIST:III]

ka-mo-   y-a   halad,   pale   ka-mo-   halad
DIR-FUT:2SG.A- 2SG.U-AUX go.straight   land.ridge   DIR-FUT:2SG.A-   go.straight

'When you come out from school, you should continue straight, continue straight along the road.'   [W20:0244]

If the subordinate clause serves to narrow down reference to some entity or individual (i.e. has a relativising function), the final demonstrative agrees in gender according to the referent, as shown by the plural demonstrative *ipe* referring to lizards in (1078).

(1078)   kunayhi   ipala-bak   nd-ah-ø-   lolo-h-a   ipe,
          [black   grass-grove LOC-DEP-3SG.A-   crawl-2|3PL.U-EXT   DIST:I/II.PL]

isahih-salisla   ipe   ta-m-ø-   y-alaw-e
small.PL-lizard.sp   DIST:I/II.PL   GIV-OBJ-3SG.A-   2|3PL.U-search-IPFV

'The black ones that crawl in the grass, those small lizards are the ones they're looking for.'   [W13:0509–0510]

Most subordinate clauses that end in a demonstrative use the Distal series. The Proximal series is used to convey that the subordinate clause refers to a referent, location or time that is in the proximity of the speaker, i.e. 'here' or 'now', as in (1073) and (1076) above.

Adding a demonstrative to mark the end of a subordinate clause is completely optional, and speakers often omit them, as seen above in (1071–1072) and (1075). The optional demonstrative and the clause-peripheral position are hallmarks that subordinate clauses share with topicalised constituents (§18.3.3), and most subordinate clauses in the corpus do indeed seem to function as topics. Following Haiman's classic observation about conditionals and topics, we can view topics and subordinate clauses in Coastal Marind as "givens which constitute the frame of reference with respect to which the main clause is either true (if a proposition), or felicitous (if not)" (1978: 564). Structural convergence between topics and subordinate clauses have been noted in the Awyu languages (de Vries 1995), spoken north of the Marind area, but appears to be unattested in neighbouring languages such as Yelmek (Gregor 2020) and the Yam languages (Carroll 2016, Döhler 2016).

20.1.1.4 Position and prosody of the subordinate clause

The subordinate clause is placed either before or after the main clause. In the preposed position, it typically patterns like a prosodically detached topicalised constituent, and forms a prosodic unit with a final falling pitch contour. It is often followed by a pause, and the pitch is reset at the beginning of the main clause. The prosodic phrasing and the presence of a pause probably correlate with the accessibility of the referent (or situation) that the subordinate clause refers to. If the speaker is unsure of whether the addressee is able to identify the intended referent, the clause can be followed by a pause and given rising intonation, which invites the addressee to give confirmation or ask for clarification, before the speaker adds the main clause.

The subordinate clause in (1079) is a typical example of a preposed, prosodically independent subordinate clause, followed by a long pause. The corresponding pitch track is given in Figure 20.1. Note how the speaker adds two more topicalised constituents ('our own [language]', 'the Marind language') after the subordinate clause, each within a separate prosodic phrase. These NPs clarify the reference of the initial subordinate clause, before the main clause concludes the utterance.

(1079)   About young people in a neighbouring village.

  epe,   *mayan*   *nama*   *ep-na-*   *lay-et*   *epe,*   *nahan a,*
  DIST:III [speech(III) now   DIST:III-3PL.A- talk-IPFV DIST:III] 1.EMPH PTCL

  malin-mayan ehe,   *menda-b-na-*   *i-kahal⟨e⟩b*
  Marind-speech PROX:III   PERF-ACT-3PL.A-   PLA-release⟨III.U⟩

  'The language that they speak, our own one, the Marind language, they've let go of it.'   [W13:0011]

The prosodic separation of the subordinate clause and the main clause clearly forms a continuum, as can be seen by comparing the detached initial clause in (1079) with the much more integrated initial subordinate clause in (1080). As seen in the corresponding pitch track (Figure 20.2), there is no pause following the subordinate clause, which is immediately followed by another (perhaps topicalised) NP showing a minimal pitch reset, and then by the main verb without any pitch reset. The speaker uttering (1080) was pointing at her mother sitting in front of her, so the relatively tight prosodic integration of the subordinate clause is probably a reflection of the high accessibility of the referent.

(1080)   *upe*   *a-n-da-h-a-*   *lay,*   *nok*   *en*   *mama,*   *upe*   *u=*
  [DIST:II   DEP-1.A-DUR-DEP-2SG.DAT- talk] 1   POSS   mother(m)   DIST:II   PROX:II=

  k-at-ø-   *mil-e*
  PRS.NTRL-PRSTV-3SG.A-   be.sitting-IPFV

  'She who I was telling you about, my mother, she's sitting there.'
                                                                                    [W13:0919]

528 — 20 Combinations of clauses

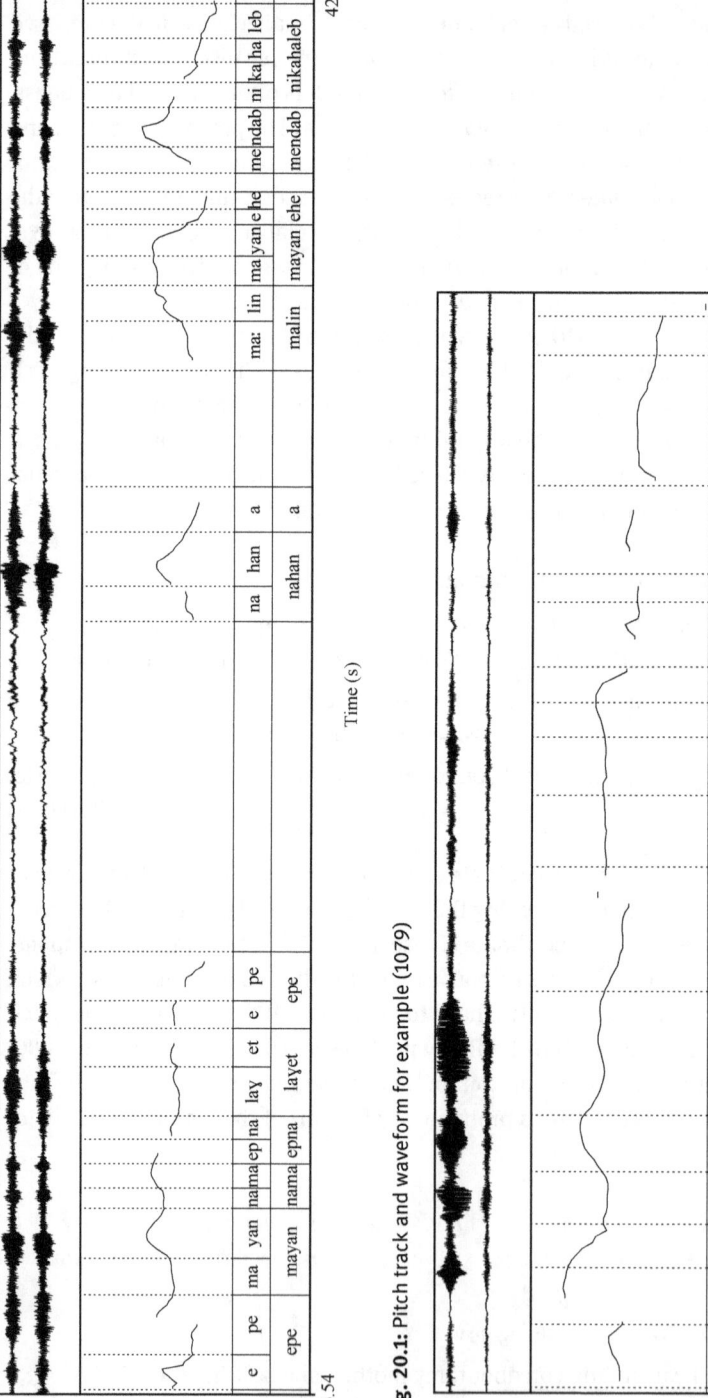

Fig. 20.1: Pitch track and waveform for example (1079)

Fig. 20.2: Pitch track and waveform for example (1080)

It is not uncommon for an initial subordinate clause to be preceded by other material belonging to the same utterance, or for a postposed subordinate clause to be followed by such material. In all cases found so far, this material is clearly extra-clausal units such as left-dislocated topics or afterthoughts, and would not constitute evidence that the subordinate clause is embedded within the main clause. See e.g. (1075) above, in which the expression 'those people' is topicalised and appears before the subordinate clause.

In conversation, it is common for subordinate clauses to be used to elaborate on a previous speaker's turn, and the subordinate clause then makes up a full utterance on its own, as in the clarifying second line of the conversation in (1081). This clause is still subordinate, albeit to a main clause in a different utterance made by another speaker.

(1081) 1. nok   nak   hindun   sa-no-d-   ka-n-alaw
            1   vine   forever   ONLY-1.A-DUR-   INESS-1.U-search

        2. ihe   tup   iha-bat-a-p-   ka-hahit-a   ihe
            [PROX:IV   rattan(IV)   PROX:IV-AFF-3SG.A-CT- INESS-put:IV.U-EXT   PROX:IV]

        1. (Pau:) 'I kept on looking for lianas.'
        2. (Mili:) '<u>The rattan canes that are up here.</u>' (Pointing above his head.)
                                                                                [W11:0759–0760]

Note that the independent verb forms formed with the Deictic prefixes described in §15.4 must have grammaticalised from the same forms used in dependent clauses, as in (1081.2), but this diachronic process does not correspond to any synchronic ambiguity. A clause like that in (1081.2) serves to describe a referent, and is often formally marked by prosody and a final demonstrative, whereas the clauses discussed in §15.4 are fully independent assertions about states-of-affairs, despite sharing the same verb form.

20.1.2 Functions of subordinate clauses

The Coastal Marind subordinate clause bears no explicit marking of the semantic relationship between the subordinate clause and the main clause (just like Warlpiri adjoined clauses, as described by Hale 1976). Thus, whether the subordinate clause restricts reference to an entity ('the one who...') or a location ('the place where...'), or provides a temporal or conditional setting ('when...', 'while...', 'if...') is determined by contextual clues. Structural features of the subordinate clause often make some interpretation more or less likely, but rarely remove all ambiguity. Subordinate clauses marked for future tense, for example, are always almost translated as temporal or conditional adverbials in the corpus ('if/when X does...'), but a relative clause interpretation is possible under the right discourse circumstances ('the one who will...').

For an illustration of the semantic underspecification of subordinate clauses, consider the corpus examples in (1082–1083). In (1082), it is unclear whether the subordinate clause narrows down the reference of the NP *pe ya epe* 'that intestine' (the relative clause interpretation), or whether it provides a locational setting for the main predication ('…is called *kukala*, where we clean…'; the locative-adverbial interpretation). The distinction has no relevance for the understanding of the utterance, and both translations work equally well.

(1082) *pe*   *ya*   *epe,*   *ep-ak-e-*   *tapid-made*   *epe,*
        intestine(III) real DIST:III [DIST:III-1.A-1PL- clean.intestine-PRS.HAB DIST:III]

  kukala   *k-a-*   Ø
  large.intestine PRS.NTRL-3SG.A- be.NPST

  'That intestine, <u>the one we usually clean out</u>, it's called *kukala*.'
  'That intestine, <u>where we usually clean out [the dirt]</u>, it's called *kukala*.'
  [W11:0908]

This contrasts with (1083), in which only the locative-adverbial interpretation makes sense. Out of context, the subordinate clause could have a relative clause-interpretation, but this interpretation is incompatible with the main predication in this utterance, because a river cannot stand (*itala*).

(1083) *kosi*   *ep-ø-*   *ka-lik-a*   *epe,*
        [small   DIST:III-3SG.A- INESS-become.river-EXT DIST:III]

  epe   *nda-d-ø-*   *kw-itala*
  there LOC-DUR-3SG.A- INESS-be.standing

  '<u>Where a small river flows</u>, he was standing there.'
  *'<u>The small river that flows</u> was standing there.'   [W02:0105]

The remainder of this section lists some functions of subordinate clauses, but it must be kept in mind that these 'functions' are primarily based on the English translations. The Coastal Marind subordinate clause does not have several different functions, only the very general function of providing a setting or frame to be interpreted in combination with the main clause.[2]

---

[2] Note that this general function of subordinate clauses is reflected in the informal variety of Papuan Malay spoken by the villagers, and which was used when annotating the corpus. This variety of Papuan Malay uses only a single general marker of subordination, *yang*, which replaces the more specific subordinators used in urban Papuan Malay (*yang* '(the one) who', *di mana* 'where', *waktu* 'when, while' etc.).

20.1.2.1 As relativising clauses

Subordinate clauses are often used to narrow down the reference of some expression in the main clause. In this section, a subordinate clause that is used with a relativising function will be referred to as a relativising clause, and a noun that refers to the same entity as the subordinate clause will be referred to as the head. There is no special marking or behaviour of the head, and there are no structural features distinguishing relativising clauses from other subordinate clauses. I use these semantic labels to make the discussion easier to follow, not because they are categories in the grammar of the language.

In the corpus data, many relativising clauses lack a head, as in (1078) above. Sometimes the head is omitted in both the relativising clause and in the main clause, as in (1072) above, or (1084) below. The omission of overt NPs follows the general tendency of omitting explicit mention of referents that are recoverable from the context.

(1084) a-n-e-   y-a   w-ahanid   sangga ipe,   ye
        [DEP-3PL.A-3PL.DAT- 2|3PL.U-AUX III.U-grasp.PLA hand(III) DIST:I/II.PL] INGRS

        ma-n-   w-amuk basik upe
        OBJ-3PL.A- 3SG.U-hit pig(II) DIST:II

        'Those whose hands had been grasped (i.e., who had been designated), they started killing the pig, [...].' [W18:0063]

When the relativising clause has a head, it remains inside the clause (and not e.g. in apposition to the relativising clause). This is shown in (1085a) by the fact that the head *nggat* 'dog' intervenes between other material that clearly belongs to the subordinate clause, viz. the temporal *wis* 'yesterday' and the verb *aho-idih* '(that) you saw it'. Like in main clauses, word order is flexible in subordinate clauses, and the speaker offered (1085b) as a synonymous alternative.

(1085) a. wis   nggat ah-o-   idih   upe,
            [yesterday dog(II) DEP-2SG.A- see:3SG.U DIST:II]

            menda-b-ø-   kahwid
            PERF-ACT-3SG.A-   die:3SG.U

        b. wis   ah-o-   idih   nggat upe,
            [yesterday DEP-2SG.A- see:3SG.U dog(II) DIST:II]

            menda-b-ø-   kahwid
            PERF-ACT-3SG.A-   die:3SG.U

            Both: 'The dog that you saw yesterday has died.'

There is no rule dictating whether an overt head is expressed in the relativising clause, or in the main clause. The general tendency is that a preposed relativising clause which introduces a referent contains an overt head, which is then taken up by zero anaphora in the main clause, as with the head *isala* 'platform' in (1086), or *anim* in (1087).

(1086) *isala   a-d-a-h-ap-   ka-tel-ti*
        [platform DEP-DUR-3SG.A-DEP-CT-   INESS-be.lying-DUR]

   ndom   ø-d-a-   kw-ehwes-a-ti
   still NTRL-DUR-3SG.A-   INESS-pile.up-EXT-DUR

   'The platform where he had been lying, it was still there.'   [W10:0429]

(1087) *ipe   anim etob ah-ø-   k-y-asib,   Wokang-duh   k-a-*
        [DIST:I/II.PL people wave DEP-3SG.A- INESS-2|3PL.U-hit] W.-beach   DIR-3SG.A-

   k-y-asib   ipe
   INESS-2|3PL.U-hit DIST:I/II.PL

   'Those people who were hit by the tsunami were hit at the beach in Wokang.'
                                                                          [D08:0047]

If the head is introduced in the main clause, as with *waninggap-aha* 'good house' in (1088), and the relativising clause is added after the main clause, then the head is not repeated in the postposed relativising clause.

(1088) *waninggap-aha   ndom   ø-d-a-p-   itala,   nahan*
        good-house   still   NTRL-DUR-3SG.A-CT- be.standing [1.EMPH

   a-n-da-h-ap-   ambad
   DEP-1.A-DUR-DEP-CT-   build.house]

   'The good house was still standing there, the one that I built myself.'
                                                                          [W12:0145]

However, these patterns are only tendencies, and there are examples in which the initial relativising clause is headless, and the head is introduced in the following main clause, as with *rusa* 'deer' in (1089).[3]

(1089) *anim   a-n-   deh,*
        [people DEP-3PL.A- shoot:3SG.U]

   upe   rusa   upe   k-e-o-p-   lemed
   DIST:II   deer(m)(II) DIST:II   DIR-2PL.A-3SG.DAT-CT-   meet

   'The one that had been shot, you met that deer.'   [W11:1198]

---

3 The bracketing of this clause is based on the prosodic phrasing in the recording, which shows that *upe rusa upe* is part of the main clause and not the relativising clause.

20.1 Subordinate clauses — 533

Tab. 20.1: Syntactic roles of relativised nominals

Example	Role in relativising clause	Role in main clause
(1072)	Possessor of S-argument of *han*	Possessor (?) of *igih* 'name'
(1073)	S-argument of *ibotok*	O-argument of *wambad*
(1074)	O-argument of *han*	Possessor (?) of *igih* 'name'
(1075)	A-argument of *hanil*	S-argument of *nayam*
(1078)	S-argument of *loloh*	O-argument of *yalaw*
(1079)	O-argument of *lay*	O-argument of *ikahaleb*
(1080)	O-argument of *lay*	S-argument of *mil*
(1084)	Possessor of O-argument of *wahanid*	A-argument of *wamuk*
(1086)	Locative adjunct	S-argument of *ehwes*
(1087)	O-argument of *yasib*	O-argument of *yasib*

The main syntactic constraint affecting relativising clauses is that they must be peripheral to the main clause, and cannot be embedded. This includes embedding under postpositions, so there is no direct equivalent of *I bought it [for the boy I saw yesterday]* in Coastal Marind, and instead one would have to use a circumlocution such as *[The boy I saw yesterday], I bought it for him*. No other syntactic constraints are known to restrict the types of roles that the head can have, in either the relativising clause or in the main clause. Table 20.1 lists some of the roles found in relativising clauses and the associated main clauses in this chapter.

20.1.2.2 As temporal and locative adverbials

Subordinate clauses are often used to specify a temporal setting for the event depicted by the main clause. There is no explicit specification of the nature of the temporal relationship, i.e. whether the events occur sequentially (*After X happened, …*) or whether they overlap (*While X was happening, …*). If the subordinate clause and the main clause both depict punctual events, they are likely to be understood as occurring in sequence, as in (1090). If both are durative, they are likely to overlap, as in (1091).

(1090) epe   kana   ah-ø-   kw-ahus   epe,
       [DIST:III egg(III) DEP-3SG.A- INESS-pull.out:III.U DIST:III]

       e=   k-a-n-   w-a   k-ihon
       PROX= DIR-3SG.A-REM- 3SG.U-AUX WITH-run:3SG.U

       'When [Stork] had taken out the sago fruit, he flew away with it.' [D02:0018]

(1091) mbya nok sa-d-a-p-   n-idih-ti,
        all   1   ONLY-DUR-3SG.A-CT- 1.U-see-DUR

   nok a-n-da-h-ap-   lu-ti   epe
   [1 DEP-1.A-DUR-DEP-CT- call:3SG.U-DUR DIST:III]

   'She just looked straight at me <u>as I was calling her name</u>.' [W10:0597]

Similarly, the habitual meaning (*Whenever...*) in (1092) is a result of the Past Habitual suffixes on the verbs, and not of any special marking of the subordinate clause.

(1092) tanama Merauke lek   a-d-ø-   ka-y-um-ma   epe,
        [again M.   from:III DEP-DUR-3SG.A- WITH-2|3PL.U-go.PLA-PST.HAB DIST:III]

   slup   ø-da-n-   ka-hwasetok-ma
   boat(m) NTRL-DUR-3PL.A- WITH-transport-PST.HAB

   '<u>Whenever they brought [goods] from Merauke</u>, they used to transport it by boat.' [W10:0099]

The order of the subordinate temporal clause and the main clause does not necessarily reflect the chronological order of the events. In (1093), the event depicted in the postposed subordinate clause (*he came*) precedes the event of the main clause (*I got startled*). The possibility of non-iconic sequencing is one feature distinguishing subordinate temporal clauses from the sequential clause linking described in §20.3.

(1093) k-ø-is-i-ap-   w-a   yuya⟨n⟩ah   ah-ø-   man-em
        DIR-3SG.A-SEP-RE-CT-   3SG.U-AUX get.startled⟨1.U⟩ [DEP-3SG.A- come-VEN]

   'I got startled <u>when he came</u>.' [W02:0033]

A subordinate clause can specify the location in which the event of the main clause takes place (1094). Again, there is no marking specifying that this subordinate clause has a locative meaning. A common sign that such clauses are intended to provide a spatial setting, and are not used to narrow down the reference of some participant, is that the Distal demonstrative *epe* 'there' is found in the pre-verbal position of the main clause, providing an anaphoric reference to the subordinate clause.

(1094) heh   inah ip-ø-   kw-ehay-a   ipe,
        [tree.sp(IV) two   DIST:IV-3SG.A- INESS-stand.PLA-EXT DIST:IV]

   epe   nda-d-ø-   ka-tel
   there LOC-DUR-3SG.A-   INESS-be.lying

   '<u>Where the two *heh* trees are standing</u>, there he was sleeping.' [W02:0060]

20.1.2.3 As conditionals

A subordinate clause can express a condition, together with a main clause that expresses the consequence. I call these the if-clause and the then-clause respectively. The General Future tense is used in conditionals expressing eventualities in the present, as in (1095),[4] or in the future, as in (1096), as well as generic truths (1097).

(1095) Addressing a witness during the settlement of a village dispute.

mayan hian a-me-ø- ø-et epe,
[speech real DEP-FUT-3SG.A- be.NPST-IPFV DIST:III]

epe ka-mo-p- y-a lay, ah-o- y-a gan epe
DIST:III DIR-FUT:2SG.A-CT- 2SG.U-AUX tell [DEP-2SG.A- 2SG.U-AUX hear DIST:III]

'If it is true, you have to tell it like you heard it.' [M05:0053]

(1096) mbya a-mo-na- kab, mano- y-amuk!
[NEG DEP-FUT:2SG.A-1.DAT- open] FUT:1.A- 2SG.U-hit

'If you don't open the door for me, I will kill you!' [D11:0016]

(1097) About the village nurse.

mbya mak-ø-am- gan, malin-mayan a-mo- ayi
NEG NAFUT-3SG.A-2SG.GEN- hear [Marind-speech DEP-FUT:2SG.A- say]

'She won't understand you if you speak in the Marind language.' [W13:0406]

Note that the if-clause and the then-clause can appear in either order, as seen by comparing (1095–1096) with (1097).

Conditionals using future tense marking are also used for situations that occurred in the past, as long as the context involves a sequence of habitually occurring events (*Whenever X happened, Y would happen*; cf. §14.2.7.6), as in (1098).

---

4 This example uses the dialect of the neighbouring Makaling village. I checked it with a speaker of the Wambi dialect who confirmed that the only difference with his dialect is the intensifier *hian*, which corresponds to Wambi *ya* 'very, real'.

(1098)   uhyub   a-p-e-   y-as   epe,
         [bird   DEP-FUT:1.A-1PL-   2|3PL.U-shoot.PLA   DIST:III]

         mboha   a-p-e-   y-as   epe,
         [magpie.goose DEP-FUT:1.A-1PL-   2|3PL.U-shoot.PLA   DIST:III]

         nda-p-o-y-   yet,   ago   amay   ay!
         LOC-FUT:1.A-3SG.DAT-ACPN-   be.moving   QUOT ancestor   VOC

         i-bat-ø-amb-   Ø-e   mboha
         PROX:I/II.PL-AFF-3SG.A-2SG.GEN-   be.NPST-IPFV   magpie.goose

         'If we shot birds, if we shot magpie geese, then I would bring them to him, saying "Hey, grandfather! Here are magpie geese for you!"'

                                                                              [W13:0761–0764]

Counterfactual conditionals are expressed by adding the Counterfactual suffix -*um*, either to the verb in the then-clause, as in (1099), or to the verbs in both the if- and then-clauses (see examples in §15.1).

(1099)   Widing ndom   ah-ø-   ola-la,
         [W.   still DEP-3SG.A-   be:3SG.U-EXT]

         mend-ø-om-   yed-um
         PERF-3SG.A-3SG.GEN-   go.straight-CTFT

         'If Auntie Widing were still alive, she would have continued it [the story].'
                                                                              [W13:0822]

All attestations of conditional clauses describing eventualities in the past are either counterfactuals, as in (1099), or describe habitual events in the past, and therefore use the Future tense, as in (1098). I have no data on non-counterfactual past conditionals (as in *If she left yesterday, then she will arrive today*).

There is no structural difference between conditionals and temporal 'when'-clauses referring to future events, so some clauses can be translated with either 'when' or 'if' (1100). The contact language used when annotating the corpus, Papuan Malay, does not distinguish the two (Malay *kalo* 'if, when') so my translations of clauses as conditionals or temporal when-clauses are entirely based on my own interpretations.

(1100)   ipe   sam   a-me-ø-   in   epe,
         [DIST:I/II.PL   big   DEP-FUT-3SG.A-   become:2|3PL.U   DIST:III]

         saley   k-ak-e-   hyamin-e
         shrimp   DIR-1.A-1PL-   call:2|3PL.U-IPFV

         'If/when they have grown big, we call them *saley* ('shrimp').'   [W13:0650]

20.1.2.4 As manner adverbials

Subordinate clauses describing the manner in which something is performed are common, and they are formed by turning the so-called Predicated Manner Construction, described in §17.3.2, into a subordinate clause. In a main clause, this construction means 'X does like this/that'. Cast as a subordinate clause, it means 'the way X does it', and functions as a complex adverbial within another clause.

The structure of the subordinate Predicated Manner construction is shown in Figure 20.3. The construction consists of the Auxiliary *wa* (§17.1) followed by a lexical verb stem, and preceded by the appropriate set of inflectional prefixes, plus one of the usual subordinating prefixes, i.e. the Dependent prefix *ah-* (if the time reference is to the non-present) or the Deictic series (if reference is to the present). Like in other subordinate clauses, a final demonstrative is optionally present.

The construction differs from its main clause equivalent (shown in Figure 17.2 on p. 465) in the absence of a demonstrative element in the pre-verbal slot, and the replacement of the Directional prefix *k-* by the subordinating prefixes.

$$\left[(\ldots) \quad \begin{matrix} \text{DEP-}\ldots\text{-} \\ \text{PROX/DIST-}\ldots\text{-} \end{matrix} \right\} \quad \text{AUXILIARY} \quad \text{VERB STEM} \quad (epe/ehe) \right]$$

Fig. 20.3: The Subordinate Predicated Manner construction

A straightforward example from my notebooks is in (1101). I had asked how we were going to get to a place outside the village, and whether we should take my motorcycle. The speaker gave the elliptical reply below, meaning that we should go by foot, like we had done the day before.

(1101) How shall we go?

    wis   a-n-da-h-e-   n-a   nayat   epe
[yesterday DEP-1.A-DUR-DEP-1PL- 1.U-AUX be.moving.PL DIST:III]

'Like we went yesterday.'

As observed above, there is no element corresponding to English *like* or *the way* in these structures. The manner component is an inherent part of the semantics of the Predicated Manner construction.

Another observed instance is in the next example. The speaker urged me and others to sit *batman* 'cross-legged', like himself. The first clause features a modifier-verb compound predicated by the Auxiliary, i.e. the structure described in §17.2.1. The second clause describes the manner, and uses one of the Deictic prefixes on the verb since the clause refers to a present situation. The Proximal form of the Deictic, as well as a

Proximal postposed demonstrative, are used because the speaker is indicating a situation that is 'here' from his point-of-view.

(1102) batman-haman ka-me- y-a yoy!
cross.legged-sit.PL DIR-FUT:2PL.A- 2|3PL.U-AUX 2PL

   eha-no- n-a mil ehe
[PROX:I-1.A- 1.U-AUX be.sitting PROX:III]

'You sit cross-legged! <u>Like I am sitting now</u>.'

The following corpus examples are slightly more complex. Example (1103) is from a description of meal preparations in a narrative. Again, the Deictic prefix is used since the manner clause refers to the present (in this case habitual present, which is clear from the context).

(1103) yal nda-d-na- og-a,
banana.leaf LOC-DUR-3PL.A- do-EXT

   namakad anep ep-ak-e- n-a og-e
[thing(III) EMPH:III DIST:III-1.A-1PL- 1.U-AUX do-IPFV]

'Then they prepared the banana leaves, <u>like we usually do those things</u>.'

[W19:0106]

In (1104) the speaker was expressing her admiration for some young men in a neighbouring village, who according to her always follow orders from elders. The Future prefixes are used here because the speaker is referring to a habitually occurring sequence of events (see §14.2.7.6).

(1104) anip a-pa-n-e- y-a lay-e epe,
[EMPH:I/II.PL DEP-FUT-3PL.A-2|3PL.DAT- 2|3PL.U-AUX tell-IPFV DIST:III]

   epe ka-p-an-o-p- y-a esoh-a
DIST:III DIR-FUT-3PL.A-3SG.DAT-CT- 2|3PL.U-AUX follow-EXT

(lit.) '<u>The way they tell them [to do something]</u>, they follow like that.'

[W19:0218]

Note that the manner that is referred to in this example is not that of the verb *lay* 'tell' (e.g. speaking loudly, or clearly), but rather the implied contents of the imagined speech event (i.e. the orders that were given).

As pointed out in §17.3.2, the use of a complex, non-compositional construction in the expression of manner is a typologically remarkable feature of Coastal Marind.

20.1.2.5 As complementising clauses

Coastal Marind lacks complement clauses, at least in the sense of clauses functioning as arguments of verbs such as *believe*, *know* or *want* (e.g. Noonan 1985). In Coastal Marind, a subordinate clause can only occur in the periphery of the clause, and cannot fill a clause-internal slot, like arguments of the verb normally can. Thus, it appears that complement clauses, in the strict sense, are impossible in Coastal Marind. However, it is not uncommon to find a perception verb ('see', 'hear') combined with a subordinate clause expressing the perceived event, as in (1105). The subordinate clause appears in the periphery of the main clause, and contains no special marking (such as a complementiser), just like all other subordinate clauses described in this section. The subordinate clause seems to fill a function similar to that of complement clauses in English and other languages, but I call subordinate clauses with this function 'complementising clauses' here, to distinguish them from complement clauses filling argument slots.

(1105) nama   bongso   epe   nd-ø-in-   w-alaw   rusa
        now   youngest.sibling(m) there LOC-3SG.A-ALL- 3SG.U-open.eyes   [deer(m)
        a-d-ø-   ku-yamat-a   epe,   mamuy
        DEP-DUR-3SG.A-   INESS-stand.PL-EXT DIST:III savanna(III)]

'Then uncle (lit. [parent's] youngest sibling) looked [and saw that] <u>there were deer standing there, in the savanna.</u>' [W01:0034]

Complementising clauses are very similar to those that were called relativising in §20.1.2.1, so that a more literal translation of (1105) would be 'Then uncle saw the deer who were standing there'. An argument for distinguishing the complementising and relativising functions is that subordinate clauses that combine with perception verbs are invariably placed after the main clause, whereas relativising clauses are often placed before the main clause. Another reason for distinguishing them is that when a relativising clause is marked by a final demonstrative, the demonstrative shows gender/number according to its head, whereas a demonstrative that marks a subordinate clause combining with a perception verb appears in the default Gender III form.

However, a fact that makes the complementising clauses similar to relativising and, perhaps most of all, temporal clauses, is that the main clause often has as its object the entity that is performing the event depicted in the subordinate clause. In (1106), the subordinate clause describes a dog chasing deer, but the dog (*Iyob*) is cast as the object of the matrix verb, and is not expressed overtly in the subordinate clause. In (1107), the source of the stimulus, *yalo* 'kookaburra sp.' is cast as the object of *gan* 'hear', and repeated again in the subordinate clause. This shows that the perception verbs take a participant of the perceived event as their object, and suggests that the subordinate clause merely adds information about that participant, rather than expressing the perceived event as a whole. If these clauses are not relativising clauses, then they can perhaps be understood as temporal clauses, as in the alternative translations below.

(1106) Iyob nahan ø-no- idih ah-ø-e- ayin epe
I. 1.EMPH NTRL-1.A- see:3SG.U [DEP-3SG.A-ACPN- run.around:3SG.U DIST:III]
'Iyob, I saw chasing [deer].'
'Iyob, I saw while he was chasing [deer].' [W11:0712]

(1107) yalo k-ak-emb-e- gan,
kookaburra DIR-1.A-2|3PL.GEN-1PL- hear

yalo ah-ø- in epe
[kookaburra DEP-3SG.A- become:2|3PL.U DIST:III]
'We heard the kookaburras calling.'
'We heard the kookaburras, when the kookaburras started calling.' [W21:0172]

Subordinate clauses are peripheral to the main clause. This means that they cannot receive constituent focus, which is expressed by placing the focused constituent in the immediately pre-verbal position (Chapter 11), i.e. a clause-internal syntactic slot. Example (1108) illustrates how to get around this restriction. A demonstrative is placed in the pre-verbal position, where it is under the scope of the Orientation prefix on the verb (here s-, marking restrictive focus, 'only'). The demonstrative refers cataphorically to the complementising clause placed after the main clause.

(1108) epe te-s-ak-omb-e- gan,
DIST:III GIV:III-ONLY-1.A-3SG.GEN-1PL- hear

derma ah-ø- og bayar epe
[alms(m) DEP-3SG.A- do pay(m) DIST:III]
'That's all we heard, that he paid the alms.' [M05:0081]

Subordinate clauses can also be used to describe the content of expressions such as *mayan ya* 'truth' (1109) and *manemna* 'story' (1110).

(1109) ehe mayan ya k-a- Ø ay, kipa ah-e-p- ol⟨e⟩b
PROX:III speech real PRS.NTRL-3SG.A- be.NPST Q [net(III) DEP-2PL.A-CT- sell⟨III.U⟩
epe
DIST:III]
'Is it the truth? That you sold the net.' [W22:0091]

(1110) manemna mak-ap-   lay-e   nok nama ehe,
        story   FUT:1.A-CT- tell-IPFV 1   now   here

   Yow a-m-bat-e-   nayat   epe nde epe
   [Y. DEP-1.A-AFF-1PL- be.moving.PL at.that.time   ]

   'I'm going to tell a story now, [about] when we went to Yow that time.'

   [W18:0003]

20.2 Clause combining by means of *ago* QUOT

While the other sections of this chapter present structures that are relatively unusual in the Papuan context, the material dealt with in this section reflects two recurring characteristics of Papuan languages: direct speech as the only available strategy for expressing reported speech (§20.2.1), and the extension of direct speech to include non-speech material such as thoughts, purpose and 'want' (§20.2.2; c.f. de Vries 1990, Reesink 1993).

20.2.1 Reported speech

Coastal Marind lacks techniques for expressing reported quotes as indirect speech, i.e. with deictics shifted according to the vantage point of the speaker who is reporting the quote. Instead, speech reports are given as if they were verbatim repetitions of the original speech event. The preference for direct over indirect speech in Papuan languages has been discussed widely in the literature (e.g. de Vries 1990, 2005, Reesink 1993, Aikhenvald 2008a).

Typically, a direct speech report is achieved by using (a) a verb representing the communicative act, usually *ayi* 'say', as in (1111), but potentially other verbs, like 'scream' in (1112); (b) the quotative index *ago* (glossed QUOT); and (c) the quoted speech itself. As in the other types of clause combinations described in this chapter, the quoted speech is always peripheral to (and, in this case, added after) the other clause, and cannot be embedded within it. In this section, I delineate the boundaries of the quoted speech by means of quotation marks "...", to make it easier to distinguish from the rest of the utterance.

(1111) epe   k-e-na-y-   aɣi   ago   "ehe mbya mank-e-   hok,
        there   DIR-3PL>1-1.DAT-1PL-   say   QUOT   here NEG   NAFUT:1.A-1PL- lie.PL

        nanggit   k-a-   Ø,   mak-e-   uma⟨n⟩ah"
        mosquito   PRS.NTRL-3SG.A-   be.NPST   FUT:1.A-1PL-   go⟨1.U⟩

'Then they said to us: "We can't sleep here, there are mosquitos, let's go".'
[W18:0294]

(1112) menda-b-na-   esol   ago   "aw! sep   menda-b-ø-   ɣahwip!"
        PERF-ACT-3PL.A-   scream   QUOT   hey   leaf.oven   PERF-ACT-3SG.A-   burn.out

'They started screaming, "Hey! The leaf oven has burned out!".' [W18:0034]

The quotative index signals to the hearer that the following material is to be interpreted as reported discourse (Güldemann 2008: 11), and is identical to the Gender III form of the multifunctional 'pro-word' *ago*, which probably derives from a manner deictic element (§4.4). The quotative index is almost always added before a quote, but is sometimes omitted, as in (1113). The presence of a speech verb and prosodic demarcation of the quote are sufficient for demarcating its boundaries.

(1113) nok   e=   k-ak-e-   n-a   aɣi, "mano-   i-sak   yoy"
        1   PROX=   DIR-1.A-2|3PL.DAT-   1.U-AUX   say   FUT:1.A-   2|3PL.U-hit.PLA   2PL

'I said like this to them: "I'm going to hit you".' [W10:0210]

Conversely, the speech verb is occasionally omitted, as the presence of *ago* signals the beginning of the quoted speech (1114).

(1114) amay   upe   ago,   "nok   nak-e-   aɣak-e"
        ancestor   DIST:II   QUOT   1   1.A-1PL-   go.inland-IPFV

'Grandma [said]: "We're going inland".' [W20:0222]

In the annotation of the Coastal Marind corpus, and in example sentences in this grammar, I have alternated freely between translating direct speech as such or rendering it as indirect speech. In some cases, it is quite ambiguous if the reported discourse is meant to convey actual speech, or if it is used in one of its extended functions (see also §20.2.2). With perception verbs, for example, reported discourse marked by QUOT is often used to express the perceived situation (as an alternative to the use of a subordinate clause, §20.1.2.5). For (1115–1116) I provide both literal translations and (more natural-sounding) free translations casting the second clauses as perception complements.

(1115) epe   k-ak-e-   gan,   ago
        DIST   DIR-1.A-1PL-   hear   QUOT

    "Romanus pula-anggay   k-ø-om-   ø"
    R.   taboo.spot-feast   PRS.NTRL-3SG.A-3SG.GEN-   be.NPST

    'Then we heard [that someone said:] "Romanus is having a mourning feast".'
    'Then we heard that Romanus was having a mourning feast.' [W18:0119]

(1116) yah   wayukli   patul   i=   ti-ø-na-   idih   ago,
        but   girls   boy   PROX:I/II.PL=   GIV:I/II.PL-NTRL-3PL.A-   see:3SG.U QUOT

    "rusa   u=   ka-hat-ø-   man"
    deer   PROX:II=   PRS.NTRL-PRSTV-3SG.A-   come

    'But then the girls and the boys saw it, [saying:] "There's a deer coming".'
    'But then the girls and the boys saw that a deer was coming.' [W10:0135]

20.2.2 *kumay-mayan* 'inside-speech': reported thought and its extensions

In Coastal Marind, like in many other languages, the strategy for reporting quoted speech is extended to express several concepts that involve no actual speech. Unsurprisingly, direct speech is used to report what Marind people call *kumay-mayan* 'inside-speech', i.e. the thoughts of oneself and others. Conincidentally, the term *inner speech* is used in the title of Reesink (1993) to refer to precisely this phenomenon (see also van Baal's discussion of the term, 1966: 931). In (1117), the narrator uses the expression to frame the following discourse as the thoughts of the protagonist.

(1117) anep   kumay-mayan   "Salibay   ka-no-   yet,   no-   uma⟨n⟩ah"
        EMPH:I   inside-speech   S.   PRS.NTRL-1.A-   be.moving 1.A-   go⟨1.U⟩

    'He [said using] inside-speech: "Here I, Salibay, am walking along, I'm going."'

More commonly, a verb such as *hwetok* marks the quote as thought content (1118).

(1118) nok   nahan   e=   ka-no-   n-a   i-hwetok-e,
        1   1.EMPH   PROX=   DIR-1.A- 1.U-AUX   PLA-think-IPFV

    ago   "mbya   malayu   a-p-a-p-   han   epe,   [...]
    QUOT   all   Indonesian(III)   DEP-FUT-3SG.A-CT-   hold:III.U   DIST:III

    'Myself, I'm thinking like this, "If only Indonesian is spoken, [then the Marind language will disappear"].' [W13:0455]

Quoted discourse is used beyond the reporting of speech and thought, to signal reasons, intentions, desire and other mental activities. As with reported speech, there is no clear boundary between thought reporting proper and the extended uses of direct speech. In (1119), the narrator is probably more concerned with providing a reason for Vitalis' actions, than reporting, verbatim, some sort of inner monologue.

(1119) *Pitalis   yohwed   ye   m-ø-o-   w-alok,   ago   "isawa   ndom*
        Vitalis   hip(III) INCPT   OBJ-3SG.A-3SG.DAT-   III.U-stab QUOT   maybe   still

        k-a-p-   w-a"
        PRS.NTRL-3SG.A-CT-   3SG.U-AUX

        'Vitalis started stabbing it in the side, [thinking]: "Perhaps it's still alive".'
        '...because he thought it was still alive.'   [W11:0885]

Coastal Marind does not have any equivalent of English *want to*+Verb. Desire in the here-and-now can be expressed by using the General Future verb forms (lit. 'I will Verb', §14.2.7.3), and such expressions can be attributed to others, or located at other moments in time, by rendering it as a direct quote with *ago* (lit. 'I, you, s/he etc. said: "I want to Verb" ').[5]

(1120) *nok   anep   ago   "pulau   Wangi-Wangi   ka-mo-   hu-n"*
        1   EMPH:I   QUOT island(m)   W.   DIR-FUT:1.A-   emerge-1.U

        'I [said/thought]: "I will go out at the Wangi-Wangi island".'
        'I wanted to go out at the Wangi-Wangi island.'   [W11:0635]

Quoted discourse provides a strategy for expressing purpose in the language. Normally, the semantics of the Future tenses (§14.2.7.3, §14.2.7.5) permits indication of purpose, but quoted discourse is used to express more complex scenarios involving purpose. Consider first the expression of negative purpose, 'lest' in (1121). The speaker wanted me to film her magpie goose, which she kept as a pet, and was trying to make the bird stand in front of the camera, which it refused to do. Her utterance can either be understood as attributing thought to the bird (as in the first translation), or, more idiomatically, as a way of expressing negative purpose (as in the second translation).

(1121) *ukna   m-a-   ka-tel-e,   ago   "mak-e-   n-amuk"*
        fear   OBJ-3SG.A- WITH-be.lying-IPFV   QUOT   NAFUT-3PL>1- 1.U-hit

        'It's lying down out of fear, [saying/thinking]: "They might hit me".'
        'It's lying down out of fear, lest we hit it.'   [W17:0011]

---

5 Note, however, that I have been unable to find a single instance in the corpus that unambiguously expresses desire, without any intention. Marind speakers seem to do without this distinction, and I would like to suggest that there is no equivalent of 'want' in the language (cf. Khanina 2008 on the universality of 'want').

The 'lest'-meaning in this example comes from the use of the Non-Asserted Future, which has apprehensive semantics in some of its uses (see §14.2.7).

The expression of positive purpose shows some additional complexity. The word *ago* is placed in the position immediately before the verb, which bears the Object Orientation prefix *m-* (§11.1.3). This use of *ago* is perhaps related to its uses as a general placeholder or 'pro-word' (§4.4). The usual reported discourse clause is added at the end, introduced by a second occurrence of *ago*, here in its normal quotative use. This structure is shown in (1122).

(1122) *anup   ago   m-an-d-in-   weheb-ti,   ago   "ndame-ø-   man"*
       EMPH:II PROW OBJ-1.A-DUR-ALL- trick-DUR   QUOT FUT-3SG.A- come
       'I was tricking [the wallaby], so that it would come.'
       '...[thinking]: "It will come".'   [W12:0204]

The pre-verbal pro-word *ago* can optionally be marked with the postposition *nanggo(l)*. The combination *ago nanggo(l)* can be placed either before the verb (1123) or elsewhere in the clause (1124).

(1123) *yah   ago   nanggol   m-ø-um-   og,   ago   "mak-ap-   i-kdahab*
       PTCL PROW   for   OBJ-3SG.A-FRUS- do   QUOT   FUT:1.A-CT- PLA-cut.off.top:III.U
       da   epe"
       sago(III) DIST:III
       'He was doing it (climbing the tree), in order to cut off the top of the sago palm.'
       '...[thinking]: "I will cut off the top of the sago palm".'   [M04:0063]

(1124) I was eliciting verb paradigms when the speaker got fed up, and suggested we move on to something else.
       mahut,   mayan   ka-p-e-p-   lay,   ago   nanggo epe,
       other.hand speech DIR-FUT:1.A-1PL-CT- tell   PRWD for   DIST:III
       oy   mayay   a-me-ø-   y-in   epe
       [2SG   able   DEP-FUT-3SG.A- 2SG.U-become DIST:III]
       'Instead, we should chat, so that you learn [the language].'

20.3 Sequential clause linkage

Coastal Marind lacks the typical clause chaining structures found in many other Papuan languages, as well as the morphosyntactic comcomitants of such systems, i.e.

switch-reference and a distinction between so-called medial verbs (lacking certain inflectional specifications, e.g. tense, mood or person) and final verbs (which have the entire gamut of features; see e.g. Foley 2000). Clause chaining and switch-reference are typical features of Trans-New Guinea languages, but do not occur in Southern New Guinea, where Coastal Marind is spoken (cf. Roberts 1997, Evans 2012, Pawley and Hammarström 2018).

Coastal Marind does, however, have a very simple system of what will be called *sequential clause linkage* here, to distinguish it from clause chaining. These structures consist of a series of (usually between one to three) clauses expressing a sequence of events, followed by one clause expressing the final event, or the culmination, of the sequence of events. In this section, the clauses preceding the last clause will be referred to as the *continuative clauses*, and the last clause will be referred to as the *culminative clause*.

The continuative clauses are marked by the presence of the Locational Orientation prefix *nd-* on the verb, and the final, culminative clause by the Directional Orientation prefix *k-*. In Chapter 11, these prefixes were described as marking the relationship between the immediately pre-verbal constituent and the verb (see §11.1.5 and §11.1.4), but in their use in clause linkage they are insensitive to the material in the pre-verbal slot, and only indicate that the verbs are part of the sequential clause linkage structure.

An illustration is given in (1125), taken from the end of a procedural text explaining sago processing. The example consists of two continuative clauses ('you come to the village', 'you put away the basket'), marked by the prefix *nd-* on the verbs, followed by a culminative clause ('with the sago, you make food'), marked by *k-* on the verb.

(1125) 1. nda-mo-   man   milah
           LOC-FUT:2SG.A-   come   village

      2. wad   nda-mo-   hwagib
          basket(III)   LOC-FUT:2SG.A-   put.away:III.U

      3. da   (.)   tamuy   ka-mo-   kama⟨y⟩in
          sago   food   DIR-FUT:2SG.A-   make⟨2SG.U⟩

      'You come to the village,
      you put away the basket,
      and [with] the sago, you make food.'   [D04:0071–0073]

Sequential clause linkage is marked prosodically, by rising "continuation" intonation on each continuative clause, and falling, "conclusive", intonation on the culminative clause. The rising intonation on the continuative clauses shows that there is more to come, and allows the speaker to pause, if needed, to plan the next clause in the sequence. Figure 20.4 provides an annotated pitch track of example (1125), which instantiates these prosodic characteristics in an unusally clear way. The speaker demarcates the end of each continuative clause by pitch excursions stretching into her falsetto

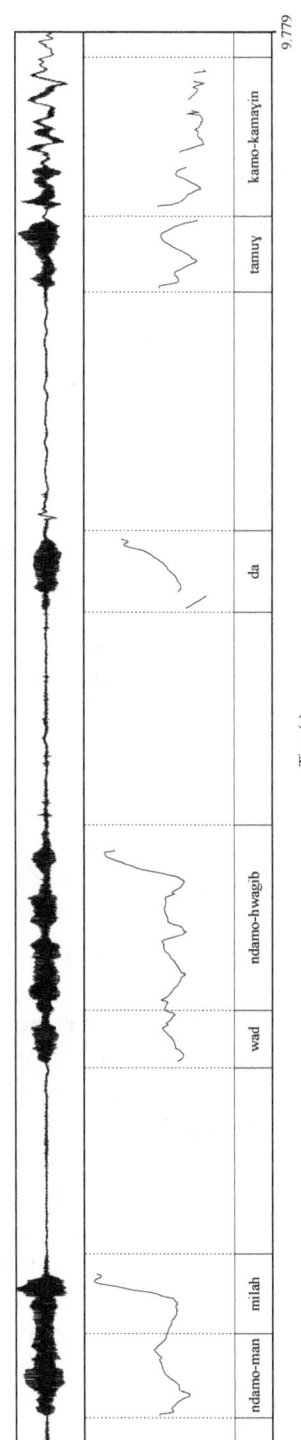

Fig. 20.4: Pitch track and waveform for example (1125), showing intonation in sequential clause linkage

range (also on the dangling topic *da* 'sago', before the last clause) and then marks the end of the sequence by falling intonation on the conclusive clause.

Almost every narrative in the corpus contains some stretches using sequential clause linkage, but this technique does not have the central importance that canonical clause chains have in languages of the New Guinea highlands. The Coastal Marind sequential linkage typically lists a couple of relatively predictable or unremarkable events, expressed by the continuative clauses, that set the stage for the event expressed by the culminative clause, which often marks the beginning of some new episode in the narrative. A standard example would be a sequence of continuative clauses expressing movement ('we walked along the swamp, then we crossed the river') and a culminative clause expressing the arrival in a new place ('and then we arrived in X'). The narrative excerpt in (1126) illustrates this pattern, with two continuative clauses expressing the trajectory towards the village, and the culminative clause expressing the arrival.

(1126) The villagers were waiting to be transported to the neighbouring village by a truck.

1. *mayay   lik   nda-d-ø-   y-ahik-a*
   front   from:I/II.PL   LOC-DUR-3SG.A-   2|3PL.U-accompany-EXT

2. *nd-ø-e-   umak-em*
   LOC-3SG.A-ACPN-   be.running-VEN

3. *e=   ka-d-ø-   luya⟨hy⟩ab*
   PROX=   DIR-DUR-3SG.A-   pour.out⟨2|3PL.U⟩

'[The truck] took the first ones,
it drove them hither,
and dropped them off here.'   [W19:0149–0150]

The clauses participating in sequential clause linkage generally show very simple syntax, and either consist of just a verb, or a verb with one or two constituents expressing participants or locations of the events. An interesting syntactic pattern is that the verb of the culminative clause, which is marked by the Directional *k-*, always has a preverbal expression realising either the O-argument of the clause, or, with a motion verb, the goal. In (1125) above, the pre-verbal *tamuy* 'food' is the O-argument, and in (1126), the Proximal proclitic *e=* expresses the goal, 'here'. If the conclusive clause does not have an overt O-argument or goal expression, a standard verb form cannot be used, and a periphrastic form must be used instead, consisting of the Auxiliary followed by the lexical verb stem. This structure is shown in the last line of (1127).

(1127) 1. *nd-an-d-e-ka-p-   hamat-a*
         LOC-1.A-DUR-1PL-PRI-CT-   sit.PL-EXT

2. roko   nd-an-d-e-p-   lahos-ti
   cigarette LOC-1.A-DUR-1PL-CT-   smoke-DUR

3. ka-p-e-   n-a   halad
   DIR-FUT:1.A-1PL-   1.U-AUX   go.straight

   'We sat there,
   we smoked,
   and then we continued forward.'   [W10:0461–0463]

The sequences depicted in clause linkage almost always feature identical S/A participants, but this is only a reflection of the types of events usually involved (e.g. sequences of movement events), and does not correspond to any rule barring switches in participants. Example (1128) shows a switch in subject between the first continuative clause, and the final culminative clause. The possibility of switches in participants, without any special verb morphology signalling this (i.e. switch-reference marking), is another aspect differentiating this simple clause linkage system to the full-fledged clause chaining structures of other Papuan languages.

(1128) 1. nd-an-ap-   lohwis   aa   makan,
          LOC-3PL.A-CT-   descend.PLA   until   ground

       2. epe   k-ø-e-   kabed [...]
          DIST   DIR-3SG.A-2|3PL.DAT-   ask

          'They climbed down to the ground,
          and he asked them: [...].'   [D01:0217]

In the following two subsections I will describe uses of the prefixes *nd-* and *k-* that are related to their use in sequential clause linkage.

20.3.1 The *epe te-nd-...- V* construction 'at that point, V'

Outside sequential clause linkage, a verb marked with the Locational *nd-* preceded by the Given prefix *te-* can be used to express 'at that point (in time), X happened' or 'that's when X happened', i.e. to express that the event described by the verb coincides with, or follows, some other event, either expressed in a previous clause or utterance, or given in the context.

This structure corresponds in meaning to the adverbial expression *epe nde epe* 'at that point (in time)' (*epe* 'there' is the Gender III form of the Distal demonstrative, and *nde* 'in' is a general locative postposition; §6.1.8).

The prefix sequence used on the verb consists of the Locational Orientation prefix *nd-* (§11.1.5) preceded by the Given *t-* and the vowel *e-* showing gender agreement (for Gender III) (see §11.4 for these prefixes). This prefix sequence is usually (but not always) preceded by the demonstrative *epe*. Example (1129) shows the construction with *epe* in the pre-verbal slot.

(1129) oso   ma-d-ø-   ihwim   katane,
        start OBJ-DUR-3SG.A-   become.dark   sun

        epe   te-nd-ak-e-   hus
        DIST:III GIV:III-LOC-1.A-1PL- cross.river

        'It was already getting dark, at that point we crossed.' [W10:0167]

There is no discernible difference in meaning when *epe* is dropped from the second clause, as in (1130).

(1130) usus   menda-b-ø-o-   w-in,
        afternoon(III)   PERF-ACT-3SG.A-3SG.DAT-   III.U-become

        te-nd-ak-e-p-   hu-n
        GIV:III-LOC-1.A-1PL-CT- emerge-1.U

        'It had already become afternoon, that's then we came home.' [W10:0619]

The temporal relationship between the two events generally depends on the aspectual value of the first clause. The event in the second clause is always subsequent to the first one if the first clause describes a punctual event, as in (1130) above. If the first clause is durative, as in (1131), the onset of the event in the second clause generally occurs within the temporal span of the first clause.

(1131) kwemek   ya   ndom   ø-d-a-   ihwim-a-ti,   tanama
        morning real still NTRL-DUR-3SG.A- become.dark-EXT-DUR   again

        te-nd-a-   umah
        GIV:III-LOC-3SG.A-   go:2|3PL.U

        'It was still early in the morning, that's when they left.' [W02:0147–0148]

20.3.2 Consequential-culminative use of Directional *k-*

The Directional *k-* is used outside sequential clause linkage to express that the action described by the verb is a consequence or culmination of some other action (described either in a previous clause or given in the discourse context). This use is quite common in corpus data, and in such contexts the Directional *k-* replaces the other Orientation prefixes described in Chapter 11, e.g. the Object Orientation *m-*.

I will illustrate this use of the Directional by a simple set of utterances, which were given to me as an illustration for when to use (and not use) this prefix, after I had used in incorrectly in conversation.

Consider first (1132). Clauses that are similar to (1132b) are common in the corpus, and I had overheard them many times, but are unacceptable without the appropriate discourse context.

(1132) Context: Out of the blue, or as an answer to 'What did you give him/her?'.

    a. *katal m-ak-o-   og*
        money OBJ-1.A-3SG.DAT- give
        'I gave him/her money.'

    b. #*katal k-ak-o-   og*
        money DIR-1.A-3SG.DAT- give
        (Intended:) 'I gave him/her money.'

One of my main teachers, Petrus Kilub, constructed the following dialogue as an example of an appropriate discourse context for the form in (1132b). The form can now be used as the second clause of B's response, because it marks a consequence of a preceding event.

(1133) 1. (A:) *awe ta   ø-b-ø-a-   og?* — (B:) *ehe   anem e=*
                     fish who NTRL-ACT-3SG.A-2SG.DAT- give   PROX:I man(I) PROX:I=

            te-ø-ø-na-   og, yah katal k-ak-o-   og
            GIV:I-NTRL-3SG.A-1.DAT- give PTCL money DIR-1.A-3SG.DAT- give

            (A:) 'Who gave you fish?' — (B:) 'This man gave it to me, so then I gave him money.'

Appendix: Texts

Text 1: The story of Mbalugyam and Ndumay (D03)

This short children's story was told by Isaias Ndiken, a school teacher from Duhmilah, in April 2015. The story relates the adventures of two tricksters pranking each other, and features several elements that are central to Marind culture, such as the Dema and their interactions with humans, the importance of inter-village travel and collaboration, and toponyms and their significance.

Some false starts and repetitions have been omitted.

1	yasti	a,	inah	yasti		Old men, [there were] two old men,
	old.man	PTCL	two	old.man		
2	Sanggahe-milah	nda-d-na-		ubun-ma		they used to camp in Sanggase.
	Sanggase-village	LOC-DUR-3PL.A-		camp-PST.HAB		
3	hyakod	Yambuti-yasti				One old man from Buti,
	one	Buti-old.man				
4	hyakod	Sanggahe-yasti				one old man from Sanggase.
	one	Sanggase-old.man				
5	ya-hwala-la	sa-d-ø-		ya-hwala		They just stayed there.
	2|3PL.U-be-EXT	ONLY-DUR-3SG.A-		2|3PL.U-be		
6	hyakodse,	inah	epe	ka-n-	ayak	One time, the two of them went inland.
	once	two	DIST	DIR-3PL.A-	go.inland	
7	milah-igih	a,	Kewel	k-a-		The name of that place [where they went] is Kewel.
	village-name	PTCL	K.	PRS.NTRL-3SG.A-		
	k-w-alin-e					
	WITH-III.U-call-IPFV					
8	namaya,	Sanggahe-yasti		ehe	a	Now, the old man from Sanggase,
	now	Sanggase-old.man		PROX:I	PTCL	
9	ndom-hwetok	epe	k-ø-in-		w-a	he got some bad ideas,
	bad-think	DIST	DIR-3SG.A-ALL-		3SG.U-AUX	
10	Yambuti-yasti	ehe				about the man from Buti.
	Buti-old.man	PROX:I				
11	ago	mak-in-		weheb	ehe	yasti	[He thought to himself:] "I'm going to trick this old man."
	QUOT	FUT:1.A-ALL-		trick	PROX:I	old.man(I)	
	ehe						
	PROX:I						

12	*epe* k-ø-o-	*aɣi*		He said to him:
	DIST DIR-3SG.A-3SG.DAT-	say		
13	*namek* *ay!*			"Hey, mate!"
	clanmate VOC			
14	*ehe* *say* *a-mo-*	*man,*		"In this place, if you come as a newcomer,"
	PROX:III place(III) DEP-FUT:2SG.A-	come		
	noɣ-mat-la-anem *ehe*			
	new-come-PTCP:I-man(I) PROX:I			
15	*kanis-dema* *e=* *nd-a-* *ø-e*			"the Betel Dema is here."
	betel-dema PROX= LOC-3SG.A- be.NPST-IPFV			
16	*yah* *namaya* *kanis* *e=* *ta-mo-*			"So now you should climb this betel tree."
	but now betel PROX= GIV-FUT:2SG.A-			
	kahek-e			
	climb-IPFV			
17	*ndamo-* *kahek-a* *lahwalah*			"You should climb to the top,"
	FUT:2SG.A- climb-EXT top			
18	*epe* *ka-mo-ka-p-* *ambid*			"and sit up there."
	there DIR-FUT:2SG.A-PRI-CT- sit			
19	*kanis-dema* *epe* *a-p-ø-a-*			"If the Betel Dema tells you to pluck, then you can pluck [betel nuts]."
	betel-dema(I) DIST:I DEP-FUT-3SG.A-2SG.DAT-			
	aɣi *katab,* *epe* *te-nda-mo-*			
	say pluck:III.U DIST:III GIV:III-LOC-FUT:2SG.A-			
	katab			
	pluck:III.U			
20	*Yambuti-yasti* *nda-bat-ø-* *w-in,* *epe*			The old man from Buti did so, and clung [to the betel tree] until he was exhausted.
	Buti-old.man LOC-AFF-3SG.A- 3SG.U-become DIST			
	nda-d-ø-o-p- *tahob-a* *aaa*			
	LOC-DUR-3SG.A-3SG.DAT-CT- cling:III.U-EXT until			
	isis *epe* *k-a-p-* *o-nggat*			
	exhaustion DIST DIR-3SG.A-CT- 3SG.U-become.PLA			
21	*menda-b-a-p-* *ɣuy⟨e⟩h*			He was already shivering,
	PERF-ACT-3SG.A-CT- shiver⟨3SG.U⟩			
22	*mig* *menda-b-ø-o-p-* *i-sak*			and the betel tree was hitting against his knees.
	knee(IV) PERF-ACT-3SG.A-3SG.DAT-CT- IV.U-hit.PLA			
	kanis *epe*			
	betel(III) DIST:III			

23	*Ndumay*	*ɣi*	*lek*	*ka-d-ø-*		*w-a*	Because he was laughing, Ndumay, um, he bent down,
	Nd.	laugh	from	DIR-DUR-3SG.A-		3SG.U-AUX	
	...	*ka-d-ø-*		*w-a*		*i-kahod-ti*	
	[hesit.]	DIR-DUR-3SG.A-		3SG.U-AUX		PLA-bend.down-DUR	
24	*emba*	*ka-d-ø-is-*		*w-alaw*		*nanih*	and turned his face away from him [so Mbalugyam wouldn't see him laughing].
	side	DIR-DUR-3SG.A-SEP-		3SG.U-open.eyes		face	
25	*hyuw*	*ah-a-p-*		*ay*			After a long time had passed,
	long.time	DEP-3SG.A-CT-		become:III.U			
26	*epe*	*te-nd-ø-o-*			*ayi*	*ago*	[Ndumay] said to [Mbalugyam]:
	DIST:III	GIV:III-LOC-3SG.A-3SG.DAT-			say	QUOT	
27	*dema*	*epe*	*menda-b-ø-ind-a-*			*tanggiɣ*	"The Dema already ordered you to pluck, so please pluck some betel!"
	Dema(I)	DIST:I	PERF-ACT-3SG.A-ALL-2SG.DAT-			order	
	katab,	*kanis*	*epe*	*ah-*	*katab*		
	pluck:III.U	betel(III)	DIST:III	IMP-	pluck:III.U		
28	*nd-a-*	*katab*	*epe,*	*k-a-*			Having plucked, he slid down the trunk all the way and landed on the ground.
	LOC-3SG.A-	pluck:III.U	DIST:III	DIR-3SG.A-			
	w-a	...	*k-a-*	*w-a*	*ɣ⟨e⟩b*		
	3SG.U-AUX	[hesit.]	DIR-3SG.A-	3SG.U-AUX	slip⟨3SG.U⟩		
	aaa	*makan*	*k-a-*	*ambid*			
	all.the.way.to	ground	DIR-3SG.A-	sit			
29	*isis*	*lek*	*k-a-*	*w-a*	*ɣali*		He fell asleep from exhaustion.
	exhaustion	from	DIR-3SG.A-	3SG.U-AUX	lie.down		
30	*nda-d-a-ka-*		*tel-ti*				He slept,
	LOC-DUR-3SG.A-PRI-		be.lying-DUR				
31	*hyuw*						for a long time.
	long.time						
32	*Ndumay*	*epe*	*k-ø-o-*		*ayi*		Then Ndumay told him...
	Nd.	DIST	DIR-3SG.A-3SG.DAT-		say		
33	*Sanggahe-yasti*	*epe*	*Ndumay*	*ø-d-a-*			That man from Sanggase was called Ndumay.
	Sanggase-old.man	DIST:I	Nd.	NTRL-DUR-3SG.A-			
	k-w-alin-ti		*igih*				
	WITH-3SG.U-call-DUR		name				
34	*namek*	*ay,*	*ago*	*tis ka*	*ay*		[Ndumay said:] "Hey mate, is that it?"
	clanmate	VOC	QUOT	that's.it	Q		

35	*ago* *tis ka* QUOT that's.it				[Mbalugyam replied:] "That's it."
36	*aw,* *mak-e-p-* *hu-n* EXCLAM FUT:1.A-1PL-CT- emerge-1.U				"Come on, let's go home."
37	*k-a-p-* *ɣ-a* *hu-h* *milah* DIR-3SG.A-CT- 2|3PL.U-AUX emerge-2|3PL.U village				They went back to the village.
38	*Yambuti-ɣasti* *epe* *ɣap* *e=* Buti-old.man(I) DIST:I night(III) PROX:I= *te-ø-a-* *ihwetok-em* *aaa,* *ehe* GIV:I-NTRL-3SG.A- think-VEN [hesit.] PROX:I *anem* *ehe* man(I) PROX:I				In the evening the old man from Buti was thinking: "This man,"
39	*ø-n-ind-a-* *weheb* *ay* 3SG.A-1.DAT-ALL-1.DAT- trick Q				"Did he fool me,"
40	*ay, mayan* *ɣa* *ma-d-ø-* *laɣ?* Q speech real OBJ-DUR-3SG.A- tell				"or did he tell the truth?"
41	*inhyakod* *ɣanid* *ah-ø-is-* *ay* three day(III) IMP-3SG.A-SEP- become:III.U				When three days had passed,
42	*epe* *ka-bat-ø-o-* *aɣi* *a* DIST DIR-AFF-3SG.A-3SG.DAT- say PTCL				he said,
43	*Mbalugyam* Mb.				Mbalugyam [said],
44	*Ndumay* *ehe* *te-ø-ø-o-* *aɣi* Nd. PROX:I GIV:I-NTRL-3SG.A-3SG.DAT- say *ago* *namek* *ay,* *nok* *nam-bat-* *dahetok-e* QUOT clanmate VOC 1 1.A-AFF- return-IPFV				he said to Ndumay: "Mate, I'm returning home."
45	*e,* *namek* *ndamo-bat-* *uma⟨ɣ⟩ah* EXCLAM clanmate FUT:2SG.A-AFF- go⟨2SG.U⟩				"Yeah, mate, you may go."
46	*nggim* *nd-a-* *owak* bracer LOC-3SG.A- wear.bracer				[Mbalugyam] put on his bracer,
47	*mih* *nd-a-* *lasan* bow LOC-3SG.A- pick.up.bow				took his bow,
48	*imadeh* *nd-a-* *elah* quiver(IV) LOC-3SG.A- hang.on.shoulder:IV.U				and hung his quiver on his shoulder.

49	*epe*	*k-a-*		*oha*		He went to the shore there,
	DIST	DIR-3SG.A-		go.seawards:3SG.U		

50	*Sanggal*	by the river Sanggal.
	S.	

51	*Sanggal*	*nd-a-*	*umuh*	*eee*	From Sanggal he went to…
	S.	LOC-3SG.A-	go:3SG.U	all.the.way.to	

52	*Kasokit*	Kasokit.
	K.	

53	*Kasokit*	*nd-ø-i-*	*umuh*	*tanama*	*Kabaim*	From Kasokit he left again to Kabaim.
	K.	LOC-3SG.A-RE-	go:3SG.U	again	K.	

54	*Kabaim*	*nd-a-*	*umuh*	*aaa*	From Kabaim he went to…
	K.	LOC-3SG.A-	go:3SG.U	all.the.way.to	

55	*Yum,*	*epe*	*k-a-p-*	*ɣali*	Yum, and there he slept,
	Y.	DIST	DIR-3SG.A-CT-	lie.down	

56	*kwemek*	until the morning.
	morning	

57	*k-a-*	*w-a*	*hus*	Then he crossed the [Bian] river,
	DIR-3SG.A-	3SG.U-AUX	cross.river	

58	*lay,*	*Hid*	to the other side, to Hid.
	side	H.	

59	*anepanda-d-ø-o-p-*		*halad-a*	He kept on going.
	CONT:I-DUR-3SG.A-3SG.DAT-CT-		go.straight-EXT	

60	*Wanggali-milah*	*ka-bat-ø-*	*ɣali*	He spent the night in the Onggari village.
	Onggari-village	DIR-AFF-3SG.A-	lie.down	

61	*Wanggali-milah*	In Onggari,
	Onggari-village	

62	*ndom-nu*	*sa-d-a-p-*	*tel*	he slept badly,
	bad-sleep	ONLY-DUR-3SG.A-CT-	be.lying	

63	*kwemek*	until the morning.
	morning	

64	*ah-ø-*	*pig*	When it got bright,
	DEP-3SG.A-	become.bright	

65	*menda-b-ø-i-*	*umuh*	he left again.
	PERF-ACT-3SG.A-RE-	go:3SG.U	

66	*Kum k-a- w-a hus*	He crossed the Kumb river.
	K. DIR-3SG.A- 3SG.U-AUX cross.river	
67	*duh ka-d-ø- lemed aaa*	He went along the beach…
	beach DIR-DUR-3SG.A- stand.PLA all.the.way.to	
68	*Kalhabob*	to Kalhabob.
	K.	
69	*Kalhabob, yahun menda-d-ø- hat-a*	In Kalhabob there was a canoe.
	K. canoe(III) PERF-DUR-3SG.A- put:III.U-EXT	
70	*kw-atin*	He went inside [the canoe],
	INESS-stand	
71	*men-ba-n-e- hus*	and was taken across the river,
	PERF-ACT-3PL.A-ACPN- cross.river	
72	*Wakin-Otih*	to Wakin-Otih.
	W.-O.	
73	*Yambuti-milah*	In Buti,
	Buti-village	
74	*namik ka-n-is-ap- y-a*	his relatives were surprised seeing him.
	clanmates DIR-3PL.A-SEP-CT- 2|3PL.U-AUX	
	yuyah	
	become.startled:2|3PL.U	
75	*a, namek a, mend-o-bat- man-em*	[They said:] "Oh, mate, you have come back."
	PTCL clanmate PTCL PERF-2SG.A-AFF- come-VEN	
76	*sapla hyuw ya nd-o-d- yet*	"You have been travelling for a very long time."
	travel long.time real LOC-2SG.A-DUR- be.moving	
	ehe	
	PROX	
77	*aa epe k-a- w-a ola,*	"Yeah, that's how it is, travelling, I was visiting my clanmates."
	EXCLAM DIST DIR-3SG.A- 3SG.U-AUX be:III.U	
	anep ago, hwil k-a- ø-et,	
	EMPH QUOT wander PRS.NTRL-3SG.A- be.NPST-IPFV	
	namik m-an-da-ka- apanawt-a	
	clanmates OBJ-1.A-DUR-PRI- visit:2|3PL.U-EXT	

78	namaya anep milah ago ø-ø-na- now EMPH village(III) PROW:III NTRL-3SG.A-1.DAT- awiɣ, anep mayay ma-no- dahetok hurt therefore OBJ-1.A- return	"Then I started feeling homesick, and because of that I returned."
79	ola-la sa-d-ø- ola eee be:3SG.U-EXT ONLY-DUR-3SG.A- be:3SG.U until hyuw ah-ø-is-ap- ay long.time DEP-3SG.A-SEP-CT- become:III.U	He just remained there, until a long time had passed.
80	menda-b-ø- pig PERF-ACT-3SG.A- become.bright	The sun was already shining bright.
81	pig-mandaw menda-b-ø- become.bright-moon(III) PERF-ACT-3SG.A- ay become:III.U	It was already the dry season.
82	namaya mamuy e= nda-bat-ø- now savanna PROX= LOC-AFF-3SG.A- ka-hwil-a, ago INESS-wander-EXT PROW:III	Now he was hunting in the savanna, in um,
83	Weda-mamuy W.-savanna(III)	in the savanna in Weda.
84	takah ye m-a- o-tad fire INGRS OBJ-3SG.A- PLA-burn	He started burning [the grass].
85	Sanggahe-namek epe k-ø-i-o- Sanggase-clanmate DIST DIR-3SG.A-RE-3SG.DAT- awiɣ Sanggahe-milah, aywa namek a, lak hurt Sanggase-village EXCLAM mate PTCL smoke a PTCL	The mate in Sanggase was missing [Mbalugyam]: "My mate, [I see] the smoke,"
86	anem pale lek a man savanna from PTCL	"[It must be] smoke from that man from the savanna."
87	ɣali s-a- w-a lie.down ONLY-3SG.A- 3SG.U-AUX	[Ndumay] just went to sleep.
88	k-a- hwehway DIR-3SG.A- put.in.order	Then he packed his belongings.
89	es nd-ø-i- w-esoh-a-m behind LOC-3SG.A-RE- 3SG.U-follow-EXT-VEN	He went after him.

90	*Mbian*	*nd-a-*	*hus,*	*laɣ*	He crossed the Bian river, to the other side.
	Bian	LOC-3SG.A-	cross.river	side	

91 *tanama epe nd-a- umuh Wanggali-milah*   He continued to Onggari, he spent
    again DIST LOC-3SG.A- go:3SG.U Onggari-village   the night there and asked [the
   k-a- ɣali, epe k-ø-e-   villagers]:
    DIR-3SG.A- lie.down DIST DIR-3SG.A-2|3PL.DAT-
   kabed ago
    ask QUOT

92 *Mbalugyam ap-e- idih yoɣ?*   "Have you seen Mbalugyam?"
    Mb. PST.Q-2PL.A- see:3SG.U 2PL

93 *ago menda-b-ø- ɣet, menda-b-ø-*   [They replied:] "He already went by,
    QUOT PERF-ACT-3SG.A- be.moving PERF-ACT-3SG.A-   he already went by."
   ɣet
    be.moving

94 *nama nda-d-ø- ɣet aaa,*   Then [Ndumay] went to the river
    now LOC-DUR-3SG.A- be.moving all.the.way.to   Kumb and crossed it.
   Kum nd-a- hus, laɣ
    K. LOC-3SG.A- cross.river side

95 *lun k-a- man-em, Dumande*   He went straight to Domande, [I
    straight.away DIR-3SG.A- come-VEN Domande   mean] to Buti.
   ... Yambuti-milah
    [hesit.] Buti-village

96 *k-ø-is-i-ap- w-a ɣuy⟨e⟩h,*   Mbalugyam got surprised seeing
    DIR-3SG.A-SEP-RE-CT- 3SG.U-AUX become.startled⟨3SG.U⟩   him.
   Mbalugyam
    Mb.

97 *aw namek ay, mend-o-bat- man-em*   "Hey mate, you already came here?"
    EXCLAM clanmate VOC PERF-2SG.A-AFF- come-VEN
   ay
    Q

98 *tis ka, hok s-a- y-a*   That's it, they just went to sleep.
    that's.it lie.down.PL ONLY-3SG.A- 2|3PL.U-AUX

99 namaya epe k-ø-o- ayi kwemek
now DIST DIR-3SG.A-3SG.DAT- say morning(III)
epe ago, yapap mak-e- ayak
DIST:III QUOT tomorrow FUT:1.A-1PL- go.inland
inah
two

In the morning Mbalugyam said: "Tomorrow morning we will go to the garden, the two of us."

100 nu nda-d-ø- hok-a ah-ø-
sleep LOC-DUR-3SG.A- lie.down.PL-EXT DEP-3SG.A-
pig kwemek
become.bright morning

They slept until it got bright in the morning.

101 oso-pig ma-n- ayak
beginning-become.bright OBJ-3PL.A- go.inland

They left for the garden as it was getting bright,

102 aaa Apata
all.the.way.to A.

to Apata,

103 dapata igih epe Apata
sago.plantation(III) name DIST:III A.
k-a- ø
PRS.NTRL-3SG.A- be.NPST

that sago plantation is called Apata.

104 yaba-bob epe nda-d-ø- hat-a,
big-swamp(III) DIST LOC-DUR-3SG.A- put:III.U-EXT
namaya menda-b-na- yokun
now PERF-ACT-3PL.A- put.inside.PLA:III.U

There used to be a swamp there, [but] now it has been filled.

105 milah otih menda-b-na- yam
house many PERF-ACT-3PL.A- build.house

They have built houses there.

106 epe k-ø-o- ayi
DIST DIR-3SG.A-3SG.DAT- say

There Mbalugyam said to Ndumay:

107 namek ay
clanmate VOC

"Hey mate,"

108 ehe ehe lek dema ehe,
PROX:I PROX:I from:I dema(I) PROX:I
kalambu-dema k-a- ø
mullet-dema PRS.NTRL-3SG.A- be.NPST

"the dema from here is a Mullet Fish Dema."

109 oy namaya, mbaymbay m-o- man-em
2SG now unable OBJ-2SG.A- come-VEN
ehe
PROX

"You came here unfamiliar with this place."

110	ah- hayok IMP- dive		"Dive into the water,"
111	kalambu hi ø-mo- amuy-e mullet like:I NTRL-FUT:2SG.A- chew-IPFV		"while opening and closing your mouth like a mullet."
112	yahaa anep dema epe, a-p-ø-ind-a- until EMPH:I dema(I) DIST:I DEP-FUT-3SG.A-ALL-2SG.DAT-		"When the dema tells you to go up from the water, then you go up."
	tanggiy y-ahwasig, epe order 2SG.U-go.up.from.water DIST:III		
	te-nda-mo- y-ahwasig GIV:III-LOC-FUT:2SG.A- 2SG.U-go.up.from.water		
113	namaya Ndumay nd-a- og now Nd. LOC-3SG.A- do		Then Ndumay did so,
114	menda-b-ø- hayaman PERF-ACT-3SG.A- enter.water		and went in the water.
115	ago kalambu hi ø-mo- amuy-e QUOT mullet like:I NTRL-FUT:2SG.A- chew-IPFV		[Mbalugyam told him:] "Open and close your mouth like a mullet!"
116	Ndumay epe nda-bat-ø- um-ti Nd. DIST LOC-AFF-3SG.A- go.PLA:3SG.U-DUR		Poor Ndumay kept going.
117	bob epe nda-d-ø- uhuk-a swamp DIST LOC-DUR-3SG.A- go.around-EXT		He swam all around the swamp...
	aaa all.they.way.to		
118	oso-pig nd-a- ahol beginning-become.bright LOC-3SG.A- swim		...he swam from the early morning...
	aaa all.the.way.to		
119	k-ø-is- w-a pig DIR-3SG.A-SEP- 3SG.U-AUX become.bright		until it was bright noon.
120	katane lahwalah s-ø-is-ap- ay sun(III) on.top ONLY-3SG.A-SEP-CT- become:III.U		The sun was right in the middle of the sky.
121	kalambu hi ø-d-a-p- amuy-ti mullet like:I NTRL-DUR-3SG.A-CT- chew-DUR		He kept swimming with his mouth opening and closing like a mullet.
122	Mbalugyam takah menda-b-ø- yus Mb. fire PERF-ACT-3SG.A- make.fire		Mbalugyam made fire.

123 | *epe k-ø-o-   aɣi, namek   ay,   ago* | Then he said to Ndumay: "That's it,
    | DIST DIR-3SG.A-3SG.DAT- say clanmate VOC   QUOT | the Dema already asked me to tell
    | *tis ka,   dema mend-a-n-ind-a-   tanggiɣ* | you to go up from the water."
    | that's.it dema PERF-3SG.A-1.DAT-ALL-1.DAT- order |
    | *ago, anam-ø-   u-hwasig   epe* |
    | QUOT JUS-3SG.A-   3SG.U-go.up.from.water DIST:I |

124 | *a-bat-   ɣ-ahwasig* | "Please go up from the water."
    | IMP-AFF- 2SG.U-go.up.from.water |

125 | *nd-a-   u-hwasig   aa* | Then Ndumay went up from the
    | LOC-3SG.A- 3SG.U-go.up.from.water   all.the.way.to | water,

126 | *bob-toh   epe   k-a-p-   haman* | and they sat down by the side of the
    | swamp-side DIST DIR-3SG.A-CT-   sit.PL | swamp.

127 | *takah epe   ...,   epe   nda-d-ø-* | by the fire um, Ndumay dried
    | fire   DIST [hesit.] DIST LOC-DUR-3SG.A- | himself there.
    | *usu-ti* |
    | heat.up:3SG.U-DUR |

128 | *ena   nd-a-   o-nggat* | He started feeling warm.
    | warm   LOC-3SG.A- 3SG.U-become.PLA |

129 | *epe   k-ø-o-   aɣi ago, mak-e-p-* | Then [Mbalugyam] said to him:
    | DIST DIR-3SG.A-3SG.DAT-   say QUOT FUT:1.A-1PL-CT- | "Let's go home."
    | *hu-n* |
    | emerge-1.U |

130 | *anem   a-d-ø-   ahol epe,   igih Ndumay* | The man who had been swimming,
    | man(I) DEP-DUR-3SG.A- swim DIST:I name Nd. | his name was Ndumay.
    | *ø-d-a-   ola* |
    | NTRL-DUR-3SG.A-   be:3SG.U |

131 | *yah bob   epe   namaya Ndumay-Ad-Amuɣ* | And now that swamp is called
    | but swamp(III) DIST:III now   Nd.-A.-A. | *Ndumay-Ad-Amugh* ['Where Ndu-
    | *k-a-   ø-et* | may opened and closed his mouth'].
    | PRS.NTRL-3SG.A-   be.NPST-IPFV |

132 | *milah-igih   epe,   Apata k-a-* | The [original] name of that place is
    | village-name(III)   DIST:III A.   PRS.NTRL-3SG.A- | Apata.
    | *ø* |
    | be.NPST |

133 | *namaya menda-b-na-   ol⟨e⟩b* | Now the name of that place has
    | now   PERF-ACT-3PL.A- change⟨III.U⟩ | been changed.

134	*Ndumay-Ad-Amuɣ* Nd.-A.-A.	*k-a-* PRS.NTRL-3SG.A-	∅, be.NPST	It's *Ndumai-Ad-Amugh*, the [current] name of the swamp.
	bob swamp(III)	*epe* DIST:III	*igih* name	
135	*nda-d-a-p-* LOC-DUR-3SG.A-CT-	*hu-h-a* emerge-2|3PL.U-EXT	*milah* village	Then they went and arrived at home,
136	*wati* kava(III)	*ka-n-* DIR-3PL.A-	*ɣi* drink:III.U	and drank kava.
137	*epe* DIST	*k-ø-o-* DIR-3SG.A-3SG.DAT-	*aɣi ago* say QUOT	Then [Mbalugyam] said:
138	*menda-b-ø-* PERF-ACT-3SG.A-	*ik-hehay* INESS-fall.PLA:III.U		"Now it's even."
139	*nok* 1	*Sanggahe-milah* Sanggase-village(III)	*epe, kanis lahwalah* DIST:III betel on.top	"I was sitting up there in the betel tree in Sanggase."
	nd-an-d-ap- LOC-1.A-DUR-CT-	*mil-ti* be.sitting-DUR		
140	*oɣ namaya, kalambu hi* 2SG now mullet like:I	*ø-o-d-* NTRL-2SG.A-DUR-		"And you, right now you were [swimming around while] opening and closing your mouth like a mullet."
	amuɣ chew			
141	*tis ka*			"That's it."
142	*mbya-hyakod* all-one	*menda-b-ø-* PERF-ACT-3SG.A-	*ay* become:III.U	"Now it's even."
143	*anim mayay* people knowing	*tapahat-ø-* PROH-3SG.A-	*in,* become:2|3PL.U	"Don't let other people know, only the two of us should know."
	nahan inah sa-p-e- 1.EMPH two ONLY-FUT:1.A-1PL-	∅ be.NPST	*nok* 1	
	mayay knowing			
144	*nda-bat-ø-* LOC-AFF-3SG.A-	*ya-hwala* 2|3PL.U-be		Having stayed there,
145	*epe* DIST	*k-inam-i-...* DIR-RCPR-RE-[hesit.]	*kuta⟨n⟩ib* get.lost⟨RCPR⟩	they um split from each other again.
146	*k-inam-i-* DIR-RCPR-RE-	*ɣ⟨i⟩da⟨n⟩awn* ⟨PLA⟩leave⟨RCPR⟩		They left each other again.

147 oɣ   namek   adeh m-o-bat-   Ø   oɣ   [Ndumay said:] "You mate, just stay
    2SG   clanmate RLQ   OBJ-2SG.A-AFF-   be.NPST   2SG   here, you Mbalugyam."
    Mbalugyam
    Mb.

148 nok no-   dahetok-e   Sanggahe-milah   "I'm returning to Sanggase."
    1   1.A- return-IPFV   Sanggase-village

149 eee!   "Goodbye!"
    EXCLAM

150 Ndumay   ka-bat-ø-   w-a   dahetok   Ndumay returned to Sanggase.
    Nd.   DIR-AFF-3SG.A-   3SG.U-AUX   return
    Sanggahe-milah
    Sanggase-village

151 mayan   e=   k-a-   hay-a   This is the end of the story.
    speech(III)   PROX=   DIR-3SG.A-   fall:III.U-EXT

Text 2: Thoughts about language shift (W13)

This extract represents the first three minutes of an hour-long discussion about various topics, recorded in September 2016. The discussion was led by Nggeh Balagaize, a man in his early 50s at the time of recording, who lives in the Kintal Misi hamlet at the border of Eastern and Western Wambi. In this extract, Nggeh is the main speaker, except for some contributions by Dina Samkakai, Ambai-Iwag Yolmend and Wakati-Iwag Kahol (as indicated). The participants talk about the centrality of the Marind language for Marind identity, how it distinguishes Marind people from Indonesians, and how they favour a village policy of bilingualism, with Marind spoken at home, and Indonesian acquired in school. Note that the statements about the obsolescence of Marind in the neighbouring Duhmilah village (lines 40–44) are somewhat hyperbolic: in fact, all generations in Duhmilah are fluent in Marind, but it is striking that younger people in Duhmilah use Indonesian amongst each other to a much larger extent than in Wambi.
Some repetitions have been omitted.

1. *wanangga mak-em- aɣi*
   children FUT:1.A-2|3PL.GEN- say
   I'm going to say something about the children,

2. *nok keti en wanangga ihe*
   1 APL POSS children PROX:I/II.PL
   our children here.

3. *wanangga mayay ipe*
   children knowing DIST:I/II.PL
   The children know [the Marind language],

4. *wanangga en wanangga ipe*
   children POSS children DIST:I/II.PL
   [but] the children of the children,

5. *nok keti en nahe ipe*
   1 APL POSS grandchildren:1 DIST:I/II.PL
   our grandchildren,

6. *alinde ka-me-ø- w-a*
   in.the.future DIR-FUT-3SG.A- 3SG.U-AUX
   ikebeh
   disappear:2|3PL.U
   in the future they will be lost.

7. *mayan m-a- ikebeh, oy*
   speech OBJ-3SG.A- disappear:2|3PL.U 2SG
   ka-p-ø-ind-a- y-a dah⟨i⟩tuk
   DIR-FUT-3SG.A-ALL-2SG.DAT- 2|3PL.U-AUX return⟨2|3PL.U⟩
   tanama, a-p-ø-um- y-alaw epe
   again DEP-FUT-3SG.A-FRUS- 2|3PL.U-search DIST
   They will lose the language, and they will turn back to you [Bruno] again, when they're trying to find it. [Referring to the dictionary that I was compiling.]

8   mbya-hyakod   k-a-   Ø   namaya,   It's all the same, in the [neighbour-
    all-one   PRS.NTRL-3SG.A- be.NPST now   ing] two villages...three,
    laɣ   kampung,   inah   kampung,   [...]
    side   village(m) two   village(m) [inaudible]
    inhyakod   k-a-   Ø
    three   PRS.NTRL-3SG.A- be.NPST

9   inahinah   kampung   four villages.
    four   village(m)

10 epe,   mayan   nama ep-na-   laɣ-et   Right, the language that they speak,
    DIST:III speech(III) now DIST:III-3PL.A- speak-IPFV
    epe
    DIST:III

11 nahan   a,   malin-mayan   ehe,   our own Marind language, they've
    1.EMPH   PTCL   Marind-speech(III)   PROX:III   let go of it, it's gone.
    menda-b-na-   i-kahaleb,   mbya
    PERF-ACT-3PL.A-   PLA-release:III.U   NEG
    k-a-   Ø
    PRS.NTRL-3SG.A- be.NPST

12 menda-b-na-   i-kahaleb   ipe   They've let go of it.
    PERF-ACT-3PL.A-   PLA-release:III.U DIST:I/II.PL

13 sam   namaɣa   malayu-mayan   k-a-p-   Now it's Indonesian that has taken
    big   now   Malay-language   DIR-3SG.A-CT-   the first spot.
    ikoheh
    go.first(?)

14 mayay   nanggo   epe   te-k-a-   That's how it will be in the future.
    front   towards   DIST:III GIV:III-PRS.NTRL-3SG.A-
    Ø
    be.NPST

15 oɣ   malin-mayan   ø-mo-   k-aɣi   You'll say something in Marind,
    2SG   Marind-speech   NTRL-FUT:2SG.A-   WITH-say

16 yah   malayu-mayan   mak-ø-a-   but the other might answer you
    but   Malay-speech   NAFUT-3SG.A-2SG.DAT-   back in Indonesian.
    ka-dhetok   tanama
    WITH-return   again

17	*yah anip mayay m-a- Ø namaya* but therefore:I/II.PL OBJ-3SG.A- be.NPST now *ehetagol ehe* like.this:III PROX:III			Because of them the situation is like this now.
18	*e= ka-mo-p- y-a kayub-a epe,* PROX= DIR-FUT:2SG.A-CT- 2SG.U-AUX guess-EXT DIST *malin-anem ø-me-ø- mil-e* Marind-man(I) NTRL-FUT-3SG.A- be.sitting-IPFV			You'll think like this: "That must be a Marind man sitting there."
19	*bawan ti anem ø-me-ø- Ø* clan with:I man(I) NTRL-FUT-3SG.A- be.NPST			"It must be a clansman."
20	*oy ago lek ka-mo-p-* 2SG PROW:III from DIR-FUT:2SG.A-CT- *unatuk-a, mayan lek, ago* not.understand-EXT speech FROM QUOT *k-a-n-i-a- w-a malayu-et* DIR-3SG.A-1.DAT-RE-1.DAT- 3SG.U-AUX speak.Malay-IPFV *ehe* PROX:III			Then you'll be confused, because of the language: "He's answering me in Indonesian."
21	*epetagol epe* like.that:III DIST:III			Like that.
22	*ehe namaya ehe wanangga epe* PROX:III now PROX:III children DIST:III *ta-m-ak-em- ihwetok-e* GIV-OBJ-1.A-2|3PL.GEN- think-IPFV			Right now, that's what I'm thinking about the children,
23	*nok en wanangga ihe* 1 POSS children PROX:I/II.PL			our children.
24	*nok mbya mank-e- lay-e malayu-mayan,* 1 NEG NAFUT:1-1PL- speak-IPFV Malay-language *nahan mayan k-ak-e- lay-motok,* 1.EMPH speech PRS.NTRL-1.A-1PL- speak-FUT.HAB *dehi* hard			(Dina:) We shouldn't speak Indonesian, we should be speaking our own language, [it's] straight [lit. 'hard, solid'].
25	*malin-mayan ka-pa-n-ap- y-a* Marind-speech DIR-FUT-3PL.A-CT- 2|3PL.U-AUX *kahuy epe malayu-mayan* speak.poorly DIST:III Malay-speech(III)			(Wakati-Iwag:) They'll speak poor Marind, [because of] the Indonesian language.

26 ka-pa-n-ap- y-a kahuy-a
    DIR-FUT-3PL.A-CT- 2|3PL.U-AUX speak.poorly-EXT
    malin-mayan
    Marind-speech

(Nggeh:) They'll speak poor Marind.

27 tanama ti a-mo-y- lay-e
    again with DEP-FUT:2SG.A-2|3PL.DAT- speak-IPFV
    epe
    DIST:III

(Wakati-Iwag:) If you repeat for them, [then they will understand.]

28 sakola a-me-ø- umah sam-sakola
    school(m) DEP-FUT-3SG.A- go:2|3PL.U big-school(m)
    epe, malin-mayan ka-me-n-
    DIST:III Marind-speech(III) DIR-FUT-3PL.A-
    y-a i-kahaleb, sam malayu
    2|3PL.U-AUX PLA-release:III.U big Malay

(Wakati-Iwag:) If they continue in school, or at university, then they'll let go of the Marind language, all [will be] Indonesian.

29 sasayi m-a- umuh-e, dapata
    work OBJ-3SG.A- go:3SG.U-IPFV sago.plantation

(Dina, commenting about a passer-by:) She's going to work, in the sago plantation.

30 a- wambad-e, wati nanggo
    3SG.A- make.plant.bed kava for

(Dina:) She's making a plant bed, for planting kava.

31 nok nahan ehe wanangga epe k-ak-e-
    1 1.EMPH PROX:I children DIST DIR-1.A-1PL-
    n-a lay-et, ago wanangga ay, yoy
    1.U-AUX tell-IPFV QUOT children VOC 2PL
    alinde epe
    in.the.future(III) DIST:III

(Nggeh:) I usually say like this to them, "You children, in the future,"

32 ndam-bat-ø- ikebeh
    FUT-AFF-3SG.A- disappear:2|3PL.U

"you will be gone."

33 ka-me-ø- w-a ikebeh,
    DIR-FUT-3SG.A- 3SG.U-AUX disappear:2|3PL.U
    ago mayan
    PROW:III speech(III)

"You will be gone, and the language,"

34 mayan k-a- ikebeh-e
    speech PRS.NTRL-3SG.A- disappear:2|3PL.U-IPFV

"you're losing the language."

35 nahan keti en mayan a-me-ø-
    1.EMPH APL POSS speech(III) DEP-FUT-3SG.A-
    ikubaya epe
    disappear:III.U DIST

"If our own language disappears,"

36	yoɣ ap epetago, ka-me-ø- w-a	"then you too will disappear."
	2PL also like.that:III DIR-FUT-3SG.A- 3SG.U-AUX	
	ikebeh	
	disappear:2|3PL.U	

37	namik i= ka-m-e-	"Then you'll bond with your mates
	clanmates PROX:I/II.PL= DIR-FUT:2PL.A-2|3PL.DAT-	over here." [i.e. with Indonesians]
	waɣuk ihe	
	join PROX:I/II.PL	

38	wagituk-tatih ti	"You'll bond with the straight-haired
	long:IV-hair(IV) with:I/II.PL	people."
	i= ka-m-e- waɣuk	
	PROX:I/II.PL= DIR-FUT:2PL.A-2|3PL.DAT- join	

39	tis ka epe, otih mbya malayu k-a-p-	That's it, then it will all just be
	that's.it DIST many all Malay PRS.NTRL-3SG.A-CT-	Indonesian.
	hat-a-motok	
	put:III.U-EXT-FUT.HAB	

40	laɣ ehan menda-b-ø- ay,	(Dina:) Over there on that side [i.e.
	side(III) REM:III PERF-ACT-3SG.A- become:III.U	in the Duhmilah village] it has
	mbya ka-n- laɣ-e epe nahan	already happened, they don't speak
	NEG PRS.NTRL-3PL.A- speak-IPFV DIST:III 1.EMPH	our language anymore.
	mayan	
	speech(III)	

41	laɣ menda-b-ø- ay	(Nggeh:) It already happened on
	side PERF-ACT-3SG.A- become:III.U	that side.

42	ka-n- y-a malayu	(Ambai-Iwag:) They just speak
	DIR-3PL.A- 2|3PL.U-AUX speak.Malay	Indonesian.

43	mbaymbay k-a- ø ipe,	(Dina:) They can't [speak Marind],
	unable PRS.NTRL-3SG.A- be.NPST DIST:I/II.PL	people from this place speak to me
	ihe lik say k-e-na-	in Indonesian.
	PROX:I/II.PL from:I/II.PL place(III) DIR-3PL>1-1.DAT-	
	y-a malayu-e	
	2|3PL.U-AUX speak.Malay-IPFV	

44	nahan mank-um-e- aɣi nahan	(Dina:) I'd try say something to to
	1.EMPH NAFUT:1.A-FRUS-2|3PL.DAT- say 1.EMPH	them in our language.
	mayan en	
	speech INSTR	

45 | nok   namaya wanangga epe   k-ak-e-   n-a
     1   now   children   DIST   DIR-1.A-1PL-   1.U-AUX
     og-e
     do-IPFV

(Nggeh:) That's how we do with our children.

46 | mend-am-b-is-e-   an⟨e⟩tok   namaya
     PERF-1.A-ACT-SEP-1PL-   divide⟨III.U⟩ now
     malayu-mayan
     Malay-speech(III)

Now we've already restricted the Indonesian language.

47 | malayu-mayan   epe   anep   sakola
     Malay-speech(III)   DIST:III EMPH:III school(m)
     ka-me-   mengerti
     DIR-FUT:2PL.A-   understand(m)

[We tell them:] "You'll pick up Indonesian in school."

48 | anep   sakola   epe   ka-me-   hwetok,
     EMPH:III school(m) DIST   DIR-FUT:2PL.A-   think
     malayu-mayan   epe
     Malay-speech(III) DIST:III

"You'll pick it up in school, the Indonesian language."

49 | nahan   aha   kumay   ehe,   anep
     1.EMPH   house(III) inside   PROX:III   EMPH:III
     malin-mayan   m-o-   lay
     Marind-speech   OBJ-2SG.A-   speak

"[Whereas] in our own house, you speak Marind."

50 | aha   kumay   lek   a-me-ø-   hawa
     house   inside from:I   DEP-FUT-3SG.A- emerge:3SG.U
     epe,   sakola   a-me-ø-   umuh   epe,
     DIST   school   DEP-FUT-3SG.A- go:3SG.U DIST
     epe   anep   a,   ndame-ø-   hwetok,
     DIST   EMPH   PTCL   FUT-3SG.A-   think
     a-me-ø-   sakola   ka-me-ø-
     DEP-FUT-3SG.A-   go.to.school(m)   DIR-FUT-3SG.A-
     hwetok, malayu-mayan
     think,   Malay-language

When [a child] leaves home, if he goes to school, indeed, he will understand it, if he goes to school then he'll understand it, the Indonesian language.

51 | namaya   epe   ta-m-k-emb-e-
     now   DIST:III GIV-OBJ-1.A-2|3PL.GEN-1PL-
     hwetok-a,   wanangga
     think-EXT   children

Now that's what we're thinking about the children.

52	*wanangga*	*se*	*mbya*	*mank-emb-e-*
	children	only	NEG	NAFUT:1.A-2|3PL.GEN-1PL-
	hwetok-a,	*es-anim*	*ap,*	*es-anim*
	think-EXT	behind-people	also	behind-people
	ihe,	*nok*	*a-nka-h-e-*	*kanam*
	PROX:I/II.PL	1	DEP-1.A-DEP-1PL-	lead.the.way
	ipe			
	DIST:I/II.PL			

We won't think this only about our children, but also about our younger siblings, those who we walk in front of.

53	*mbya*	*k-e-na-y-*	*wayuk-e*	*namaya*
	NEG	PRS.NTRL-3PL>1-1.DAT-1PL-	join-IPFV	now

They aren't bonding with us anymore.

54	*ago*	*ehe*	*imimil*	*k-a-* Ø
	QUOT	DIST:I	elder.sibling	PRS.NTRL-3SG.A- be.NPST

[They might say:] "There's my elder brother,"

55	*mat-o-*		*wayuk,*	*mayan ndap-a-na-p-*
	HORT-3SG.DAT-		join	speech FUT-3SG.A-1.DAT-CT-
	lay			
	tell			

"I'll join him, he'll have a chat with me."

56	*isawa*	*waninggap-manemna*	*ndap-a-na-p-*
	maybe	good-story	FUT-3SG.A-1.DAT-CT-
	lay		
	tell		

"Maybe he'll tell me a good story."

57	*ago*	*adeh*	*m-a-*	*hamat-a* *ipe*
	QUOT	RLQ	OBJ-3SG.A-	sit.PL-EXT DIST:I/II.PL
	anip			
	EMPH:I/II.PL			

[But in fact they say:] "Let them remain there."

58	*nahan*	*e=*	*ta-ma-no-*	*uma⟨n⟩ah-e*
	1.EMPH	PROX=	GIV-OBJ-1.A-	go⟨1.U⟩
	eyal-milah		*ehan*	*[...]*
	PRNM:III-village(III)		REM:III	[inaudible]

"I'll go to such-and-such place [...]" [i.e. instead of joining the mates]

59	*mend-u-bat-ap-*	*gat-a*	*epe*	*mayan*
	PERF-2SG.A-AFF-CT-	hear-EXT	DIST:III	speech(III)
	epe			
	DIST:III			

Now you've already heard about that.

60	*epe*	*te-ka-hat-ø-*	Ø,
	DIST:III	GIV:III-PRS.NTRL-PRSTV-3SG.A-	be.NPST
	ipe	*Wambi-agi*	
	DIST:I/II.PL	W.-PROW:I/II.PL	

That's what they are like, the Wambi villagers.

Bibliography

Aikhenvald, Alexandra Y. 2008a. "Semi-direct speech: Manambu and beyond". In: *Language Sciences* 4 (30), pp. 383–422.
Aikhenvald, Alexandra Y. 2008b. *The Manambu language of East Sepik, Papua New Guinea*. Oxford: Oxford University Press.
Aiton, Grant. 2016. "A grammar of Eibela: A language of the Western Province, Papua New Guinea". PhD thesis. James Cook University.
Andersen, Torben. 2015. "A ternary voice-like system in Nilotic". In: *Studies in Language* 39.3, pp. 508–554.
Arka, I Wayan. 2012. "Verbal number, argument number, and plural events in Marori". In: *Proceedings of the LFG12 Conference*. Ed. by Miriam Butt and Tracy Holloway King. Stanford: CSLI Publications, pp. 23–43.
Arka, I Wayan. 2015. "Constructed middle in Marori: An LFG analysis". In: *Proceedings of the LFG15 Conference*. Ed. by Miriam Butt and Tracy Holloway King. Stanford: CSLI Publications, pp. 26–46.
van der Auwera, Johan. 1998. "Phasal adverbials in the languages of Europe". In: *Adverbial constructions in the languages of Europe*. Ed. by Johan van der Auwera and Dónall P. Ó Baoill. Berlin: Mouton de Gruyter, pp. 25–145.
van Baal, Jan. 1984. "The dialectics of sex in Marind-anim culture". In: *Ritualized homosexuality in Melanesia*. Ed. by Gilbert H. Herdt. Berkeley: University of California Press, pp. 128–166.
Baerman, Matthew. 2014. "Suppletive kin term paradigms in the languages of New Guinea". In: *Linguistic Typology* 18.3, pp. 413–448.
Bauer, Laurie. 2001. "Compounding". In: *Language typology and language universals: An international handbook*. Ed. by Martin Haspelmath, Ekkehard König, Wulf Oesterreicher, and Wolfgang Raible. Berlin: de Gruyter. Chap. 51, pp. 695–707.
Bickel, Balthasar and Fernando Zúñiga. 2017. "The word in polysynthetic languages: Phonological and morphological challenges". In: *The Oxford handbook of polysynthesis*. Ed. by Michael Fortescue, Marianne Mithun, and Nicholas Evans. Oxford: Oxford University Press, pp. 158–185.
Bittner, Maria and Kenneth L. Hale. 1995. "Remarks on definiteness in Warlpiri". In: *Quantification in natural language*. Ed. by Emmon Bach, Eloise Jelinek, Angelika Kratzer, and Barbara H. Partee. Studies in Linguistics and Philosophy 54. Dordrecht: Kluwer, pp. 81–106.
Bloomfield, Leonard. 1933. *Language*. New York: Holt.
Bloomfield, Leonard. 1962. *The Menomini language*. New Haven: Yale University Press.
Brown, Dunstan and Marina Chumakina. 2014. "Rethinking adposition agreement: The Archi postposition *eq'en*". Presented at *Rethinking comparative syntax* (ReCoS), Cambridge, May 9–10.
Bruce, Leslie. 1984. *The Alamblak language of Papua New Guinea (East Sepik)*. Pacific Linguistics C 81. Canberra: Department of Linguistics, Research School of Pacific Studies, Australian National University.
Butt, Miriam. 2010. "The light verb jungle: Still hacking away". In: *Complex predicates: Crosslinguistic perspectives on event structure*. Ed. by Mengistu Amberber, Brett Baker, and Mark Harvey. Cambridge: Cambridge University Press, pp. 48–78.
Bybee, Joan L., Revere Perkins, and William Pagliuca. 1994. *The evolution of grammar: Tense, aspect, and modality in the languages of the world*. Chicago: University of Chicago Press.
Carroll, Matthew J. 2016. "The Ngkolmpu language: With special reference to distributed exponence". PhD thesis. Australian National University.

Carroll, Matthew J., Nicholas Evans, I Wayan Arka, Christian Döhler, Eri Kashima, Volker Gast, Tina Gregor, Julia Miller, Emil Mittag, Bruno Olsson, Dineke Schokkin, Jeff Siegel, Charlotte van Tongeren, and Kyla Quinn. 2016. *Yamfinder: Southern New Guinea lexical database*. Accessed: August 20, 2017. URL: http://www.yamfinder.com.

Chafe, Wallace L. 1980. "Consequential verbs in the Northern Iroquoian languages and elsewhere". In: *American Indian and Indoeuropean studies: Papers in honor of Madison S. Beeler*. Ed. by Katherine Klar, Margaret Langdon, and Shirley Silver. The Hague: Mouton, pp. 43–49.

Cheng, Lisa. 1991. "On the typology of *wh*-questions". PhD thesis. Cambridge, Massachusetts: MIT.

Chumakina, Marina and Oliver Bond. 2016. "Competing controllers and agreement potential". In: *Archi: Complexities of agreement in cross-theoretical perspective*. Ed. by Oliver Bond, Greville G. Corbett, Marina Chumakina, and Dunstan Brown. Oxford studies of endangered languages. Oxford: Oxford University Press, pp. 77–117.

Chumakina, Marina, Oliver Bond, and Steven Kaye, eds. Forthcoming. *Agreement beyond the verb: Unusual targets, unexpected domains*. Oxford: Oxford University Press.

Comrie, Bernard. 1976. *Aspect*. Cambridge: Cambridge University Press.

Comrie, Bernard. 1982. "Grammatical relations in Huichol". In: *Studies in transitivity*. Ed. by Paul J. Hopper and Sandra A. Thompson. Syntax and semantics 15. New York: Academic Press, pp. 95–115.

Comrie, Bernard. 2003. "When agreement gets trigger-happy". In: *Transactions of the Philological Society* 101.2, pp. 313–337.

Comrie, Bernard, Martin Haspelmath, and Balthasar Bickel. 2015. *The Leipzig Glossing Rules: Conventions for interlinear morpheme-by-morpheme glosses*. Revision of May 31, 2015. URL: https://www.eva.mpg.de/lingua/resources/glossing-rules.php.

Corbett, Greville G. 1991. *Gender*. Cambridge Textbooks in Linguistics. Cambridge: Cambridge University Press.

Corbett, Greville G. 2000. *Number*. Cambridge Textbooks in Linguistics. Cambridge: Cambridge University Press.

Corbett, Greville G. 2006. *Agreement*. Cambridge Textbooks in Linguistics. Cambridge: Cambridge University Press.

Corbett, Greville G. 2007. "Canonical typology, suppletion, and possible words". In: *Language* 83.1, pp. 8–42.

Corbey, Raymond. 2010. *Headhunters from the swamps: The Marind Anim as seen by the Missionaries of the Sacred Heart, 1905–1925*. Leiden: KITLV Press, C. Zwartenkot Art Books.

Creissels, Denis. 2014a. "Cross-linguistic variation in the treatment of beneficiaries and the argument vs. adjunct distinction". In: *Linguistic Discovery* 12.2, pp. 41–55.

Creissels, Denis. 2014b. "Functive phrases in typological and diachronic perspective". In: *Studies in Language* 38.3, pp. 605–647.

Creissels, Denis. 2018. "Current issues in African morphosyntactic typology". In: *The languages and linguistics of Africa: A comprehensive guide*. Ed. by Tom Güldemann. Berlin: De Gruyter Mouton, pp. 712–821.

Cristofaro, Sonia. 2004. "Past habituals and irrealis". In: *Irrealis i irreal'nost'* [Irrealis and irreality]. Ed. by Yury A. Lander, Vladimir A. Plungian, and Anna Ju. Urmanchieva. Issledovanija po teorii grammatiki 3 [Studies in the theory of grammar 3]. Moscow: Gnosis, pp. 256–272.

Crysmann, Berthold and Olivier Bonami. 2015. "Variable morphotactics in information-based morphology". In: *Journal of Linguistics* 52, pp. 311–374.

Cysouw, Michael. 2003. *The paradigmatic structure of person marking*. Oxford studies in typology and linguistic theory. Oxford: Oxford University Press.

Dahl, Östen. 1979. "Typology of sentence negation". In: *Linguistics* 17.1–2, pp. 79–106.

Dahl, Östen. 1985. *Tense and aspect systems*. Oxford: Blackwell.

Dahl, Östen. 2000. "Animacy and the notion of semantic gender". In: *Gender in grammar and cognition*. Ed. by Barbara Unterbeck. Berlin: Mouton de Gruyter, pp. 99–115.

Dahl, Östen. 2004. *The growth and maintenance of linguistic complexity*. Amsterdam: Benjamins.

Dahl, Östen. 2015. *Grammaticalization in the North: Noun phrase morphosyntax in Scandinavian vernaculars*. Studies in Diversity Linguistics 6. Berlin: Language Science Press.

Dahl, Östen and Eva Hedin. 2000. "Current relevance and event reference". In: *Tense and aspect in the languages of Europe*. Ed. by Östen Dahl. Berlin: Mouton de Gruyter, pp. 385–402.

Dahl, Östen and Maria Koptjevskaja-Tamm. 2001. "Kinship in grammar". In: *Dimentions of possession*. Ed. by Irène Baron, Michael Herslund, and Finn Sørensen. Amsterdam: Benjamins, pp. 201–225.

Dahl, Östen and Bernhard Wälchli. 2016. "Perfects and iamitives: Two gram types in one grammatical space". In: *Letras de Hoje* 51.3, pp. 325–348.

Daniel, Michael and Edith A. Moravcsik. 2013. "The associative plural". In: *The world atlas of language structures online*. Ed. by Matthew S. Dryer and Martin Haspelmath. Leipzig: Max Planck Institute for Evolutionary Anthropology. URL: http://wals.info/chapter/36.

Davies, John. 1981. *Kobon*. Lingua Descriptive Studies 3. Amsterdam: North-Holland.

de Vries, Lourens J. 1990. "Some remarks on direct quotation in Kombai". In: *Unity in diversity: Papers presented to Simon C. Dik on his 50th birthday*. Ed. by Harm Pinkster and Inge Genee. Dordrecht: Foris, pp. 291–308.

de Vries, Lourens J. 1995. "Demonstratives, referent identification and topicality in Wambon and some other Papuan languages". In: *Journal of Pragmatics* 24.5, pp. 513–533.

de Vries, Lourens J. 2005. "Towards a typology of tail-head linkage in Papuan languages". In: *Studies in Language* 29.2, pp. 363–384.

DeLancey, Scott. 1997. "Mirativity: The grammatical marking of unexpected information". In: *Linguistic Typology* 1.1, pp. 33–52.

Diessel, Holger. 1999. *Demonstratives: Form, function, and grammaticalization*. Amsterdam: Benjamins.

Diessel, Holger. 2003. "The relationship between demonstratives and interrogatives". In: *Studies in Language* 27.3, pp. 635–655.

Dingemanse, Mark. 2012. "Advances in the cross-linguistic study of ideophones". In: *Language and Linguistics Compass* 6.10, pp. 654–672.

Dixon, Robert M. W. 1977. *A grammar of Yidiɲ*. Cambridge Studies in Linguistics 19. Cambridge: Cambridge University Press.

Dixon, Robert M. W. 1994. *Ergativity*. Cambridge Studies in Linguistics 69. Cambridge: Cambridge University Press.

Dixon, Robert M. W. 2002a. *Australian Languages: Their nature and development*. Cambridge Language Surveys. Cambridge: Cambridge University Press.

Dixon, Robert M. W. 2002b. "The eclectic morphology of Jarawara, and the status of word". In: *Word: A cross-linguistic typology*. Ed. by Robert M. W. Dixon and Alexandra Y. Aikhenvald. Cambridge: Cambridge University Press, pp. 125–152.

Dixon, Robert M. W. 2003. "Demonstratives: A cross-linguistic typology". In: *Studies in Language* 27.1, pp. 61–112.

Dixon, Robert M. W. 2004. "Adjective classes in typological perspective". In: *Adjective classes*. Ed. by Robert M. W. Dixon and Alexandra Y. Aikhenvald. Explorations in Linguistic Typology. Oxford: Oxford University Press, pp. 1–49.

Dixon, Robert M. W. and Alexandra Y. Aikhenvald. 1997. "A typology of argument-determined constructions". In: *Essays on language function and language type: Dedicated to T. Givón*. Ed. by Joan Bybee, John Haiman, and Sandra A. Thompson. Amsterdam: Benjamins, pp. 71–114.

Döhler, Christian. 2016. "Komnzo: A language of Southern New Guinea". PhD thesis. Australian National University.
Donaldson, Tamsin. 1980. *Ngiyambaa: The language of the Wangaaybuwan*. Cambridge: Cambridge University Press.
Donohue, Mark and Lila San Roque. 2004. *I'saka: A sketch grammar of a language of north-central New Guinea*. Pacific Linguistics 554. Canberra: Australian National University.
Drabbe, Petrus. n.d. "Gegevens over drie talen met praefixale vervoeging op Nederlands Zuid-Nieuw-Guinea: Jaqaj, Marind, Boazi *[Data on three languages with prefixal inflection of Dutch South New Guinea: Yaqay, Marind, Boazi]*". Unpublished manuscript.
Drabbe, Petrus. 1947. "Marind woordenlijst: Boven-Bian-dialect, Nieuw Guinea *[Marind wordlist: Upper Bian dialect, New Guinea]*". Unpublished manuscript.
Drabbe, Petrus. 1950. "Talen En Dialecten Van Zuid-West Nieuw-Guinea: Deel I *[Languages and dialects of Southwest New Guinea: Part I]*". In: *Anthropos* 45.4/6, pp. 545–574.
Drabbe, Petrus. 1954. *Talen en dialecten van Zuid-West Nieuw-Guinea* [Languages and dialects of Southwest New Guinea]. Microbiblioteca Anthropos 11. Microfilm. Posieux/Fribourg: Instituut Anthropos.
Drabbe, Petrus. 1955. *Spraakkunst van het Marind: Zuidkust Nederlands Nieuw-Guinea* [Grammar of Marind: South coast of Dutch New Guinea]. Studia Instituti Anthropos 11. Wien-Mödling: St. Gabriël.
Dressler, Wolfgang U. 1968. *Studien zur verbalen Pluralität: Iterativum, Distributivum, Durativum, Intensivum in der allgemeinenen Grammatik, im Lateinischen und Hethitischen*. Wien: Böhlaus.
Dressler, Wolfgang U. and Lavina Merlini Barbaresi. 1994. *Morphopragmatics: Diminutives and intensifiers in Italian, German, and other languages*. Berlin: Mouton de Gruyter.
Edwards-Fumey, Deborah. 2005. "The Absolutive marker in Kuni". Bachelor's Thesis. Bern University.
Enfield, Nick J. 2003. "Demonstratives in space and interaction: Data from Lao speakers and implications for semantic analysis". In: *Language* 79.1, pp. 82–117.
Evans, Nicholas. 1992. "'Wanjh! bonj! nja!': Sequential organization and social deixis in Mayali interjections". In: *Journal of Pragmatics* 18.2, pp. 225–244.
Evans, Nicholas. 1994. "The problem of body parts and noun class membership in Australian languages". In: *University of Melbourne working papers in linguistics* 14, pp. 1–8.
Evans, Nicholas. 1995. *A grammar of Kayardild. With historical-comparative notes on Tangkic*. Berlin: Mouton de Gruyter.
Evans, Nicholas. 2000. "Family portrait: Iwaidjan, a very un-Australian language family". In: *Linguistic Typology* 4, pp. 91–142.
Evans, Nicholas. 2008. "Reciprocal constructions: Towards a structural typology". In: *Reciprocals and reflexives: Theoretical and typological explorations*. Ed. by Ekkehard König and Volker Gast. Trends in Linguistics 192. Berlin: Mouton de Gruyter, pp. 33–103.
Evans, Nicholas. 2012. "Even more diverse than we had thought: The multiplicity of Trans-Fly languages". In: *Melanesian languages on the edge of Asia: Challenges for the 21st century*. Ed. by Nicholas Evans and Marian Klamer. Language Documentation & Conservation Special Publication No. 5. University of Hawaii, pp. 109–149.
Evans, Nicholas. 2015a. "Inflection in Nen". In: *The Oxford handbook of inflection*. Ed. by Matthew Baerman. Oxford: Oxford University Press, pp. 543–575.
Evans, Nicholas. 2015b. "Valency in Nen". In: *Valency classes in the world's languages*. Ed. by Andrej L. Malchukov and Bernard Comrie. Berlin: De Gruyter Mouton, pp. 1069–1116.
Evans, Nicholas, I Wayan Arka, Matthew Carroll, Yun Jung Choi, Christian Döhler, Volker Gast, Eri Kashima, Emil Mittag, Bruno Olsson, Kyla Quinn, Dineke Schokkin, Jeff Siegel, Philip Tama, and Charlotte van Tongeren. 2018a. "The languages of Southern New Guinea". In: *The languages*

and linguistics of the New Guinea area: A comprehensive guide. Ed. by Bill Palmer. Berlin: De Gruyter Mouton, pp. 641–774.

Evans, Nicholas, Henrik Bergqvist, and Lila San Roque. 2018b. "The grammar of engagement I: Framework and initial exemplification". In: *Language and Cognition* 10.1, pp. 142–170.

Evans, Nicholas, Janet Fletcher, and Belinda Ross. 2008. "Big words, small phrases: Mismatches between pause units and the polysynthetic word in Dalabon". In: *Linguistics* 46.1, pp. 89–129.

Evans, Nicholas and Julia Colleen Miller. 2016. "Nen". In: *Journal of the International Phonetic Association* 46.3, pp. 331–349.

Fedden, Sebastian. 2011. *A grammar of Mian*. Berlin: Mouton de Gruyter.

Feldman, Harry. 1986. *A grammar of Awtuw*. Pacific Linguistics B 94. Canberra: Australian National University.

Fillmore, Charles J. 1968. "The case for case". In: *Universals in linguistic theory*. Ed. by Emmon Bach and Robert T. Harms. New York: Holt, Rinehard and Winston, pp. 1–88.

Fillmore, Charles J. 1970. "The grammar of *hitting* and *breaking*". In: *Readings in English transformational grammar*. Ed. by Roderick A. Jacobs and Peter S. Rosenbaum. Waltham: Ginn, pp. 120–133.

Foley, William A. 1986. *The Papuan languages of New Guinea*. Cambridge Language Surveys. Cambridge: Cambridge University Press.

Foley, William A. 1991. *The Yimas Language of New Guinea*. Stanford: Stanford University Press.

Foley, William A. 1999. "Grammatical relations, information structure, and constituency in Watam". In: *Oceanic Linguistics* 38.1, pp. 115–138.

Foley, William A. 2000. "The languages of New Guinea". In: *Annual Review of Anthropology* 29, pp. 357–404.

Geniušienė, Emma. 1987. *The typology of reflexives*. Berlin: Mouton de Gruyter.

Geurtjens, Hendrik. 1926. *Spraakleer der Marindineesche taal* [Grammar of the Marind language]. Verhandelingen van het Koninklijk Bataviaasch Genootschap van Kunsten en Wetenschappen 67. The Hague: Martinus Nijhoff.

Geurtjens, Hendrik. 1933. *Marindineesch-Nederlandsch Woordenboek* [Marind-Dutch dictionary]. Verhandelingen van het Koninklijk Bataviaasch Genootschap van Kunsten en Wetenschappen 71. Bandung: Nix.

Gibson, Hannah, Andriana Koumbarou, Lutz Marten, and Jenneke van der Wal. 2016. "Locating the Bantu conjoint/disjoint alternation in a typology of focus marking". In: *The conjoint/disjoint alternation in Bantu*. Ed. by Jenneke van der Wal and Larry M. Hyman. Berlin: De Gruyter Mouton, pp. 61–99.

Gil, David. 2015. "The Mekong-Mamberamo linguistic area". In: *Languages of mainland Southeast Asia: The state of the art*. Ed. by Nick J. Enfield and Bernard Comrie. Berlin: De Gruyter Mouton, pp. 266–355.

Gil, David. 2017. "Roon *ve*, DO/GIVE coexpression, and language contact in Northwest New Guinea". In: *NUSA: Studies in language typology and change* 62, pp. 43–101.

Gregor, Tina. 2020. "A documentation and description of Yelmek". PhD thesis. Australian National University.

Guillaume, Antoine. 2016. "Associated motion in South America: Typological and areal perspectives". In: *Linguistic Typology* 20.1, pp. 81–177.

Guillaume, Antoine and Françoise Rose. 2010. "Sociative causative markers in South-American languages: A possible areal feature". In: *Essais de typologie et de linguistique générale. Mélanges offerts à Denis Creissels*. Ed. by Franck Floricic. Lyon: ENS, pp. 383–402.

Güldemann, Tom. 2008. *Quotative indexes in African languages: A synchronic and diachronic survey*. Empirical Approaches to Language Typology 34. Berlin: Mouton de Gruyter.

Haas, Mary R. 1941. "Tunica". In: *Handbook of American Indian languages: Vol. 4*. Ed. by Franz Boas. New York: Augustin, pp. 1–143.

Haiman, John. 1978. "Conditionals are topics". In: *Language* 54, pp. 564–589.

Hale, Kenneth L. 1976. "The adjoined relative clause in Australia". In: *Grammatical categories in Australian languages*. Ed. by Robert M. W. Dixon. Canberra: Australian National University, pp. 78–105.

Halliday, Michael A. K. 1967a. "Notes on transitivity and theme in English: Part 1". In: *Journal of Linguistics* 3.1, pp. 37–81.

Halliday, Michael A. K. 1967b. "Notes on transitivity and theme in English: Part 2". In: *Journal of Linguistics* 3.2, pp. 199–244.

Harris, Alice C. 2002. *Endoclitics and the origins of Udi morphosyntax*. Oxford: Oxford University Press.

Harris, Alice C. 2016. "Understanding multiple exponence: How can diachronic linguistics contribute to understanding morphology?" Presented at Anamorphosys: Analyzing Morphological Systems, Université Lyon 2.

Haspelmath, Martin. 1993. "More on the typology of inchoative/causative verb alternations". In: *Causatives and transitivity*. Ed. by Bernard Comrie and Maria Polinsky. Studies in Language Companion series 23. Amsterdam: Benjamins, pp. 87–120.

Haspelmath, Martin. 1994. "Passive participles across languages". In: *Voice: Form and function*. Ed. by Barbara Fox and Paul J. Hopper. Amsterdam: Benjamins, pp. 151–177.

Haspelmath, Martin. 2015. "Transitivity prominence". In: *Valency classes in the world's languages: A comparative handbook*. Ed. by Andrej L. Malchukov and Bernard Comrie. Berlin: De Gruyter Mouton, pp. 131–147.

Haspelmath, Martin and Oda Buchholz. 1998. "Equative and similative constructions in the languages of Europe". In: *Adverbial constructions in the languages of Europe*. Ed. by Johan van der Auwera and Dónall P. Ó Baoill. Berlin: Mouton de Gruyter, pp. 277–334.

Heath, Jeffrey. 1981. *Basic materials in Mara: Grammar, texts and dictionary*. Pacific Linguistics C 60. Canberra: Department of Linguistics, Research School of Pacific Studies, Australian National University.

Heath, Jeffrey. 1991. "Pragmatic disguise in pronominal-affix paradigms". In: *Paradigms: The economy of inflection*. Ed. by Frans Plank. De Gruyter Mouton, pp. 75–90.

Heath, Jeffrey. 1998. "Pragmatic skewing in 1<->2 pronominal combinations in Native American languages". In: *International Journal of American Linguistics* 64.2, pp. 83–104.

Herring, Susan C. and John C. Paolillo. 1995. "Focus position in SOV languages". In: *Word order in discourse*. Amsterdam: Benjamins, pp. 163–198.

Himmelmann, Nikolaus P. 1996. "Demonstratives in narrative discourse: A taxonomy of universal uses". In: *Studies in anaphora*. Ed. by Barbara A. Fox. Amsterdam: Benjamins, pp. 205–254.

Himmelmann, Nikolaus P. and Eva Schultze-Berndt. 2005. "Issues in the syntax and semantics of participant-oriented adjuncts: An introduction". In: *Secondary predication and adverbial modification: The typology of depictives*. Ed. by Nikolaus P. Himmelmann and Eva Schultze-Berndt. Oxford: Oxford University Press, pp. 1–67.

Hisa, La, Agustinus Mahuze, and I Wayan Arka. 2017. "The ethnobotanical-linguistic documentation of sago palms: A preliminary report from Merauke". Presented at Workshop on the languages of Papua 4, Manokwari, Indonesia.

Hockett, Charles F. 1958. *A course in modern linguistics*. New York: Macmillan.

Hofherr, Patricia Cabredo and Brenda Laca. 2012. "Introduction: Event plurality, verbal plurality and distributivity". In: *Verbal plurality and distributivity*. Ed. by Patricia Cabredo Hofherr and Brenda Laca. Berlin: De Gruyter, pp. 1–24.

Honeyman, Thomas. 2017. "A grammar of Momu, a language of Papua New Guinea". PhD thesis. Australian National University.

Horvath, Julia. 1986. *Focus in the theory of grammar and the syntax of Hungarian*. Dordrecht: Foris.

Inkelas, Sharon. 1993. "Nimboran position class morphology". In: *Natural Language and Linguistic Theory* 11.4, pp. 559–624.

Jendraschek, Gerd. 2009. "Clause linkage in a language without coordination: The adjoined clause in Iatmul". In: *Form and function in language research: Papers in honour of Christian Lehmann*. Ed. by Johannes Helmbrecht, Yoko Nishina, Yong-Min Shin, Stavros Skopeteas, and Elisabeth Verhoeven. Trends in Linguistics Studies and Monographs 210. Berlin: De Gruyter, pp. 139–148.

Kamp, Hans and Antje Rossdeutscher. 1994. "DRS-construction and lexically driven inference". In: *Theoretical Linguistics* 20.2-3, pp. 165–235.

Kashima, Eri. 2020. "Language in my mouth: Linguistic variation in the Nmbo speech community of Southern New Guinea". PhD thesis. Australian National University.

Keenan, Edward L. 1976. "Towards a universal definition of 'subject'". In: *Subject and topic*. Ed. by Charles N. Li. New York: Academic Press, pp. 303–333.

Kemmer, Suzanne. 1993. *The middle voice*. Typological Studies in Language 23. Amsterdam: Benjamins.

Khalilova, Zaira. 2009. "A grammar of Khwarshi". PhD thesis. Utrecht: LOT.

Khanina, Olesya. 2008. "How universal is wanting?" In: *Studies in Language* 32.4, pp. 818–865.

Kim, Alan Hyun-Oak. 1988. "Preverbal focusing and type XXIII languages". In: *Studies in syntactic typology*. Ed. by Michael Hammond, Edith Moravcsik, and Jessica Wirth. Amsterdam: Benjamins, pp. 147–169.

Kim, Yuni. 2010. "Phonological and morphological conditions on affix order in Huave". In: *Morphology* 20.1, pp. 133–163.

Kittilä, Seppo. 2005. "Recipient-prominence vs. beneficiary-prominence". In: *Linguistic Typology* 9.2, pp. 269–297.

Knauft, Bruce M. 1993. *South coast New Guinea cultures: History, comparison, dialectic*. Cambridge Studies in Social and Cultural Anthropology 89. Cambridge: Cambridge University Press.

Koch, Harold. 1984. "The category of "associated motion" in Kaytej". In: *Language in Central Australia* 1, pp. 23–34.

van de Kolk, Joseph and Petrus Vertenten. 1922. *Marindineesch woordenboek* [Marind dictionary]. Weltevreden: Landsdrukkerij.

König, Ekkehard and Martin Haspelmath. 1997. "Les constructions à possesseur externe dans les langues d'Europe". In: *Actance et valence dans les langues d'Europe*. Ed. by Jack Feuillet. Berlin: Mouton de Gruyter, pp. 525–606.

Kriens, Ronald. 2003. *Report on the Kumbe River survey: South coast of Irian Jaya, Indonesia*. SIL International.

Krifka, Manfred. 2008. "Basic notions of information structure". In: *Acta Linguistica Hungarica* 55 (3-4), pp. 243–276.

Kroeger, Paul. 2017. "Frustration, culmination, and inertia in Kimaragang grammar". In: *Glossa* 2.1, p. 56.

Kuroda, Sige-Yuki. 1972. "The categorical and the thetic judgement: Evidence from Japanese syntax". In: *Foundations of Language* 9, pp. 153–185.

Kuteva, Tania. 1998. "On identifying an evasive gram: Action narrowly averted". In: *Studies in Language* 22.1, pp. 113–160.

Lambrecht, Knud. 1994. *Information structure and sentence form: Topic, focus and the mental representation of discourse referents*. Cambridge Studies in Linguistics 71. Cambridge: Cambridge University Press.

Lebold, Randy, Ron Kriens, and Peter Jan de Vries. 2010. *Report on the Okaba subdistrict survey in Papua, Indonesia*. SIL International.

Lee, Jenny. 2016. "Pluractionality in Ranmo". In: *Oceanic Linguistics* 55.1, pp. 25–51.

Levin, Beth. 1993. *English verb classes and alternations: A preliminary investigation*. Chicago: The University of Chicago Press.

Lichtenberk, Frantisek. 1983. *A grammar of Manam*. Oceanic Linguistics Special Publication 18. Honolulu: University of Hawaii Press.

Lichtenberk, Frantisek. 1995. "Apprehensional epistemics". In: *Modality in discourse and grammar*. Ed. by Joan L. Bybee and Suzanne Fleischman. Amsterdam: Benjamins, pp. 293–327.

Lichtenberk, Frantisek. 2000. "Inclusory pronominals". In: *Oceanic Linguistics* 39.1, pp. 1–32.

Lindsey, Kate L. 2019. "Ghost elements in Ende phonology". PhD thesis. Stanford University.

Malchukov, Andrej. 2008. "Split intransitives, experiencer objects, and 'transimpersonal' constructions: (Re-)establishing the connection". In: *The typology of semantic alignment*. Ed. by Mark Donohue and Søren Wichmann. Oxford: Oxford University Press, pp. 76–100.

Malchukov, Andrej, Martin Haspelmath, and Bernard Comrie. 2010. "Ditransitive constructions: A typological overview". In: *Studies in ditransitive constructions: A comparative handbook*. Ed. by Andrej Malchukov, Martin Haspelmath, and Bernard Comrie. Berlin: Mouton de Gruyter, pp. 1–64.

McDonough, Joyce. 2000. "On a bipartite model of the Athabascan verb". In: *The Athabascan languages: Perspectives on a Native American language family*. Ed. by Theodore B. Fernald and Paul Platero. Oxford: Oxford University Press, pp. 139–166.

McGregor, William B. 2003. "Aspect, time, and associative relations in Australian languages". In: *Tidskrift for Sprogforskning* 1.1, pp. 151–175.

McGregor, William B. 2013. "Grammaticalisation of verbs into temporal and modal markers in Australian languages". In: *Diachronic and typological perspectives on verbs*. Ed. by Folke Josephson and Ingmar Söhrman. Amsterdam: Benjamins, pp. 107–132.

McGregor, William B. 2017. "Unusual manner constructions in Shua (Khoe-Kwadi, Botswana)". In: *Linguistics* 55.4, pp. 857–897.

Merlan, Francesca. 1983. *Ngalakan grammar, texts and vocabulary*. Pacific Linguistics B 89. Canberra: Australian National University.

Merlan, Francesca. 1985. "Split intransitivity: Functional oppositions in intransitive inflection". In: *Grammar inside and outside the clause: Some approaches to theory from the field*. Cambridge: Cambridge University Press, pp. 324–362.

Mithun, Marianne. 1991. "Active/agentive case marking and its motivations". In: *Language* 67.3, pp. 510–546.

Moravcsik, Edith A. 2003. "A semantic analysis of associative plurals". In: *Studies in Language* 27, pp. 469–503.

Mushin, Liana. 1995. "Epistememes in Australian languages". In: *Australian Journal of Linguistics* 15.1, pp. 1–31.

Muysken, Pieter. 1986. "Approaches to affix order". In: *Linguistics* 24, pp. 629–643.

Nedjalkov, Vladimir P. 1988. *Typology of resultative constructions*. English translation ed. by Bernard Comrie. Amsterdam: Benjamins.

Newman, Paul. 1990. *Nominal and verbal plurality in Chadic*. Dordrecht: Foris.

Nichols, Johanna. 2005. "A bipartite stem outlier in Eurasia: Nakh-Daghestanian". In: *Proceedings of the 29th meeting of the Berkeley Linguistics Society*. Ed. by P. M. Novak, C. Yoquelet, and D. Mortensen. Berkeley: Berkeley Linguistics Society, pp. 321–334.

Nichols, Johanna, David A. Peterson, and Jonathan Barnes. 2004. "Transitivizing and detransitivizing languages". In: *Linguistic Typology* 8, pp. 149–211.

Noonan, Michael. 1985. "Complementation". In: *Language typology and syntactic description, Vol. 2: Complex constructions*. Ed. by Timothy Shopen. Cambridge: Cambridge University Press, pp. 42–140.

Nose, Masahiko. 2009. "The expression of comparative and similative in Oceanic and non-Oceanic languages: A typological study". In: *Language and Linguistics of Oceania* 1, pp. 45–62.

Noyer, Rolf. 1994. "Mobile affixes in Huave: Optimality and morphological wellformedness". In: *Proceedings of the 12th West Coast Conference on Formal Linguistics*. Ed. by Erin Duncan, Donka Farkas, and Philip Spaelti. Stanford: CSLI, pp. 67–82.

Obenauer, Hans-Georg. 2004. "Nonstandard wh-questions and alternative checkers in Pagotto". In: *Syntax and semantics of the left periphery*. Ed. by Horst Lohnstein and Susanne Trissler. Berlin: Mouton de Gruyter, pp. 343–384.

Olsson, Bruno. 2013. "Iamitives: Perfects in Southeast Asia and beyond". Masters thesis. Stockholm University.

Olsson, Bruno. 2015. *Coastal Marind recordings*. Digital collection managed by PARADISEC. URL: https://catalog.paradisec.org.au/collections/BRO1.

Olsson, Bruno. 2017. "The Coastal Marind language". PhD thesis. Singapore: Nanyang Technological University.

Olsson, Bruno. 2019a. "The Absconditive revealed: Attention alignment in the grammar of Coastal Marind". In: *Open Linguistics* 5.1, pp. 136–155.

Olsson, Bruno. 2019b. "The gender system of Coastal Marind". In: *Grammatical gender and linguistic complexity, Vol. 1: General issues and specific studies*. Ed. by Francesca Di Garbo, Bruno Olsson, and Bernhard Wälchli. Berlin: Language Science Press, pp. 197–223.

Olsson, Bruno. 2021. *Petrus Drabbe's Coastal Marind texts: Edited and annotated by Bruno Olsson*. Parts I & II. Language & Linguistics in Melanesia: Texts in the Languages of the Pacific series. URL: https://www.langlxmelanesia.com/tilp.

Olsson, Bruno and Timothy Usher. 2017. "On the history of Marind verb stems". Presentation given at the 4th Workshop on the Languages of Papua, 23–26 January, Manokwari, Indonesia.

Oswalt, Robert L. 1961. "A Kashaya grammar (Southwestern Pomo)". PhD thesis. University of California, Berkeley.

Overall, Simon E. 2017. "A typology of frustrative marking in Amazonian languages". In: *The Cambridge handbook of linguistic typology*. Ed. by Alexandra Y. Aikhenvald and Robert M. W. Dixon. Cambridge University Press, pp. 440–476.

Pawley, Andrew, Simon Peter Gi, Ian Saem Majnep, and John Kias. 2000. "Hunger acts on me: The grammar and semantics of bodily and mental process expressions in Kalam". In: *Grammatical analysis in morphology, syntax and semantics: Studies in honor of Stanley Starosta*. Ed. by Videa P. De Guzman and Byron W. Bender. Oceanic Linguistics Special Publications 29. Honolulu: University of Hawai'i Press, pp. 153–185.

Pawley, Andrew and Harald Hammarström. 2018. "The Trans New Guinea family". In: *The languages and linguistics of the New Guinea area: A comprehensive guide*. Ed. by Bill Palmer. Berlin: de Gruyter, pp. 21–195.

Peterson, David A. 2007. *Applicative constructions*. Oxford Studies in Typology and Linguistic Theory. Oxford: Oxford University Press.

Reesink, Ger P. 1987. *Structures and their functions in Usan*. Studies in Language Companion Series 13. Amsterdam: Benjamins.

Reesink, Ger P. 1993. "'Inner speech' in Papuan Languages". In: *Language and Linguistics in Melanesia* 24, pp. 217–225.

Reesink, Ger P. 2013. "Expressing the GIVE event in Papuan languages: A preliminary survey". In: *Linguistic Typology* 17, pp. 217–266.

Reid, Nicholas. 1997. "Class and classifier in Ngan'gityemerri". In: *Nominal classification in Aboriginal Australia*. Ed. by Mark Harvey and Nicholas Reid. Amsterdam: Benjamins, pp. 165–228.

Rice, Keren. 2000. *Morpheme order and semantic scope: Word formation in the Athapaskan verb*. Cambridge Studies in Linguistics 90. Cambridge: Cambridge University Press.

Roberts, John R. 1997. "Switch-reference in Papua New Guinea: A preliminary survey". In: *Papers in Papuan linguistics No. 3*. Ed. by Andrew Pawley. Pacific Linguistics A 87. Canberra: Australian National University, pp. 101–241.

Ross, Malcolm. 2002. "The history and transitivity of western Austronesian voice and voice-marking". In: *The history and typology of western Austronesian voice systems*. Ed. by Fay Wouk and Malcolm Ross. Pacific Linguistics 518. Canberra: Australian National University, pp. 17–62.

Ross, Malcolm. 2005. "Pronouns as a preliminary diagnostic for grouping Papuan languages". In: *Papuan pasts: Studies in the cultural, linguistic and biological history of the Papuan-speaking peoples*. Ed. by Andrew Pawley, Robert Attenborough, Jack Golson, and Robin Hide. Pacific Linguistics 572. Canberra: Australian National University, pp. 15–66.

Russell, Kevin. 1999. "The 'word' in two polysynthetic languages". In: *Studies on the phonological word*. Ed. by T. Alan Hall and Ursula Kleinhenz. Amsterdam: Benjamins, pp. 203–221.

San Roque, Lila, Lauren Gawne, Darja Hoenigman, Julia Colleen Miller, Alan Rumsey, Stef Spronck, Alice Carroll, and Nicholas Evans. 2012. "Getting the story straight: Language fieldwork using a narrative problem-solving task". In: *Language Documentation and Conservation* 6, pp. 135–174.

Sapir, Edward and Harry Hoijer. 1967. *The phonology and morphology of the Navaho language*. University of California publications in linguistics 50. Berkeley: University of California Press.

Sasse, Hans-Jürgen. 1987. "The thetic/categorical distinction revisited". In: *Linguistics* 25.3, pp. 511–580.

Sasse, Hans-Jürgen. 2002. "Recent activity in the theory of aspect: Accomplishments, achievements, or just non-progressive state?" In: *Linguistic Typology* 6, pp. 199–271.

Schultze-Berndt, Eva and Nikolaus P. Himmelmann. 2004. "Depictive secondary predicates in crosslinguistic perspective". In: *Linguistic Typology* 8, pp. 59–131.

Shagal, Ksenia. 2019. *Participles: A typological study*. Empirical Approaches to Language Typology 61. Berlin: de Gruyter Mouton.

Shibatani, Masayoshi and Prashant Pardeshi. 2001. "The causative continuum". In: *The grammar of causation and interpersonal manipulation*. Ed. by Masayoshi Shibatani. Amsterdam: Benjamins, pp. 85–126.

Siegel, Jeff. 2019. "The relative pronoun strategy: New data from southern New Guinea". In: *Studies in Language* 43.4, pp. 997–1014.

Siewierska, Anna. 2003. "Person agreement and the determination of alignment". In: *Transactions of the Philological Society*. Vol. 101. 2, pp. 339–370.

Siewierska, Anna. 2004. *Person*. Cambridge Textbooks in Linguistics. Cambridge: Cambridge University Press.

Smith, Carlota S. 1997. *The parameter of aspect*. 2nd ed. Studies in Linguistics and Philosophy 43. Dordrecht: Springer.

Sohn, Myo-Sook, Randy Lebold, and Ron Kriens. 2009. *Report on the Merauke Subdistrict survey: Papua, Indonesia*. SIL International.

Stassen, Leon. 1997. *Intransitive predication*. Oxford Studies in Typology and Linguistic Theory. Oxford: Oxford University Press.

Stolz, Thomas. 2001. "Comitatives vs. instrumentals vs. agents". In: *Aspects of typology and universals*. Ed. by Walter Bisang. Berlin: Akademie Verlag, pp. 153–174.

Stump, Gregory T. 2001. *Inflectional morphology*. Cambridge Studies in Linguistics 93. Cambridge: Cambridge University Press.

Suter, Edgar. 2018. "Comparative morphology of the Huon Peninsula languages (Papua New Guinea)". PhD thesis. Cologne University.

Tatevosov, Sergej. 2002. "The parameter of actionality". In: *Linguistic Typology* 6.3, pp. 317–401.

Tent, Jan. 1998. "The structure of deictic day-name systems". In: *Studia Linguistica* 52.2, pp. 112–148.

van Tongeren, Charlotte. 2015. "Suki". Presentation given at the Languages of South New Guinea meeting, Australian National University, March 13, 2015.

Treis, Yvonne. 2017. "Similative morphemes as purpose clause markers in Ethiopia and beyond". In: *Similative and equative constructions: A cross-linguistic perspective*. Ed. by Yvonne Treis and Martine Vanhove. Amsterdam: Benjamins, pp. 91–142.

Tsunoda, Tasaku. 1985. "Remarks on transitivity". In: *Journal of Linguistics* 21.2, pp. 385–396.

Ultan, Russell. 1975. "Infixes and their origins". In: *Linguistic Workshop III*. Ed. by Hansjakob Seiler. Munchen: Fink, pp. 157–205.

Usher, Timothy. 2020. *newguineaworld*. URL: https://sites.google.com/site/newguineaworld.

Usher, Timothy and Edgar Suter. 2015. "The Anim languages of Southern New Guinea". In: *Oceanic Linguistics* 54.1, pp. 110–142.

van Baal, Jan. 1966. *Dema: Description and analysis of Marind-Anim Culture (South New Guinea)*. KITLV Translation Series 9. The Hague: Nijhoff.

van den Heuvel, Wilco. 2016. *Aghu: Annotated texts with grammatical introduction and vocabulary lists*. Asia-Pacific Linguistics 33. Canberra: Australian National University.

Van Valin, Robert D. and Randy J. LaPolla. 1997. *Syntax: Structure, meaning and function*. Cambridge Textbooks in Linguistics. Cambridge: Cambridge University Press.

Voorhoeve, C. L. 1975. "Central and Western Trans-New Guinea phylum languages". In: *New Guinea area languages and language study Vol. 1: Papuan languages and the New Guinea linguistic scene*. Ed. by Stephen A. Wurm. Vol. 38. Pacific Linguistics C 38. Australian National University, pp. 345–460.

Wälchli, Bernhard. 2006. "Typology of heavy and light *again* or the eternal return of the same". In: *Studies in Language* 30.1, pp. 69–113.

Weber, David J. 1989. *A grammar of Huallaga (Huánuco) Quechua*. University of California publications in linguistics 112. University of California Press.

Wilkins, David P. 1991. "The semantics, pragmatics and diachronic development of 'associated motion' in Mparntwe Arrernte". In: *Buffalo Papers in Linguistics* 1, pp. 207–257.

Windschuttel, Glenn A. 2018. "Object verbs: Link from Timor-Alor-Pantar to Trans-New-Guinea. An exploration of their typological and historical implications". PhD thesis. University of Newcastle.

Wirz, Paul. 1922/1925. *Die Marind-anim von Holländisch-Süd-Neu-Guinea, I–IV* (Vol. 1–2). Abhandlungen aus dem Gebiet der Auslandskunde, Band 10/16: Reihe B, Völkerkunde, Kulturgeschichte und Sprachen. Hamburg: Friedrichsen.

Woodbury, Anthony C. 1998. "Documenting rhetorical, aesthetic, and expressive loss in language shift". In: *Endangered languages: Current issues and future prospects*. Ed. by Lenore A. Grenoble and Lindsay J. Whaley. Cambridge: Cambridge University Press, pp. 234–258.

Wurm, Stephen A. 1982. *The Papuan languages of Oceania*. Ars linguistica 7. Tübingen: Narr.

Xrakovskij, Viktor S. 1997. "Semantic types of the plurality of situations and their natural classification". In: *Typology of iterative constructions*. Ed. by Viktor S. Xrakovskij. München: LINCOM, pp. 3–68.

Yokoyama, Masako. 1951. "Outline of Quechua structure I: Morphology". In: *Language* 27.1, pp. 38–67.

Yu, Alan C. L. 2007. *A natural history of infixation*. Oxford Studies in Theoretical Linguistics. Oxford: Oxford University Press.

Index

1pl indexing, 217–218

Actor indexing, 187–204, 297, 299–301, 304, 307
adjectives
– description of, 49–51, 58–61
– gender agreement, 58–60
adverbials
– locative, 88, 133–135, 269, 276–277, 285–286, 516–517, 533–534
– manner, 95, 136, 329, 464–466, 519–520, 537–538
– temporal, 133, 266, 277–278, 533–534
adverbs, 61, 487–493
Aktionsart, 354–361
alignment, 188
allegro speech, 44, 94, 293
Anim languages, 1, 5–6, 55, 101, 105, 189
applicatives, 256, 259, 263, 319–344
apposition, 61, 159
argumenthood, 479–481
aspect, 54, 276, 354–395, 451, 490, 550
assimilation, 192, 513
associated motion, 450
Associative Plural *ke/keti*, 161–162, 220
Australian languages, 60, 98, 111, 169, 460, 529
Austronesian languages, 253

benefactive, 211, 319, 480
Bian Marind, 7–14, 17–18
Bitur, 101, 105
Bulaka River languages, 14, 68
Bush Marind, 7–14, 17–18

causatives, 353
clans, 16–17, 145
classifiers, 62
clause chaining (absence of), 545
code-switching, 14, 62, 136
colour terms, 59
completion, *see* telicity
compounds, 26, 39, 68–75, 97, 174
conditional clauses, 396–397, 535–536
consonant clusters, 12
consonants, 24–31
constituent order
– in clauses, 254, 470, 482–493, 531

– in noun phrases, 146–154
copula, 175, 258, 366, 467–474

Dative indexing, 187–190, 204–212, 299, 305, 308, 311
deictics, 53, 86–90, 149, 152, 418, 438, 448, 524
demonstratives, 86–95, 146, 149–154, 156, 291, 294–296, 491–492
dialects, 9–12, 26, 28, 32, 43, 398, 441, 461
dual number, 12

engagement, 396
epenthesis, 34, 37–38, 231, 233, 293

focus, 253, 280–283, 459, 479, 482–485

gender
– agreement controllers, 118
– agreement targets, 113–115
– assignment, 12, 48, 101, 104–110
– defaults, 87, 95, 101, 115, 119, 526, 539
– exponence, 102–104
– overt gender, 48, 54–57, 110–111
Genitive indexing, 187–190, 212–217, 309, 312

habituality, 368, 381–384, 393–395
headhunting, 16

ideophones, 57
imperatives, 398, 500–508
indexing vs. agreement, 187
Indonesian, *see* Malay
infixes, 40, 218, 231–240, 426–427
Inland Gulf languages, 6
instruments, 256, 259–260, 310
interjections, 143–145, 392
Ipiko, 101, 448

kinship terms, 63–68
Kuni, 345

Lake Murray languages, 5
loanwords, 14, 24, 26, 36, 108, 204, 297
Lower Fly River languages, 6

Maklew, *see* Bulaka River languages
Malay, 8, 14, 20, 21, 28, 51, 57, 62, 108, 144, 161, 227, 297, 434, 565–571
malefactive, 211

Marori, 14, 305
mass nouns, 53–54, 364
metathesis, 46, 240
middle verbs, 198–201, 223–224, 304–305, 307–308, 467
motion verbs, 125, 127, 221, 264, 269, 276, 320, 330, 331, 336, 339, 355, 409, 415, 435, 438–439, 448–449, 492, 548

negation, 256, 289, 290, 391, 404, 488–489
noun phrases, 146–154
nouns
– description of, 48–84
– temporal, 53, 168, 266, 526
number
– and gender agreement, 102–104, 113–115
– marking in nouns, 54–57
numerals, 61–63, 127, 154–156, 279, 430, 496

Ok languages, 6
orthography, 24, 33, 46, 173, 186, 293

participant indexing, 12, 187–252, 297–317
participles, 76–84
particles, 137–143, 164
phonotactics, 12, 233–234, 240, 293
placenames, 98
Plosive Nasalisation, 41–42, 192
pluractional verbs, 250–252, 423–433
position verbs, 332–335, 415, 439
possession
– and body parts, 160–161
– and kinship terms, 63–68, 159–160
– attributive, 131, 158–160
– predicative, 473–474
postpositional phrases
– as adverbials, 125, 134, 157, 265
– as attributive modifiers, 123, 127, 146, 158–159
– as secondary predicates, 123, 125, 260
– description of, 156–158
postpositions
– description of, 120–135
– gender agreement, 121–123, 125–130
prefixes
– mobility of, 178–183
– multi-class, 176
– ordering of, 176–184
prenasalised plosives, 1, 24–27, 36, 41, 193, 213
prepositions, 135–137

prohibitives, 504–507
pronouns, 12
– emphatic, 85–86
– interrogative, 95–97
– personal, 84–85
proper nouns
– dog names, 17
– person names, 49, 99
– place names, 107
purpose expressions, 99, 265, 338, 544–545

quantification, 132, 165–170, 496
questions
– content, 20, 95–97, 281, 329, 405–406, 466, 483, 511–521
– polar, 414, 436, 508–511

reason expressions, 124, 266
reduplication, 57–58, 427
reflexives, 304, 351–353
relativisation, 479, 531–533, 539
repair sequences, 98, 139
reported speech, 4, 52, 541–545

scope, 129, 132, 137, 140, 164, 167, 279, 402, 459, 489, 525, 540
secondary predication, 260, 263, 493–497
serial verb constructions (absence of), 5
stress, 1, 35–36, 174
subordinate clauses, 5, 135, 140, 147, 181–183, 392, 522–541
suffixes
– outer, 185–186, 366
– Undergoer, 240
suppletion, 57, 60, 63–66, 82, 115–117, 199–201, 239, 240, 244–252
switch-reference (absence of), 5, 546
syllable structure, 33–34
syncope, 38–39, 234
syncretism, 197, 204, 205, 250, 259

telicity, 355–357
thetic sentences, 461–464
topics, 283–284, 474, 485–487
Trans-New Guinea languages, 1, 6, 189, 546

Undergoer indexing, 187–190, 221–252, 301, 304

verb stems
- alternating vs. invariant, 221, 224–227, 249
- derivation, 173, 184–185
verbs
- ditransitive, 205, 262–263, 271–272, 310–312
- intransitive, 114, 188, 204, 212, 215, 221, 223, 226, 300–306, 499
- labile, 312–317
- patientive, 52, 188, 198, 222–223, 257, 301–304, 316–317, 476, 478, 502
- pseudo-transitive, 309
- transitive, 212, 222, 226, 306–309, 370, 499
vocatives, 137

vowel gradation, 39–41, 231, 234, 377
vowel length, 1
vowels
- combinations of, 32, 45–46
- description of, 31–33

Warkay-Bipim, 5

Yam languages, 14, 53, 68, 305
Yaqay, 5, 189, 448
Yelmek, *see* Bulaka River languages

zero verb stem, 160, 175, 467, 482

www.ingramcontent.com/pod-product-compliance
Lightning Source LLC
Chambersburg PA
CBHW081822230426
43668CB00017B/2344